The Sage of Jasper

Gus Nichols: A Biography

Scott Harp

Layout
Tom Childers
www.friendsoftherestoration.com

Author
Scott Harp
www.therestorationmovement.com

Copyright 2019

Publisher information
Cobb Publishing
704 E. Main St.
Charleston, AR 72933
CobbPublishing@gmail.com
CobbPublishing.com
(479) 747-8372

ISBN 978-1-947622-28-9

Table of Contents

Acknowledgments vii
Dedication ix
Preface x
Foreword xii
Early Childhood 1
Iron Mountain Schoolhouse 8
A Congregation Planted 16
Learning To Walk 20
An Help Meet For Him 25
The Winds Of Change 31
Striving For Masteries 41
Inspiration From The West 51
Staying The Course 60
Cordova 65
A New Work In Jasper 77
Mission Work In Lamar 85
A New Voice 94
Workers And Works 99
Struggle And Joy 107
Building Up The House 113
Happy Days Are Here Again 124
Under The Master's Tutelage 134
Publishing The Word Throughout The Land 138
A Full-Time Preacher 146
Relationships That Make Life Greater 155
The Heart Of Compassion 166
Unity: Challenges And Victories 177
Stand-Patters and Stay-Putters 189
New Roles And New Threats 198
From Co-Editor To Editor 209
Rising To The Defense Of The Gospel 219
Montgomery Bible College 232
On The Go And On The Air 238
The Mighty Pen 247
The Dean 256
Breaking Down Prejudices 265
Childhaven 277
Broadening Influence 287
My Choice Hobby 296
A Special Family 303

Speaking The Truth In Love	311
I Discovered Gus Nichols	328
Stalwart Defender Of The Faith	341
Where The Savior Trod	361
Where The Nichols Boys Go, Things Grow	375
Solid Affiliations	387
Controversy	395
Mr. Walking Bible	407
Brother Horton	416
A Master Preacher	423
These Old Soldiers	434
The Octogenarian	444
The Sage Of Jasper	452
Honor To Whom Honor Is Due	462
A Servant Goes Home	470
His Works Do Follow	481
Thank God For Brother Nichols	493
Addendum #1	499
Addendum #2	517
Addendum #3	521
Addendum #4	526
Bibliography	532

Photographs

Frederick and Mary Wyers 1
Willie and Lizzie 2
1918 William Henry & Mary Francis Singley Nichols 3
Singing School at Iron Mountain Schoolhouse 9
Gus at 20 years-old 20
Matilda Brown at 18 years-old 25
Alexander Campbell 34
1917 Ordination Papers 35
WWI Draft Card 41
F. D. Srygley 42
Flavil Hall 43
Alabama Christian College 46
Barton W. Stone 51
Austin McGary 52
David Lipscomb 52
G. A. Dunn 54
J. B. Nelson 55
J. D. Tant 56
Gus - young preacher 60
J. M. Barnes 61
T. B. Larimore 63
1905 - Tom Evans Baptizing 66
Early Nichols Family Photo 68
1906 - Chautauqua Tent Meeting 69
1925 - Gus Nichols at Posey School 79
1924 - Family at Millport 85
1923 - N. B. Hardeman 95
Hardeman Nichols 95
Foy and Hardeman 96
W. A. Black 99
The Gospel Way 100
Millport Trade Street 107
The Lamar Democrat, 28 Aug. 1929 108
1930 - The Gus Nichols Family 113
Fifth Avenue Church Building in Jasper, Alabama 125
G. C. Brewer 129
Cecil Newcomb and Gus Nichols 130
1930s - Gus Nichols 134
John T. Lewis 142
1936 - Birthday for Lucendy Calloway 148

B. C. Goodpasture and Avery Fike	150
The Nichols Boys Playing Marbles	152
1939 - Bertha Nichols, FHC Student	178
1939 - Flavil Nichols, FHC Student	179
G. H. P. Showalter	180
1938 - Mary Hardin, FHC Student	185
1938 - Flavil Nichols, FHC Student	185
1937 - Vodie Nichols, *Treasure Chest*	*186*
1940 - Gus Nichols	190
C. M. Pullias	192
1946 - *The Port Arthur Newspaper* Ad, October 6	194
Gus Nichols- Cane Ridge	203
Gus Nichols, E. R. Harper, Guy N. Woods	211
George W. DeHoff	213
Gus Nichols' Office Over His Garage	216
1943 - Nichols-Weaver Debate Book	221
1943 - FHC *Sky Rocket*, November	228
C. Leonard Johnson and Gus Nichols	232
Gus Nichols	238
Bertha Nichols Blackwood and Uncle Pervie Nichols	240
Gracie Nichols Young	243
1945 - Gus Nichols	247
A New Book Printed	248
Business Card	251
Sermons by Gus Nichols	260
1950 - Nichols-Holder Debate	273
Wendell Winkler, Gus Nichols, S. F. Hester	278
Newspaper clipping - Childhaven	279
John T. Lewis	280
Newspaper clipping - Home at Cullman	281
R. H. Boll	288
Mr. and Mrs. N. B. Hardeman	292
1951 - Lectureship Day Speakers	293
The 500 Club	299
1950s - Gus and Matilda	303
1960 - Nichols Family Photo	304
David Paul Young	306
Bertha Nichols Blackwood	306
Gus with Eddie and Karen	307
N. B. Hardeman	311
N. B. Hardeman Revival and Radio Ad	312
1950s - Gus Nichols	313

1955 - Willard Collins	314
1956 - Gus Nichols	315
Ground Breaking for Jasper Church Building	317
Sixth Avenue Church Building	318
Sixth Avenue Church History	319
1957 - FHU Annual Bible Lectureship	320
Gus Nichols, B. B. James, H. A. Dixon	324
Gus Nichols and a brother	328
1959 - Herald of Truth Dinner	329
1959 - Four Preachers	330
Nichols at John Dillinger's Grave	331
Crown Hill Cemetery, Indianapolis	331
Friday Night Classes	337
Gus Nichols	341
Marvin Bryant, Gus Nichols, V. P. Black	342
The Lecturer	345
Gus Nichols' 77th Birthday	347
Gus Nichols	349
The Gus Nichols Story	351
Gus and Matilda at Blue Ridge	353
Blue Ridge Encampment Attendees	354
Attendees at Blue Ridge Encampment	354
26th Annual Lectureship, *Skyrocket*	362
1962 - *Christian Chronicle,* Feb. 23	363
Chart painted by W. G. "Pem" Pemberton (1886-1962)	376
1963 - Christian Service Award	377
Speaker at ACC Elders' Workshop	379
1963 - 50th Wedding Anniversary	382
1963 - *Daily Mountain Eagle* Report	383
Glenn A. Posey	387
Glenn Posey Family	388
Gus and Glenn at a Gospel Meeting	389
Mr. and Mrs. B. C. Goodpasture	392
Guy Nichols and Guy Woods at FHC Open Forum	397
Lectures on the Holy Spirit	399
The Answer Man	407
Gus Nichols Library and Learning Center	411
James A. Horton	416
Gus and Matilda at the New Preacher's Residence	417
Gus Nichols	423
Matilda and Gus - His 77th Birthday	428
Gus Nichols at Library Dedication	429

1969 - Gus and Matilda Nichols 431
1971 - Church Photo 434
Gus Nichols Sunday School Class 436
Gus Nichols and Billy D. Hilyer 437
Gus and sister Hazey Dozier and Zella Windham 439
1972 - Gus at 80 Years of Age 444
1972 - Gus and Matilda Nichols 445
80th Birthday Celebration 445
1972 - FHC Lectures 446
News Clipping - Serving on the Board at Alabama Christian College . 448
Gus, Matilda, Karen, Eddie 452
1973 - Sister Nichols Honored at IBC, August 453
Lectures on the Holy Spirit 455
Ray Dutton 457
"Grace" 459
Brother and Sister Nichols 462
7:30 at Bader Gym - FHC Lectures 463
Sixth Avenue Church Members 465
25 Years on the Radio 466
Mr. and Mrs. Gus Nichols 470
B. C. Goodpasture and Gus Nichols 474
J. M. Powell and Gus Nichols 474
Blue Ridge Encampment 474
The Nichols Bible Hour 475
Charlie R. Nichols 477
Daily Mount Eagle: Report on the passing of brother Nichols 491
Levi Sides - Nichols Cottage 494
Gospel Advocate Gus Nichols Issue 495
Indian Creek Hall of Fame 496
1976 - Open House - Nichols Library 496
1975 - Last Known Photo of Brother Nichols 535

Acknowledgments

The people who have contributed to the production of this volume are very difficult to list completely. From my childhood, Gus Nichols was a household name. Preachers I heard all my life recalled things brother Nichols said or did. Those recollections, as much as any, are acknowledged as making contributions to this book.

Then there was brother Nichols himself. I heard him preach, and his sons preach. They were family friends. Gus Nichols did not keep a running diary of his work over the years. But, in the early years of his ministry he sent in reports to brotherhood journals. In later years, when his reports were fewer and fewer, his fame caused those with whom he worked to report on his efforts with them. So, his presence in the press, especially the *Gospel Advocate* and the *Firm Foundation,* has made this book possible.

Since 2009 I have been researching this project. Imagine going through thousands of feet of microfilm of back issues of all the newspapers and brotherhood journals that brother Nichols either wrote reports to or articles for over the span of his career. Assisting me in this project to access the material with greater ease were men like Dr. Barry Jones, Tom L. Childers, Bennie Johns, and Charlie Wayne Kilpatrick, to name a few.

Thousands of miles and hundreds of hours have been spent in courthouses, libraries, knocking doors where brother Nichols' influence was felt, as well as phone calls to people who might have stories to tell. Hundreds of conversations with preachers, requests for recollections of things they heard brother Nichols say or do in their presence were necessary to make this work come to fruition.

There have been so many interviews. Over the years, I have had occasional dialogs with brother Nichols' children, Flavil, Bertha, and Hardeman. These were more than interviews; they were life highlights that will go with me to my grave. What a great part they played in helping me write this work about their father! Other family members, like Nick Hamilton, Peggy Champion, Betty Beck, Aubrine Nichols (1918-2013), James Wyers, and others made great contributions with stories they recalled. I had meaningful and informative interviews with Glenn Posey (1935-2018), James Horton, Ray Dutton, and Levi Sides, all former co-workers of brother Nichols. They knew the man potentially better than anyone. Others who helped include John Ancil Jenkins, E. Claude Gardner (1925-2017), Alan Highers, Gary Hampton, Robert R. Taylor, Jr., Ken Joines, Dr. Sam Hester, Jeff A. Jenkins, and Dr. David Hester, to name several.

Special thanks must go to Vicki Blackwood. Like the rest of her cousins, she loved her "Granddaddy," and honors his memory. Vicki spent hours searching for information, supplying photographs for scanning, reading manuscripts, and putting up with what seemed like endless emails and text messages that helped clarify family information.

When the manuscript of the book was complete, those who proof-read and helped to check grammar, fact-check, and even fill in gaps and make corrections were James Horton, Vicki Blackwood, Levi Sides, my father, Richard T. Harp, and Alice Holton.

Many, many thanks are extended to Tom L. Childers who worked so many hours in setting up the book and preparing it for print. His love for brother Nichols has been recalled in many of our conversations over the years. He encouraged me in the writing of the book, and he has assisted me in seeing it to its final stage.

I could not have produced this volume had it not been for an understanding, loving, and devoted wife. Jenny has endured nearly ten years of what some might consider an obsession. Enduring the miles, waiting while I traipsed through grave yards, interviews, and the like, her understanding has been nothing short of extraordinary. What a trooper!

There are others who made this book possible, and while they may not have been mentioned here by name, their part has been vital and much appreciated.

Dedication

They brought me into the world.
She has nurtured me from the start.
He has always been my preacher.
They have shown me the picture
of what true Christianity is like
by the example of their lives.
They introduced me to Gus Nichols
when he stayed in our home.
It is for this reason that this book
is dedicated to my parents,

Richard Turner Harp
and
Dixie June Baldy Harp

Preface

In September 2009 I spent two weeks at the Grand Eastern Hotel in Labasa, Vanua Levu, Fiji Islands. It was not a vacation as evenings were devoted to teaching Pacific Islands Bible College classes at the local church of Christ. The days were mine to plan and contemplate. Besides a tsunami that hit the island while I was there, and one of my students being mugged on the way to class one night, having to be rushed to the hospital, everything was relatively calm and event-free.

Prior to my departure to the islands, a fresh new bundle of scans of old *Gospel Advocates* were added to my laptop thanks to a joint effort with a few of my preacher friends,[1] and I was looking forward to perusing the old issues. But, I needed a project—a focus of sorts, to dig into something historical, something relevant.

Gus Nichols has always been a fascinating giant among preachers in my estimation. The times I had heard preachers whom I respect say, "brother Nichols once said. . ." or "Gus Nichols taught. . ." are more than I could count. In recent years, reference to him has been less and less, but back in the day, the man was a household name among churches of Christ.

Adding to this is the proximity of his influence. Winston County, Alabama, the home of my birth and ancestry, borders Walker County to the south, where Gus Nichols was born, raised, and the point from where his greatest influence emanated. My family knew and respected him, so I thought everybody felt the same way.

He helped my family. When my father, Richard T. Harp, graduated from David Lipscomb College in 1960, his first mission effort was in the small town of Lancaster, South Carolina. The small struggling church needed a new building, and he was determined that, God willing, the structure would become a reality. Brother Nichols set up some appointments in the area around Jasper, and invited him to come stay in their home as long as he needed to raise the funds necessary for the work. That building became a reality, thanks in part to brother Nichols.

When I was a young teenager, brother Nichols came to Atlanta and preached a meeting at the Forest Park congregation where my dad was preaching at the time. Staying in our home, we have photos of him holding my little brother, Victor, on his lap. We had a bedroom with bunk beds, and so brother Nichols and I shared the space that week. I heard him sleep deeply only a few feet away. I remember watching him change his hearing aid batteries, and still have the ones he discarded in a box somewhere. What I remember most was his interest in me and my spiritual walk. One night we sat on the edge of our beds for over an hour studying the Bible together after everyone else had gone to bed. Even in his 80s, he was amazingly focused on my well-being and growth as a young Christian. It has been over forty years since, but his sage advice still rings in my ears.

While in high school, I had the privilege of traveling with my dad to Freed-Hardeman College, now University, for the annual lectureship. I remember well attending brother Nichols' 7:30 a.m. session in Bader Gym, and seeing the friendly banter that he and brother Woods exchanged on the subject of the Holy Spirit during the Open Forum. The influence of these men in my life led me to attend FHU after finishing high school.

Over the years, it has been my privilege to read biographies of many great preachers and church leaders. I have always wondered why one was not written about brother Nichols. The research and preparation for this volume over the last decade has made me understand why. The man did so much, and that is putting it mildly.

Just a few words about the book itself. I chose to use chapter endnotes in this volume. While footnotes have always been a favorite of mine, burying them in the back of a book is almost a certainty they will be ignored. Be sure and glance at each endnote when you see one noted in the text. It may be that the note will give you added information to the story that I felt was unnecessary in the text. Also, the chapter endnotes make it possible for researchers in the future to "dig where I dug," and of course, to make the telling of brother Nichols' story even more accurate.

I commend to you the life and times of the man I call, *The Sage of Jasper: Gus Nichols*.

Scott Harp
1 January 2019

ENDNOTE
1 Special thanks to Tom L. Childers, Bennie Johns, Barry Jones, and others who have taken it upon themselves to digitize many of our old Restoration Movement papers.

Foreword

Gus Nichols Appreciation Dinner
Freed-Hardeman College
February 1962[1]

In 1940, I crossed the Mississippi River for the first time and landed in Henderson, Tennessee, to participate in the lectures at Freed-Hardeman College. At this time, I was unknown except by name, to anyone connected with the school, other than N. B. Hardeman. I was relatively a young man, and the names of the men with whom I was associated cast in me no little fear. H. Leo Boles was teaching a class. N. B. Hardeman was teaching a class. Gus Nichols was teaching a class and conducting the Round Table discussions. These classes were conducted from eight o'clock in the morning until after the Round Table in the afternoon, with lectures again that night for a period of two long weeks. Of course, I had heard and read about Gus Nichols, but until January 1940, I had never met him. My first time to see him was when he stood to speak—a young man of only forty-seven years, tall, dark, and handsome. He had the bearing of a man of greatness and gave the impression of one who would be a leader in any group and who would grace the Senate of the United States. His manner of speaking was impressive. He was very firm, kind, and spoke distinctly. We had no public address system, but he could easily be heard in every nook and corner of the auditorium. People listened with rapt attention.

G. K. Wallace

At this meeting, twenty-three years ago, a friendship was begun that has lasted over the years. For twenty-three years, including this year, I have worked with and listened to this great man of God. I have been amazed at his vast accumulation of knowledge on almost every Bible subject. In his classes and in the Round Table discussions, there was no topic that arose for which Brother Nichols did not have a ready answer and a quotation from the Bible. Sometimes in these rough and tumble arguments, when great issues were before the church; such as premillennialism and the orphans' home question; I have seen him pressed hard by those who would have their own way in preference to the way of the Lord. Not one time did he ever lose his composure, his temper, nor speak an unkind word. Even though Brother Nichols has come to lecture at Freed-Hardeman College every year for twenty-six years, he never hesitates to repeat great truths that young people need to know. He seems to take for granted that every new group of young people in college ought to learn basic Bible principles and that older brethren who come here for study need to be reminded again of the fundamentals of the gospel.

Brother Nichols is a man of great mental activity, which is so vital in an age when the champions of error are giants in intellect and scholarship. He knows how to meet and vanquish such men and still maintain truth high and above danger. Brother Nichols has no fear of the opponents of truth. He can brush away error with a hand velvety as down itself. However, when need so demands, he can saber down the haughty foe of truth with a blade broad, keen, and irresistible.

Brother Nichols is a man whose art in logic is unmatched, whose kindly manner and subtle persuasion overpower the enemies of Christ. He is a man who is a master in the art of preaching and debating.

Brother Nichols has been strong physically with a bright intellect, blended with deep-glowing thought and never-flagging energy. He is a man whose heart is sweet and fathomless with love and whose whole nature is mellowed with piety. He is a man whose spirit has been broken with grief, and in whose heart stands great wells of sympathy for ruined humanity. The man to whom we pay tribute today can speak truth, sparkling as it falls like drops of dew, and yet, he can still clothe his thoughts in words a child can understand.

To a man who has lived such an exemplary life, raised such an illustrious family, written so many great sermons and articles, and helped train and direct so many, many young preachers we now pay tribute. A great man, a great soldier, a great leader, in the house of God is among us today. To him and to his family we wish the best and pray that his years may be multiplied to serve the cause we all love best.

G. K. Wallace (1903-1988)

ENDNOTE

1 G. K. Wallace, "Brother Gus Nichols," *Gospel Advocate*, 1 July 1976, p. 424. Note: In February 1962, Freed-Hardeman College honored Gus Nichols at their first annual Appreciation Dinner. G. K. Wallace (1903-1988) was not initially scheduled to appear on the program but was slotted in at the last moment. His speech at the dinner appeared verbatim in the pages of the *Gospel Advocate* the summer after the passing of brother Nichols. To my knowledge, it is the only speech from that memorious occasion that has been preserved. In all the things this author has read about brother Nichols, there has been nothing that introduces the man any better. Though brother Wallace is now with the Lord, I am sure he would have been honored to have the opportunity to introduce Gus Nichols to you in this volume.

- 1 -

Early Childhood

For thou hast possessed my reins: Thou hast covered me in my mother's womb. I will praise thee; for I am fearfully and wonderfully made: Marvelous are thy works; And that my soul knoweth right well.

—David, Psalm 139:13-14

Greatness has often been clothed in humble beginnings. For all that can be said of the enormity of Presidents Abraham Lincoln, James A. Garfield, and Andrew Jackson, their ascension to the height of public leadership is only enhanced by their modest log-cabin entrances into the world. The same is true of Gus Nichols. Born on a small farm about twenty-five miles west of Jasper in Walker County, Alabama, he was the first of twelve children born to Will and Lizzie Nichols.

Officially, he was given the name Bunion Augustus Nichols.[1] Regal sounding when said out loud, however it was never a name by which he was known. When asked in later life as to why he did not go by his given name, he explained that his first name was painful to him because it was descriptive of an unbearable inflammation people received in their feet. His second name, he did not care for because it was after a great,

Frederick and Mary Wyers

but merciless and evil Roman emperor. So "Gus" was his preference all his days.

The paternal heritage of the Nichols family stretches back to around the turn of early 18th century Ireland. His father, William Calvin "Will" Nichols was born in Selma, Alabama the 12th of March 1868. He was the ninth of twelve children born to William Henry "Bill" Nichols (1829-1905) and Mary Francis Singley (1833-1904).

Bill Nichols, a South Carolinian by birth, was one of eleven children born to Arthur Nichols (1807-1862) and Mary Ann Sanders (1807-1860). Arthur's parents were John Nichols (1795-1850) and Jane Simpson (1787-1860) of Belfast, Laurens, South Carolina. Irish sounding, is it not? It is little wonder as John's parents were James T. Nichols (1737-1810) and Elizabeth Green (1739-1814), both of whom were born in Ireland, and married there in 1760. They migrated to the American colonies, landing at Charleston, South Carolina in 1767. James' father was Allen Nichols, born in Ireland in 1715 and lived there all his life.

The maternal ancestry of the Nichols goes nearly as far back, at least to the same region of the eastern U.S. coastal states. The mother of Gus Nichols was Velma Elizabeth "Lizzie" Wyers, born the 19th of November 1873, in Fayette County, Alabama. Her father was known as "Singing" John Frederick Wyers (1840-1924), a Confederate soldier during the Civil War.[2]

Willie and Lizzie

John Frederick's father was also John Wyers (1810-1870), born in Newberry, South Carolina. John's father, and the great, great grandfather of Gus, was Joseph Wyers (1774-1819), who was born in Newberry, North Carolina, and died in the same town in South Carolina.[3] After his death, his widow, Elizabeth, and most of the children migrated to Perry County, Alabama in the 1830s.[4]

Bill Nichols was born in South Carolina in 1829, but settled with his family in Perry County, Alabama at a young age. Farming was his trade, and he raised his family to understand the need to work and provide. By the time Will was only a couple of years into this world the family's net worth was about $250.00. However, the land upon which they were farming was worth about $300.00.[5] It was a family business. With eleven brothers and sisters, children learned early that work was as much a part of life as eating and sleeping. The regimen for every day was assigned. Expectation was high that each was to carry his or her own weight of responsibility.

When Will was released from the mastery of his father, he took a job for a time at a paper mill in Tuscaloosa, Alabama. At about the age of twenty, he made his way into the northeast section of Fayette County to a farming community on the North River. Located just a few miles south of Carbon Hill in Walker County, he began working as a farm hand for John F. Wyers. This is where he became most interested in the eldest daughter of John and Mary Susan Doss Wyers, Lizzie.

The reasons for Will's move from Tuscaloosa to a farm in northeast Fayette County are unknown. However, tracking the family ancestry of both the Wyers and the Nichols, it is easy to assume that the families knew each other for generations. Earliest available details reflect that both

Early Childhood

lived in South Carolina around the same time not more than thirty miles apart. Both families migrated to Perry County, Alabama in the 1830s. As farming was the trade of both families, it is easy to think that Bill Nichols and John F. Wyers may have known each other from their youth. Thus, for Will to have traversed fifty miles of farming country, and ending up on a section owned by John Wyers, is not far-fetched.

Will and Lizzie fell in love, and receiving the blessings of her parents, were married on the 23rd of November 1890. They settled on a small farm of their own in the community of Kansas, in the western part of Walker County.[6] A small cabin made of logs was where the couple spent their early years, and a little over a year after their nuptials their humble home was blessed with the birth of a bouncing baby boy.

1918 William Henry & Mary Francis Singley Nichols

Gus, born the 12th day of January 1892, was the first of ten children to live to adulthood. Within nearly ten months, his first brother, Charlie R. was born on the 3rd of November 1892. A third child, Carey Columbus, came on the 18th of December 1896. A bond was sown early in life that led these three lads on similar paths all their days, although one arose to wider fame.

Several stories have survived over the years of things that happened when Gus was a youth. One told by his son expressed the lesson young Gus learned about the importance of respecting property owned by others. Flavil related,

> When he was about five, Gus Nichols returned from a visit to his grandparents (about three miles through the woods) with six new shiny "cut" nails in his pocket. His maternal grandfather was putting some new shingles on his roof, and those were the first new nails he had ever seen. His mother made the lad walk back—alone—to return them, and to ask his grandfather's forgiveness for "stealing" them. He said he ran most of the way back home, because he wanted to get out of the forest before dark. But from that experience he learned honesty, and to control his "wants." He never again had "sticky fingers" and taught us not to steal.[7]

In later life, Gus reflected on several events in his youth that he used to illustrate important applications about spiritual things. For instance, once he reflected on a song he sang in his youth that helped him to look for the good in all things. He said, "When I was a boy we often sang the song: 'There is a glory side to the cloud we fear.' There is a glory side to every cloud. The sun is always shining above the clouds in the daytime. So, it is with all our problems in life; they have their brighter side."[8]

Familiarity with one's surroundings, or the lack thereof, can have a long-lasting effect on a boy. Living in the wide expanse of a rural setting, he learned early that he must be careful in his wanderings. In another lesson entitled, "What If I Am Lost?" he shared a childhood experience that had long stayed with him. Illustrating the despair of being a lost sinner he explained,

> Have you ever been physically and literally lost? When I was a lad of a boy I was lost from my mother in the woods. I was gathering huckleberries and lost my way in a forest of hundreds of acres. The trees were up to about a hundred feet high, and the bushes and the undergrowth were so thick that one could see only a short distance. The last thing I remembered was that I was frightened almost to death, and was running, perhaps in the wrong direction, and was crying and calling my mother. O! It is a terrible feeling to find that you are lost![9]

Schooling in western Walker County was available to the Nichols children, but only in a somewhat limited way. Just a couple of miles south of Carbon Hill is the community surrounding what at one time was known as Iron Mountain Schoolhouse.[10] Overtaken by nature, today there is little evidence, other than a small spring nearby, that there ever was a school on Iron Mountain. The original structure was a one-room building made of logs and later covered by white-washed clapboard. It served for many years as a multi-purpose venue for society life. During the winter months, the children of the area attended the school there. It had one teacher who served all ages. As soon as Gus was old enough to go, he began making his way to the old schoolhouse for his daily ration of "book learning." Though a setting far less advanced than city schools, he was treated to the opportunity of learning how to read and write, the basics of arithmetic, the rudiments of music, the significance of history, and most of all, an appreciation for the power of knowledge.

Meanwhile, the family continued to grow. Just a week after his sixth birthday, Gus and his brothers received a great family surprise when Lizzie gave birth to her fourth child, the boys' first sister Zora, on the 18th of January 1898. Then, on the 10th of May 1900, another sister, Hazey Mae, entered the world. Still later, another sister arrived, Velma Virginia, on the 22nd of February 1903.

Early Childhood

At the turn of the 20th century, farm living in northwest Alabama relied heavily upon the contributions of child labor, especially boys. When planting time arrived in the spring of 1904, twelve-year old Gus was the eldest of six Nichols children. With growing demands at home, some practical decisions had to be made. While "book-learning" had its place, survival trumped over scholastic proclivity. Thus, having only completed the sixth grade, he was forced to withdraw from school in view of full-time work on the land.

All of the teen years of his life were spent outside the classroom, but to say his education took a hiatus is far from the truth. Setting in crops behind a mule-driven plow, caring for animals, repairing barbed-wire fences, and other routine daily chores, served to instill within the young man a deep sense of responsibility and tenacity toward achievement of anything to which he turned his hand.

Learning to read in those early years of school planted deeply within Gus Nichols a heart of inquiry. He read whatever printed material upon which he could lay his hands. He read newspapers, the Farmer's Almanac, and he even read the Ladies Birthday Almanac.[11] He was a seeker of knowledge. His interests were wide and varied, and such an appetite for learning from an early age initiated a life-long starvation for the wisdom of the ages.

By the time Gus was sixteen, the family had grown to ten including his parents. Brother, William Archie was born the 23rd of January 1906, and Katie Ozella rounded out the junior eight when she arrived the 16th of February 1908. Two more brothers, Clarence, born in 1910 and Troy, in 1911, died in infancy. Pervie was born the 18th of October 1912, and the youngest, Hubert Titus, was born the 19th of December 1916.

More mouths to feed called for inventive measures. Purely for economic reasons, Will began hiring Gus out to labor and sharecrop on other farms in the area. At times, he was hired out to dig ditches, and when things were quiet around the farm he worked as a hand in a sawmill for $1.00 per day.[12] In the spring of 1908 he, "worked on a farm for an uncle, M.O. Wyers, for $12.50 per month and his board. In 1910, he farmed for Lewis Cunningham for $20.00 per month and board. In 1911, he farmed for "Lige" Cunningham for $25.00 per month and board. In the years of 1912 and 1913 he farmed "on the halves."[13] For all practical purposes, his trade was set. Farming was in his blood. Sowing and reaping was an honorable labor. It was the work of his father and his father's father before him. A worthier pursuit was impossible to imagine. But, God had other plans!

ENDNOTES

1 Note: Various spellings of the name appear in different documentation. In an unpublished document entitled, *Arthur Nichols, A Biographical And Genealogical Record*, by John T. Nichols, the name is spelled, "Bunyan Augustus 'Gus' Nichols." In the Twelfth Census of the United States in 1900, the eight-year-old was listed as "Bunyan" and his mother was listed as "Velmer." With Census records there is always a question as to whether the entry spelling was provided by the family member, or from the census taker. In June 1917, he appeared before the draft board and signed his name as "Bunion Augustus Nichols."

2 Note: John Frederick Wyers served in the army of the Confederate States of America during the Civil War. According to records held at the Alabama Department of Archives and History, he was a part of the 40th Alabama Regiment. He was an infantryman, and served in companies D & H. He enlisted in Marion County, Alabama in September 1862, and was discharged as part of the surrender at Salisbury, Durham Station, North Carolina, the 26th of April 1865.

3 Note: The city of Newberry was part of the section cut out of North Carolina when South Carolina received statehood, the 23rd of April 1788. This was how John Wyers could be born in one state and die in another yet stay in the same town all his life.

4 Note: The Wyers name spelling varies the further back you go in the ancestry of Lizzie Wyers. According to documentation provided by genealogists, Edward Wyers on Ancestry.com, records have shown alternative spellings for Lizzie's great grandfather, Joseph Whyer/Wier/Wire. The 1840 U.S. Census for Perry County, Alabama includes as head of the home Elizabeth Wires, Sarah Wire, Frederick Wires, and John Wires, and that the family spread north and west from there.

5 1870 U. S. Census for Perry County, Alabama.

6 Aubrine A. Nichols and Dessie Ree Nichols, *Will and Lizzie Nichols Family Roster*, Unpublished document, 1995.

7 Flavil Nichols, *Freed-Hardeman Lectures*, 1990, pp. 193-94.

8 *Speaking The Truth In Love*, Sixteen Full-Length Sermons and Three Lectures To Bible Classes presented by Gus Nichols: In a meeting at Lamesa, Texas, 4-11 March 1956, p. 80.

9 Ibid., pp. 183-84.

10 Flavil H. Nichols, ed., *Words of Truth*, Vol. 22, Number 46, Friday, 15 November 1985, p. 1. Note: Several articles on the life of Gus Nichols include the humble settings of his early education.

11 Basil Overton, ed. *The World Evangelist*, December 1975, p. 3.

12 *Speaking The Truth In Love*, Sixteen Full-Length Sermons and Three Lectures To Bible Classes presented by Gus Nichols: In a meeting at Lamesa, Texas, 4-11 March 1956, p. 7.

13 Marvin Bryant, "New Library Learning Center To Be Named In Honor Of Gus Nichols," *Words of Truth*, Friday, 13 May 1966, p. 2. Note: "the halves" was of old English terminology to describe sharecropping on land owned by others.

- 2 -

Iron Mountain Schoolhouse

> He maketh me to lie down in green pastures:
> He leadeth me beside the still waters. He
> restoreth my soul: He leadeth me in the paths
> of righteousness for His name's sake.
> —David, Psalm 23:2-3

When Alabama received statehood on the 14th of December 1819, it was the 22nd region of the United States of America to be so recognized. Just five years later, the state legislature designated a section, which, "lay in the corner of the territorial boundaries of the Creek, Cherokee, and Chickasaw nations of the Native American peoples who first inhabited this country."[1] Cut from Marion and Tuscaloosa Counties, that part of the country was a lush farmland area, rich in forestry and minerals. It was named for the President of the Constitutional Convention that framed Alabama's first constitution, John Williams Walker (1783-1823), of Huntsville, Alabama.

In the western part of the county, Carbon Hill came into existence just six years before Gus was born. It was a farming area, for the most part, until the Kansas City, Memphis, and Birmingham Railroad, (later Frisco Railroad) laid tracks through the community. A post office was established there in 1887.

Soon after, churches began appearing. The Methodists arrived in 1888, and the Baptists settled in 1892. In 1890, the population of Carbon Hill was 568. By 1900, the town had grown to 830, and nearly doubled in the next ten years.[2] Just two miles west, the railroad ran through the little community of Kansas where Gus was born. A little over three miles south of Kansas on the Haleys Bottom Road was the Iron Mountain Schoolhouse.[3]

School sessions lasted two and one-half to three months during the winter.[4] When school was not in session, the building was used for community gatherings, religious revivals, Saturday singing schools, and other things. Music was the center of country life. In the days preceding radio and television, a Saturday night gathering at the Iron Mountain Schoolhouse brought in musicians from all over the area. From early life experience of seeing people play, hearing the blending of voices, and learning the basics of music in his schooling, Gus took to music with a passion. There was not an instrument he could not play. When A. J.

Showalter's book on practical rudiments of music became the textbook for Saturday singing schools, he memorized the whole volume.[5]

Within Gus, there seemed to be a genetic love for music, singing and playing, for it came so naturally to him. His mother's people were musically inclined as well. His grandfather was known in the area as "Singing" John Wyers. Sam Wyers, John's youngest, was a talented song leader and taught singing schools.[6] Eight years Gus' senior, he saw in his nephew the ability to follow his footsteps to become a teacher of music. The two often conducted singing schools together.[7]

Singing School at Iron Mountain Schoolhouse

Will and Lizzie Nichols raised their children to be good citizens. Community demanded the need to know your neighbors and help one another in times of difficulty. Social gatherings in rural regions were regularly enjoyed in tandem with spiritual awakening when news came of a visit from a traveling preacher. Attending a brush arbor revival meeting in a grove, a mountain hollow, or in a schoolhouse was an opportunity for saint and sinner to commune in these sterile, and for the most part, safe venues.

Both parents answered the call for religious experience while their children were young, and they were accepted among the fellowship of the Missionary Baptist Church nearby. They were described as being "strict moralists, but did not regularly attend worship services."[8] However, their influence was strong enough to make sure their children received proper spiritual training. In 1908, sixteen-year-old Gus satisfied the demands of entrance into the denomination and acceptance into the church followed.[9]

As with everything he committed himself to, Gus took very seriously his relationship with God. He involved himself in the promotion of the good news of Jesus any way he could. Worship gatherings afforded him the opportunity to use his talents in leading the singing in his church. In time, he became known as one of the best singers in the area.

In the fall of 1909,[10] and upon the completion of another singing school session conducted by Gus and his uncle Sam, an announcement was made that the following night C. A. Wheeler intended to "run"[11] a meeting in the schoolhouse.

Charlie Alexander Wheeler (1851-1937), a "Campbellite"[12] from Lamar County, was a most successful itinerant preacher. An evangelist, debater and church planter, he was known widely for his fairness and firmness in Biblical exposition.

There were a few members of the church of Christ in the area when brother Wheeler arrived. In the course of organizing the meeting, "He told them that if someone would lead the songs, they could sing 20 or 30 minutes before he preached, but that he could not sing."[13] As there were none who felt confident in carrying out such a task, it was suggested that he might approach either Sam Wyers or Gus Nichols. When he asked who of the two was the best singer, the feelings were that the younger man had the better voice.[14] The only problem was that the seventeen-year-old was a member of the Missionary Baptist Church.

Wheeler, considering the effects of a meeting without singing, versus one with singing, was prepared to make some concessions with stipulations. When approaching Gus, he was told that all he needed was to have him sing with the people, and that in return Wheeler intended not to be controversial or attacking in nature, only to preach the Scriptures. To this, the young singer responded that he would assist in the meeting.

From the beginning, the preaching of Charlie Wheeler was different than any commonly heard in that section of the country. The Scriptures were being revealed in such a clear, loving, and rational manner that it soon caused Gus to sit up and take notice. Wheeler's teaching on the subject of baptism for the remission of sins was not a new subject for the young Baptist singer.

The previous year, when Gus was considering becoming a Baptist, a cousin, Larkin Wyers, took the opportunity to sit down with him to study what the Scriptures reveal on the subject of salvation. He shared with him that the Bible teaches that immersion in water, while trusting in God's power to save, was essential in bringing about the forgiveness of sins. This was contrary to what his cousin had been taught in the church of which his parents were members.

Back when Gus was searching for the truth on the subject, he spoke with his parents' Baptist preacher who dismissed the idea that baptism was for salvation. He had also been approached by an older uncle who said he wanted to talk to him about baptism. He told the receptive youth to look at 1 Peter 3:21 which says, "The like figure whereunto even baptism doth also now save us (not the putting away of the filth of the flesh, but the answer of a good conscience toward God,) by the resurrection of Jesus Christ."[15] From this passage, he explained that baptism was a figure. Then, he held his hand up to the sun so as to cast a shadow and said, "Gus, now you step on that shadow. You cannot mash blood out of that shadow. Why? Because it is a shadow, and not the real thing." Again, he said, "Baptism is a figure, a mere shadow! You have got to get the blood of Jesus to save you, and you will not get it from baptism."[16] This explanation seemed to have set the searching mind at ease when Gus became a Baptist the year before. However, the preaching he was hearing from C. A. Wheeler was causing the old controversy to arise once again.

One lesson entitled, "Walking By Faith," especially challenged his thinking about needing to place his trust in God, and making the choice of doing exactly what the Bible said to do in full confidence. Gus discussed this with different people. A young lady to whom he was close at the time, by the name of Salina Brown, began noticing how the lessons were impacting him. Why, he seemed to her to be drawn to the Bible messages like a dry sponge to water! One night she told him that she thought he would become a "Campbellite." He was surprised at her charge stating that as far as he could see, the Bible had been preached, "just as it was written in his own Bible."[17]

Night after night the Baptist song leader walked the three miles home to the family farm, thinking deeply about what he heard in the sermons, seeing that what preacher Wheeler taught was the truth. By the end of the meeting, the decision was made, and with a few others, the schoolhouse emptied toward the water's edge. Upon his simple confession of Christ as Lord, Charlie Wheeler baptized Gus Nichols into Christ for the forgiveness of his sins. With the new life in Christ that followed, a fresh resolve to serve God in a better, and more Biblical way, was at the forefront of his mind. He read and studied day after day what the Bible taught. Similar to another young man nearly 2000 years previous, Gus "increased in wisdom and in stature, and in favor with God and man."

WHY I AM A CHRISTIAN
By Gus Nichols

Peter says I am to give a reason,
When its requested, and this in season,
For the hope I have in Jesus the Christ,
Who died for me and was sacrificed.
(1 Pet. 3:15 — Heb. 2:9)

I am a Christian because I believe,
No unbeliever can this Christ receive.
I believe in Christ, for he rose again,
After suffering and dying for my sin.
(Acts 10:43 — 1 Cor. 15:1-26)

This faith came by hearing the word of God,
Who created me from the dust of the sod.
The gospel's the world's best good news story;
It tells of Christ who came down from glory.
(Rom. 10:17 — Jn. 6:38, 63)

The gospel proves that Christ rose from the dead,
That we can believe every word he said.
He tells us of God and the heaven above,
And about his amazing and wonderful love.
(Rom. 1:1-4 — Jn. 3:16)

This faith turned me from iniquity and sin,
Made me desire a new life to begin.
One must be converted (turn face about)
In order to have his sins blotted out.
(Acts 3:19,26 — Acts 17:30-31)

One must believe in the Christ that God sent
Strong enough to turn from sin and repent,
Then be baptized for the remission of sins.
It's after baptism that the new life begins.
(Acts 2:38 — Rom. 6:3-4)

I know I obeyed all this from the heart,
And that I have lovingly done my part.
T'was by God's grace my sins were forgiven,
And I know I'm on my way to heaven.
(Rom. 6:16-18 — Eph. 2:8)

I know I'm a Christian - living that life –
And that I am now free from sin and strife.
I love the Lord and do his blessed will.
And shall always strive his word to fulfill.
(Acts 11:26 — 26:26-28)

The gospel has often been proven true –
I believe in Jesus Christ - why not you?
Our world knows Christ was not a deceiver—
God would not have deceived the believer.
(Acts 8:35-39 — Mt. 3:13-17)

Our world admits that Jesus lived and died,
The fact that He rose was tested and tried.
Many who were with him unto the end,
Said that he rose, and they saw him ascend.
(Mt. 16:13-18 — Acts 1:26; Acts 1:5-11)

Great multitudes did he miraculously feed,
And were witnesses of his mighty deeds.
His apostles were with him day and night,
Even when he ascended out of their sight.
(Mt. 15 — Heb. 2:1-4)

He had healed their sick and had raised their dead,
Thus confirming every word he had said.
He fulfilled his word that he would arise,
And ascend unto God beyond the skies.
(Jn. 20:30-31 — Acts 1:1-5)

We know that Christ arrived up in heaven,
For he fulfilled a great promise given,
That when he arrived he'd send the Spirit,
Upon his apostles - men of merit.
(Jn. 3:5 — Acts 2:30-39)

And when the Spirit came on Pentecost,
The gospel was revealed to sinners, lost.
Three thousand obeyed when the facts they searched,
The Lord saved and added them to the church.
(Acts 2:22-41 — v. 47)

The church of Christ was established that day,
With Christ head over it in a wonderful way.
He is still the head of his spiritual body,
His church is important, not something shoddy.
(Mt. 16:18 — Rom. 16:16)

These are some reasons why I'm a Christian,
And why I'm not an alien Philistine,
And why of Christ I am not ashamed,
But as a Christian wear his holy name.
(Acts 11:26 — 1 Pet. 4:16)[18]

ENDNOTES

1 *The Heritage of Walker County*, Heritage of Alabama Series, 1999, p. 1.

2 Ibid., p. 46.

3 Note: The Iron Mountain Schoolhouse is no longer extant. The GPS location of the old building is: Decimal Degrees - 33.877365,-87.581448.

4 Basil Overton, "Farewell, Soldier of Christ," *The World Evangelist*, December 1975, pp. 1, 3.

5 Phone interview with Hardeman Nichols, 3 November 2009.

6 Note: Part of the singing school experience was learning Sacred Harp music. Often referred to as "Fa-So-La" singing, it involved the study of shape-notes, used in religious hymnals. All day singing schools concluded with a concert for the community where demonstrations of singing the shape-notes of familiar songs entertained the crowd. Gus was a master of Fa-So-La singing and could sing the notes as easily as anyone could sing the words.

7 Phone interview ith Hardeman Nichols, 3 November 2009.

8 Flavil Nichols, ed. "In Memoriam: Gus Nichols," *Words of Truth*, Vol. 22, Number 46, 15 November 1985, p. 1.

9 Willard Collins, "The Gus Nichols Story, Part 1," *Gospel Advocate*, 2 March 1961, p. 136.

10 Gus Nichols, art. "A Fifty-Year-Old Decision," appearing in *The Beacon*, weekly bulletin for Bellview Church of Christ, W. S. Cline, ed., Vol. 4, No. 26, 26 June 1975.

11 Phone interview with Hardeman Nichols, 3 November 2009. Hardeman emphasized that Brother Wheeler never did "hold" meetings. He always said he intended to "run" a meeting.

12 Note: "Campbellite" is a derogatory designation of members of churches of Christ who acknowledge the early leadership in the American Restoration Movement of Alexander Campbell (1788-1866) of Bethany, West Virginia. Campbell was among others in his generation who stressed a return to the Bible for authority in all religious practice.

13 Flavil Nichols, ed. "In Memoriam: Gus Nichols," *Words of Truth*, Vol. 22, Number 46, 15 November 1985, p. 1.

14 Phone interview with Hardeman Nichols, 3 November 2009.

15 1 Peter 3:21, King James Version.

16 Phone interview with Hardeman Nichols, 3 November 2009.

17 William Woodson, ed., "Dedication To Gus Nichols," *Freed-Hardeman Lectures*, 1976, pp. 2-5.

18 Gus Nichols, "Why I Am A Christian," *Words of Truth*, Vol. 9 No. 37, 28 March 1975, p. 4.

- 3 -

A Congregation Planted

I have planted, Apollos watered; but God gave the increase.

—Paul, 1 Corinthians 3:7

The presence of New Testament Christianity at Iron Mountain Schoolhouse may have been new to rural west Walker County in the fall of 1909, but it was not original to that part of the state.

About fourteen miles southwest of the Nichols family farm, down in Fayette County, was the Berea church of Christ. Pronounced "Old Breer" by those who have called it home, the congregation was planted in 1845 under the preaching of pioneers John Taylor (1808-1885) and Jeremiah Randolph (1808-1894) and continues to the present. It is believed to be the oldest church in that part of the state of Alabama. Both these men were instrumental in planting churches all over northwest Alabama. Churches still exist in Lamar, Fayette, and Walker Counties who felt the influence of these great servants of the Lord.

John Taylor

The life and work of John Taylor is both colorful and stirring in nature. He and his wife, Mary, moved to Marion County from South Carolina in 1827. His conversion to New Testament Christianity can only be summed up as a tribute to the power of the pure gospel of Christ. Failing in his struggle to "get religion," according to Primitive Baptist teaching, led him to a destructive path, giving up religion all together for the bottle. At the admonition of his wife, he made an effort once again. When he heard a Baptist preacher read Acts 2:38, he realized what he must do. Weighing out that simple passage, he reasoned that salvation was not to be found in some Holy-Spirit-induced experience, but in the simple obedience to the gospel through repentance and baptism for the forgiveness of his sins.[1]

Taylor's work in Colbert, Franklin, and Lauderdale Counties in the late 1860's led him into co-labor with a young preacher by the name of T. B. Larimore. Theophilus Brown Larimore (1843-1929), of the Cumberland Gap in south central Tennessee, moved into the Tennessee Valley of north Alabama in early 1868.[2] Within two years of his arrival, he married and started a school to train preachers in Lauderdale County, just north of

A Congregation Planted

Florence. Beginning in January 1871, Mars Hill College served young men from several states in preparing them for the ministry. Two of its fifteen years of service allowed for the presence of a young student from Lewis County, Tennessee, by the name of Joseph H. Holbrook (1841-1905).[3]

Upon completion of his studies, Holbrook moved to New River in Fayette County, Alabama. He "preached extensively through Fayette, Lamar, Tuscaloosa, Walker, Marion, Lawrence, Franklin and Colbert counties, Alabama and...also made preaching tours to Tennessee, Mississippi, Missouri, Arkansas and Texas."[4] His work was vast, but concentrated and effective. Hundreds came to the Lord as a result of his efforts.

In 1880, the work at Union was organized just east of Vernon, Lamar County, Alabama.[5] Shortly after, J. H. Holbrook held a meeting there. One of those responding to the call of the gospel was Charlie A. Wheeler (1851-1937).[6]

So impressed he was with the message, Wheeler intended to begin preaching the good news of Christ. Being a humble farmer all his days called for very little book learning. Thus, illiteracy impeded his progress. Eagerness to learn and preach was his motivation. So, his wife took the Bible and taught him how to read and write. In a short time, he was not only able to read, but to study and memorize great portions of the Biblical text.

Much like his father in the faith, Charlie Wheeler began preaching all over the area. He debated the gainsayers. He continued farming as his main source of income, which was very little. When harvest was in, preaching season led him to travel far and wide, preaching the gospel. Never having owned a vehicle, he relied heavily on riding the train, or a good brother going his way in a wagon. Most of the time he walked, sometimes fifty or sixty miles to an appointment.

Charlie Wheeler

Around the turn of the 20th century he settled on a small farm in Walker County, just south of Jasper in what is now the Midway community. This remained his home for the rest of his life. When he arrived at Iron

Mountain Schoolhouse in the autumn of 1909, the preacher had planted many congregations.[7] Thousands of people were immersed into Christ by his hands.[8] Thus, his knowledge of the Scriptures, along with his practical experience of how to organize a congregation, was essential to the survival of the few that had been baptized during that meeting.

Consequently, a congregation was organized at Iron Mountain Schoolhouse, with the promise that brother Wheeler would try to visit at least once per month for preaching and encouragement.

GIVE ME TRUTH
Gus Nichols

"Give me truth! It I will do!
For in John eight, verse thirty-two.
Our Savior said, as you may see,
It is the truth that maketh free."
—First poem.[9]

ENDNOTES

1 Note: The life and work of John Taylor among churches of Christ has remained in relative obscurity until the last few years. In 2010, author Earl Kimbrough released a fine biography entitled, *John Taylor: The Life and Times of A Backwoods Preacher 1807-1885*. For further information see *Alabama Restoration Journal*, Volume 3, Issue 2, August 1, 2008.

2 F. D. Srygley, *Larimore and His Boys*, 1889, p. 94.

3 Note: Variations in the spelling of Holbrook appear in different reports. Sometimes the rendering is Halbrook, as in the case of F. D. Srygley's references. However, the grave markers of he and his two wives render the spelling, "Holbrook."

4 F. D. Srygley, *Larimore and His Boys*, p. 153.

5 The name "Union" was later changed to Bethel church of Christ, and was the home church for Charlie Wheeler and his extended family.

6 Note: Sometime between 1880 and 1885 is when Charlie Wheeler became a Christian. This is evidenced by the fact that the Bethel church, formerly Union, in Lamar County was organized in 1880, according to church records. Further, the obituary for Jesse J. Wheeler, the father of Charlie Wheeler, states that he had been converted under the preaching of his son ten years before his death in 1895. (*Gospel Advocate*, 23 January 1896, p. 61). Thus, C. A. Wheeler was baptized sometime between 1880 and 1885.

7 Note: C. A. Wheeler died in 1937 and was buried in Dutton Hill Baptist Church cemetery, near his old home place, just south of Jasper, Alabama. Gus Nichols preached his funeral, and his son Flavil was one of the pallbearers. His monument records, "C. A. Wheeler, January 2, 1851, April 29, 1837, Evangelist, Church of Christ 63 Years, Baptized 6000 Souls, And Established About 100 Congregations, His Influence Abides With Us While His Spirit Is At Rest."

8 Note: The family of the author of this book is deeply indebted to C. A. Wheeler. It was by his hands that my paternal great-grandmother, Leona Fell Harp Turner, was immersed into Christ during a tent meeting between Thorn Hill and Haleyville in Marion County, Alabama in 1915. She was the first of our family heritage to leave denominationalism to practice Christianity after the Ancient Order of the New Testament. She said that she asked him personally what she should do. He told her to go home and read Matthew, Mark, Luke, John to learn about Jesus, and Acts to see how people became followers of Him. Then she was to come back and tell him what she should do. She said she read all night long by the light of a coal-oil lamp. The next night she responded to the invitation saying she needed to be baptized in order to be forgiven of her sins. Elders, deacons, teachers, preachers, and life-long faithfulness to Christ have come about because of her decision those many years ago.

9 Flavil Nichols, *Freed-Hardeman Lectures*, 1990, p. 191.

- 4 -

Learning To Walk

As newborn babes, desire the sincere milk of the word, that ye may grow thereby: If so be ye have tasted that the Lord is gracious.
—Peter, 1 Peter 2:2-3

Still clothed with the moisture that had just embraced him into a relationship with Christ through faith, Gus left the baptismal pool with a sense of newness that was enhanced by the belief that he had simply done what God's Word prescribes. He had been called by the gospel and had answered that call in fullness of faith. Descending the one hundred feet of elevation that led from Iron Mountain Schoolhouse to his Kansas farm home that night, the mind raced with anticipation and excitement. Over and over, the sense of surety of faith that came from the Word of God set him at ease with his decision. The flame in his heart was fanning toward greater knowledge and understanding.

The scheme of God's plan had been clearly displayed in the preaching of his newly found friend and father in the faith. Forty-one years his senior, brother C. A. Wheeler had quickly moved from stranger to rescuer, and from obscurity to key player in the formation of Gus' maturity. But, not only was he affected by the simple gospel message, his brothers Charlie and Carey soon followed their older brother's example by being immersed into Christ.

Gus at 20 years-old

In the days that laid ahead, anticipation brought questions, and questions needed answering. If the message that had been taught Gus in the denomination he left had been proved wrong, what else did the Good Book have to say about things he had assumed were correct? The desire to learn had long been a fixture in his psyche. But now, absorbing biblical truths was the natural progression, with greater purpose. There was a tenacity about him. The flame of faith, having been kindled, led him to every opportunity possible to absorb more and more knowledge.

Necessity has a force all its own when centered on the idea that the church Jesus established can and does exist in the present age. Apostolic authority in the Scriptures demands following God's will implicitly, not only in what one must do to be saved, but also in church organization and in worship. The Lord's church was established at Iron Mountain Schoolhouse. Quickly, Gus and the few other men of the congregation were thrust into early and defining leadership roles. Being the good singer he was, even a small group of disciples could draw and enthuse the occasional passer-by. Very quickly, he learned to teach classes and to fill in the gaps with the other men who kept things going from week to week when brother Wheeler was away.

Gus sought every opportunity he could to hear the message preached. He did not mind walking several miles, if necessary, in order to attend a meeting being held somewhere. Dedication knows no boundaries! About six months after he obeyed the gospel, begging leave from his farm duties for a day, he set out about four o'clock one morning and walked about fifteen miles to where a meeting was being conducted by brother Wheeler. He spent the day hearing the message preached and fellowshipped with his newly found brethren, and after the evening session, began the fifteen-mile journey back. He arrived at home at eleven-thirty that night.[1] When other occasions arose, he made similar efforts.

As his family and many of his friends were still among the Baptists, from time to time Gus attended meetings held by various denominations, but from a different perspective. Seeking always to be prepared for a defense of his newly found faith in Christ, it was helpful to attend these meetings, for one never knows when one might be afforded the opportunity to defend the faith.

Many years later, he was writing a response to a question someone sent into the *Gospel Advocate* about women testifying. In the process, he recalled an occasion shortly after becoming a Christian when he was visiting a "denominational prayer meeting," and was called upon to "testify." In the third person Gus recalled,

> He arose, thanked them for the opportunity of saying a few words, then stated that he had believed the testimony of the apostles, who were the inspired witnesses of Jesus; and thus having believed the gospel, and having believed on Christ through the apostles' word (John 17:20-21), he had repented of all sins (Acts 17:30; 3:19), and that he had confessed his faith in Christ

as did the Ethiopian eunuch of Acts 8:37-39, and, like him, was immersed in water, trusting the promise of the Lord, saying, "He that believeth and is baptized shall be saved" (Mark 16:16), and the promise of the apostle who said: "Repent, and be baptized every one of you in the name of Jesus Christ for the remission of sins, and ye shall receive the gift of the Holy Ghost." (Acts 2:38.) The writer further stated that, like the eunuch, he did not join any denomination, was not voted upon nor received into any denomination; that he did not subscribe to any human creed or to any human religious name, but had striven to be simply a Christian, a member of the church to which the Lord adds all the saved (Acts 2:47); and that he was worshiping and serving the Lord according to the New Testament teachings without addition or subtraction, and was striving to get all other people to simply follow Christ, simply as Christians and members of the church of Christ, without any denominational affiliation, to the end that the Lord's prayer for unity might be answered. (John 17:20-22.) Whereupon an old lady broke the silence that followed by saying: "May the Lord have mercy on that poor and lost young man."[2]

He further noted that the woman's attitude represented most of those in denominations who refuse to give up the "experience of grace, for all that the Bible says."[3]

It was about this time, in 1910, that Gus was taken very ill. The young eighteen-year-old spent many days in the sick bed, and his life, for a time, was in the balance. The doctor was called to come to see about him. The finding was not good—*pneumonia!* For many, the diagnosis was nothing less than a death warrant. It would be another eighteen years before Alexander Fleming would discover penicillin. At eighteen years of age, Gus was faced with the reality that one out of every three people die of this dreaded illness.[4] His life in the balance, a fight for survival was on his hands. With a good mother as nurse, in time, he began showing signs of improvement. Many years later, an x-ray revealed a scar on his lungs "as big as a dollar," that came about due to this traumatic experience.

The next couple of years were spent doing his father's bidding, whether it involved farm work at home, or being hired out to others. Always faithful to his assigned tasks, his mind actively pursued knowledge. Farming duties may have prevented regular appearances in a school classroom, but Gus was intent on learning. Brother Wheeler lived nearly thirty miles away from his home, a little south of Jasper. While the Frisco railroad ran through Kansas, the train stopped at Carbon Hill, about two or three miles away. Occasionally, he would leave early in the morning and walk to the train station with an empty suitcase. He then boarded the train for

Jasper. Upon arrival, he would begin the three-mile walk to the Wheeler farm. This afforded him the opportunity to spend a good part of the day asking questions and studying the Bible with the elder preacher.

Brother Wheeler did not have a large library, but the books he had were very helpful. He was good to loan Gus whatever volumes he thought would benefit him. So, regularly, he filled the empty suitcase with books like "McGarvey's *Commentary On Acts*, Lard on *Romans*, Milligan on *Hebrews*, *The Gospel Plan Of Salvation* by Brents, Campbell's, *The Christian System*, the *Campbell-Rice Debate*, and other such books as would help him discern truth from error."[5] Then, he carried the weighted bag back to the train in Jasper that headed toward home late in the evening. His studies often kept him awake on into the night. He burned pine-knots in the fire to help him see the pages. When his eyes got tired, he closed one eye, covering it with one hand, while the other was left open as he read the print in the dim light.

Gus celebrated his twentieth birthday, Friday, the 12th of January 1912. Seeing he was an adult, and must make a life for himself, his father set him free to pursue his own goals. Immediately, he returned to the old schoolhouse where classes were already in session. Within six weeks he completed the requirements for the seventh, eighth and ninth grades.[6]

When the school closed for the spring, he boarded a train for Herrin, Illinois, for work and schooling, but was only there for a few months.[7]

When he returned home, Gus was given the opportunity to continue high school studies, and even teach two children's classes to pay for his tuition.[8]

A fuller house and education had all the makings of departure to a life on his own.

Enter Matilda Brown.

ENDNOTES

1 *Speaking The Truth In Love*, Sixteen Full-Length Sermons and Three Lectures To Bible Classes presented by Gus Nichols: In a meeting at Lamesa, Texas, 4-11 March 1956, p. 8.

2 Gus Nichols, "Questions Answered," *Gospel Advocate*, 6 October 1949, p. 629.

3 Ibid.

4 Gus Nichols, *Lectures On The Holy Spirit*, Plainview: Nichols Bros. Publishing Co., 1967. p. 24. Note: One would assume he was speaking of a "silver" dollar which was in wide circulation in the early to mid-part of the 20th century.

5 Flavil Nichols, "In Memoriam: Gus Nichols," *Words of Truth*, Vol. 22, No. 46, November 15, 1985, p. 1.

6 Ibid.

7 William Woodson, *Freed-Hardeman Lectures*, 1976, p. 3. Note: Very little information is available as to what school Gus Nichols attended or the work he did while in Herrin, Illinois. It is known that for a time, he worked as a railroad hand, and during the year of 1912 a railroad was being laid between Carbondale and Herrin, Illinois in an effort to connect the Illinois-Central line to Chicago. Also, similar to Walker County, Alabama coal mining was plentiful in Herrin, so there may have been the potential of mining that drew him there.

8 *Speaking The Truth In Love*, Sixteen Full-Length Sermons and Three Lectures To Bible Classes presented by Gus Nichols: In a meeting at Lamesa, Texas, 4-11 March 1956, p. 8.

- 5 -

An Help Meet For Him

He who finds a wife finds a good thing and
obtains favor from the Lord.
—Solomon, Proverbs 18:22

Matilda Francis Brown entered the world the 29th day of March 1894 on a small farm in northern Fayette County, Alabama. She was the youngest of five children born to William Christopher Columbus Brown (1856-1934) and Naomi Caroline Kitchens (1853-1952), and the youngest of five, which grew to adulthood.[1] She was named for her father's sister, Alcy Matilda, and his maternal grandmother, Francis P. Brown Randolph (1796-1849), who was born on Cane Creek, Walker County, Alabama.

The ancestry of the Browns is not known past William Brown's father, Robert S. Brown (1833-1870) of Georgia. His mother was Lidy Ann Randolph (1831-1881) of Walker County, Alabama.[2] William's maternal grandfather was John Daniel Randolph (1798-1870), born in Greenville, South Carolina. John Daniel's father was John Abraham Randolph (1773-1837), born in Edgecombe County, North Carolina. John Abram's father was James Richard Randolph (1770-1796), born in Caswell, North Carolina. His father John Randolph (1742-1775) was born in Henrico, Virginia, and died in Roanoke, Bedford County, Virginia. His father, Richard Randolph (1686-1748) was born at Turkey Island, Henrico, Virginia, and died at Curl's Neck, in the same region. His father, William Randolph (1621-1678) was born in Warwickshire, England, and died at Henrico, Virginia, USA. Thus, Matilda's ancestry through her maternal grandmother is known back eight generations.[3]

Matilda Brown at 18 years-old

The Browns and the Nichols lived about three miles from each other. They attended the same Baptist church. When Matilda was old enough to go to school, the nearest was Iron Mountain Schoolhouse, where she went along with the Nichols boys and others in the community.[4]

Two years her senior, Gus represented leadership in her church. She and the other young teens in the congregation looked up to him. When C. A. Wheeler preached at the schoolhouse in the autumn of 1909, the eyes of the close community were on their prized song-leader as he considered defecting to the "Campbellites." When he told Matilda he was contemplating conversion to see what she thought, her response was, "You can do what you want, but I'm not going to do that."[5] Even some in his own family members were deeply concerned at his decision. When he converted, his own mother called him "a turncoat."[6]

Religious differences notwithstanding, within a couple of years, the relationship between Gus and Matilda matured into a deeper and abiding love. Her unwillingness to convert to New Testament Christianity did not hold him back from his relentless pursuit of her. They spent as much time together as possible. He even attended the services of the Baptist church on occasion, even though he had been withdrawn from after his baptism.[7]

When his father "set him free," he began to lay plans for their marriage. By planting time, the following year, he had secured a humble house and a few acres on the "Shaw place"[8] in the Howard Community, near Carbon Hill. He put in cotton on the land he sharecropped that year in view of making his home complete with Matilda as his wife. Plans were set to make it official shortly after harvest.

In keeping with honorable traditions, Gus approached Matilda's parents with respect, but with persistent expectation. He explained to them how well his crops had done, along with how many bales of cotton and bushels of corn he had harvested. He explained how he had saved the seed of three bales of cotton for planting the following year. To this her mother responded, "You don't think 'Tildie' can eat cotton seed, do you?"[9] Standing his ground, he respectfully engaged by saying that he thought that if he had to do it, she could as well.

Permission was finally granted, and the date of the nuptials was set. On the 30th of November 1913, in the Brown family home, Gus married Matilda Brown. Brother Wheeler officiated in a ceremony that lasted about an hour.

The only wedding gift they received was a kerosene lamp with a globe.[10] Lamps of this sort were fairly common in those days, but most came with no globe. This was a pretty special gift to a couple whose only sources of brightness of light in the night were burning pine-knots. To them it was like receiving a bar of solid gold. In it was the expression of the humble beauty of innocence, love, and the radiance of their happy union. Its illumination was a symbolic manifestation of what was forthcoming to the world through their lives. Imagine the possibilities with this one gift!

A TRIBUTE TO MY WIFE
By Gus Nichols

Matilda Francis Brown was born
On a very cold and snowy morn,
Snow remaining in a normal way,
March 29, (1894) was the day.

The baby was the last of five,
To live on and remain alive.
The others have all passed away,
But Matilda is alive today.

As time passed by, it was not long,
Until she was growing very strong.
One eye was larger than the other,
Soon it was normal as her brother's.

She went to school three months a year—
Had a one room school, so I hear,
With different grades and many classes,
Composed of children, boys and lasses.

The Browns were poor, but that's no harm,
So Matilda worked on her father's farm.
Though she was tanned in the hot sun,
She loved to work, and had lots of fun.

However, she was beautiful and fair,
With her ribbons and long flowing hair.
She was tall and slim at twenty,
And weighed about one hundred and plenty.

Many good graces she did inherit,
Among them was a lovely spirit.
However, of boys she was very shy,
If strangers, she passed them by.

But when I was a boy about eleven,
One night about half past seven,
She with relatives visited us
We played games and she called me Gus.

I called her Tilda, and could see,
That I liked her, and she liked me.
Though they stayed until it was late,
I followed along to the gate.

That night I dreamed we were to marry,
(But eleven more years we had to tarry).
For when I went to ask Mrs. Brown,
She insultingly turned me down.

I dreamed she was feeding the chickens,
And made me feel mean as the Dickens.
She said we were just children, then,
And Matilda was only ten.

She told me to leave—ran me off.
She did nothing but rave and scoff.
When I awoke it was only a dream.
But dreams are not what they may seem.

I'd never been in love before,
Had never met such a girl to adore.
I felt like crying—perhaps I should;
But I thought it wouldn't do any good.

I cherished that dream for eleven years,
Often thought of it with fright and fears.
Though boy after boy came along,
None of them had the right love song.

But the years passed very slowly by,
And my boyish love did not die.
I tried to dream of her at times,
But somehow the bells would not chime.

We often met, and dated some,
But the hour of my dream had not come.
Finally I went to ask Mrs. Brown
And sure enough she turned me down.

She said I couldn't her daughter feed,
Since I had only some cotton seed.
I said she could eat what I could,
And the Lord would provide, surely would.

But that old dream really bothered me,
As on my way Mrs. Brown to see.
If some of it was true—the best—
What of the chickens and the rest?

But thanks to Goodness, she gave in,
And I don't think it is a sin,
For me to believe the good in dreams,
That the bad is not what it seems.

When this girl was leaving her teens,
In early Nineteen and Thirteen,
Both of us were almost ready,
And so we started going steady.

On the twenty-second day of June
We were engaged to be married soon.
Then on Thirtieth of that November,
We took those vows to remember.

And that girl has filled my very life,
Made me happy, been a good wife.
She is trustworthy, as pure as gold,
Though tried by years and growing old.

She has worked very hard, been no drone,
Been the power behind the throne—
Been a good help meet through the years,
Sharing my burdens, joys and tears.

She must have been born for my day,
To serve in a wonderful way,
Just for such a time as has been,
To help me and ours in fighting sin.

Thank God that Matilda was born,
On that cold day and snowy morn,
And that she has been a super wife,
And has so richly blessed my life.[11]

ENDNOTES

1 Gus Nichols, "A Tribute To My Wife," *Words of Truth*, Friday, 16 May 1975, p. 2.

2 Note: Discovering Matilda's paternal grandmother being a Randolph, it is easy to assume she may have been related to the Randolphs of Fayette County who planted and strengthened churches of Christ in the 19th century. But no connection has been discovered.

3 Note: These links in ancestry were made available through Ancestry.com.

4 Willard Collins, "An Outstanding Christian Family—The Gus Nichols, of Jasper, Ala.," *Gospel Advocate*, 19 May 1955, p. 387.

5 Hardeman Nichols, Phone Interview 3 November 2009.

6 Neil Anderson, "Trailblazers: 100 Servant Leaders In The Church During The 20th Century," *Gospel Advocate*, November 1999, p. 29.

7 William Woodson, "Dedication To Gus Nichols," *Freed-Hardeman College Lectures*, 1976, p. 3.

8 Ibid.

9 Flavil Nichols, "In Memoriam: Gus Nichols," *Words of Truth*, Volume 22, Number 46, 15 November 1985, p. 1. Note: The name "Tildie" or "Tilda" was what Matilda was known by from her childhood. Often, in interviews with her children, they well recalled their father affectionately calling their mother "Tilda." However, in public, brother Nichols referred to her as either "Matilda," or "sister Nichols."

10 Gus Nichols, *Speaking The Truth In Love*, Fort Worth: Nichols Brothers Publishing Co., 1956, p. 8.

11 Gus Nichols, "A Tribute To My Wife," *Words of Truth*, Friday, 16 May 1975, pp. 2, 4. Note: There is a question as to when this poem was written. One source says Gus wrote this poem and read it to Matilda at their 50th wedding anniversary. Another says it was written for their 59th anniversary gathering on 13 November 1972 (WOT, 06.06.1975, p. 2). It was also read in 1973 at the appreciation evening at International Bible College for Matilda Nichols by her son, Flavil.

- 6 -

The Winds Of Change

> The wind blows where it wishes, and you hear its sound, but you do not know where it comes from or where it goes. So it is with everyone who is born of the Spirit.
>
> —Jesus, John 3:8

There is nothing like farm life. It is hands-on in a way like no other. The return on the investment of time is never immediate. Not like most jobs, there are no paychecks to be cut at the end of a work-week. Life centers around planting and harvesting. A good plow, a hearty animal, a strong back, and sheer determination are essentials. So many variables are at play in the effort to bring about success. Extreme weather conditions such as drought, flooding, strong head winds, and the like can take its toll on a farmer and his family. Even the best of crops in a tough economy can add difficulty to survival. It is a place where improvisation is always a necessary ingredient to achievement. A broken implement or tool could bring production to a stand-still. In those days, the Farmers Co-op, the Land Agent, and the latest copy of the Farmer's Almanac were all basic necessities of farming life.

Groomed for this kind of existence, Gus and Matilda worked together on their small piece of sod-laden land to make the best possible living. This meant that every day, except the Lord's Day, was a mutual effort toward survival. The first week of their marriage, they finished the remainder of the harvest for the year. When crops were laid by, and with the onset of the shorter days of winter, the demand for income caused Gus to turn to coal mining.

At the turn of the 20th Century, Walker County, Alabama was the largest coal-producing county in the state.[1] "The original drift of Carbon Hill,"[2] was discovered by the Kansas City Coal and Coke Company, and entered upon in the 1880's. English-born entrepreneur, Robert Galloway, purchased rights to the mine during that decade, and with it the founding of the Galloway Mining Company. By the year 1910, Galloway Mining Company was the third largest producer of commercial coal in the South.[3]

By the time that Gus began spending winter months in the mines, he was one of over three thousand co-laborers working in eight different mines in five counties in the state. The Carbon Hill drift was an electricity mine, with a maze of different smaller shafts that descended several miles underground.

Leaving his farm home in the pre-dawn hours, the typical day involved walking three to four miles to the entrance of the mine, and then descending another three miles into the maze of shafts, where he would finally arrive to begin his twelve-hour shift. With a pick and a shovel, he began breaking and loading the coal, one shovel at a time. By the end of his shift he had shoveled through twenty-one tons of coal, plus several tons of rock. At the end of the day, he reached home having never seen the light of it. Yet, the work was reliable, and the $1.10 per day's wage helped to, as he said, "Keep the wolf away from the door."[4] In later life, it was often recalled among his children that during the coal-mining periods of the year, after the crops were laid by in the summer and during the winter months, he would not see his family awake except for his only day off, Sunday.[5]

The day of rest offered little time for relaxation, however the spiritual devotion offered great refreshment. In the early days of their marriage, Gus and Matilda rose up early on the Lord's Day to make their way to Iron Mountain Schoolhouse for worship. Matilda maintained her membership in the Baptist church but was taught early in life to support the spiritual leadership of her husband. Willing to attend the worship services of the church of Christ with him, little by little, opportunities availed themselves for spiritual growth for both of them.

By planting time in the spring of 1915, the birth of Gus and Matilda's first child was drawing near. On the 27th of April, little Gracie Nichols adorned the family with her presence. Just seventeen months later, a little sister entered the family fold when Vodie was born the 10th of September 1916.

When planting season arrived in the spring of the following year, the young farmer had much on his mind. Breaking ground behind mule and plow had more significance than ever before. With every passing row and every seed planted, a man has plenty of time to plan and dream of what can be accomplished for his family. Added to his thinking were the needs of the small and struggling church that existed on Iron Mountain. The church needed more teaching than what he could do in a Bible Class, and so much more than brother Wheeler was able to provide on his regular monthly visits. The elder preacher's example loomed greatly in his thinking as he moved slowly under the increasing temperature of the sun's radiant glow. Brother Wheeler was a farmer, yet he still had time to travel and to be at the disposal of so many. But then, entertaining as to whether he could follow the older preacher's example stood in conflict with present family needs. There was never a desire to be rich. Such was unrealistic and foolish. But, could he make enough to support his family,

The Winds Of Change

and still serve the Lord like he believed he should, was his continued inner struggle.

THE STORM

Walker County lies in the middle of a particularly tumultuous weather pattern. Similar to the "tornado alley" reputation of the mid-western region of the United States, the potential for severe storms and tornadic wind activity have plagued the area for generations. Most weather systems come out of the southwest and move in a northeasterly direction. Because of it, an integral part of farm-living is the necessity of a fallout shelter. Often dug into the side of a bank, or a fruit cellar somewhere under the floor of the house, it was called upon as the family retreat on days of severely inclement weather.

Like most Sundays, the 27th of May 1917 began with the routine gathering of the saints at Iron Mountain Schoolhouse. The afternoon lent itself to uncertain weather activity that forced the small family of four into their storm shelter. At about 8:45 that evening, a tornado entered through the southwestern end of the county, passing through Howard, and within a few moments, Carbon Hill, leaving a path of devastation seventeen miles in length.

When the tornado hit the farm, Gus hurriedly helped Matilda and the girls into the dugout fruit cellar beneath the kitchen floor. Just as the winds were beating upon the house, the diligent father still had not lowered himself entirely into the cellar. A beam from above fell and hit him on the head, knocking him out, and into the cellar floor. Matilda recalled that the blow left a knot on the back of his head "as big as a goose egg." They said the experience was like, "taking a box of kitchen matches and throwing them into the air."[6]

In the aftermath, it was reported that the storm was an F3 on the Fujita-Pearson scale with winds from 158-205 miles per hour. Two citizens died in the storm's path in Kansas, and six were killed in Carbon Hill. Over 100 people were injured, and a total of nine fatalities were reported in the area. Fifty people lost their lives state-wide during the severe weather that day.[7] The storm left a path of devastation which destroyed crops, over 200 buildings and homes toppled, and many families experiencing shattered lives due to the mayhem.

After a night in the fruit cellar, and rising to a new day, the Nichols witnessed the fullness of their plight. The house was demolished; furniture strewn, clothing hanging in trees, and the tender shoots of their growing crops were gone. Years later the harrowing experience was recalled, "In the year 1917 a tornado destroyed our home, blew us away and ruined our crops out on a farm before it tore into Carbon Hill, Alabama and left the dead and the homeless in its wake. But we did not give up and quit."⁸

In the days ahead, many decisions had to be made. Protective accommodations and food was the immediate concern. Coal mining the remainder of the year was going to be financially essential. But another issue seemed more pressing to Gus than ever before—preaching. He recalled reading about how Alexander Campbell (1788-1866) supported himself in the gospel by farming. This led him to think that he could do the same.⁹ Talking to Matilda about what his heart was telling him to do brought a surprising response. She said, "Don't make a two-by-four preacher, but be a good one."¹⁰ To her it was essential that he be the best he could be if he was going to devote his life to preaching. After two or three hours of debating it in his head, he determined he was going to preach.¹¹

Alexander Campbell

Nearly forty years later, Gus was speaking to a group of teenagers in a Saturday morning youth rally in Lamesa, Texas, on the subject of making good choices in life, when he said,

> We are creatures of choice. I am standing before you this minute because of a choice, which I made one day in 1917. I decided to give my life to the preaching of the gospel. While I had been considering the matter for some time, the choice was made in a single day, in fact within two or three hours. I prayed over the matter and decided that regardless of what the results might be, the rest of my life would be spent in preaching the gospel of the Son of God.¹²

BEGINNING TO PREACH

It was the second Sunday in June; just fourteen days after his life-threatening experience that he stood before the brethren to present his first sermon. Approaching the makeshift lectern, he held in his hands a cumbersome outline of seven pages full of notes. There were no topic headings, nor were there any numbered points. He had just filled each page with text. When he started speaking, he quickly realized that his effort to make good eye contact with his audience caused him to lose

> We the members of the Church of Christ, worshiping at Iron Mountain School-house in Walker County, Ala. do herby indorse and set apart brother Gus Nichols as a preacher of the gospel and herby state that he has been set apart or ordained as such.
>
> Done by order of said church, Sept IX 12, 1917.
>
> _C. A. Hulse_, Pastor.
> _John Sparks_
> _Sam Poe_, Deacons.
> _Mack McDonald_, Elder
>
> State of Alabama.
> Walker County.
>
> I, E. W. Long, Judge of Probate in and for said State and County do hereby certify that the above was filed for record in this office on the 13th day of September 1917 and was duly recorded in Miscellaneous record 160 page 190. This the 13th day of September 1917.
>
> _E. W. Long_, Judge of Probate.

1917 Ordination Papers

his place in his outline. Thus, he folded his notes and placed them in his pocket and proceeded to speak the word from memory.[13]

His preaching was well received by those in attendance, though a neighbor who was there asked him if he remembered fiddling with the buttons on his jacket while he was preaching. Having not realized it, the fellow proceeded to tell him he had buttoned and unbuttoned his jacket fifty-seven times.[14] He was already learning the value of criticism as well as encouragement in the work of an evangelist.[15]

Within a short time, he began to be called upon for speaking appointments. His first meeting was at Dogtown, a little congregation that met a few miles northwest of Carbon Hill.[16]

The summer of 1917 was filled with opportunities to travel to different sections in the area where gospel meetings were taking place. One in particular was under way in Eldridge, about seven miles northwest of their home. Like most churches in the area, it was small. But, a good group came out to hear John T. Lewis who was preaching in the meeting.

A Tennessean by birth, John Thomas Lewis (1876-1967) was a graduate of the Nashville Bible School. He moved to the city of Birmingham after graduation and had been there a little over ten years.[17] He was credited as having started over fifty congregations of churches of Christ in the course of his tenure in Jefferson County, Alabama.[18]

John T. Lewis

Attending each session, the power of the gospel was realized among the hearers, especially Matilda. At twenty-three years of age, she had already experienced many changes in her life that were quite different from her youth. Since childhood, she had stayed true to her Baptist roots. However, her husband had for several years been a member of a different church. While she wanted to honor her husband and support him by attending with him, she had been true to her own commitments. But, much had happened in the last couple of years. She had given birth to two children, maintained her duties on the farm, narrowly escaped death in the storm that took most of her earthly possessions, witnessed her husband make a crucial transition toward preaching, and the question still at issue for her was, am I saved? Truly saved? The preaching of the Birmingham minister challenged the answer to those questions in a thought-provoking way like never before. She and Gus had discussed it in the past, but he never pressured her to make a change. This was something she had to determine on her own. With each passing lesson, the message knocked heavily upon the door of her belief system, and it was found wanting; upon her heart, and it was now softening.

At the close of the meeting, Matilda was troubled deeply within herself. The walls of resistance fading away with such Scriptural confrontation, she waited for the next visit of brother Wheeler at Iron Mountain Schoolhouse. There she responded to the invitation of Christ and was baptized by brother Wheeler in the same place where her husband had been immersed several years previous.[19]

Such jubilation! Such excitement! The family was now united in Christ. A clear direction was now firm, and solidarity now in place for both Gus and Matilda Nichols to change the world for Christ.

Many years later, Gracie related her memories of her mother's baptism. Though very young, she remembered seeing her mother being baptized, and recalled being fearful that she might drown when she was submerged below the water. Some time passed when one day Gracie and Vodie were left playing on the front porch of their house. Their mother had strictly forbidden the girls from leaving the porch while she went down and worked in the garden. As they were looking around for something to do, a hen came up on the porch. Following her were her baby chicks. The girls got the idea to go and get the pan of drinking water on the shelf at the end of the porch. In it was a drinking ladle, just the perfect size to serve as a baptistery for the prospects of saving the unsuspecting little chicks. Some time passed when their mom returned from the garden to check on the girls. When she got to the porch she asked the girls what they had been doing with those little chicks? Gracie piped up, "We were practicing baptizing, and when we would baptize one it would want to take a nap, and we would just let it." Unbeknownst to the girls, the chicks did not survive their well-intended acts of kindness.[20]

Over the years, the girls remembered many precious things. They loved to tell that when they were little they would hear the song at church, "I will give you grace and glory." They thought they were singing, "I will give you Gracie and Vodie."

BUT NOT ON SUNDAY NIGHT
By Gus Nichols

I love the church that Jesus built,
And know that it is right.
I go there every Sunday morn,
But not on Sunday night.

I love to sing the songs of God;
Such worship must be right.
And this I do on Sunday morn,
But not on Sunday night.

I love to hear the Gospel too,
It gives me pure delight.
I hear it every Sunday morn,
But not on Sunday night.

And may God bless our preacher too,
And give him power and might,
And put a sinner in my place
At worship Sunday night.

It's true, the church can save the world,
If good light shines bright;
I help it every Sunday morn,
But not on Sunday night.

Yes, all of us must one day die,
I hope I'll be doing right;
So may I die on Sunday morn,
But not on Sunday night![21]

ENDNOTES

1 Ethel Armes, *The Story of Coal and Iron In Alabama*, Birmingham: Published under the auspices of the Chamber of Commerce, 1910, p. 488.

2 Ibid, p. 497.

3 Ibid.

4 Allen Pettus, "Gus Nichols 1 of 14 Preachers In Family; Group Has Baptized 17,956 in 182 Years," *Nashville Tennessean*, Sometime in 1951. Note: (Exact date unknown – article found in 6th Avenue church of Christ scrapbook. He conducted a meeting at Charlotte Avenue church in Nashville, Tennessee in the fall of 1951. The specific dates are unknown.) In the article Gus related the history of the hard first years of his preaching.

5 Flavil Nichols, "Gus Nichols As A Father," *Gospel Advocate*, 25 March 1976, pp. 196-97.

6 Dr. J. D. Thomas, "Interview with Hardeman Nichols," Unpublished, at Freed-Hardeman College, 4 February 2003, p. 4.

7 Note: These statistics were gleaned from records kept by the National Weather Service. The web address for the Southern Regional Headquarters is http://www.srh.noaa.gov.

8 Gus Nichols, "Try Beginning Again," *The World Evangelist*, November 1974, p. 5.

9 Dr. J. D. Thomas, "Interview with Hardeman Nichols," Unpublished, at Freed-Hardeman College, 4 February 2003, p. 4.

10 Obituary, *Daily Mountain Eagle*, November 18, 1975; reposted in *Words of Truth*, 21 November 1975, Volume 11, Number 26, p. 2.

11 Gus Nichols, *Speaking The Truth In Love*, Sixteen Full-Length Sermons and Three Lectures To Bible Classes presented by Gus Nichols: In a meeting at Lamesa, Texas, 4-11 March 1956, pp. 156-57.

12 Ibid.

13 Note: In some of the reporting on the first time Gus Nichols preached, the date of June 1916 has appeared in several publications. The June 1917 date is preferred as Flavil later wrote, "Dad began preaching in 1917, two years before I was born." *Gospel Advocate*, March 25, 1976, p. 198. Also, in *Words of Truth*, November 15, 1985, on page 1, he gave the second Sunday in June 1917 in his article entitled, "In Memoriam: Gus Nichols." Over the course of Gus' preaching career, memorizing his sermons, and presenting them without notes became his way of delivery. Sometimes he jotted down his main points so as get the order in his head, and to make sure he covered everything he intended throughout the course of his sermon. Then, putting it in his pocket, he preached "from the overflow" of his vast knowledge of the subject.

14 Flavil Nichols, "In Memoriam: Gus Nichols" *Words of Truth*, 15 November 1985, p. 2.

15 Note: Gus earned $5.00 for his first year of preaching according to Basil Overton in Mule Musings Series, *The World Evangelist*, September 1997, p. 8.

16 Larry Whitehead, "Gus Nichols: Gospel Preacher 1892-1975," in the regular column, "They Being Dead Yet Speak," *Alabama Restoration Journal*, Volume 1, Number 4, p. 7.

17 Otis Castleberry, *He Looked For A City: A Biography of John T. Lewis*. p. 2. Note: He came to work at the end of 1907 with the Fox Hall church in Birmingham. Later the church was known as West End, and still later after his death, the Palisades church of Christ.

18 Ibid. p. 12.

19 William Woodson, "Dedication To Gus Nichols." *Freed-Hardeman Lectureship*, 1976 pp. 2-5.

20 Telephone interview with Hardeman Nichols the 3rd of November 2009.

21 Gus Nichols, "Not On Sunday Night," The *Words of Truth*, 3 July 1997, p. 4. Note: Several adaptations of this poem have appeared over the years in different publications. It is uncertain as to who authored the first variation.

7

Striving For Masteries

And if a man also strive for masteries, yet is he not crowned, except he strive lawfully.
—Paul, 2 Timothy 2:5

On the 2nd of April 1917, President Woodrow Wilson asked the U.S. Congress for a declaration of war against Germany, and on the 6th it became official. The nation was at war.

It was the 5th of June when Gus Nichols appeared before the Walker County Draft Board to register for military service. His registration card shows that he was 25 years of age. He claimed exemption from service on the grounds of having a wife and two children dependents. He was described as being tall, slender, with brown eyes and black hair. His occupation or trade was listed as "Farming." He signed his name, Bunion Augustus Nichols.[1]

Within ten days of the storm that turned their world upside down, the Nichols family moved to a farm about seven miles northwest of the Howard community in the vicinity of Eldridge. Their address was RFD, No.1, Eldridge, Alabama.[2]

WWI Draft Card

Throughout the summer and latter part of the year, Gus spent his time studying the Bible and reading books that could help him firm up his ability to defend the faith. He made a decision to spend at least five hours a day in personal study. Such a regime demanded getting up well before daylight and studying the Bible along with all the scholarly helps he could find. This was his course for the remainder of his life, with very few exceptions.[3]

The preacher at Winfield at the time was W. W. Gaddis (1885-1968).[4] He spent time studying with Gus on the purpose of baptism. Also, a brother

Russell, "who had studied under F. D. Srygley (1856-1900)[5] at Mars Hill, helped him concerning Holy Spirit baptism, instrumental music, and other controversial subjects." [6]

Meanwhile, he continued his weekly grind in the coal mines. Between 1917 and 1919, when not farming, or preaching, the mines were where he devoted most of his time. Once, while working in the mines, he lost his way. Years later, in a sermon, he recalled it in view of illustrating the horrible existence of being outside of a relationship with Christ,

> O! It is a horrible feeling to find that you are lost! I also was lost in a coal mine once. My light went out as I was going in by myself following an old man-way, and I could not get my carbide lamp to burn again. I had to feel my way for perhaps a quarter of a mile in the blackness of darkness. How I would have welcomed a guide and a light! I was in danger of straying off into some old worked-out entry where there was no fresh air, and where the top would be falling in, and where I might starve to death. The joy I had when I finally found my way to the trap-door into the main entry where there were beautiful electric lights was surpassed only by my salvation from my sin when I obeyed the gospel, and, like the Eunuch, went on my way rejoicing.[7]

Years later, he recalled going to work one Saturday when all the workers were called together by the foreman and told they had to work the following day. As the men began to disband to start the day's activities, Gus went to his boss and told him that he had other responsibilities on Sunday that demanded his time. To this, he was told that if he did not show up for work at the appointed time he need never come back. Walking away with a deep sunken feeling in his heart, he went about his assigned tasks. What was he going to do? Sunday is the Lord's Day, and the brethren would be counting on him to preach. In the hours that followed, he prayed fervently that the Lord would find a way to get him to his Sunday appointments. At one point late in the day he and his foreman crossed paths when as if out of the blue, he was told not to worry about coming in on Sunday as one who was supposed to be away had decided he could work after all. This was always a sign to Gus that the Lord was truly making a way for him.[8]

F. D. Srygley

A good crop was planted in the spring of 1918, and preaching opportunities continued to avail themselves over the course of the year.

The more Gus had the chance to preach, the more he desired to give himself totally to the work of evangelism. Both he and his brother Charlie were preaching where they could. Not far behind them was younger brother Carey.

During the summer, Matilda learned that she was to have another child early in the following year. The fateful day arrived on the 2nd of February 1919 when a little boy entered the Nichols home. The name given him represented all the Nichols knew to be good among those who proclaimed the message of Christ during that day. Not only was the man from Halls Valley, Georgia, a great preacher, but Flavil Hall was also known as a great singer, composer of songs, editor of hymn books, and teacher of singing schools. He was the consummate preacher of the day in their thinking, and one worthy to adorn the identity of their first-born son, Flavil Hall Nichols.

Flavil Hall

By the spring of 1919, both Charlie and Gus were in full-swing seeking opportunities to preach where they could. The March issue of the *Firm Foundation* carried the report, "Brother Charlie Nichols of Carbon Hill, Alabama writes that he will do a considerable amount of mission work this year. Brother Nichols should be encouraged in this work by the churches."[9] Three issues later the first report known to have been sent in by Gus appeared. It said,

> Brother Gus Nichols writes from R. F. D. 1, Eldridge, Alabama date of March 11: "I want to hold gospel meetings from July to November. Any congregation wanting my services in such meetings, or knowing where I may hold one or more mission meetings, please write me at once. I have arranged to preach at about seven different places monthly, some of them are mission places. Brethren, let us see that the gospel is preached wherever man is found."[10]

The load between the congregations began to be shared evenly between the two brothers. By late May, Charlie was preaching three Sundays a month at Galloway, Dun Schoolhouse, at Berea down in Fayette County, and was looking for an additional place to fill his monthly circuit.[11] In July, he held his first debate with a Nazarene by the name of a Mr. Plunkett at Eldridge on the subject of "Sinless Perfection."[12]

The first additions Gus sent in appeared in the pages of the *Firm Foundation* later in the summer after some work he had done in Fayette County. Stated was the good news, "Brother Gus Nichols of Eldridge, Alabama reports seven baptisms at New River, where he has preached several times recently."[13]

ALABAMA CHRISTIAN COLLEGE

About twenty-five miles south of Eldridge, the little Fayette County town of Berry is situated on the old Georgia-Pacific Railway line between Birmingham, Alabama and Columbus, Mississippi. There was a school there run by the brethren called Alabama Christian College.

Opening its doors in June 1912, the college was operated under a board of trustees. The founding president was G. A. "Gus" Dunn, Sr. (1876-1967).[14] He continued as head of the school through the end of the 1914-1915 school year. The following year, J. Paul Hanlin (1884-1972) served as president, but by the fall of 1916, another Texas preacher and educator, Hal P. McDonald (1879-1959), became president, and maintained that position for the duration of the school's existence.[15] The institution offered training on several levels, and included a wide-range of academics.

> The College was composed of a Primary, Intermediate, Academic, Collegiate, Music, Expression and Art Department. Emphasis was placed on the teaching of the Bible with every student attending a daily class. In the advanced classes, Latin, Greek, French and Philosophy were offered along with English, History and a complete business course. Tuition ranged from $12 for Primary to $20 for College, per term.[16]

The influx of Texas influence continued under McDonald's leadership when he introduced annual lectureship programs and protracted meetings, inviting men like, J. D. Tant (1861-1941), Joe S. Warlick (1866-1941), Foy E. Wallace, Jr. (1896-1979), L. R. Wilson (1896-1986), and others.[17]

For some time, the Nichols boys had been discussing the need for more education. John T. Lewis (1876-1967), who was instrumental in the founding of the school, had suggested to Gus that attending would be good for him and his brother.[18]

Charlie married a young lady by the name of Lillie Hayes a few years earlier. They had given birth to a son, Curtis, who died. A daughter, Opal, was born the 21st of October the previous year.[19] Deciding to go at least a year, they moved to Berry and rented a house in time for the October 1919 session.[20]

When Gus and Matilda packed up the family to move to Berry, all their earthly possessions were able to be fit into a single wagon. With their plowing mule, Kate, pulling, and their milking cow following behind, they made the slow two-day journey to their new home, spending one night with Matilda's sister along the way. Arriving in Berry, a house was rented where they stayed for a couple of months, when severe leaking in the roof caused them to have to move into another rental house. Finally, they were able to purchase seven acres on the east side of town on Fenton Street, at the end of the road leading behind the building of the Berry church of Christ.[21]

Most of the acreage was used for planting crops, but Gus built a house and a barn on the property.[22] The house was a wooden structure with a central dog-trot type "hall-way" in the middle with two rooms on each side.[23] And, after surviving the 1917 tornado, he also dug a storm cellar large enough to protect all the members of his family. Shelves were added all around serving double duty as a fruit cellar.[24] When he built the house, he determined to build something that would be long-lasting and secure. In previous years, he had worked for a time as a lineman on the railroad and had learned how to preserve crossties with creosote. Made of distilled coal tar, creosote "has an odor that is far from pleasing."[25] So, beginning at the rear of the house, he painted it with the preserving liquid. While this served to both paint and preserve, it added a most unappreciated and disturbing smell to those who lived inside the dwelling for quite some time. For many years after the children recalled how funny their dad was for painting the house with creosote, though at the time it was anything but a laughing matter.

This is but a taste of the ingenuity in this young farmer. His clever skills helped when Frank Baker (1871-1928),[26] a teacher, preaching associate, and dear friend, needed part of a hill flattened for the building of his house. Gus rigged a mule-drawn slip-scoop to flatten the area. Later, when needing to carve out a drive to his own house he used the same technique.[27]

He built his own refrigerating system by constructing an icebox. He lined it with galvanized metal to prevent rusting, and packed sawdust between the metal and the outer shell. When the ice wagon came around, he would buy an ice-block, put it in the icebox, and it kept things refrigerated for several days.[28]

Stories were more than a few through the years about Kate, the trusty mule who brought the family to Berry. She led Gus down many a row, on the acreage that backed up to the railway line that followed the back of the property. She helped Gus with his preparation and delivery of sermons. How? Perhaps, she assisted in more ways than one might imagine. One way was in the field. Early on in his development as a preacher, he carried a pocket New Testament in his bib-overalls. When out plowing with Kate, he often began a row by stopping for a moment to read a passage of Scripture. Then, while Kate pulled the plow down to the end of the field, Gus repeated the passage over and over in his mind until he finally memorized it. At the end of the row, he would stop and check

Alabama Christian College

his memory against the Word and read another verse before turning her around and heading back down the next row. In this way Kate helped him to learn the Scriptures.[29]

Another way she assisted is by pulling a buckboard-type wagon to and from places Gus preached. When the family was in town, they were able to walk to the church building, which was at the end of their street. But, when Gus was preaching over at New River, Pea Ridge, up at Iron Mountain Schoolhouse, and the like, Kate was called upon to deliver him to his meetings and back home. Sometimes late at night after preaching, they traveled down many a long and lonely lane, just the two of them in the moonlight; the noise of crickets, the creaking of the wooden wheels, and the sound of the occasional stream along the way. After a long day's work and night of preaching, and still several miles away from home, Gus would say, "Home Kate! Take us home!" Then, he would fall asleep only to be awakened as Kate stopped in front of the home place.[30]

The summer after the first term of school brought opportunity to widen his field of influence in preaching. Reports to the *Firm Foundation* included work in a meeting at Friendship, in Steens, Mississippi, with no additions, but plenty of interest.³¹ During the month of August, he held meetings at New River in Fayette County, at Kingsville, about eight miles north of Kennedy over in Lamar County, and at Berea near Glen Allen. He reported forty-three baptisms and nine restorations in these meetings.³²

Potentially, the first mention of Gus Nichols in the pages of the *Gospel Advocate* appeared at the end of the summer in a report from C. C. Tomlin,

> Kennedy, August 17. -Our six-days' meeting with the church of Christ at Liberty, which resulted in fourteen baptisms, closed last Friday at the water's edge. Brother Gus Nichols did the preaching. We had two services each day, with dinner on the ground. Good crowds attended. Everyone seemed to rejoice at the success. The church was strengthened in other ways.³³

By the time the October 1920 session of Alabama Christian College began, Gus Nichols had reported in brotherhood papers of over fifty baptisms and many restorations during the summer and fall meeting season. Schooling was a change in effort, but the pace with classes and fulfilling assignments stayed the same. Gus was offered a wide range of study in his college classes, including business, typing, English, debate, and of course Bible. Some of his children's earliest memories included their daddy sitting at the kitchen table learning to type on an old manual typewriter where he practiced "typing with a metal cover over the keyboard, but they also observed that on occasion he could not resist 'peeping' for a particularly stubborn letter."³⁴

That year the college advertised in a circular listing "him and his brother Charlie as being on opposite sides in a debate on giving the vote to women. Gus Nichols was in the negative."³⁵ As women had received the right to vote in the passing of the Nineteenth Amendment to the U.S. Constitution the previous August, it would appear that Charlie's arguments carried the day.

Just about the time classes began, Matilda delivered their fourth child, Bertha, on the 1st of October. Their third daughter, she was a precious addition to a growing family.

As the year drew to an end, the family saw itself as most blessed with health and happiness. A father was maturing, a preacher was preparing, and a brotherhood was being introduced to a man named Gus Nichols.

ENDNOTES

1 Registrar's Report, Precinct 25, Walker County Draft Board, 5 June 1917.

2 Ibid.

3 Reports of Gus Nichols studying between four and six hours a day have appeared from various sources over the years. Most accept that five was the actual average of daily hours of study. Willard Collins in *Gospel Advocate*, 1961, 2 March issue, p. 136, said that it was five hours. Again in 1968, in the 11 January issue, p.26 he wrote of Gus Nichols, "The author has been averaging five hours a day in Bible study for fifty years." In the *2000 Florida School of Preaching Lectures*, p. 54, Tom Holland, on the subject of a preacher's need to grow, noted that Gus Nichols studied five hours per day, and Franklin Camp studied six hours a day." In the *2006 FSOP Lectures*, J. Brooks Boyd, Jr. said, "This writer recalls Franklin Camp's explanation for spending the first seven hours of his day (from 4:00 to 11:00 a.m.) in personal Bible study. He knew that Gus Nichols studied for six hours every day, and that if it took Gus Nichols that much time to be able to preach as he did, it would take Franklin Camp at least seven." Neil Anderson, under title, "Trailblazers" in the November 1999 *Gospel Advocate*, p.3, said, that Gus Nichols studied four hours per day. Hugo McCord, in his article "Gus Nichols," appearing in *Hammer and Tongs*, January-February 1999, p. 4, said that he studied "four hours per day."

4 William Wesley Gaddis (1885-1968) was born and raised in Marion County, Alabama. He preached the gospel in several places in Alabama, Tennessee and Texas. Reports of his local and evangelistic labors appeared in both the *Firm Foundation* and the *Gospel Advocate*. At Carbon Hill in the second decade of the 20th century, he lived at Cordova in 1925, at Waterloo, Alabama in 1927, at Florence, Alabama in 1928, and at Town Creek, Alabama between 1933 and 1934. In 1938 he preached at the author's home congregation, South Haleyville in Winston County, Alabama. Between 1938 and 1941 he preached in Combes, Texas. He moved from there to Selmer, Tennessee, and back to Vernon, Alabama by 1951. His last days were in the northern Walker County, Alabama town of Nauvoo. He passed from this life 31 January 1968. His remains were planted in the Fernwoods Cemetery. He was a long and endeared friend to the Nichols family, and to the Lord's church in Northwest Alabama.

5 Fletcher Douglas Srygley (1856-1900) was from Rock Creek in Colbert County, Alabama. He was a student at Mars Hill with C. F. Russell. Srygley was a capable gospel preacher, prolific writer, and served for a time on the editorial staff of the *Gospel Advocate* before his untimely death in 1900. He was laid to rest in Nashville, Tennessee, at Mt. Olivet Cemetery.

6 William Woodson, Freedom: Heritage, Accomplishments, and Prospects in Christ, *Freed-Hardeman College Lectures*, Henderson Tennessee, 1976, "Dedication To Gus Nichols," p. 4. Note: Woodson only referred to these men by their last names. In his book, *Larimore and His Boys*, F. D. Srygley entered the name of C. F. Russell, who was a student at Mars Hill. C. F. Russell may have been the preacher Woodson was recalling in his dedication. There was a Cornelius Frank Russell (1868-1943) who died in Killen, Alabama near Florence,

and was buried in the Harrison Cemetery. It is assumed that this was the preacher who influenced young Gus Nichols.

7 *Speaking The Truth In Love*, Sixteen Full-Length Sermons and Three Lectures To Bible Classes presented by Gus Nichols: In a meeting at Lamesa, Texas, 4-11 March 1956, p. 184.

8 Note: Story related to the author in 2015 by John Ancil Jenkins as having heard from the lips of Gus Nichols.

9 Charlie Nichols, "News And Notes," *Firm Foundation*, 25 March 1919, p. 4.

10 Gus Nichols, *Firm Foundation*, 15 April 1919, p. 4.

11 Charlie Nichols, *Firm Foundation*, 3 June 1919, p. 4.

12 Ibid., 8 July 1919, p. 4.

13 Gus Nichols, "News and Notes," *Firm Foundation*, 26 August 1919, p. 4.

14 Note: Gustus Albert "G. A." "Gus" Dunn (1876-1967) was born, educated, and did some of his earliest preaching in and around Readyville, Tennessee. However, he moved to Texas in 1904 to preach in Cleburne. In 1907 he moved back to Memphis, Tennessee where he lived at the time of his call to Highland Home College south of Montgomery, Alabama. Later, after leaving Alabama Christian College in 1915, he moved to preach for the Central church of Christ in Houston, Texas, and lived the remainder of his life in that state. Though technically he could be called a Tennessee preacher, he spent most of his years in Texas, and was long recognized as a Texas preacher. After his death in 1967, burial followed in the Laurel Land Cemetery in Dallas, Texas.

15 Herbert Newell & Jeanie Newell, eds., *History Of Fayette County, Alabama*, Southern Historical Press, 1960, p. 105.

16 Larry Whitehead, ed., *Alabama Restoration Journal*, Volume 1, Number 1, 1 November 2005, p. 2. Note: Special thanks to Earl Kimbrough who painted the likeness of the ACC school building and gave permission for its use.

17 A. M. Plyler, *Historical Sketches of the Churches of Christ in Alabama*, p. 58.

18 Larry Whitehead, *Alabama Restoration Journal*, Volume 1, Number 4, Nov. 1, 2006, p. 7.

19 Aubrine A. Nichols and Dessie Ree Nichols, *Will and Lizzie Nichols Family Roster*, Unpublished document, 1995.

20 "News And Notes," *Firm Foundation*, 14 October 1919, p. 4.

21 Basil Overton, "Mule Musings And Other Matters," *The World Evangelist*, September 1997, p. 8.

22 Note: The Global Positioning Satellite Location of the Berry House, D.d. 33.66201,-87.596046.

23 Conversation with Flavil Nichols, March 22, 2011. Flavil recalled the house had four steps leading to the "hall-way" in the middle where he and the other children played many games when he was a little boy.

24 Flavil Nichols, "Gus Nichols As A Father," *Gospel Advocate*, 25 March 1976, p. 197.

25 Earl Kimbrough, "Gus Nichols' Home At Berry, Alabama," *Alabama Restoration Journal*, Volume 2, Number 1, 1 February 2007, p. 22.

26 Frank Baker (1871-1928) was a Missouri-born preacher. He spent many of his early years evangelizing in Texas, Oklahoma and Arkansas. He moved to Berry, Alabama from Village, Arkansas in late 1911 to assist in the planting of Alabama Christian College, and to evangelize in the region. In the mid 1920s, he began making evangelistic trips to Florida, but due to a development of high blood pressure, his health declined, and he had to return to Berry. After several months of ill health, he suffered a massive heart attack, and perished 22 October 1928. His remains were laid to rest in the Berry Cemetery.

27 Flavil Nichols, "In Memoriam: Gus Nichols," *Words of Truth*, November 1985, p. 2.

28 Flavil Nichols, "Gus Nichols As A Father," *Gospel Advocate*, 25 March 1976, p. 197.

29 Basil Overton, "Mule Musings And Other Matters," *The World Evangelist*, September 1997, p. 8.

30 Ibid. Note: Basil Overton referred to this in his article. But, I still recall as a teenager, sitting around the table in our kitchen with my parents and Flavil Nichols, not long after his father died, telling us the story about old Kate bringing his daddy home after those meetings in the early days.

31 "News And Notes," *Firm Foundation*, 27 July 1920, p. 4.

32 Ibid., Three straight issues, 10, 17, and 24 of August.

33 C. C. Tomlin, *Gospel Advocate*, 26 August 1920, p. 842.

34 William Woodson, "Freedom: Heritage, Accomplishments, and Prospects in Christ," *Freed-Hardeman College Lectures*, Henderson Tennessee, 1976, "Dedication To Gus Nichols," p. 4.

35 Ibid.

8

Inspiration From The West

He that hath pity upon the poor lendeth unto the Lord; And that which he hath given will He pay him again.
—Solomon, Proverbs 19:17

The Texas connection with Alabama churches is worthy of far more than a passing notion. There was a steady flow of input from Texas preachers at the turn of and during the first thirty years of the twentieth century. To appreciate the fuller picture of western influence, the proverbial expression, "what goes around comes around" enters the mind in explaining the more than apparent symbiotic relationship between the two states.

Before Alabama reached statehood in 1819, some early converts of Kentucky reformer, Barton W. Stone (1771-1844), moved into the northern district. Former Indian Scout, and later Christian preacher, Benjamin Lynn (1750-1814) and his wife, Hannah, entered Madison County with their two daughters and their families, Rachel and Marshall D'Spain, and Esther (1780-1852) and John Chisholm (1775-1847) in 1810.[1] When both parents died in 1814, the children began thinking of a westward move.

Barton W. Stone

Fort Hampton, set at the edge of Indian lands to prevent white settlers from entering the region, was abandoned in 1816 after the Chickasaw Indians ceded their lands in the Shoals to the United States. This allowed the Chisholms to settle in what is now north Florence, while the D'Spains continued to the northwest corner of Lauderdale County. In Waterloo, they were joined by the families of Ephraim Moore (1784-1859), Mansell Matthews (1806-1891), and many others, to make up a sizeable congregation of the church of Christ in that region.[2]

The westward pull of early pioneer days led this group to move in that direction in the fall of 1835. Traveling in wagon-train formation, they were led as far as Memphis by Davy Crockett (1786-1836) and his Tennessee Volunteers. Crossing the Mississippi and Red River to enter the Lone Star State, this body of believers were among the earliest New Testament

Christians on Texas soil. Arriving at Clarkesville on the 17th of January 1836, the settlers began influencing their neighbors for a return to the Scriptures for authority in religion.[3] For the next fifty years the cause of Christ spread throughout the state.

THE FIRM FOUNDATION

When the *Firm Foundation* was established by Austin McGary (1846-1928) in Austin, Texas in 1884, almost immediately it was being promoted east of the Mississippi.[4] Reports were soon sent in from evangelistic labors in Alabama, Tennessee and Georgia. In time, invitations for western preachers to come east gave rise to subscriptions to the paper.

The presence of this Texas journal also gave rise to concern over the subject of salvation, in particular the acceptability of denominational baptisms. David Lipscomb's (1831-1917) paper, the *Gospel Advocate*, a time-honored tradition among Christians in the South since 1855, began to show signs of weakness in Austin McGary's thinking, and the feelings were spreading. Lipscomb believed and taught that if a person had been immersed in the belief that he or she was obeying God, it was sufficient for acceptance into the fellowship of believers, even if they did not acknowledge at the time of their immersion that their baptism was for the forgiveness of their sins. McGary did not agree.

Austin McGary

It was Lipscomb's "shaking them in"[5] theology that, in part, sparked the beginning of McGary's paper, and in short order, found a place for discussion in many issues for over fifteen years. Written debates between McGary and Lipscomb on the subject were hashed out in both journals in the 1890s. The *Firm Foundation* printed a written debate between McGary and James A. Harding (1848-1922), who held to Lipscomb's view.

Austin McGary succeeded in making his point in Alabama. In the summer of 1889, associate editor Elijah Hansbrough (1824-1896) and his wife conducted a preaching tour through North Alabama and Tennessee emphasizing, as part of his preaching, the essentiality of baptism for the remission of sins.[6] The paper, along with Hansbrough's visit, served to make its mark, as most congregations of churches of Christ today hold to McGary's thinking on the subject. Tuscumbia, Colbert

David Lipscomb

County preacher, L. C. Chisholm, summarized McGary's teaching when reporting in the *Firm Foundation*,

> I believe there are preachers that preach Acts 2:38 who do not believe what they preach. Actions speak louder than words. The gospel is God's power to save those that believe the gospel; it will save no others. Jesus said, "He that believeth (the gospel) and is baptized shall be saved." The gospel requires men to be baptized for the remission of sins. There are scores of men who will preach Acts 2:38 and at the close of the sermons invite and accept men and women into full fellowship in the church of God as pardoned whom they know were never baptized for pardon of sins, much less believe it. They will take those who say positively that they never heard the gospel before in their lives. If they have been immersed is all they ask. Can such preachers believe baptism is for the remission of sins? Surely not.[7]

E. J. Penegar (1875-1961) of Cordova, Walker County, added, "Brethren, let us be true to the teaching of the gospel and be consistent. If we receive sectarian baptism, let us receive their faith and confession also."[8]

TEXAS PREACHERS IN ALABAMA

In time, western preachers heeded the invitations, coming to Alabama for debates, protracted meetings, and for educational purposes. C. R. Nichol (1876-1961) of Clifton, Texas[9] held the first of eleven debates with Baptist champion Benjamin Marcus Bogard (1868-1951) in Millport, Alabama in April 1908.[10]

In 1910, G. A. Dunn, Sr. (1876-1967) came to Alabama to serve as president of Highland Home College in Montgomery County.[11] Founded out of the old Strata Academy by J. M. Barnes (1836-1913) in 1856, it had served the lower part of the state for many years as an educational institution. Two years later, he was invited to take the presidency of the new Alabama Christian College in Berry, a position he held until the end of 1915, as has been noted.

Other Texas preachers, Frank Baker (1868-1928) and J. B. Nelson (1877-1940), joined brother Dunn in building up the school. They also did much preaching in the area when not teaching. For instance, J. B. Nelson conducted a meeting in Oakman, Walker County, Alabama in April 1913 reporting it as, "the place where we made a hard fight against the innovators."[12] The six main points of his first lesson entitled, "The New Testament Church," were there enlisted. Frank Baker lived, worked, and preached throughout the area during the entire life of the college. His family lived in Berry and had a home just across the road from Gus and Matilda Nichols.

J. D. Tant (1861-1941),[13] a Texas preacher who had early declared his support of McGary on the baptism issue, answered the call for help in Alabama in deliberate fashion. He made several trips to Berry and other Alabama towns for debating and extended meeting work. He held a debate with Primitive Baptist, C. H. Cayce (1871-1945) in August 1920 in Fayette County. It was stated, "Cayce is considered the strongest Primitive Baptist in America, but Brother Tant gained a great victory for the truth."[14]

Tant openly espoused the need for churches to take responsibility for educating its members for the ministry. In so doing, he wrote often in both the *Firm Foundation* and the *Gospel Advocate* of his concerns over the "Church College" concept. As vocal as he was, he shunned not to come to the aid of works when they were in trouble and helped get them on what he believed to be the best possible track.

G. A. Dunn

FINANCIAL TROUBLES IN THE SCHOOL

When Gus Nichols entered his third year at Alabama Christian College in the fall of 1921, the school was in deep financial crisis. School president, and Texan, Hal P. McDonald (1879-1959), made several appeals in brotherhood papers for students and financial support. The previous year, he wrote a lengthy report on the college in the *Firm Foundation*, and shared a dream of building another campus in a different location where he could "accommodate 100 students," if he could just get the support.[15] Some time later, McDonald did secure a thousand acres of property several miles north of Berry on Ford's Mountain, where he built a school building, calling it "The Temple Of Knowledge."[16] The enterprise never truly got off the ground.

The invitation was extended to J. D. Tant to come and preach a meeting at Berry in the early part of 1922. On the 1st of February, Frank Baker wrote, "Our meeting with J. D. Tant to lead in the strong drive for the school and to strengthen the things that remain, will begin February 26th."[17] In his typical sharp and aggressive way, Tant had his own view of what the meeting was to accomplish. He wrote,

> It seems that the desire of this meeting is not only to arouse an interest in the church to teach the gospel in Berry, but it is to arouse a general interest among the people all over Alabama and see if we shall build up a first-class educational institution in Alabama where our boys and girls who go from home to school and have religious influences and Bible training while preparing

themselves for usefulness in life; or shall we spend our money to build barns for our horses, sheds for our cows, and pens for our hogs, and let our children drift on the infidel wave that now permeates many of our leading schools.

Brethren, there are enough of your boys and girls wanting to make life a success to put four hundred students in Berry College each year, and enough money spent by my brethren for moonshine whiskey and tobacco to keep them there, and we hope to make some change for the good of all and we plead with the brethren in reach of Berry to attend the meeting and let us see what can be done.[18]

During the meeting, brother Tant made eight different recommendations that, in his thinking, could save the school. These suggestions included changes in the organization of the school so as to distance itself from any connection with the church. He went as far as to say the name "Christian" should be removed from the name of the institution, and that Bible classes should be offered but not compulsory. These measures were in view of being able to get public moneys allotted for free education. In essence, he thought it best to build a state college operated by Christian people, but not by the church.

J. B. Nelson

The suggestions had a practical flavor to them, but in the long-run proved too little, too late. Money was still owed on the school building, even though trustee and financier, J. C. Shepherd (1895-1949), was willing to forgive a $16,000 debt on the schoolhouse and grounds if a girl's dormitory were to be built by the Board and the Berry congregation.[19]

As of April, reaction to the meeting was still very positive, and the hopes for the school very strong. Frank Baker, taking a therapeutic approach to Tant's capabilities reported,

Our home work is growing, and we expect to continue to grow. If your congregation is on the sick list and in a manner dead, send for J.D. Tant, if it is wide awake send for him anyway. He will do you good. Berry is blessed with five gospel preachers, a good house of worship, a fine school building, and we hope to have a fine school here in another year. Any brother who wants a home in a good country where he can have good health, raise everything in the vegetable line, drink the purest of water, you find all this at Berry, Alabama.[20]

A couple of issues later, Gus Nichols weighed in on the home front's effort of putting on a brave face and pressing forward. He wrote,

> The church at Berry is doing very well. We have an interesting Bible study every Wednesday night, also a class in Tant's "Bible Studies" every Lord's day night. This is in addition to the regular Lord's day service. Some of those baptized by brother Tant in our meeting will pray in public. We have several preachers here, and I believe all of them are unselfish and without prejudice.[21]

Subsequently, efforts to save the school were discarded by the end of the school year. Her president abandoned the institution when Hal P. McDonald moved to Walker County and began preaching for the Liberty Hill church south of Oakman.[22] The school property and buildings were sold to the county for the purpose of conducting a high school that continues to this day.

TIME TO PRESS ON

Thus, with the close of the 1922 school year, Gus Nichols completed his third and final year of formal training at Alabama Christian College and was unleashed upon the world to make his way. As in the days of the Messiah's ministry, the fields were "white unto harvest."[23] The thirty-year-old was already living the Lord's vision and was ready to walk through any door God opened for him and his family. Clearly, pressing forward was the right thing to do.

Preachers in that day had great challenges before them, not only to preach the unsearchable riches of Christ, but also to earn enough earthly wages to survive. For most, the challenge of balancing the two was a daily struggle.

Having worked in the Alabama vineyard for nearly a dozen years, Frank Baker summarized his concerns for the lack of help in preaching. In his own unique fashion, he saw a similarity of the preacher's struggle to that of the Levites of old when he wrote,

J. D. Tant

> Much has been said in the past year about the dearth of preachers. My observations of the cause are today very much as it was in the days of old. 'And I perceive that the portions of the Levites have not been given them: for the Levites and the singers, that did the work, were fled every one to his own field.' (Neh. 13:10). I know

of at least four gospel preachers of no mean ability all within a short distance of Berry, who have had to pattern after the Levites, some to work on the railroad as section hands and other like public work. If we are the church of the New Testament, this is not as it should be.[24]

Tim Walker (1885-1967) was a Fayette County, Alabama-born preacher, who spent most of his years in Texas, but worked in Berry and vicinity for a time. He moved to Haleyville in Winston County in early 1922 and spent several years building up the church in that area.[25] In February, he wrote to the *Gospel Advocate* of his previous year's work, and essentially explained the situation in Alabama at the time of Gus Nichols' departure from the school in Berry. He summarized,

> During the year, I conducted two mission meetings, preaching to audiences that never before heard the true story of the cross; operated a sawmill to the extent of cutting fourteen million feet of lumber; traveled over fifteen hundred miles to preach the gospel; paid more than fifty dollars in cash for the cause of Christ; received one hundred and ten dollars and seventy-five cents, a balance of sixty dollars and seventy-five cents to support my family (wife and four children) made a crop: one hundred and fifty bushels of corn and one bale of cotton; and almost completed a six-room bungalow house. I hope to go farther and preach more in 1922 than ever before. Brethren, do not be discouraged at this and other reports coming from Alabama. We have some very godly men and women in Alabama. Alabama has about three and one-half million people, only seventy-four white preachers, five colored ones, that stand for apostolic worship. Alabama stands as the third cotton state in the Union; some of the greatest railroads in the United States are in Alabama; the greatest coal fields in the South are in Southern Alabama. There are scores of cotton mills, and the greatest iron works in the South are found in Alabama. A number of other good things could be said, but this is sufficient at present. Alabama is a fertile field for the gospel. Preacher, will you please pitch your tent this way and help evangelize this great State and build up the church of God?[26]

ENDNOTES

1 George William Beattie and Helen Pruitt Beattie, "Pioneer Linns of Kentucky," *Filson Historical Club Quarterly*, John Chisholm Letter, Vol. 20, April 1946, p. 156.

2 Note: On page 380 of the December 1832, issue of the *Christian Messenger*, Barton W. Stone and John T. Johnson, editors, reported, "Also, we have sent 300 Hymn Books to Waterloo, Alabama consigned to James Witherspoon for Elders James E. and Mansel Matthews of Bartons, Lauderdale Co. Alabama." This suggested a large representation of New Testament Christians living in the northwest corner of the state of Alabama.

3 Stephen Daniel Eckstein, Jr., *History of the Churches of Christ In Texas, 1824-1950*, Austin: *Firm Foundation* Publishing House, 1963, p. 8.

4 Note: In the fourth issue of the *Firm Foundation*, listed as "Authorized Agents for the *Firm Foundation*" in Alabama were R. H. Gibson of Cedar Plains, J. D. Wade of Pruitton, and H. H. Turner of Florence. December 1884, p. 22.

5 Note: "Shaking them in" was a phrase coined by those who held to the essentiality of baptism for the remission of sins. It was a slight against those who believed that a person who had been immersed in a denomination did not need to be baptized again to come into the fellowship of the church.

6 *Firm Foundation*, 2 May 1889, p. 2, also 9 May 1889, p. 4.

7 L. C. Chisholm, "The Cause In Alabama—No. 1," *Firm Foundation*, 1904, Vol. 20, No. 42, p. 2.

8 E. J. Pinegar, *Firm Foundation*, 22 November 1904, Vol. 20, No. 47, p. 3.

9 Note: Charles Ready Nichol (1876-1961) was born in Readyville, Tennessee. It could be said that he was a Tennessee preacher, but he spent most of his life working in Texas. He was an extraordinary debater and writer. He was not related to Gus Nichols, but they were very close friends and co-workers. He died at Clifton, Texas, and is buried in the Clifton Cemetery.

10 C. R. Nichols, *C. R Nichol: A Preacher Of Righteousness*, Clifton: The Nichol Publishing Company, 1952, p. 105.

11 "G. A. Dunn, "President of Highland Home College," *Firm Foundation*, 20 December 1910, Vol. 26, No 51, p. 5.

12 J. B. Nelson, "Outlines of Sermons Preached at Oakman, Alabama," *Firm Foundation*, 27 May 1913, p. 5. Note: James Bridges Nelson was born in Readyville, Tennessee, in the same community as the Dunn family preachers and C. R. Nichol. Related to the Dunns, he preached, but was mainly supported by teaching school. He conducted meetings all over the south. He was administering the Boles Children Home in Dallas, Texas, when on April 24, 1940 he was involved in an auto crash, being hit by a train at a crossing. His body was laid to rest in Laurel Land Cemetery in Dallas.

13 Note: Jefferson Davis Tant (1861-1941) was born in Cartersville, Georgia. He was a colorful and skilled preacher in the area of debate. His tenacious spirit

was brisk in the eyes of most, but none doubted his commitment. He died 1 June 1941 and is buried in the Cleburne, Texas, Memorial Cemetery.

14 W. H. Gurganus,, *Gospel Advocate*, 16 September 1920, p. 905.

15 Hal P. McDonald, *Firm Foundation*, 20 July 1920, p. 5.

16 Larry Whitehead, "Alabama Christian College," *Alabama Restoration Journal*, Vol. 5 Issue 1, 30 April 2011, 20-22.

17 Frank Baker, *Firm Foundation*, 14 February 1922, p. 5.

18 J. D. Tant, "Work At Berry, Ala." *Gospel Advocate*, 16 February 1922, p. 163.

19 Ibid. *Gospel Advocate*, 23 March 1922, p. 284.

20 Frank Baker, *Firm Foundation*, 18 April 1922, p. 5.

21 Gus Nichols, *Firm Foundation*, 2 May 1922, p. 5.

22 Frank Baker reported in the pages of the *Gospel Advocate* on the 1st of June that he had just finished a meeting at Liberty Hill, and added, "This is now the home congregation of Brother Hal P. McDonald, a splendid man and a good gospel preacher." 1 June 1922, p. 526.

23 John 4:35, King James Version.

24 Frank Baker, *Gospel Advocate*, 5 May 1922, p. 424.

25 Note: While Tim Walker lived in Haleyville, he planted the church in Double Springs, Alabama and sometime around 1933 or 34 moved to Texas. He preached at Littlefield and for a time at Anton. He ended up in Dallas, preaching at the Page Street church in 1941. He died in March 1967, and burial followed in the Laurel Land Memorial Park in Dallas.

26 Tim Walker, "Encouraging Words From Alabama," *Gospel Advocate*, 23 February 1922, p. 186.

- 9 -

Staying The Course

But continue thou in the things which thou hast learned and hast been assured of, knowing of whom thou hast learned them.
—Paul to Timothy, 2 Timothy 3:14

The closing of Alabama Christian College was a setback for Christian education in Alabama. Joining the ranks of other such failed institutions like: the 13-year program (1868-1881) at Mountain Home School in Lawrence County operated by J. M. Pickens (1836-1881); the 16-year program (1871-1887) at Mars Hill College in Florence, conducted by T. B. Larimore (1843-1929); and the state's longest running institution of 59 years (1856-1915), Highland Home College in Montgomery County, led by J. M. Barnes (1836-1913); the school at Berry went the way of the world after its eleventh year of operation.

Gus - young preacher

As it is the duty of education not to teach all there is to know, but to equip one with the tools necessary for a lifetime of accessing information, Gus Nichols' experience at Alabama Christian set him on the road to self-discovery in a most remarkable way. Knowing there would be no classes to attend in the fall of 1922, he devoted himself to his newly acquired skills. He observed in view of the transition in status,

> I have preached more thus far than ever before having had more time to study, I am better prepared for my work than I have been in the past on account of some changes. I desire to hold some meetings somewhere the second and third Lord's day in July, and the second Lord's day in August.[1]

Other than his farming duties, he maintained a busy schedule into the fall, preaching and teaching as far north as Iron Mountain Schoolhouse, as far east as Cordova, and as far west as Bethel, near Vernon in Lamar County. In September, he reported that he had received what may have been his first invitation for a distant meeting. A Christian woman at a mission point in Batson, Texas, near Houston, wrote him saying they had about a "dozen members," had "secured a house," and were "anxious for a meeting."² Nothing ever appeared to show that he answered this call, but within a few years, people from Texas and beyond came to appreciate his talents.

J. M. Barnes

Education helped him early on to value the printed page. The Berry church served as a great testing ground for materials that had been written to enhance Bible knowledge. In addition to *Tant's Bible Studies*, Gus took advantage of the *Gospel Advocate's Advanced Quarterlies* or *Lesson Helps* by F. W. Smith (1858-1930). Toward the end of the year, the *GA* advertised the *Lesson Helps* in an article showing the written endorsements of twenty-five preachers. Gus Nichols' support appeared as,

I regard your Bible Lesson Helps as being as good as the best. I simply see no room for improvement. I have been using my influence for this literature ever since I first saw them and shall continue to do so. I will try to introduce it in as many places where they do not use "literature" as I possibly can.³

The year 1922 came to a close with the belief that he had done what he could for the cause of Christ. He had spoken publically, "two hundred and fifteen times, besides funerals and other short talks."⁴ He had baptized thirty people into Christ and assisted in the restorations of about seventy souls.

1923

With the onset of a new year came new challenges and responsibilities. There was a call from churches in Marion County looking to have a man in the field for evangelistic work. The Nichols were invited, and Gus had a great desire to heed the call, but Matilda was struggling with some health issues that prevented his ability to take the work. This was probably due to the fact that she was in the last stage of carrying her fifth child, who was due in March. Carrie was born the 11th of March. She was Gus and Matilda's fourth daughter. They had always planned to have four sons and then four daughters. Except for Flavil, it had the appearance of coming about the opposite way.

Contacting his brother Charlie, who had left ACC after a year's study for the work in Parrish, in Walker County, the offer was made to him to go to Marion County. He accepted the opportunity and moved there in February 1923. Excited to get busy for the work he wrote, "I am giving all my time to the evangelistic work in Marion County. I will visit every home in the county."[5] He even worked for the *Firm Foundation* as a field agent to increase subscriptions.[6] On the 20th of April, Charlie reported on a most hectic schedule in the first twenty days of the month in Marion saying,

J. M. Pickens

> During the month of April, I preached forty-one sermons, visited ninety-five homes and talked to three hundred forty people on Bible subjects and baptized one. My meeting at Concord school house closed Saturday night with more than five hundred present. I began last night at the Tirey school house. The mission work in this county (Marion) is in fine condition. The brethren are standing by the work. Preach the word.[7]

While Charlie seemed to be "shaking the bushes" with success in Marion county, his elder brother was bearing the burden of the loss of the school, and the toll it was taking on the Berry congregation. Putting forth a positive spin on an otherwise discouraging setting he observed,

> The church here is doing very well. However, since we lost our school (the Alabama Christian College) the interest is not what it once was. We have some fine brethren here, but some are not as faithful as they could be. A number have moved away, leaving about one hundred members, all poor and in bad condition financially, except one or two. I have never seen a church which I loved more than this one. All of our preachers have moved away, except Frank Baker and me. —Gus Nichols[8]

Staying the course of commitment provides the balm of relief often needed when struggle strikes. Maintaining a presence among the Berry congregation was important to Gus, but the burden for the lost grew in his heart with every passing day.

Other works he assisted continued to receive regular attention. In May, he went back over into Lamar County to preach his third straight meeting at Kingsville. On May 7th he wrote,

> I preached at Kingsville yesterday where we have some of the best people in the country. Probably every young man in the church has taken some part in conducting the services at some time. Three years ago, there were not more than one or two who would lead in prayer. I have held their meetings and preached

monthly for them for three years. Have baptized about thirty. They are at peace.⁹

With his reputation increasing, the summer months took Gus a little farther afield than normal. He preached meetings as far east as Antioch near Altoona, Alabama, and Cleveland, southeast of Cullman, and as far west as Macedonia, Alabama near the state line closest to Columbus, Mississippi. Closer to home, he had success at New River in Fayette County, near Oakman in Walker, and near home at Pea Ridge, Clover Hill, and Iron Mountain Schoolhouse. He reported results of all of these to the papers, and of the Clover Hill meeting he commented,

> Today I closed one of the best meetings of my life at Clover Hill with sixteen baptized and about fifty restored. This church was in a serious condition. Many of the members here were bootleggers, moonshiners and drunkards and the community and church were practically ruined by whisky and its evils. These brethren agreed to clean up the church and meet every Lord's day for worship.¹⁰

Meeting work presented many obstacles that had to be overcome. The prayer of the righteous always seeks God's providence to give the proper answer for the reason of one's hope. In one meeting Gus was preaching under a brush arbor, there were some hecklers close by repeatedly calling out to him during his sermon to produce a miracle. Such distractions were more common in those days. Finally, he answered their jeers, "No, but if you don't quit disturbing this meeting we will cast out the devils."¹¹

T. B. Larimore

Throughout the year of 1923, Gus reported around seventy baptisms, over fifty restorations, and continued his monthly circuit with Kingsville, Pea Ridge, Iron Mountain Schoolhouse, and his home church in Berry.¹²

ENDNOTES

1 Gus Nichols, *Firm Foundation*, 27 June 1922, p. 5.

2 Ibid., 12 September 1922, p. 5.

3 Gus Nichols, "Commendations of Lesson Helps," *Gospel Advocate*, 30 November 1922, p. 1137.

4 Ibid., 15 March 1923, p. 256. and *Firm Foundation*, 20 March 1923, p. 4.

5 Charlie Nichols, *Firm Foundation*, 6 March 1923, p. 5.

6 Ed., *Firm Foundation*, 20 March 1923, p. 4.

7 Charlie Nichols, *Firm Foundation*, 5 May 1923, p. 5.

8 Gus Nichols, *Gospel Advocate*, 17 May 1923, p. 494.

9 Gus Nichols, *Firm Foundation*, 22 May 1923, p. 5.

10 Ibid. 25 September 1923, p. 5.

11 Note: This story was shared with me by Bertha Blackwood October 10, 2011. It was in the form of an old clipping from a Bulletin Digest article that said the story was contributed by Henry Herron of Birmingham, Alabama.

12 Note: Gus Nichols sent in several reports to both the *Firm Foundation* and *Gospel Advocate* of meeting work results. The numbers mentioned above are cumulative from the reports sent of his work in the fall of 1923.

- 10 -

Cordova

> And a vision appeared to Paul in the night; There stood a man of Macedonia, and prayed him, saying, "Come over into Macedonia, and help us." And after he had seen the vision, immediately we endeavoured to go into Macedonia, assuredly gathering that the Lord had called us for to preach the gospel unto them.
>
> —Luke, Acts 16:9-10

Winding through the hills and valleys of Alabama is the beautiful and peaceful Black Warrior River. Named for the great Mississippi Indian chief, Tuskaloosa,[1] this 178-mile waterway begins in the Cumberland Plateau and empties into the Tombigbee River. Its continuous flow finds its way to the Gulf of Mexico at Mobile Bay. Major tributaries of the river, the Sipsey Fork from the west and Mulberry Fork from the east, merge in Walker County. One of the settlements that sits on the Mulberry Fork of the river is Cordova.[2] Located in the south-central part of the county, it served as a shipping point for river trade for many years leading up to the turn of the 20th century.

In 1898, the Nashua Manufacturing Company of Nashua, New Hampshire, opened the Indian Head Textile Mill that provided growth and revenue in the township for over sixty years.[3] With 4,649 of the county's 50,593 population in 1920, Cordova was the second largest town with just a little over a thousand less than her bigger sister-city to the north, Jasper.

The earliest activity of restoration preaching in the county took place just a few miles up the river and along the banks of the Sipsey Fork. "There was a family of Randolphs who came to Alabama from Kentucky by way of a sojourn in Warren County, Tennessee. They settled first in Morgan County, Alabama where they conducted camp meetings and established churches."[4] Elisha Randolph moved to work about sixteen miles east of Jasper in 1832 and preached in the area for about nine years. He and his sons, Jeremiah, Lorenzo Dow, and Simeon, evangelized all over the region, but considering the county to be "unhealthy,"[5] they moved down into Fayette and Lamar counties and established works there.

Baptized In 1905

At an old-fashioned baptism in August of 1905, Lee Powell and Dow Wade were baptized by Tom Evans in Wolf Creek while members of the congregation looked on. The baptism, held at Wethington Ford near the Jess Davis home, brought the two into membership of Liberty Hill Church of Christ south of Oakman. The two men still live in Walker County.

1905 - Tom Evans Baptizing

Over the next fifty years, more productive works developed in various parts of the county, like the one started on Cane Creek a few miles southeast of Jasper, and another on Lost Creek, later called the New Hope church of Christ, about six miles southwest of Jasper.[6]

Things so progressed that by "1920 there were only about fifteen small congregations in the county."[7]

There was an Alexander family who were members of the church living in Cordova in the 1890s.[8] An organized effort finally appeared around the turn of the century.[9] It was started by John Gurganus (1852-1932), his wife Amanda Evans (1855-1935), and about ten others. They began meeting in the Masonic Hall above Dr. Miller's drugstore in 1899. The work continued through 1904, when a building was built for worship. John's family along with some of the others moved down to the southern part of the county to begin a new work at Liberty Hill, later known as Central church of Christ.[10] It is worth mentioning here that several members of the Liberty Hill group were Amanda Gurganus' siblings, including her younger brother Thomas Marion "Tom" Evans (1878-1915), "a gospel preacher, who was killed in Madisonville, Texas, while reading in his home. It seems, his murderer had been infuriated over the advertisement of a gospel meeting."[11] Another brother was Jabe D. Evans (1874-1967). A great church leader in his own right, one of his daughters, Mary Evelyn Evans (1919-1978), became the wife of Pervie Nichols (1912-1984). Another daughter, Dona Evans (1903-1995), was the wife of longtime elder in the church at Jasper, C. M. Karrh (1902-1970).

However, a small group continued in the building at Cordova. One early member of the congregation, who preached in the area somewhat, was E. J. Pinegar (1875-1961).[12] He sent in several reports of his efforts as well as others in the area, like James K. Hill (1872-1908), then of Oakman, who came to preach occasionally for the small congregation in 1905.[13] A successful meeting took place in 1910 with John T. Hinds (1866-1938) doing the preaching. He reported, "The writer of these notes is now at Cordova, Ala., in a meeting. The meeting has been in progress about two weeks. Seven baptized and two restored are the results up to the present, so far as we can see."[14] Other preachers who helped in the work during those early years of development were William H. Gurganus (1872-1940), Frank Baker (1868-1928), Charlie Nichols (1892-1975), and Hal P. McDonald (1879-1959).

While living in Oakman, brother McDonald opened a School of Business in Cordova and worked in the congregation as much as possible to build it up. The school ran in ten-week intervals during the summer and the fall. A very good report by one of his associates, J. L. Hunter, was made in early 1922,

> Coming to Cordova the first of last September to teach in the Cordova School, I found a live, active congregation of Christians, numbering about one hundred and forty members. This is the result of the labors of Brethren G. C. Brewer, C. R. Nichol, John T. Hinds, John T. Lewis, Charlie Nichols, A. D. Dies, J. H. Murrell, G. A. Dunn, O. C. Lambert, and others. These people have built and seated their house of worship, almost altogether of their own means at a cost of about three thousand dollars, which teaches a good lesson to many congregations that rely too much on outside help. The contributions for 1921 was $1,173.11, which was somewhat less than in 1920. The church paid out last year $1,173.10 paying for building, seats, helping the poor, etc. This congregation is blessed with a large number of male members who take a public part in the Lord's day worship and in the prayer meeting. The prayer meeting is not nearly so well attended as it should be; however, the interest seems to be growing. Brother A. R. Hill, on his way back to David Lipscomb College, stopped over and preached two good sermons on New Year's Day. —J. L. Hunter[15]

With no regular preacher in place, the occasional visiting evangelist ignited life and increased fellowship among the brethren. With an extra bedroom open, the members vied for position to be the host family. In 1923, while enjoying a brief visit with the good brethren in Cordova, Frank Baker wrote, "It is a pleasure inexpressible to me at least to meet and enjoy the kindness of such Christian homes and especially those whom I have known so long."[16]

Early Nichols Family Photo

The growth and development of this congregation, without the benefit of a local worker, served to attract the Nichols to that work. Reports from his brother Charlie, Frank Baker, and others, led them to consider what could be if they had a worker in the community long-term. Cordova needed help, and an invitation was extended to the young family to come over and assist in their work.

Thus, at the beginning of 1924, the family committed itself to the selling of the farm in Berry and moving the thirty-mile distance to Walker County's river town. Determined to express to the world his commitment, he sent word to G. H. P. Showalter (1870-1974), "Please state in the *Firm Foundation* that I have changed my address from Berry, Alabama to Cordova, Alabama. I will do what I can for the cause here and elsewhere. The interest here is growing."[17] A similar message appeared in the *Gospel Advocate*.

Excitement immediately spread throughout the congregation as the Nichols settled near the banks of the Black Warrior. The name of God was now being proclaimed from her shores, spreading throughout the county, and into all the world. Within weeks, the message to the brotherhood was, "The interest here is growing. We are planning to build a new house, as our old one is too small."[18]

Soon after arriving, the opportunity arose for Gus to purchase his first automobile. For the price of $685, the four-door Model-T sedan had plenty of room for the whole family. It made travel to distant locations much easier, but as the rural roads were not much more than wagon tracks, it made the ride somewhat rough. In later years, the older children recalled often how that as they traveled down those little roads, occasionally, they came upon a farmer with his wagon and team. When the farmer saw them coming, he would quickly jump down from his seat and stand in front of his team to try and keep them from getting spooked while the noisy vehicle passed.[19]

Around the end of May, a Radcliffe Chautauqua[20] tent was placed in the community for its annual social activities. When the town committee determined how to best use it for spiritual encouragement, the name of Gus Nichols arose as a potential guest speaker. On Sunday night, the first of June, the tent was filled to capacity with all religious and non-religious persuasions in attendance as the young

1906 - Chautauqua Tent Meeting

preacher for the church of Christ mounted the platform. His "gospel discourse to the sinners" was entitled, "The Gospel Of Christ." He said, "I preached a full gospel and it seemed to be enjoyed by all."[21]

The summer was filled with preaching opportunities in the region as well as a little help from outside. Cordova's gospel meeting began the 7th of July and was conducted by Kentucky preacher, J. Petty Ezell (1885-1934).[22] In anticipation of his coming, Nichols taught the congregation through musical "drilling in song service, advertising, preparing for the crowds, etc."[23] The meeting ran for ten days with three baptisms after the first day. By the end, ten had been baptized and two were restored.[24] Following the meeting, Gus preached meetings at Mars Hill in Franklin County, Antioch in Blount County, and at Mount Pleasant near Millport in Lamar County. The Antioch meeting was reported in this way, "I baptized eighteen on Sand Mountain. Pray for us."[25] Twenty-two baptisms and nine restorations resulted in the Lamar County meeting.

While at Mount Pleasant, an appeal was made by the churches of that region for a man who might move into the area and become a county evangelist. Being in the new work in Cordova prevented him from being able to make such a commitment himself. Thus, he determined to promote the idea among the brotherhood. He wrote,

> The few brethren in Lamar County are planning to put a man in the county for mission work. One hundred and fifty men who will give a dollar per month can support a preacher for full time and enable him to buy a car in which to do the traveling. Some can do many times that much. How is your county brother? Are you doing your best?[26]

Little did he know that within two years, he would be that man.

Back home in Cordova, the crowds were enthusiastically turning out to hear his preaching. A fall meeting was set to begin Sunday, the 28th of September with their home preacher. For fifteen days, the gospel was preached to a full house of members, and the community, resulting in ten baptisms and eight restorations. The crowd was so big the last night that some were turned away, unable to find a seat. Quite confident of the way things were heading, Gus admonished, "Pray for us and watch us grow!"[27]

The fall of the year brought joy to the Nichols family in the birth of another precious child. The family plan of four girls had been achieved. Having four boys was the challenge, and a second son was the gift. Like his older brother Flavil, he too deserved a name in tribute to a loyal and faithful man of God. The Wallace family preachers were highly known and respected in the brotherhood in those days. Among them were, "Foy E. Wallace, Sr., and his sons, Cled E., Foy E., Tom and Paul. G. K. and Glenn Wallace, well-known as gospel preachers,"[28] were their cousins. Most beloved and respected of that generation, was the elder, Foy E. Wallace, Sr. (1871-1949),[29] and most esteemed by the Nichols. Thus, Foy Wallace Nichols[30] was the name given to their sixth child on the day of his birth, the 15th of October 1924. Of all the children, it was often said in life that Foy looked most like his father.[31]

In November, Gus was able to preach in another meeting in Blount County with the Antioch church on Sand Mountain. This resulted in another two baptisms, bringing a total of twenty baptisms that year to add to the ten members that were meeting there. He followed this effort with a mission meeting in Cullman, Alabama using the building of the Primitive Baptist church. Then, he hurried back home just to follow up with a short meeting at New River in Fayette County.

The Thanksgiving Day issue of the *Gospel Advocate* reported the sad news of the passing of one of Walker County's finest Christian ladies.

Nancy Wheeler, the aged wife of its oldest and most respected preacher, Charlie A. Wheeler, died on the 18th of November. Speaking to a large group of mourners, Gus "tried to comfort the heartbroken relatives and to admonish all the great host of friends who were present at the funeral service to prepare to meet God and to make their calling and election sure."[32]

The way of the preacher of brother Wheeler's day was hard. With little support from meeting work and other ministerial labors, provision for a preacher's family often fell far short of what was necessary to provide for their needs. The Wheelers were very poor, and expenses to provide a proper burial were nearly impossible. Such pathos and nurturing surrounded the heart of young Gus to such a degree that he felt the need to both console and assist the grieving widower. His pen, extended with entreaty, wrote,

> Brother C. A. Wheeler is, no doubt, one of the greatest preachers in the South. He has given his life for the gospel, which he so much loves. He is now more than seventy years old and can no longer do hard work and preach at his own expense. He needs sixty-five dollars to meet burial expenses. Brother, can you help bear this burden? Will you do it? If more than sixty-five dollars is received, it would still prove to be a blessing to our dear brother in his few remaining days.[33]

To the end of his life, brother Wheeler continued to be a mainstay among the brethren in Walker County, and a frequent guest in the Nichols family home, as well as a focal point of their benevolent care.

Having Gus Nichols working in the county served to be a shot in the arm for the tender work. Before the end of his first year, he sent a report to Joe S. Warlick (1866-1941), Texas preacher, and the editor of the Dallas based paper, *Gospel Guide*. Warlick observed,

> Bro. Gus Nichols, of Cordova, Ala., writes us with his renewal. He says he has had a good year, and some sixty have been baptized, and much other good accomplished. Gus is a good boy, and safe in every way. He has one of the best women for a preacher's wife that ever lived. I can prove this by Bro. Frank Baker, who knows her well.[34]

ARE YOU MAKING THE WORLD BETTER TODAY?
By Gus Nichols

Let's make our world better each day,
By all that we think, do and say.
That God made it "good," makes us glad,
Sin has ruined it, and we are sad.

How about making it over again,
By turning it away from sin?
Don't get mad, shake your fist and hiss;
And waste your life in things like this!

Is your very life being mis-spent?
Wasted in sin and discontent?
Why not straighten up: live for others?
Think of them as earthly brothers?

Resolve to help all whom you meet;
Speak kind words to all whom you greet.
Tell them Jesus can show the way;
Begin this very hour and day.

Remember to start this very day;
Hours and days are passing away!
The world needs the truth about Christ,
Who for our sins was sacrificed.

Let's get our world to give up sin,
Doctrines and commandments of men;
Return unto New Testament times,
Then look ahead to better climes.

How can you sleep all night in bed,
When not a good word you have said?
Having ignored God and his plan,
To evangelize the world thru man?

Show your faith, demonstrate your love,
For Christ, our Lord, in heaven above.
If you possess nothing to share,
It may be because you don't care.

Learn the truth, win souls for your prize,
For "He that winneth souls is wise."
"GO" - don't waste another minute!
Do your best - put everything in it!

Then when you close your eyes tonight,
You can say, "I've treated others right,
I've followed Christ, walked in his way;
I've made the world better today!"[35]

ENDNOTES

1 Note: Chief Tuskaloosa, his name meaning "Black Warrior," was the ancestral high chief of the Mississippian Indian nations who fought against Hernando DeSoto at the battle of Mabila in 1540. The Mississippian Indians were likely the ancestors of the Choctaw and Creek Indian nations.

2 Note: Named by Captain Benjamin M. Long in 1859, after a city in Mexico where he was stationed during the Mexican War. Previously called, "Dent" or "Dent's Place," the city was a shipping point with access from the Gulf of Mexico.

3 Note: John T. Hinds held a twenty-day meeting in Cordova in June of 1910. On the front page of the July 19th issue of the *Firm Foundation*, under the title, "Small Things," he reported on the effort, but focused in detail about his tour through the Indian Head Textile Mill in Cordova. In it he discussed his impressions of the 500-employee factory with its huge looms that worked at maximum speed. He drew some spiritual comparisons by the fact that such a massive machine will automatically come to a halt if one little strand of string breaks in a loom.

4 Earl Kimbrough, "Elisha Randolph." *Alabama Restoration Journal*, Vol. 2 No. 2, p. 28.

5 L. D. Randolph, "The Bible Alone In North Alabama. When and by Whom," *Gospel Advocate*, 3 June 1891, p. 339.

6 Ibid.

7 A. M. Plyler, *Historical Sketches of the Church of Christ in Alabama*, Hester Publications, p. 102.

8 Note: Queries appeared in the 6 March 1894 issue of the *Firm Foundation* from G. T. Alexander of Cordova, Alabama, and also 5 August 1902 from G. W. Alexander. No mention is made of an organized work in those submissions.

9 A. M. Plyler, *Historical Sketches of the Churches of Christ In Alabama*, Hester Publications, p. 95.

10 V. Q. Gurganus, Unpublished brief history on the Cordova Church of Christ, Vertical Files in the Genealogy Room at Carl Elliott Regional Library in Jasper, Alabama.

11 Willard Collins, "Our Christian Families: The Jabe D. Evans Family, Oakman, Ala.," *Gospel Advocate*, 8 September 1955, p. 798. Note: Little is known of the circumstances surrounding the death of Tom Evans. He was buried in the cemetery at Liberty Hill, on Pleasantfield Rd. south of Oakman, Alabama.

12 E. J. Pinegar, *Firm Foundation*, 18 April 1905, p. 8. Note: Elda Joseph Pinegar (1875-1961) reported in several issues of the *Firm Foundation* in 1910 and 1911. He also wrote a couple of articles that appeared in the *Gospel Advocate* in 1909, on pages 479 and 704. He was a gospel preacher in the area. His brother was a Baptist debater by the name of Ernest Pinegar. E. J. traveled, preached, and reported on meeting work he did in Tennessee and Mississippi.

Little is known after 1911 of his work among churches of Christ. He died 25 July 1961 and is buried in Hueytown, Alabama's Valley Creek Cemetery.

13 Note: James K. Hill (1872-1908) was from Lebanon, Tennessee. He preached much in south central Tennessee around Winchester and spent some time in North Alabama in both Walker and Winston Counties. He moderated in a debate with G. C. Brewer in Walker County in 1906 and was long remembered for his contributions to the discussion. (Hill reported on that debate in the *GA* 6 December 1906, p. 782. and it was recalled in detail by G. C. Brewer in his book *Forty Years On The Firing Line*, chapter 1.) Brother Hill suffered from rheumatism, and it cut his life short as he passed at the young age of 35, 23 February 1908. He was buried in the Bethlehem Cemetery, just west of Lebanon, Tennessee.

14 John T. Hinds, "Arkansas Notes," *Firm Foundation*, 19 July 1910, p. 1.

15 J. L.Hunter, *Gospel Advocate*, 26 January 1922, pp. 92-93.

16 Frank Baker, "News And Notes," *Firm Foundation*, 27 March 1923 p. 5.

17 Gus Nichols, "News And Notes," *Firm Foundation*, 18 March 1924 p. 5.

18 Gus Nichols, *Gospel Advocate*, 24 April 1924 p. 397.

19 Phone conversation with Flavil Nichols, 22 March 2011. Note: Flavil reflected with fondness his memories of this car. He said it had three doors, two in the back, and the driver entered from the passenger side. The driver's side had no door, for on the outside of the car was a three-feet tall hand-break that blocked the way for a possible driver's side access. He said that sometimes, especially if his mom was in the car, his daddy would use the hand crank starter in the front of the vehicle to get it started. Then, he would climb through the window to sit behind the steering wheel. Under the steering wheel was a fuel-flow lever that allowed his dad to turn the fuel off while going down long hills. Riding in this car was one of the children's favorite memories.

20 Note: The Chautauqua movement was an adult education crusade that began in the last quarter of the 19th century in America. Its purpose was to promote the talents of the American people in communities all over the country. The Radcliffe Chautauqua System had a characteristic appeal for smaller localities, where sometimes annually, they would put up a large tent in a field close to a township for a period of several days. Each community had a committee whose job it was to organize musical, dramatic, religious, and other educational and entertaining activities for the time made available by the national organization.

21 Gus Nichols, "News And Notes," *Firm Foundation*, 10 June 1924, p. 5.

22 Note: J. Pettey Ezell (1885-1934) was a Kentucky preacher who was very popular among churches in the south. He met an untimely death in a bus accident while making his way back to Nashville, Tennessee after a quick trip over to Crossville to baptize a hospital patient. He was the only person on the bus to die. His remains were planted at Bowling Green, Kentucky's Fairview Cemetery.

23 Gus Nichols, "News And Notes," *Firm Foundation*, 1 July 1924, p. 6.

24 Ibid., 29 July 1924, p. 7.

25 Gus Nichols, "Our Messages," *Gospel Advocate*, 14 August 1924, p. 777.

26 Gus Nichols, "News And Notes," *Firm Foundation*, 2 September 1924, p. 5.

27 Ibid., *Firm Foundation*, 21 October 1924, p. 5.

28 Noble Patterson and Terry J. Gardner, *Foy E. Wallace, Jr., Soldier of the Cross*, Fort Worth: Wallace Memorial Fund, 1999, p. vi.

29 Note: Foy Edwin Wallace (1871-1949) was a Texas-born preacher of the gospel. He was a missionary to the Indian territory in the 1890s. He was a debater, and a good writer. He passed from this life 21 November 1949, and is buried in the cemetery in Georgetown, Texas.

30 Note: Unpublished interview with Hardeman Nichols, by J. D. Thomas, Tuesday, 4 February 2003. Transcribed by Jennifer Gravelle, Freed-Hardeman University Historical Room, p. 5. Also note, that the transcription denotes "Wallace" as being spelled "Wallis." However, "Wallace" is the correct rendering.

31 Note: Phone conversation with Glenn Posey, 2 November 2009.

32 Gus Nichols, *Gospel Advocate*, 27 November 1924, p. 1152.

33 Ibid.

34 Joe Warlick, *The Gospel Guide*, October 1924. As reported by Don Deffenbaugh in *Four State Gospel News*, Neosho, Mo., March 1980.

35 Gus Nichols, "Are You Making The World Better Today?" *Words of Truth*, Vol. 10 No. 16, 12 September 1975, p. 4.

- 11 -

A New Work In Jasper

The Lord hath brought forth our righteousness: come, and let us declare in Zion the work of the Lord our God.
—The Weeping Prophet, Jeremiah 51:10

The work in Jasper, Alabama can trace itself back to the 19th century. The Randolphs held brush-arbor meetings in the area, but no serious and long-term effort came about until the turn of the 20th century. A small group was established in town and was set to prosper in many ways. Due to the influence of some of the prominent members in the congregation, instrumental music was introduced into the worship, resulting in the refusal by some of its members to attend.

For the next twenty years, no established work after the Ancient Order existed in Jasper, but a number of congregations were situated in the county. With nowhere to attend, members who lived in Jasper traveled out of town when they could to worship with the saints.

During the school year of 1921-22, students came into Jasper from various rural locales to attend Walker County High School. Among them were children of families that attended the rural congregations. Florence Plylar of Parrish; Irene Grace, Clarence Mullinax, and Dona & Ezra Evans of Oakman; and the Gibson children—Malcomb, Pauline and Hugh, were all students looking for a place to worship. The Gibsons allowed them to worship in their home some, and at other times they met in the Avery Fike family home.[1]

In the fall of 1924, a few of the Christians living in Jasper were the Robinson and Oakley families. Forney Robinson and his wife had for some time traveled to Cordova for worship but wanted intensely to have a place to worship in Jasper. Several others living in the vicinity, unaware of each other, were worshipping elsewhere.

When Forney Robinson approached Gus Nichols about the need to plant a strong congregation in Jasper, he seemed very excited and willing to help. If a hall could be obtained, he promised brother Robinson that he would come and hold a meeting to see what could be done.

A hall was located in the Phillips-Stanley building in downtown Jasper, and a date was set for the meeting. Reporting on his schedule Gus wrote, ". . .I go next to Jasper, Alabama to the I.O.O.F. Hall, and will continue there indefinitely. We hope to establish a scriptural church there, after the New Testament Pattern. Please pray for me."[2]

As the early October meeting approached, flyers were produced and posted around town as well as advertisements in the *Mountain Eagle*, Jasper's local newspaper. Attempts were made to connect with members of the Christian church as well.

Avery Fike was one of the Christians living in Jasper, and he was unaware of the intentions to plant a new work. In later years, he fondly recalled how he discovered the meeting that was planned,

> Wednesday after the meeting started, I was walking down the street and in front of the Christian Church, I saw an arrow drawn on the sidewalk with crayon, which said, "GOSPEL MEETING, FOLLOW THE ARROWS." This had an interesting ring to it, and through curiosity, I followed the arrows around the block to the foot of the stairs where the arrow pointed upstairs. I followed on, and wound my way around, and around, until I came to a door upon which was tacked a notice which said, "GOSPEL MEETING— SERVICES 7:30 P.M. each evening. WELCOME. Gus Nichols Minister, Cordova Church of Christ." I departed and passed down by the Post Office and received a card from Brother Nichols stating that he had heard I was a member of the Church of Christ and it contained an invitation to come to the meeting. That night my wife and I and our three babies were at the meeting. That night marked the beginning of my connection with the congregation and the work here.[3]

It seemed that Gus was willing to do anything necessary to make a success of the meeting, even if he had to get on his hands and knees with a crayon to draw arrows to the location from the front door of the Christian Church building.

The meeting was not well attended by the community, but the gospel message was preached to those in attendance. The result was that a good solid group of about thirty people committed to organize themselves into a congregation. Brother Nichols promised to come and preach for them on Sunday afternoons as well as conduct a regular Tuesday night leadership training class to help the brethren learn how to lead in all areas of congregational activity.

One of the original members was a daughter of C. A. Wheeler, Della Deason.[4] Her involvement meant that her father visited from time to time when he was able to be away from his work at Shiloh (later Midway church of Christ). He preached for the church on those occasions.

Thus, the workload for Gus increased with the planting of the church in Jasper. Several attempts were made to attract those of the Christian Church, but most of his concentration was on preaching to anyone in the area who would come to listen.

Soon after the church began meeting regularly, they met their first challenge on a very cold Sunday afternoon in the early part of 1925. When the church turned up at their rented hall for worship, they noticed that the location had been turned into a dance hall, and the church had been expelled from meeting there. Standing in the corridors and looking to Gus for direction, he suggested that they go downtown and conduct their service on the courthouse grounds.

1925 - Gus Nichols at Posey School

Just as they gathered themselves on the cold and windy lawn, Walker County Sheriff, Farm Kilgore, came by to see what was happening. He encouraged the group to get out of the cold by going indoors to meet in the large courtroom for worship. Soon after, the church was given the opportunity to begin worshipping in the smaller courtroom regularly until a permanent location could be found.

At the end of March, Gus made a quick train trip up to Murray, Kentucky, to attend a debate between C. B. Douthitt (1896-1971), then of Martin, Tennessee, and Missionary Baptist, R. L. Riley of Arlington, Kentucky. It was a four-day discussion on the subject of baptism. "This was Brother Douthitt's first discussion. His arguments were clear, convincing, and persuasive."[5] The time was well spent in support of the cause of Christ, giving Gus better exposure to the greater brotherhood, and contributed to the honing of his own skills for the numerous occasions when he engaged in similar debating opportunities.

Upon his return to Cordova, Gus began making preparation for a big gospel meeting in Jasper to give the fledgling congregation a boost. To do so, he was able to acquire the assistance of Gus A. Dunn, Jr. (1904-1994), for a gospel meeting. The name "Dunn" was as well known in the brotherhood as any preacher. Though in his early twenties, this young preacher was already making a reputation for himself as strong and persuasive, much like his father and his uncles.[6]

Beginning the 19th of April, the teaming effort of Gus Nichols leading the singing, and Gus Dunn, Jr., doing the preaching, served to be a great combination to attract attendance. People came in from at least three counties to support the effort. Dunn wrote a letter the following day to the *Firm Foundation* stating,

> Yesterday, our meeting began here with three services, with people present from Cordova, Benoit, Summit (sic, Sumiton), Parrish, Oakman, Berry, Bankston, Millport, Carbon Hill and Winfield. We have only a handful of members meeting in the courthouse. Brother Gus Nichols is certainly working for the meeting.[7]

During the series, efforts were made to reach out to the "instrumental brethren" in town in the interest of breaking down barriers and uniting their efforts. Referred to as "digressives," brother Dunn was asked to preach one of his sermons on the reasons why the use of instrumental music in the worship was without the authority of the Scriptures, and therefore to be rejected. At the end of the meeting, Gus reported,

> Brother G. A. Dunn, Jr., recently held a twelve-days' meeting at Jasper, in the courthouse, in which the writer led the song service. Six were baptized and eight became identified with the congregation as the result of the meeting. Two or more were from the "digressives," who have a church in Jasper. One afternoon we went to Coal Valley and baptized a lady who had been taught the truth by her mother-in-law, but who had never heard a gospel preacher. After Brother Dunn was gone, the digressive preacher tried to reply to Brother Dunn's discourse on the music question. I think it did us more good than harm, for it was the weakest thing I ever heard. He took the erroneous position that God's word does not require Christians to sing in church worship and said many things equally as absurd. After the services I had a conversation with him, in which he contended for instrumental music as an aid to the singing or to lead the songs. I suggested that they get a graphophone to lead the prayers. He said it would be all right. I suggested that we have a friendly discussion on the music question, but he would not accept.[8]

Other efforts were made in time to break down barriers with the instrument-using brethren, but the resolve to continue using the instrument kept the congregations from being able to work together.

As the meeting season began in the early summer, Gus' schedule kept him very busy. He wrote, "I recently baptized a fine young man here. My time is all taken till late in the fall. I begin at Millport, Ala., on June 24."[9]

This meant others were needed to assist in the work at Jasper. Tim Walker (1885-1967) of Haleyville, John K. McClesky (1896-1968) of Parrish, and a former schoolmate at Alabama Christian, W. A. Holly (1911-2003), filled in with great success.[10]

During the twelve-day meeting at Millport, "two were baptized and one was restored."[11] The pitch was made yet again for the desperate need for someone to come and be the county evangelist. The promise for support was confirmed, and the right man, like Gus Nichols, was needed to make it happen. As the summer was just beginning, and meeting work was before him, it was impossible for Gus to make a commitment then, so he continued on his path, praying all the time for the Lord to direct his steps in doing what was best for the cause of Christ.

In July, he traveled back over to Blount County to preach his annual meeting at Antioch on Sand Mountain. He reported having some of the best attendance they had ever enjoyed over the years. Seven made the good confession and were baptized, and the work was left on a positive track.[12] It was followed by a meeting at Shiloh back in Walker County, where C. A. Wheeler was preaching. The church had been having some disunity, and the presence of brother Nichols assisted in bringing unity back in place. He also reported "twenty-two baptisms and about as many restorations"[13] by the end of the meeting.

He followed with an eleven-day brush-arbor meeting at Dixie Springs where there were, "twelve baptisms and a number of others persuaded to be Christians."[14] Subsequent meetings in September brought about twenty-five baptisms at Cleveland over in Fayette County, and sixteen at Mount Pleasant over in Lamar. Then, there were four baptisms at Key Schoolhouse near Cordova, followed by seven baptisms at Pea Ridge near Berry.

Significant to the Mount Pleasant meeting was the conversion of one young man by the name of Willet A. Black (1904-1980).[15] In years to come, W. A. Black was to become one of Lamar County's leading evangelists.

A story about the Cleveland, Alabama meeting was reflected upon several years later in an article written in the *Gospel Advocate* by F. B. Srygley (1859-1940) on the history of the work in Fayette County. The setting was to show the history behind Gus Nichols being the first speaker in the new church house in Cleveland in 1926. Leading up to its building and dedication was the meeting that Nichols preached in August of the preceding year. He wrote,

> I understand that the first house was an old log house. Gus Nichols was to go there for a meeting in 1925, I believe, but the elders and the other brethren thought they were not ready for

a meeting and that they could not support Brother Nichols, and wrote him to that effect. The ladies took the letter out of the box, and Brother Nichols came. They had one of the greatest meetings in the history of the church, which resulted not only in many obeying the gospel, but in the new building.[16]

Challenging the thinking of his readers, Srygley followed with the question, "Did the ladies do right?"[17]

At the end of October, Gus held a meeting at his home congregation at Cordova where he announced to the brethren of his intentions of going into the mission field of Lamar County. He put pen to paper on October 31st and submitted for publication,

> I recently closed a nineteen-day meeting with the church at Cordova, with eight baptisms and four restorations. The bad weather hindered much, but the interest was good, and we had additions even down to the last service. I will close my work here and go to Lamar County about the first of the year, if the Lord wills. I am to do mission work next year.[18]

The rest of the year, Gus had two or three meetings to attend to, but his main focus was on transitioning his emphasis toward the move to Millport, and at the same time preparing the brethren at Cordova and Jasper to continue in the work on their own.

A meeting was called in December of all the congregations in Walker County to come to Cordova for a discussion on the work in the county. Representatives from most every congregation were in attendance. The name of Hal P. McDonald (1879-1959) was put forward as a potential candidate for becoming a county evangelist for the following year. If the churches would support him, he intended to buy a tent and set it up all around the county for evangelistic purposes. At the end of the following year it was reported, "During the year of 1926 he bought a tent and conducted 26 gospel meetings, and baptized about one hundred and fifty people that year."[19]

The Nichols' last Sunday at Cordova was a day of mixed emotions. Many life-long friendships had been made over the two years of their sojourn there. One lady responded to the invitation that day, and she was taken to the water. He later remarked, "Yes, the water was a little cold and icy; but when one's heart is right, the water is always warm enough."[20]

In the days that laid ahead, the Nichols family packed up their belongings, and began making their journey seventy miles westward to Lamar County, Alabama. On the 4th of January he penned from Millport,

A New Work In Jasper

Last Lord's day in December closed my last with the congregation at Cordova. We baptized a fine lady in the afternoon. I am now located at Millport where we have some very fine brethren who plan to assist me in doing some mission work in this county during the year. Our aim is to establish some new congregations in the county, if the Lord wills. I spoke three hundred fifty-four times and baptized one hundred twelve last year.[21]

ENDNOTES

1 Avery Fike, "A Brief History of the Fifth Avenue Church of Christ," Unpublished paper read at the mortgage burning of the Fifth Avenue church of Christ, Vertical Files, Genealogy Room, Carl Elliott Library, Jasper, Alabama. No Date.

2 Gus Nichols, "News And Notes," *Firm Foundation*, 25 November 1924, p. 5.

3 Ibid.

4 Note: Sometimes written, "Delia."

5 Coleman Overby, "Riley-Douthitt Debate," *Gospel Advocate*, 7 May 1925, p. 456.

6 Note: There were five brothers in the Dunn Family who preached. John Evans (1867-1932), James Sterling (1874-1922), Jasper William (1878-1964), Thomas Franklin (1872-1948), and Gustus Albert (1876-1967), Gus Jr.'s father. Most spent their years preaching in Tennessee and Texas, but were from Readyville, Cannon County, Tennessee.

7 Gus Dunn, Jr. "Notes and News," *Firm Foundation*, 28 April 1925, p. 6.

8 Gus Nichols, "From The Brethren," *Gospel Advocate*, 28 May 1925, p. 525.

9 Gus Nichols, *Gospel Advocate*, 4 June 1925, p. 537.

10 Unpublished historical data on the history of "The Church" in Jasper, in the Vertical Files, Genealogy Room, Carl Elliott Library Jasper, Alabama. No Date. No Author.

11 Gus Nichols, *Gospel Advocate*, 16 July 1925, p. 681.

12 Gus Nichols, "Notes and News," *Firm Foundation*, 11 August 1925, p. 5.

13 Ibid.

14 Ibid. 25 August 1925, p. 5.

15 Recording, "Gus Nichols: A Great Man." W. A. Black, speaking at the funeral of Gus Nichols on 19 November 1975, opened his speech by saying, "It was fifty years ago, this past summer that brother Gus Nichols converted me, baptized me into Christ, unto the remission of my sins." This places his baptism during the Lamar County meeting of the summer of 1925.

16 F. B. Srygley, *Gospel Advocate*, 3 September 1936, pp. 845, 853.

17 Ibid.

18 Gus Nichols, "Notes and News," *Firm Foundation*, 5 November 1925, p. 5.

19 A. M. Plyler, *Historical Sketches of the Church of Christ in Alabama*, Hester Publications, pp. 101-02.

20 Gus Nichols, *Gospel Advocate*, 14 January 1926, p. 33.

21 Gus Nichols, "Notes and News," *Firm Foundation*, 12 January 1926, p. 5.

- 12 -

Mission Work In Lamar

> Also I heard the voice of the Lord, saying, Whom shall I send, and who will go for us? Then said I, Here am I; send me.
>
> —Isaiah, Isaiah 6:8

Amidst the forests of western Alabama lies the county of Lamar. Cut from parts of Marion and Fayette counties, the area was formed February 4, 1867 as Jones County. In 1868 the region was reorganized as Sanford County. Then, in 1877, it was again renamed Lamar. Adjacent to Fayette County to its east and the Mississippi state line to the west, its rural charm and rich farm land has for generations been home to some of the state's finest citizens. The region's earliest influence for New Testament Christianity pre-dates the original designation.

The Randolphs were among the first to labor in the Lord's vineyard in this area. In the 1840s, Jeremiah Randolph (1808-1894) and his family spent some time living there and made efforts to plant congregations. His son, Virgil (1847-1906), grew to be a great preacher in his own right.

1924 - Family at Millport
Bertha with hands at her face, Gracie, Flavil, Vodie,
Matilda holding Foy, Gus holding Carrie

The first solid work in the county, appearing sometime in the 1850s, was on the Luxapalila River. The younger brother of Jeremiah, Lorenzo Dow Randolph (1833-1907), planted that work. Soon after the Civil War, reporting from Millport, Jones County, Alabama under the title, "Report From Ala." he wrote, "There are 2 congregations of the brethren in the vicinity, numbering 50 members each, known as the Luxapalila and Antioch Churches. To these congregations, there were some 15 accessions last year by my humble labors. Here is a large field for gospel laborers."[1] In that same report, he suggested that he was the only worker within thirty-five miles of his home, "laboring for the Bible alone." The Luxapalila work was later known as Mt. Pleasant church of Christ.

L. D. Randolph was also instrumental in the founding of the Union congregation in about 1880. Located a few miles east of Vernon, this little congregation thrived under Randolph's influence. He taught in Bethel Schoolhouse. Later, the congregation's designation was changed to Bethel church of Christ, and it has continued to the present. As has been noted, later in the century, when Joseph H. Holbrook (1841-1905) was preaching a meeting at Bethel, a young farmer of that community responded to the invitation by the name of Charlie Alexander Wheeler (1851-1937). The church has been known far and wide for producing great leaders and preachers of the gospel for several generations. Many of the Hester family preachers claim roots at Bethel.

In mid-1890, while living at New River in Fayette County, J. H. Holbrook spent about two weeks in Lamar County preaching to three of the eleven churches for which he was serving as primary minister. During this time, three works were in place in the county. Two of them had recently built meetinghouses, and were funded, as he put it, "without the aid of any missionary society."[2]

Originally known as Lick Skillet, the little settlement of Millport is located in the southern part of the county on the main trunk line of the Georgia Pacific Railroad. A congregation of the Lord appeared there sometime around 1899 or 1900, though L. D. Randolph had made preliminary efforts there when he reported to the *Gospel Advocate* on the history of the work in Alabama in 1891.[3] A building was built in 1904 and served the congregation until a new one was built in 1954. It was here, where in April 1908, C. R. Nichol (1876-1961) held the first of the eleven debates he would eventually engage in with the renowned Baptist debater, Ben M. Bogard (1868-1951).[4]

When the Nichols family moved to Millport in January 1926, there were five other churches in place in the county in addition to Millport, Mt. Pleasant, and Bethel. There was the Ole Liberty church that began in 1868 in the Kingville community. "The Kingville congregation grew out of

Mission Work In Lamar

the Ole Liberty church in the early 1900's."[5] Separate from Kingville was the Kingsville church. There was also the Antioch church that began in 1880, the Mount Olive congregation that began in 1909, and the newest work, in Vernon, which began in 1917.[6]

Three of the congregations, Mount Pleasant, Kingsville, and Millport, agreed to support the Nichols family while Gus served as a county evangelist.[7] His responsibilities included preaching for these churches in a monthly circuit, strengthening other churches, and evangelizing throughout the county in the hopes of establishing new congregations.[8] The other congregations had help from others, such as Gus' brother Charlie who, living over in Clay County, Mississippi, had been making trips over to help the Antioch church for a couple of years.[9]

His familiarity with churches in Lamar County gave Gus a great head start in assisting in their needs. He had held meetings in these congregations in the past, and now working among them, he was able to dive in and give each the personal attention they so desperately needed. As with every spring, he put in a garden for the family to live off of in the summer and following winter. But, most of his time was devoted to visiting weak church members and setting a solid foundation in each congregation through continued teaching and preaching. Had he been in Walker County, several meetings would have been added, but focusing specifically on what was going on in Lamar led him to report, "We have had no series of meetings. However, we baptized two on Saturday and then two more on Sunday, one from the Baptists. Interest is growing all the time in the country."[10]

Being free on fifth Sundays, Gus made a quick trip over to Walker county in May, where he proceeded to pack in as much activity as possible. That day he preached at Carbon Hill, Cordova, and at Zion. At the latter, one lady responded to the invitation for baptism, but was not able to be immersed until the following Tuesday. Staying over for the baptism, and as it was to take place over near Iron Mountain Schoolhouse, he took the opportunity to preach that night at Eldridge on his way back home.[11] This typifies the work ethic that existed in the young preacher. He was obsessed with serving God in any capacity in which he was providentially directed, and an opportunity to visit the old home place and to enjoy some of his momma's home cooking did not make the stay over any less pleasant. Returning home, he spent the rest of the summer in mission work in Lamar County.

DEBATES

Much excitement in the county centered around the occasional debate. Such were nearly as much a societal magnet as a religious one. Sometimes these discussions were called "union meetings," where attempts were made on the part of all involved to see what barriers could be broken down in the interest of spiritual oneness. By the summer of 1926, Charlie Nichols' reputation was increasing rapidly as a good debater, and one who represented well the truths of Scripture. Beginning the first Sunday in July, he started one such "union meeting" with Luther Hollis, a Free-Will Baptist.

The discussion was hosted about five miles south of Vernon at the Mount Harmony Baptist Church, a location that was central, and also one in which Charlie was familiar. For back in December of the previous year he had conducted a debate there with J. R. Clark, a Missionary Baptist minister from Martin, Tennessee.[12] Attempts had been made by the brethren to repeat the debate with Clark, but he refused to debate Nichols. The Baptists felt that Hollis was the man that could handle the young preacher from the church of Christ, as Charlie reported, "The debate is the cause of the Baptists, being anxious for the union meeting."[13] Older brother Gus, along with brethren from all over the region, supported the effort, and all were pleased with Charlie's success.

With the call for a third debate at Mt. Harmony in September, Charlie decided to move his family to Vernon. He was already preaching in the county one Sunday on his monthly circuit, and it seemed fitting to live closer to the action. The prospect of working closer with Gus was appealing as well. They were already supporting each other's meetings, and leading singing while the other preached.[14] Invitations for the debate appeared in the *Firm Foundation* and in the *Gospel Advocate*, in which he wrote,

> I baptized twenty-four persons during the meeting with the Pumpkin Center Church. I will begin a six-days' debate with W. C. Austin (Freewill Baptist), at Mount Harmony Baptist Church, five miles from Vernon, on September 27. Visiting brethren may write me at Vernon, and I will make ready for their coming. Get off the train at Millport Ala. I am now in my tenth meeting for the season.[15]

Meanwhile, Gus' own work was keeping him very busy. Extended meetings in churches that supported Gus brought good results. In mid-August he reported, "Five were baptized at Mount Pleasant; ten at Kingsville and ten confessions to date at Millport's Out-door services. We are having great crowds and interest."[16] Millport had a good facility for worship, but being far too small to host the crowds, evangelistic efforts were often held in a nearby open field.

The *Firm Foundation* seemed to be the journal of choice for reports in the summer and fall with twenty-six baptisms being reported from a meeting at the Cleveland church in Bankston, over in Fayette County. It was his eighth such meeting for that congregation where O. C. Dobbs (1875-1960) served as the regular preacher.[17] In the following issue, Gus reported on a meeting at Bethel, near Vernon, where he worked with local preacher D. B. Salter. Brother Salter had formerly preached and even debated for the Baptists but had been converted a few years previous. That meeting brought about five baptisms and four confessions.[18]

Later in October, tents were pitched in evangelistic efforts. About twelve miles northwest of Millport on Hwy. 12 is the Fernbank community. Some Christians were already living close by, so it seemed a good place to plant the first congregation of Gus' mission in the county. The meeting produced seven additions at the water. These were joined by several others to start a congregation with about 20 members.[19] A similar effort in the Crossville community, a few miles east of Vernon, proved less successful, with no additions.

Evangelistic activity always leads to interesting interactions with people from all walks of life. All who come to the table of reason have their own unique twist of understanding the Bible. While preaching a meeting at Kennedy, just a few miles east of Millport, Gus came across an interesting fellow who seemed to be very close to the truth. He wrote,

> I found a man at Kennedy who has been isolated, I think, from all denominations and teaches the true plan of salvation, even as we do; but he contends for "divine miraculous healing," foot washing in the worship, and a few other such things. We hope to convert him from his error and start him to preaching the truth in full.[20]

The last effort of 1926 reported by Gus Nichols involved a trip back over to Sand Mountain in Blount County in the latter part of October to preach for the Antioch church of Christ. It was his third meeting for the congregation, and the results of his campaign away from home were six baptisms. He said, "The people came through the cold and rain to hear the sweetest story ever told."[21]

1927

On the 12th of January 1927, Gus Nichols turned thirty-five years of age. He, Matilda, and their six children had fulfilled the first of seven years they would spend in Lamar County, Alabama. The first year had been hard—groundbreaking, if you will—and the work was still so much in its early stages that it was difficult to measure its success.

Some things he had going for him was that he was a student by nature. The culture in which he lived, rural and farming, was the most basic to his natural makeup. He still wanted to know more, and the farmer's almanac was part of his choice reading. He knew the Word of God, and his daily devotion to the study of it led him to grow day by day. He was driven by the challenge of his commitment to three congregations in the county to truly make a difference. Churches had been planted in the first year, but they were fragile, so very fragile.

There were some logistical issues that made the situation even direr in nature, like weather, access, location and finance. Questions like, what community might be most open to the gospel? If we have one in the winter, how will people get to a meeting? Access was always a concern, as there were no paved roads in Lamar County in 1927; bad weather could cripple attendance. Then, if a meeting was planned, where will it be possible to run it? Brush arbors worked well in the summer, but in the winter, it was highly susceptible to cold and rain to drown out the crowd. The city of Vernon had a tent that had been loaned to Gus from time to time, but the availability of it was always a question. They needed a tent, but from where would the funds come to acquire it? Discussing it with the brethren, an appeal was made to purchase a tent that would adequately support the work. The Lord provided through those generous brethren, and by spring, the cloth pavilion was purchased and in place for use.

Beginning in April, Gus became entrenched in tent-meeting work. He put up the tent and preached in it night after night. The meetings continued as long as there was sufficient interest. When the interest waned, he folded the tent and moved it to another part of the county and put it up, never missing a night of preaching and teaching. For six months he shunned not to declare the whole counsel of God, strengthening the church, and evangelizing throughout the area.[22] He was so busy that he barely had time to stop and rest. Only three reports appeared in the brotherhood papers during the year. On the 11th of June he penned the following,

> I baptized a fine young lady here last Lord's day. I shall begin tonight under a big new tent near Vernon. I closed a three-weeks' night song drill here last night. Best wishes to the *Gospel Advocate*, which is very fine and helpful to those who desire the ancient church and worship.[23]

The following week another report appeared in the pages of the *GA* of the help in the work being done by his brother, "Charlie Nichols and the writer recently closed a good meeting at Furnace Hill under the big tent belonging to the county, in which we had five baptisms and a splendid interest manifested otherwise. I am now near Vernon at another mission point."[24] With two Nichols men under tents in the county, there was sure to be plenty of good preaching and teaching.

By the end of his second full year of labor, Gus reflected on the success of his labors by penning,

Mission Work In Lamar

I have completed my second year's work with three of the churches in Lamar County. These three churches supported me to work with them and also do mission work in the county. We conducted five Bible classes each week during winter months and held more than a half dozen mission meetings under our big tent during the summer. We preached regularly at several mission points also. I spoke about three hundred and thirty-six times during the year. I shall work again this year with the same churches and do more mission work. Five other churches in the county are also busy and prosperous.[25]

The five congregations included Vernon, Mt. Olive, Liberty, Antioch, and Bethel. O. C. Dobbs, Charlie Nichols, and W. A. Black, among others, were assisting these congregations in rotation with their other works.

ENDNOTES

1 L. C. Randolph [sic], "Report From Ala.," *Gospel Advocate*, 10 October 1867, pp. 816-17. Note: The *Gospel Advocate* misspelled his initials in this report as "L. C. Randolph." It should have been "L. D. Randolph."

2 J. H. Halbrook, *Gospel Advocate*, 9 July 1890. p. 446.

3 L. D. Randolph, "The Bible Alone In North Alabama. When and by Whom," *Gospel Advocate*, 3 June 1891, p. 339.

4 Maude Jones Underwood, *C. R. Nichol: A Preacher Of Righteousness*, Clifton, Texas: The Nichol Publishing Co., 1952, pp. 105-06. Note: This most noted debate was widely attended. Even the local schools were let out, so the students could attend. Ben M. Bogard was said to have been so explosive that at one point in the debate he reached over and knocked a book out of his competitor's hands. In the process he scratched brother Nichol's hand, drawing blood. Nichol took the opportunity to show the bloodstained handkerchief and castigated Bogard for his aggressive tactics.

5 Terry W. Stubblefield, "Some History of the Church of Christ in Lamar County, Alabama," *World Evangelist*, August 2001, p. 16.

6 Note: Gleanings of historical data on Lamar County churches came from a variety of sources, but mainly *The Heritage of Lamar County, Alabama*, Heritage Pub. Consultants, 2000 ed.

7 A. M. Plylar, *Gospel Advocate*, 8 December 1927, p. 1161.

8 Gus Nichols, *Firm Foundation*, 12 January 1926, p. 4.

9 J. M.Adair, "Nichols-Clark Debate," *Gospel Advocate*, 25 February 1926, p. 185.

10 Gus Nichols, *Firm Foundation*, 11 May 1926, p. 5.

11 Gus Nichols, *Gospel Advocate*, 24 June 1926, p. 585.

12 J. M. Adair, "Nichols-Clark Debate," *Gospel Advocate*, 25 February 1926, p. 185.

13 Charlie Nichols, *Gospel Advocate*, 27 May 1926, p. 489.

14 Charlie Nichols, *Firm Foundation*, 27 July 1926, p. 6.

15 Charlie Nichols, *Gospel Advocate*, 16 September 1926, p. 893.

16 Gus Nichols, *Firm Foundation*, 31 August 1926, p. 6.

17 Ibid., 21 September 1926, p. 6.

18 Ibid., 28 September 1926, p. 6.

19 Ibid., 2 November 1926, p. 5.

20 Gus Nichols, *Gospel Advocate*, 11 November 1926, p. 1065.

21 Gus Nichols, *Firm Foundation*, 24 November 1926, p. 5.

22 Flavil Nichols, *Words of Truth*, 2 November 1985, p. 2.

23 Gus Nichols, *Gospel Advocate*, 7 July 1927, p. 632.
24 Ibid., 14 July 1927, p. 657.
25 Ibid., 2 February 1928, p. 105.

- 13 -

A New Voice

*The voice of him that crieth in the wilderness,
Prepare ye the way of the Lord, make straight in
the desert a highway for our God.*
—The son of Amoz, Isaiah 40:3

The 1920s were mighty times for presenting the gospel of Christ. Of the grand group who proclaimed the message, the traveling meeting preacher was especially known for his ability to move people into the aisle. All throughout the brotherhood there were many greats. The "old-guard" of powerful evangelists were men like T. B. Larimore (1843-1929), Foy E. Wallace, Sr. (1871-1949), G. Dallas Smith (1870-1920), James A. Harding (1848-1922), J. D. Tant (1861-1941), R. W. Officer (1845-1930), and Hall L. Calhoun (1863-1935), to name a few.

The new generation of meeting preachers were men like, C. R. Nichol (1876-1961), G. C. Brewer (1884-1956), S. H. Hall (1877-1961), John T. Lewis (1876-1967), C. M. Pullias (1872-1962), and B. C. Goodpasture (1895-1977); along with the Wallace, Dunn and Lemmons family preachers. In 1928, any list of the veritable who's who among powerful evangelists was incomplete without the name, N. B. Hardeman (1874-1965). He was not only one of the champions of Christian education, being president of Freed-Hardeman College in Henderson, Tennessee, but he was more widely known for his preaching and debating skills.

Nicholas Brodie Hardeman was born in a small cabin north of Milledgeville, Tennessee, on the 18th of May 1874. His mother died when he was two years old, but as his father was a doctor, provision was adequate. He attended West Tennessee Christian College in 1890, and graduated under the college's new president, A. G. Freed (1863-1931), in 1895. He returned to the college after the name had changed to Georgie Robertson Christian College as a graduate student and teacher in 1897. When the school became known as Freed-Hardeman College in 1919, he served as vice president under the leadership of A. G. Freed. After a short departure in 1923, he returned to co-chair the presidency of the college with Hall L. Calhoun in 1925. When Calhoun left in 1926, N. B. Hardeman was in complete control of the college. This position he held until his retirement in 1950.

In 1922, he began his first of three evangelistic series of sermons that decade in Nashville's Ryman Auditorium. Estimates of between 6,000 and 8,000 people were in attendance, with 2,000 to 3,000 being turned away due to filled capacity. Twenty-two lessons preached led to 200 baptisms and 30 restorations. Of the fifty congregations in the Nashville area, forty united their efforts in bringing about the meeting. Stenographers from two newspapers, *The Tennessean* and the *Nashville Banner*, transcribed the lessons word-for-word and inserted them in the following day's issues; the papers claiming a combined readership of over 80,000.[1] The sermons were later included in a series of numbered volumes entitled, *Hardeman Tabernacle Sermons*.

1923 - N. B. Hardeman

The following year, Hardeman returned to the Ryman three times for various and similar activities. In April, the second "tabernacle"[2] series took place with over 7000 in attendance the last two nights. Beginning on 31 May, thousands again came to the Ryman for a debate between Hardeman and the champion debater among the Christian Church, Ira M. Boswell (1866-1950), on the subject of instrumental music. For six nights he and Boswell spoke, again and again to capacity crowds. He ended the year of 1923 with another series in the Ryman to preach and teach about the summer he spent traveling through the Holy Lands, 18-20 December.

N. B. Hardeman began connecting more with brethren in Northwest Alabama when he preached a meeting for the young work at Jasper. In August of 1926, a tent had been pitched across from the Collins Hotel in town, and he preached for two weeks under the open-air shelter with good results. "Thirty-seven additions,"[3] gave the church such growth that the brethren were forced to escalate their efforts of procuring a building of their own. Until that time, the small group had been meeting in the courthouse.[4] A lot was purchased on 5th Avenue, and construction began in August of the next year. When the building was completed two months later, the dedication was set for the first Sunday in October. In the meantime, L. R. Wilson (1896-1986) had moved to Jasper at brother Hardeman's suggestion, and had become its part-time preacher. The college president was present to preach at the afternoon building dedication. On that occasion he was noted as saying, "If Jasper, Alabama is ever saved it will be through the Church."[5]

Hardeman Nichols

It is unclear as to when Gus Nichols and N. B. Hardeman met. However, a life-long friendship ensued after their meeting. Hardeman spent time in the home of the Nichols as early as 1931 when he preached the commencement exercises at the Lamar County high schools of both Millport and Kennedy, the next town east, on the 11th of May.[6]

By the spring of 1928, the name of N. B. Hardeman was appearing in most issues of the *Gospel Advocate*. He was serving in gospel meetings, debates, and "tabernacle meetings" all over the country. At least three books were selling like hotcakes at the time, one from the Boswell debate, and the other two from the previous tabernacle series. Just two days prior to the opening of his third series of evangelistic meetings at the Ryman in Nashville, a little boy entered the world in Millport, Alabama. A new voice for God began to be heard the 16th day of March, when the seventh child and third son of Gus and Matilda Nichols arrived. His name was Hardeman.[7]

Foy and Hardeman

I WILL GO VISITING
Gus Nichols

I must go visiting, as in Isaiah two;
For many don't know what to do—
I must force myself at first, I guess—
But I'm going to do my very best.

Many around me are lost in sin—
Don't know what to do, nor where to begin—
But we're not wise unless we win souls,
And have teaching others as our goals.

Sinners are in danger of damnation,
And the gospel's the power unto salvation.
Surely, I can show one what to do,
Regardless of what he is, and who.

3000 obeyed in Acts, chapter two,
Learned in few minutes what to do.
We should now teach them before too late,
What to do, as in Acts two-thirty eight.

We are not as Peter and inspired men,
But we can show SINNERS where to begin,
By showing them every verse and line,
And win THEM TO BE CHRISTIANS now—IN TIME![8]

ENDNOTES

1 N. B. Hardeman, *Hardeman Tabernacle Sermons*, Vol. 1, Henderson: Freed-Hardeman College, 1990, pp. 9ff.

2 Note: Tabernacle meetings were different from regular Gospel Meetings. Coined from the Ryman Meeting, they were generally meetings held in various parts of the country where several congregations went together to bring N. B. Hardeman in for joint gospel meeting efforts. Tabernacle meetings were held in several locations in the 1920s and 1930s across the brotherhood.

3 James Marvin Powell and Mary Nell Hardeman Powers, *NBH: A Biography of Nicholas Brodie Hardeman*, Nashville: Gospel Advocate Company, c.1964, p. 226. Note: Hardeman recorded 37 additions, which corresponds to another, unpublished history of the Sixth Ave. Church. However another unpublished history by Avery Fike, an original member, said that there were 22 baptisms during the meeting.

4 Avery Fike, *Unpublished History of Sixth Avenue Church of Christ*, Vertical Files, Genealogy Room, Carl Elliott Regional Library, Jasper, Alabama.

5 Ibid.

6 James Marvin Powell and Mary Nell Hardeman Powers, *NBH: A Biography of Nicholas Brodie Hardeman*, Nashville: Gospel Advocate Company, 1964, p. 228.

7 Aubrine A. Nichols and Dessie Ree Nichols, *Will and Lizzie Nichols Family Roster*, Unpublished document, 1995.

8 Gus Nichols, "I Will Go Visiting," *Words of Truth*, Vol. 10 No. 8, 18 July 1975, p. 4.

- 14 -

Workers And Works

Thou therefore, my son, be strong in the grace that is in Christ Jesus. And the things that thou hast heard of me among many witnesses, the same commit thou to faithful men, who shall be able to teach others also.
—Paul, 2 Timothy 2:1–2

Passion for lost souls drew Gus Nichols to Lamar County in 1926. Walker County seemed to have plenty of Kingdom laborers in place to do the work. Capable men like Charlie Wheeler (1851-1937), Hal P. McDonald (1879-1959), William H. Gurganus (1872-1940) and others were more than qualified to meet the challenges there. But Lamar needed workers. The churches in the county were weak. For Gus, moving there meant new souls for Christ, and potentially vibrant congregations. But, it had to start with developing workers from within; congregations training their own to preach the word. In his thinking, help was needed—his help was needed—to initiate that much-needed maturing.

THE GOSPEL WAY

Soon after arriving in the county, Gus learned of the opportunity to purchase a "foot-operated, manually-fed, printing press,"[1] with ten trays of moveable type. The large contraption was easy to operate, but time consuming when it came to placing each letter and space in the exact order necessary to produce one page of religious material. On it, he generated a little paper he called, *The Gospel Way*. Distributing it free of charge to as many people as would take it, he wrote with great fervor, and spent many hours in the production of the material in order to get the gospel message into their hands.

W. A. BLACK

One promising nugget of gold in Gus Nichols' thinking was the budding of one young man he had converted in a previous meeting. As has been noted, during the August meeting he preached at Mount Pleasant in 1925, several responded to the

W. A. Black

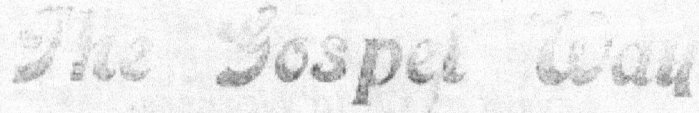

The Gospel Way

invitation. Of that group, one was a youthful twenty-one-year-old by the name of Willet A. Black.

Willet Anderson Black (1904-1980) was the oldest of ten boys in the Black family home. The potential from this one family made the move to Millport that much more promising. From the start of his new walk in Christ, he showed the signs of being just what the work required. But he needed refining. In short term, W. A. began spending many hours in the Nichols' home. It was said that when he preached his first meeting, that he spent the week with the Nichols. Every day he studied with the elder preacher concerning the points he was developing, and then he went that night to preach the sermon upon which they had co-labored.[2] Other than his influence on his brothers, Carey and Charlie, W. A. Black was the first preacher that was developed by Gus Nichols. And from W. A.'s conversion only eternity will know the wealth of goodness that was done through him and his brothers who preached like, Plato (1914-1986), V. P. (1918-2007), Warren (1923-2003), and Jack. W. A. would later raise four sons who also preached.

In one of his earliest reports, he wrote from Steens, Mississippi, to the *Gospel Advocate*,

> 13 July— I am to close a very good meeting at Friendship, near here, tonight. I baptized a fine lady yesterday. The interest has been good throughout the meeting. I shall begin at Pea Ridge, near Berry, Ala., next Sunday. Gus Nichols has done most of the singing.[3]

On the same page another report appeared showing his excitement to be among great men and doing many things for the Lord,

> Beginning on Thursday before the third Sunday in June and continuing over Lord's day, C. A. Wheeler, Gus Nichols, Charlie Nichols, and I were with the Antioch church of Christ in Jefferson County, Ala. We had two or three sermons at each service, day and night. Much good was done. Three were baptized from the sectarians and one from the world. A like meeting was announced for the same time next year.[4]

The year 1928 was a blessed time for the work of the Lord in Lamar County. Early on Gus wrote,

> I am now having three Bible classes each week and preaching at nine different points monthly—two discourses at four of the places. I have three other places to visit when spring opens up. The brethren in these parts have opened up their hearts and pocketbooks and are determined to send the truth to those who have it not. —Let others do likewise.[5]

The same day he wrote the *Firm Foundation* and explained his plans for the spring and summer, "We have a big tent and hope to do more mission work than ever this year. All congregations in the county seem happy and prosperous."[6] And, in April, the "big tent" was set up at the first of several places it was seen throughout the meeting season.

CHRISTIAN CHAPEL CHURCH OF CHRIST

Sometime in the mid-summer, Gus began conducting weekly classes in the home of Golden and Ruby Curry. The previous summer they had been converted during the six-month stretch of meetings where he preached somewhere in the county every day. In that particular evangelistic effort, Gus had pitched his tent on "McDaniel's Fish Pond,"[7] a few miles south of Vernon. It was the hotbed of Baptist influence in the county, being the area where Mt. Harmony Free-Will Baptist Church stood.

The Nichols name was a household word among the people surrounding, since in just a few weeks, Charlie was to hold his third debate there in ten months. Adding to this, was the overwhelming success of his older brother in the county as well. This had the making of drawing a good crowd from the neighborhood. In the course of this meeting, the Currys and a few others were converted.

The Currys had a farm not too far away, located on the main road between Millport and Vernon. For the first year or so, they attended the Kingville church in the Kingville community close by. But there was a strong resolve in their hearts to have a congregation in their own neighborhood. Thus, arrangements for regular meetings in their home began. Gus promised to come and teach classes in their home every Thursday evening, but he suggested they needed to have W. A. Black come and preach on Sundays.

Through the years, it was often reflected upon as to how those gatherings were conducted in the early days. During the warmer and dryer weather, Golden Curry set up a makeshift outdoor worship setting right in front of his house. He took crudely milled boards and set them across wooden blocks to accommodate the brethren and friends in attendance.

In the wintertime, worship and classes were conducted in the Curry home. As the inclement weather made for impassable roads, it was often difficult for Gus to make the trip up from his Millport home for the Thursday night classes. The suggestion was made to take advantage of the "party-line" phone system. All the neighbors shared the same phone line, and each person had their own set of ring combinations to know who was being called. What was meant to be an honor system among neighbors to respect each other's privacy, turned out to be a perfect avenue, not for the gossip, but for the gospel. So, all the neighbors were told that on Thursday nights, brother Nichols would crank the old phone on the wall in his kitchen, and with Bible in hand would proceed to speak into the fixed microphone of the phone box for a period of Bible study. All those who were interested picked up the phones in their homes and listened. As radio was still in its early days of production, this made for a pretty good way to utilize the technology of the day.

Another story that has been told about those early days centered on a three-week meeting that Gus Nichols held in the Curry's front yard. Flavil wrote the following,

> Good crowds attended the meeting in Golden Curry's yard night after night, the uncomfortable and tiresome seating arrangements non-withstanding! One reason crowds were so large at religious services then is that there was nowhere else to go and no dependable way to get there! Being social creatures, people came, but also there is a stirring appeal of the gospel when it is tenderly urged upon human hearts. And Gus Nichols spoke the truth in love (Eph. 4:15).
>
> Brother Curry found it necessary to go into town after the service one night. Dad had preached and preached and preached! And brother Curry dreaded the round-trip of about twenty miles after the service. After the invitation song, while Dad announced the service for the next night, brother Curry pulled out his pocket watch and calculated how long the particular service had lasted. Just as he tucked his watch back into his pocket, Dad called on him to dismiss the service with prayer.
>
> Like many Christians, brother Curry often said in such dismissals, "Our Father, we thank thee for this hour we have spent in Thy service." But having noted the length of the particular service, he blurted out, "Holy Father, we thank Thee for this two hours and fifty-seven minutes we have spent in Thy service!!!"[8]

This story captures the down-home humanity, and maybe a little sense of humor, enjoyed among those who enter fellowship in the presence of a loving God.

Within a few short years, land was given by the Currys for the purpose of a permanent structure. They, along with many others, gave lumber and much labor for their first little building. When it was finished, they approached brother Nichols about what name should be used to capture the spirit of the work. He suggested they name themselves Christian Chapel church of Christ. When the name seemed favorable to all he announced to the brotherhood,

> A new congregation has been established in Lamar County on the Vernon-Millport Highway. Having done much to assist in starting this work, I was given the honor of naming the meeting place, where a splendid house has been built and is almost paid for. It will be known as Christian Chapel. Golden Curry is the efficient leader.[9]

While many churches were planted during the seven years of his labor in Lamar, Christian Chapel stands to this day as a crowning decorum to the sacrifice of Gus Nichols and his years of labor in that section of the country. To this day it serves as a beacon to the community, county, and to the world as a voice for the gospel of Christ.

The small cemetery that was planted adjacent to the church building there many years ago serves as the final resting place for many of Lamar's great and dedicated preachers and their families. Among the many faithful of Christian Chapel's rich history buried there are the families of W. A. Black (1904-1980), Plato Black (1914-1986), S. F. Hester (1908-1982), Benny Hester (1940-2012), Giles Hester (1945-2003), Jeremiah Jones (1933-2003), John L. Wheeler (1926-1992) and others.

CHALLENGES IN THE WORK OF AN EVANGELIST

Often times in his preaching schedule, Gus made his way to the railroad ticket office with barely enough money for passage on the train to and from an appointment. Traveling miles and miles he arrived at his destination and walked several miles before reaching the intended location. Brethren were not always dutiful when it came to being hospitable to the visiting preacher.

Years later, Flavil recalled one most difficult Sunday in his father's life. He remembered,

> After riding the 7:30 train one Sunday morning perhaps twenty-five miles, he walked two or three miles from the depot to his appointment. Arriving long before the local members, he studied his lessons, and read other Bible passages while awaiting the time for the service. All knew he was to preach again that night, and that his train back home did not run till after four o'clock the next morning—yet not one person invited him to go home for lunch! No one even mentioned it! Left alone at the meetinghouse, he read the Bible, and studied again his sermon for that night. Drawing several buckets of water from the well in the church yard, he drank plenty of fresh water! Confident that other members had slept on those benches, he used his briefcase for a pillow, and took a nap. As time for the night service approached, people again congregated—but not one soul inquired where he had eaten lunch, nor where he had spent the afternoon! Following the night service, not a soul invited him to sleep a few hours at his house, nor offered to take him on horseback (nor a wagon, or buggy), to the depot the next morning. All the saints simply went home, leaving the young preacher alone at the meetinghouse! He again slept on the pews a few hours, then walked back to town, and caught the train home.[10]

From the event, he and Matilda determined never to allow such a thing to happen to any person they had the opportunity to assist by way of hospitality. It would be impossible to count how many times perfect strangers ate at their table, as well as a host of others they greatly loved and appreciated. If Gus brought someone home unexpectedly, she was known to say, "We'll just put more water in the soup!"

While this experience was most unforgettable, it was the exception. Most brethren tried to do what they could. Very little did the brethren have to give, and when the collection was added up it only amounted to a little more than a few coins. This, they gave to the preacher if they could. When he had a way to get it home, he might get a sack of potatoes here and there, or some other vegetables for his efforts. But, he never complained to the brethren. He worked for the Lord and depended on Him for his provisions.[11]

A great deal of propriety and reverence for all things godly accompanied him in all his travels. Even the most devout of men were targeted by the devil to test their resolve for faithfulness. On one occasion, Gus was away in a gospel meeting. As it was the custom for preachers to stay in the homes of the members, this occasion was no different. The family who hosted him was a working household. Like most men, the head of the house worked away from home during the day. One morning, a knock came at his bedroom door. Answering, he was met by the wife of his host completely unclothed. Perplexed by this unexpected and disconcerting predicament, he fell to his knees and began praying. His hands perfectly folded under his chin, and eyes tightly closed, he cried out to God on behalf of this woman and her family. He prayed for her faith to live right and look to God for overcoming temptations. He prayed—and he prayed! After a good long while, he opened his eyes to see an empty hallway, much to his great relief. Years later, he often told this story to young preachers to advise faithfulness for the times when the devil would, like a "roaring lion," seek to devour them while serving the Lord.[12]

ENDNOTES

1 Flavil Nichols, "Lessons I Learned From My Father, Gus Nichols," *The Spiritual Sword*, Volume 26, No. 2, January 1995, p. 12.

2 Basil Overton, ed. *The World Evangelist*, Quoting from the memories of Flavil Nichols in an obituary at the passing of W. A. Nichols. June 1980, p. 8.

3 W. A. Black, *Gospel Advocate*, 2 August 1928, p. 728.

4 Ibid.

5 Gus Nichols, *Gospel Advocate*, 23 February 1928, p. 177.

6 Gus Nichols, *Firm Foundation*, 28 February 1928, p. 7.

7 "Christian Chapel Church of Christ," *The Heritage of Lamar County, Alabama*, p. 53.

8 Flavil H. Nichols, "Christian Chapel Church Of Christ—This Hour We've Spent In Thy Service," *Lamar County Heritage Book*, p. 110.

9 Gus Nichols, *Gospel Advocate*, 7 June 1934, p. 552.

10 Flavil Nichols, "Lessons I Learned From My Father, Gus Nichols," *The Spiritual Sword*, Volume 26, No. 2, January 1995, p. 12.

11 Note: Recollections of Flavil H. Nichols in the summer of 1976, during a gospel meeting in Forest Park, Georgia.

12 Note: Gus related this embarrassing story at different times through the years. In later years, his sons, similarly, recalled how their father was tempted, using the incident to admonish preachers in their many trials to remain faithful. The first time your author heard it was from another of Sixth Avenue's great line of faithful preachers, Glenn Colley.

- *15* -

Struggle And Joy

> These things I have spoken unto you, that in Me ye might have peace. In the world ye shall have tribulation: but be of good cheer; I have overcome the world.
> —Jesus, John 16:33

The months leading up to the national presidential election of 1928 were such that the Republican candidate, Herbert W. Hoover (1874-1964), appeared to be a shoo-in for victory. Wealth and prosperity in the land was at an all-time high. Republican presidents had been in the White House for two terms, and post-world war America looked as if she was unstoppable while continuing in her stride through the industrial age. No one could have foreseen that within less than a year of the election the nation would be hurled into the deepest financial depression in its history.

Millport Trade Street

Hundreds of miles away from the hustle and bustle of Wall Street, the distant western region of Lamar County, Alabama was conducting life as usual. Riches there were not so much counted in dollars and cents as in health and well-being. If you had a bit of land on which to plant a crop, a job to attend, and peace in the place where you hung your hat, you considered yourself a pretty wealthy man. By national standards, however, this area of the country was relatively poor. Gus reflected on his financial station by noting, "Three poor congregations in Lamar county are supporting me in mission work...The brethren in Lamar county have their hearts and pocket books in this mission work and are, therefore, happy and at peace among themselves."[1] And, this was the case a full year before the stock market crash of October 1929.

After the crash, things were even more difficult. The brethren had promised the Nichols $100 per month when they moved to Millport. For the first couple of years, things went well with support. But, with severe economic decline of the country, their income began to be adversely affected. Some months, "he received only $80.00, and sometimes only $60.00 a month!!!"[2]

At the end of three years in this mission field, Gus reported,

> I have just closed my third year with the churches and mission work in Lamar County and entered upon the fourth year. Kingville, Mount Pleasant, and Millport give me a regular support. I preach for them during the winter months and leave them and go out with the tent into mission work in the county as early as possible in the summer. These three churches still support me through the summer. Vernon and Bethel assisted in a mission meeting each last year. What is lacking on the part of all others is always supplied by the Millport church, which gives most of my support. Our interest is good and our work is growing. We now have nine congregations in the county. A new house is being erected at Detroit, and we have a lot for a building at Fernbank. I spoke two hundred and ninety-four times last year, baptized forty-seven persons, and restored twenty-four. We are united and happy in our work.[3]

Sometime in the summer of 1929, the Nichols family was struck suddenly with the news that Charlie, who was living in Vernon at the time, suffered a severe accident. In the days previous to modern electric clothing irons, there was a phase of development of the iron where gasoline, coal oil, or sometimes alcohol was added to a small reservoir in irons. On the end was a wick that when

Meeting Closed At Church Of Christ

The Rev. Gus Nichols of Millport closed a series of meetings at the Vernon Church of Christ Tuesday night. The meeting was held in a large tent placed on the grounds at the church. Large crowds attended the services which were held at 3:00 and 7:30 p.m. each day, with three services on Sundays.

The meeting was very successful, twenty-five members being added to the church here. After the baptising services this (Wednesday) morning Mr. Nichols left for Kennedy where he will hold another series of meetings under the tent, beginning tonight.

NOTICE

The Lamar Democrat, 28 Aug. 1929

lit, heated the element in the iron, similar to a gas stove. It happened that while he was ironing some of his clothing that the gas iron exploded. The clothing he was wearing immediately caught flame and was soon spreading throughout the house. Very quickly, the flames from his body were extinguished. But the damage was severe. He was immediately taken to the hospital in Birmingham where he underwent several treatments for burns all over his body. Breaking the news to the brotherhood, his brother reported,

> Brother Charlie Nichols is suffering from a severe burn which occurred when a gas iron exploded and burned all he had, his clothing and his books. His expenses will be heavy. Write him at the Baptist Hospital, 2nd Avenue, West End, Birmingham, Alabama. He is expected to be out of the hospital in 20 days. Send him any good book you can spare and help replace his library. Any fellowship will be appreciated at this time. His friends are requested to act in accordance with the golden rule (Matt. 7:12).[4]

After many weeks of treatment, he was able to return to Lamar County. But, as his family's personal effects were lost in the fire, he had to move into his older brother's home in Millport for a time. Convalescence continued at a slow pace, as he had lost much of the mobility in his legs. In his own hand he recounted, "My burns are healing very well, but I preach sitting down. I can walk only a few steps. The doctor says I will never be able to walk much."[5]

With the help of family, Charlie gave himself to the Lord, and sought to get back to preaching as soon as he was able. Gus provided him with much encouragement, and even changed his own schedule so as to attend to preaching appointments with him. Their multiple talents made it possible to take turns preaching and leading the singing.

Before the end of the summer, Charlie preached a meeting back at Lone Oak in Steens, Mississippi. He needed a meeting to build his confidence back, and this church was a most loved and familiar one to him, as it had been the church where he preached his first gospel meeting nine years previous. Fifteen were added to the Lord in that meeting.

Another big test for Charlie came in the way of a debate. Back in June, and just before the accident, Gus had entered upon a discussion with a Holiness preacher in the county by the name of R. E. Higdon. Earnest Higdon lived in Millport but preached for a little Holiness church in Kennedy. In the debate, "He affirmed the direct work of the Spirit in conversion, the continuation of miracles, signs of healing etc., that the Spirit directly dwells in and guides the child of God, independent of the Word."[6]

The debate was said to have been well attended, and the return event, this time with Charlie in the exchange with Higdon, was set for the Fall. After the accident, fulfilling his commitment to take part in this discussion was an appointment he was determined to keep. With the assistance of his older brother, the debate took place over one full week in October. At the end of the event, Gus baptized one person who attended.[7]

Over the course of the next several years, Earnest Higdon continued to be a foe upon the polemic platform in the county. Gus eventually debated him on seven different occasions. In addition to his exchanges with Charlie, he also met W. A. Black (1904-1980) in a discussion in January 1934.

Fulfilling the duties of the work, the Nichols brothers continued their co-labor through to the end of the year. Reports were sent in to reflect their efforts. Gus wrote the following, "We recently closed a meeting at Kennedy, with one man being baptized. Brother Charlie Nichols led the song service. On last Friday night we closed at Fernbank, with five baptized and some funds raised with which to build a house. Charlie did the preaching and I led the song service."[8]

With several other meetings in the county finished, Gus ended the year by reporting,

> I am closing my fourth year with the brethren in Lamar County. I have agreed to stay here another year. This year I preached in thirteen meetings, having spent the winter months with three congregations and some mission points. I spoke about three hundred and ten times, baptized about eighty-six, and had a few restorations. About one hundred and thirty-four discourses were delivered at mission points. Brethren nobly supported me in this work. We hope to do a great work next year. W. A. Black, Charlie Nichols, and I have baptized more people than all our denominational friends claim to have baptized in the county this year. We have only nine congregations, but they believe in preaching the gospel.[9]

In another report, he added that he had "conducted two discussions, and attended another."[10] Worthy of note are the typical calls that came to him in the way of assistance in weddings and funerals. In May, Gus was called upon to preside in the marriage of W. A. Black and "Miss Mattie May Golden, a fine Christian young lady, also from Millport."[11]

Sadly, a call of a different kind came on the 28th of October from the family of James M. Wade (1845-1929), who was one of the last of the "old guard" of preachers in Fayette County. He had traveled in the early days of the Restoration Movement with John Taylor (1807-1885), planted many churches, and was a gifted steward of the people of God. He was a close friend and co-worker with the Randolphs, and had, himself, been called upon to preach the funeral for Jeremiah Randolph when he passed away the 24th of April 1894. The call to New River church of Christ was familiar to all in the region; the old cemetery already being the resting place for some of the greatest workers for God in that section's history. There, Gus Nichols stood before the grave of death's newest victim to recall with praise the greatness of the man, and the dedication of his call in Christ Jesus. With praise he later recalled,

> Brother James Wade, a faithful gospel preacher, of Fayette County, Ala., recently passed into the great beyond. Brother Wade lived above reproach and was loved by all who knew him. He had no children, but was a great lover of children. He supported himself and his faithful wife and did much preaching among the poor. He loved the church and did much to develop the members, where he labored in purity of life. Brother Wade was eighty-four years old. The writer spoke at the funeral a few words of comfort. — Gus Nichols.[12]

What greater gifts might be given to preachers of the gospel than the joy of marrying two Christians who desire to commit to God and to one another for life, or the honor of standing before a grave imparting words of comfort to a family of a dearly departed old soldier of the cross? Perhaps even greater might be the blessing of baptizing one of your own children into Christ. For such was the joy of Gus Nichols on the second Lord's Day in December 1929, when his eldest son, Flavil, "unexpectedly came forward with tearful eyes desiring to obey the Master."[13] At just a few weeks shy of his eleventh birthday, he told his dad that he intended to dedicate his life to preaching the gospel.[14]

Thus, for the people of rural northwest Alabama 1929 came to an end with little or no fanfare resulting from the stock market crash on distant Wall Street, New York City. News of people casting themselves out windows of skyscrapers and plunging headlong to their death over financial ruin made its way to the ears of those in the country, but those kinds of things yet seemed to be far removed from their present reality. However, in a short time, the area, like all other parts of the nation, were to feel the struggle as America entered into several years of economic depression.

ENDNOTES

1 Gus Nichols, *Firm Foundation*, 18 September 1928, p. 6.
2 Flavil Nichols, *Words of Truth*, November 1985, p. 2.
3 Gus Nichols, *Gospel Advocate*, 24 January 1929, p. 81.
4 Gus Nichols, *Firm Foundation*, 2 July 1929, p. 5.
5 Charlie Nichols, *Gospel Advocate*, 5 September 1929, p. 853.
6 Gus Nichols, *Firm Foundation*, 25 June 1929, p. 4.
7 Gus Nichols, *Gospel Advocate*, 24 October 1929, p. 1024.
8 Ibid.
9 Ibid., 26 December 1929, p. 1232.
10 Gus Nichols, *Firm Foundation*, 7 January 1930, p. 13.
11 Ibid., 4 June 1929, p. 4.
12 Gus Nichols, *Gospel Advocate*, 2 January 1930, p. 22.
13 Gus Nichols, *Firm Foundation*, 7 January 1930, p. 13.

Note: All the boys, from early age, heard their father encourage them to grow up and preach the gospel. It was often recalled that when Flavil was little, his daddy would carry him while greeting people at church and would say, "Son, tell our friends what you want to be when you grow up!" Flavil would respond slowly and succinctly, "A gos-ple pree-cher!"

- 16 -

Building Up The House

For every house is builded by some man; but he
that built all things is God.
—The Author, Hebrews 3:4

Matilda Nichols was just three months away from of her thirty-sixth birthday when the calendar rolled over to 1930. She was the wife of a missionary, gospel preacher, teacher, debater, farmer, and an exceptional father. Her life's work was the raising of seven growing girls and boys. But, there was more! For, the last several months she had been carrying another child that was to be born sometime before the end of January.

Back in the days before the ultrasound, and when most children were born at home, the child had to be born before the family knew if it was a boy or a girl. The present concern was that of a name. Gus had "put in his order" for four boys and then four girls. As has been noted, the order seemed to have nearly reversed itself with most of his first children being girls except for Flavil. They now had four girls and three boys. If a boy, what name might worthily be placed upon such a potentially powerful force for God? If the first three boys were named for great gospel preachers of their day, certainly the same must be done for the fourth.

1930 - The Gus Nichols Family
L-R: Foy, Bertha, Carrie, Flavil, Hardeman
Back: Gracie, Matilda, Hudson, Gus, Vodie

In the thinking of the expectant parents, during that day, no greater name in the brotherhood was to be known than John Allen Hudson (1893-1962). Immerging from humble beginnings, brother Hudson hailed from Cold Water, Mississippi. He was schooled in Texas, and attended Cordell Christian College in Cordell, Oklahoma. At just a year younger than Gus, brother Hudson was a most successful gospel preacher. He wrote much for the *Firm Foundation* and the *Gospel Advocate*. His articles were solid and sound in the faith. He preached all over the country, living in Oklahoma, Washington D.C., and later in Los Angeles, California. He was the consummate preacher of the day, with a name certainly worthy in Gus and Matilda's minds to be given to one of their sons.

But, then, equally powerful to brother J. A. Hudson, was the up and coming Willett Anderson Black (1904-1980). W. A. was to Gus what Timothy was to the apostle Paul. Already, his heart was full for this young and growing preacher of the gospel. In him was the drive of intensity he saw in himself, and certainly answered to a name worthy to grace the life of his natural-born son if God so chose to bless him in that way.

Thus, as the course of time was realized an eighth child was born to Gus and Matilda Nichols on the 29th day of January 1930. He was named Willett Hudson Nichols. Hudson's birth brought to fruition the plan of his father, and the joy of his mother. Soon after his birth, and for many years thereafter, Gus fondly surmised that the Lord had blessed him with "forty cents worth of Nichols."[1]

GROWTH IN WRITING

The printed page was something that was attractive to the 38-year-old missionary to Lamar County. Since the beginning of his ministry, he was faithful to report to the religious papers of the day of his various and sundry ministerial activities. His earliest reports were sent to the *Firm Foundation*, and a few years later, he began writing of his activities to the *Gospel Advocate*. They were usually brief and to the point. In time, the *GA* became the journal of choice to post his endeavors for Christ.

Beside his continued effort with his little paper, *The Gospel Way*, what appears to have been one of the first, if not the earliest full article Gus Nichols contributed to brotherhood papers came about as a result of a trip he made to Henderson, Tennessee, to the campus of Freed-Hardeman College.[2] The occasion was the May Commencement exercises in 1930. It was a brief presentation and worthy of inclusion here. He wrote,

MY VISIT AT FREED-HARDEMAN COLLEGE
BY GUS NICHOLS

I visited Freed-Hardeman College at Henderson, Tenn., during their commencement week, and was so delighted with all I saw and experienced that I wish to make a statement concerning the school and the impressions made on my mind while there.

The town of Henderson is a most beautiful little city, located in what appears to be a very healthful section. It has many beautiful homes and is well kept. The college is well located in the city. I found that the brethren had been very conservative in their statements concerning the school and what they have. The buildings were far more beautiful and more modern than I expected to find them.

I have never met a more friendly and hospitable people anywhere than there. They seemed to be living largely for the school and for the benefit of the young people who are away from home and loved ones seeking wisdom and knowledge. The good ladies served meals, free to all, and all did everything possible to make the occasion a happy one. The very atmosphere seemed to be filled with the sweet fragrance of Christian influence. The programs were spiritual and uplifting. I saw nothing which, in my judgment, was questionable. Brother G. C. Brewer delivered the class address, which was as good as the best. The students seemed to be happy and holy. They were friendly and courteous, and each one seemed to be a booster for the school. I think no sacrifice, however great, has been made for them in vain.

Brethren, I want to urge you to help support such schools by sending your children to them and in every other way possible. Some of our young people attended the State University and went off with the "digressives" the first year. This would not have happened at Freed-Hardeman or any other school of like nature. Lot pitched his tent toward Sodom and lost most of his family because of its evil influence. He only considered the fertile valleys and good pastures, and took no thought it seems, for the spiritual welfare of his family. It is far more important that we put our children under Christian influence than many seem to think. The finest cherries in the nation are now being grown by a gentleman who first canvassed the whole nation before selecting a site for his orchard. He knew his healthy trees would not do well unless planted in the right soil and climate. Paul says: "Evil companions corrupt good morals." But the rule works both ways; therefore, good companions correct bad morals. This is why we are called "the salt of the earth" and "the light of the world."

If at all possible, let us send our sons and daughters to college next year where they will be under Christian influence, where they may obtain an education which includes the knowledge of that Book which is a "lamp unto our feet" and a "light unto our path."[3]

The imagery in the article demonstrated a most pleasant and beckoning call to all people with spiritual inclination to consider heavily the need for Christian education. His writing style was illustrative, easy to read, and most inviting. His points were clear, portraying the idea that spiritual development, alongside training for any worldly pursuit, should be accomplished through Christian education. The trust he placed in schools like Freed-Hardeman College was in view of his strong belief that such schools were seeking to follow Scriptural directives as a foundation upon which all other educational instruction should be built.

After his visit, he admonished W. A. Black to attend school there. He was the first of many, over the years, who sat at the feet of Gus Nichols, and heard within the scope of that training of the need to go to Freed-Hardeman College, and later Alabama Christian College, and similar schools for further preparation. His own children followed this course when their times arrived to enter that level of education.

His visit to Henderson was the first of many such trips over the next forty-five years. The relationship he enjoyed with N. B. Hardeman (1874-1965) and the school's subsequent leadership in his lifetime was solid, and clearly visible to all who knew of him and the college. There developed a symbiotic relationship that existed between the two that caused many who knew both to think of the other when either was mentioned in conversation.

GROWTH IN THE WORK

Meanwhile, the local work continued to develop splendidly. Gus wrote, "We are gaining in numbers and influence in Lamar County each year. We recently had three restored at Mount Pleasant. All is at peace among us."[4] This growth was not without its challenges. Denominational bias and prejudice served to impede his efforts. One example of this was seen in an effort he was involved in back over in Walker County near his home in Kansas, Alabama. There was a small group of Christians meeting in homes there. In early May, they invited Gus over for a meeting, but they needed a location large enough to accommodate the potential crowds. The local Baptist church was approached for permission to use their meetinghouse. However, when some of the members strongly protested it, the meeting was moved to a local, and more spacious schoolhouse. He said, "our crowds increased to overflowing, and where we taught 'much people' the way of God more perfectly!"[5] In the end, there were no conversions reported from the meeting. But, excitement was in the air. Beyond capacity crowds provided a wonderful way to overcome temporary setbacks brought on by losing a meetinghouse in which to preach Christ. He observed, "I have never seen better interest than we had when no one obeyed the gospel. I hope to return later and reap what we have sown there."[6]

No responses in one place, a few here and a few there, or many conversions and restorations in others, demonstrates the inability to calculate the results a meeting will bring forth. One would think that the same preacher with the same message in relatively the same time period should get similar results in meeting work. However, planting and watering provides very little accuracy for detailing absolute reactions people will make when considering the increase of God's provision. As with all things, the gospel planted brings forth fruit all in His time. For instance, Gus preached a meeting among his old home brethren at Howard near Carbon Hill in late June where there were four baptisms reported.[7] The next week, he preached a meeting at Flat Creek near Millport, and the result was twenty-one baptisms and two restorations.[8] In August, eleven were baptized in a meeting at Bethel, near Millport.[9] Eleven more obeyed the gospel at Mount Pleasant, and six were converted at Millport in a meeting with J.D. Tant (1861-1941) before the end of the month.[10] Later in September, Gus baptized six during a meeting at Vernon, with three restorations.[11] From there he went back to Walker County and preached a meeting in Cordova at the end of September. Thirty were baptized in that meeting, "one taking fellowship, one reclaimed, and more than twenty confessing their faults."[12] Next, he preached a meeting at Kennedy, back in Lamar County, where there were, "no visible results."[13] Rounding out the month of October were meetings at Altoona,[14] near Gadsden, and Waterloo in Lauderdale County, Alabama with one baptism reported.[15] In November, one was restored in a meeting at Antioch, in Lamar County, and one was baptized,[16] and three were reported baptized from within his local work at Millport.[17]

Gus' year of meeting work came to an end with a visit to the church he planted while living in Cordova. The church in Jasper had been growing since his departure from the area in 1926. A warm reception among friends, along with his thoroughness in proclaiming the message, made for a wonderful reunion among the people. As was his habit, upon returning home, he dropped in the mail the following note,

> I recently closed a good meeting at Jasper with one baptism and two confessions of faults. These brethren have a new and modern meeting house which is a credit to the city and the cause of Christ in general. While they are burdened with debt they are hopeful, united and happy.[18]

At this stage of the Lamar County mission, one has to begin discerning the weight of pull that might have been cultivated during this Jasper meeting. It had been his first return to preach among these brethren since leaving the area. L. R. Wilson (1896-1968) had been preaching for the church for the last three years but had departed the previous June due to graduating from the college he had been attending in Birmingham. They had a new building that was a financial burden to the small group. They needed development in the leadership, and growth in the body. They needed a regular preacher to assist them in these and many other specific areas of their lacking. The pull to be in several places at one time was often most dissettling to the responsible and devoted Gus Nichols. Adding to this was the economic weight being placed upon the shoulders of a father of eight children who was feeling the challenge of difficult economic times brought on by the Great Depression. After the Jasper meeting, how often might the questions have arisen over the following two years, "Should I stay in Lamar and continue this track I am on, or move my family back to Walker County?" Only time would tell.

But, before making any decisions about a move, he was committed steadfastly to the work at hand. The year 1931 had been a typical twelve months of work with fewer reports on meeting work than in previous years. One report in July recapped several weeks of work,

> I have conducted meetings this season at Guin, Cordova, Kansas, and Flat Creek with twenty-two baptisms in all the meetings. Our meeting at Millport has just closed with two baptisms and fine interest and attendance throughout. Brother Chester Estes of Winfield did the preaching. I am now at Bethel near Vernon.[19]

Though successful as in the past, fewer reports appeared in the fall and winter, and no annual reports materialized with summary totals as in previous years.

At the end of the year, Gus' attention again turned toward Walker County. He felt deeply responsible for the welfare of his "father in the faith" back on that small farm south of Jasper. Sister Wheeler had been with the Lord for several years, and the winter had been hard on brother Wheeler's health. He wrote an appeal for assistance both through prayer and financial consideration for this old champion of the faith. He said,

Brother C. A. Wheeler of Jasper, Alabama is sick with pneumonia, but will perhaps recover. However, his doctor thinks he will not be able to preach this winter. Brother Wheeler has been preaching over fifty years. Now that he is unable to work this winter, let us help to pay his doctor's bill and tide him over this winter. I personally know that he needs our sympathy and prayers. Write him a comforting letter today, and enclose a free-will offering.[20]

Gus returned to Jasper for a quick fifth Sunday meeting in January 1932. The day was successful with one lady being baptized into Christ after the evening service.[21] Then, in April, he was called back to Jasper quickly upon receiving the news of the death of brother Wheeler's daughter. He reported,

I was called to Jasper last week to speak at the funeral of Sister Delia Deason, who was a daughter of our beloved Brother C. A. Wheeler. Sister Deason was a good and faithful member of the church of Christ in Jasper, was a teacher of a children's class, all of whom wept like they had lost their best friend. Sister Deason leaves her husband and her daughter, Gertrude, and many other relatives to sorrow over her departure, but not as those who have no hope. The overflow attendance at the funeral and the fine floral offering was an evidence of much respect.[22]

Delia Deason had been one of the founding members of the Jasper congregation. Her passing was not only felt by the Jasper work but was a great loss to all the Christians in the county and beyond.

During the meeting season, some of the greatest successes of Gus Nichols' career were experienced. If successes are gauged in responses, perhaps the most successful meeting of his life took place just out of Parrish, Alabama in mid-June at the Aldridge congregation. He noted, "Just closed at Aldridge with fifty-five being baptized and forty-three confessing their faults. Brother A. M. Plylar assisted in prayer and song. I promised to return for a week this fall. In the last thirty days we also baptized two at Winfield and eleven at Baileyton."[23] A meeting at Bethel in Marion County rendered ten baptisms and three restorations to their "first love."[24] Then two meetings back-to-back in Lamar County followed. Eleven were won to Christ, with two restorations at Mount Pleasant in late July. This was the ninth meeting he had preached for that congregation.[25] Seven more were added to the Lord and one restored at Kingville at the end of July.[26]

Then, it was back to Walker County for a gospel meeting at Carbon Hill which closed with eleven baptisms and five or six restorations. It was followed by a meeting just down the road at Eldridge where nineteen were immersed into Christ and two came back to the Lord.[27] His thirteenth meeting of the season closed at Steens, Mississippi on the 11th of September with no additions.[28]

The fall of the year continued to keep Gus busy in meeting work, where he enjoyed great response. He preached a meeting at Pleasant Hill in Jefferson County that ended with fifteen baptisms. In the report of its success, he gave the name of the young preacher there that he met and who assisted him in the meeting; his name—Rex Turner (1913-2001).[29]

Many years later that same preacher, then the Alabama Christian School of Religion president, reflected on that meeting when he wrote of brother Nichols,

> He came to the Pleasant Hill Church, near my home, for a gospel meeting. Our daughter Jackie had just been born, but I managed to attend all the services, none-the-less. One of the first sermons that I heard him preach in that meeting—perhaps the first—was on the subject of the Holy Spirit. My! What a sermon! I knew absolutely nothing about the subject, and I had wondered what was meant by the statement, "baptizing them into the name of the Father and of the Son and of the Holy Spirit." The Father I knew and the Son I knew, but the Holy Spirit I did not know. When his sermon was over, I knew essentially what I know today, and I have preached that sermon that I heard from him hundreds of times since.[30]

The year began winding down as Gus Dunn, Sr. (1876-1967) held a meeting at Millport, culminating in ten baptisms, included a schoolteacher from the local high school.[31] Immediately after, Gus Nichols left for a meeting at Cordova, in Walker County, where eleven were baptized and thirty were restored.[32]

On the 28th of November he penned the following to the readers of the *Gospel Advocate*,

> I have arranged to begin work in Walker County the first of the new year, and will be located at Jasper, where I am to work part time with the church. I am finishing my seventh year at Millport. I have worked outward through Lamar and adjoining counties, doing much mission work. During the seven years spent here I delivered two thousand five hundred discourses and baptized more than one thousand souls, this year being our most successful year, with two hundred and twenty-eight baptized to date. Surely there are no better people than those who have supported this work. They are at peace. It is painful and sad to leave this people; but their invitation to stay came four days too late, as I had already agreed

to go to Jasper. They tried to get a release, but failed. Thank God for such friends.

Two more were baptized by the end of the year, bringing the total of two hundred thirty souls being added to the Lord's church in 1932.[33]

Thus, seven years of faithful service came to an end very quickly. The Nichols left Lamar County on good terms, with a good reputation among the churches. Gus was to spend the remainder of his life supporting the work in that region as best he could, preaching countless meetings, and being called for many weddings and funerals for life-long friends over the years. The church was left in good hands with W. A. Black moving back to Millport to take the work.

Thus, with their departure, the Nichols family entered upon a new field with the potential for new relationships in Walker County.

ENDNOTES

1 William Woodson, "In Memoriam," *Words of Truth*, 25 October 1991, p. 1.

2 Note: Commencement exercises at Freed-Hardeman College, now University, were a week full of events beginning on Sunday, May 25th with a Baccalaureate address by F. W. Smith (1858-1930), the senior editor of the *Gospel Advocate*. Events followed each evening to display the talents of the students from the Literary Societies to the Music and Expressions Departments. It culminated Thursday morning with the Graduation Exercises. There were thirty-four graduates in 1930 according to the school's newspaper, *The Skyrocket*, Vol. 7, No. 9, May 1930, p. 1.

3 Gus Nichols, "My Visit At Freed-Hardeman College," *Gospel Advocate*, 3 July 1930, p. 639.

4 Ibid., 17 April 1930, p. 317.

5 Gus Nichols, *Gospel Advocate*, 15 May 1930, p. 465.

6 Ibid.

7 Ibid., 10 July 1930, p. 656.

8 Ibid., 14 August 1930, p. 781.

9 Ibid., 21 August 1930, p. 800.

10 Ibid., 4 September 1930, p. 849.

11 Ibid., 25 September 1930, p. 934.

12 Gus Nichols, *Firm Foundation*, 14 October 1930, p. 5. Note: A similar report was in the *Gospel Advocate* on the 9th of October 1930, p. 969. However, it was a recap, and not the actual report Gus Nichols made. That report said there were "more than fifty addition-baptisms."

13 Gus Nichols, *Gospel Advocate*, 16 October 1930, p. 1008.

14 Ibid., 23 October 1930, p. 1017.

15 Ibid., 30 October 1930, p. 1041.

16 Gus Nichols, *Firm Foundation*, 18 November 1930, p. 6.

17 Gus Nichols, *Gospel Advocate*, 20 November 1930, p. 1124.

18 Gus Nichols, *Firm Foundation*, 16 December 1930, p. 5.

19 Ibid., 11 August 1931, p. 5.

20 Ibid., 15 December 1931, p. 6. Note: A similar report appeared in the *Gospel Advocate*, 10 December 1931, p. 1553.

21 Gus Nichols, *Gospel Advocate*, 18 February 1932, p. 216.

22 Ibid., 28 April 1932, p. 542.

23 Gus Nichols, *Firm Foundation*, 5 July 1932, p. 5.

24 Gus Nichols, *Gospel Advocate*, 4 August 1932, p. 883.

25 Ibid., 11 August 1932, p. 908.
26 Ibid., 18 August 1932, p. 932.
27 Ibid., 8 September 1932, p. 1003.
28 Ibid., 29 September 1932, p. 1077.
29 Ibid., 27 October 1932, p. 1172.
30 Rex Turner, "Gus Nichols as I Knew Him," *Sound Doctrine,* November/December 1975, p. 2.
31 Gus Nichols, *Gospel Advocate*, 3 November 1932, p. 1197.
32 Ibid., 17 November 1932, p. 1243.
33 Gus Nichols, *Firm Foundation*, 13 December 1932, p. 6.

Happy Days Are Here Again

> Because I said unto thee, I saw thee under the fig tree, believest thou? Thou shalt see greater things than these.
> —Jesus, John 1:50

Described by many as one of the most difficult years in all American history, 1933, entered with the sound of the promise of prosperity once again. The race for the White House had been up for grabs for several previous months. Herbert Hoover (1874-1964) was in the fight for his political life to hold onto the presidency, but the up and coming New Yorker, Franklin D. Roosevelt (1882-1945), had waged a stronger battle. Making use of the song, "Happy Days Are Here Again" as his theme, Roosevelt won the election, and took the oath of office on the 4th of March.

A new president hardly made a dent in the nation's unemployment of over 25% that year. That is one in every four people out of work! Americans left their homes in droves as they moved wherever they heard there was a possibility of employment. By the following year, severe drought in the Midwest led to extreme dust storms in the beginning of the period known as the Dust Bowl era.

Jasper, Alabama was a typical southern town with their fair share of economic struggles. The average laborer's wage was about $20.00 per week. The average home cost around $5,750 dollars to build. You could buy a Plymouth 6 automobile for $445.00. A loaf of bread was seven cents, a pound of hamburger meat eleven cents, and a gallon of gasoline would cost you a dime.[1]

The home of the Bankhead family was Jasper, Alabama. A strong political force both in the state and the nation, John Hollis Bankhead (1842-1920) was born in present day Lamar County. He served in the Civil War for the Confederacy and reached the rank of Captain. After the war, he began involving himself in state politics. Then he served twenty years in the U.S. House Of Representatives. Finally, he was appointed a U.S. Senator, and continued in that role for several years. He moved to Jasper in 1910 and built a home there, which he called Sunset. After arriving, he and his sons purchased Caledonia Coal Company, and renamed it Bankhead Coal Company. Two of his five children were in politics. Senator John Hollis Bankhead II (1872-1946) was a Jasperite who assisted Franklin D. Roosevelt in the New Deal early in its process. John's brother, William

Brockman Bankhead (1874-1940), was for several years Speaker of the U.S. House of Representatives. William's daughter, Tallulah (1902-1968), was a Hollywood actress, and was known for her frivolous lifestyle, and like many of her relatives, was politically active. Others in the Bankhead family were lawyers and business owners in the region, and were well-known in society.[2] Since 1943, a large 181,230-acre forest region a few miles north of Jasper has been called the William B. Bankhead National Forest.[3]

Fifth Avenue Church Building in Jasper, Alabama

The first day of January 1933 fell on Sunday. It was a great way to start the year with the small church of Christ meeting on Fifth Avenue in Jasper. The Nichols family entered the still very recently built church house on Fifth Avenue with great anticipation and excitement. Meeting them there was a congregation whose members were equally filled with thanksgiving at their arrival. On the 4th, Gus penned these words,

> After bidding farewell to friends and brethren at Millport, who for seven years had been faithful and true, in sickness and in health in adversity and in prosperity, we turned our tearful eyes toward Jasper, where we received a hearty welcome. On the Lord's Day we had a fine attendance at both services. We expect to have four or five services here each week. Already there is much enthusiasm manifested. We are planning greater things for

God in and around Jasper. I have arranged to be in a service every night. Please pray for us in this new work.[4]

The church owned a house next door to the building that was sufficient to house the new preacher and his family. Over the garage, adjacent to the home, Gus made an office for his books. It was a great place to start each day with study. The expectations of Jasper's new preacher were to work part-time for the congregation. Somewhat reverse of seven years previous, he was now preaching the first and third Sundays with the Jasper church. On the second Sunday of the month, he preached for his old congregation at Cordova. On the fourth Sunday, he preached at Carbon Hill. Through the week he taught five night classes, and spoke four times over the weekends. Adding to this were numerous calls for funerals, weddings, gospel meetings, and the occasional debate.

Though the excitement was high, several of the brethren in the congregation were out of work. This led to the strained feeling over paying what was due on a church building that was a little over five years old. Gus voiced their concern by saying, "We have a splendid building, and we feel confident that if the depression does not continue too long, and it is the Lord's will, we can save it to the glory of God."[5] Historian and elder of the congregation Avery Fike, wrote that when brother Nichols arrived,

> The depression was at its worst, and everything looked gloomy ahead. Brother Nichols went to work to train leadership, hold missions meetings, and preach in weak places. All were taught and encouraged to give and work and pray to pay off our indebtedness regardless of the sacrifices to be made. We were cheerful and hopeful, but with nearly all our members out of employment, and starvation and suffering all around us, we could do little more than hope and pray for better days.[6]

Most of the year's activities surrounded his monthly circuit among the churches of his labor. However, during summer, he was able to preach in a few mission-meetings. In late July he wrote, "I recently baptized seven at Carbon Hill, three at Cordova, six at Eldridge, and closed today at New Bethel with fourteen baptisms. I go next to Flat Creek."[7] Gardner S. Hall (1906-1978) of Birmingham held the May meeting at Jasper. There were six baptisms and several in the congregation were said to be "almost persuaded" to obey.[8] Hugo McCord (1911-2004) was invited to preach the August meeting. Brother McCord recalled this meeting nearly fifty years later. Remembering with fondness the encouragements of brother Nichols he wrote, "Lois and I were privileged to be in a gospel meeting there August 13-23, 1933, soon after the Nichols family arrived. He encouraged young preachers. When I was in a meeting at Parrish, some 15 miles away, he was in the audience nearly every night."[9] Gus attended many meetings where he did not preach, and even then, he was making a difference, if for no other, to express to preachers and all in attendance of his love and support for the gospel being preached in every place. Similar to McCord, another young preacher, Hoyt Bailey of Haleyville, from up in Winston County, looked to men like brother Nichols for motivation and wrote,

> I have been preaching for one year. During that time, I have established one congregation, and have preached for fifteen others scattered over Marion, Walker, Lamar, and Fayette Counties. I have walked approximately seven hundred miles filling my regular appointments. W. A. Black, Millport, Ala., and Gus Nichols, Jasper, Ala., have encouraged me much in my work.[10]

However, preaching was Nichols' great strength for bringing revitalization among all the communities around the area. Before the end of August, he had preached meetings at Flat Creek where there were six baptisms, and one at Cleveland, Fayette County, "which resulted in two being baptized and about fifty confessions of faults. This was a great 'revival' in the proper sense of the word."[11] Again, he sent reports on the 4th and the 5th of September to tell of successes at Macedonia, near Townley where he had "six baptisms and twenty-two confessions of faults."[12] Then he was at Baileyton, near Arab, where he reported, "Frank Moody lives there, and is loved by all the people. Oran Boulding also lives there and preaches much. We baptized twenty-seven, and about fifty others responded to the invitation, confessing their faults."[13]

SETTING FORTH A DEFENSE

A steady eye open for problems in the region, Gus had reported early in the year of trouble from the Christian church that met in Jasper. He said, "Our digressive brethren are soon to begin a series of meetings, with a woman preacher assisting their pastor."[14] He long sought to meet the preacher in debate, but invitations were generally ignored. The end of the year's activities centered around debate opportunities. He reported having two debates on four different subjects. He wrote,

> On December 7 and 8, I met "Rev." J. L. Scott, D.D., of Chattanooga, Tenn., in debate at Carbon Hill, Ala. We discussed Holy-Ghost baptism and signs and miracles. Mr. Scott is a nice man in debate, and has had many debates in the past, but for some reason had "quit debating" until his brethren urged him into this one, which I think will be his last. He is an editor of their "Sunday-school literature," and has been editor of one of their religious papers, which is suspended because of the depression. He claimed to belong to the "Original Church of God." Alva Ganey moderated

for Mr. Scott, and Huston Haney moderated for me the first night and John McCleskey the last night. Great crowds attended.[15]

Again, on the 13th of December, Gus wrote of a series of three different debates he had with the same denominational preacher,

> I recently met E. Wright, of Dora, Ala., in three discussions—the first at Cordova and the last two at Dora. Large audiences attended, and good order prevailed in each discussion. We discussed the design of baptism at Cordova, and Holy Ghost baptism, spiritual gifts, and sinless perfection at Dora. Mr. Wright is a very weak man in debate, and only furnishes an occasion for us to reach many people whom we could not induce to hear the truth in any other way. We have no congregation at Dora but hope to hold a mission meeting there next spring.[16]

1934

In January 1934, Gus headed back to Millport to moderate for W. A. Black (1904-1980) in a debate with R. E. Higdon. Higdon had already debated both Gus and his brother, Charlie, several times in the past and was trying out the new kid on the block, so to speak. He reported,

> On January 11 and 12, W. A. Black engaged R. E. Higdon in debate at Millport on the establishment of the church. Brother Black kept the proper division of the word of God before the audience and exposed the absurd conclusions and contradictions of his opponent to the satisfaction of the church at Millport, and, no doubt, to the satisfaction of most *of* the "outsiders" present. Large audiences attended, and good order prevailed at all times. The writer kept time for the disputants.[17]

On the 17th of March, Gus wrote of his intentions to meet a Missionary Baptist by the name of B. G. Dodd in a three-night discussion beginning the 29th of that month. The series was to be held at Old Macedonia, on Black Water Creek, just north of Jasper about ten miles. Speaking of Dodd, he said, "He is to affirm the direct work of the Spirit in conversion, and salvation by faith in answer to prayer before baptism. I am to affirm the possibility of apostasy."[18]

A GREAT MEETING

The work in Jasper received a great boost in the summer of 1934 by way of a gospel meeting. It was to be a two-week effort involving three Sundays "beginning the second Lord's day in July and running over the fourth Lord's day."[19] The preaching was to be done by the nationally acclaimed and respected evangelist, G. C. Brewer.

A Tennessean by birth, Grover Cleveland Brewer (1884-1956) began his preaching career at the age of twenty-two while living in the Shoals area of Lauderdale County, Alabama. For many years he served as a staff writer for the *Gospel Advocate* and more than a few of those years he edited the "Queries and Answers" department for the paper. His preaching took him to all "the States in the Union except the States along the Canadian border."[20] However, he had a love for Alabama like no other. Interestingly enough, he had only been preaching a matter of weeks when he held his first debate in Walker County.

G. C. Brewer

Having spent the summer of 1906 preaching in the deep forest region of the southern part of the county in and around the old Liberty Hill church of Christ, Brewer had created much havoc among the denominations in the area. This led to being challenged to a debate by Baptist preacher, L. H. Baker. He referred to the 22-year-old Brewer as the "beardless boy" preacher, obviously to cast doubt that one of such youth could be trusted to accurately interpret the Scriptures. However, nothing about G. C. Brewer's command of the Word of God could be said to be immature. He took to Baker's teachings like a lion out of a cage. More than once he was verbally attacked by Baker's moderator, a Baptist preacher by the name of Ernest Pinegar. No less than twice James K. Hill (1872-1908), moderator for Brewer, and a gospel preacher living in Oakman, had to get between the two to keep them from going at one another with fisticuffs. Finally, Pinegar's anger got the best him. He got up from his seat and headed toward the "beardless boy" and they, "went together like dogs."[21]

The debate was long recalled by people in the county, though it had been twenty-eight years previous to his visit to Jasper in 1934. The meeting was well attended by brethren from all over the region, as well as good representation from the community around the building. Cecil Newcomb of Winfield came over and led the singing each evening, and Gus assisted in every way possible. There were "eighteen baptized and four were restored."[22] In August, an extended article appeared in the pages of the *Gospel Advocate* on the work in Jasper by brother Brewer. Among many reminiscences of the early days he reported on the current meeting saying,

> There are now about thirty-two congregations in Walker County. There are some ten or a dozen preachers in the county, but only

two or three of these are supported for full-time work, and their support is not what it should be....

We now have a good church at Jasper. They have a good brick house, well located, and the church is growing. In our recent meeting—held out of doors—our audiences ran between eight hundred and a thousand each night.

Gus Nichols deserves much credit for the success of the work at Jasper, and also for the success of our meeting. He is a prayerful, consecrated man, and a hard-working, faithful gospel preacher. I shall always love Walker County, Ala.[23]

MAINTAINING A BUSY PREACHING WORK SCHEDULE

Just before the Brewer meeting, Gus reported on the success of a meeting he began at his old home church at Howard. He started the meeting and brother Charlie Wheeler finished it. The younger preacher baptized four, and his older counterpart baptized five more.[24] Gus then followed with a quick meeting at Nauvoo where they, "had eight restored and the church was seemingly strengthened very much by the preaching."[25] Almost immediately after the meeting, he headed to Hackleburg in Marion County with, "twenty-five baptized and forty-three confessions of faults," reported.[26] Then, it was to Joppa in Morgan County, where he preached a meeting for the Hebron church. He told of, "nine baptisms and about forty confessing their faults."[27] In mid-September, he conducted a meeting at Boston, near Brilliant, in Marion County, with two baptized and three restored."[28] On October 1st he wrote, "We closed a good meeting yesterday afternoon at Zion, near Parrish, with two baptized and three restored. I am now at Flat Creek, with good audiences at the night services. I go next to North Birmingham, then back to my local work for the winter."[29]

Cecil Newcomb and Gus Nichols

There were three baptisms at the Flat Creek meeting,[30] and the North Birmingham where Gardner S. Hall was preaching brought about eleven baptisms and two restorations.[31]

Having concluded two years in the work at Jasper, Gus reported a summary of his 1934 efforts saying that he had, "conducted 452 services, including 126 Bible classes, 286 discourses, and 40 funerals. Some visible results were: 182 responded to the invitation—68 for baptism and 114 to confess their faults and for restoration."[32]

ENDNOTES

1 Gleanings from http://www.thepeoplehistory.com/1933.html.

2 Gleanings from *Encyclopedia of Alabama*, an on-line Encyclopedia of historical facts pertaining to the people, places, and things of Alabama.

3 Online resource, http://en.wikipedia.org/wiki/William_B._Bankhead_National_Forest.

4 Gus Nichols, *Gospel Advocate*, 26 January 1933, p. 91.

5 Ibid., 23 March 1933, p. 283.

6 Avery Fike, Unppublished document. *A Brief History of the Fifth Avenue Church of Christ.* This document was read at the mortgage burning of the Fifth Avenue Church, pp. 6-7.

7 Gus Nichols, *Gospel Advocate*, 10 August 1933, p. 762.

8 Ibid., 15 June 1933, p. 572.

9 Hugo McCord, *Words of Truth*, October 2002, p. 7.

10 Bailey, Hoyt, *Gospel Advocate*, 4 January 1934, p. 25.

11 Gus Nichols, Gospel Advocate, 7 September 1933, p. 860.

12 Ibid., 21 September 1933, p. 906.

13 Ibid.

14 Gus Nichols, *Gospel Advocate*, 23 March 1933, p. 283.

15 Ibid., 11 January 1934, p. 49.

16 Ibid.

17 Gus Nichols, *Gospel Advocate*, 25 January 1934, p. 97.

18 Ibid., 29 March 1934, p. 314.

19 Gus Nichols, *Firm Foundation*, 3 July 1934, p. 6.

20 Gussie Lambert, *In Memoriam*, Shreveport: Gussie Lambert, 1988, p. 34.

21 G. C. Brewer, *Forty Years On The Firing Line*, Kansas City: Old Paths Book Club, 1948, p. 24.

22 Gus Nichols, *Firm Foundation*, 3 July 1934, p. 6.

23 G. C. Brewer, "The Work In Walker County, Alabama." *Gospel Advocate*, 16 August 1934, pp. 780, 797.

24 Gus Nichols, *Gospel Advocate*, 19 July 1934, p. 696.

25 Ibid.

26 Gus Nichols, *Gospel Advocate*, 6 September 1934, p. 864.

27 Ibid., 20 September 1934, p. 916.

28 Ibid., 4 October 1934, p. 960.

29 Ibid., 11 October 1934, p. 984.

30 Ibid., 1 November 1934, p. 1058.
31 Ibid., 1 November 1934, p. 1061.
32 Ibid., 7 February 1935, p. 136.

- 18 -

Under The Master's Tutelage

The Lord God hath given me the tongue of the learned, that I should know how to speak a word in season to him that is weary: he wakeneth morning by morning, he wakeneth mine ear to hear as the learned.
—The Prophet, Isaiah 50:4

Understanding and strength of service in the Kingdom of heaven is a learned behavior. The all-empowering Word of God gives strength to the hearer and establishes the advocate of His grace. In the day of the Scriptures, ". . .holy men of God spake as they were moved by the Holy Spirit," 2 Peter 1:21. Yet, in these last days, though we have a completed message, the people continue to suffer for lack of knowledge.

In the fall of 1934, Gus Nichols laid a plan through which he might empower those who wanted to grow and develop themselves for leadership. Living through the economic crisis invading the land during that period, the idea of sending members to Freed-Hardeman College, David Lipscomb College, or Harding College was out of the question. Yet, the problem remained; the people needed educating. The church at Jasper needed elders and deacons, Bible class teachers, men who could lead singing, and other aspects of worship. The brethren needed to learn to teach cottage meetings and basic Bible studies.

1930s - Gus Nichols

Compounding the issue at hand for the Walker County preacher was the growing pressure from within his own family. He needed to challenge his young sons who were up and coming into their own.

In May of that year, Flavil had preached his first sermon on the front porch steps of the Walter Gurganus home in the Dovertown community. His sermon was entitled, "God's Plan For Man." He later recalled that he thought he could "go with it 25 or 30 minutes. . .. He started the sermon with Adam, touched all the major players in the Old Testament, the birth, life and crucifixion of Christ and ended with the instructions for the apostles to evangelize the world, all in 17 minutes."[1]

Through his father's tutelage, he learned quickly the importance of multi-tasking in the work as well as reporting on his efforts. Flavil's first report of work came as a result of fulfilling his first real assignment on July 29th. He wrote,

> Last Lord's day I filled my first appointment and made my second effort as a preacher at Brock meetinghouse, in Marion County. I am fifteen years of age and have been making talks a little more than a year. I hope to hold a few meetings next year. I taught a children's class daily during a ten days' meeting, in which my father, Gus Nichols, did the preaching, at Bethel, closing last night with two baptisms and one restoration. We will begin at Hackleburg August 12.[2]

Gus began looking around to see what was successful in other areas. In Birmingham, John T. Lewis (1876-1967) had started a training school for the brethren and was having some good success. Upon later reflection on this period of his ministry he recalled Lewis' example saying, ". . .I got the idea from him and started a class like that."[3] Twenty-seven years after starting the class he was asked about why the class was begun. To this he explained,

> We didn't have any elders, so I organized the class just for men and boys. I felt the need of training elders. I started it with the idea of its being a training class for the local congregation only, but soon, to my surprise, people were coming in from round about until it has grown now to sometimes sixty or seventy preachers.[4]

The nature of the class took on a basic format that involved coming to the church building on Friday evenings at around seven p.m., and the class would generally go to about nine-thirty or ten. He further explained the evenings as being that,

> Preachers come in from far and near. I make sermon outlines and discuss them as though I were preaching them, stopping along the way for illustrated material from the class, comments, or questions. We spend forty minutes at least on each outline. They get so full of that subject that they know what to do with it. They go back and remake it and rebuild it so they can preach it. They take my illustrations and comments which have been offered in the class and build them into their own outlines.[5]

For many of these preachers, it was the best help they could receive, because most of them worked in secular jobs through the week. By the time the weekend arrived, it was a mad dash to get themselves ready for a Bible Class and a sermon or two for Sunday. Some of these fellows were preaching for two or more congregations each week as well. Through this class setting, many churches heard Gus Nichols' sermons on any given Lord's Day.

So, beginning in 1934, he started around the first of September each year, the sessions generally running for six months, through the fall and winter. The Friday night classes became a core ingredient of his ministry long-term. In 1965, a "free all-day school"[6] on Saturdays was added. For 43 years, he educated the brethren at Jasper as well as giving training to above 500 preachers. Today, the school is still operated by the leadership of the Sixth Avenue congregation under the name, *Gus Nichols School of Biblical Studies.*

ENDNOTES

1 Christopher Wood, *Daily Mountain Eagle*, 13 May 1993, p. A7.

2 Flavil Nichols, *Gospel Advocate*, 16 August 1934, p. 795.

3 Ottis L. Castleberry, *He Looked For A City: A Biography of John T. Lewis*, Fairmount: Cogdill Foundation Publications, c.1980, p. 221. Note: The relationship Gus Nichols had with John T. Lewis was always kind and loving. In the late 1940s and early '50s their relationship was publicly strained because of the sides upon which they each fell over the support of children's homes from the church treasury. However, through it all, they always maintained an amicable relationship. See pages 182ff as evidence of this. He said, ". . .they remained the closest of friends until the death of Brother Lewis."

4 Willard Collins, "The Gus Nichols Story, Part II" *Gospel Advocate*, p. 216.

5 Ibid. Note: This event was not just for preachers. Men and boys were invited to come as well. Many teenage boys who later became preachers and teachers can recall going to this wonderful Friday evening class.

6 Marvin Bryant, *Gospel Advocate*, 26 May 1965, p. 325.

- 19 -

Publishing The Word Throughout The Land

The light of the eyes rejoiceth the heart: and a
good report maketh the bones fat.
—Solomon, Proverbs 15:30

When Gus celebrated his forty-third birthday, he had just begun his third year of toil with the Fifth Avenue church in Jasper. The variety of demands of this effort kept him constantly on the go. Though cares of the local saints were his primary focus, his influence throughout the area continued to expand. His was truly a county effort.

That which stimulated his broadening reputation could be seen on several fronts. Most prominently, was his preaching. Several hours of daily Bible study, mixed with a driving passion for the souls of people, proved to energize the man by sheer necessity. People need good preachers, and Gus was certainly one of the best, if not the best the region had to offer. And, he was in demand! Sundays were filled with going to support the works of his regular circuit. Reporting on his efforts in January he wrote, "One restored in Carbon Hill recently, and eight confessed their faults at Boston the second Lord's day. We recently baptized a lady here, (Jasper) and another came from the digressive church last Lord's day."[1] In the same issue he said, "I preached at Howard last Saturday night. The little band of disciples there are planning to build a modest meetinghouse soon. . .I was at Carbon Hill last Lord's Day and spoke to good audiences morning and evening. Carbon Hill Church is growing rapidly."[2]

Placing one's self in the lives of so many people, there are plenty of celebrations of success, but all too often he received calls to bear the suffering of the weak. One such occasion arose early in February when he reported, "We had a good service and attendance here Lord's Day, notwithstanding the tragic death of one of our members, who was killed Saturday night in a wreck."[3] Most Sundays involved speaking at least three times, especially when he was over in the western part of the county at Boston or Carbon Hill, he might be speaking in the afternoons at Howard or Gold Mine or Brilliant up in Marion County. Later in the year, he began preaching Monday evenings at Manchester and Tuesday evenings at Carbon Hill, all the while conducting two mid-week services at Jasper.[4] Then, on Friday nights he conducted his training class at the Fifth Avenue church building.

Another way his reputation continued to expand was through his son, Flavil. Following in his father's footsteps, very quickly he was in demand,

and with him the Nichols name continued to make its mark. Flavil reported in March, "Since October I have spoken somewhere every Lord's day. I have preached at Manchester, Dora, Gorgas, Eldridge, Berea, Oak Grove, Flat Creek, Bethel, and Winfield. Several have been restored and one baptized."[5]

Congregational growth continued to be a blessing at Jasper, and while the members of the church were still feeling the deep struggles of the national economic crisis, they were fulfilling their obligations. On March 4th Gus updated,

> We had two good services here yesterday. We have maintained the unity of the Spirit at all times in work and worship, and enjoyed a fellowship one with another, which makes our work as pleasant as it is successful. Our debt is being paid as due, and everyone seems to be happy to have a part in the work of the church.[6]

In early March, W. A. Black (1904-1980), then living and preaching a few miles south in Parrish, traveled with Gus over to Lamar County to support one of his Walker County preacher boys who was engaging in a debate. James Garland Pounds (1914-1991) was born in Cordova, and was one of the young men who, growing up in the congregation there, was greatly influenced by brother Nichols. He had assisted him some time previous to go to Detroit in Lamar to work with the small band of Christians in that town. On the occasion, Pounds met a young Baptist preacher by the name of J. D. Hankins. Previously, he had met another Baptist by the name of C. C. Clark, and was to meet him again, but "the Baptists changed men and put up J. D. Hankins."[7] W. R. Willcutt (1882-1946) from over at Fulton, Mississippi came over to moderate for brother Pounds.[8] The debate was well attended, and the cause of Christ was upheld in the debate.

In April, Gus participated in a lectureship over in Hamilton. Lindsay A. Allen (1907-1999),[9] the preacher there at the time, organized the forum and included his Jasper colleague in the Saturday evening program. Gus spoke on the subject, "A Bible Home." The lesson was so well received that opportunities presented themselves for him to be able to present the lesson at several other venues.[10]

The summer gospel meeting season opened at Alabama City, near Gadsden, in mid-May. Gus conducted a twelve-day meeting resulting in thirteen baptisms. The preacher there, William Floyd (1906-1975), traded pulpits with brother Nichols during the meeting when he preached at Jasper "the third Lord's day in May."[11] The success of the meeting was so great that they asked Gus to come back and preach another meeting the following year. This meeting was followed by a good mission effort back in one of Walker County's oldest works on Flat Creek. On the 5th of July he wrote, "I closed a week's meeting at Flat Creek on Saturday night, with thirteen baptized and one restored."[12]

For the work in Jasper, the big meeting for the summer was an attempt to recreate the fervor and excitement they had the previous year when twenty responded to the gospel call. G. C. Brewer (1884-1956) agreed to come again and preach a two-week meeting beginning the first Sunday in July. On the last day of the meeting Gus sat down and penned the following for the readers of the *Gospel Advocate*,

> Our series of meetings, in which G. C. Brewer did the preaching and Cecil Newcom directed the song service, came to a close today. At the last baptismal service two grown people made the good confession. There were eleven baptized and four restored during the meeting. The attendance was good! Perhaps the audience ran as high as a thousand at some of the evening services. From one hundred to four hundred heard the gospel every evening who were not members of the church of Christ. Also, the day services were well attended. Our services were conducted out in the open air. Brother Brewer was with us in just such a meeting last year. The church has been strengthened and edified in the meeting, and sinners were taught the way of salvation. We are planning to have a like meeting again next year.[13]

In August, Gus made his way over to Munford, Alabama to participate in a gospel meeting. The work there had long been a hotbed of restoration activity that ran back to the late 1870s when J. M. Joiner (1843-1921) planted New Testament Christianity in Talladega County's Hopeful Community. One of his first converts there was a Baptist by the name of William Joseph Camp (1847-1934). Joe and his wife Elizabeth Smith (1843-1927) raised six sons and one daughter. Joe preached in the area and planted churches in several locations. One of his sons, Benjamin Franklin "Frank" (1876-1941) also entered the ministry and had great success in the region.

About three months before Gus' arrival for the meeting, one of Frank's boys, Joseph Franklin (1915-1991) preached his first sermon for his home congregation. Young and impressionable, hearing Gus Nichols made a profound impact on his life. Many years later, Franklin Camp reminisced about this meeting in glowing terms saying,

> I recall vividly the first time I ever saw brother Nichols. It was the third Sunday of August 1935. . . . The first service began at 11:00 A.M. At about two minutes before eleven, he walked through the door and down to the front of the building. Only one person

in Munford had ever heard him preach before this time. When the first service was over, those who had never heard him before realized that they had been privileged to hear one of the great preachers of all time. The meeting lasted two full weeks with services twice each day. The crowds grew; the house ran over; people were standing; children were sitting around the rostrum and people were outside listening through opened windows. Thirty-seven people obeyed the gospel during the meeting. He stayed in our home and a friendship began which was to grow through a period of forty years.[14]

    The young preacher was so impressed with the older. His demeanor, the way he emphasized the Scriptures and the like, made its impact. Adding to this first meeting, he further recalled when brother Nichols, "stated that he had studied the Bible five hours a day for twenty years. I realized that if a man like him needed to study five hours a day, I'd need to study even more."[15] For a generation, the greatness of Gus Nichols and Franklin Camp[16] was in part signified in countless sermon illustrations by restoration preachers that brother Nichols studied five hours a day, and brother Camp studied six. Working companions for life, during subsequent years the leadership of both these men made them household names throughout the brotherhood.

A FAMILY IN TRANSITION

    Some changes in the Nichols household happened in early September. The oldest of Gus and Matilda's children, Gracie, had finished her high school activities the previous May, and was now ready to spread her wings. She boarded the train leading to Henderson, Tennessee, where she was to begin her studies under N. B. and Mrs. Jo Hardeman at Freed-Hardeman College. Seeing the train disappear in the distance, there was a certain sense of mixed emotion as the family, now with one member missing, left the rail platform that day to return to their Fifth Avenue home. There is just something about that first one who leaves home. Despite the emotion, life does find a way to continue.

DEBATE IN LAMAR COUNTY

    Resumed efforts in mission meetings kept Gus busy into the fall of the year. On October 22nd, he headed over to Lamar County once again to engage an old rival in a religious discussion. R. E. Higdon had once again sounded the battle cry and found a ready foe in the preacher from Jasper. Both he and Charlie had met Earnest Higdon on several occasions. This debate took place over the space of four days and each night was devoted to different topics. On Tuesday night the discussion was on the subject "of the establishment of the church."[17] On Wednesday evening the two preachers debated on the subjects of Holy Ghost baptism and miracles. On Thursday, they squared off on the use of instrumental music in worship, and on Friday, they closed the appointment with opposing views over "feet washing."[18]

TRUTH IN LOVE

The work in Birmingham during the 1930s was enjoying an impactful gain of strength due to the long-time efforts of John T. Lewis (1876-1967). A Tennessean by birth, he had moved to Birmingham after completing his studies at Nashville Bible School in 1906. Upon arrival in Alabama's most central city, he set himself to the work of building upon the foundations of a generation's worth of evangelism that preceded him in the efforts of J. M. Barnes (1836-1913).[19] Lewis believed that every community needed its own congregation of the Lord's people, so within a couple of decades congregations sprung up throughout the city.

John T. Lewis

By the mid 1930s, two young preachers in Birmingham were enjoying exceptional success in their respective congregational efforts. Jack D. Meyer (1914-1972) was working with the city's oldest congregation, West End. In early 1936, he announced that the church would begin using the new technology of radio to evangelize in the city. Under the title "Birmingham On Air," he wrote:

> Beginning February 2 and concluding June 28, West End Church broadcasts a studio sermon every Sunday afternoon, at 4:30 to 4:45 o'clock, over station WAPI, 1140 kilocycles, a 5,000-watt station. In this major evangelistic endeavor, we only ask for announcements of churches, especially in this area, and that members especially induce friends of the world to listen.[20]

Very soon the crowd at West End increased to over 400 in weekly Sunday attendance. The radio program continued for several years as a joint effort among churches of Christ in the city.

Just up the road, north of the city, was Gardner Sewell Hall (1906-1978), who was in his sixth year of working with the North Birmingham congregation.[21] Gardner was the son of brother Flavil Hall (1876-1952) of Halls Valley, Georgia. The Halls were already held in high esteem by the Nichols, as their eldest son bore the name of the elder Hall, as has been noted. The younger Hall was coming into his own success as a preacher of the gospel and was doing a fine work in the north Birmingham area. They had Gus Nichols for a gospel meeting in October 1934 with good success.

It was around this time that discussions began to arise around the idea of publishing a journal that would meet the needs of a growing church in the state and around the country. In the clime of other very successful efforts in the past, this paper needed to be informative of efforts being done as well as instructive in the teachings of the Scriptures.

The two younger preachers looked to Gus for his expertise in this field. Already, Gus had enjoyed some success with the little paper he produced during his days at Millport, *The Gospel Way*. Also, not long after moving to Jasper he was editing another paper called, *The Gospel Standard*.[22] All three men had been submitting reports to the *Gospel Advocate* for quite some time, and so it seemed good to them to enter into a joint editorship of a new paper they called, *Truth In Love*.

The first issue of *Truth In Love* appeared in November 1935. Within a short time, a fourth editor was added, John Dee Cox (1908-1964). John was from up in the Shoals area, of the little town of Killen. He had completed his training at David Lipscomb and had been preaching in locations in Tennessee and Mississippi. When Gardner Hall left North Birmingham in 1937 for the West Hill church in Pensacola, Florida,[23] Cox filled the vacated pulpit, and joined the editorial staff of *Truth In Love*. He continued co-editing for a little over four years. He later recounted, "During that four years, the circulation increased from 7,000 to 25,000."[24]

Meanwhile, Gus continued sending a few reports to the *Gospel Advocate* during the fall and early winter of 1935. He had good results in a meeting at Carbon Hill, a congregation where he preached every fourth Sunday of the month and every Tuesday night, "with four baptized and one making the good confession, who became ill and is to be baptized later."[25] Around the first of November, he preached a two-week mission in the Pleasant Grove community, about seven miles west of Jasper. The meeting was held under an arbor, and the crowds were between six and eight hundred in nightly attendance.[26]

In December, an opportunity arose for Gus to go to Birmingham and do something he had never done before. The potential to speak to thousands of listeners at once came when he was invited to speak over the radio. He quickly dispatched a telegram to the *Gospel Advocate* saying, "I will speak over *WBRC*. Birmingham, December 15, at 4:30 pm."[27] This introduction sparked what led to an era of outreach that continues to the present day. But, more will come to describe its progress.

ENDNOTES

1 Gus Nichols, *Gospel Advocate,* 7 February 1935, p. 136. Note: The "digressive church" in Jasper referred to is the First Christian Church of Jasper, Alabama (Disciples of Christ) located on W. 18th St.

2 Ibid.

3 Ibid., 14 February 1935, p. 160..

4 Ibid., 26 December 1935, p. 1243.

5 Flavil Nichols, *Gospel Advocate,* 14 March 1935, p. 258.

6 Gus Nichols, *Gospel Advocate,* 14 March 1935, p. 258.

7 J. G. Pounds, *Gospel Advocate,* 21 March 1935, p. 283.

8 Note: William Riley Willcutt was an accomplished preacher and debater among churches of Christ in Mississippi. He preached many years around Columbus and Fulton. On 19 May 1946, while traveling over to West Point for a preaching appointment, brother Willcutt was tragically killed in a car crash. A longtime friend of Gus Nichols, he was asked to come over and preach the funeral. Brother Willcutt was buried in the little cemetery at Lone Oak church of Christ in Steens, the same cemetery where Gus' younger brother, Charlie, and his family would be buried several years later. Brother Willcutt's obituary is in 27 June 1946 issue of the *Gospel Advocate,* p. 619.

9 Lindsay Allen, "Lectureship At Hamilton," *Gospel Advocate,* 18 April 1935, p. 377. Note: Lindsay Anderson Allen was born in Lynn, Winston County. He became a Christian under the influence of C. R. Nichol in a meeting in Russellville, Alabama while in his teens. L. A. Allen attended David Lipscomb College and Harding College. He supported himself as a schoolteacher while preaching in several different locations. Mostly, his preaching work was in north Alabama, Mississippi and Tennessee. He spent the last years of his life in the Shoals area where he passed from this life the 11th of July 1999. He was buried in the Tri-Cities Memorial Gardens in Florence. A brief biographical sketch appeared in the 20 February edition of *Gospel Advocate,* 1941, p. 183. Also, an obituary appeared in the Birmingham News 14 July 1999, p. 05-C.

10 Chester Estes, *Firm Foundation,* 14 May 1935, p. 7.

11 Gus Nichols, *Gospel Advocate,* 13 June 1935, p. 570. Note: George William Floyd was born near Sparta, Tennessee, the 6th of January 1906. He attended David Lipscomb and Vanderbilt University, and preached in Attalla, near Gadsden, Alabama for several years. He spent most of his years in Texas. He finished his earthly vigil in Sherman, Texas, the 3rd of April 1975. His body was returned to Sparta where interment followed in the Floyd Cemetery a few miles west of town.

12 Gus Nichols, *Gospel Advocate,* 1 August 1935, p. 739.

13 Ibid.

14 Franklin Camp, "Brother Nichols," *The Word of Life,* Vol. 5, No. 1, January 1976, p. 1.

15 Ibid.

16 Note: Your author was greatly impacted by the preaching of Franklin Camp. During a gospel meeting he conducted the first week in June 1968 at the Chisholm church of Christ in Montgomery, Alabama, this young ten-year-old was so impressed upon with the need to obey the gospel that he was baptized on Wednesday night of the meeting, 5 June 1968.

17 Gus Nichols, "Do The Scriptures Authorize Instrumental Music," *Words of Truth*, 29 May 1969, p. 2. Note: This article was based on an article that originally appeared in a little-known paper that Gus Nichols edited in 1935 called, *The Gospel Standard*.

18 Ibid.

19 Note: Justus McDuffie Barnes (1836-1913) was one of Alabama's early and great evangelists. Born to a wealthy landowner south of Montgomery, he was trained by Alexander Campbell at Bethany College beginning in 1854, and devoted his life to strengthening and planting churches in Alabama. His life was prematurely cut short in a freak car accident the 28th of April 1913. He was buried in Montgomery's Greenwood Cemetery.

20 Jack Meyer, *Gospel Advocate*, 23 January 1936, p. 89.

21 Gardner S. Hall, *Gospel Advocate*, 4 July 1935, p. 642.

22 Gus Nichols, "Do The Scriptures Authorize Instrumental Music," *Words of Truth*, 29 May 1969, p. 2.

23 Gardner S. Hall, "Hall to Pensacola, Fla.," *Gospel Advocate*, 2 September 1937, 834.

24 John D. Cox, *A Word Fitly Spoken*, Nashville: Gospel Advocate Company, 1962, 47.

25 Gus Nichols, *Gospel Advocate*, 21 November 1935, p. 1120.

26 Ibid. Note: The Pleasant Grove meeting was reported on 15 November and appeared on the same page in a separate entry.

27 Gus Nichols, *Gospel Advocate*, 12 December 1935, p. 1243.

- 20 -

A Full-Time Preacher

> I know both how to be abased, and I know how to abound: every where and in all things I am instructed both to be full and to be hungry, both to abound and to suffer need. I can do all things through Christ which strengtheneth me.
> —Paul, Philippians 4:12–13

The sixth year of the century's third decade entered with the nation still deeply entrenched in economic crisis. Many western states were continuing to experience the effects of the Dust Bowl where thousands were driven from their homes to seek work and shelter in less impacted areas. A national election was to be held later in the year, but the popularity and help attained through Roosevelt's New Deal seemed to make his re-election nothing less than expected. While several of the brethren at Jasper were still out of work, others were getting assistance through the President's back-to-work programs.

THE PROVIDENCE OF GOD

When the Fifth-Avenue building was completed in 1927, the church was left with a debt of a little over $10,000.00. A fifteen-year note had been worked out with a mortgage company to pay back $8,000, and the other $2000 had been made possible through personal loans. For the first half of the life of the loan, most of the money paid back was interest, and very little toward the principle. The church had made their payments regularly, but barely. It was around this time when the church was contacted by their lien holders who, themselves, were in desperate need of freeing up cash. In a speech made during the Freed-Hardeman College Lectures several decades later, Flavil reflected on the providential way in which God blessed the work at Jasper during this most difficult time saying,

> The mortgage company notified the church that it would accept $4,000 cash by a certain date as full payment for a balance of $7,000. A $3,000 gift offer!...Dad preached two Sundays on prayer and asked the elders and their wives to join him and mother in prayer every hour, daily, for two weeks—to pray fervently that God would lead them to someone with $4,000 the church could borrow. After this period of prayer, on Monday morning before the deadline, Dad told Mother he did not intend to return home until he had found that needed loan. She remarked that he *could not* go very far, because she knew he did not have money to buy

much gasoline. He replied that he was not going in the car, but on foot—and kissed her goodbye.

Walking toward the business district he passed one office where the black janitor was sweeping the sidewalk. The second man he saw that morning was a judge on the courthouse steps. Exchanging greetings, my father remarked that the judge seemed unusually happy that morning. Cheerfully, he explained that he had a special reason to be happy—he had just paid off his $3,000 mortgage!

Entering the courthouse together, he remarked that the agent did not like it because he had paid it off ahead of schedule, and the out-of-state lender had been depending on the interest it was earning. Inside his office, Dad stated that no doubt God had providentially led him to the judge that morning. Upon hearing his mission, by phone the judge made an appointment for Dad immediately, and he soon returned to report that the agent agreed to let the church borrow that $3,000. Now, could the judge suggest a source for the other $1000? A widow who lived in another town was employed in the courthouse and had overheard at least part of their conversation. She spoke up and proposed that *she* would lend the church $1,000 if Dad would personally sign the note with the elders. Dad was back home well before noon with assurance of the needed funds for the church. He always believed that their prayers had availed with God.[1]

With such a visible example of God's providence before them, the church and its preacher pressed on with the work at hand. In January, he put the final touches on his first gospel tract and followed it up with an advertisement in the *Gospel Advocate* with the details. "'What Must I Do To Be Saved?' By Gus Nichols—A 32-page tract: A sermon on the plan of salvation—interesting and convincing. Order from the author, Jasper, Ala. Price, 10 cts. each; $1.00 a dozen."[2]

As with the previous winter, while the work continued to be blessed, it was not without its setbacks. Twice in February, he reported funerals he had to preach. One of particular note he conveyed involved a severe loss to one family in the congregation. Writing February 3rd,

> Last Saturday, Sister Elmer Kimbrell's home here was destroyed by fire, burning her three children to death. The mother had gone to get a pail of water at a neighbor's home nearby, and upon returning found her home enveloped in flames. The children had been locked inside. Their ages were four months, two years, and

four years. I preached the funeral of the three children Sunday afternoon.³

Later in the spring, reminiscence emerged for the people of the area of the devastation suffered nearly twenty years previous when on April 5th, a weather system passed through Tupelo, in Lee County, Mississippi, killing 216 and injuring over 700. The storm passed north of Walker County, killing eight people in Red Bay, in Franklin County, Alabama. The following day, that same system brought devastation to the city and region around Gainesville, in Hall County, Georgia, where 203 died and over 1,600 suffered injuries. The two days of calamity through the southeastern United States produced twelve different tornadoes, killing 454 people, and became the second worst tragedy of its kind in U.S. history.

1936 - Birthday for Lucendy Calloway

People are resilient in the face of severe tragedy. The human spirit engages when devastation hits, and those left behind rebuild. Putting your best foot forward demands faith in He who is not seen, as a Father who will help His children overcome. Setting their focus on what they could do, the church at Jasper stepped out in faith to commit their support to mission work. Brother Nichols reported in the Texas paper,

> The church in Jasper has arranged to support its minister for a month of mission work this year, the work to be done near enough to Jasper that the church here can keep in touch with the congregations which we hope to establish until they may become strong enough to take care of themselves. We have several young preachers who go out and assist weak congregations in teaching the truth in their respective communities. This work is done at a sacrifice on the part of those young brethren, and proves their unselfish interest in the church of our Lord. The writer is preaching half time in Jasper and one Lord's day per month at Carbon Hill and Boston, respectively. We are certainly increasing in every good word and work in this section.⁴

A few weeks later, good spirits and positive thinking continued to be expressed for the work that was being done as demonstrated in the following,

> Our congregations near here are in the best condition they have ever been. Peace and harmony prevail among the brethren. More efforts are being put forth to spread the gospel than usual. We have several splendid young preachers being rapidly developed. More people are reading good papers and religious literature. Perhaps ten sermons are delivered now in this section to where one was delivered a few years ago. Several new congregations have been added to the list making about thirty now in existence in Walker County.[5]

Knowing the readership of the brotherhood papers among the locals, he attempted to rally the congregations in the area to get behind the young preachers he was training when he made a third appeal, this time in the *Gospel Advocate*,

> We have some splendid young preachers near here who want to get into the harvest fields and begin to gather precious sheaves for the Master this summer. May I suggest that congregations which feel unable to support an experienced preacher would do well to arrange with these young brethren and stand by them in some mission meetings. I know they can preach the truth.[6]

As Gus was gearing up for the summer meeting period, he was called upon by some of the schools in the region to speak at their graduation exercises. On April 19th, he had the privilege of preaching the graduation sermon at the Kennedy High School, over in Lamar County.[7] Some of the students in the graduation class were from congregations in the area, among whom he had assisted personally in previous years. Again, on the 26th he preached the commencement sermon at the Hubbertville High School in Fayette County.[8] Then, on Sunday night the 17th of May he preached the commencement sermon at the High School in Oakman, a few miles south of Jasper.[9] After a good mission meeting in West Jasper at the end of May, Gus made his way back over to Alabama City, near Gadsden, to begin a thirteen-day preaching series the first Sunday in June. He had been there the previous year where the response to the preaching of the gospel had been good, and the brethren were hoping for similar results by a return engagement. At the end of the month he reported having enjoyed his efforts working alongside their minister, William Floyd (1906-1975). "Fifteen were baptized, two restored, and two became identified with the congregation during the meeting."[10]

B. C. GOODPASTURE

Returning home quickly after the meeting, he had but a few days to prepare the area for what had become the great annual summer meeting at the Fifth Avenue church. During the last couple of years, they had enjoyed the preaching of G. C. Brewer (1884-1956), but this year a relatively unknown young preacher was to visit the small Walker County town; his name, B. C. Goodpasture.

A Tennessean by birth, Benton Cordell Goodpasture (1895-1977) had preached in his home state, a short time in north Alabama, and was at that time the preacher for the Seminole Avenue church of Christ in Atlanta, Georgia. In later years, as *Gospel Advocate* editor, he remembered with fondness his first preaching in Jasper and how engaged its preacher was with his preaching. He said, "I have never seen anyone who enjoyed hearing the gospel preached more than Brother Nichols. He listened as if he had never heard 'the sweet story' before."[11]

B. C. Goodpasture and Avery Fike

Equally impressed with the Atlanta preacher, many years later Gus recalled with glowing tribute,

> He was then considered as a young preacher of rich and mellowing experience. He had formerly delivered a high school commencement address at Fayette, Alabama the echo of which had reached us at Jasper, an adjoining county. The people of Fayette had "never heard a man his equal" for such an occasion. Having heard of the "great man of God," we wanted him for a meeting. We asked brethren G. C. Brewer and H. Leo Boles if they had ever heard of the great preacher from Atlanta. They highly recommended him. The meeting began on a Lord's day morning. None of us had ever seen the preacher before. After a brief introduction, Brother Goodpasture arose to speak. The house was so crowded that I had to sit on the platform with the speaker. The large audience was tense and almost breathless as the speaker rose to address them. "Surely no one could possibly live up to the background commendations and the introduction given to the strange, but handsome young man," the audience seemed to say in tense expressions on their very faces. But within sixty seconds, every one was completely relaxed, and seemed to feel at ease in the presence of a great personality who had come to us on the level of a friend and brother in the Lord.

After the meeting that morning, visitors from Haleyville, Birmingham, Fayette, and other places too numerous to mention, said in substance, "That is the best preaching that we have ever heard." We moved out into the open space beside the meeting house for the evening services where we had provided a platform and lights with seats enough for 1000 people. Before the meeting closed we had more than that number present. Many obeyed the gospel and many others were restored to their first love during the meeting.[12]

Goodpasture reported early on, "I am here in Jasper in the first week of what promises to be a good meeting. Large crowds and one confession to date."[13] The talents of the young preacher, along with such positive response from the community, led to other opportunities in later years for him to return to Jasper for other preaching engagements.

His biographer, J. E. Choate (1916-2013), recalling these later visits said,

> Something came out of that Jasper meeting that never happened to Goodpasture anywhere before or since. When he returned later for a second meeting, on the first Sunday of the meeting, Gus Nichols told Goodpasture the elders would like to meet him in a Sunday school room. So, he went into the room where the elders were. They asked him if he still had the sermons that he preached in the previous meeting. And he told the elders that he thought he had the sermons. Then they said, "We want you to preach those same sermons in this meeting." Several years later, Goodpasture returned for a third meeting in their new meetinghouse, and they asked him to preach the identical sermons again and he did.[14]

MORE SUMMER MEETING WORK

During the weeks ahead, Gus Nichols continued to indelibly imprint the mark of his passion upon the lives of countless individuals in the region. He reported nine baptisms and eight restorations in a meeting at Brush Pond in Walker County on August 29th.[15] In the same report, he mentioned one baptism at Liberty Hill, in a week's meeting in the southern part of the county, and thirteen baptized at a meeting in Hodges, in Franklin County. He followed a month later with reports of eleven baptisms and several restorations in a series at Eldridge back near home.[16]

Another meeting in early September was held down toward Birmingham in the community of Morris in north Jefferson County. The church there had been a plant of the North Birmingham congregation through the efforts of Gardner S. Hall (1906-1978). There were several interesting things about the meeting to capture the imagination of the modern reader. As the work in Morris was still very much a fledgling effort, their numbers being few, it was essential to carry out the assemblies each evening under a brush arbor. The North Birmingham brethren, and the community supported it very well. "It was said that so many people had not attended a meeting of any kind in Morris in twenty-one years."[17] One other interesting thing Gus reported on the meeting was that four ladies were baptized, two of them were twin sisters. He said, "We buried and raised them in the same baptismal act."[18]

FULL-TIME

There was a transition in the congregation at Jasper that began sometime in October. The elders approached brother Nichols about becoming a full-time preacher. Up to that time, as has been stated, he was half time with the brethren at Jasper and was on a circuit to other churches the other half of the time. Knowing the present economic stress on the church, along with a mortgage they were paying, it was a real step in faith to commit themselves financially. They committed $100 per month to the Nichols family, and promised to increase it as opportunity arose. Avery Fike, one of the elders, later recalled, "We increased his support as we could, but still he has made a financial sacrifice to stay with the work."[19]

The Nichols Boys Playing Marbles

At the age of forty-four, Gus commented to the brotherhood, "I am giving full time to the work here now, whereas in the past I only gave half time. We are growing in every good work."[20]

Full-time work at Jasper hardly changed any aspect of Gus' work schedule. Jasper may have paid him for the work, but his ministry went far beyond that of the city limits, and the auspices of the local church. He was a people person. Folks in the town knew him, and he was respected among the community at large. His home was filled with children, but never too full to be a support for others. The table was seldom spread without an extra place-setting or two for visitors.

A Full-Time Preacher

A fatherly sense of duty to his fellow church workers in the area enlisted one more message to the *Firm Foundation* before the end of the year. In it, he gave a list of the preachers who had moved around to different locations, so they would be able to continue receiving the paper,

> My address will be the same next year as this, 1405 Fifth Avenue, Jasper, Alabama. The phone number is 225-J. Flavil Nichols is the same as mine. Brother J. G. Pounds has moved from Detroit, Alabama to Jasper, Alabama, Route 4. Brother A. P. Jones has moved from Jasper, Alabama, Route 5, to Quinton, Alabama, Route 2. Brother Willie Holley, Parrish, Alabama is a splendid preacher and I believe his name has not been in the preacher list. Rex Turner has gone from his former address to Route 3, Box 309, Montgomery, Alabama. W. A. Black has moved from Millport, Alabama to Booneville, Mississippi. Brother Chessley Cranford should be on the list. He is at Route 1, Breeman [sic, Bremen], Alabama. Brother C. A. Wheeler of Jasper, Alabama, Route 5, should be added to the list. He is eighty-five years old.[21]

ENDNOTES

1 Flavil Nichols, *Freed-Hardeman University Lectures*, 1990, p. 195-96.

2 Advertisement, *Gospel Advocate*, 6 February 1936, p. 142.

3 Gus Nichols, *Gospel Advocate*, 20 February 1936, p. 186.

4 Gus Nichols, *Firm Foundation*, 10 March 1936, p. 6.

5 Ibid., 19 May 1936, p. 7.

6 Gus Nichols, *Gospel Advocate*, 21 May 1936, p. 498.

7 Ibid., 7 May 1936, p. 449.

8 Gus Nichols, *Firm Foundation*, 26 May 1936, page 7.

9 Ibid.

10 Gus Nichols, *Gospel Advocate*, 9 July 1936, p. 665.

11 B. C. Goodpasture, ed., *Gospel Advocate*, 25 March 1976, p. 194. Note: This issue of *Gospel Advocate* was dedicated to Gus Nichols in honor of his, then, recent passing. B. C. Goodpasture's reflections were in the opening editorial, where he reported the meeting as taking place in the spring of 1934. In his biography, *The Anchor That Holds*, J. E. Choate records on page 117 that the meeting was held in the summer of 1934. However, Nichols always reported on the meetings in Jasper during that time. He reported that G. C. Brewer held the meetings at Jasper in the summers of 1934 and 1935. It was not until the summer of 1936 when the first Goodpasture meeting took place. Also, Goodpasture reported being in Jasper in a meeting in the 16 July edition of *GA*, 1936, p. 688. The visual behavior in Nichols became a most striking consistency in his life. Many through the years reflected similarly when being in an audience with brother Nichols. No matter the subject preached or the eloquence or fame of the speaker, when Gus Nichols was in the audience, he engaged as if the message being spoken was the first time he had ever heard it.

12 Gus Nichols, "B. C. Goodpasture In The Pulpit," *Sermons And Lectures*, Chapter VII, pp. 29-31.

13 B. C. Goodpasture, ed., *Gospel Advocate*, 16 July 1936, p. 688.

14 Ibid.

15 Gus Nichols, *Gospel Advocate*, 10 September 1936, p. 882.

16 Ibid., 24 September 1936, p. 928.

17 Ibid., p. 930.

18 Ibid.

19 Avery Fike, Unpublished. *A Brief History of the Fifth Avenue Church of Christ*, p. 7. The document is located in the Jasper Public Library in their Genealogy Room.

20 Gus Nichols, *Gospel Advocate*, 29 October 1936, p. 1048.

21 Gus Nichols, *Firm Foundation*, 15 December 1936, p. 7.

- 21 -

Relationships That Make Life Greater

A man that hath friends must shew himself friendly: and there is a friend that sticketh closer than a brother.
—Solomon, Proverbs 18:24

SPECIAL COURSES AT FREED-HARDEMAN COLLEGE

It has been said by those who knew Gus Nichols best, something to the effect that he was a living, breathing, sponge for knowledge. For years, he devoted himself to several hours a day in the study of the Word of God, but there was always more to learn, more to know, and more to understand. In later years, he was asked if there were any regrets in his life, and he responded that his greatest sorrow was that he did not know more of the deep treasures of the word of God. He was a teacher of preachers. Yet, this teacher desired to be taught, and opportunities to expand his horizons were ever in his thoughts.

A little less than 150 miles northwest of Jasper is the small college town of Henderson, Tennessee. Freed-Hardeman College was, in those days, a two-year school primarily devoted to schoolteacher preparation. The nationally known preacher and college president, N. B. Hardeman (1874-1965) desired to expand assistance to preachers, and the development of preachers in his program. He determined to begin offering special courses to preachers from far and wide during the month of January. The first such courses began during the first month of 1937.[1]

Gus and Flavil Nichols made their way to attend the Special Courses series that first Tuesday of the new year. The courses were to take place throughout the month. Sessions began on Tuesdays and finished on Saturdays in time to allow preachers to get back to their regular preaching assignments, and then classes would resume again on Tuesday of the following week. There was no charge for tuition, and room and board was only one dollar per day. The *Gospel Advocate* ran this first promotion of the program,

> The special courses given at Freed-Hardeman College are now in progress. There is a large attendance—more than sixty-five have been enrolled for these special courses. This does not include the group of young preachers who are regular students. There are about thirty regular students who are preachers of the gospel; with faculty members, about one hundred preachers are taking

these special courses. There are seventeen states represented by those who have come for the special courses. Others are expected to come for the latter part of the courses. There are to be four weeks given to these special courses. Special courses are given in "The Bible," "Bible Geography," "Evidences of Christianity," "Church History," "English," "Sunday-School Work," "Preparation and Delivery of Sermons," "Religious Errors and How to Meet Them," "Singing," etc. H. Leo Boles is assisting the faculty of Freed-Hardeman College in presenting these courses; he is also preaching—each evening—in a series of meetings for the church. Other special teachers and preachers have been invited to supplement the courses. Among those invited brethren are: F. B. Srygley, Foy E. Wallace, Jr., Clarence Cook, B. C. Goodpasture, Batsell Baxter, E. H. Ijams, C. R. Nichol, J. T. Lewis, J. F. Cox, J. T. Hinds, E. R. Harper, J. N. Armstrong, and I. A. Douthitt.[2]

Ninety preachers from several states attended the special courses series during its first year.[3] In future years, Gus Nichols increased his involvement extensively in the program, but for the present, his blessing was to soak up the experience, drink in the Word being taught, and every week, carrying with him a veritable treasure trove of ideas to initiate in his own ministry.

CHARLIE ALEXANDER WHEELER

As Paul was to Timothy, so was Charlie Wheeler to Gus Nichols. Since his baptism in the fall of 1909, his and brother Wheeler's lives enjoyed an interweaving adventure in Christian living that surpasses the best of relationships among men. Several vignettes of antiquity might be used to describe the relationship that existed between these two soldiers of the cross. Their friendship was like that of David and Jonathan. They loved each other dearly. Their ministry was often like that of Paul and Silas in that they studied together, traveled, preached, and planted works together. Theirs was like John, the Baptist and Jesus, when John said, "He must increase, but I must decrease" (John 3:30). Seeing Gus develop into a powerful voice for Christ was one of Charlie Wheeler's greatest delights. Watching Gus evolve, as a preacher of the gospel, beyond the sphere of his influence and preeminence among the brethren, was as great a blessing to the older brother as any other thing of

C. A. Wheeler
Nancy Adeline Dodson

which he could imagine in life. To Wheeler, Gus was more than a feather in his cap; he was a star in his crown of glory.

For Gus, the feelings of respect were mutual. Words could not be found to describe the depth of love, veneration, and honor for the elder brother. Not only did he baptize him, but also he trained him. Hours and hours these two men spent together studying the deep treasures to be found in the Word of God. Brother Wheeler fed the continuous hunger pains for knowledge that seemed to envelope the heart of the younger man. He was Gus Nichols' friend and confidant, truly a father in the faith. The direction of the older preacher was always a pleasure to hear. The wisdom of his years supplanted any foolishness that might be found in the younger to make him strong in the Lord, and in the power of His might.

This relationship evolved deeply into the family life of both men. As has been mentioned, Charlie Wheeler baptized Matilda, and performed the ceremony when she and Gus were married. When sister Wheeler, and later their daughter, Della Deason, passed away, it was Gus who preached their funerals. To the Nichols children, brother Wheeler was as much a fixture in their home as anyone could be. Many were the meals where brother Wheeler sat with the family around the table. Often the children have recalled having had brother Wheeler participate in the family devotionals when the children would say their memory verses, their father would quote the verse before it in the Bible, and brother Wheeler would quote the verse after it.[4]

Suffice it to say, Gus felt deep respect for brother Wheeler in his later years. On February 18, 1937 an open letter to the brotherhood appeared on in the pages of the *Gospel Advocate* on behalf of his old counterpart. It appeared under the heading, "C. A. Wheeler Now Eighty-Six—Gus Nichols," and said,

> C. A. Wheeler, of Route 5, Jasper, Ala., is well known in North Alabama. He is now in his eighty-seventh year, and is no longer able to preach the gospel. Brother Wheeler says he has preached for more than sixty years, and has baptized about six thousand people. He has established many congregations in North Alabama and labored most of his life with weak congregations and in places where there were no churches after the New Testament order. Of course this type of work did not bring him wealth. He barely obtained the necessities of life while he was strong and able to bear the burden and the heat of the day. Now that he has passed the high mark of eighty-six years of age, he is no longer able to earn anything whatsoever. He is living with one of his granddaughters, and will never lack for personal attention.

However, his expenses have increased, and he is in need. Those who for a few years have sent regularly to his assistance have ceased to remember him in a practical way until he receives only two or three dollars per month. He needs medical attention more often than he did a few years ago. He needs money with which to buy fruits and the kind of food prescribed by the doctor. I have learned that he has gone lacking for such essentials in the recent past. For a time he obtained what he needed and paid for it with funds received from those who promised to send a dollar per month. Now that he receives very little in this way, he owes some bills, which he hopes to settle before going hence.

C. A. Wheeler is known and loved by our outstanding preachers everywhere. G. C. Brewer wrote to the *Gospel Advocate* concerning the life and work of Brother Wheeler while here in a meeting a few years ago, and, if I remember correctly, Brother Wheeler received fifty or seventy-five dollars in response to that letter. About a year ago Brother Wheeler wrote what he thought might prove to be his last article to the *Advocate*, pointing out the nature of his work of faith and labor of love. His needs were again immediately supplied. Now, let all those who know of his sacrifices for the cause—those who love him for his work's sake—send him a small contribution that his needs may be supplied. Judging from past responses, I think no church or individual need send more than a dollar. Surely this will not be a burden to any congregation knowing of his work and success as a loyal and able defender of the faith at a time when such noble characters were so sorely needed. Many individuals could send one dollar and not make much of a sacrifice. Let us send him a shower of dollars to take care of his needs during the few remaining months of his earthly pilgrimage. If you are one of his friends and cannot send anything, please write him a letter, anyway, and comfort his tired and weary soul. We would not wish to be neglected and forgotten when we become old and feeble and no longer able to fight in the battle. Send your letters to C. A. Wheeler, Route 5, Jasper, Ala. He will see that all contributions are acknowledged.[5]

Within ten weeks of the appearing of this article, the elder Wheeler was at rest with his fathers. The bitter-sweet news that calls Christians together for memorializing the dead was sounded forth on the 29th of April 1937. The following day, several preachers of the region carried the mortal remains of the most beloved preacher, one of whom was young Flavil Nichols.[6] As they stood upon the mound at Dutton Hill Cemetery, Gus recalled with fondness the blessings of the older brother's life. Then, that which returns to dust was eased into the earth, next to that of his wife, Adeline, to await the coming of the Lord.

THE WORK AT JASPER GROWS

The work in Jasper enjoyed a continuous activity of growth during the spring in spite of inclement weather and sickness in the congregation. Anticipation of being more active as the seasons produced a warmer and dryer climate seems to be a motive in the following update,

> We believe our work here is producing good results. Our membership is certainly growing in faith and in all good works. Several members who have moved in recently have become identified with the congregation and gone to work with us. We are having preaching full time. The interest and attendance have been exceptionally good until a recent epidemic of "flu" broke out among us. The *Gospel Advocate* is now a weekly visitor in most of our homes. We are at peace among ourselves and happy. We hope to hold several mission meetings around us as soon as the weather will permit outdoor services. We have the singers and preacher, the seats, songbooks, etc., and the members need the blessings which such work brings to the laborers in a perishing, wasting harvest. In addition to our mission meetings, I have permission to assist some congregation in a spring meeting elsewhere if wanted and needed.[7]

Opportunities were forthcoming, and the forty-five-year-old Jasper preacher was able to conduct some of those meetings, while continuing to assist in the building of the work on the home front.

One of the most impactful talents of Gus Nichols was his ability to present the truth of the Scriptures in a simple, yet profound way. His success in the pulpit, the classroom, under a brush arbor, and upon the printed page, was because of his amazing ability to relate even the hardest subjects in the simplest terms. A short article appeared in the *Gospel Advocate* that demonstrates this remarkable aptitude to relate by comparing the miraculous age of the gospel with the creation of a full-grown oak tree. Under the title, "The Miraculous Age," he wrote,

> Everything began in miraculous power. The first man had no mother; neither did the first oak come from an acorn. But God does not make men and trees today as he made the first. Yet God has not changed. It was never his purpose to do anything needlessly. The church first passed through a creative age. Its first preachers had to be inspired. The apostles were baptized with the Holy Spirit to qualify them to reveal and confirm the gospel, which is the power of God unto salvation. (Acts 2:1-4; Rom.

1:16.) The Spirit guided them into all truth. (John 16:13.) They were also given power to confirm the word which they preached. (Acts 1:8; Luke 24:49.) The work which they did by miraculous power was for the benefit of all future generations, as well as for the people then living. The gospel which they revealed and confirmed by the power of the Holy Spirit in the first century will never have to be revealed and confirmed again. They wrought in our behalf. We have the New Testament which they gave unto mankind. The New Testament is to us what inspiration was to the people of that age. The masses then had to learn the truth from the inspired apostles and teachers, and we learn the same truth from the same teachers today in the New Testament. We need no new apostles nor new gospel; neither does the gospel of the New Testament need any new confirmation by apostolic signs and miracles. The miraculous gifts of the Spirit then were to confirm the word which was then being revealed for all ages. (Heb. 2:3,4.) We have this word today. It has not lost any of its power. It carries its confirmation with it. It is as much the seed of the kingdom now as when it first fell from the lips of inspired men. An acorn today has as much power to produce an oak as did the acorns which fell from the first oak in the long ago. "The seed is the word of God" (Luke 8:11). Let us not worry about the miraculous, but believe in the power of truth, and sow this country down with the word this year, and some day go home rejoicing, bearing precious sheaves.[8]

The summer preaching efforts brought about good results, and with a thrust further south. The community of Aldridge, just south of Parrish, was a place where the preaching of Gus Nichols always seemed to enjoy good results. He reported "thirty restorations and twelve baptisms"[9] in that meeting and told of one young lady who had wanted to be baptized, but her father refused to allow her to do so. After this meeting, he ended the month with preaching a short series at West Jasper.

A TRIP TO MONTGOMERY

Then, he headed south to Montgomery where he was engaged in a gospel meeting for the Chisholm congregation, beginning the 4th of July. Located in the Chisholm community on Park Avenue, the church was one of the oldest of the four churches in the city.[10] The year before, this church had invited the talented Rex A. Turner (1913-2001) to become their regular preacher. The preaching duties were shared with C. Leonard Johnson (1910-1994). As Turner was one of brother Nichols' preacher boys,[11] it was only a matter of a short time before brother Nichols was invited for a meeting.

In January 1937, the Montgomery preacher announced to the brotherhood that the Chisholm church had begun a radio program on WSFA every Sunday morning from 8:15 to 8:30.[12] Before brother Nichols arrival, Turner sent in the following to tell how this way of broadcasting the gospel was being expanded. He said,

> The Chisholm Church broadcasts over WSFA daily. The time of the broadcast is 8:15 A.M. each weekday and 7:45 A.M. on Sunday. WSFA comes over 1,410 kilocycles. . .Gus Nichols, of Jasper, Ala., will begin a meeting at Chisholm on July 4, and will continue through two weeks. Brother Nichols will speak over the radio while he is here.[13]

The meeting continued for two weeks in which Gus spoke every morning at 10:00 and every evening at 7:45.[14] Adding to this were his morning radio lessons. At the close of the meeting, both he and Turner reported the success of the engagement with seventeen baptisms.[15]

GUS A. DUNN, SR.

Brother Nichols returned to Jasper just in time for the summer meeting to be held at Fifth Avenue church of Christ with brother Gus Dunn, Sr. Gustus Albert Dunn (1876-1967) was born in Readyville in Cannon County, Tennessee. He was raised in a family of nine children, five of whom devoted themselves to the preaching of the gospel of Christ. He began preaching in his home state, but for the last forty-five years of his life he lived in Texas. Most considered him a Texas preacher, but he held meetings all over the south, baptizing hundreds of people into Christ.

When beginning his meeting at Jasper, he penned the following to the *Firm Foundation*, "On the 15th I closed a meeting in Nacogdoches, Texas, with six baptisms. I am now in a meeting in Jasper, Alabama with larger crowds at night than the seating capacity of the house, hence we are outdoors, using a loud speaker."[16]

At the end of the meeting, Gus sent a report to tell of its success,

> G. A. Dunn, Sr., closed our meeting here last night, with more than fifty having responded to the invitation, twenty-six for baptism. The church has been greatly revived and strengthened, and the people around have been taught the way of the Lord more perfectly. The attendance was good, and the interest was at a high pitch from the very first. The meeting was conducted out in the open air, where the large crowds could be seated and keep cool. A public address system was used to enable all to hear. The preaching was uncompromising in its nature, yet it was done in love and kindness.[17]

BUSY MEETING SCHEDULE

After brother Dunn's meeting, Gus continued his meeting schedule with plans to go to Blessing, near Albertville, Alabama the first week in August.[18] Nineteen obeyed the gospel in that meeting.[19] He went from there to Christian Chapel, near Amory, Mississippi, where sixteen responded in obedience to the gospel, and "about 40 confessions of faults. Most of those confessing faults had either quit or neglected the worship because of some trouble in the church."[20] He followed with a week in Fayette County, Alabama with the Hubbertville church. Because of scheduling, J. G. Pounds (1914-1991) had to start the meeting because brother Nichols could not arrive until Wednesday. In the end, ten were baptized and seventeen were restored.[21] He went from this church to Munford, Alabama where he preached "twenty-seven sermons and baptized twenty-seven people."[22]

In the same report, he spoke of completing another shorter meeting at Fulton, Mississippi, where one was restored and four were baptized. Two weeks later, he reported on a good meeting at Alabama City where there were nine baptisms. While there he conducted, "two-fifteen minute programs daily over the local radio station during the meeting."[23]

DUNN-DAVIS DEBATE

Brother Gus Dunn, Sr. returned to the area in late November to engage in a debate with a Primitive Baptist by the name of W. C. Davis. The discussion began in Parrish on the evening of the 15th and continued for four days, on the subject of the plan of salvation. Brother Nichols moderated for the elder challenger and later reported overwhelming success by the Texas preacher. He said,

> Great crowds attended from the first service to the last one, at which time Brother Dunn delivered one of the most wonderful speeches this writer ever heard fall from the lips of man. Mr. Davis' last speech was simply pitiable. Every word of it showed signs of conscious defeat.[24]

He also conveyed his feelings that in spite of Mr. Davis' pitching "his part of the discussion on a very low plane," the brethren believed that the debate did much more than could have been accomplished in a protracted meeting.

ANOTHER CHANGE IN THE NICHOLS HOME

The growth and development of Flavil Nichols since he began preaching in early 1934 was nothing short of remarkable. The young man remained very busy in the kingdom of the Lord. Throughout the year he, like his father, sent reports into the *Gospel Advocate* to tell of the successes of his labors. He was no longer the little boy Gus chased around the yard where when they came up to the trailer hitch he would jump over it, and Flavil would run under it, as he recalled in later years. It was time for him to spread his wings, and fly. As Gracie had finished her studies and was home, the visit to the train platform in Jasper that day was to see Vodie off, who was entering her sophomore year at F-HC, and her little brother Flavil who was to begin his studies there. On the 30th of September the following appeared in the brotherhood journal,

> Flavil Nichols, Freed-Hardeman College, Henderson, Tenn., September 20: "I closed my last meeting for this season last Friday night at Morris, Ala., with fair crowds and interest, but no additions. I am here to better prepare myself for life on earth and in heaven."[25]

ENDNOTES

1 E. C. Gardner, *Gospel Advocate*, 25 March 1976, p. 202. Note: Gardner claimed that the Special Courses began in 1937, and that Gus Nichols attended every session for the remainder of his life.

2 "Special Courses Draw Many," *Gospel Advocate*, 14 January 1937, p. 44.

3 "Calendar," *Treasure Chest*, 1937 Freed-Hardeman College Yearbook, p. 19.

4 From interviews with Flavil Nichols and Hardeman Nichols.

5 Gus Nichols, *Gospel Advocate*, 18 February 1937, p. 165.

6 Note: One summer day in 2001, your author and his father, Richard T. Harp, spent a day with Flavil and Mary Nichols. We visited the graves of many of those who blessed our lives, including the graves of C. A. and Adeline Wheeler. One of my most prized photographs is one where Flavil was standing by the grave of brother Wheeler, one hand resting on his cane, the other resting on the grave marker. I will never forget that when the camera clicked, he snatched his hand back and said in his loving voice, "Oh, I've ruined your picture." Very quickly I responded, "Oh, brother Nichols, you did not ruin it, you made it!"

7 Gus Nichols, *Gospel Advocate*, 25 March 1937, p. 284.

8 Gus Nichols, "The Miraculous Age," *Gospel Advocate*, 8 April 1937, p. 318.

9 Ibid., 1 July 1937, p. 619.

10 Fred Little, "Preparations Are Being Made For A Great Meeting In Montgomery, Alabama," *Gospel Advocate*, 21 February 1929, p. 171. Note: Fred M. Little reported that Chisholm was one of four congregations in the city—Catoma Street, Highland Avenue, West Montgomery, and Chisholm. Of these four churches were an aggregate membership of about 800 Christians. The congregation moved from Park Avenue to a new building a couple of blocks further north on Lower Wetumpka Highway in the 1940s. Today this congregation has moved again and is known as the Eastern Meadows church of Christ. Between 1965 and 1968 your author's father, Richard T. Harp, was the minister for this fine congregation. Some of my earliest memories are of the great families of this church, the Nortons, Jones, Hicks, Brannons, and several others who attended in those days.

11 Note: Rex Allwin Turner (1913-2001) was born, raised, educated, and preached most of his life in Alabama. Soon after he began preaching in 1932, he was admonished by the brethren to go back to school. Years later, in an article he wrote in *Sound Doctrine*, Vol. 1, No. 4, November/December 1975, pp. 2, 14, under the title, "Gus Nichols As I Knew Him," he explained that a brother Hood Florence suggested that he go and study under brother Gus Nichols. So, he caught a ride to Jasper, and proceeded to knock on his door. He said, "Brother Nichols happened to be in, and I announced that I had come to study under him—all of this without an invitation, mind you! Brother and Sister Nichols greeted me and extended their hospitality to me as if I had been their grandson whom they had not seen in a long time. The depression was on, and the Nichols had eight children at home—only eight, mind you!" Turner later became one of

Alabama's great educators, co-founder of what was to later become Faulkner University, and founder of what is now Amridge University. He served for a time as president of both colleges. He passed from this life 16 January 2001 at the age of 87. His remains were interred in Montgomery's Greenwood Cemetery.

12 Rex Turner, *Gospel Advocate*, 14 January 1937, p. 42.

13 Ibid., 1 July 1937, p. 621.

14 Advertisement, *Truth In Love*, 1937, Vol. 1, No. 9, p. 5.

15 Rex Turner, *Gospel Advocate*, 29 July 1937, p. 713. Note: Gus Nichols' report appeared on p. 714.

16 Gus Dunn, *Firm Foundation*, 10 August 1937, p. 4.

17 Gus Nichols, *Gospel Advocate*, 12 August 1937, p. 762.

18 Ibid.

19 Ibid., 26 August 1938, p. 808.

20 Gus Nichols, *Firm Foundation*, 14 September 1937, p. 4.

21 Gus Nichols, *Gospel Advocate*, 2 September 1937, p. 835.

22 Ibid.,30 September 1937, p. 932.

23 Ibid., 14 October 1937, p. 977.

24 Ibid., 21 April 1938, p. 371.

25 Flavil Nichols, *Gospel Advocate*, 30 September 1937, p. 929.

- 22 -

The Heart Of Compassion

And Jesus, when He came out, saw much people, and was moved with compassion toward them, because they were as sheep not having a shepherd: and he began to teach them many things.
—Mark, Mark 6:34

Fifteen years previous to the 1938 Special Courses at Freed-Hardeman College, N. B. Hardeman (1874-1965) and Ira A. Douthitt (1891-1975) conducted, "a three-months' tour of Europe and the Bible Lands."[1] After their return, Hardeman conducted his third series of events for the year at Nashville's Ryman Auditorium, lecturing on the things he witnessed on his Middle East tour.[2] Thousands poured into the arena on the nights of December 18-20, 1923, to hear his addresses on "Egypt and the Holy Land."[3]

The next session of the Special Courses began at 8:30 on the 4th of January on Henderson's college campus. N. B. Hardeman's course was entitled, "The Lands of the Bible." In the audience were Gus and Flavil Nichols, as well as a host of other very capable preachers of the gospel. Other sessions included a class by brother Hardeman on "Denominational Arguments, with their Refutations." Evenings were devoted to preaching by H. Leo Boles (1874-1946). Boles also taught classes during the day sessions on the Holy Spirit. Other classes were taught by David H. Bobo (1910-1985), L. O. Sanderson (1901-1992), Foy E. Wallace, Jr. (1896-1979), L. L. Brigance (1879-1950), and John T. Lewis (1876-1975).

GROWTH IN THE COUNTY

The work in Jasper during this time was producing deeper roots in the community than ever. Ten years after the congregation began meeting in their Fifth Avenue building, the attendance was running around 250 at their Sunday gatherings. This was attributed much to the hard work of a strong leadership of elders and preacher. In the five years Gus Nichols had been their preacher, the church had been introduced to growth opportunities, and the people had a will to broaden their horizons and apply themselves. The Friday evening classes continued to supply an increase in knowledge and training. Their support of brother Nichols in mission meetings in the county were producing new congregations, and those being trained in his school were going out to help these fledgling works develop further. At this point in time, there were thirty-two congregations of the Lord's church in the county, and Fifth Avenue was providing a great example for the brotherhood to follow.[4]

GOOD READING AND SINGING MATERIAL

Promoting good reading material for Christians was ever in the thoughts of the Nichols. All the members of the congregation were encouraged to subscribe to the *Gospel Advocate* and other brotherhood journals. Gus' own editorial skills continued to enjoy a cultivating of interest within the public arena. His co-labor with some of the Birmingham brethren on the paper, *Truth In Love*, was enjoying dramatic growth in wider circulation. In an early year report, fellow editor, Jack Meyer (1914-1972) revealed, "Our monthly gospel journal, *Truth in Love*, now fifteen months old, is growing and regularly has a circulation of 11,000 in bundles to churches."[5] Meanwhile, Flavil was doing his best to increase readership of the *Gospel Advocate* as a student on the Freed-Hardeman campus. The paper reported that he had "raised the largest club during the third period which ended on January 31."[6]

In the same encouraging vein, Gus wrote an endorsement for *The Bible Banner*, a new paper produced by Foy E. Wallace, Jr. (1896-1979) out of Fort Worth, Texas, in which he said,

> *The Bible Banner* is as good as the best. It is bound to accomplish great good in staying off departures from the Old Paths. God bless you, and keep you bold and courageous, active and clean, to do a work for the defense of the truth for many years which none other can do so well.[7]

He also put his stamp of approval on a hymnal that was newly published by Marion Davis (1906-1979) in Fayette, Alabama.[8] The book, *The Complete Hymnal* was advertised in the brotherhood journals along with the added words, "'It's a good book!' – Gus Nichols, Jasper, Alabama."[9]

Much of the spring was devoted to mission meetings in the region. Gus always sought ways to include and insert young men he had the opportunity to develop as preachers. In one two-week effort in Townley, a few miles west of Jasper, most of the meeting was conducted by Nichols except for a few of the gatherings toward the end where he involved some other preachers like, Crawford Allen, J. G. Pounds, E. W. Guttery and G. W. Hall. "Five were restored during the meeting."[10]

ASSISTING OTHERS IN THE WORK

During the summer, Gus was called on once again to assist a young preacher who found himself in unfamiliar territory. Many years later, a much tried and tested Hugo McCord recalled how the Jasper preacher came to his aid. He said,

About 30 miles from Jasper is Carbon Hill. When I was in a tent meeting there the pastor of the Nazarene Church, on the night of July 3, 1938, was in the audience. In the sermon I had mentioned that babies are born sinless, that they do not inherit Adam's sin. The pastor spoke up from his seat and said I was wrong. I asked him publicly to come back the next night and we would divide the time, and he agreed.

I was a scared young preacher, 27 years old. Gus Nichols was in the audience, and immediately after the dismissal prayer, I went to him, asking him to sit with me the next night to help me. He said he had an appointment the next night at Christian Chapel in Mississippi, but when he saw how nervous I was, he said, "I'll send Flavil [his eldest son] to fill the Mississippi appointment, and I'll be here in the morning and study all day to get ready for the debate."

In the morning brother Gus came, and had brought black oil cloth and white paint, and soon he had prepared some charts for me to use. In the course of the Nazarene pastor's speech, he said the fact that a baby cries shows he is a sinner. Brother Gus leaned over to me, saying, "That makes Jesus a sinner—Jesus wept, John 11:35." When I repeated brother Gus' words publicly, the answer so demoralized the visiting pastor that he got up and walked out.[11]

This much-appreciated assistance was never forgotten, and further assists the reader to appreciate how the making of Gus Nichols was so deeply entrenched in the making of others. In all that he did, he sought to help the brotherhood be both practical and powerful in the pursuit of promoting the gospel.

For instance, he was particularly impressed with the design of one church building in which he preached a meeting in Baileyton, Alabama. The brethren had built a new church house, for the most part, from a large financial gift by one of the members. He described the building as a great option for brethren considering the need for building or expanding in the most practical way. He described it in this way,

> The building is so designed that the audience enters through cloak rooms at the front of the 40x60 foot building, the pulpit also being in this end of the building. There are four class rooms in the rear end of the building made by raising the floor and lowering the ceiling at that point so that the rooms may be cut off from the auditorium by curtains. The partitions making the rooms are pointed directly toward the pulpit so the speaker

and those in the class rooms can see each other during the sermon. This conserves space by turning the class rooms into the auditorium when needed. It is a good idea for those wishing to build economically.[12]

His eyes were always open for struggling areas that needed help. Reporting to the papers was his way to get the message to the brotherhood. For instance, he had a meeting at Clanton, Alabama where he baptized six and, as he put it, "some confessed wrongs who had been out of duty for some time."[13] He went on to describe how there was much discouragement in the congregation because they did not have an evangelist to work full-time in that, "mission territory. We might as well expect to grow a crop without sowing as to expect spiritual results without plenty of sound preaching."[14]

Gus closed a meeting on the 11th of September at the White's Chapel church in Fayette County. This congregation was close to his boyhood home, and several of his mother's family, the Wyers, were members there. It was truly a homecoming for him. The meeting was successful with twenty-seven baptisms and many restored. He recalled with warmth his life-long affection for this church, and especially one of its leaders, who, in his early days of determining what he wanted to do with himself in life, helped direct his path. He recalled,

I worshiped regularly there for many months when I was a young man. Billy Erwin, with whom I worked some in those days, was largely responsible for my preaching. He encouraged me to go to school, regardless of the hardships, and carry out my desire to preach. Let us not be sparing with our encouragement, but provoke "unto love and good works."[15]

He conducted a meeting in Pensacola, Florida, in the fall. The West Hill congregation where Gardner S. Hall (1906-1978) had just left before moving to Tuscumbia, Alabama had invited Gus for a meeting. He was greatly impressed with the strength of the church there, even though there were no additions. One of the treats of this trip was to enjoy his first opportunity to visit the Gulf of Mexico.[16]

A VISIT TO DEATH ROW

Other efforts for the year were reported to the brotherhood papers, but of note are a couple of visits he made to Montgomery, one for a debate with a Mr. Casey in November. Not much information about the debate was preserved other than a report on its success from J. O. Jones (1910-1968), a Fayette County preacher who attended, saying,

I was privileged to attend the Hardeman-Bogard debate, also the Wallace-Tingley discussion. I have just returned from a week's visit in Montgomery, where I heard Gus Nichols debate with Mr. Casey. I think the truth won victories in each of these debates.[17]

The other trip to Montgomery was in the way of another visit to the Chisholm congregation for a gospel meeting. The previous year, he had enjoyed good success at the reception of the brethren there. Two preaching services a day took place, one in the morning at 10am, and the other in the evening at 7:00 pm. The attendance was good throughout the meeting. One of the preachers, C. Leonard Johnson (1910-1994) reported two baptisms during the dates of the 14th through 26th of the August series.[18]

On Thursday the 18th, after the evening worship services, brothers Nichols and Johnson had another appointment to attend to, the experience of which left their lives never the same. Compassion, self-sacrifice, love for the gospel, and the souls of men were among the motives these men shared in making their way to their point of call that evening.

A little north of town, there was a place where no man or woman wished to go, nor to experience. It was a housing facility for the hardened criminals of the state of Alabama. The Kilby State prison was a 2,550-acre penitentiary that was built in 1922 and 1923. At the center of its various levels of incarceration was a room that held its most feared form of justice. "Yellow Mama,"[19] was a chair no criminal ever wanted to sit in, or even see.

Two men on death row in the prison were Curtis Cobb and Willie J. Whitfield.[20] Both men were found guilty of heinous crimes, and immediately after midnight they were to be executed.

Late into the early morning hours, so far from the innocent environs of his Jasper home, a changed man penned the following in a letter to Matilda and his children. It is preserved as follows,

> Friday, August 19, 1938
>
> Dear Ones,
>
> I do not feel well this morning, though I am not sick. It is about 6:30, and I have slept only a few minutes—did not sleep a wink until break of day. I was nervous because of what I had seen and witnessed. You know I am not very excitable, yet I witnessed the saddest scene of my life just after midnight.
>
> Yesterday I noticed that two convicts were to be electrocuted at Kilby Prison about midnight, and decided I wanted to witness that scene. By phone I obtained permission for myself and brother Leonard Johnson to see it.

The Heart Of Compassion

After preaching to a fine audience we had "supper" (about 9:30), and arrived at the prison about eleven o'clock. The Guard at the great iron gate at the entrance to a massive building (which appears to cover several acres) opened, and we were locked inside.

We waited in the broad open space of a large and beautiful hall for a while, and were finally seated in the Warden's office by a kind-hearted and friendly Guard, who informed us the Warden would soon be in. We were already in a serious strain of conversation, talking of the joy of being free and able to go where we pleased in life—when we suddenly realized that we were in fact right then locked in prison! We still felt that we were free men, however; but were sorry for the more than fifteen hundred white men (plus many negroes) inside the prison! We planned to try to warn more earnestly of the "wages of sin"—the thing which took away the liberty and freedom of those inside!

Many big burly guards with guns walked down the hall. We joined them to see what they were talking about. At 11:30 the Assistant Warden motioned for us to come to him behind another great iron gate down the spacious hall. Others preceded us; but (not being preachers) they were turned through a door to the left, and were searched. Even some of the Guards had their guns taken. We were "trusties," [sic] and hence were not searched—not then, nor later. Upon being admitted through the gate, we proceeded toward another one about fifty yards ahead. Passing through it, we turned up a flight of stairs to one of the many stories of the great building.

Now we are in the Death Territory. This hall is about 25 x 40 feet, and several condemned to die in the near future are on either side of us. The Assistant Warden beckons for a preacher of the Salvation Army, and the white Chaplain, and also the old negro who is the colored Chaplain, and we are introduced. They led us to the end of this hall, to the last cell on the left, where one of the young men doomed to die in a few minutes has knelt by his cot, and is praying. He assaulted a ten-year-old girl in Birmingham, and must soon pay with his life.

Wishing not to disturb his prayer, we pass into a narrow hall, but only a few feet away; and on the right is the other condemned prisoner, who murdered a Montgomery merchant with an axe, for only a few dollars of money on his person. He, too, must pay with his life. Through the strong steel lattice door we see him pacing back and forth. He is singing (or chanting) over and over:

> I have a little sister gone on,
> And I was left alone;
> And now I am going home!
> I've made peace with Jesus!
> He says, "I go to prepare,
> And will come after you."
> He died for me—and I'm so glad!

The Salvation Army preacher asked him how he feels, and he is claimed to be ready. But he asks who we are; and upon learning that brother Johnson and I are gospel preachers, he wants us to pray for him.

The short prayer over, we go back to the other prisoner, who is now sitting flat on the floor. Upon arising he is directed by the Salvation Army preacher to repeat the prayer:

"God, be merciful to me, a sinner, And save my poor soul," which he does recite. He picks up a ten-cent New Testament from his cot and says, "If it was not for this little book, I'd be ruined!"

They now are told to pray hard, for they have only a few more minutes. They saunter around and around, praying and chanting in a half-conscious manner, not noticing anybody. Now the other one wants brother Johnson to pray for him. When this short prayer is over, they want us to sing. "In The Sweet Bye And Bye" is the first song; then, "Nearer, My God, To Thee," and then, "Love Lifted Me."

There comes a great company of men—guards, doctors, news reporters, and others. With them we move on down the narrow hallway, past the electric chair, where we hope to see clearly. We are now by the door, just in the hall, and within ten or twelve feet of the death chair. Being taller, I am looking over brother Johnson's shoulder. We are sad—occasionally feeling rather "mean" for being there; then we remember that we helped sing, and prayed, and tried to lend comfort to the condemned men— for whom we feel very sorry, regardless of their guilt.

There they are with the murderer. He is being strapped hard and tight in the great wooden chair. All are as silent as death. —Now the prisoner is saying:

> I killed a man, and must pay for my deed!
> I love everybody. And now I'm going home.
> (They are strapping the cup on his head through which the 'lightning' will run through his body.)
> I want to meet my Savior.

The Heart Of Compassion

> Mr. Warden, tell Eleanor "Hello" for me.

All is ready, and we are almost holding our breath. Brother Johnson is crying, while I (being older) am choking back all I can.

The Chaplain reads: In my Father's house are - - -

—and, Oh my! Ugh!—The current has come! Suddenly, he has been lifted by it just as high as the straps will let him rise! His neck veins are protruding, and his hands are drawn as tight as a wrench!

This continues for about a minute, then is turned off at about the same length of time.—But now it comes again! Up he rises again! Now the smoke is coming up from his head, and from his leg! The burning flesh is making an awful scent! The "sizzling" and "buzzing" noise of the current is so loud it could be heard several blocks away!

Now it is off again. The doctors go forward. They listen to his heart, but soon say: "He is dead." The stretcher is just behind me, coming in for him. I have moved to the other side of the door; now he is brought out.

In a moment everything is ready again, and the other prisoner, about seventeen years of age, is brought in. He, too, is walking glibly, and also has tearful eyes. As they are strapping him, he breaks the deathly silence:

> The strap under my chin is too tight!
> Lord, have mercy on me! —Tell everybody
> 'Goodbye!' Oh, Me! Lord, Take me! —
> That strap is too tight!—Only another
> minute, and I'll be long gone! Just
> another moment! Lord, Have mercy! —But
> I must go; I can't stay! —I am ready
> to die for my fault!

The colored Chaplain begins to read, and the boy begins to repeat after him:

> The Lord —
> The Lord is my Shepherd; I—I—I—Eigh—I

But the "buzz" is on him! He, too, rises up! And he dies about as the other did. He is pronounced "Dead," and all is over.

"He has paid an awful price for assaulting a white girl, about ten," said a man behind me, who broke the silence.

But we are put forward, and are coming down. Some are laughing and talking, some crying; one (at least) choking, and thinking that he wished his boys could see this. Silently I pray that they may be good, and control the flesh, that they may not thus have to reap!

On our way "home" we speak very little. I find my key, and open the door to my room;—am now about to go to bed, but I am not a bit sleepy! Now I am musing: "Well, I am a MAN; I can forget all of this, and sleep soundly." But no! I am rolling and turning! Something is wrong! Maybe I am too hot?? I turn on the fan — but that's not the trouble! I am tired, but not sleepy! As I close my eyes, I can "see" but one thing—and that's that chair!

My effort to sleep began about 12:35; now it is 2:00 A.M. I get up and read until 3:05—but no sleep will come! I can still "see" those boys when my eyes are closed!—Now the chickens are crowing for day; I pull down the shades, and slip away for about an hour; then try and try to sleep—but can't! I read; then begin this letter .... (Emphasis his).

Breakfast is over, and I feel all right; but I may get very sleepy today. I know, without waiting to find the facts, that brother Johnson did not sleep a wink!

Pray for our dear children, and for me. Let us be a model family, and do a great work. God bless you every one.

I must get ready to preach on the radio, then go to lunch, and will get back to my room (as usual) about three or four o'clock this afternoon.

I love each of you lots,

(Signed)

Gus [21]

ENDNOTES

1 James Marvin Powell and Mary Nelle Hardeman Powers, *N.B.H.: A Biography Of Nicholas Brodie Hardeman*, Nashville: Gospel Advocate Company, c.1964, p. 216.

2 Note: 1923 was N. B. Hardeman's busiest year. See chapter 13 for a fuller description.

3 James Marvin Powell and Mary Nelle Hardeman Powers, *N.B.H., A Biography of Nicholas Brodie Hardeman*, Gospel Advocate Company, 1964, p. 293. Note: These lectures were recorded by a stenographer and appeared daily in *The Tennessean*, one of Nashville's daily newspapers. Later the lectures were included in a volume similar to that of the *Hardeman Tabernacle Series* made available to the brotherhood.

4 Gus Nichols, *Gospel Advocate*, 9 October 1938, p. 946.

5 Jack Meyer, *Gospel Advocate*, 6 January 1938, p. 16.

6 "Still Climbing," *Gospel Advocate*, 17 February 1938. p. 165.

7 Gus Nichols, *The Bible Banner*, November 1938, p. 16.

8 Note: Francis Marion Davis (1906-1979) was a capable song director. He traveled and led singing for Gus Nichols, Foy E. Wallace, Jr. and several other meeting preachers of his day. He operated a printing business in Fayette, Alabama. For a time, he served as owner of *Truth In Love*, the brotherhood paper that Gus Nichols edited and co-edited for at least two different periods. Davis was a leader in the church in Fayette, where he passed away in 1979. His remains were planted in the city cemetery there.

9 Advertisement, *Firm Foundation*, 28 June 1938, p. 6. Note: Similar advertisement appeared in the *Gospel Advocate* in the 26 May issue, p. 496.

10 Gus Nichols, *Gospel Advocate*, 26 May 1938, p. 493.

11 Hugo McCord, *Words of Truth*, October 2002, p. 7.

12 Gus Nichols, *Firm Foundation*, 7 June 1938, p. 6.

13 Gus Nichols, *Gospel Advocate*, 6 October 1938, p. 946.

14 Ibid.

15 Ibid.

16 Gus Nichols, *Gospel Advocate*, 27 October 1938, p. 1018

17 J. O. Jones, *Gospel Advocate*, 8 December 1938, p. 1153.

18 C. Leonard Johnson, *Gospel Advocate*, 8 September 1938, p. 852.

19 Note: "Yellow Mama" is the nickname given to Alabama's electric chair, which was used for executions from 1927-2002. It was first installed at Kilby Prison in Montgomery, Alabama. It acquired its yellow color when painted using highway-line paint from the adjacent State Highway Department lab. The chair was built by a British inmate in 1927 and was first used to execute Horace

DeVauhan that same year. World Wide Web: http://en.wikipedia.org/wiki/Yellow_Mama.

20 Alabama Department of Corrections Website - http://www.doc.state.al.us/Executions.aspx

21 Gus Nichols, Unpublished, Personal correspondence with his family. This experience made a lifetime impression upon Gus. He referred to the event many times in sermons and in the company of the many preachers and Christian brethren he had the opportunity to influence throughout the remainder of his life.

- 23 -

Unity: Challenges And Victories

Can two walk together, except they be agreed?
—The Herdsman Prophet, Amos 3:3

The history of the Restoration Movement in the United States is replete with occurrences of great success—and unfortunately—failure. The resounding cry of early reformers to go back to the Bible for authority in all religious practice was heard in many places. The thought of participating in first-Century Christianity as opposed to the quagmire of religious division in their day was met with wide acceptance. Initially, uniting on the basis of the Scriptures was a challenge in view of generations of discord brought on by man-made creeds and denominational division. When objective truth was applied, and unity was achieved, it was both precious and fragile.

In time, the process of experimentation with all things biblical, especially when laid within the scope of the practical, forced the authority of the Scriptures to take a back seat. On such occasions divisions followed. Most noted as departures from the simple plan of the Word were things like the introduction of a man-made system for evangelism in the 1849 founding of the American Christian Missionary Society. Unity was further broken with the addition of the instrument of music in worship in various locations. These and other departures from the simple New Testament pattern placed the unity movement on track for ultimate failure in many congregations of the Lord's people. When the U.S. Census of 1906 was published, clear delineation between the instrumental and non-instrumental brethren was visible in the designations of churches of Christ and Disciples of Christ (Christian Church), although the labels were never fixed across the brotherhood.[1]

All along the way, several efforts, some on a grander scale and some lesser, were made to continue dialogue between the divided groups with the hopes of re-unification. Claud F. Witty (1877-1952), a preacher in Detroit, Michigan, led an effort in the 1930s to reach out to splintered groups for the purpose of helping to break down barriers and reunite brethren. He was praised in 1936 for his efforts in assisting two congregations merge in Beamsville, Ontario, Canada, who had been splintered for over 25 years.[2] This success set him on a path to reach out on a grander scale to induce unity among all divisions among restoration churches. On Easter Weekend in 1936, Witty organized several gospel meetings to begin among churches of Christ in Detroit.[3] Coinciding with the meetings, a large unity gathering was planned for Sunday afternoon and evening at the West Side Central building where he was the regular minister. H. Leo Boles (1874-1946), John Hardeman (1893-1963), and Ben F. Harding (1882-1944), who were preaching meetings in the area, came and preached at the evening unity sessions, and it was reported as being a most successful venture.[4] All three names had history on most sides within Restoration-related churches, which contributed to the great support it received.

In the spring of 1937, Witty and Christian-church-preacher James DeForest Murch (1892-1973) organized two meetings, one in Cincinnati, and the other in Indianapolis. These meetings were on a grander scale than previous meetings, involving many Christian church leaders. Also attending were leaders of the premillennial movement in Louisville, Kentucky, with E. L. Jorgenson (1886-1968) and others present. Later meetings followed in "Akron, Ohio; Los Angeles, California; and Columbus, Indiana."[5]

1939 - Bertha Nichols, FHC Student

This meeting however, led to criticisms that sounded in the pages of several brotherhood journals. The concerns, for the most part, were in two different areas. One thing was that no matter how many representatives of the divisions of the Restoration Movement were in attendance, they only truly represented themselves and not the church at large. Thus, unity on any level was going to be limited. The other issue was that the things that led to the divisions in the first place had not changed. Missionary societies, instrumental music in worship, pastoral systems, denominational union meetings, and the like, were always going to prevent re-unification on any scale.

Unity: Challenges And Victories

Another unity meeting was planned for early May 1939, this time in Indianapolis. Ahead of the event, Witty was invited to Freed-Hardeman College's Special Courses to explain his purposes for the unity meeting. An advertisement in the official newsletter for the college appeared in the issue leading up to the event with the following caveat,

> Brother Claude Witty has sprung a new proposition upon the brotherhood in recent months in an effort to unite the divided forces of the "Restoration Movement." We have not indorsed [sic] his position in this matter, but we want to hear his own explanation and "justification."[6]

And, explaining was his encounter. H. Leo Boles took the lead in an open forum setting in asking Witty several questions that forced him to be straight forward in his response. Questions were asked like, "Are you not a self-appointed representative of the churches of Christ?" and "Have you told Murch and his brethren there can be no unity until he puts the organ aside and gives up the missionary societies?"[7] Other equally pointed questions followed.

Meanwhile on the home front, Gus Nichols had made numerous attempts since the founding of the Jasper congregation to reach out to the Christian Church in town in hopes of breaking down barriers and unifying on the basis of the Scriptures. Offers for open dialogue, discussion, debate, or any other platform had been presented, but all appeals had fallen on deaf ears. Over the years, some had left the Christian Church to join forces with the Fifth Avenue brethren, but they were few and far between. In May he reported, "We have recently had five new members come among us and become identified with the congregation. Last Lord's day one lady came from the Christian Church."[8]

1939 - Flavil Nichols, FHC Student

Another controversial visitor to the F-HC campus that year was Daniel Sommer (1850-1940). Long known as an opponent against the "Christian College" approach to education,[9] his visit to the school just thirteen months before his death was an indication of a softening of his sternness of earlier years. It was also a great welcome to all those in attendance. Like Witty, his visit invoked similar qualification,

Frankness requires us to say that we have not agreed with Brother Sommer on the "Bible School" question but we recognize his ripe scholarship, his broad knowledge of the Bible, his ability as a speaker and writer and his long and eventful career as a preacher of the gospel.[10]

Thus, the Special Courses held great anticipation to the Jasper preacher as he joined two of his children on campus beginning the 3rd of January 1939. Flavil was there, and Bertha had left home the previous fall to begin her college experience.

At the close of the series in Henderson, Gus made his way down to Starkville, Mississippi, to be involved in a lectureship that began on the fifth Sunday in January. A new congregation had been planted near the state college the previous October, and he had been invited to speak, along with, "Robert Box, Columbus, Miss.; John Cox, Birmingham, Ala.; and Howard White, Charleston, Miss."[11]

A call from southeast Texas followed soon thereafter. Edd Holt (1906-1985) was a North-Alabama-born preacher who was minister at the time for the Eleventh Street church in Port Arthur, Texas. He invited Gus down for a two-week meeting that began in mid-March. On the 14th Gus penned a note to the *Advocate* stating that two had been baptized in the first two days of the meeting.[12] A fuller account followed on the 1st of April where he reported nineteen baptisms, three of whom had been Catholics.[13]

While in the area, he had an occasion to hear one of Texas' great traveling preachers, Horace W. Busby (1884-1965), who was preaching in Beaumont in a meeting. Also, he had the opportunity to go over to visit the Sixth Street church in Port Arthur where O. C. Lambert (1890-1972), another Alabamian, was the preacher. Foy E. Wallace, Jr. (1896-1979) was engaged in a meeting there at the time. He said, "At this meeting I met, among other gospel preachers, G. H. P. Showalter. The brethren in Port Arthur are not ashamed of the gospel. They love the truth and are spreading it abroad orally, on the printed page, over the radio, etc."[14]

G. H. P. Showalter

George Henry Prior Showalter (1870-1954) was born and raised in Snowville, Virginia. He preached in Virginia and West Virginia until 1897 when he moved to Texas to become the president of Sabinal Christian College. In 1908, he became the editor of the *Firm Foundation*. When Gus Nichols met brother Showalter it was a dream come true. Since his earliest recollections as a Christian, he had been encouraged by brother Wheeler to read the brotherhood papers. And, as has already been demonstrated, Gus had been writing letters to brother Showalter ever since he began his preaching career. The opportunity to finally meet the Texas editor was truly a highlight.

Upon returning home, Gus was met with a couple of pleasant surprises, as he penned the following on the 1st of April,

> One was baptized here last Lord's day night. Our interest and attendance are still growing. While I was away at Port Arthur, Texas, in a meeting, the brethren here built another classroom for our Bible-school work and made other needed improvements. Leon Fike, one of our young men, spoke one Lord's day while I was away, and Judge Clark, from Birmingham, spoke the next. H. Leo Boles will preach in our meeting, beginning July 2.

The mention of H. Leo Boles as being the featured speaker at the summer meeting at Jasper is worthy of greater focus in lieu of the present discussion. Henry Leo Boles (1874-1946) was born in Gainesboro, in Jackson County, Tennessee. His father, Henry Jefferson Boles (1845-1923), was a gospel preacher. His paternal grandmother was the daughter of the early restoration preacher most affectionately known as "Raccoon" John Smith (1784-1868).[15]

1939 - Port Arthur, Texas March Meeting
L-R: O. M. Reynolds, Edd Holt,
O. C. Lambert, ???, Gus Nichols,
Horace W. Busby

In 1939, perhaps no more powerful voice among restoration churches for the old paths was that of H. Leo Boles. For over forty years of his life, he wrote for the *Gospel Advocate* as staff writer and served as editor for part of that time. He served as president of Nashville Bible School, later David Lipscomb College, on two different occasions, and taught classes there for many years. Since its inception, Boles had been a featured speaker each year at the Special Courses at Henderson, and it is assumed that this was where Gus Nichols met the esteemed elder preacher. As noted, Boles was involved in Claud Witty's first unity meeting in Detroit a couple years earlier. For the May meeting being planned in Indianapolis, again Boles consented to be a participant.

From the Indiana meeting it was reported that, "the preachers who stood up to be counted numbered 148,"[16] but the total registered were said to be 196. These were just the preachers. The estimates put the "Wednesday night attendance at 800 to 1000."[17] Speeches from both sides were made during the two-day event of May 2-3. However, when it became Boles' turn to approach the speaker's stand, the crux of the matter of unity was spelled out in no uncertain terms by way of a speech that lasted no less than one and one-half hours.

In his discourse, Boles set out an apologetic that explained the history of the restoration movement in America, and the strong desire all had in common to follow the order set out in the Scriptures. He discussed what was considered "common ground" between the groups, especially that the gospel must be obeyed through belief, repentance, and baptism into Christ. He identified other commonality in the mutual belief in the need to follow the New Testament implicitly in all work and worship, and that our lives must be governed by it. He then showed how this ethical approach to interpreting the Scriptures was demonstrated in the 1832 unity meeting that took place in Lexington, Kentucky, between the forces of Barton Stone's Christian movement, and Alexander Campbell's Disciples. Though Boles did not mention it in the speech, most there knew that Campbell's representative, and speaker for the reform movement in Kentucky at that meeting was none other than his great-grandfather, "Raccoon" John Smith.[18]

He further explained how this unity prevailed until 1849 when the American Christian Missionary Society was founded. Signified as a "departure," two other subsequent things were similarly identified, one with the introduction of instrumental music into the worship, and finally the denominational behavior of the Christian church as it interacted socially and in worship with the denominations. He followed with a resounding appeal, "Brethren, put away the organ and you will be where the pioneers first stood when the unity of God's people was enjoyed." Similar appeals followed concerning the other departures.

What followed the meeting were reports in brotherhood journals from every side represented. Christian church leader A. T. DeGroot (1898-1982) reporting in *The Christian-Evangelist* said, "The strongest language employed at the conference, other than in the expected warmth of some exchanges in the open forums, came in the address of H. Leo Boles, of Nashville, Tenn."[19] *The Christian Standard* reported that Boles was "outspoken in argument."[20]

Ten weeks following the Indianapolis meeting, the sixty-five year old Tennessee church leader headed to Walker County, Alabama to preach the summer meeting for the Fifth Avenue church. His stay in the home of the Nichols during that meeting presented both men the opportunity to discuss at length the events of the last several months, and in particular the efforts being made in Jasper to tear down the barriers that then had long existed between factions within Restoration churches.

On the 5th of August Gus penned the following to the *Gospel Advocate*,

> H. Leo Boles recently closed a good meeting here in which there were seven baptized, three placed membership, and four were restored. The preaching was as good as I have ever heard. The church was well pleased with the sound gospel lessons given by Brother Boles. The meeting did much good among the outsiders, and the members were edified and strengthened by the great sermons delivered. I, too, believe that we should have a volume or two of sermons by Brother Boles. Many of his sermons should be passed on to future generations in the most permanent form possible. They are simple enough for a child and profound enough for a philosopher to learn wisdom from them.[21]

The year of evangelism was fast paced as usual for Gus Nichols. About fifteen baptisms appeared in reports to the *Gospel Advocate* over the summer months with meetings at Mount Pleasant in Lamar County, at Howard near home, at Brookside down in Jefferson County, and at Clanton in Chilton County between Birmingham and Montgomery. Gus sent in a lengthy report of successful work on the 19th of September,

> The meeting at Bulah, near Cullman, Ala., resulted in two or three baptisms and several restorations. Good crowds, but almost all were members. James Benson works for this church and has been supported by the congregation in much mission work. One member contributed a tent for such work. Every church should have a preacher and a tent kept busy in evangelizing near-by communities. The devil is not lacking in men, money, and means. The meeting at White's Chapel, in Fayette County, resulted in fifty baptisms and fifty-six confessing sins and being restored. There were many outsiders as well as members from many congregations. Many of those who were restored were from near-by congregations. The windows were taken out for better ventilation and better vision of those outside. Some of those responding to the invitations came from the outside audience. I have just closed a mission meeting in the open air at Drummonds' Schoolhouse, about fifteen miles east of Jasper, in which seventeen were baptized and a new congregation

established. They met for worship on Lord's day during the meeting and have arranged to continue the work. They plan to build a meetinghouse in the next few weeks. The church at Jasper will oversee the work until the leadership is trained to carry on. Flavil and Pervie Nichols and Gilford Dobbs started the meeting and continued several nights until I could close the extended meeting in Fayette County. I begin Friday night of this week in the Theater Building at Empire, in the extreme eastern part of Walker County. We hope to establish a congregation there.[22]

At the end of September, Gus held the Empire meeting as just noted. No church had been previously planted there. He took his tent and set it up and preached to all who would come. The results were very good. He reported,

I closed the mission meeting at Empire, Ala., Saturday night, with only one baptized, but with more than a dozen members who had obeyed the gospel elsewhere beginning to worship "as it is written." Walker Davis, one of the number there, is a trained leader who formerly worshiped at Dora, Ala. They had a fine attendance Lord's day and are sure to succeed. This is the second congregation I have started in the last month. On Lord's day afternoon I preached at Howard and baptized three, and one of the number was an old lady eighty-two years of age. One was restored at the same service. We had a good day here in Jasper on Sunday; also Cecil Sanford baptized one here in the afternoon.[23]

A few days later a report followed in the *Firm Foundation*, "I have just established a congregation at Empire, Alabama. There are about twenty-five members. The attendance is about forty each Lord's day."[24]

Gus continued to preach into the fall in tent meetings and every place it was his opportunity to go. His last report for the year appeared in the pages of the *Gospel Advocate* as follows,

I recently closed a tent meeting about three miles out of Jasper in a community where we have a few members who have been worshiping in another community. The interest was good, and seven backsliding members confessed their faults. Members from all near-by congregations attended. We want to build a house for the convenience of the more than twenty members who go elsewhere to worship. Several have been restored and placed membership here this fall.[25]

FIFTEEN CENTS WORTH OF NICHOLS WEDDINGS

Gus and Matilda's oldest daughter, Gracie, finished her studies at Freed-Hardeman at the close of the 1936 school year. She had returned home for a time. While in school she met and fell in love with a Tennessean by the name of Frank D. Young (1909-1989). Raised in Nashville, Frank was baptized by Jesse P. Sewell (1876-1979) in September 1924. He attended Freed-Hardeman in the years 1933-1936. While in school he became a close friend to an Arkansas preacher student by the name of George W. DeHoff (1913-1993). After finishing school, DeHoff assisted Frank in getting preaching opportunities in Arkansas and other places. He lived for a time in Brush Creek, Tennessee. Then, he moved to live a short time later in Scottsville, Kentucky. Late in 1938, Frank moved to Humble, Texas. In all these places he was attached to local works, but preached gospel meetings in several locations. In early May the following year he and Gracie were married. The report appeared in the "News and Notes" section of the *Gospel Advocate* which read, "Frank D. Young, who preaches for the church at Humble, Texas, and Miss Gracie Nichols, daughter of Gus Nichols, of Jasper, Ala., were married at the bride's home in Jasper on May 3, with George W. DeHoff officiating."²⁶

1938 - Flavil Nichols, FHC Student

Nine weeks after Gus presented his eldest in holy matrimony, once again he was called upon to give another of his precious daughters in marriage. While a student at Freed-Hardeman, Vodie had met a young preacher

1938 - Mary Hardin, FHC Student

student by the name of A. J. Kerr (1916-1999). Born in Brookport, Illinois, A. J. was baptized by Floyd A. Decker (1898-1960) in July 1930. Within a few years, he began preaching in his hometown. Very soon after arriving at F-HC, he met Vodie, also a member of his Freshman class. Soon their friendship blossomed into romance, and the couple wed at her parents' home on the 6th of July 1939.

Like most Christian colleges, Freed-Hardeman has long been known for being a haven of marriage-making. Other than Gracie and Vodie, Flavil, too, found the love of his life while a student there. Mary Elizabeth Hardin was born just a month after her husband-to-be in Marmaduke, Arkansas, on the 7th of March 1919. Her parents, H. R. "Bud" and May Hardin, raised her in the town of Rector. From there she entered F-HC in the fall of 1936 in view of preparing herself for teaching school. She graduated in the spring of 1938, and for a time taught in a one-room school. Flavil, intending to continue at F-HC for the third-year preacher's track, cut it short, when brother Hardeman suggest he should take the work at Tuckerman, Arkansas. At 8:00 a.m. on the November 28th he and Mary were united together as husband and wife in the home of her parents in Rector. Traveling from Alabama for the event were Flavil's sisters, Bertha and Carrie, along with their father, who performed the ceremony. Over the years they recalled often how all went to a restaurant for lunch that day and Mary noticing that she still had rice in her hair.[27]

1937 - Vodie Nichols, *Treasure Chest*

The family was growing, and through it all God was being glorified. His Kingdom was increasing and his servants, the Nichols, continued to be a force for His cause.

ENDNOTES

1 Note: The designations of "Churches of Christ," "Christian Church," and "Disciples of Christ" were interchangeable among all groups in the Restoration Movement for most all the 19th Century. Though churches of Christ became most known after 1906 as being non-instrumental, many churches of Christ, who were so designated before the 1906 Census, had already introduced the instrument of music in their worship assemblies, and kept their name. Thus, designations were not hard and fast.

2 S. H. Hall, *Gospel Advocate*, 23 July 1936, p. 699.

3 Claud F. Witty, *Gospel Advocate*, 19 March 1936, p. 285.

4 Ibid., 7 May 1936, p. 448.

5 J. E. Choate, *The Anchor That Holds: A Biography Of Benton Cordell Goodpasture*, p. 147.

6 *Skyrocket*, Vol. 16, No. 3, December 1938, pp. 1-2.

7 Leo Lipscomb Boles and J.E. Choate, *I'll Stand On The Rock: A Biography of H. Leo Boles*, p. 250.

8 Gus Nichols, *Gospel Advocate*, 25 May 1939, p. 494.

9 Note: Daniel Sommer was considered to be one of the most powerful voices among Restoration Churches at the turn of the 20th century. Born in Maryland, educated at Bethany College, and at that time the nationally known editor of Benjamin Franklin's (1812-1878) *American Christian Review*, he devoted his life to fighting for the cause of Christ set out in the Scriptures. He was the leader at the great Sand Creek, Illinois, meeting in August 1889 where 6,000 determined to stand against the "digressions" of the day. Within a couple of years of his visit to Freed-Hardeman, he passed from this life, the 19th of February 1940, in Indianapolis, Indiana. Burial followed at Crown Hill Cemetery in that city.

10 *Skyrocket*, Vol. 16, No. 3, December 1938, pp. 1-2.

11 Crawford Allen, *Gospel Advocate*, 26 January 1939, p. 90.

12 Gus Nichols, *Gospel Advocate*, 23 March 1939, p. 281.

13 Ibid., 13 April 1939, p. 356. Note: A similar report appeared in the *Firm Foundation*, 2 May 1939, p. 5.

14 Ibid.

15 Note: H. Leo Boles' paternal grandmother was one of two daughters of John Smith and his first wife, Anna Townsend Smith, who escaped a terrible home fire that took the lives of two of their children. Their oldest son Eli, who was seven, and daughter Elvira, who was five, perished in the fire. Within days their mother died of a broken heart. The surviving children were three-year-old Jane, sometimes called "Jenny," and Zerelda Ann, an infant. This happened while they lived in a small cabin north of Huntsville, Alabama in 1815. Jane grew up to marry Thomas Jefferson Boles. Their only child, Henry Jefferson Boles married Sarah Smith, a distant cousin. They were the parents of H. Leo Boles.

16 R. H. Boll, ed., *The Word and Work*, June 1939, p. 124.

17 Ibid.

18 Note: Those in attendance at that meeting would have also known the great sacrifice made by Boles' great-grandfather in the years that followed the New Year's Day 1832 unity meeting at Lexington, Kentucky. For, "Raccoon" John Smith traveled with John Rogers, the appointed representative of the Stone movement, for the space of three years in efforts to assist churches across the land to unite on the basis of New Testament principles.

19 B. C. Goodpasture, ed., "H. Leo Boles' Speech at the 'Unity Meeting,'" *Gospel Advocate*, 25 May 1939, p. 476.

20 Ibid.

21 Gus Nichols, *Gospel Advocate*, 17 August 1939, p. 778.

22 Ibid., "Prospering Work," 28 September 1939, p. 926.

23 Ibid., 12 October 1939, p. 970.

24 Gus Nichols, *Firm Foundation*, 24 October 1939, p. 5.

25 Gus Nichols, *Gospel Advocate*, 16 November 1939, p. 1090.

26 "News And Notes," *Gospel Advocate*, 25 May 1939, p. 492.

27 Peggy Champion, daughter of Flavil and Mary Nichols. From email correspondence 24 January 2015.

- 24 -

Stand-Patters and Stay-Putters

That we henceforth be no more children, tossed to and fro, and carried about with every wind of doctrine, by the sleight of men, and cunning craftiness, whereby they lie in wait to deceive; But speaking the truth in love, may grow up into him in all things, which is the head, even Christ.
—Paul, Ephesians 4:14–15

SPECIAL COURSES

The annual Freed-Hardeman Special Courses were reduced from three weeks to two weeks beginning Tuesday, the 9th of January and running through the 19th, 1940. Again, Gus Nichols was in attendance for this, the fourth such series. H. Leo Boles (1874-1946) was once again utilized to take a leading role in teaching courses on "Homiletics and Christ" and "His Church." Others who appeared included G. A. Dunn (1876-1967), B. C. Goodpasture (1895-1977), G. K. Wallace (1903-1988), C. L. Wilkerson (1888-1949), and college president, N. B. Hardeman (1874-1965).

The addition of B. C. Goodpasture to the official program was far from incidental that year.[1] Two years previous, the managing editor of the *Gospel Advocate*, John T. Hinds (1866-1938), died of a stroke on the evening of 1 January 1938. Leon B. McQuiddy (1887-1950) was, at that time, the publisher of the *Advocate*. He and business manager, L. O. Sanderson (1901-1992), entered upon an effort to find a qualified replacement. After a year of searching, B. C. Goodpasture was announced as the new editor on 1 March 1939. His presence on the platform and in the classroom during the Special Courses the following year was both an effort to engage the *Advocate's* support of the school as well as N. B. Hardeman's (1874-1965) blessing upon the selection of the paper's new editor. It also afforded the brotherhood a better opportunity to meet the man.

On Friday of the first session, Gus Nichols celebrated the completion of forty-eight years on God's green earth. Part of the day was spent with his daughter, Bertha, who was in her last year at F-HC, as well as time with Flavil, who drove over from Arkansas for the series.

Gus had already developed a friendship with the *Gospel Advocate's* new editor, as B. C. had preached a meeting in Jasper four years previous. So, it was a reunion of sorts between the two men. In the course of time, an invitation was extended to Gus to submit a brief biographical sketch and a sermon outline to be featured in a future edition of the *Gospel Advocate*. Featuring gospel preachers of growing influence had been a time-honored tradition in the brotherhood papers for several years. For Gus to be highlighted was truly an honor he regarded highly. The 18 April issue of the *Advocate* devoted page 373 under the heading, "Gus Nichols."[2] The brief sketch is entered here in full,

> Gus Nichols was born in Walker County, Ala., January 12, 1892. He was reared under Baptist influence, and nearly all of his relatives were members of the Baptist Church. At the age of seventeen he went to the "mourner's bench," and was persuaded that he had forgiveness of sins before he had obeyed any command of God. He joined the Baptist Church and was prejudiced in behalf of it. He read the New Testament, and hoped that the Lord would call him to preach the Baptist doctrine. He became disturbed because he could not find the Baptist Church in the New Testament. He was told that it was a branch of the church of the New Testament. He heard C. A. Wheeler preach the gospel, and learned the truth from him. He was baptized upon confession of his faith for the remission of sins.

1940 - Gus Nichols

> Brother Wheeler suggested to him that he ought to preach the gospel and teach his people the truth. Brother Nichols began teaching the adult Bible class in his community and to take a leading part in the worship. He was encouraged to preach the gospel, and began doing so. His education was limited. He had a large family to support. He studied the Bible at home. He began preaching in 1917. In 1919 he moved to Berry, Ala., and attended Alabama Christian College there for two years. He preached at Cordova for two years, and then in 1926 moved to Millport, Ala., where he spent seven years preaching for the church. In 1932 Brother Nichols moved to Jasper, Ala., where he still lives and labors. He has done much mission work in Alabama and has been successful. He has done evangelistic work in Mississippi, Texas, and Florida. He has held a number of public debates, and is well

qualified to meet any opponent of the truth at any time. He is one of the editors of *Truth and Love* [sic].³

Following the sketch was a seven-point outline under the title, "Things By Which We Are Saved." Each point was basic to the truth, and well-fortified with Scripture references. Only eternity knows how many times and in how many places that sermon was preached around the world.

The mention in the sketch about his co-editorship of *Truth In Love* cannot be underestimated. The paper was enjoying its fourth year of production and reported an average circulation for the first half of 1940 of 22,928 copies per month.⁴ The success and strength of the paper prompted Foy E. Wallace, Jr. (1896-1979) to write in his paper, *The Bible Banner*,

> Exchanging compliments, let me say that *Truth In Love* is one of the best mediums of truth, serving the purpose of disseminating the first principles of the gospel and the duties of the Christian life among unconverted people. The men who write for it, including Gus Nichols, of Jasper, Alabama, are stand-patters and stay-putters for the truth in love. Some men chatter about "the truth in love" who have neither truth nor love. Not so with Jack Meyer's *Truth In Love*, they have both, and their paper is being distributed in bundles by churches all over the south and west, "accenting" the truth in love.⁵

In his most inimitable way of expressing praise, being called "stand-patters and stay-putters" was Wallace's stamp of approval on the editorial staff of the Birmingham paper.

GROWTH AT HOME

Throughout the spring, the labor at Fifth Avenue continued to enjoy increase and peace within its ranks. A little over mid-way through May Gus penned the following about the work and immediate plans of the Jasper congregation,

> We have recently baptized eight here, and our general interest is the best in the eight years of my work in Jasper. C. M. Pullias will do the preaching in our meeting this year, beginning the first Lord's day in July. We want to start the meeting with all day services and basket dinner. Our meetinghouse debt has been reduced since I have been here from about $10,000 to about $3,000. Our contributions are going above our budget. Perfect peace prevails, as far as I know, and has from the first. Spiritually, our membership is far above the average. With few exceptions, the members live above suspicion and reproach. Still there is much room for improvement.⁶

The next week, he was so excited to report the success of a unique conversion. The 6th of June issue of the *Gospel Advocate* carried the heading, "Baptist Preacher Baptized." Explaining he said,

> Last week we baptized a man here who had been a Baptist preacher. He now wants to preach the gospel without addition or subtraction. I am now preaching in a meeting at Townley, where there is a very small group struggling for assistance. There have been no additions to date.[7]

As introduced above, the summer meeting at Fifth Avenue was to be preached by C. M. Pullias. Charles Mitchell Pullias (1872-1962) was born and reared in Trousdale County, Tennessee. He was twenty-two years of age when he was baptized by L. S. White (1867-1949). Born of Italian parents and with a deep voice, he was in great demand as a preacher in most places he traveled. He wrote much for the brotherhood papers, and in the early days of radio he was among the first to use its power in spreading the gospel while living in Dallas, Texas. In 1922, when the churches of Nashville were organizing the first Ryman Tabernacle Series, his name arose first as potential speaker before N. B. Hardeman was finally selected. In the end, Pullias led the singing for the meeting. By 1940, he was one of the most beloved and influential preachers of his day. His visit to Walker County, Alabama in the summer of that year was most welcome and much anticipated. Gus wrote:

C. M. Pullias

> Our meeting will begin the first Sunday in July, with C. M. Pullias doing the preaching. There will be an all day service, with good singing, the first day of the meeting. We invite all our friends everywhere to come and spend the day and enjoy the sermons and singing. We will be out in the beautiful shade by the meetinghouse on Fifth Avenue during the meeting, unless weather conditions drive us into the house.

The meeting was completed on the third Sunday in July. During Pullias' visit, seven were baptized and five were restored.[8] Immediately after the meeting Gus conducted a meeting over at Eldridge. The preacher, Johnie Payne (1910-1992) reported, "Our meeting here was one of the best in the history of the congregation. There were twenty baptisms and ten restorations. There were additions at almost every service. Gus Nichols did the preaching."⁹

NICHOLS-LODGE DEBATE

About forty-five miles northeast of Jasper is the little town of Vinemont, Alabama. This Cullman County township played host to a debate under an open-air tent on the nights of 10 and 11 September 1940. One of the participants was O. G. Lodge, a preacher for the Church of God from High Point, Georgia. His opponent in the discussion was Gus Nichols. A good report of the debate was sent in to the brotherhood papers by the former preacher for the church there, Horace A. Holt (1912-2003). In part he described,

> In the first session Brother Nichols ably affirmed the usual church proposition. He set forth in a clear, forceful manner the teachings of the New Testament on the church. Mr. Lodge did not attempt to refute a single argument or answer a Scripture used by Brother Nichols in the first night of the debate. Instead of taking notes and trying to answer the arguments made by Brother Nichols, Mr. Lodge spent sixty minutes running back and forth before the audience, jumping up and down, keeping the audience in an uproar most of the time. The second night Mr. Lodge was supposed to affirm the same proposition concerning his church. His efforts were very little better than the night before. He did not define his proposition, even after Brother Nichols asked him to do so. His speeches were made up of unreasonable assertions, which he did not even attempt to prove. Brother Nichols answered every Scripture he used and turned them all against Mr. Lodge, showing that they taught just the opposite to what he was trying to prove. He showed that Mr. Lodge contradicted himself a number of times and made him admit twice that he had knowingly perverted the Scriptures. Before the debate started, Mr. Lodge said they should have four nights. The second night he asked Brother Nichols to allow each speaker to have an extra twenty minutes in order to get through. At the end of Brother Nichols' third speech, Mr. Lodge wanted to call off the last speeches. Brother Nichols would not agree to this, but did agree to cut them to ten minutes. Mr. Lodge used only five of his ten minutes in his last speech. He gave as the reason that the people were getting cold in the open air. It was obvious to almost everyone present that it was the extreme portion of Mr. Lodge's anatomy that was getting cold. Close to a thousand people heard the gospel during this discussion, and it is sure to do a world of good. To anyone desiring the truth humbly proclaimed and false teaching exposed I recommend Brother

Nichols. I believe him equal to any situation calling for a forceful, convincing debater. Following the debate, I preached Thursday and Friday nights. The writer acted as moderator for Brother Nichols and a Mr. Ben Izibell moderated for Mr. Lodge.[10]

EVANGELISM ABROAD AND AT HOME

In early October, Gus and song leader, M. L. Johnson, who lived over in Lamar County, traveled down to Port Arthur, Texas for another gospel meeting effort similar to the one he held there the previous year. The meeting began the 6th of October and continued through the 20th. On the 30th of the month he reported,

> I recently returned from Port Arthur, Texas, where I preached in a three-Lord's-day meeting with the Eleventh Street Church,

The Church of Christ, 3548 Eleventh Street, invites you to hear Evangelist Gus Nichols, of Jasper, Alabama, in a series of meetings, October 6-20. Services twice daily, 10 a. m. and 7:45 p. m. Come and hear sin condemned, Christ and His Church exalted and the plan of salvation proclaimed.

1946 - *The Port Arthur Newspaper* Ad, October 6

> for which Edd Holt preaches. Three were baptized and one or two restored. M. L. Johnson, of Vernon, Ala., directed the song service. Brother Johnson has labored with me in this capacity more or less for twenty years, and I wish to commend him to any church wanting a clean and efficient teacher of songs or director for a meeting. The Eleventh Street Church, in Port Arthur, is doing much to spread the gospel. It is training young men to preach the

word and supporting Brother Holt in much mission work; also it is supporting a preacher full time in the state of Louisiana.[11]

With his return home, this concluded his mission work for the year. Yet, Gus lost no steam in plowing right back into the local work. Within days he stated,

> Since returning to regular local work, four have been baptized here. Last week I spent five days with the Mount Olive Church, in Fayette County, and baptized three. One of the number had not heard me preach. One afternoon I taught a young lady, who decided to be baptized "immediately," and while she went home to prepare extra clothes, the sisters where I had lunch carried me out to talk to her mother, and in less than an hour she, too, wanted to be baptized that afternoon. One of the four baptized here recently came to my home Tuesday of this week and asked some questions. Being fully satisfied with Bible answers, he was immediately baptized. Our prospects here are growing brighter all the time.[12]

THE CHRISTIAN RACE
By Gus Nichols

All who would enter Heaven by grace,
Must enter and run the Christian race.
One must have Heaven as his goal,
Or he'll lose his immortal soul.
(Heb. 12:1-2; Mt. 16:26.)

Yes, the way is very rugged and rough,
But faith can make one strong and tough.
By all who enter and patiently run,
The crown of life will surely be won.
(1 Cor. 9:24-26; 2 Tim. 4:1-8)

We've never heard of one's winning a crown,
Who spurned the rules and wore a frown.
Such examples one can't defend;
One must run lawfully on to the end.
(2 Tim. 2:1-5; 2 Jn. 9; Mt. 24:13.)

To win this race, one must first start,
Be a Christian and do his part.
One can't win on faults of others,
Or, just by criticizing his brothers.
(2 Cor. 6:2; Phil. 2:12; Jn. 21:20-22.)

So, why do you wait, my dear friend?
You cannot begin at the end!
The crown of life you cannot win,
Unless you first of all begin!
(Rev. 2:10; Rom. 2:4-11.)

So start right in this very minute.
You can't win unless you're in it.
You've already failed unless you try:
You can't win by just standing by.
(Prov. 27:1; Heb. 3:7-8; Mk. 16:15-16.)

If you had a hundred years to wait,
You might still be outside the gate,
For every day you fail to start,
You further harden your calloused heart.
(Heb. 3:7-8; I Tim. 4:1-3)

Why stand here idle, my fellow man?
You ought to begin, while you can.
The race you cannot ever win,
Unless you first of all begin.
(Matt. 20:1-16; Mt. 25:1-46)[13]

ENDNOTES

1 Note: According to the biography of H. Leo Boles, *I'll Stand On The Rock*, p. 248, B. C. Goodpasture was in attendance at the 1937 series of the Special Courses in a speaking role along with several others who were not a part of the official program. However, Goodpasture's first official designation was at the 1940 series.

2 *Gospel Advocate*, 18 April 1940, p. 373.

3 Ibid.

4 "A Sound Policy," *Gospel Advocate*, 25 July 1940, p. 715.

5 Foy E. Wallace Jr., *The Bible Banner*, June 1940, p. 10.

6 Gus Nichols, *Gospel Advocate*, 23 May 1940, p. 497.

7 Ibid., 6 June 1940, p. 544.

8 W. E. Brightwell, *Gospel Advocate*, 22 August 1940, p. 812.

9 Johnie Payne, *Gospel Advocate*, 22 August 1940, p. 812.

10 Horace A. Holt, *Gospel Advocate*, 26 September 1940, p. 931. Note: A similar report appear in the *Firm Foundation*, 22 October 1940, p. 8.

11 Gus Nichols, *Gospel Advocate*, 7 November 1940, p. 1077.

12 Ibid., 14 November 1940, p. 1096.

13 Gus Nichols, "The Christian Race," *Words of Truth,* 13 October 1967, p.3.

- 25 -

New Roles And New Threats

But sanctify the Lord God in your hearts: and be ready always to give an answer to every man that asketh you a reason of the hope that is in you with meekness and fear.
—Peter, 1 Peter 3:15

"MY DADDY"

Twelve days into 1941, Gus Nichols completed his forty-nineth year. Crossing the threshold into a new decade of life brought much promise for himself, his family, and a loving church. In honor of the occasion, Flavil wrote the following:

> My dear Daddy, you have helped me many a day
> In the path of the Lord and Savior to stay.
> Before me daily you have done all you could
> To set an example of how to be good.
>
> You have taught us children to reverence God
> And in Christ's holy way to always trod.
> We bring you our problems, and you treat us grand!
> Your influence leads us to a better land.
>
> Many know this is true, and seek your advice
> When Satan has worked some wicked device.
> You, Daddy, always give ear to their troubles
> And often they vanish like huge soap bubbles!
>
> You have been faithful to sound out God's Word
> In many weak places where it had not been heard.
> You often have, both by word and by deed,
> Caused many lost sinners God's truth to heed.
>
> Regardless of where I may chance to stay,
> I'll appreciate your influence to my dying day!
> But there are two more words that I just must say
>
> To you, Dear Daddy: "HAPPY BIRTHDAY!"
>
> —Flavil H. Nichols, Jan. 12, 1941.[1]

SPECIAL COURSES

During the weeks leading up the 1941 Special Courses series at Freed-Hardeman College, advertisements appeared in brotherhood papers to the effect that a new face was to appear on the rostrum involved in various roles. The *Firm Foundation* tendered the event to be 14-23 January with courses being taught by H. Leo Boles (1874-1946), John T. Lewis (1876-1967), and N. B. Hardeman (1874-1965). Also scheduled under the heading, "Discussions," set for Tuesday was, "Does the Holy Spirit operate directly upon the heart of the sinner in conversion?" C. D. Plum (1898-1977) was to represent the affirmative side and Gus Nichols, the negative. Then on Thursday, "Is Baptism essential to salvation?" B. L. Douthitt (1899-1989) was to affirm, and Gus Nichols again, to take the negative position.[2]

The practical aspect of offering mock debates as a part of the Special Courses was due to the wide use of debating in evangelism among Restoration preachers during that era. At a time when the polemic platform was the place where Biblical questions were openly discussed, the importance of preparing the young preacher for this venue was paramount. The capable debater had not only the potential of exposing the masses to truth, but through its reasonable display, bring about life-changes among many hearers at one setting.

Of the several great and successful debaters in the brotherhood during that period, Gus Nichols ranked among the most accomplished. His vast knowledge of denominational doctrines made him the most qualified to take the lead in representing the negative in the mock discussions. If fact, he knew the doctrines of the gainsayers so well, having held many debates with denominational preachers, that he gave the young preacher in the crowd the best opportunity to hear both sides of the topic being discussed. After all, knowing your opponent's doctrine better than he does most certainly gives you the better advantage. Having Nichols on the platform was a "feather in the caps" of the program's planners, however there were some things he brought to the table that had not been anticipated.[3]

It happened at the Thursday exchange with Boone L. Douthitt (1899-1989)[4] that questions began to arise in the mind of N. B. Hardeman (1874-1965) as to whether this format should be continued. One of the teachers in the school who was present at this event was C. P. Roland (1893-1985).[5] He explained the concern as it unfolded in an interview several years later. He recalled,

> So brother Boone had the Bible truth, and the right side of it. Brother Nichols had a few keen points that he supposed he would use on him, and so he told brother Boone the afternoon before,

> said, "Boone hadn't we better go over my notes, here, so that you'll be familiar with some of these things that you might not have run into in your discussions." And said, "I had to do a lot of study on some of these myself, so if you'd like to, we'll just go over my notes." And brother Boone, egotistically in a way, said, "No, brother Nichols, they can't bring up—I don't think you can bring up anything that I haven't already heard in a debate."[6]

Underestimating the expertise of the Alabama disputant proved to be folly on the part of brother Douthitt. Clearly recalling the exchange that took place nearly forty years previous, Roland explained Nichols' offensive,

> That night the debate went on, brother Nichols advanced on, I believe, on Galatians 3:26-27, and said, "Now, you just can't read the Bible, Boone, brother Douthitt." He said, "You haven't read that. It says we're all children of God by faith. We're all children of God by faith." And said, "Of course, then, anyone who is a child of God by faith then, since he wants to obey the Lord, then he will be baptized. So, it wasn't essential to Salvation, you already had Salvation, you can see that in the passage, anybody can see that and study the passage." "Well—he was a child of God, and then he'd do what any child of God would do, go ahead and obey the Lord in whatever He told you to do." So, therefore he told them, "You are a child of God by faith in Christ Jesus, so all of you children of God need to be baptized if you haven't been," and so on. And he just made that so strong that it confused Boone, and in his last speech, which was—in his last speech, he had realized it so keenly, and the audience had become humiliated because it had been presented so strongly, and he couldn't answer it—hadn't any answer for it, and so on. And he said, "Now, if there's anybody in this audience that's not satisfied..." He readily admitted his own defeat in supporting the truth, because he said, "If there's anybody in this audience that's not satisfied with that, you come around and see me later."[7]

The following day, Gus was able to explain his arguments and shared how he would respond if he encountered the particular argument he had used to tie up his opponent the night before. The outcome of the mock debate left organizers concerned that the very thing they were intending to do in helping prepare preachers to debate could also be a venue for promoting falsehood as well, which defeated the intended goal. Within a few years, the mock debates were discontinued for a time.

At the end of the month, H. Leo Boles (1874-1946) reported the success of the series saying, "These courses proved helpful to the young preachers.

Gus Nichols conducted a query-box discussion one hour each day, and another hour was given to young preachers in the discussion of different topics."[8] This was the first of such sessions that later became known as the very popular daily Open Forum during the annual lectureship program at Freed-Hardeman University.

INCREASED INFLUENCE

The growing popularity of Gus Nichols was making its mark on the lives of so many individuals. Young preachers who had the opportunity to study at his feet in the Friday night classes, the young men who heard him preach during gospel meetings, and the reputation that continued to win the hearts of the brotherhood, caused many to want to follow in his footsteps.

For instance, Hoyt Bailey (1913-1994) was one such preacher who found inspiration in brother Nichols and other greats of his day.[9] Around that time, the *Firm Foundation* ran a regular column entitled, "Getting Acquainted With Our Preaching Brethren." The 11 February 1941 issue featured brother Bailey and spoke of what inspired him to preach. Among several facts related, it was said "upon hearing Brother Dunn, Brother W. A. Black, Brother Chester Estes, and Brother Gus Nichols in meetings, and having studied the sermons of outstanding preachers, Hoyt was inspired to start proclaiming the news of salvation."[10] This story was repeated time and again all over the country with other young preachers.

During the spring of 1941, Gus continued a busy schedule at home and on the road. He participated in a lectureship at the Sherrod Avenue church of Christ in Florence, Alabama in mid-March. Appearing with him on the forum were Gardner S. Hall (1906-1978), Jack R. Hackworth (1905-1993), Leon C. Burns (1906-1984), and B. L. Douthitt (1899-1989). On Thursday evening, Gus spoke on, "The Establishment of the Church."[11]

On the 6th of April he switched pulpits with J. O. Jones (1910-1968) of Winfield over in Marion County to make it possible for Gus to preach the commencement sermon for the local high school. Jones said, "Everyone thought Brother Nichols' sermon could not be surpassed by anyone, and that it was superior to any ever heard."[12]

As the summer meeting work was drawing near, the Fifth Avenue brethren determined to purchase a new tent to assist in the evangelistic work of their preacher. The brethren believed in mission work and often underwrote Gus' preaching endeavors not only in Walker County but wherever the brethren were in need. At the end of April, they paid for him to go to Fort Payne, Alabama to preach a mission meeting for the small congregation that existed there. He said, "We have a few brethren who are faithful and determined to build a nice but modest house of worship.

I preached the last few days of the meeting in the courthouse and had a fairly good attendance."[13]

THE TINGLEY DEBATE

At the end of May, Gus participated in a debate with Glenn V. Tingley. A member of the Christian Missionary Alliance, Tingley had debated John T. Lewis (1876-1967) in Birmingham in 1935. He also had met Foy E. Wallace, Jr. (1896-1979) there in September 1938 on the subjects of Baptism, Premillennialism, and Holy Spirit Baptism. Advertising the event, Gus wrote,

> Beginning May 26 and continuing for six nights, I am to meet Mr. Glenn V. Tingley, of Birmingham, Ala., in a discussion at Oak Grove church of Christ, near Flat Creek, Ala. Mr. Tingley affirms the direct operation of the Spirit in conversion, and salvation by faith alone before and without water baptism. I affirm that water baptism is a condition of salvation or remission of sins to alien sinners. Two night sessions of two hours will be given to each proposition.[14]

In attendance at the debate was J. O. Jones who said, "This was the greatest debate that I have ever heard. The propositions were "The Work of the Holy Spirit and The Plan of Salvation!" Brother Nichols presented the truth, then whipped Tingley with his own logic!"[15]

The preacher from Brilliant in Marion County at the time, James G. Pounds (1914-1991), in glowing terms added,

> I have attended many debates, but never did I hear the truth better defended and error more defeated. In every speech Brother Nichols manifested the spirit of great conviction, hatred for error, and love for truth and the souls of men. Mr. Tingley tried to discard such plain passages as Mark 16:16 and Acts 2:38 by bringing up cases where "great" men this side of New Testament times died without baptism. Brother Nichols showed that to fail to comply with God's commands did not make them of none effect, and that every commandment could be discarded the same way. While debating the Holy Spirit question, Mr. Tingley had Cornelius a bad sinner and the Spirit falling upon him to convert him; but when he came to discuss baptism, Cornelius was a saved man before baptism and before the Holy Spirit fell upon him. Many gospel preachers attended this debate. W. A. Black, of Alabama City, Ala., moderated for Brother Nichols, and did a splendid job of it. Thanks be to God for the sword of the Spirit and men like Brother Nichols who can use it.[16]

W. A. Black reported, "There were sixteen gospel preachers who attended the debate. If there were any preachers that believed like Mr. Tingley that attended the debate, I failed to get acquainted with them."[17] As for some of the argumentation used in the discussion Black followed with,

> Mr. Tingley gave Cornelius as an example of the Holy Spirit operating directly upon an alien sinner to convert him. Then when they came to baptism, Mr. Tingley took the position that Cornelius was a saved man when the Spirit fell on him. Of course, Brother Nichols exposed him on this and on every other argument that he tried to make. Mr. Tingley was so hard pressed that he claimed that the Spirit operated upon dogs and mules. Many times in the debate Mr. Tingley would make a bold assertion that the Bible said thus and thus, when the Bible did not say it. Among the assertions that he made are the following: "Paul prayed for a direct operation of the Spirit on alien sinners." "You believe into Christ." Brother Nichols challenged him to read the above statements out of the Bible and he would acknowledge defeat and quit the debate. Of course the debate continued. I have attended several debates, and I think that Brother Nichols did the best job in exposing error and upholding the truth in this discussion that I have ever heard. So well pleased were the brethren with the debate that Howard Horton, of Bessemer, Ala., asked them to repeat it in Bessemer this fall. So I suppose that we can look forward to another great debate if Mr. Tingley does not back down. Debates like this one do good. Let us have more of them.[18]

AMONG EARLY HEROES OF THE RESTORATION MOVEMENT

Soon after the debate, Gus was off to Lancaster, Kentucky for a gospel meeting. The small church there was special to him, not only for the opportunities for the gospel message, but also because Vodie and A. J. worked with that congregation.

Living just thirty-five miles south of Lexington, the Kerrs were very close to many sights of the early days of the Restoration Movement in Kentucky. While in the area, they took Gus to visit the old Lexington Cemetery, with it towering monument and burial place of the great Kentucky statesman, Henry Clay (1777-1852). While there

Gus Nichols- Cane Ridge

they stood near the graves of great restoration preachers like, "Raccoon" John Smith (1784-1868), John T. Johnson (1788-1856), Robert Graham (1822-1901), Robert Milligan (1814-1875), Isaiah Boone Grubbs (1833-1912), and John W. McGarvey (1829-1911). One day they made their way out beyond Paris, Kentucky, to Cane Ridge, touring the old meetinghouse, and stopping at the grave of the great revivalist, Barton W. Stone (1772-1844).

Gus Nichols and A. J. Kerr
at J. W. McGarvey's Grave

Amongst a great cloud of witnesses, for twelve days, Gus preached the message of truth under a big tent on Campbell Street in Lancaster to large crowds.[19] At the close of the meeting, A. J. Kerr sent in the following,

> Last Friday night Gus Nichols, of Jasper, Ala., closed the best meeting in Lancaster, which this congregation has ever had. The attendance, interest, and results were above expectation. The congregation was strengthened both spiritually and in numbers. Seven were baptized and four restored (three from the Christian Church). At the morning service last Sunday another gave up the error of the Christian Church.[20]

"THESE TRYING TIMES"

As was commonplace for Gus, at the close of the meeting in Kentucky, he hurried back to Jasper to make final preparations for the annual July meeting at Fifth Avenue. Returning for the second year in a row was C. M. Pullias (1872-1962). The meeting the previous year had been so successful that it was determined that the big new tent should be set up under the shade trees in anticipation of the large crowds that were sure to come. And come, they did. On the 31st of July, Gus penned the following,

> Our meeting closed with a great crowd present last Sunday night. C. M. Pullias did the preaching, and gave us some of the best lessons that we have ever heard. The church was greatly strengthened by the wonderful sermons, which were largely adapted to the church members and to our needs in these trying times. I am to begin at White's Chapel, in Fayette County, the second Sunday in August.[21]

As Gus mentioned, these were "trying times" in the world. The nations of Europe were at war. Adolph Hitler had become a household name everywhere. While the U.S. was making a diligent effort to stay out of the war, many Americans were fearful that the day was coming that they must begin sending their husbands and children off to fight on foreign soil as they did less than a generation before in the Great War.

The fear of warfare was but a fraction of the concern of people on the home front. The war that Satan was unleashing upon the brethren was of constant concern. Discouragement comes while standing for God in a world that is deeply resentful of all things right and holy. These kinds of things played heavily upon the mind of the preacher of the Fifth Avenue church of Christ. Feeling these life-threats, he wrote an article and submitted it to the *Gospel Advocate* on the subject, "Peter Encourages Suffering Christians." It was a study on 1 Peter, and it appeared under the regular column, "The Uniformed Lesson—August 17, 1941."[22] Within just a few weeks, this article proved to be more essential than anyone would have thought.

The fall of the year introduced some suffering on a personal level to the Nichols family. In early September, Gus found himself in the hospital in Jasper having to undergo surgery. An operation was performed, the nature of which is unspecified. It was serious enough that a prayer request was sent to the brotherhood under the title "Nichols Has Operation." It said, "J. G. Pounds, Brilliant, Ala., September 10: 'Gus Nichols, of Jasper, Ala., has just undergone an operation in the Walker County Hospital. His condition is reported good. We pray that he may speedily recover.'"[23]

Within a few days he was able to return to his regular duties.[24] However, extreme illness returned to the Nichols home very quickly as about six weeks later a telegram appeared at the offices of the *Gospel Advocate* with an alarming appeal for intercession on Matilda's behalf. It read, "Gus Nichols, Jasper, Ala., November 10 (telegram): Mrs. Nichols is improving. Pneumonia followed ruptured appendix operation Friday. Please pray for recovery."[25]

The sickness was so severe that Gus had to excuse himself from a gospel meeting in Steens, Mississippi, in order to stay with her. Flavil was sent in his stead to conduct the meeting, but the illness appeared to be so severe that his father called him to his mother's bedside. Others completed the meeting in their stead.[26] Within four days of the previous telegram a follow-up message was sent to the *Advocate*,

> Mrs. Nichols is much better. It is believed that she is out of danger now. Though she is still under the oxygen tent and has special nurses, her temperature is about normal and she is improving every hour. She will no doubt be in the hospital at least another week or more. God be thanked for her progress.[27]

The year closed with some of America's darkest hours. Fears of the threat of war became a reality when the U.S. Naval forces were attacked on Sunday morning, the 7th of December, on the small Pacific island of Oahu, Hawaii. Pearl Harbor was mercilessly bombed in multiple waves of Japanese attacks, leaving a total of 2,403 military and civilians dead. It was the single worst tragedy in U.S. history to date. Within hours the citizens of Jasper, Alabama, like all those across the nation, heard the words of President Franklin D. Roosevelt of a declaration of war that forever changed the course of American history.

ENDNOTES

1 Flavil H. Nichols, "The Editor's Pen," *Words of Truth*, 19 August 1988, p. 1.

2 Advertisement, *Firm Foundation*, 19 November 1940, p. 5. Note: Similar announcements appeared in the *Gospel Advocate*, 14 November 1940, p. 1097, and repeated 19 December 1940, p. 1219. Also, the *Bible Banner*, December, p. 9.

3 Note: For quite some time, there were Thursday night mock debates at the Jasper church building, where preachers in the area, wanting to hone their skills, asked brother Nichols to assist them. He planned the sessions and assisted the preachers with their propositions. Then they would debate each other for an hour. At the end, he would mount the platform for the next 90 minutes to 2 hours with critical input and some preaching. He would explain the topic more fully, revealing further arguments, so as to prepare the preachers for debate encounters. It was a veritable college course in debate procedures and skills.

4 Note: Boone Lawrence Douthitt (1899-1989) was considered a Kentucky preacher. Two of his brothers, Ira A. (1891-1975) and Cecil B. (1896-1971) were well-known preachers in the brotherhood. Boone was a graduate of Freed-Hardeman College, and preached primarily in Kentucky, Alabama and Tennessee. He preached the gospel for over 70 years and was a disputant in about 65 debates. He passed from this life September 25, 1989, and was interred in the Woodlawn Cemetery in Nashville, Tennessee.

5 Note: Clifford Paul Roland (1893-1985) was born the 4th of July 1893 in Essary Springs, Hardeman County, Tennessee. He attended Freed-Hardeman College in 1910 when it was called National Teacher's Normal And Business College. He finished at Memphis State University in 1916. In 1931, he received his Masters degree from Vanderbilt University. He served as principal in two schools before returning to F-HC in 1921. He served the school as Faculty Member, Business Manager, Dean, and later Vice-President. He served as an elder of the Henderson church, and preached all over the country during his lifetime. It was a privilege of your author to have known him when attending F-HC in the 1970s, a dear and respected man. He passed from this life 11 December 1985, his body being interred in the Henderson Cemetery.

6 Richard Corum, "Richard Corum's Interview With C. P. Roland: The Old Main Administration Building," November 29, 1979, Tape two, unpublished transcriptions by Amy D. Gaskin, 22 June 2002.

7 Ibid.

8 H. Leo Boles, "Freed-Hardeman Special Courses," *Gospel Advocate*, 30 January 1941, p. 113.

9 Note: Hoyt Bailey was born 27 February 1913 in Marion County, Alabama near the town of Haleyville. He was the middle child of nine. He grew up at the Whitehouse church of Christ and began preaching in 1932. He walked to most all his appointments, as was noted earlier. One year he reported having walked over 700 miles in the work of his ministry. He did some studies at Harding

College and about six months of preacher courses at Freed-Hardeman. Bailey preached in Arkansas, Mississippi, Alabama, Tennessee, New York, and other places. He did radio work in the early days of that form of media. His last years were spent in Huntsville, Alabama where he worked among the churches. He passed from this life 1 February 1994 just a few days shy of his 81st birthday. He was buried at Maple Hill Cemetery.

10 "Getting Acquainted With Our Preaching Brethren," *Firm Foundation*, 11 February 1941, p. 3. Note: This may have been the first time Gus Nichols' name appeared alongside other great preachers of note among the brethren. In later years, his name was categorized alongside the greatest preachers of his day.

11 "News And Notes," *Gospel Advocate*, 20 March 1941, p. 285.

12 J. O. Jones, *Gospel Advocate*, 17 April 1941, p. 377.

13 Gus Nichols, *Gospel Advocate*, 15 May 1941, p. 472.

14 Ibid., 8 May 1941, p. 451. Note: A similar report appeared a couple days before in the *Firm Foundation*, 6 May 1941, p. 5.

15 J. O. Jones, *Gospel Advocate*, 12 June 1941, p. 568. Note: A similar report appeared in the *Firm Foundation* 17 June 1941, p. 5.

16 James G. Pounds, *Gospel Advocate*, 19 June 1941, p. 595.

17 W. A. Black, *Gospel Advocate*, 17 July 1941, p. 691.

18 Ibid.

19 A. J. Kerr, *Gospel Advocate*, 19 June 1941, p. 593.

20 Ibid., 10 July 1941, p. 668.

21 Gus Nichols, *Gospel Advocate*, 31 July 1941, p. 739.

22 Ibid., 7 August 1941, p. 756.

23 J. G. Pounds, *Gospel Advocate*, 18 September 1941, p. 904.

24 Pryde E. Hinton, *Gospel Advocate*, 9 October 1941, p. 983. Note: Hinton reported that Gus was involved in preaching a funeral just three days after his surgery, (13 September) saying, "Gus Nichols made a fine talk, and I led the prayer and concluded the service."

25 Gus Nichols, "Asks Prayer For Wife," *Gospel Advocate*, 13 November 1941, p. 1101.

26 Jean Thornton, *Gospel Advocate*, 20 November 1941, p. 1121.

27 Gus Nichols, "Mrs. Nichols Improves," *Gospel Advocate*, 20 November 1941, p. 1125.

- 26 -

From Co-Editor To Editor

> Or saith he it altogether for our sakes? For our sakes, no doubt, this is written: that he that ploweth should plow in hope; and that he that thresheth in hope should be partaker of his hope.
>
> —Paul, 1 Corinthians 9:10

Among the many reports sent in to the Austin, Texas, offices of the *Firm Foundation*, editor G. H. P. Showalter (1870-1954) closed the first issue of 1942 observing,

> Another Gospel paper of merit is "*Truth In Love*" published from Birmingham, Alabama. Its editors are J. D. Cox, Jack Meyer, G. S. Hall, and Gus Nichols. Its eight pages come filled with good matter. This monthly, like the *Gospel Proclaimer*, is concerned with the fundamentals of the Gospel, and is widely circulated.[1]

In its first six years of production, *Truth In Love* continued to enjoy a growing influence among the brotherhood. With a solid editorial force, its reputation for soundness was nothing short of excellent. However, little did Showalter know at the time that changes on the editorial staff of *Truth In Love* had already been put in motion.

After nearly four years at the North Birmingham congregation, co-editor John D. Cox (1908-1964) cast his eyes toward the Chattanooga, Tennessee, area in view of working with the St. Elmo congregation there. Jack D. Meyer (1914-1972) had been with the West End church in Birmingham since August of 1935 but was eager to answer the call of the brethren at the Heights congregation in Houston, Texas.[2] Gardner S. Hall (1906-1978) had moved away from the area in 1937 to work in Pensacola, Florida.

Since its inception in November 1935, *Truth In Love* was primarily known as a Birmingham paper even though Gus Nichols had never lived there. At the time, there were twenty congregations of the Lord's people in the growing metropolitan area, and there was need for a paper to be produced in the area.[3]

Another of the local preachers in the city was William Carlos Graves (1886-1946). W. C. Graves was converted in a gospel meeting preached by S. H. Hall (1877-1961) in 1912 at East Point, Georgia.[4] At Hall's insistence, he attended Nashville Bible School. After his schooling, he moved to

Birmingham, where he began working closely in association with John T. Lewis (1876-1967) in the planting and building up of the churches in that city. In 1921, he was financially responsible for bringing in and assisting Marshall Keeble (1878-1968) with the planting of the city's first black work.

In the early 1920s, Graves began a paper for the churches in Birmingham under the designation, *Truth In Love*. Its focus was more of sharing and spreading news of the works going on among the congregations in the city. The paper had ceased publication several years when the present paper, under the same title, began to be produced. Through the years, he contributed articles for publication to the *Gospel Advocate*, and was serving as the front-page editor of *Sound Doctrine*, the Montgomery paper founded by C. Leonard Johnson (1910-1994), and Rex A. Turner (1913-2001). When it became known to Graves that transition in editorship was needed due to the departure of its present staff from the region, he determined to purchase the paper and continue its good work. Its readership had reached above 20,000 subscriptions, and he deemed it essential to continue the work. So, W. C. Graves began editing *Truth In Love* in the fall of 1941. In his first article, he promised to continue in the same vein of quality writing that had been in place previously, and all the former co-editors promised to continue sending articles in for publication.

SPECIAL COURSES AT F-HC

Gus was called upon for the second year in a row to assist in the Special Courses series at Freed-Hardeman College. In the six years of its running, it continued to grow in popularity among preachers. L. L. Brigance (1879-1950)[5] reported the success of the event,

> The best series of special courses at Freed-Hardeman College came to a close January 15. This was the sixth of these courses, with greater interest and enthusiasm than any of the preceding ones. Altogether, there were one hundred fifteen visiting preachers from all parts of the country. Fifteen states and the Dominion of Canada were represented. It was an ascending climax from beginning to end, reaching the peak at the close of the last session in a debate on the premillennialism question between E. R. Harper, of Little Rock, Ark, and Gus Nichols of Jasper, Ala. The last session closed with an overflowing crowd. Numbers were standing around the walls and adjoining hall during this last session. There was not a discordant note from beginning to end, but complete harmony and cooperation prevailed throughout. The debates on live religious questions seemed to create more interest than any other feature of the program. Both sides of these questions were presented in the strongest possible way.

These discussions were of great value to all who heard them, but especially to the young preachers. This series will long be remembered by all who attended. It was announced that unless some unforeseen situation arises on account of the war, these courses will be repeated next January. Complete announcement will be made at the proper time.[6]

Rex A. Turner was present at the event and followed with a report in his paper *Sound Doctrine* with, "Leo Boles lectured daily, along with N. B. H. and Bro. Dixon."[7] He added,

> The debates were fine; especially the last one, when Brother E. R. Harper affirmed Premillennialism against Brother Gus Nichols, and quoted as his authority for this heresy the writings of Dr. Brents, C. H. Robertson of Abilene Christian College, and J. N. Armstrong, Dean of Bible at Harding College.[8]

Gus Nichols, E. R. Harper, Guy N. Woods
FHC Annual Bible Lectureship

A GROWING SCHEDULE

Lectureships followed in February and March. The first series took place at the South Parkway church of Christ in Memphis. Gus spoke twice during the week of 16-19 February on the subjects of "Is Bible Study An Act Of Worship?" and, "Woman And Her Work In The Church."[9]

The other lectureship Gus attended was in Anniston, Alabama beginning the 22nd of March. The Noble Street church advertised that the speakers were, "B. C. Goodpasture, Frank Pack, J. Leonard Jackson, H. Clyde Hale, and Gus Nichols."[10] Gus closed the sessions on Friday speaking twice on the subject of "The Divinity of the Bible." Each session was concluded with a period of audience questions and answers.

In April, he headed to Georgia to preach a gospel meeting in the city of LaGrange. The local preacher, A. C. Dreaden (1903-1974) reported of the meeting,

> Gus Nichols closed our meeting April 16. We had a great meeting, with eleven baptized and five restored. Brother Nichols' preaching was powerful. He preached over the radio, and a great interest was aroused by his lessons. In addition, his teaching in private was most effective. Often this is a preacher's greatest opportunity while in a meeting. Our crowds have been better at all services since the meeting than before. One was restored the following Sunday. Park Avenue is doing a great work, and the denominational folks are taking notice and talking the work for us.[11]

In late May, Gus returned to the campus of Freed-Hardeman College in order to preach at the Henderson church and then stand before the graduating class at the college to give the Commencement Speech. While there, he was given a room in Paul Gray Hall. E. Claude Gardner (1925-2017), then a freshman in school, and a resident of the dormitory, recalled brother Nichols' visit to the campus that weekend. Seventy-three years later, he specifically remembered the industrious ways in which brother Nichols devoted his time. He said that he and his fellow students could easily hear when the senior preacher was in his room by the continuous sound of his portable typewriter at work.[12] Soon after his return home, Gus sent in the report,

> I preached for the church at Henderson, Tenn., May 24, then delivered the commencement sermon Sunday night to a fine group of graduating students of Freed-Hardeman College. It is an injustice to young people for their parents to send them off to infidel schools and rob them of the fine environment and godly instruction afforded at Freed-Hardeman College. Every young man and young woman should urge it upon his parents to put God and interest in the soul first when it comes to the choice of a school for the higher training of young people. Vanderbilt Black preached at Jasper last Lord's-day morning and evening. Our meeting begins at Jasper on June 7, George DeHoff preaching.[13]

The summer meeting at Jasper regularly appeared sometime in July, but this year the month of June worked better with everyone's schedule. At a little shy of 29 years of age, George Washington DeHoff (1913-1993) was a younger preacher than most of Fifth Avenue's previous speakers for their summer meeting. However, the Arkansan and Freed-Hardeman College graduate was a growing powerhouse for the gospel, and the church in Jasper was all about giving him the pulpit for reaching out to the community. Following the meeting, a very pleased Gus Nichols followed with glowing praise,

> Our meeting with George W. DeHoff preaching came to a close last night with eleven having been baptized and two restored. Brother DeHoff did some of the finest preaching that it has ever been my good fortune to hear. The whole church was highly pleased with the strong and sound gospel sermons delivered. A fine interest was manifested by those who heard.[14]

George W. DeHoff

DeHoff gave his own thoughts that included high praise for working with the esteemed Walker County preacher. He said, "At Jasper, Ala., where Gus Nichols is the regular preacher, with nine baptisms and two restorations. I feel that we do not have a better-informed man in the brotherhood than Gus Nichols; so naturally it was a treat to be with him."[15]

TWO DEBATES

Of note, two discussions were held in the summer. In June, Gus traveled down to the southwest part of Alabama's largest city to meet a Holiness preacher by the name of O. G. Lodge. Reflecting on the particulars of the "discussion" early in July, Gus summarized,

> Some few weeks ago I was invited by the Bessemer Church to come to Powderly (Birmingham) and debate four nights with O. G. Lodge, a so-called Holiness, who challenged us for a debate. The discussion was arranged and conducted in the usual way. Mr. Lodge was weak in argument and easily exposed before an audience. The attendance was good and the crowds were orderly. The debate was conducted in the Church of God (or Holiness) meetinghouse. All the preachers in the Birmingham district who were not engaged in meetings attended the discussion. Flavil Nichols, of Tuscumbia, Ala., moderated for me. Brethren attended the discussion from a distance of one hundred miles or more; yet we had only a few days in which to announce the discussion. All seemed highly pleased with the discussion.[16]

A couple of weeks after this report, Gus was involved in another debate, this time with a Baptist. The discussion took place in Huntsville, Alabama. The new preacher at the Lincoln congregation, W. Gaddys Roy (1916-2009), sent in a quick overview of how the debate proceeded under the big tent,

> Several weeks ago, Charles V. Headrick, a Baptist preacher, Huntsville, Ala., challenged the churches of Christ to meet him in debate. He had said that we were afraid to meet him. The Lincoln Church, in Huntsville, accepted the challenge, and invited Gus Nichols, Jasper, Ala., to meet him. The debate was held in the Lincoln Church building July 14 to 17. Two propositions were discussed—baptism as a condition of pardon and the prayers of alien sinners being heard without baptism. The debate was very orderly. The writer and Mr. Morrison had but little to do as moderators. Mr. Headrick made about all the usual quibbles against water baptism, but these were all ably met by Brother Nichols. The public was accommodated with loud-speakers, which could be heard for a great distance. Hundreds heard the debate, and the churches of Christ were well pleased with the results.[17]

EDITORSHIP OF TRUTH IN LOVE

With the September issue of *Truth In Love*, news was released of changes once again in the editorship of the Birmingham paper. W. C. Graves had purchased the journal in the fall of the previous year and had put out the first ten issues. But due to some unexpected personal problems, Graves determined he was unable to continue.

A businessman of Fayette, Alabama Marion Davis (1906-1979), was a member of the Fayette congregation and most known for his song-leading abilities. He taught singing schools and traveled with several preachers to lead singing for them in gospel meetings including Gus Nichols, Foy E. Wallace, Jr. (1871-1949), and several others. He also operated a publishing company, and as has been noted, in 1940 had co-edited a songbook with brother Wallace under the title, *Complete Christian Hymnal*.[18]

W. C. Graves approached Davis to see if he would be interested in purchasing and publishing the paper. The interest was there, but the editorship was something that Davis knew needed the expertise fitting for such a journal. Gus Nichols was the obvious person for the role of editor. Entered into to the pages of the Volume 6, Number 11 issue of *Truth In Love*, Gus wrote,

Graves Sells Truth In Love

Truth In Love has changed hands again. Brother W. C. Graves, of Birmingham, Ala., has been the sole editor and publisher of *Truth In Love* for nearly a year. Conditions recently developed over which Brother Graves had no control, making it necessary for him to give up the responsibility of editing and publishing the paper. Brother Graves kept *Truth In Love* on a very high plane and gave us a good paper. Through its columns the truth went out to bless the lives of many people.

Davis Buys Truth In Love

Brother Marion Davis, of Fayette, Alabama bought *Truth In Love*. Brother Davis is known all over the nation as one of our best evangelistic singers. He is a teacher and writer of vocal music, and also is editor of song books second to none in the brotherhood. Brother Davis will publish *Truth In Love* in the future. His past experience guarantees that all business matters connected with the paper will be handled with efficiency and care. Brother Davis will edit a page of *News and Notes* which should be of general interest among preachers and churches.

The New Editor

I have accepted the responsibility of editing *Truth In Love*, and have been left free under Christ to perform my task as I see fit. While Brother Davis has assumed all financial responsibility connected with the paper, I alone may be held responsible for what is taught in its columns. I am happy to be associated with Brother Davis in this worthy endeavor, which is to be a work of faith and labor of love. I was one of the original editors of *Truth In Love* from 1936 until Brother Graves took over the paper in the fall of last year. I shall appreciate the co-operation of those good brethren whose untiring efforts helped to make *Truth In Love* the great paper it is.

Policy Of Truth In Love

I see no reason for changing the original policy of *Truth In Love*. It has ever been the purpose of its editors to keep it true to its name—*Truth In Love*. To teach the *truth* is to teach the whole truth about whatever issue may need discussion, and nothing but the truth. To teach the truth in *love* is to teach the truth in love of the truth, and in love of all those who need the truth. Of course, love for the truth, and for those to be taught, will manifest in loyalty to both the truth and all men.[19]

Gus Nichols' Office Over His Garage

TRUTH IN LOVE

Published first of each month at Fayette, Ala.

Gus Nichols .... Editor
Marion Davis .... Publisher and Owner

SUBSCRIPTION RATES

Single Subscription .... 25c Per Year

BUNDLE RATES

25 Copies, to one address .... 50c Per Month
50 Copies, to one address .... 50c Per Month
75 Copies, to one address .... $1.00 Per Month
100 Copies, to one address .... $1.35 Per Month
500 Copies, to one address .... $6.50 Per Month
1000 Copies, to one address .... $12.50 Per Month

All Subscriptions Payable In Advance
Application for Entry as Second Class Matter is Pending.
—Advertising Rates Sent Upon Request—
Address all communications to

TRUTH IN LOVE
Box 518, Fayette, Alabama.

ENDNOTES

1 *Firm Foundation*, 6 January 1942, p. 8.

2 Ibid., 24 March 1942, p. 6.

3 W. C. Graves, "Sound Doctrine," *Truth In Love*, 10 January 1942, p. 5. Note: This total of congregations mentioned was taken from Graves' summary of 14 congregations "within the city limits and nearby," and "six colored congregations within the city limits."

4 Note: This meeting served to spur the founding of the East Point congregation. In subsequent years, this church planted several other churches in the southern part of metropolitan Atlanta.

5 Note: Leonard Lee Brigance (1879-1950) was born in Scotts Hill, Henderson County, Tennessee. A cousin to N. B. Hardeman, he was educated at Georgia Robertson Christian College at Henderson, Tennessee. Later, he received the M.A. at National Teachers Normal and Business College, also there at the Henderson campus. He preached in Florida for a time but returned to Henderson and worked as head of the English Department. He served as manager of advertising for the school. His special emphasis was upon Restoration History and served the brotherhood for decades with research articles in several brotherhood papers. He developed diabetes in 1926 but suffered through it to do his work. He passed from this life 4 February 1950 and was buried in the Henderson City Cemetery.

6 L. L. Brigance, *Gospel Advocate*, 22 January 1942, p. 93.

7 Rex A. Turner, Sound Doctrine, 10 February 1942, p. 4.

8 Ibid.

9 Advertisement, *Gospel Advocate*, 29 January 1942, p. 117.

10 Ibid., 19 March 1942, page 285.

11 A. C. Dreaden, *Gospel Advocate*, 7 May 1942, p. 448.

12 E. Claude Gardner, phone interview with the author 2 November 2015. Note: Still as sharp in his memory at nearly 91 years of age as ever, the former president of Freed-Hardeman recalled with great fondness the time when Gus Nichols came to the campus of the college while he was a student there. Many thanks to brother Gardner's son-in-law Sam Hester for making the interview possible. Long time president of Freed-Hardeman and a dear friend to the Nichols family, brother Gardner passed away, 31 December 2017, and was buried in the Henderson Cemetery, Tennessee.

13 Gus Nichols, *Gospel Advocate*, 4 June 1942, p. 545. Note: The record of his presence is also recorded in the 1942 F-HC *Treasure Chest*, p. 66.

14 Gus Nichols, *Gospel Advocate*, 2 July 1942, p. 642.

15 George DeHoff, *Gospel Advocate*, 17 September 1942, p. 910.

16 Gus Nichols, *Gospel Advocate*, 2 July 1942, p. 640.

17 W. Gaddys Roy, *Gospel Advocate*, 6 August 1942, p. 762.

18 Advertisement, *Sound Doctrine*, 25 May 1942, p. 8. (Also appeared again in the 10 September issue, p. 8.) Note: The advertisement added, "Letters of commendation have come from such men as L. L. Brigance, G. A. Dunn, Sr., Jasper Dunn, E. R. Harper, O. C. Lambert, C. R. Nichol, Tillit S. Teddlie, Austin Taylor, N. B. Hardeman, Chester Estes, Rex Turner, Jack Meyers, W. C Graves, C. M. Pullias, Gus Nichols, Dr. B. H. Murphy, Eugene Smith, Clarence Cooke, and many others." Advertisements also appeared in the *Bible Banner*.

19 Gus Nichols, *Truth In Love*, Vol. 6, No. 11, September 1942, p. 4.

- 27 -

Rising To The Defense Of The Gospel

> Some indeed preach Christ even of envy and strife; and some also of good will: The one preach Christ of contention, not sincerely, supposing to add affliction to my bonds: But the other of love, knowing that I am set for the defense of the gospel.
> —Paul, Philippians 1:15–17

It was known by many among restoration churches that no man was more knowledgeable of the teachings and practices of the Pentecostal movement in America during the 20th century than Gus Nichols. The events surrounding his work in the early-to-mid 1940s was probably the reason for such claims. His research and study on the work of the Holy Spirit made him an authority on the subjects of the Godhead, Biblical Authority, and the assimilation of a Biblical time-line for the miraculous and non-miraculous activities of the Trinity's third person.

Early in 1943, he made his third appearance on the Freed-Hardeman Special Courses series. Advertised that year as the "Freed-Hardeman Lectureship," the topics of discussion assigned to him on 14 and 15 January were, "Holy Rollers, Pentecostians, and Nazarenes."[1]

The Pentecostal movement was on the rise in America at that time. Several articles in the *Gospel Advocate* were devoted to a proper understanding of the work of the Holy Spirit. In February, an article by West Virginia preacher, C. D. Plum (1898-1977), appeared entitled, "Some Things We Believe About The Holy Spirit."[2]

On the last page of the last issue of the *Advocate* for 1942 there was an announcement of the release of a new volume written by H. Leo Boles (1874-1946) called, *The Holy Spirit, His Personality, His Nature, And Works*.[3] Its contents were the assignment for brother Boles at the F-HC Lectures a couple weeks later. Then the following April, Gus wrote a letter commending the volume with,

> I wish to say to the readers of the *Gospel Advocate* that they should not fail to get H. Leo Boles' new book on *The Holy Spirit*. Perhaps every passage in the Bible giving any information about the Holy Spirit has been either discussed in this book or at least referred to by Brother Boles. A fine sermon outline, so simple that it may be used by any speaker, precedes the matter making

up each chapter of the book. The reader is constantly referred to the Scriptures as the last word of authority on the subject. No one could write so large a book on 'The Holy Spirit,' and discuss all the Bible says about the Spirit, without contradicting the opinion of some other Bible student on some point. Yet, Brother Boles has adhered so closely to the facts and statements of the Scriptures on the subject that, in the main, his positions are not to be questioned. The book manifests back of it a long life of painstaking study of the subject treated. There is nothing like it, and no substitute for it in all the realm of our literature. It breathes the spirit of reverence so manifest in the life of its author, who is one of the greatest Bible scholars now living.[4]

There is little doubt that the volume assisted Gus in his preparation for a debate that was to take place in early May in Huntsville, Alabama. As has been noted, in July, the previous year, Gus had gone there to meet Baptist preacher, Charles V. Headrick, in a discussion on salvation issues. This dispute was to be with a Holiness preacher by the name of C. J. Weaver.

Charlie Joseph Weaver (1895-1963) was from among the "largest branch of all the Holiness movement in the United States."[5] Living in Sheffield, Alabama at the time, he was making somewhat of a name for himself as a champion defender of the Holiness cause. A challenge went out for anyone who might be willing to meet him in a debate. Congregations of churches of Christ answered that call in the person of Gus Nichols. In anticipation of the event a brother wrote,

> Beginning Monday night, May 3, and continuing through May 7, there will be a debate conducted by Gus Nichols, Jasper, Ala., and Charles Weaver (Church of God), Sheffield, Ala. The debate is to be conducted at the Merrimack church of Christ, Huntsville, Ala. The time is 7 P.M. to 9 P.M. This debate will be broadcast over station WBHP (1220 kilocycles on your dial). Arrangements have been made to accommodate all visiting preachers, but please bring your ration book.[6]

As was mentioned, this was potentially one of the largest religious debates ever to be held in north Alabama. After a brief visit to the Georgia town of LaGrange for a gospel meeting, Gus made his way to the city of Huntsville to participate in the debate.[7]

For five nights, the two men met to discuss several topics. Each man assigned to affirmative and negative was given three opportunities to discuss his understanding of the Scriptures in light of the given subject. On Monday evening the first proposition presented was, "The Scriptures teach that baptism with the Holy Ghost is for the sanctification of all Christians, the eradication of evil nature, or inborn sin, and is to continue throughout the gospel dispensation, or Christian age."[8] C. J. Weaver took the affirmative and Gus Nichols was in the negative.

1943 - Nichols-Weaver Debate Book

On Tuesday evening, the 4th of May, once again the men squared off at the Merrimack church building. The second proposition was, "The Scriptures teach that the signs and miracles done by the apostles and other disciples, as recorded in the New Testament, were to cease, or to be done away, at the close of the apostolic age, or by the time the complete will of God was revealed and confirmed in the New Testament."[9] Gus filled the roll of the affirmative for this discussion. Again, both men were given three times to affirm or negate the other's input.

On the third evening the subject was, "The Scriptures teach that water baptism to a penitent believer of the gospel is unto the remission of alien sins or is a condition of salvation from past sins."[10] Again, Gus took the affirmative and Mr. Weaver denied.

On the fourth evening the subject changed yet again, "The Scriptures teach that alien sinners are saved from their past sins upon the conditions of repentance, confession of sins, and faith, before and without water baptism."[11] Mr. Weaver affirmed this position, and Gus denied.

Friday evening brought a dialogue on the following proposition, "The washing of the saints' feet, as an act of worship in the church (in connection with the Lord's Supper or other such items) is authorized in the Scriptures."[12] Again, Weaver took the affirmative and Gus the negative.

Following the debate, the *Truth In Love* editor gave his own overview of the previous activities along with plans for the future in view of them.

> May 3rd to 7th I engaged Elder C. J. Weaver of the "Church of God," (Gospel Trumpet Holiness) in debate at the Merrimack Church of Christ, Huntsville, Alabama. The discussion was very pleasant, and our people were more than well pleased with my defense of the truth. Elder Weaver was selected as a representative debater who has had "much experience" in debating preachers of the church of Christ over a period of many years. His people said they were getting their best debater and wanted us to put up one of our strongest men. For some reason our people selected the editor of *Truth In Love*. It was the general comment among them after the discussion that we would never get another debate out of the "Holiness" people in Huntsville. Elder Weaver belongs to the largest branch of the "Holiness" in the nation.
>
> **Broadcast Over Radio**
>
> The local radio station in Huntsville was engaged to broadcast the debate. The announcement of this broadcast was made for weeks before the debate, and interest in this feature ran very high. Our people in the Muscle Shoals area were so highly pleased with my defense of the truth the first three nights of the discussion that they arranged and had the last two nights broadcast over the Northern Alabama Net-Work that it might be heard in the Tri-Cities. Some preachers estimated that fifteen thousand people heard the discussion. Loud speakers also carried the discussion to those out of the meeting house who could not get inside.
>
> **To Be Published In Book Form**
>
> When the discussion was first planned, the "Holiness" people talked about having the discussion published, but soon this plan failed. Brethren then wrote me to make the necessary plans and have the debate put into book form. I accepted this suggestion and had them engage an expert court reporter to take the speeches in short hand and make a transcript of the debate as delivered for publication.[13]

A year passed before the volume finally appeared in print. In the meantime, it was business as usual for the Jasper preacher. The summer was moving ahead quickly. Meetings were already set and being reported.

During the first week of June, Gus headed north to Danville, Illinois, to preach in a twelve-day meeting in the congregation where Vodie and A. J. Kerr had moved to work.[14] Afterward, he again made his way back home to prepare for Fifth Avenue's annual summer meeting. Again, the services of Arkansas preacher, George DeHoff (1913-1993) were engaged for the second year in a row. On the 24th of June, Jasper's *The Mountain Eagle* newspaper carried an advertisement for the event in which was added, "The Fifth Avenue Church of Christ has installed large ceiling fans to cool the auditorium so that everyone may be comfortable in the hottest of weather."[15]

As announced, the Jasper meeting began on the 27th of June and ran for twelve days. With the following Sunday falling on the nation's birthday, the newspaper continued its promotion, "On the afternoon of the Fourth of July, N. B. Hardeman, President of Freed-Hardeman College, and B. C. Goodpasture, editor of the *Gospel Advocate*, are expected to be with us and speak."[16] What an exciting Sunday it must have been, both for the congregation and the community, to have such esteemed speakers representing the gospel of Christ.

In early August, Gus went to Winfield, over in Marion County, for a meeting where seven were baptized. The preacher, J. O. Jones (1910-1968), surmised, "The meeting in Winfield was one of the best known to the congregation."[17] From Winfield, Gus went just a few miles west to Guin where he continued the good work of the Lord in preaching the message. W. A. Holley (1911-2003) was the preacher there at the time. Of the meeting he recounted,

> On August 15 we closed one of the best meetings in the history of the Guin Church. In spite of war conditions, we had splendid crowds at every service. Gus Nichols, of Jasper, Ala., preached, while Brother Dickinson directed the song service. There were nine responses to the invitation—seven baptisms and two confessed faults. I believe we will be stronger in the Lord and in the power of his might as a result of this great gospel meeting. Brother Nichols never did better preaching in his life.[18]

Throughout the remainder of the year, Gus continued editing *Truth In Love*. It was around this time that he also began regularly submitting sermon outlines to the local *The Mountain Eagle* newspaper for distribution in the community. Articles he authored appeared in other brotherhood papers as well. The *Firm Foundation* entered a brief sermon outline of his in July entitled, "New Testament Worship,"[19] wherein he listed five basic points categorizing worship as teaching, fellowship, communion, prayer, and singing.

These were the war years. Budgets were tight. People needed the fundamentals of the Scriptures, and Gus Nichols knew no better path to take than to reveal the hidden treasures of God to the people of his day. He was, at this point, at the height of popularity among the brethren. The demand was never greater to have him come speak on a lectureship or in a meeting. He spent every waking hour in devotion to the Lord's cause, and the brotherhood knew it. Perhaps his fame among the churches might be demonstrated in an advertisement for a song book that appeared in the December issue of Foy E. Wallace's (1896-1979), *Bible Banner*. The book, *The Complete Hymnal,* produced by Wallace and Marion Davis (1906-1979), added as part of the advertisement endorsements from a veritable who's who among gospel preachers of that day. It said,

> Commended by leading evangelists. Letters of commendation have come from such men as L. L. Brigance, G. A. Dunn, Sr., J. W. Dunn, E. R. Harper, O. C. Lambert, C. R. Nichol, Tillit S. Teddlie, Austin Taylor, N. B. Hardeman, Chester Estes, Jack Meyers, W. C. Graves. C. M. Pullias, Gus Nichols, Dr. B. H. Murphy, Clarence Cooke and many others.[20]

THE DEBATE IN PRINT

The year 1944 began in typical fashion with another visit to Freed-Hardeman College for the annual lectureship. This session of the program took place 11-20 January. On Tuesday the 18th, Gus spoke on the subject, "Sanctification or Holiness."[21]

Several weeks passed when the *Gospel Advocate* editor, B. C. Goodpasture (1895-1977), made two announcements consecutively concerning the work of Jasper's talented preacher. First, under the title, "Brother Nichols To Write For Advocate," he declared,

> We are glad to announce that Gus Nichols, of Jasper, Ala., has been added to our staff of regular writers. Brother Nichols is one of the best-known and ablest preachers in the entire brotherhood. He is an experienced debater and a ready writer. For the past twelve years he has labored with the congregation in Jasper, Ala. His articles will be strong, scriptural, and practical. Our readers will profit by a careful perusal of anything he writes.[22]

Following this announcement, under the title, "Nichol-Weaver Debate,"[sic][23] were the words,

> Within a few days we hope to have ready for delivery an outstanding debate on the differences between the churches of Christ and the Church of God (Holiness). Gus Nichols represented the former, and C. J. Weaver, of Sheffield, Ala., represented the latter. This discussion will fill a long felt and vital need. The price,

cloth, is $1.50. Almost one thousand copies have already been sold. These orders will be filled as soon as possible.[24]

Another announcement followed early in June proclaiming, "This is the best discussion of some of the differences between the church of Christ and Holiness church that we have seen."[25]

Finally, the book began being advertised as released and ready for sale.[26] Within weeks, articles appeared both explaining the value of the printed debate, as well as praise being poured upon brother Nichols for his eloquence in defending the truth. Nationally acclaimed debater and Texas preacher C. R. Nichol (1876-1961), wrote,

> I have just read with interest the 'Nichols-Weaver Debate.' Good only will come for the truth where this debate is read with a desire to know what the Bible teaches on the subjects discussed. I wish for the book a wide circulation. I can but wonder if Mr. Weaver will not revise his views on some points when he has read the book carefully.[27]

This was followed by a lengthy article by G. C. Brewer (1884-1956) where he reminisced on his long-term familiarity with Gus, and the pleasure he had enjoyed in seeing him develop to this point. In part he wrote,

> I have known Brother Nichols for many years, and I count him my friend as well as a brother in Christ. I knew him and knew of him when he first learned the way of the Lord and began "to preach the word." I have known him through the years. He has reared a family of eight children. His son is a preacher, and his daughters have married preachers. He sent these children to Christian schools. He has labored incessantly for the Lord, and often with very little financial support. He has preached to the poor and often in hard places. He has grown marvelously since I have known him. He has been a diligent student, and he is now one of the best informed Bible preachers living. Truly the word of Christ dwells in him richly. He has had to meet the various errors of sectarianism in their most stubborn and fanatical form—often among very ignorant people. It would be hard to find a man who can more successfully refute and correct these errors than Gus Nichols can on a moment's notice. This is attributable to three things: (1) His thorough knowledge of God's word; (2) his familiarity with these errors and with the quibbles that men use to uphold them; (3) his natural kindness of disposition and his evident sincerity and his courteous treatment of and sympathy

for those who hold these errors. These are the things that I would say make him a master in debate.[28]

He continued to give a good breakdown of the debate with much reminiscence of his own work in that region of the country for over forty years. His final words in the article speak of the integrity and candor in which Gus conducted himself in this debate. He extolled Gus with,

> One point in this debate deserves to be especially mentioned. In discussing the Holy Spirit or any phase of His work, or in considering the question of divine healing or of a miraculous or a mystical conversion, it is hard for any of us to avoid appearing to be legalistic, irreverent, and unbelieving to those who hold the position that Mr. Weaver holds on those that are similar. But if Brother Nichols did not succeed in avoiding this attitude or in escaping this impression, none of the rest of us need to try.[29]

In similar fashion, H. Leo Boles (1874-1946), gave a good breakdown of the debate. As the discussion was stenographically reproduced, he explained that the error presented by C. J. Weaver was emphatically revealed along with the truth. He said,

> Nearly every denominational preacher represents error and must deny the truth in order to maintain his position. This debate has this quality. It has as strong an exponent of error as could be found in that section of the country. Those who read the debate may be assured that error is presented in as strong light as it can be. The truth was upheld in a very dignified, Christian-like, way by Brother Nichols. He not only upheld the truth on the propositions, but he met in detail each of the errors presented by his opponent. . .Brother Nichols' presentation of the truth is so simple, logical, and scriptural that the ordinary reader can appreciate the truth. It is commended to all who want to know the truth on these subjects and who need to refute the errors of the Holiness sects.[30]

Under the title, "Concerning New Books" section of the *Firm Foundation*, Tennessee preacher, Leslie G. Thomas (1895-1988), promoted the printed debate in part with,

> It is doubtful if there is a man among us who is better prepared or who can do a better job of representing the truth regarding these issues than Brother Nichols. Mr. Weaver is also a good debater; and those who read this book may expect to understand the truth regarding the subjects discussed. The truth never suffers in Brother Nichols' hands.[31]

A young West Tennessee preacher, Guy N. Woods (1908-1993), weighed in on the volume by saying,

> I have this moment completed the reading of 'The Nichols-Weaver Debate,' held at Huntsville, Ala., May 3-7, 1943, between Gus Nichols, of Jasper, Ala., and C. J. Weaver, of Sheffield, Ala., on "some of the differences between the churches of Christ and the Church of God (Holiness)," and lately published by the *Gospel Advocate* Company. Five propositions were discussed, touching "Divine Healing," "The Design of Baptism," and "Foot Washing," including many collateral questions. The stenographic report thereof makes a book of approximately 225 pages. The book is neatly and durably bound, and pictures of the disputants appear therein. Brother Nichols' defense of the truth is simply superb. Mr. Weaver's utter bewilderment is manifest on every page. The discussion was launched and maintained on a high plane, and the published report is very readable. This volume supplies a long-felt want in our literature. Widely circulated, it will be the means of leading many out of fanaticism into the truth.[32]

This debate is how Woods became aware of the quality person Gus Nichols truly was for the cause of Christ. Through the years, no greater friendship existed than was held between these two great church leaders. When Gus stepped down from conducting the Open Forum during Freed-Hardeman College's annual lectures, Woods took on the role, and continued it for over twenty years, but most considered that it was a role he shared with Gus in many respects. More on this relationship is to come.

In later years, Woods published two volumes from questions that were asked during the Open Forum period during his tenure. In Volume One, he dealt with the question, "What books have you found to be most helpful to you in your work as a preacher of the gospel? List those books which you feel all preachers and serious students ought eventually to obtain."[33] In answering the question, he listed over a hundred volumes that he classified in different categories. In the category of, "Debates and Controversial Materials," he listed the following:

> Campbell-Owen Debate; Campbell-Purcell Debate; Campbell-Rice Debate; Lard's Review of Jeter; Brents-Herod Debate; Woods-Nunnery Debate; Warren-Ballard Debate; Woods-Cogdill Debate; Boles-Boll Debate; Canright on Adventism; Baptist Blunders, by Joe S. Warlick; *Nichols-Weaver Debate* (a magnificent effort by brother Nichols, and a total, complete triumph for truth).[34]

Of the hundreds of debates that have been produced during the 19th and 20th centuries, it is easy to see how highly Woods considered brother Nichols' effort in the debate with C. J. Weaver.

Around the middle of the 20th century, perhaps no one in the brotherhood was more widely read than *Gospel Advocate* editor B. C. Goodpasture (1895-1977). His own personal library contained many

1943 - FHC *Sky Rocket*, November

thousands of volumes. At the encouragement of N. B. Hardeman (1874-1965), Goodpasture produced his own list of the top one hundred books that all preachers should have in their library. Initially, it was released to the several hundred preachers that attended the Freed-Hardeman College Lectures, but it was also reproduced in an issue of the *Gospel Advocate*. Appearing at number 39 was the "Nichols-Weaver Debate."[35]

Sales of the book were so good that within four months of its release it was reported, "The Nichols-Weaver Debate is enjoying a splendid sale. At the rate it is going, it will soon be sold out."[36] By the end of the year the book was completely sold out. In early 1945 the first reprint went into circulation.

ENDNOTES

1 Advertisement, "Freed-Hardeman Lectureship Soon," *Gospel Advocate*, 7 January 1943, p. 18.

2 C. D. Plum, "Some Things We Believe About The Holy Spirit." *Gospel Advocate*, 11 February 1946, p. 133.

3 Advertisement, *Gospel Advocate*, 31 December 1942, p. 1245.

4 Gus Nichols, "Rates Book Very Highly," *Gospel Advocate*, 8 April 1943, p. 332.

5 Gus Nichols and C. J. Weaver, *Nichols-Weaver Debate*, Nashville: *Gospel Advocate*, p. 3.

6 Gordon Slatton, *Gospel Advocate*, 29 April 1943, p. 401. Note: The reference to bringing a ration book was in view of the economic situation in America at the time. The high demand for products to support the war effort meant shortages, hence rationing was essential.

7 Gus Nichols, *Gospel Advocate*, 29 April 1943, p. 402.

8 Gus Nichols and C. J. Weaver, *Nichols-Weaver Debate*, Nashville: *Gospel Advocate*, p. 7.

9 Ibid., p. 55.

10 Ibid. p. 95.

11 Ibid. p. 141.

12 Ibid. p. 187.

13 Gus Nichols, *Truth In Love*, June 1943, p. 4.

14 A. J. Kerr, *Gospel Advocate*, 10 June 1943, p. 535.

15 "Church of Christ To Have Revival," *The Mountain Eagle*, 24 June 1943, p. 5.

16 Ibid.

17 J. O. Jones, *Gospel Advocate*, 26 August 1943, p. 773.

18 W. A. Holley, *Gospel Advocate*, 16 September 1943, p. 844.

19 *Firm Foundation*, 6 July 1943, p. 15.

20 J. O. Jones, December 1943, p. 8.

21 Advertisement, *Firm Foundation*, 11 January 1944, p. 6.

22 B. C. Goodpasture, ed., *Gospel Advocate*, 27 April 1944, p. 282.

23 Note: Several times in Gus Nichols' life his last name appeared in print without the last letter. The obvious typographical error was most confusing, especially since the brotherhood already had a prominent preacher with similar talents in the person of C. R. Nichol. In fact, the two were so often confused by the brethren that the works of one occasionally was mistakenly attributed to the other. For instance, C. R. Nichol produced a pocket encyclopedia that was distributed widely. Many incorrectly ascribed the work to Gus Nichols. Alan Highers once observed, "I met C. R. Nichol on one occasion. Someone asked

Rising To The Defense Of The Gospel   231

if he was related to Gus Nichols. He said, 'No, he is Nichols, I am Nichol.' 'Oh,' they said, 'he is many, you are just one.' Brother Nichol replied, 'No, I am the Nichol from which Nichols are made!'" (Facebook, Friends of the Restoration, 15 January 2015.)

24 Advertisement, "Nichol-Weaver Debate," *Gospel Advocate*, 27 April 1944, p. 282..

25 B. C. Goodpasture, ed., "Office Note," *Gospel Advocate*, 8 June 1944, p. 390.

26 Note: Ads appeared in the *Gospel Advocate* in the 22 June and 6 July issues.

27 C. R. Nichol, *Gospel Advocate*, 27 July 1944, p. 502.

28 G. C. Brewer, *Gospel Advocate*, 3 August 1944, p. 508. Note: When brother Nichols died in 1975, William Woodson (1931-2010) recalled and read these words at the funeral service.

29 Ibid.

30 H. Leo Boles, *Gospel Advocate*, 24 August 1944, p. 566.

31 Leslie G. Thomas, *Firm Foundation*, 17 October 1944.

32 Ibid. p. 565.

33 Guy N. Woods, *Questions And Answers: Open Forum-Freed-Hardeman College Lectures*, Volume 1, Henderson: Freed-Hardeman University, c.1976, p. 313.

34 Ibid., p. 316.

35 B. C. Goodpasture, ed., *Gospel Advocate*, 6 February 1947, p. 108.

36 Advertisement, *Gospel Advocate*, 5 October 1944, p. 661.

- 28 -

Montgomery Bible College

> To know wisdom and instruction; to perceive the words of understanding; To receive the instruction of wisdom, justice, and judgment, and equity; To give subtlety to the simple, to the young man knowledge and discretion. A wise man will hear, and will increase learning; and a man of understanding shall attain unto wise counsels.
>
> —Solomon, Proverbs 1:2–5

The strength of the Lord's church in Alabama can be attributed to many factors. Leading in the building up of the body in that part of the nation was a body of believers dedicated to the promoting of the gospel of Jesus. As has already been observed, the impact of Christian education under girded the skills of these people to defend the faith and build upon the foundations of others. By the fall of 1942, T. B. Larimore's (1843-1929) school, Mars Hill, had been closed for 55 years. J. M. Barnes' (1836-1913) school at Highland Home had been gone for 27 years, and the doors of Gus Nichols' alma mater, Alabama Christian College at Berry, had been closed for two decades.

C. Leonard Johnson and Gus Nichols

The first advertisement to appear for a new school in the state's capital city appeared in the 25 April 1942 edition of *Sound Doctrine*. It read, "Announcing The Opening Of Montgomery Bible School, September 14, 1942."[1] The plan included a three-year high school, and first year college. The institution was to provide training for Business, Public Speaking and a "Special Preacher's Course."[2]

The school was the brainchild of Joe B. Greer (1908-1995), C. Leonard Johnson (1910-1994) and Rex A. Turner (1913-2001). All three were members of the Chisholm congregation in Montgomery. Their relationship spawned many good works for the Kingdom of Christ throughout the city and the state, but their mutual interest in this educational venture served to be the crowning jewel of their numerous collaborations.

Joe Greer was a local farmer, businessman, entrepreneur, and dedicated member of the church. His family had planted the Chisholm work, and since its existence had promoted the cause of Christ with any and every means available to them. He served as president of the board of trustees for the school for many years. Also, he assisted in the purchase of a two-story building and 26 acres of land at 914 Ann Street in the spring of 1942. It served as an administration building and campus for the school's planned beginning in the fall. It had the potential of adequately facilitating up to a hundred students.[3]

Both Johnson and Turner were gospel preachers and educators. In the beginning, the former served as principal of the school, and the later the head of Bible training.

Many of Montgomery's dedicated brethren were on hand on its inaugural day in September. Several preachers were also there including,

> Brethren G. A. Dunn of Dallas, Texas; John T. Lewis of Birmingham; J. R. Ezell of Birmingham; Chester H. Cranford of Coffeeville, Alabama; J. S. Moores of Wetumpka, Alabama; I. L. Boles of Montgomery, Alabama; H. C. Green of Montgomery; and our colored evangelist, Sutton Johnson of Montgomery, Alabama. Several of these men delivered addresses filled with wise counsel and inspiration.[4]

Included on that day was a significant speech by C. Leonard Johnson. His purpose was to establish the intentions of the school's leadership in conducting the school. In part he included,

> The Montgomery Bible School and schools like it are the outgrowth of the far-reaching vision of J. A. Harding and David Lipscomb, who saw a need in the education of youth that was not being met by the already established institutions of learning.

> The supreme purpose of the Montgomery Bible School is to build men and women of character. A vital element of genuine character is the religious and moral nature.

> Hence the Montgomery Bible School will teach the Bible as the most effective means of cultivating the moral and spiritual nature. It is desired as Lipscomb and Harding expressed it, "to teach the Bible as the recorded will of God to man and as the only sufficient rule of faith and practice, and to train those who attend in pure Bible Christianity." To this work we dedicate ourselves and our fortunes.[5]

The school began with 24 enrollees that fall. By the first of the following year, 40 were enrolled, half of whom were in the college program.[6] At the same time the name was changed to, "Montgomery Bible College because in its first year the decision was made to add a second year of college and become a junior college."[7] Becoming a college, the roles of leadership also changed. C. Leonard Johnson and Rex Turner then began serving as co-presidents.

The following May, the first lectureship series was conducted with several speakers involved each day. John T. Lewis (1876-1967), conducted round-table discussions an hour before noon each day, and spoke every evening throughout the week.

From its inception, Montgomery Bible College had no greater proponent for its significance in the state of Alabama than Gus Nichols. His inability to attend the first lectureship was due to the fact that at the same time of its meeting, he was conducting his debate with Holiness preacher, C. J. Weaver in Huntsville. Otherwise, he would have been in attendance, and would have most certainly participated in some way.

NICHOLS-HOLDER DEBATE

Just a month prior to the 1944 Montgomery Bible College Lectureship, the college Co-President, Rex Turner, served as moderator for Gus in a debate. The discussion was held about 35 miles east of Montgomery in the small town of Tallassee. J. D. Holder (1898-1978), a Primitive Baptist from Tupelo, Mississippi, represented his denomination's position on matters of salvation. In a lengthy report, James S. Benson gave a detailed account of the proceedings in the next issue of *Sound Doctrine*. He recalled,

> From March 6 to 9, 1944, Brother Gus Nichols of Jasper, Alabama met in debate J. D. Holder, Primitive Baptist of Tupelo, Mississippi. For the first two nights of the discussion at the church of Christ at Tallassee, Alabama, Brother Nichols ably affirmed: "The Scriptures teach that Christ died for all the sinful race of Adam, and that he offers the remission of alien sins, or salvation, to all alike upon the conditions of Faith, Repentance, Confession, and Baptism."
>
> Brother Rex Turner moderated for Brother Nichols; J. M. Bullard, a member of the Mississippi House of Representatives, moderated for Mr. Holder. Mr. Drew Redden, a Missionary Baptist, acted as chairman moderator the first night and the last night of the debate. Good order prevailed throughout. Large crowds attended every night—even the first night when a heavy rain was falling. The last two nights were conducted at the meeting house of the Primitive Baptists, where Mr. Holder affirmed that: "The Scriptures teach that all for whom Christ died will be saved, or receive remission of sins, without the preached or written word, or any condition on their part."

Brother Nichols used a number of charts which effectively set forth the truth of his proposition. He showed that all nations were to be blessed through Christ, Abraham's seed. Gen. 28:14; Gal. 3:16. He showed that God is no respecter of persons; that Christ died for all the dead, 2 Cor. 4:14-15; that he is the propitiation for "our sins"—those of the elect—and not for ours only, but also "for the sins of the whole world," 1 Jno. 2:2. He made the strong point that God commands all men everywhere to repent in view of the righteous judgment of God, and that repentance could not benefit anyone at the judgment unless Christ had died for him, Acts 17:30-31. It was also shown that those for whom Christ died could be destroyed or perish, Rom. 14:15; 1 Cor. 8:11. The word "perish" in the last passage is the same one that occurs in Jno. 3:16.

From Mark 3:28-29, it was shown that Christ died for "all the sons of men" or else the "elect" could commit the sin against the Spirit and be lost. From Jno. 12:47, 48 it was shown that the wicked could not "reject" Christ if he were not offered to them. Jno. 3:17 indicated that the world "might" be saved through Christ; Brother Nichols challenged Holder to give a passage in which the word "world" refers to the elect only, or where the elect are ever spoken of as the "world." From 2 Pet. 2:1 it was shown that false prophets, preaching "damnable heresies," would deny the Lord that bought them and receive destruction. Holder insisted that the word translated "Lord" or "Master" in this passage referred to a master of slaves and was different from the word translated Lord. Brother Nichols showed that the word was used in prayer to God—Acts 4:24; and (if I remember correctly—J. M. B.), the word is used seven times in the New Testament to refer to God or Christ and four times to refer to masters of slaves. Holder complained that his opponent used too much scripture; Nichols answered that the Germans and Japanese probably think that the United Nations are using too many soldiers, bullets, airplanes, and bombs in the present war. Mr. Holder said that Cornelius was already "cleansed" and "accepted" with God before he was baptized. Brother Nichols showed that all Gentiles were cleansed in the sense that Cornelius was, i.e., Jewish gospel preachers could associate with them and preach the gospel to them, or else the expression would mean universal salvation. Further, he showed from the Revised Version that Cornelius and the Gentiles were "acceptable" to God on conditions;—not already accepted.

Brother Gus Nichols was kind, yet firm and impressive; he is far superior in ability and thoroughness to most debaters this writer has heard. Of all our splendid debaters, not one excels him.

Many gospel preachers attended the discussion, including Brethren Gaddys Roy, Guntersville, Ala.; John McCleskey, Parrish, Ala.; Plato Black, Cordova, Ala.; Joe S. Hyde, Parrish, Ala.; Herman Black, Oakman, Ala.; W. A. Holley, Guin, Ala.; Flavil Nichols, Tuscumbia, Ala.; Ellis Holly, Parrish, Ala.; Rex Turner, Montgomery, Ala.; W. O. Norton, Montgomery, Ala.; Pervie Nichols, Selma, Ala.; Leonard Johnson, Montgomery, Ala.; Homer Reeves, Auburn, Ala.; Willard Willis, East Tallassee, Ala.; Morgan Buffington, Montgomery, Ala.; William Earl Lybrand, Talladega, Ala.; Thomas D. Weaver, Montgomery, Ala.; Lewis Casey, Excel, Ala; and Brother Moores of Wetumpka, Ala. In addition to these, all the preacher boys from Montgomery Bible College with many of the other students attended regularly.

Great good will surely result from such a discussion, since many outsiders heard the truth who could not have been reached otherwise; and, also our hands are clean from the blood of the Primitive Baptists in this community, since God's truth in its purity has been presented to them."[8]

Within a few weeks, Gus Nichols returned to the area to be on Montgomery Bible College's second annual lectureship. Each morning between the 4th and 7th of April Gus opened each day's program with lectures on "Religious Errors and How To Meet Them." This was followed by John T. Lewis speaking on "Abrahamic Problems." Each evening was topped off, as at the previous series, with Lewis speaking on "Living Issues."[9]

From this first official visit to the college campus, Gus and the school continued to build a closer and more binding relationship with each other. For the remainder of his life, he supported the college with his livelihood, his talents, his wisdom, and his leadership. No volume about the life of this man would be complete without including the events that led to his initial visit to the campus of Montgomery Bible College.[10]

ENDNOTES

1 Advertisement, *Sound Doctrine*, 25 April 1942, p. 8.

2 Ibid.

3 "The Montgomery Bible School Purchases Permanent Location," *Sound Doctrine*, 25 June 1942, p. 7.

4 Arthur L. Butler, "Many Attend The Opening Of Montgomery Bible School," *Sound Doctrine*, 25 September 1942, p. 4.

5 Ibid.

6 Arthur L. Butler, *Sound Doctrine*, 10 January 1943, p. 5.

7 Ken Randolph, The *Alabama Restoration Journal*, 1 April 2009, p. 9.

8 James M. Benson, "The Nichols-Holder Debate," *Sound Doctrine*, Vol. 4, No.3, 10 April 1944, p. 1.

9 Advertisement, *Sound Doctrine*, 25 March 1944, p. 8.

10 Note: Initially, the school was called Montgomery Bible School. Very soon it became known as Montgomery Bible College. A number of years later, a new name was given, Alabama Christian College. Today, Faulkner University serves the state and brotherhood by offering the highest quality in Christian education. Several colleges operate under the auspices of its title including, College of Arts and Sciences, V. P. Black College of Biblical Studies, College of Business and Executive Education, College of Education, Thomas Goode Jones Law School, and Kearley Graduate School of Theology.

- 29 -

On The Go And On The Air

> And the lord said unto the servant, Go out into the highways and hedges, and compel them to come in, that my house may be filled.
> —Jesus, Luke 14:23

It has been rightly said that change is life's only true constant. With the growth and influence of the Nichols family continuing to expand, the church was the recipient of the blessings. Gus had four brothers in the ministry, three of whom were in the general area. Charlie lived and worked with churches in eastern Mississippi. Around the spring of 1944, he started a weekly radio broadcast from 9:45 to 10:00 every Sunday morning on WCBI in Columbus.[1] He was also involved in much meeting work. Carey lived in Fayette County, Alabama. He was a farmer and preached among local churches in the area. William Archie lived for a time in Arkansas, but later lived in the Birmingham area. He worked as a farmer, stave mill worker, at a cotton mill, and was an industrial worker. He also preached like his older brothers. Pervie's work was wider and more far-reaching. In the early 40's, he was in Mobile, Alabama preaching primarily for the Oakdale church of Christ. In late 1943, he moved to Selma and began working with the church in that city.[2]

Gus Nichols

Gus and Matilda's children were on the move as well. Flavil and Mary moved to Tuscumbia, Alabama in January 1942. Early in 1944 he reported,

> January 1 marked the beginning of my third year here. There were two restorations and four baptisms during January and February. The church here plans to support me during three months of mission work this summer and plans to get some other young preacher to come here during that time. When the church *members* are at work, the *church* is at work; hence, we

should all become busier than ever that the *church* may be able to accomplish more.³

When they had been there for five years, Flavil received a call from a relatively new work in Birmingham, known as the Fairview church of Christ. This was John T. Lewis (1876-1967) country, where the philosophy was that when outgrowing your building, rather than expansion, you plant new congregations in the next community closest to you. After moving there, Flavil reported these sentiments saying,

> The Fairview congregation is less than nine years old, but has already outgrown its present building and is planning to "swarm" by planting a church after the New Testament pattern in Belview Heights, about one-and-one-half miles west of our present location. Already the fund for this project totals more than $4,000. We have to use additional chairs on Sundays, and two have been baptized since my coming.⁴

For the first couple of years of the decade, Gracie and Frank were working with the church in Hartsville, Tennessee. In 1944, they moved to Memphis, Tennessee, where he preached for the Seventh Street congregation. While there, they gave birth to Gus and Matilda's first grandchild, Paul, on the 1st of October 1945. In 1946, the Youngs moved to work with the church for a time in Carthage, Tennessee.⁵

Vodie and A. J. started the decade working with the Maple Street congregation in Lancaster, Kentucky, but moved to work with the church in Danville, Illinois, in 1942. In 1945, the Kerrs moved to Wyandotte, Michigan, where they began working with the Oak Street church of Christ.

Youngest son, Hudson, made his declaration for the pulpit in 1944. At the age of fourteen, he preached his first sermon at his home congregation. His older brother, Foy, entered Freed-Hardeman the fall of that year and began his two-years of study. While willing to preach from time to time, he did not make a life-long commitment to full-time ministry like his other three brothers.

While Carrie was attending college in Henderson, Tennessee, she met a young man by the name of W. T. Hamilton (1921-1986). W. T. was born in Goree, Texas. It was during a gospel meeting in his hometown, that Burton Coffman (1906-2006) baptized him into Christ. He was fourteen years of age. Several years later, he attended Freed-Hardeman College. After graduation in 1943, he returned to Texas where he began preaching for the church in Bowie. He and Carrie were married on September 18, 1945, at her Jasper home. Settling in Bowie, nearly eleven months passed when Carrie gave birth to Gus and Matilda's second grandchild, Kathy, July 30, 1946.

Just a few weeks before Kathy's birth, her uncle Foy finished his studies at F-HC. Around the same time, her uncle Hardeman was being graduated from Walker County High School. Incidentally, another senior in his class was a young aspiring actor by the name of George Lindsey.[6] As with most friends in a high school setting, their pursuits took on far different courses. Hardeman had originally thought he might become a doctor. However, when he had an opportunity to preach in a prison he determined to follow the path of his father and older brother, Flavil, in preaching the gospel. In the fall of 1946, as with all his elder siblings, he entered Freed-Hardeman to begin his college studies.

At the end of the year, another wedding took place in the Nichols household. When Bertha returned to Jasper after completing her college experience, she did some secretarial work for a time. She was employed by E. R. Mattingly Ford Dealership as a bookkeeper, and did some legal secretary work for Pennington, Tweedy and Beech Law practice. It was around this time that she met George Rile Blackwood (1914-1999), a young man from Parrish. His parents, John and Ida Blackwood, were members of the church in Parrish. During the war, Rile served in the US 8th Air Force, increasing to the rank of Corporal. He spent most of the war years in England. When his tour of duty was complete he returned to Walker County where he landed the job of county agent. The two were married by her daddy in the Fifth Avenue church building on the 12th of December 1946. Rile was the only son-in-law who did not preach. It was often said among the family that it did not bother them that he was an insurance agent. Somebody in the family had to make a living.[7]

Bertha Nichols Blackwood and Uncle Pervie Nichols

Upon completion of Hardeman's studies at Freed-Hardeman, he returned to Walker County and began preaching for the church at Cordova where his father had preached nearly a quarter of a century previous. He had met a young lady of great interest to him while in college—her name, Virginia Montgomery. The two were married on the 5th of August 1948.

WWWB

In early 1946, Jasper, Alabama had no regular news service of its own. *The Mountain Eagle* newspaper was the best resource for receiving important information. However, daily distribution was still several years from being published.

Walter Will Bankhead (1879-1988) was a Jasper-born-and-bred entrepreneur. He was the son of John H. Bankhead II, grandson of John H. Bankhead, and nephew of William B. Bankhead, the U.S. congressman from Alabama. A lawyer by trade, he served for a time in the U.S. Congress, was chairman of the board for Bankhead Mining Company, and Bankhead Development Company.[8] He was also a good friend to Gus Nichols.

In a brief exchange one day as Bankhead was out for a stroll near the Fifth Avenue building, he mentioned to Gus about his intentions of beginning a radio station in Jasper. To this the preacher responded, "I want to be on it the very first day."[9]

Plans were already in motion to apply for FCC licensing and station development. Initially, the Bankhead Broadcasting Company broadcasted with 250 watts of power on 1240 kHz.[10] The call letters selected for the company were the initials of its owner, W. W. Bankhead. WWWB began broadcasting on the 2nd day of November 1946 at 6am. At the beginning of the third hour on the air that morning, the program, "The Gospel Broadcast," was introduced with its speaker, Gus Nichols.[11]

The thirty minutes that followed included a mix of local news, advertisements for church related events, and a segment devoted to Scriptural exhortation. When asked about the program several years later Gus said,

> Well, we do have a very popular radio program seven days per week from eight o'clock in the morning until eight-thirty. We come on the air with some good recorded singing and follow that by ten or fifteen minutes of news during which time we announce free of charge for all people, regardless of religious affiliation, births, illnesses, hospitalizations, deaths, funerals, injuries, or anything else which would be in keeping with the nature of a gospel broadcast. We announce only our own gospel meetings and religious services. Otherwise, we make almost any kind of announcement which is requested. We also wish many people a happy birthday on our program. All of this popularizes our program and attracts a large number of listeners.[12]

Very early on, "The Gospel Broadcast" became a mainstay to the community. In the days before two-way radios and cell-phones the program proved to serve the area as a way to communicate. One morning a severe illness in one Jasper home caused an interruption in that morning's broadcast. A woman became very ill after her husband had departed for work in Birmingham. Knowing her husband would be listening to the radio on his way to work, the message was delivered to the station, and over the air, Gus called the man back home to take care of his family crisis.

Before long, Gus was getting several calls in a day to make announcements of different kinds. He quickly explained to his audience that he would take calls an hour and a half before the broadcast. So, like clockwork, the phone calls began pouring in about 6:30 every morning, and he would add the announcements to be delivered when he began his program.

The impact of the daily show cannot be fully estimated. Radios within a 100-mile radius could pick up the program. This included all of Walker County, and it could also be heard in border counties of Fayette, Winston, Marion, and in the northern part of Jefferson. Literally, thousands of citizens woke up each morning to hear the voice of Gus Nichols. Only eternity will bear out the untold number of people who were able to know the good news of Jesus Christ because of "The Gospel Broadcast."

The program served to demonstrate the caring side of the Jasper preacher. His passion for people who suffered came through in many ways. E. R. Brannan wrote,

> Literally hundreds of requests went out over his radio program to help people in need. Often tears coursed down his cheeks as he told of the calamity befallen some neighbor in the community. The community responded generously because of their respect for this great man of God, and they knew his own personal gift would probably be the first given.[13]

The program served as an outstanding venue for the gospel of Christ. Telling the story of Jesus was the greatest delight of the evangelist from Walker County. Hours of study, committing much Scripture to memory, and being ready at a moment's notice to defend the faith, helped him greatly to spread the message of the gospel in a genteel, yet forceful way. He never resorted to name calling. On Saturday mornings he conducted a quiz program where people were encouraged to call in with their Bible questions, and he answered them on the spot—clearly, concisely, and most of all, biblically.[14]

Sitting at the desk day after day, week after week, he proclaimed the good news professionally, always wearing his suit and tie. He never took notes with him to the microphone; he would often teach a biblical topic that had numerous points. One of several of his young protégés through the years, Ray Dutton, fondly recalled,

One day brother Nichols began the biblical part of his program on a topic in which he related numerous points. After several moments of speaking and giving point after point after point, he paused and quite unexpectedly said, "Brother Dutton, give us a point!" As I never knew what brother Nichols was planning to speak on, and the fact that he never used notes of any kind, I had no idea of what point to add. However, being put on the spot, I was able to quickly come up with an additional point to add to the study.[15]

The air waves became a grand venue for discerning truth and error. Several debates were conducted over the years, many times unplanned nor prearranged. Soon after WWWB went on the air, several of the denominations in the region also had shows, sometimes before and after the Fifth Avenue church program. Several challenges to Gus Nichols for debate came from denominational preachers during their particular shows. Sometimes calls for formal debates came, but often comment or criticism materialized in reference to brother Nichols' most recent broadcast. Then, when Gus returned to the air, it became his duty to respond to the comments and accusations that were being made against him or the truth. He conducted radio debates with preachers from the Church of God, the Nazarenes, and even with some of his brethren who, in his estimation, veered away from the truth.

Gracie Nichols Young

Several humorous things happened over the years. Hardeman recalled a funny thing that happened in later years. By then, Gus had developed some hearing loss, and it happened one day that a woman called in while he was doing his program. As his secretary was away, he told the radio audience that he needed to answer the call just in case there was some important news. He lifted the receiver and the woman told him her issue. The listening audience could hear him tell the woman that he would ask his listeners to be on the lookout. Returning to the microphone he explained that Mrs. _____ called and said she had lost her *teeth* somewhere between the post office and her place of work, and if anyone saw them to call her. In a matter of seconds, the phone began ringing. Again, he told his hearers that this might be an update the woman's teeth, so he needed to take the call. Leaving to answer, it could be heard over the airways, "Uh, yes! I need to let them know that. I'll sure do it. Thanks for calling." Returning once again to the microphone he explained that it was not her *teeth* she lost, but her *keys!*[16]

For years, the local Ford, Buick, Pontiac and Cadillac car dealer, Mr. Buddy Franklin (1913-2007), had a fifteen-minute sports show that followed brother Nichols program. Many times, over the years while "The Gospel Broadcast" was on the air, Franklin would send word to the speaker that he was giving his time so preaching could continue an extra twelve or thirteen minutes. Flavil later said, "Only eternity can reveal how much time he has paid for and given for our use. Although he is a Methodist, there are absolutely no strings attached to his gift, either."[17]

It is easy to see that "The Gospel Broadcast" became another powerful platform available to the man of God from Jasper. It became one of the most potent weapons in his arsenal in presenting the gospel plea. With it he was able to continue his efforts to slay the giants of infidelity throughout the remainder of his days.

ENDNOTES

1 Charlie Nichols, *Firm Foundation*, 20 June 1944, p. 6.

2 Pervie Nichols, "Nichols to Selma," *Gospel Advocate*, 13 January 1944, p. 39.

3 Flavil Nichols, *Gospel Advocate*, 16 March 1944, p. 195.

4 Ibid., 13 February 1947, p. 146.

5 Batsell Barrett Baxter and M. Norvel Young, eds., *Preachers of Today*, Volume 1, p. 382.

6 Note: George Smith Lindsey (1928-2012) was born in Fairfield, Jefferson County, Alabama. He was raised in Jasper. He later became a Hollywood actor making small appearances in television shows. Beginning in 1964, he became best known for his role at "Goober Pyle," the slow-witted cousin of Gomer Pyle (Jim Nabors) on The Andy Griffith Show. Lindsay passed from this life 6 May 2012 in his Nashville home. His body was laid to rest in the Oak Hill Cemetery in his hometown of Jasper, Alabama.

7 Interview with Bertha Blackwood October 10, 2011. Note: Sister-in-law Marilyn Nichols and longtime friend and preacher, Levi Sides, were present at the interview that took place in Bertha's home in Jasper. In later years, Rile ran a successful insurance business for 43 years in Jasper.

8 Ancestry.com, Note: In his lifetime, W. W. Bankhead served as vice chairman, board of directors, First National Bank of Jasper, was a long-time resident of Jasper, and died there in November 1988.

9 Jennifer Williams, "Words of Truth," reporter, quoting Levi Sides, *Daily Mountain Eagle*, 4 August 2008, p. 1a.

10 "Directory of Standard (AM) Broadcasting Stations of the United States," Broadcasting-Telecasting 1949 Yearbook. Washington, D.C.: Broadcasting Publications, Inc. 1949., p. 70. Note: According to an Online Wikipedia article, the station got a construction permit in 1956 and increased its wattage to 1,000 watts. It was then that the FCC allowed the station to move to its present 1360 kHz broadcasting frequency. The station was known as WWWB all of brother Nichols' life. In March 1986 the station was sold, the call letters changing to WZPQ. The station changed ownership a few times over the years. On 6 July 2005 the station received its present call letters of WIXI.

11 Note: Gus was given the choice of times in the daily schedule from the first. He chose the 8:00-8:30 am time. Over the next several decades the program changed stations four different times, but always maintained the same time-slot. Some years later, after brother Nichols began his paper, "*Words of Truth*," the elders at Jasper determined that all press from the church would be referred to as "*Words of Truth*." Hence, the radio program is called "*Words of Truth*," to this day. It is the oldest continuous running religious radio program in Alabama. At the time of this writing, the program is heard over station AM 1240, WJLX.

12 Willard Collins, "The Gus Nichols Story," *Gospel Advocate*, 2 March 1961, p. 136.

13 E. R. Brannan, "Gus Nichols, The Man," *Gospel Advocate*, 25 March 1976, p. 196.

14 Batsell Barrett Baxter and M. Norvel Young, eds., *Preachers of Today*, Vol. 1, Nashville: The Christian Press, Williams Printing Company, 1952, p. 250.

15 Phone interview with Ray Dutton, 10 April 2015.

16 Hardeman Nichols, Freed-Hardeman University Lectures, unpublished speech on his father's life at the Friends of the Restoration Luncheon, 2 February 2012.

17 Flavil Nichols, *Words of Truth*, 13 June 1986, p. 2.

- 30 -

The Mighty Pen

For whatsoever things were written aforetime were written for our learning, that we through patience and comfort of the scriptures might have hope.
—Paul, Romans 15:4

When *Gospel Advocate* editor, B. C. Goodpasture (1895-1977) announced that Gus Nichols was to become a staff writer for the paper, the demands of the role led him to determine that some things needed to change. A busy preaching schedule, meetings, debates, and other pressing commitments, led him to give editorship of *Truth and Love* back over to its publisher and owner Marion Davis (1906-1979) in the summer of 1944. Soon, the paper transitioned to its new editor—Springfield, Missouri, preacher, lawyer, and church leader, Roy E. Cogdill (1907-1985).[1]

1945 - Gus Nichols

By the end of the year, no less than five articles written by Gus Nichols appeared in the pages of the *Gospel Advocate*. Nearly that many more appeared in the journal in the first three months of the following year. The increase in popularity may be marked up to several reasons. The Gospel Advocate Company had recently published brother Nichols' debate with C. J. Wheeler, and the sales had been out of the roof. Within nine months of its original release it was being reordered from the printers. The second release in the following spring came with the advertisement, "A new edition of the 'Nichols-Weaver Debate' came off the press recently. The price remains $1.50. This is one of our best-selling debates."[2]

Another reason for his growth in fame could be supported by the fact that brethren further afield were calling for his services. In December, he headed out to Texas to preach a meeting for the brethren in Longview. The preacher there, Cecil E. Hill (1904-1988) sent in a report saying, "Gus Nichols did a most helpful work here in a recent meeting. Thirty have been added, half of whom were baptisms."[3]

Adding to this, in the new year, he began to be regularly scheduled on three different college lectureship programs. Early in January, he was at Freed-Hardeman College for their annual lecture program.[4] Then, he made his first appearance on the David Lipscomb College Lectureship series that was conducted the week of the 28th of January. During this forum, he led a daily class for preachers each morning from 11:20-12:20.[5] Finally, in May, he was to make a trip to Montgomery to appear on the annual program at Montgomery Bible College. But, at the last minute he became ill and was unable to attend. The brethren quickly contacted G. A. Dunn, Sr. (1876-1967) as a replacement. The only way he could make it in time was to fly. Brother Dunn later related, "I went over by request in an airplane, and in a way enjoyed it, but I am afraid of the air travel."[6]

WHY I AM A MEMBER OF THE CHURCH OF CHRIST

For a few years already, Gus' name and comments had been appearing in various advertisements in brotherhood publications to sign off on books, tracts, songbooks, and other useful helps to the church. His advice was often sought in the publication and critique of books well before going to press. Potentially, one of the greatest books to hit the market in the 20th century from among the brethren was written by Leroy Brownlow (1914-2002), and released in May 1945 under the title, "Why I Am A Member Of The Church of Christ." In its very first advertisement for sale, the *Firm Foundation* added the following from the pen of Gus Nichols,

> You have done the cause of Christ a great favor in bringing out this new book. It is the best thing that I have ever seen to pass on to outsiders and young members of the Church. . .There is nothing like it in print. . . I predict that it will live and have a place among our literature a hundred years from now."—Gus Nichols. (Brother Nichols read and criticized the manuscript before the book was printed.)[7]

A New Book Printed

In a later advertisement, he was recorded as saying concerning the volume, "'It fills a place all its own. There is nothing like it in print. It gives a bird's eye view of the church in a most interesting manner.' —Gus Nichols."[8]

HITLERISM IN RELIGION

The *Gospel Advocate*, like most brotherhood journals, has been known to pull out articles of the past and re-publish them for a particular reason always as it serves the purposes of its editor. However, in the spring of 1945, one of Gus' articles appeared twice in about a month's time. The first to appear was in the April 5th edition. Then, a re-written version, with some changes, appeared under the same title four issues later in the 3rd of May release. The title of both articles was, "Hitlerism in Religion."

The articles were cleaver efforts on the writer's part to invoke the ways of the world's greatest villain at that time, Adolf Hitler, for the purpose of making a most Biblical and pertinent application to that day's religious discord. The first article opened with,

> It is strange that so many people who condemn Hitlerism in politics endorse the same principles in religion. Hitler is afraid for his people to know the whole truth about the war. Long ago he confiscated radio receiving sets, and outlawed the reading of leaflets dropped from our planes. His people are required to accept what they are told by the German leaders. They are not permitted to listen to world news. Hitler is afraid for them to hear the whole truth. They are given only one side of the news— Hitler's side. Free and open information is opposed by Hitlerism.[9]

What followed were several challenges to the lack of religious freedom among the Christian world of the day. He spoke of a "certain church" that forbids their members from reading and studying the Bible, and that open and honest Bible study was a closed subject to their adherents. He further applied Hitlerism to the denominations, saying that their members are told to steer away from those who question their doctrines, and admonish their members not to be concerned when told that doctrine has something to do with their salvation. He further compared,

> Hitlerism opposes open and free discussion. Perhaps we would not have had this war if Hitler had freely discussed the principles of right and justice, all down the line, with other nations. When he started the war, Mr. Chamberlain[10] went to see him a second time, but he did not want to talk with him at all. He did not believe in, listening to, or even considering, what others had to say. His mind was made up; and though he did not know a lot of things, one thing which he did know was that he was not

going to change his mind, regardless of the facts. In our country, we propose to hear all sides. Anyone for or against a bill on the floor of the house is given a hearing in open debate. This has been our safeguard all along the line. It has held us very close to the principles of the Constitution. Every one of our laws has been hammered out in the heat of free and open controversy. However, Hitlerism in religion opposes religious discussion, in which the people can hear both sides. They brand all controversy in religion as un-Christian. But the Bible says: "Debate thy cause." (Prov. 25:9.)[11]

This was a powerful expulsion of both Hitlerism and the continuous challenge among the brethren to get the message out to the world, especially in the debating arena. Many denominations were beginning to shy away from engaging preachers from churches of Christ in public debate. Denominations were losing their members in droves to the concept of New Testament Christianity. This article was a cry against Hitlerism, Romanism, denominationalism, and any other kind of "ism" that stood between people and a better knowledge of the truth.

In short, the appearance of the article served to be prophetic. Hitlerism was rapidly on the downturn in worldly affairs. The United States and the other members of the Allied Forces where making headway into every German stronghold. The world began to believe that an end to the "war to end all wars" might be in sight. In this way, the article was a perfect admonition to the forces of the Lord to be on the move toward affecting a similar type decline among those who were under religious "Hitlerism" in the world.

In another sense, the release of the article was a bit premature. On the 28th of April, Italy's Fascist leader, Benito Mussolini, was executed by a firing squad. Two days later, Germany's Adolf Hitler was reported as committing suicide in his Berlin bunker. The leading editorial for the following issue of the *Gospel Advocate* was "Mussolini Is Dead."[12] The front page article by Gus Nichols was—once again, "Hitlerism In Religion." It was very similar to the initial article four weeks prior, but with stronger language. Again, there was an appeal to Christians to see how Hitler's oppressive tactics to shelter his people from the truth were similar to the efforts among denominational leaders to keep their members from taking a critical look at their own teachings in comparison to the truth of the Scriptures. He closed his thoughts with,

> The church of Christ stands for free speech, open and honorable controversy, and is not afraid of the light. This is not true of any other religious body known to this writer. It is the exception to the rule for denominational preachers to seek a full and fair

investigation of all they teach. They want people to take what they teach without question. This is Hitlerism in religion.[13]

HENRY LEO BOLES

When Gus, Pervie, and Flavil converged in Henderson, Tennessee, for the 1946 annual Special Courses/Lectureship series, they arrived to the news that brother H. Leo Boles (1874-1946) had taken to his sickbed at his Nashville home.

Since the previous November, he had complained of severe pain in his leg. At seventy-two years of age, the doctors initially thought that it had something to do with the length of time he spent on his feet, but later concluded that it was a case of phlebitis. The day before he was to depart for Henderson, brother Boles developed pneumonia and was put to bed.

Immediately, the Nichols preachers sent a telegram from Henderson stating their love, affection and their desire for a return of good health. Prayers reached toward heaven from all over the brotherhood in the days that laid ahead. Yet, recovery was not to be. Brother Boles passed from this life at 10:30 on the morning of the 7th of February.[14] News spread quickly through the many brethren he touched, leaving all in deep sorrow. When hearing of his passing, Gus sat down and inscribed the feelings of his heart at the loss of his dear friend. Though lengthy, it illustrated the deep pathos felt by an adoring brotherhood. He wrote,

Business Card

> The church of our Lord sustained a very great loss when H. Leo Boles left us and went home to God. I knew Brother Boles through the last eighteen or twenty years of his stay on earth. He stayed in our home at Jasper, Ala., while preaching there in a meeting a few years ago. I have also heard him speak several times daily in the lecture courses conducted at David Lipscomb College and at Freed-Hardeman College since these courses were inaugurated. I have read his articles in the *Gospel Advocate* since I was a young preacher. I also have his various books and have used his Bible-school commentaries since he began to write them. I reached the

conclusion some years ago that Brother Boles was the greatest man known to me in all the brotherhood; I thought of him as the best all-around man among us. He was highly endowed by nature, had a wonderful mind, and was a profound scholar. With his powerful mind he could see through a problem or a proposition, clearly define the issue, and make the truth to shine as bright as day, while others were wasting time with technicalities. His sermons were beautiful and powerful in their simplicity. All could easily understand any argument that he made on any subject. He could state the truth on any question in few words; and when he stated any proposition, he clearly defined the terms used and presented the truth from so many angles that the force of his arguments were irresistible. He was just and fair in dealing with men and issues. He never intentionally misrepresented anyone to obtain the advantage in argument. Like the Master himself and the apostles, Brother Boles was a controversialist. He had deep and abiding convictions, knew what he believed, and why he believed as he did. He could give a reason for the hope that was in him. He was as "bold as a lion" in defense of the truth. He knew the word and will of God, and feared no man who would dare raise his voice against the truth. He loved men, especially his brethren, but he put the truth above all men. Yet, he was as humble and gentle as a little child. The light of Christ and his gospel was brightly reflected in the character and life of Brother Boles. I thought of him as being more nearly perfect than any man living.

Upon our arrival at Freed-Hardeman College in January, Flavil Nichols, Pervie Nichols, and the writer sent Brother Boles a telegram, closing with the words: "We love you." No mother ever expressed her love for her darling babe with more tenderness of feeling than the love which stated these endearing words unto the bedside of Brother Boles in that telegram. Perhaps he was loved by more people than any man in the church. He was growing old most gracefully. One's life was deeply enriched by hearing him for a single day. I learned many wonderful truths from Brother Boles, but his life did as much, or more, for me than his teaching. His life, though to some extent imperfect, was a living sermon. I shall always feel indebted to Almighty God for the providence which brought his life in touch with mine. At times I could feel myself drinking in his Christ-like spirit.

There are many things in Brother Boles' life which if imitated would bring about a wonderful change in this old world. He was free from prejudice, envy, and jealousy. He loved all faithful gospel preachers, everywhere, and often said, "More power to them!" in the great work, which they were doing. It was his practice never to allow any brother to rise to speak a word in behalf of the truth that he did not first breathe a prayer for him in his efforts to teach the truth. Often, the preacher feels that his audience has come as spectators to find fault and to criticize rather than to find strength for the trials ahead. It would give the poor, stumbling, faltering preacher more power to know that his audience is praying for him in his difficult task. We need more piety and goodness in the church. We need more preachers like Brother Boles. He stood foursquare against modernism, denominationalism and all digression from the truth as it is in the New Testament. He was ready to meet any man on earth who would dare to lift his voice against the truth. He was aware of the fact that the truth of God has no voice of its own with which to defend itself when blasphemed, defamed, and cast down as damnable heresy. Hence, like Paul, he was "set for the defense of the gospel." He earnestly contended for the faith once delivered to the saints. Many "isms" and theories arose to challenge the truth, but he was never carried away with any of them. He was no hobby rider nor fanatic. He never caused trouble in the church by speculating and theorizing. I went to see him a few days before his passing, and he referred to a certain brother of fine ability as a hobby rider, because he was teaching a new "ism" to the disturbance of the peace and harmony among brethren.

Brother Boles was like Paul in that he labored more abundantly than the rest of us. He did an enormous amount of work in his day. He was "always abounding in the work of the Lord." But his work on earth is done, and his works will follow him, for he died in the Lord. Brethren, let us imitate all the good in his life and stand for the truth, which was dearer to his heart than all earthly things combined. Let others rise up and qualify to take his place. Let us cherish his memory, perpetuate his work, and so live that we may meet him and all the faithful on that golden shore where sorrow and pain can never come. Let us be ready unto every good work, lest we lose what Brother Boles won for the cause at great cost and sacrifice. Thank God for such a man and what he meant to me![15]

Evaluating the impact of the loss felt by the brotherhood in the passing of H. Leo Boles may never be fully calculated. However, the weight of significance the brotherhood felt toward both he and Gus Nichols at this time might be demonstrated in the words of Restoration Movement historian L. L. Brigance (1879-1950) when he said,

For ten years, Freed-Hardeman College has conducted a series of courses of study and lectures during the month of January. Each of these series has been carefully planned, and we have tried to secure the best talent in the brotherhood to conduct them. In nine of them, H. Leo Boles was the principal instructor, and was preparing to start to Henderson for the tenth when he was taken ill and had to go to the hospital instead. Gus Nichols, of Jasper, Ala., has played an important part in every one of the ten. Many others have rendered important service on these programs, but none have done so much of it as the two mentioned above.[16]

ENDNOTES

1 "Cogdill To Edit *Truth In Love*," *Gospel Advocate*, 17 August 1944, p. 550. Note: Roy Edward Cogdill was born in Hobart, Oklahoma, 24 April 1907. A lawyer as well as preacher, editor, and over-all church leader, Cogdill was a powerful force in the non-institutional movement among churches of Christ from the early 1950s until his death. He passed from this life 13 May 1985. Burial followed in his home town of Hobart in the Hobart Rose Cemetery.

2 Advertisement, *Gospel Advocate*, 8 March 1945, p. 152.

3 Cecil E. Hill, *Gospel Advocate*, 4 January 1945, p. 12. Note: a similar report appeared in the *Firm Foundation*, 21 December 1944, p. 14.

4 Note: Gus was not a featured speaker in 1945. However, at this point in its history, he had become a mainstay to the success of the program. The 3:30 p.m. time slot during this session was designated as "Informal Discussions" where it is assumed he contributed greatly. In future sessions, this period was designated as "Roundtable Discussions" with Gus Nichols, and later called, "Open Forum."

5 Advertisement, *Gospel Advocate*, 18 January 1945, p. 46.

6 Gus Dunn, *Firm Foundation*, 15 May 1945, p. 10.

7 Advertisement, *Firm Foundation*, 15 May 1945, p. 14.

8 Ibid., 3 July 1945, p. 13.

9 Gus Nichols, "Hitlerism in Religion," *Gospel Advocate*, 5 April 1945, pp. 196-97.

10 Note: Neville Chamberlain (1869-1940) was the British Prime Minister when the United Kingdom entered World War II in 1939. He served in the role from May 1937 to May 1940. He was followed by Conservative Party leader, Winston Churchill (1874-1965).

11 Gus Nichols, "Hitlerism in Religion," *Gospel Advocate*, 5 April 1945, pp. 196-97.

12 Editorial, "Mussolini Is Dead," *Gospel Advocate*, 3 May 1945, p. 242.

13 Gus Nichols, *Gospel Advocate*, 03 May 1945, p. 245.

14 Leo L. Boles and J. E. Choate, *I'll Stand On The Rock: A Biography Of H. Leo Boles*, p. 257.

15 Gus Nichols, *Gospel Advocate*, 28 March 1946, p. 306-07.

16 L. L. Brigance, *Gospel Advocate*, 17 October 1946, p. 996. Note: These sentiments were repeated in the *Firm Foundation*, 24 December 1946, p. 7.

- 31 -

The Dean

> For so is the will of God, that with well doing ye may put to silence the ignorance of foolish men: As free, and not using your liberty for a cloke of maliciousness, but as the servants of God. Honour all men. Love the brotherhood. Fear God. Honour the king.
> —Peter, 1 Peter 2:15-17

When Gus was entering his mid-fifties, he was already a seasoned and respected preacher. Looking back over his career, he had seen so many changes since his decision to preach the unsearchable riches of Christ. At the beginning, there were only fifteen congregations in Walker County. Now there were forty, much attributing to his efforts along with several others. Asa M. Plyler (1902-1991) confirmed their contributions writing,

> Gus Nichols has spent more than twenty of his thirty years as a preacher in this part of the country. H. P. McDonald lived and preached for a number of years among us. John McClesky has spent more than fifteen years in this county doing a splendid work with the congregations with whom he labored. W. A. Black lived with the church in Parrish for several years and has done much preaching throughout the county. Sherley F. Hester is living with the church at Short Camp and doing full time work in his section of the master's vineyard. Plato Black lives and works for the church in Cordova. John Wheeler is also doing a splendid work supported by the church at Zion. All these together with a host of others who labor with their families through the week go out on Lord's days to tell the glad story of the cross and encourage the brethren in weak places. To this class of preachers we should show the highest appreciation. They are not men who preach to make a living, but rather, men who make a living to preach. They preach not because they are supported for such work but they preach because they love the truth and have a longing and joy in the salvation of lost souls.[1]

Gus' activities at this time were full on, fast going and much further reaching than the region surrounding his home. Writing for the papers, preaching in the many meetings, and serving on all the lectureships was taxing, but rewarding. In his thinking, he was serving the Lord and His Church. Congregations from far away called him often for his help and attention. For instance, there was a meeting he held in October 1946 in Longview, Texas, where the brethren were making a concerted effort toward organization. He had been there in a gospel meeting a couple years prior, but his return was much needed in view of addressing their leadership development. The results were great, the local preacher reporting,

> Brother Gus Nichols of Jasper, Alabama recently closed a very successful meeting here. He delivered his lessons in such a way as to make them effective. Four were baptized and the congregation was greatly edified. One of the main objectives of the meeting was selection and appointment of elders and deacons. I am happy to report that this was accomplished in a very successful manner. Brother Nichols and Brother Foy E. Wallace, Sr., are to be commended for their wisdom in dealing with the situation. The church now has three elders and six deacons.[2]

Calls continued to come from far and near. As time would allow it, Gus was determined to be available in any way the brethren could use him. When he was not preaching or debating, he was aiding in some other capacity. For instance, he assisted with the Porter-Tingley Debate in Birmingham from the 24th of February to the 1st of March 1947. Gus had faced off against Glenn V. Tingley (1901-1988) in May of 1941. This time he served as moderator for the seasoned debater, W. Curtis Porter (1897-1960). The Arkansas preacher was well prepared to meet the Calvinist on the subjects of the Holy Spirit's activity in conversion, Baptism, and Faith Only doctrines. The discussion was held in the building of the Central church of Christ, with 1200 to 1500 in attendance each night, including "several hundred preachers from several states."[3] Among them was George W. DeHoff (1913-1993), who came with SoundScriber© equipment in hand to record the proceedings. Later, he published the discussion in a volume entitled, *Porter-Tingley Debate*.[4]

Gus baptizing a Baptist Preacher Clifton Bighurat

ANOTHER TRIP TO TEXAS

After baptizing five during a two-week meeting in Tarrant City, Alabama in early April,[5] Gus and Matilda headed out to the little town northwest of Fort Worth, Texas, called Nocona. James C. Bays (1913-1998) was the young preacher there and had organized a lectureship for the week of the 13th through the 18th. As Nocona was just up the road from Bowie where Carrie and W. T. were living, the Nichols were able to spend some quality time with their little nine-month-old grandbaby, Kathy, during the lectureship.

Gus closed the series out on Friday night on the subject, "Dangers Facing the Church." This subject had been his focus for the last several months. Since his time in Longview, Texas, back in the fall assisting that congregation in the appointment of elders, he had been thinking about the troubles that were facing the church through a lack of leadership and the much-needed respect for it. Back in January, he had discussed several dangers at length during the Queries and Answers sessions of the Freed-Hardeman College Special Courses, and the same title was given to his daily classes at the David Lipscomb College Lectures.[6]

The church was in need of teaching on the most basic fundamentals of New Testament Christianity. Seven articles on various subjects appeared during the first six months of the year in the pages of the *Gospel Advocate*. Various topics were discussed like "Some Church Problems," that appeared in the last issue in January. In it, he expressed that the church was not evangelizing as it should, and that elders were not leading in the process. He further taught the need for churches to have qualified men to serve in the role of elder, and that once in place they should be respected by all if they were serving in keeping with the will of God.[7] Other articles that appeared in sequence were, "The Church of Christ,"[8] "Problem of Discipline,"[9] "The Change of Heart,"[10] "False Worship,"[11] "Out Of The Overflow,"[12] "Jurisdiction of Elders,"[13] and "Bible Colleges."[14]

In the latter article, he expressed his concern at the lack of encouragement of young people among the churches to attend the Bible Colleges. But the point most strongly made was that the Bible Colleges were, in fact, under the oversight of local elders in the sense that if colleges did not do as they should biblically, that local elders could admonish families under their oversight to refuse to allow their children to attend. He said, "It seems to me that this is a strong safeguard thrown around the schools."[15] He applied this reasoning to religious papers or any other thing with which members of the local congregation might be involved.

Upon completion of the Nocoma Lecture program, Gus began a meeting at Bowie. Montague County was a mission field that was, "bearing much fruit,"[16] according to W. T. Hamilton, who had already made a good effort evangelizing in the county since graduating from F-HC. The meeting with his father-in-law was both meaningful, and a great encouragement to his young family. He wrote, "Last week we closed one of the best meetings we have ever had in Bowie. Gus Nichols preached. A new Bible-study record was set the second Sunday of the meeting. During the meeting there were four baptized and two placed membership."[17]

DEAN OF THE GROUP

When Gus attended his eleventh session of the Freed-Hardeman College Special Courses in January 1948, he was seen as one of the top contributors in the leadership of the forum. On the front page of the next edition of the school's paper, *The Sky Rocket,* under the title, "January Visitors Warmly Welcomed," a report of the role of his and others were expressed in the following,

> A great number of visitors attended our recent January courses and added to the pleasures of that week. Many are newcomers, while many are "January Alumni" of several years' standing.
>
> The "January Faculty," this year was composed of Brethren W. O. Davis, of Memphis, G. K. Wallace, of Wichita, Kansas, James A. Allen, of Nashville, George DeHoff, of Murfreesboro, Tenn., Earl West, of Indianapolis, and Gus Nichols, of Jasper, Alabama. Brother Nichols is the dean of the group, with a continuous record of January attendance since 1937; Brother Wallace is next, with several years of January teaching to his credit.[18]

Gus' lead in the forum forced him into a level of leadership he did not seek, yet by design of role, was the obvious outcome. He knew the Bible and how to apply it to the present needs of the church. Yet, the pressure of fielding the many questions that were asked in the daily Round-Table Discussions was a challenge that few people in the brotherhood other than Gus could handle. L. L. Brigance (1879-1950) defined his work as, "the hardest job of all."[19]

Again, Gus made his presence known at the David Lipscomb College Lectures series at the end of January. This was the second year of its running, and as part of its festivities was the sale of its first volume of the previous year's forum. Three of Gus' lessons on dangers in the church appeared in the volume.[20] This year, he closed the lectureship with the Friday evening discourse on the subject, "Hatred." The lecture was so well received that he was asked by B. C. Goodpasture (1895-1977) to write a series of articles on the subject for his paper. With the July 15th issue of the *Advocate*, four articles in the series had appeared describing the sin of hatred and its disturbing effect on the home, the church, and the world. The series also included several things that *should* be hated, like sin, division in the body and home, and the like.[21]

BOOK OF SERMONS

As early as 1943, Gus began submitting sermon outlines and articles to *The Mountain Eagle* newspaper. Blanketing the region with solid Biblical topics served to get the message through doors that otherwise would not be accessible. Some of the submissions found their way into the hands of soldiers on foreign battlefields. Each lesson was intended to correct real and present needs at the time. While evangelistic in thrust, they were intended to be an apologetic for the truth of the gospel. They fulfilled their intended purpose, for lives were changed through them. It was reported, "We have learned of several people who were converted by these sermons. Bro. Joe S. Hyde baptized a whole family of six who learned from our sermons in the paper."[22]

During the year of 1947, the Fifth Avenue church paid nearly a thousand dollars to see that articles were placed in every issue. Many thought it would be a good idea to gather a selection of his best entries and put them into a volume for mass distribution.

B. C. Goodpasture, under the title, "Office Notes," included amongst other things the following note,

Sermons by Gus Nichols

> A copy of "Sermons," by Gus Nichols, Jasper, Ala., has just come to our attention. While we have not had time to read this book, we do not doubt that it is sound in teaching. It contains sixty-six short sermons, which Brother Nichols originally prepared for the local paper. The book is privately printed, bound in paper, and sells for $1.[23]

GUS NICHOLS TO CONDUCT QUERY DEPARTMENT

One of the most significant divisions at the *Gospel Advocate* was the Query Department. This time-honored post began in the early days of the paper when Tolbert Fanning (1810-1874) and David Lipscomb (1831-1917) were the editors. Over the years, enlisted were the talents of a veritable who's who among leaders in the American Restoration Movement. When Gus began reading the paper, J. C. McQuiddy (1858-1924) was the editor of the queries that were sent in for discerning and biblical responses. Other subsequent queries editors were E. A. Elam (1855-1929), H. Leo Boles (1874-1946), John T. Hinds (1866-1938), R. L. Whiteside (1869-1951), and G. C. Brewer (1884-1956).

A demonstration of the esteem held for Gus Nichols by the paper's editor came with the following in the December 2nd edition, "With this issue Brother Nichols of Jasper, Ala., will answer queries addressed to him or the *Gospel Advocate*. Brother Nichols is one of our best-informed and soundest gospel preachers. He needs no introduction to the readers of this journal."[24]

The rise in prominence never seemed to affect the humility of Jasper's preacher. He continued being the most genial and approachable person. His daily work was always in view of building up the church and through it, the community. Adding to this were the many calls for conducting weddings and funerals alike. One of the several funerals he conducted during 1948 was for an old sister who had been a charter member of the Winfield congregation. "Sister Martha Caroline Vickery"[25] was said to have been present at the first meeting of the congregation when Charlie Wheeler (1851-1937) started the church the first Sunday in August 1895 and was the last surviving member. Her desire was always that Gus Nichols would conduct her funeral, which he did in January.

His meeting schedule seemed always to be filled. In the spring, he preached a meeting at Woodbury, Tennessee where twenty were added, nine of whom were baptized.[26] Then, in June, he conducted a tent meeting in Paducah, Kentucky.[27] Finally, in October he was called up to Lincoln Park, Michigan for a meeting where seven were baptized and two were restored. The preacher there, Roy K. Akers (1906-1997) commented, "It is a real privilege to be associated with brethren like Brother Nichols. His love for the truth, his sincerity and zeal, his splendid ability to preach in his humble way were a real blessing to us."[28]

RICH MAN AND LAZARUS
By Gus Nichols

If you will turn to Luke, chapter sixteen,
You will find it revealed and clearly seen;
That in God's sight there's a difference in men.
One was righteous; the other died in sin.

There is also a difference after death:
Lazarus was comforted after his last breath,
In hell the rich man lifted up his eyes,
And the world can still hear his cries.

ATHEISM is here completely denied,
And all those who have the Bible defied,
Saying we might as well live in sin and strife,
Denying that there is any future life.

UNIVERSALISM is also here refuted;
And the "No hell" theory is disputed.
The rich man landed in a fiery hell,
Where nothing ever any more went well.

MODERNISM is also herein exposed:
Here Jesus the inspired scriptures proposed
As the only hope for the lost brothers,
And therefore the only hope for others.

"CHRISTIAN SCIENCE" too, is exposed in this record,
With false doctrine woven in and checkered.
It denies sin, and pain, death, and sores;
If right, Lazarus should have stayed on these shores.

SPIRITUALISM too is herein proven untrue;
For it also can deceive quite a few.
No one could be sent to warn earthly kin,
Lest they live on and die in their sins.

MATERIALISM is denied in this story.
They think the dead are unconscious in glory.
Think the dead are like the little dog Rover,
And that when they die they die all over.

CATHOLICISM is denied on "purgatory."
They claim to pray them up into glory;
But the rich man in hell suffered in grief,
And could not get any sort of relief.

MORMONS claim there is a chance after death.
But opportunity ended with the man's last breath.
His brothers could not obey God for him,
And there was no way by which to reach them.

CALVINISM could not have helped the brothers,
Neither has it ever saved any others.
They were told to hear the scriptures they had;
To expect a miracle would be too bad!

THE DEAD did not come back to preach on earth
To the five brothers needing a new birth.
But they must be persuaded by the word,
Which by all must be loved and heard.[29]

ENDNOTES

1 Asa Plyler, *Historical Sketches of Churches of Christ in Alabama*, Henderson: Hester Publications, p. 102.

2 Cecil E. Hill, *Firm Foundation*, 6 November 1945, p. 13.

3 A. E. Emmons, Jr., *Firm Foundation*, 27 April 1948, p. 15.

4 W. Curtis Porter and Glenn V. Tingley, *Porter-Tingley Debate*, Murfreesboro: DeHoff Publications, 1947.

5 Raymond H. Crumbliss, *Gospel Advocate*, 24 April 1947, p. 298. Note: From this meeting it was said of Gus, "Those who heard him before said that Brother Nichols was at his tiptop best." Later in the summer, Crumbliss reported in the 24 July issue, "In all, this adds up to six baptisms and three restorations since the Gus Nichols' meeting early in the year."

6 Willard Collins, "Southern Opens Lecture Series," *Gospel Advocate*, 23 January 1947, p. 73.

7 Gus Nichols, *Gospel Advocate*, 30 January 1947, pp. 85, 93.

8 Ibid., 6 February 1947, p. 116.

9 Ibid., 20 February 1947, p. 159.

10 Ibid., 6 March 1947, p. 201.

11 Ibid., 3 April 1947, p. 253.

12 Ibid., 15 May 1947, p. 337.

13 Ibid., 13 June 1947, p. 406.

14 Ibid., 26 June 1947, p. 435.

15 Ibid.

16 W. T. Hamilton *Gospel Advocate*, 6 March 1947, p. 206.

17 W. T. Hamilton, *Firm Foundation*, 20 May 1947, p. 12. This was also reported in the *Gospel Advocate*, 15 May 1947, p. 351.

18 Ed., "January Visitors Warmly Welcomed," *The Sky Rocket*, Volume 25, Number 4, January 1948, p. 1.

19 L. L. Brigance, *Gospel Advocate*, 22 January 1948, p. 91. Note: This note also appeared in the *Firm Foundation*, 24 February 1948, p. 7.

20 Advertisement, "Lipscomb Lectures, Volume I Ready For Delivery," *Gospel Advocate*, 19 February 1947, p. 187. Note: The lessons included in the volume by Gus Nichols were "Dangers Facing the Church," "More Dangers Facing the Church," and "Danger of Premillennialism."

21 Gus Nichols, "The Awful Sin of Hatred," *Gospel Advocate*, 6 May 1948, p. 444, 17 June 1948, p. 583, 1 July 1948, p. 637, 15 July 1948, p. 685.

22 Gus Nichols, *Sermons*, Jasper: Gus Nichols, 1948, Introduction.

23 B. C. Goodpasture, ed., "Office Notes," *Gospel Advocate*, 25 March 1948, p. 305.

24 B. C. Goodpasture, "Gus Nichols To Conduct Query Department," *Gospel Advocate*, 2 December 1948, pp. 1156, 1165.

25 H. H. Camp, "At Rest," *Gospel Advocate*, 3 June 1948, p. 550.

26 Billy Nicks, *Gospel Advocate*, 24 June 1948, p. 621.

27 Alonzo Williams, *Gospel Advocate*, 17 June 1948, p. 591.

28 R. K. Akers, *Gospel Advocate*, 11 November 1948, p. 1124.

29 Gus Nichols, "Rich Man And Lazarus," *Words of Truth*, 8 December 1972, p. 4.

- 32 -

Breaking Down Prejudices

> Therefore, my beloved brethren, be ye stedfast, unmoveable, always abounding in the work of the Lord, forasmuch as ye know that your labour is not in vain in the Lord.
> —Paul, 1 Corinthians 15:58

The power of the pen is most impactful in the molding of the thinking of its readers. Among churches of Christ, particularly in the South, no more powerful pens were wielded than those that contributed to the production of the brotherhood papers. The *Gospel Advocate* and the *Firm Foundation* were chief among the many that spanned the country with their research and expositions of the Scriptures.

Sitting in the query editor's seat of the *Gospel Advocate* was not only an honor for the preacher from Jasper, Alabama but it was also a position of great influence. Nearly half the weekly issues released in 1949 included a column entitled, "Questions Answered," by Gus Nichols. He dealt with a wide range of topics addressing questions about such things as celebrating Christmas, the qualifications of elders, divorce and remarriage, and women wearing veils. He addressed worship issues like the breaking of bread, instrumental music, and tithing. Praise for his adequacy in the job came from his predecessor in the Query Department, G. C. Brewer (1884-1956), when he encouraged people to send their questions to Gus Nichols as he was, "thoroughly capable and conscientious."[1]

In the first issue of February, he dealt with a question on a subject that eventually would lay claim to a great deal of his time and devotion over the next twenty-five years. Billy Nicks, of Woodbury, Tennessee asked the question, "Can a congregation send money to another congregation, scripturally, to support a mission field?"[2] The answer to the question was brief—only one paragraph—in which Gus explained that while it was certainly scriptural for a congregation to send money to a worker in the mission field that, "Several congregations may cooperate in doing what one congregation alone is unable to do," and that all this is possible without developing an "ecclesiastical organization tying the congregations together."[3] Within a short time, he was to endure a firestorm of criticism from some of his brethren on these simple views on the subject of church cooperation.

But, at the turn of the fifth decade of the century, among the brotherhood, there was a solid trust in the Nashville paper. One brother from Middletown, Ohio expressed the general consensus saying, "As long as the *Gospel Advocate* has its writings in the hands of capable men, such as its editor, Gus Nichols, Guy N. Woods, G. W. DeHoff, Earl West, C. D. Plum, and the host of others, it will be my favorite paper, because it will soundly be proclaiming truth in love."[4]

PROMOTER OF GOOD WORKS

Leadership within the brotherhood demanded Gus' attention and praise for the works of others. This was something he never considered a chore, on the contrary, it was an honor.

For instance, when the dynamic educator and preacher, James R. Cope (1917-1919) was drafted by N. B. Hardeman (1874-1965) from David Lipscomb's Bible Department during the summer of 1944, it was believed by many that Cope was being bred to take the helm someday when Hardeman retired, and was even chosen by the Board of Freed-Hardeman to be Vice-President at the beginning of the 1949-1950 session.[5] But, when he announced that he was going to take the presidency of Florida College in Temple Terrace, Florida, many were surprised, but supportive. A dear friend of Cope's, brother Nichols, applauded in the *Advocate*, "I wish to congratulate you upon having such a fine president as you have in Brother Cope. He is every inch a man, and is equal to the task, great as it is."[6]

Other opportunities to lend support came through signing off on new literature arriving on the brotherhood scene. The preacher from the Central congregation in Tuscaloosa, Alabama at that time, Paul M. Tucker (1914-2000), released a new tract in the spring of 1949 entitled, *Undenominational Christianity*. In an advertisement in the *Gospel Advocate*, both Guy N. Woods (1908-1993) and Gus Nichols commented on the value of the work. Gus said, "This is the best thing of its kind that I have ever seen. It should be in every home, given out by every congregation, and could be profitably read and studied by every accountable person in the nation."[7]

Later in the summer when Earl I. West (1920-2011) released the first volume of, *The Search For The Ancient Order*, Gus read it with "great delight and profit" commenting,

> This is a wonderfully fine book, and ought to be in the hands of every gospel preacher and other leaders in the church. It is written in a most fascinating manner, and contains much information about the Restoration Movement that is not accessible unto the masses of the people. I feel indebted to Brother West for his painstaking efforts in getting out this book. It contains biography

written in such a fashion as to make the book an inspiration unto young people as well as others.[8]

Another advertisement including a Nichols endorsement was for a book that had been out for a short time by D. M. Canright, *Seventh-Day Adventism Renounced*. The Gospel Advocate Company, selling the book for $3.00, enjoyed promotion by the old guard, G. C. Brewer (1884-1956), the late H. Leo Boles (1874-1946), and Gus Nichols who called it, "The best thing on the subject."[9]

Two of his own works were also released during this time in subsequent fashion. As has been noted, a volume of sermons had been released in the spring of 1948. They were a compilation of the sermons that had appeared in the local newspaper, *The Mountain Eagle*. In the spring of 1949, another volume of *Sermons* was released having been self-published by the author. An ad appeared in the *Advocate* in May with the following, *Sermons*, Volume 2, by Gus Nichols and others, contains thirty-one sermons by Brother Nichols and one each by G. A. Dunn, Sr., R. H. Crumbliss, W. A. Holley, Gardner S. Hall, John T. Lewis, and W. T. Hamilton. This is a worthy companion to Volume 1. Price, $2."[10] The following year, he released a third volume under a similar title, *Sermons*, Volume 3," selling it for a dollar.[11]

GOSPEL MEETINGS WITH C. L. OVERTURF

Illinois preacher, Charles Logan Overturf (1905-1995), was the minister for the college church that met on the campus of David Lipscomb College. Later known as the Granny White church of Christ, he had been there since mid-1944, and had for many years made quite a reputation for himself as a powerful evangelist on the gospel meeting circuit. The church in Jasper secured his services for their summer meeting in 1946 where it was recorded that, "twenty-eight" responded, including nineteen baptisms and nine were restored.[12] He returned to preach in the summer meetings at Fifth Avenue over the next three years and did successful work each time. After the 1949 effort Gus reported, "Our meeting has just closed, with thirteen baptized and two restored. C. L. Overturf preached. This was his fourth meeting with us, and he is to return 2 years from now."[13]

WILLIAM C. NICHOLS OBEYS THE GOSPEL

How does a preacher spell success? He may baptize many in his lifetime, but what of his own family? A play on the memorable words of Jesus might express it best, "What does it profit a man if he gains the whole world" for Christ, and loses his own family, or at least some of them, to the world? Such for years had been the concern of Gus and his siblings for their father, William Calvin Nichols. Not long after Gus obeyed the gospel, his mother, Lizzie, did the same. But, his father held back and refused to accept the way of truth. Breaking down prejudices was a family effort for years, but to no avail.

However, in the late summer of 1949, Gus' young brother, Pervie, had been living in Sylacauga, Alabama and was in the process of moving to a new work over in Greenville, Mississippi. At the end of August, he preached some meetings near his old Walker County home. One was at Davis Chapel, near Bankston where four were baptized and one was restored. Another was down at Hauch Chapel near Fayette where four were baptized. One day while in his parent's home, he took the opportunity to try to convince his father of the need to obey the gospel. He wrote,

> One of the most joyous occasions during my visit in that section was when I had the opportunity to assist my eighty-one-year-old father in obeying the gospel. I believe that my brother, Gus Nichols, through his radio program, did much to break down prejudices and bring about his conversion.[14]

Twelve years later, Gus recalled the day with great clarity shedding further light on the background of the occasion. He rehearsed,

> Well, my father was at first a member of the Baptist Church. I was the oldest child, and I can remember when he joined the Baptist Church. He later became a Fatalist, thinking that one had to succeed in living a perfect and sinless life in order to be a Christian, and since he did not know of any such perfect characters, he often said that there were no Christians on earth. Later he embraced the theories of Russellism and of Jehovah's Witnesses. At the age of eighty-one I baptized his oldest brother-in-law and wife. He—his brother-in-law—had been a Free Will Baptist preacher. This, most of all, challenged my father's attention to the power of the simple gospel of Christ. Knowing that he was much interested in the gospel—that he knew the truth—I sent my brother, Pervie, who is a gospel preacher and next to the baby child, to persuade him to obey the gospel that very day, and I started warming the water in the baptistry. And sure enough, at noon the great event for which we had hoped and prayed for more than forty years had taken place.[15]

WILLIAM WOODSON OBEYS THE GOSPEL

Walker County boy, William Edgar Woodson (1931-2010), grew up on Fifth Avenue in Jasper. As a lad, he attended the Pentecostal church on Fifth Avenue. At about the age of thirteen, he began attending the Northside Baptist Church, also located on Fifth Avenue. He was a bright young student, having graduated as president of his Walker County High

School class. It was not long after this time that he began dating a young lady who attended the church of Christ on Fifth Avenue. She began strongly challenging the doctrines of his church. While he had never been immersed into the Baptist Church, he still felt they were all right. So, he purchased a little pocket New Testament, to look up the verses she referred to, in hopes that he could answer his girlfriend's many challenges. He also went with her to the worship services of the Fifth Avenue church of Christ. Week after week, he heard Gus Nichols preach. And, week after week, he studied his little Testament to see if the things he heard were so. On the last Saturday in July 1950, the young man presented himself to brother Nichols determined to be baptized into Christ for the forgiveness of his sins.

After his baptism, Gus gave him copies of his first two books of sermons. In the opening of the first he inscribed the words, "With best wishes of Gus Nichols to William Woodson on this his birth day into the Kingdom of God - July 29, 1950."[16] These books, and later the third when released, remained treasured volumes in his library all his days. In his thinking, no greater influence for the good of his life was to be found than in his father in the faith, Gus Nichols.

Seeing the potential of this young man, just six weeks after his baptism, he was encouraged to preach a sermon. Woodson recalled,

> The first sermon I preached, September 9, 1950, was prepared for me by Gus Nichols. It was entitled "What Must I Do To Be Saved." He folded a sheet of typing paper, typed the headings, pasted 72 verses at the appropriate places, said I should learn all of these, then I was to come and preach the sermon before him until he was sure I was ready to preach it in a meeting he was holding—but he had to perform a wedding that night.[17]

Many years later, William was given the task of speaking in a Restoration Unity Forum held on the campus of Freed-Hardeman College. Hardeman Nichols served as the moderator. During brother Woodson's summation at the end of the forum he recalled his baptism, and the books brother Nichols had given him. Holding the inscribed volume in his hand, he expressed the following,

> I have carried this with me through all these years. Often in graduate school, after I had been taught by liberal teachers, I would go home and read my Bible and pray, and I would check this book again, and I would say, "Do I believe still what I believed the day I was baptized? Am I standing where I was then?" In five campaigns into England, Scotland, and Ireland, I have carried this book. In numerous, numerous instances, I have turned to it.

On page 14, concerning the churches of Christ, that good man said, "Any now who preach, believe, and practice identically what inspired teachers believed, taught, and practiced in the first century, without addition or subtraction or any other change, will be nothing but Christians and the church of Christ in a given community." [He says,]. . .neither can any man, or set of men, ever produce a denomination, or anything, but churches of Christ by assembling all the parts of his doctrine, as he gave it, and putting all items of his teaching in worship into loving obedience on the part of the people in a given community. [He says,] Any desire, or attempt, to change the church from what it was in the New Testament times shows one to be dissatisfied with the church as Jesus built it (Matthew 16:18). Christ has given no man any authority whatsoever to change his church from what it was when he built it. . . .

This book does not authorize anything "churches of Christ." Only such congregations as are patterned after the "churches of Christ" in the New Testament are "churches of Christ" now. A church will cease to be "of Christ" when it ceases to be fashioned by the will and authority "of Christ." A thing cannot be of God or of Christ which is contrary to the will of God and of Christ. A Masonic Lodge is built upon the principles and teachings of Freemasonry, not upon those of the Odd Fellows or the Elks. All depends upon the old, or original. It is not proper to compare a given congregation with congregations of the days of Luther or Calvin or Smith or Wesley. This is sure to lead into error. The only comparison that is proper is—is the church of which I am a member in my community identical with "the churches of Christ" in the days of the apostles? "Make all things according to the pattern."

That is where I have stood. I am not the standard. The last conversation I had with brother Nichols, brother Flavil was there. That good man looked at me, and he said, "Be true, teach young men the truth, and all will be well," and I said, "I will do that."[18]

MEETINGS

A busy schedule for any preacher is to have two or three gospel meetings to preach every year. But Gus Nichols was not just any preacher. He was in high demand. Other than his annual appearances on the college Lecture forums, he preached a good number of gospel meetings throughout the year. January always began with his responsibilities on the Freed-Hardeman College Lectures. In March, he was again at Montgomery Bible College for the annual lectures, speaking each day on, "The Great

Commission."[19] He preached a meeting at Lincoln Park, Michigan, beginning in late May 1949.[20] After that, he was planning to make his way over to Atlanta to preach a meeting at the Northwest congregation, but was waylaid with a brief illness that prevented him from making the trip.[21]

He was at the Central church in Memphis, Tennessee, the following September.[22] The preacher there, Buford Holt (1910-2001), later reported over twenty congregations to have been represented from the area who attended the meeting, "and as many as twenty-six preachers." He followed with an announcement of their plans for having him return in 1951 saying, "All who know brother Nichols know we had the very best preaching for the meeting."[23]

In early October, Gus participated with several other preachers in the Birmingham area in a meeting at the Berney Pointe congregation. "The speakers were: Franklin T. Puckett, C. L. Overturff, John T. Lewis, Howard Horton, Gus Nichols, and Maurice Howell."[24] He then preached a meeting in Woodbury, Tennessee, resulting in six baptisms and six restorations.[25] This was followed by a trip out to Oklahoma to where Carrie and W. T. were working, the Fifteenth and Balsam church in Frederick. It was a ten-day meeting where he spoke on the local radio station at 8 a.m. each morning, then preached at the church building at noon, and followed up each evening at 7:00 p.m. with another message.[26]

In 1950, after doing his questions-and-answers work at Freed-Hardeman, he was involved in a dedication Sunday for a new building at the church of Christ in Pell City, Alabama. He and John T. Lewis (1876-1967) were the speakers.[27] He returned there in September for a gospel meeting.[28] At the March lectureship at Montgomery Bible College he spoke daily on "Religious Errors."[29] In April, Gus made his way over to Salisbury, North Carolina, for a meeting with eleven baptisms being reported.[30] Later in the spring, he had a meeting at Oxford, Alabama.[31] The result of the effort was eight being baptized with "large crowds assembled each night, and extra chairs" being used.[32] From there, he went over to Lewisburg, Tennessee where he preached a meeting at the Water Street congregation. Thirteen were reported to have been baptized in this meeting with one restoration. Added were the words of praise, "Gus Nichols preached the gospel in that soul-stirring manner characteristic of him, and wonderful good was done. . .those who could not get into the building last night used folding chairs out in the yard and in the basement."[33]

THREE DEBATES

The year 1950 might be surmised as the year of the debate. Three discussions were conducted between mid-May and mid-September, all with denominational preachers.

The first discussion was held in Pensacola, Florida, against Pentecostal (Holiness) preacher, David Lamar Welch (1905-1994). Welch championed the "Oneness" view of the Godhead and had encountered debates with several of the brethren. This debate was somewhat unexpected because W. A. Black (1904-1980), at the time the preacher in Alabama City, Alabama was schedule to meet Welch, but became ill. At the last minute, Gus traveled down to Pensacola to face the Pentecostal.[34] Local preacher, Howard A. Blazer (1909-1995) sent in the following account,

> A public discussion between Mr. D. L. Welch (Pentecostal Holiness) and Gus Nichols was conducted in Pensacola, Fla., May 15-19. The subjects for the first two nights were concerning the baptism of the Holy Spirit and miracles. The two following nights were on the godhead. The last night Mr. Welch affirmed that mechanical instruments of music are acceptable in the worship of the church today. The crowd was estimated at about fifteen hundred each evening. Mr. Welch is the Pentecostal's champion debater in these parts, but Brother Nichols did such a wonderful job of pressing him from the first until by the last night he seemed to have lost most of his zeal in his efforts to uphold his doctrine. We feel that the cause of truth has been greatly strengthened here, and that the forces of error will not be so bold in challenging the church in this section for many years to come. Flavil Nichols did a fine job in moderating for his father. Gus Nichols plans to publish this discussion in book form in the near future. He also plans to be with us next spring for a meeting. One who was influenced by the debate was baptized and one restored at our morning service last Sunday. One other was baptized and one restored recently here at Brownsville. We had a very large number of local visitors last Lord's day.[35]

The second debate took place the following month in Greenville, Mississippi. As was mentioned, Pervie moved there a little less than a year before and had arranged for his older brother to face another Pentecostal by the name of Wes Busbee. He recounted,

> Gus Nichols of Jasper, Ala., engaged Mr. Wes Busbee of the Pentecostal Holiness Church, of Meridian, Miss., in a debate, June 26-29. This discussion was held under a large tent in Greenville, Miss. The first night Mr. Busbee affirmed that the baptism of the Holy Ghost, with the evidence of speaking in tongues, is essential to the new birth and is for us today. The second night Gus Nichols affirmed that there are three persons in the godhead—the Father, the Son, and the Holy Ghost. The third night my brother affirmed that water baptism should be performed in the name

of the Father, the Son, and the Holy Ghost (as stated in Matt. 28:19.) The fourth night Mr. Busbee affirmed that the scriptures authorize the use of mechanical instruments of music in Christian worship. Flavil Nichols moderated for his father, and a Mr. Stokes was the moderator for Mr. Busbee. Although we had only one week in which to advertise this discussion, approximately five to eight hundred attended every night. As many as ten preachers (including denominational preachers) were present some of the time. Mr. Busbee never attempted to examine more than half of Gus Nichols' arguments. His failure to meet the issue and sustain his position could be seen by all except the most prejudiced.

1950 - Nichols-Holder Debate

On the third night Mr. Busbee urged everyone to return and hear the discussion on the music proposition, and concluded that Mr. Nichols was really going to "skin" him on that. I never saw a false teacher defeated as badly as was Mr. Busbee. Good order prevailed throughout the debate, which proved that such discussions can be carried on in a decent and orderly way. Many members of the church say that this debate has strengthened their faith, and many of our religious neighbors say that they were greatly impressed with the truth. This proves that debates have not ceased to do good. We believe that the church in this mission field will be benefited. A wire recording was made of the entire discussion.[36]

The third debate took place in September with a man he had faced in March of 1944, Primitive Baptist, J. D. Holder (1898-1978). This was a four-night discussion that began on the 11th of September in the church of Christ in Medina, Tennessee. Each speaker took the affirmative two nights each, and the main points of the debate were over conditional versus unconditional salvation, whether God saves sinners separate and apart from the word of God, and whether or not atonement is universal.

The first night, the church house of the brethren was filled to overflowing. Loud speakers were used to accommodate those who could not get into the building. The last three nights the discussion was moved to a large shed that could seat over seven hundred. Basil Overton (1925-2013) was one of many preachers in attendance during that debate. Years later, he recalled being in the old pack shed when a bug flew into the mouth of brother Nichols as he was speaking and defending the gospel. Brother Nichols hardly missed a moment of speech. He said, "I remember well his saying of that bug, 'He was a stranger, and I took him in; he was lukewarm and I spewed him out.'"[37]

It was estimated that above 3,000 attended the discussion. The debate was recorded by C. A. Brannon with the intentions of publishing it.[38] One candid reviewer wrote in and said, "We heard part of Gus Nichols debate with Holder recently, and I have never heard a man get a harder 'skinning' in all my life than did Holder."[39] The Nichols-Holder Debate was finally published in 1954.

ENDNOTES

1 G. C. Brewer, *Gospel Advocate*, 3 February 1949, p. 67.

2 Gus Nichols, *Gospel Advocate*, 3 February 1949, p. 66.

3 Ibid.

4 Hubert Brandenburg, *Gospel Advocate*, 7 September 1950, p. 578.

5 C. Owings, *Firm Foundation*, 12 April 1949, pp. 2-3.

6 Gus Nichols, *Gospel Advocate*, 12 May 1949, p. 290.

7 Advertisement, *Gospel Advocate*, 19 May 1949, p. 313.

8 Gus Nichols, *Gospel Advocate*, 18 August 1949, p. 523.

9 Advertisement, *Gospel Advocate*, 4 May 1950, p. 294.

10 Ibid., 19 May 1949, p. 313.

11 Ibid., 26 October 1950, p. 694.

12 Gus Nichols, *Gospel Advocate*, 4 July 1946, p. 646.

13 Ibid., 7 July 1949, p. 424.

14 Pervie Nichols, *Gospel Advocate*, "Nichols To Greenville, Mississippi," 15 September 1949, p. 588.

15 Willard Collins, *Gospel Advocate*, "The Gus Nichols Story," 2 March 1961, pp. 136-37.

16 William Woodson, Private Papers, "Did Churches of Christ Originate In The Restoration Movement," unpublished, p. 9.

17 William Woodson, "Reflections: My Life In Preaching I and II," Unpublished, 28 August 1997, p. 3.

18 William Woodson, *The Restoration Movement And Unity, Freed-Hardeman College, Preachers And Church Leaders Forum*, October 12, 1985, Henderson: Freed-Hardeman College, 1986, pp. 137-38.

19 Advertisement, *Gospel Advocate*, 3 March 1949, pp. 138-39.

20 R. K. Akers, *Gospel Advocate*, 30 June 1949, p. 413. Note: Three baptisms and one restoration in the Lincoln Park meeting.

21 Paul Hunton, *Gospel Advocate*, 16 June 1949. p. 380.

22 Buford Holt, *Gospel Advocate*, 22 September 1949, p. 633.

23 Buford Holt, *Firm Foundation*, 25 October 1949, p. 14.

24 Farris J. Smith, *Gospel Advocate*, 27 October 1949, p. 682.

25 Billy Nicks, *Gospel Advocate*, 3 November 1949, p. 698.

26 W. T. Hamilton, *Gospel Advocate*, 27 October 1949, p. 682. Also reported in *Firm Foundation*, 25 October 1949, p. 11.

27 Joe S. Hyde, *Gospel Advocate*, 23 February 1950, p. 123.

28 Ibid., 3 August 1950, p. 497.

29 Advertisement, "The Lecture Program Of The Montgomery Bible College, (March 6-10)" *Gospel Advocate*, 2 March 1950, pp. 141-42.

30 J. G. Binkley, *Gospel Advocate*, 27 April 1950, p. 274.

31 W. Gaddys Roy, *Gospel Advocate*, 27 April 1950, p. 272.

32 Ibid., 29 June 1950, p. 416.

33 E. W. Guthrie, *Gospel Advocate*, 29 June 1950, p. 417.

34 Note: It might be good to insert here that a follow-up debate between Nichols and Welch took place in Montgomery, Alabama, the 20th through the 23rd of February of the following year. This debate was conducted in the City Auditorium and was widely supported by the brethren. Rex Turner (1913-2001) reported on the success of this discussion in *GA* 17 May 1951, p. 315 saying, "Brother Nichols defended the truth in a masterful way. He did not let a single argument pass. We are fortunate to have men like Brother Nichols who can so ably defend the truth. The propositions discussed were concerning the Holy Spirit and the Godhead."

35 Howard A. Blazer, *Gospel Advocate*, 8 June 1950, p. 373. Note: An abbreviated report was sent to the *Firm Foundation*, 6 June 1950, p. 9.

36 Nichols, Pervie, "Nichols-Busbee Debate," *Gospel Advocate*, 20 July 1950, page 469.

37 Basil Overton, ed., *The World Evangelist*, December 1975, p. 3.

38 Earl Fly, *Gospel Advocate*, 2 November 1950, p. 707.

39 C. C. Jones, *Gospel Advocate*, 5 October 1950, p. 642.

Childhaven

> Pure religion and undefiled before God and the
> Father is this, to visit the fatherless and widows
> in their affliction, and to keep himself unspotted
> from the world.
> —The Brother of the Lord, James 1:27

Benevolent care for orphans and widows has long been a concern for Christians. Its tie to "pure religion" as recorded by the New Testament writer James has made such duty essential. Within churches of Christ, the earliest of the homes instituted in the 20th century for this purpose was the Tennessee Orphan Home that began in September of 1909. By 1950, there were twelve known entities among the brotherhood for the sole purpose of caring for the needs of orphaned children.[1]

Long had there been a desire among many brethren for Alabama to have a home to take care of needy children. As far back as the early 1920s in Berry with Gus Nichols' associations with Frank Baker (1868-1928), Hal P. McDonald (1879-1959), and others, were there discussions about the need for just such an organized program in the state.[2] Gus long believed in and supported the children's home concept, having promoted them and utilized their services in the past.[3]

An advertisement under the title, "A New Home For Homeless Children," appeared on the back page of the 15 December 1949 issue of the *Gospel Advocate*. What followed was an explanation of how a contract had been signed on the 17th day of November for the purchase of a 349-acre tract of land with buildings in rural Cullman, Alabama for the purpose of establishing a children's home. The main property had served as a children's home operated by the Independent Order of Odd Fellows but had been closed for several years. The property sold for $50,000.00, with earnest money being paid in advance in the hopes of raising $30,000.00 over the next 90 days to pay off the debt.

The Board of Trustees included a list of seventeen men from various parts of the state of Alabama. All were members of churches of Christ and most were businessmen. Several were deacons and elders of different congregations in the state. Two of the men on the board were preachers, Rufus David Underwood (1908-1955) at that time, of the Central congregation in Huntsville, and "Gus Nichols, Evangelist, Jasper, Alabama."[4]

On the back page of the first issue of the *Advocate* in January 1951 was another advertisement under the title, "Childhaven (Orphan Home) Cullman, Alabama." In it, Gus introduced the family of brother J. L. Brock, who was to be superintendent of the institution. The article was an appeal for support with several passages of Scriptures used to admonish brethren as to the need to, "Remember The Poor."[5]

Wendell Winkler, Gus Nichols, S. F. Hester
Goodsprings Church of Christ

Further, Gus made an appeal to those in attendance at his sessions at the Freed-Hardeman Lectures. Building a case for the need for this and all of the brotherhood homes he enquired, "What are we going to do with all the illegitimate children born in the world?"[6] Again, in the Lipscomb Winter Lectures he made an appeal in his discourse entitled, "The Christian Life in the New Testament Church."[7]

The first to raise a concern over church support of Childhaven, and orphanages in general, was by the preacher at Woodlawn in Birmingham, Hershel Erwin Patton (1917-2010). Under the title, "Have We Been Preaching the Wrong Thing?" he questioned doing benevolent work beyond the local church and taking special collections in the Bible Class setting for special works, like Childhaven, in addition to the regular Sunday collection.[8]

"CHILDHAVEN" FOR 100 HOMELESS—This is the I. O. O. F. Home located two miles from Cullman on U. S. 31 which has been purchased by Alabama members of the Church of Christ for a home for homeless children. A drive to raise $117,000 to renovate the property is now underway.

Church Of Christ Purchases Site Near Cullman For Children's Home

CULLMAN, Ala., Dec. 10—The I. O. O. F. Home located off U. S. 31 some two miles from here, has been purchased by Alabama members of the Church of Christ for children's home.

The home will be known as "Childhaven" and is expected to be opened next September with an enrollment of 100 children.

The Board of Trustees of the home Saturday launched a drive to raise $117,000 for renovation of the present buildings on the site here. T. E. Gossett, chairman of the finance committee, said about 20 per cent of the needed funds already has been spoken for.

"Funds," he said, "are being accepted from friends who have a desire to be a part of this great humanitarian and Christian work. While business houses are not solicited for contributions, voluntary offerings of equipment will be gladly accepted."

MR. GOSSETT asked all contributions be sent to "Childhaven," P. O. Box 142, Birmingham.

Members of the Church of Christ in Alabama have for more than a year been working on plans to provide a facility for homeless children.

A non-profit organization was formed and chartered under state laws, and a Board of Trustees was formed.

Mr. Gossett said the trustees at first planned to build a home. But that the original intention was changed when it was found that the I. O. O. F. property here was up for sale and that it had been built for an orphan's home.

Children between the ages of 2 and 12 will be accepted. They will be kept at "Childhaven" until they are through high school.

The trustees plan to help the grown youngsters get a start in college or in the world of business, as is the case.

IN ADDITION to administrative offices and reception rooms, there will be a dining hall, a kitchen, manual training shops and sewing rooms.

The basement will be turned into indoor play rooms and will include manual training shops and sewing rooms.

A dairy barn on the property will be renovated to care for some 20 cows. A laundry building will be reconditioned to meet the needs of the new home.

"Childhaven" will make use of the enclosed swimming pool located some 200 yards south of the main building and fed by an all-year-round spring.

There are two other springs on the property and it is planned to build a lake and stock it with fish.

Mr. Gossett said the farm facilities on the site will be used "in every possible way to produce food and income for the home." He said the trustees contemplated hiring a farm manager.

The home, located near Cullman city limits, is serviced with city water and also has a deep well on its grounds.

* * *

AT A RECENT meeting of the trustees, a building committee was selected to guide the renovation of the property. The group will select an architect shortly.

Members of the "Childhaven" board of trustees are:

Dr. Glenn D. Davis, Montgomery, president; Mr. Gossett, Birmingham, vice president; W. Ralph Wharton, Birmingham, secretary-treasurer; Dan P. Barber, Birmingham, counsel; Gus Nichols, Jasper; A. C. McGinn, Jasper; Dr. M. E. Barrett and Murry Dodd, Decatur; Rufus D. Underwood, Huntsville; K. L. Heflington and M. L. McCain, Arab; Leonard W. Thompson, Cullman; Leo King, Florence; C. H. McDonald, Mobile; Judge J. O. English, Elba, and W. B. Jeffres, Dothan.

Mr. Thompson is chairman of the building committee. Other members are Dr. Barrett, Mr. King and Mr. Heffington.

Newspaper clipping - Childhaven

The first critical attack on the newly proposed children's home came from the pen of John T. Lewis (1876-1967). Long-time friend, confidant, and supporter of Gus Nichols, the Birmingham preacher came to the discussion with deep dissatisfaction with the plan. Otis Castleberry (1921-2007), biographer of the life of brother Lewis, related a story from around this time recalled to him by Flavil. He recounted how that,

> He and brother John T. Lewis went to call on Ben Horton, following the death of Brother Horton's mother. When they returned from their hurried visit to the Hortons, Flavil stopped the car in front of the Lewis' home. It was pouring rain, and Brother Lewis hesitated for a moment. "Flavil are you in a hurry?" "No!" "Kill the motor." "Now, Flavil, your dad's on this board to organize an orphan's home," Brother Lewis said, "I'm against it. I think he is wrong, dead wrong. I'm going to do some writing about it. I'm going to call his name in it, but I know Gus Nichols; its not going to alienate him and me. We'll still be friends when it is all over, and it won't make any difference between you and me, unless you want it too." Flavil assured him that he certainly didn't "want it to make a difference."[9]

What followed was an eight-article series written by Lewis that appeared in the local newspaper in the Ensley, *Steel City Star*, under the heading "Childhaven."[10] Throughout this run of articles the name of Gus Nichols appeared no less that thirty-five times in light of the older preacher's disagreement with the proposed children's home.

John T. Lewis

Copies of some of the articles were picked up and reproduced in Roy E. Cogdill's (1907-1985) Texas paper, *The Gospel Guardian*, and other papers. The *Gospel Advocate* reproduced Lewis' third article in the 26 April 1951 edition. The article was mainly a treatise on Lewis' understanding of 1 Timothy 5:1-16. At the end of the piece he rhetorically questioned, "Is this Somerite foam? Borrow brother Gus Nichols' glasses and see if you can see 'Childhaven' in these verses."[11]

G. C. Brewer (1884-1956), a long-time supporter of the idea of churches supporting Christian Colleges and Children's Homes led a counter-attack in the pages of the *Gospel Advocate*. While Lewis' article, mentioned above, appeared beginning on page 265, Brewer's article, under the title, "Brother Lewis and Childhaven" appeared beginning on page 263. Though friends with Lewis since college days at Nashville Bible School, Brewer's irritation at the whole matter led him to characterize Lewis' article as not being "Somerite foam," but said, "I can testify that it is a Ketcherside fallacy, one hundred percent perfect!"[12]

Newspaper clipping - Home at Cullman

In brief, brother Brewer's allusion to "Somerite Foam" was a reference to the late Indiana preacher/editor Daniel Sommer (1850-1940) and his reputation for wielding a fiery pen when encountering various adversaries. The "Ketcherside fallacy" comment was in view of Missouri preacher, William Carl Ketcherside's (1908-1989) reputation during that time for his legalistic tendencies. He had been stirring the orphan home controversy for several years, having debated Roland Rue Porter (1890-1967) on the subject in Ozark, Missouri, in March 1937.

Of course, Lewis responded three weeks later saying that Brewer's comment left him, "flat as a flounder."[13] He went on to explain that he had determined to take all his articles on Childhaven and put them in a tract for free distribution to the brotherhood. Brewer continued to address the issue on into July by saying that he had not seen Lewis' tract but initiated his intentions of taking it point by point and responding to his arguments in a tract of his own.[14]

Meanwhile, Gus carried on with his work. His assigned topic for the February 1952 David Lipscomb College Lectures was, "The Gospel And The Care Of Orphans."[15] Other opportunities to discuss the topic were presented in several places and in different formats. But for certain, he was a man of integrity. He was the veritable student of the Word! He believed he was right in his understanding of the Scriptures on the subject. There was no relenting with Gus Nichols when he believed a thing to be true. He intended to support and promote Childhaven, and for him there was no turning back. When the March financial statement for the institution was posted, there were several names of the trustees who loaned or contributed money to assist in getting the home off the ground. Included in the list was an entry for trustees A. C. McGlaun and Gus Nichols having loaned $2,000.00.[16]

To say the orphan home issue took its toll on the brotherhood is an understatement. While questions over church-supported Christian colleges, orphanages, and homes for the aged had long been discussed and debated in several locales in previous decades, the reaction to Childhaven brought the dispute to a head in brotherhood discussions like it never had until that point. Over the next twenty years a strong vibrant church was made weaker through division and separation into smaller, and less productive fellowships. Divisions over how to take care of orphans and widows became so sharp that congregations split, and families were divided. The Nichols family was not left untouched by the divisions. Relationships were strained even between Gus and his brothers, Charlie and Carey, over the subject. Others in the Nichols family were affected in dramatic and hurtful ways. In the end, many men went to their graves in deep sorrow over broken relationships that came about as a result of this dispute.[17]

Despite the controversial nature of supporting Childhaven, Gus never flinched in promoting the work. Later his son, Flavil, joined the board of directors of the institution as well. In later years, Childhaven honored brother Nichols by naming one of its newly built homes, the Gus Nichols Cottage.

MUTUAL LOVE
By Gus Nichols

I love you. I love you because your very heart is so much like my own, but my greatest need and joy of life is to ever have you by my side.

I love you because your very presence makes me happy and your voice, to my ear, is sweeter than the melody of song or the music of the violin.

I love you because your high ideals match, and even surpass my own. You have been able to reach down deep into my heart and discover lovely virtues which no other looked quite deep enough to find.

I love you because you are the inspiration which I need and because your countenance drives away darkness as the glowing light of the morning sun.

I love you because you have a sympathetic understanding of all my weaknesses; and yet, you love me despite them all. Your love for me is cherished far above all earth's silver and gold.

I love you because you have already made me very happy and enriched my soul with a joy which only you can impart, and you have done it without any effort, without a word; by simply being yourself. Your natural goodness, loving spirit, have been more than enough for the longings of my heart, for someone who could fill it and bless it with a fragrance of love divine.

I love you more than ever before because I'm now to take you to be with me and to be mine; to live in my heart and in my life; to be a part of me and all that I am or ever shall become, as long as we both shall live in this beautiful, wonderful world.

In a word, I love you because you are you, and because God drew us to each other and brought us to this hour and to this alter, where we, like two rippling rivers, are to become united and submerged, each losing itself in the other, to ever afterward flow on together toward a silvery sea of a glorious eternity.

We're now to become one flesh, one heart, and one soul, with a stream of our life ever deepening and widening to the enrichment of that nobler life which we together are to make more abundant and sweet for ourselves.

Only God can know all the reasons why I love you; but since you are giving me the rest of your life, may I just say now, with all my heart, I love you—and then spend the rest of my life proving I do![18]

ENDNOTES

1 Harold G. Hunt, *Firm Foundation*, 1 November 1966, p. 695. Note: The Hunt report added that there were eight orphan homes before 1940, six before 1930, and two before 1920. According to the 1966 article, there were sixty such institutions to date.

2 Baker, Frank *Firm Foundation*, 20 June 1922, p. 5. Note: Baker sent in a report about a brother who had produced a tract and was selling it for 25 cents each saying that, "the proceeds will go to building up an orphan home in Alabama."

3 Note: In November 1947 Gus had the young men of the Tennessee Orphan Home come to Jasper to conduct the worship services at Fifth Avenue in his absence one Sunday (*GA*, 27 November 1947, p. 978). The following year Gus had sent five brothers and sisters from one family to the Children's Home in Spring Hill, Tennessee, after he had preached the funeral of their young mother. (*GA*, 19 February 1948, p. 187.)

4 Advertisement, "A New Home For Homeless Children," *Gospel Advocate*, 15 December 1949, p. 800.

5 Ibid., "Childhaven," *Gospel Advocate*, 4 January 1951, p. 16.

6 John T. Lewis, *Childhaven*, Birmingham: Star Publishing Co., p. 6.

7 Advertisement, *Gospel Advocate*, 11 January 1951, p. 28.

8 H. E. Patton, *Gospel Advocate*, 22 June 1950, pp. 397-98.

9 Otis L. Castleberry, *He Looked For A City*, Fairmount: Cogdill Foundation 1980, pp. 182-83.

10 John T. Lewis, "Brother Lewis And Childhaven," *Gospel Advocate*, 17 May 1951, p. 309.

11 John T. Lewis, "Childhaven," *Gospel Advocate*, 26 April 1951, p. 265.

12 G. C. Brewer, "Brother Lewis And Childhaven," *Gospel Advocate*, 26 April 1951, p. 263.

13 John T. Lewis, "Brother Lewis And Childhaven," *Gospel Advocate*, 17 May 1951, p. 309.

14 G. C. Brewer, "The Review Is Forthcoming," *Gospel Advocate*, 12 July 1951, p. 440.

15 Advertisement, *Firm Foundation*, 8 January 1952, p. 9.

16 W. H. Camp, *Firm Foundation*, 5 August 1952, p. 14.

17 Note: These sentiments were seen in an interview with Flavil. In 2015, while visiting him in the home of his daughter, Peggy Champion, we were discussing various things about his father's life. When I asked him a question about how the cooperation issues affected his family, he looked down at the floor. After many seconds of silence, I asked if he was OK. At that, he looked at me and said, "It still hurts too much!"

18 Note: This poem was contributed by the Nichols' granddaughter, Vicki Blackwood. It is thought that Gus wrote this in 1959 at the request of a young man who wanted something special to be read at his wedding. Over the next several years, Gus read this poem at the weddings he performed for his own grandchildren. After his death, others in the family read the poem at the weddings of the Nichols' great-grandchildren. On page 4 of the 9 June 1971 issue of *Words of Truth*, the poem was published under the title, "I Love You."

- 34 -

Broadening Influence

Wisdom crieth without; she uttereth her voice in the streets: She crieth in the chief place of concourse, in the openings of the gates: in the city she uttereth her words.
—Solomon, Proverbs 1:20-21

THE GALLATIN-NASHVILLE DISCUSSION

Arguably, the most renowned proponent of premillennialism among churches of Christ in the early 20th century was Louisville, Kentucky, preacher Robert Henry Boll (1879-1956). Beginning in 1909, Boll was the front-page editor for the *Gospel Advocate*. His published views on eschatology led to his departure in 1915. Taking the editorship of the paper, *Word And Work*, in 1916, he was able to continue to promote his premillennial views. During the year 1927, the *Gospel Advocate* served as venue for a written discussion between R. H. Boll and H. Leo Boles (1874-1946), the President of David Lipscomb College. The following year, the *Advocate* published the work under the title, *Unfulfilled Prophecy: A Discussion On Prophetic Themes*. But, to most it became known as the Boles-Boll Debate.

H. Leo Boles

When the opportunity to meet Gus Nichols in an oral debate arose, brother Boll initially accepted the challenge. To this point, he had never entered the verbal platform for debating purposes. While he did not mind defending his views, face-to-face debating was not his preferred mode of doing so.[1] Efforts were made to organize a discussion between Boll and Nichols in July 1952. The plan for each participant was to preach six times, three evenings of which were to be held in Gallatin, Tennessee, followed by three scheduled evenings in Nashville. As announced, "The doctrine of the premillennial coming of Christ will be discussed, also related subjects such as: the kingdom of God, the throne of David, the resurrection, the thousand years, is the second coming of Christ imminent? Does God have a special program and purpose for Israel?"[2]

After several weeks of planning, R. H. Boll cited an "awkward time arrangement," as the reason he would not attend to the appointed effort. Wanting to see the debate go on, he reached out to Frank M. Mullins (1901-1964),[3] the preacher for the Fair Park church of Christ in Dallas, Texas, to step in and defend the premillennial position. Mullins had been connected with Boll and his *Word And Work* paper since the late 1920s and served as its queries editor for a time. In light of his inability to attend, Boll wrote, "I trust you will not think that I am in any wise afraid or ashamed to stand up for my beliefs and convictions, either on the questions in dispute among us, or any other line of the Bible's teaching. I never have been nor intend to be so."[4]

R. H. Boll

Billed the "Gallatin-Nashville Discussion," the initial meeting took place at the Gallatin High School Hall on the nights of 7-9 July and concluded the last three nights at the building of the Charlotte Avenue church of Christ in Nashville, the 10th-12th. Each speaker alternated in order each night, Gus Nichols being the first speaker on "Monday, Wednesday and Friday."[5]

In the crowd, for some part of the week was Louisville preacher, and co-editor of *The Word And Work*, Elmer Leon Jorgenson (1886-1968). He reported that, "The all-round behavior and courtesy of the brethren who attended, and of those who were in position of hosts to the meetings, was, of course, beyond all criticism."[6] He spoke highly of Mullins' defense of the premillennial position, expressing his demeanor as leaving, "an impression upon all, I think, in complete harmony with his settled character as a clean-thinking, high-toned, spiritual man of God."[7] Jorgenson's observations toward the competitor were less glowing. Referring to him as "Gus Nichol of Jasper, La.," [sic] he said,

> The other speaker, though not unbrotherly in companion with some we have heard on these lines, seemed to look upon the meetings as more of the nature of a debate, and spent much time in rebuttal—not only against what Mullins was saying, but against the many things—true or untrue—that the brethren of "the premillennial view" have been reported to believe. But this difference in the approach of the two speakers is, of course, only a reflection of their different attitudes—the one believing that our prophetic differences are not rightfully a bar to fellowship;

the other of the view, apparently, that the lines have been drawn and must still be justified.[8]

The outcome of the discussion proved convincing to some, as it was reported that three deacons and an elder left the old congregation in Gallatin where premillennialism had become the prevalent view and joined themselves with the new work that began on South Waters Avenue. The work there had been established the previous April, with about forty-six members, but after the debate the church swelled to "eighty members," many of whom had come from the premillennial group.[9]

It was not until 1954 that Gus was able to come back to South Waters Avenue for a strengthening and evangelistic effort. Virgil R. Richie (1913-2004)[10] was the minister there at the time, and more than happy to have the debater come and assist in solidifying the work. A new building had just been built, and in the new environment there was a wonderful spirit of unity. At the close of the effort Richie reported,

> Gus Nichols has just closed one of the best meetings this church has ever had. There were fourteen baptisms and four to place membership. One has been baptized since the meeting. Brother Nichols did some of the best preaching I have ever heard. The building was filled almost every evening. The church here is making more progress than ever since the new building has been completed.[11]

CLUBS AND SUBSCRIPTION DRIVES

For many years of its existence, the *Gospel Advocate* enjoyed a great increase in influence due to a great marketing plan. They encouraged readers, especially gospel preachers, to build clubs, or cluster groups of subscriptions. Meeting preachers often went into different areas for their preaching opportunities and would promote the paper in order to add subscriptions to a club drive being done in a particular time period. Very few in the brotherhood were any better at promoting the *Advocate*, than Gus Nichols. For several years, reports were given of his sending in subscription numbers from time to time. His brothers and sons were good at promoting the paper as well. One of the biggest records set for sending in subscriptions was for a club that was noted in April 1952. Nearly two pages were devoted to the long list of those who sent in subscriptions, and at the top of the list was Gus Nichols. His picture was included with the following,

> This Is It!! From week to week we have been calling attention to a large club that was in the making. This week the big club has been received. Gus Nichols, from Jasper, Ala., sends us three hundred sixty-seven subscriptions. This is the largest club that we have

received during this pre-price-increase drive for subscriptions. So far as we know it is the largest club that the *Gospel Advocate* has ever received. Brother Nichols has set a high standard. Who will surpass what he has done? Would you like to try? Frankly, we should like to see this record broken. Brother Nichols writes: "I always enjoy working for the *Advocate*. Like its writers, it is not perfect, but it is sure to be a blessing to all homes in which it is read."[12]

LECTURES ON PREACHING

Abilene Christian College began a series in late 1951 called, "Lectures on Preaching." The first series was held in December, and the guest speaker for the event was long-time preacher for the Skillman Avenue church in Dallas, Texas, John H. Banister (1910-1995).[13] The second annual event was held from 8-12 December 1952. The guest speaker was Gus Nichols. The program was "designed particularly for students, but preachers and other interested persons"[14] were invited. His schedule for the event included addresses on, "Preachers and Preaching" (I and II); "The Preacher's Manner of Life," "The Call To Preach," "Preaching Out of the Overflow" (V and VI); "The Sermon," "The Material of the Sermon" and "The Delivery of the Sermon" (IX and X).[15] It is interesting to note that the following year, B. C. Goodpasture (1885-1977) served as the school's third person to conduct the "Lectures on Preaching."

MONTGOMERY BIBLE COLLEGE GETS A NEW NAME

Gus Nichols' connection with Montgomery Bible College went back to its early days of existence. By the mid-1940s, he was making regular trips to the campus to assist in the annual lecture program.

At the December 1952 meeting of the Board of Trustees, various questions arose on the viability of the school, and as to whether it was meeting the needs of the state of Alabama in the best possible way. Leading up to the meeting, brother Nichols had been asked his impressions of what could be done to make the school more viable and useful to the brethren. In the exchange, he expressed his concern at the limited appeal regionally for the college. In his thinking, as it was the only college among churches of Christ in the state, the institution should appeal to the people of the whole state. Remembering his days as a student of the then defunct Alabama Christian College in Berry, it was his estimation that the present name of the Montgomery-based college should be replaced with the more inclusive and wide-spread appealing designation, Alabama Christian College. The suggestion was met with positive response by the members of the Board of Trustees. The result was a unanimous decision to raise the banner of Alabama Christian College once again.

Announcements were forthcoming in brotherhood journals. A full-page advertisement appeared early in 1953 in the *Firm Foundation* revealing in bold print,

> Now Alabama Christian College, formerly Montgomery Bible College. In order to more adequately reflect the territory and scope of work at the Montgomery Bible College, The Board of Trustees voted in their quarterly meeting—December 19—to officially change the name of the school to Alabama Christian College.[16]

Six years later, when an opening on the Board of Trustees for the college came vacant, board member, Joseph Franklin Camp (1915-1991) proposed the name of Gus Nichols as a practical and enterprising choice. Representing his fellow leaders, he approached Gus about joining the board. Thrilled at the opportunity to help the college in this capacity, he accepted the invitation with great humility. Beginning in 1958, he served on the Board of Trustees for Alabama Christian College and continued in that role for the remainder of his life.[17]

A YEAR OF PREACHING AND TEACHING

The year of 1952, like so many before it, was filled with activity for Gus Nichols and his family. At the early January session of the annual lectures at Freed-Hardeman, the queries part of the program was handed over to Guy Napoleon Woods (1908-1993), due largely to the fact that Gus was known for his voluminous dealings with each topic that arose for discussion. In other words, he took too long, not allowing for many questions to be handled during each session. Woods had a legal background and was able to move more rapidly through the questions. However, Gus Nichols' presence was most certainly felt. If questions arose that he deemed necessary to weigh in on he was always given right-of-passage to the podium.

Most noted of issue between Nichols and Woods was their differing views on the work of the Holy Spirit. Nichols held to the personal indwelling of the Holy Spirit, while Woods held to the influence of the Holy Spirit being through the Scriptures alone. Their opposing views on this subject allowed for friendly banter between the two for many years. While they both were most sincere in their beliefs on the subject, their repartee was often a highlight of the annual program among those in attendance. That year, Gus' assigned topic was on the subject of "Basic Denominational Errors."[18]

In the previous chapter, it was noticed that Gus spoke on the David Lipscomb College Lectures in February 1952 on the subject, "The Gospel And The Care For Orphans." He also dealt with the topic, "The Gospel And

The Education Of Youth."¹⁹ In March, he lectured daily on the Alabama Christian College Lectures on, "Paul's Epistles."²⁰ "In April, he headed out to Gainesville, Texas, to preach a meeting at the Commerce Street church. W. T. and Carrie were living and working there at the time.²¹ Toward the end of the month, N. B. Hardeman (1874-1965) made his way to Jasper for the spring gospel meeting. Closing on the 27th, Gus penned the following,

> He did some of the best preaching I have ever heard. He is now at his best. All know that he has been a preacher, second to none in power and ability. Notwithstanding his great preaching in past years, he never could preach quite so well and so powerfully as now. We feel fortunate to have had him with us and that Sister Hardeman could be with him.²²

Mr. and Mrs. N. B. Hardeman

In May, Gus headed back out to Texas to preach a meeting at the Tenth and Broad Street church in Wichita Falls. Then, in July, he was in Anniston, Alabama at the Central congregation where seven obeyed the gospel.²³

The fall meeting at Jasper was attended to by Nashville preacher, Herbert Ernest Winkler (1889-1983). After the meeting he sent in a report

Gus and Matilda Nichols
with other family members

Broadening Influence

expressing, "On August 31 I preached at Jasper, Ala., the home of Gus Nichols. Brother Nichols held one of the best meetings in my memory last fall at Charlotte Avenue in Nashville, my home congregation."[24]

Day Speakers on the Lectureship

Frank VanDyke
G. K. Wallace
Earle West
Gus Nichols
Kelley Doyle
Frank Pack

1951 - Lectureship Day Speakers
FHC *Treasure Chest* Yearbook

Day Speakers

Gus Nichols
Guy Woods
Homer Hailey
Frank Van Dyke
G. K. Wallace

1952 Lectureship Day Speakers
1952 FHC *Treasure Chest* Yearbook

Thus, the broadening influence of the preacher from Jasper continued to be felt in several areas in the brotherhood. In 1952 he made three trips to Texas, at least three trips to Tennessee, and to several places in Alabama for meetings, lectures, and debates.

ENDNOTES

1 Note: On page 32 of the February 1936 issue of *The Word And Work*, R. H. Boll wrote an article entitled, "About Religious Debates." The first sentence begins, "So far as my acquaintance with religious discussion goes, there is no poorer method of seeking to arrive at truth than a debate, especially oral debate." In Boll's opinion, oral discussions had little value, however there were "some advantages" in the written debate.

2 A. K. Gardner, *Gospel Advocate*, 12 June 1952, p. 388.

3 Gordon R. Linscott, ed., *The Word And Work*, June 1964, p. 156.

4 R. H. Boll, as reported by A. K. Gardner, *Gospel Advocate*, 3 July 1952, p. 436.

5 Ibid.

6 E. L. Jorgenson, "The Gallatin-Nashville Discussion," *The Word And Work*, August, 1952, p. 175.

7 Ibid.

8 Ibid.

9 Robert Dixon, *Gospel Advocate*, 2 October 1952, p. 644.

10 Note: Virgil Richard Richie (1913-2004) was born and reared in Atlanta, Georgia. He was converted at the old West End congregation under the preaching of brother Henry Clyde Hale (1901-1979). Hale encouraged him and his brother, Charlie, to preach at a young age. Brother Richie attended David Lipscomb College in the early 1950s, and his first work was at Gallatin. In later life, he worked many years at Riverdale, Georgia. His last years were at Fayetteville, Georgia, where he served as an elder under which your author served as minister. I was honored later to preach his funeral. Virgil loved brother Nichols. When Gus Nichols died in 1975, B. C. Goodpasture was in the middle of a gospel meeting at the Riverdale church. The meeting was completed by Richie when Goodpasture departed to preach brother Nichols' funeral in Jasper, Alabama.

11 Virgil R. Richie, *Gospel Advocate*, 9 September 1954, p. 717.

12 B. C. Goodpasture, ed., *Gospel Advocate*, 10 April 1952, p. 226.

13 "Named Pastor Plans Talk, Abilene," News Report, *The Odessa, Texas American*, p. 2. Note: A more lengthy report also appeared in *The Abilene Reporter-News*, under the title, "'Preach Christ And Not Selves,' Ministers Admonished At ACC," 9 December 1952, p. 6-B.

14 Walter E. Burch, "Gus Nichols Guest Speaker At Abilene Christian College," *Gospel Advocate*, 11 December 1952, p. 812.

15 Advertisement, *Gospel Advocate*, 3 December 1953, p. 832.

16 Announcement, *Firm Foundation*, 13 January 1953, p. 15. The announcement also appeared in *Gospel Advocate*, 15 January 1953, p. 32.

17 *The Alabama Christian Reporter*, December 1975, Volume 21, Number 5, p. 3.

18 W. A. Bradfield, "Freed-Hardeman Lectureship," *Firm Foundation*, 1 January 1952, p. 14.

19 Willard Collins, "Program Announced For Lipscomb Winter Lectures," *Gospel Advocate*, 3 January 1952, p. 11.

20 Rex Turner, "Montgomery Bible College Lecture Program," *Gospel Advocate*, 7 February 1952, p. 94.

21 W. T. Hamilton, *Gospel Advocate*, 31 January 1952, p. 75. Note: Notice and report on the annual success of W. T.'s labors appeared in the *Firm Foundation*, 4 February 1952, p. 10.

22 Gus Nichols, *Gospel Advocate*, 19 June 1952, p. 402.

23 W. Douglas Harris, *Gospel Advocate*, 30 October 1952, p. 706.

24 Herbert E. Winkler, *Gospel Advocate*, 30 October 1952, p. 708.

- 35 -

My Choice Hobby

> The Lord gave the word: great was the company of those that published it.
> —David, Psalms 68:11

Throughout the 1950s, the *Gospel Advocate* knew of no greater supporter than Gus Nichols. He and its editor, B. C. Goodpasture (1895-1977), shared a mutual admiration that was clearly seen in most every issue. As the magazine moved closer and closer to its centennial year of production, a campaign to boost subscriptions to 50,000 was implemented. To meet the new goal of increased circulation, a friendly competition was set among the friends of the brotherhood paper.

As has already been noted, in 1952, Gus sent in a very large subscription list. Spring boarding from it, a good write-up appeared on the 2nd of April the following year with his photo under the title, "Brother Nichols' Club and Letter." Congratulatory remarks followed for sending in a whopping 330 subscriptions during the first quarter of the year, a little shy of the 367 he sent the entire previous year. In the letter brother Nichols sent with the club of subscriptions, he explained his success in distributing the paper as an evangelistic tool. He said,

> It has been a joy to get these subscriptions. It is my choice hobby, and I believe a good work which will live on. If the Lord wills, I shall send in other lists before long. I send the paper free to at least twelve persons each year, then check results. Through this means I have led several friends to obey the gospel, and others who formerly were very prejudiced against the truth are now friendly toward the church. After reading the paper for only one year, a denominational preacher began sending us an occasional contribution to our radio program. I think yet he will obey the gospel.
>
> If every gospel preacher would send in a large list of subscriptions from the field where he labors, his own work would be made much lighter by the weekly visits of the *Gospel Advocate*, and we would go above the 50,000 subscription goal set for the one hundredth anniversary of the *Gospel Advocate*. I think it a mark of distinction to be a subscriber to a religious paper and especially the *Gospel Advocate*.[1]

My Choice Hobby

In April of 1954, he sent in still another grand list of subscriptions. Under the title, "Brother Nichols Goes Over The Top," it was said,

> Gus Nichols, of Jasper, Ala., sends us a club of two hundred ninety-six and writes: "It is always a joy to influence people to subscribe for the *Gospel Advocate*. I have known of many persons who were converted to the truth in this section by reading this paper. I try to be just as zealous in teaching through the printed page as orally from the pulpit. I now think that the *Advocate* is going to every family thought to be faithful in the Fifth Avenue church of Christ (Jasper). . . .Many of our members subscribe for other people whom they either hope to convert or strengthen in the faith." Well done, Brother Nichols! May your tribe increase! We are grateful to all who have made this fine list possible.[2]

Throughout the year, more subscriptions were turned in, and the numbers continued to increase. In August, he sent in fifty-eight subscriptions stating his intended goal of sending in 500 by the end of the year.[3]

The centennial year of the existence of the *Gospel Advocate* was 1955. A goal was initially set for 50,000 subscriptions to be added to its present circulation. Response was so good by the brotherhood that by April the goal was doubled to 100,000.[4] Gus was doing his part, as the following issue reported that he had sent in 533 more subscriptions.[5] After receiving his copy of the centennial edition of the paper in July, he penned the following,

> I shall strive for the 2,000 by April 1, 1956. It is a great joy and a wonderful favor to get the *Gospel Advocate* started into any home. It is a pity that more people have not experienced the joy and satisfaction that comes from increasing the circulation of this paper. I am already sixty-three years of age and fully realize that at best, most of my life on earth has passed and gone, but since the century edition of the paper came out, I shall feel during the rest of my days that the *Gospel Advocate* will be a more sacred visitor into our home than ever before. Just as the ground on which Moses stood was holy ground because of God's presence and blessing, so the *Gospel Advocate* has taken on a more holy and sacred aspect because God's truth has been disseminated through its pages for the past 100 years. The deepest of emotions well up in my soul as I think of the multiplied thousands of people who have been blessed, made better, and many of them saved through the influence of this medium of divine instruction. Thank God for the *Gospel Advocate*, and all other good religious papers

likewise standing for the truth, promoting peace and good works in the church of our Lord."

After its centennial celebration year, the *Advocate* initiated a "Second Century Drive." Beginning January 1 and ending on April 1, it was followed by an awards banquet that took place in the gymnasium on the campus of David Lipscomb College. There were 350 who attended the ceremonial dinner. It was announced that during the centennial year, subscriptions had increased 344%, and that the Second Century Drive had already seen 62,000 subscriptions turned in since the drive had gotten under way. Four cash prizes were presented to the highest contributors. The top contributor of more than 600 subscriptions was Gus Nichols. He received a $100 prize that was presented to him by editor, B. C. Goodpasture.[6]

THE GOSPEL ADVOCATE FIVE HUNDRED CLUB

In late March 1956, the *Gospel Advocate* released a volume in honor of the paper's celebration of being in existence for 100 years. *The Gospel Advocate Centennial Volume* contained photos, biographical sketches, and articles written by all eleven of its past editors. These included Tolbert Fanning (1810-1874), William Lipscomb (1829-1908), E. G. Sewell (1830-1924), J. C. McQuiddy (1858-1924), A. B. Lipscomb (1876-1940), H. Leo Boles (1874-1946), James A. Allen (1884-1967), Foy E. Wallace, Jr. (1896-1979), John T. Hinds (1866-1938), as well as the current editor.

Beginning on page 274 of the volume was a chapter acknowledging the successes of the men who excelled in contributing above 500 subscriptions during the centennial effort to add 100,000. Called the "Five-Hundred Club," the list included Roy H. Lanier (1899-1980), Price Billingsley (1877-1959), Willard Collins (1915-2007), Ira North (1922-1984), Batsell Barrett Baxter (1916-1982), G. K. Wallace (1903-1988), Athens Clay Pullias (1910-1985), George Benson (1898-1991), and Guy N. Woods (1908-1993). But, the first to be listed was Gus Nichols.[7] His photo, along with a brief biographical sketch, was entered. Also, reference was made to a 1953 newspaper article that appeared in the Jasper local paper, *Mountain Eagle*. In it, the editor had commented on Gus' twenty years of serving the community by writing,

> During the score of years, he has comforted the bereaved, and has rejoiced with those who have recovered from serious illness or met with good fortune. In his bigness of spirit, unhurried way, and love for his fellow men and women, this man represents much that is finest in Jasper. Wouldn't it be appropriate for the people of Jasper to express their appreciation of this man in an appropriate way? He will probably be surprised at the foregoing suggestion, and may say he doesn't deserve any special recognition, but the people of Jasper know that he does.[8]

Chapter XIII
MEMBERS OF THE GOSPEL ADVOCATE FIVE HUNDRED CLUB

These have secured five hundred, or more, subscriptions to the Gospel Advocate since the Centennial Drive began. We appreciate their outstanding service in extending the circulation of the Advocate. All honor to them!

GUS NICHOLS
JASPER, ALABAMA
WILLARD COLLINS

When Gus Nichols was walking ten miles each day to work in a coal mine at approximately six dollars per week, he had no

GUS NICHOLS

Further expressed, was the great growth and influence Gus had given to his family. Sixteen preachers in the Nichols' immediate family were in the pulpit. Also revealed, was that he had conducted over 100 debates in his years in the ministry and had been a staff member for the *Gospel Advocate* since 1944. The article closed with,

> Gus Nichols wants to go to heaven and he lives accordingly. He has a very big heart, a wonderful knowledge of the scriptures, and he makes those in his audience determine to live a better life. Any person who has heard him preach on "The Blood of Christ," "The Love of God," or "The Faith of Abraham" must have left the service with more faith to live the Christian life.[9]

His ties to the *Advocate* arguably did more for his brotherhood-wide reputation than any other single work in which he labored. However, as has been seen, it was but one of the many ways in which he served in the Kingdom of his Lord at home and across the nation.

PROMOTING THE GOSPEL ADVOCATE

Gus saw writing in such a favorable light! Next to preaching, he envisaged the printed page, with its ability to engage a wide circulation, to be the best way to publish the gospel message. He loved writing for the *Gospel Advocate*. During the centennial-year drive, he wrote several times through the year to encourage people to subscribe to the paper, but in the process, he let all know his passion for it. In one report he said,

> I count it a great privilege as well as a distinct honor to have a part in the circulation of a paper so true to the Old Paths and to the word of God as is the *Gospel Advocate*. I am fully convinced that it is a great blessing to any family or individual to have the *Gospel Advocate* come as a weekly visitor to teach, and to encourage in the way of the Lord. It is next to having the great gospel preachers and writers of the paper sit down and discuss with us matters pertaining to our soul's welfare and the kingdom of God. I am positive in the conviction that the circulation of papers like the *Advocate* is the best and most effective way to spread the word through the printed page. It is a distinct honor in the first place to be a member of the church of our Lord, and to do what we can for the advancement of that church. It is also a mark of distinction to be a reader of a paper which has weathered the storms for one hundred years, as has the *Advocate*.[10]

Over the next few weeks, other passionate appeals appeared to convince readers to buy subscriptions. One most powerful push came in the way of a true-to-life illustration of the potential of using the paper in evangelism. He wrote,

R. F. Kilpatrick, Gurley, Ala., who is a fine gospel preacher, told me the following story: When he had been a member of the church only a few years but had never heard of the *Gospel Advocate* or any other religious paper published among churches of Christ, a very prominent Baptist preacher asked him one day if he had seen a certain article in the latest *Gospel Advocate*. He informed the preacher that he did not take the paper nor had he ever heard of it before. The Baptist preacher told him about the *Advocate* and offered to pay for it for Brother Kilpatrick, which he did. In the next few years Brother Kilpatrick had learned enough about the Bible to discuss religion with the preacher. As a result of the influence of the *Advocate* and Brother Kilpatrick's teaching, the preacher was convinced of the error of his way and gave up his position as a preacher in his denomination. There must be millions of people whose hearts are sick of religious divisions and in whose honest hearts there is a constant longing for a better knowledge of pure, simple, New Testament Christianity, without any mixture of the commandments of men, or of denominationalism. It is wonderful to be a simple New Testament Christian! A subscription to the *Gospel Advocate* will always help the honest heart. Don't be afraid to send it to your neighbor.[11]

ENDNOTES

1 B. C. Goodpasture, ed., "Brother Nichols' Club and Letter," *Gospel Advocate*, 2 April 1953, pp. 194, 204.

2 Ibid., "Brother Nichols Goes Over The Top," *Gospel Advocate*, 22 April 1954, p. 318.

3 Ibid., 12 August 1954, p. 638.

4 Ibid., 7 April 1955, p. 266.

5 Ibid., 14 April 1955, p. 301.

6 Ibid., 3 May 1956, p. 411.

7 Willard Collins, *The Gospel Advocate Centennial Volume*, Nashville: Gospel Advocate Company, 1956, p. 274.

8 "Editorials," *Mountain Eagle*, Thursday, 5 March 1953, p. 2a.

9 Willard Collins, *The Gospel Advocate Centennial Volume*, Nashville: Gospel Advocate Company, 1956, p. 276.

10 Gus Nichols, *Gospel Advocate*, 14 April 1955, p. 301.

11 Ibid., 26 May 1955, p. 410.

- 36 -

A Special Family

Behold, children are a heritage from the LORD, the fruit of the womb a reward. Like arrows in the hand of a warrior are the children of one's youth. Blessed is the man who fills his quiver with them!
—Solomon, Psalm 127:3-5

Eight children were gifts from God to Gus and Matilda. They thought that in them they understood the fullness of family joy. But, then, the grandchildren began coming along. As noted, the next generation of Nichols started in the mid 1940's with the birth of Gracie and Frank's son, Paul, October 1, 1945. Over the next eighteen years little Nichols grandkids sprung up all over the place. As was mentioned, Carrie and W. T.'s daughter, Kathy, was born the following year on the July 30th.

1950s - Gus and Matilda

Sometime that same year, Foy married Sarah Ann McCullough, a young woman from Townley. Their first son, Eddie, was born on June 22, 1947. They had a daughter the following year, Karen, born on July 11th. Gus Nichols "Nick" Hamilton was born June 11, 1949, and Gracie had a daughter, Janet, at the end of that same year on the 20th of December. Hardeman and Virginia had Judy, September 10, 1950. Rile and Bertha had Vicki early in the new year, February 6, 1951. Flavil and Mary followed with their first child, Jimmy, on May 3rd that year, and a daughter, Peggy, at the end of the following year, December 15, 1952. Ahead of Peggy in the count was Beth Nichols, born to Hardeman and Virginia, on May 7th that same year. In 1955, Vodie and A. J. welcomed their daughter, Pam, December 13th. Then, the Blackwoods gave Vicki a little brother, John, March 19, 1960.

While Hudson was attending Freed-Hardeman College, he began dating a young lady by the name of Marilyn Harwell. She and her twin sister, Carolyn, were from Corinth, Mississippi. The two were in the Sigma Rho

Club,[1] and sang together in the A Cappella Chorus. In due time, they fell deeply in love, and were married, October 8, 1950. Two years later, the two were deeply saddened at the birth of their first child. She delivered a little boy that perished in childbirth, November 9, 1952. The baby was laid to rest at Oak Hill Cemetery just north of Jasper. A daughter, Sharon, entered the world on December 18, 1954. Two boys followed, Ray, April 14, 1959, and Joe, April 24, 1963.

1960 - Nichols Family Photo

Altogether, sixteen grandchildren grew to maturity in and out of the Nichols family home.[2]

Fun and amusement are but a couple of words to describe the years of joy the grandchildren had when visiting Granddaddy and Grandmother Nichols. In the summer of 1958, the congregation at Jasper purchased the old Brown Funeral Home that stood on the west corner of 15th Street and 6th Avenue. The white three-story house had served grieving families in the community for many years, but being sold to the church, it was quickly transitioned to a home for the preacher and his family. Gus told his *Gospel Advocate* readers, "after twenty-five years at the same address I have moved just one block so as to be just across the street from our new meetinghouse."[3]

A Special Family

The move had some interesting twists. The old funeral home had an upstairs apartment. Living there at the time of the purchase was Oxford Myers, the preacher of the Bible Missionary Church, which had purchased the old Fifth Avenue building. Unbeknownst to Matilda, Gus was on the radio one day and announced that the Nichols and Myers were switching homes. Within days the Nichols had to load up everything and move into their new home.

The funeral home presented a few new problems for the aging couple. Even though there was a perfectly good apartment on the top floor, Matilda had bad knees, making it impossible to traverse the stairwell daily. So, the family had to make do with living on the main floor with its vast visiting parlors. They made their bedroom in the casket display room. As the room had no closets, makeshift armoires were made out of casket shipping crates. They stood the crates on end, and galvanized pipe was run through the tops, making it possible to hang up their clothes.

Grandchildren
L-R: Paul Young with hand on hip. Janet Young Watson, dark hair-Karen Nichols, holding doll, Peggy Nichols Champion, sucker in mouth, Jimmy Nichols, and Vicki Blackwood. Adults in back: Flavil Nichols with camera and A. J. Kerr. Note: The girls all had on dresses to play in; no pants or shorts.

As Gus and Matilda's children had families of their own at the time, it was very easy to be overwhelmed at the size of the dwelling. For several years, Foy's children, Eddie and Karen, lived with their grandparents. Added to the more regular mix were Vicki and John who lived just up the street. When all the families came together, the old white house became a veritable playhouse to the grandchildren. Plenty of room was available for a good game of hide and seek, and other diversions. The basement floor of the house had in older days been used as a large garage for hearses that brought bodies in and out for funerals. The Nichols grandkids used it as a place for skating, indoor ball games and simply a fun place to play inside on rainy days.

While at play with neighborhood children, the grandkids were known to charge their curious friends a dime to tour the embalming room that they said still had blood-stains in the sink from years of use. The kids loved going up and down the old rope-pulled elevator from floor to floor, and when it was bedtime, their grandmother would bed them all down in the big visitation parlor. There were three large couches, all of which would pull out to make beds. The little ones were always amazed that the room was so big that when all the beds were pulled out, there was still plenty of room to run around easily and play games.[4]

During the 1960s, the Nichols moved down the road into temporary housing for a few months. This was in anticipation of moving into a new house that was to be constructed. The old funeral home they lived in had reached the point that it was far past the ability to repair, and the elders determined that it should be demolished, and a home built in the same location. When the house was completed, the Nichols moved in very quickly. Facing the church building, the house became a most cherished and enjoyed location for the remainder of brother Nichols' life.[5]

Bertha Nichols Blackwood

Growing up in and around the Nichols' family home presented the little ones a grand opportunity to behold the man in his truest form. To the brotherhood, Gus Nichols was so many things, but to the children he was Granddaddy. For them, he was no ordinary grandfather, as in him dwelled the spirit of all things good and holy. His expertise and dedication to Christ could always be seen. Why, he even mowed the lawn wearing a clean white shirt and tie.

Lest one think his professionalism kept him from being able to connect with children, think again! He had a wonderful gift of entertaining children through sleight of hand. Magical tricks were often used to amuse and even to teach spiritual lessons.

David Paul Young

A Special Family

He always saw the spiritual side to everything. This is illustrated in a particular memory of grandson, Nick Hamilton. Growing up for the most part in Texas, his times in Jasper were generally seldom, but lengthier when they did take place. In later years, Nick would often go with his grandfather to attend gospel meetings and the like. Some of the best training he ever received as a gospel preacher was the summer times he spent shadowing his granddaddy.

One memory he had was an occasion sometime in the fall of 1974. He recalled one Sunday afternoon watching the Dallas Cowboys play football. At the end of the game, placekicker Efren Herrera, kicked a walk-off field goal to bring his Texas team to victory. His granddaddy had not watched the game but was walking through around the time when the ball went through the uprights for the win. Nick was most excited, and said, "Granddaddy! Watch this replay!" After stopping to see the replay he observed, "Well, I'll declare! What an amazing God we serve who made that man with a leg that could kick a ball so far as to get it through those uprights!" His grandson recalled, "This is just how my granddaddy thought of everything—all in terms of how it connected with God."[6]

Gus with Eddie and Karen

Holiday occasions were special when much of the family came together in the Nichols family home in Jasper. Many times, the grandchildren remembered the room being full of Nichols relatives, with everyone engaged in conversation, that they could look over and see Granddaddy, with his hearing aids out of his ears and sound asleep in his easy chair. Yet, at other times he would be the life of the party. Other than the gospel, his presence among them was the glue that held them all together.

GRIEF AND LOSS

Sadness came to the Nichols family in the summer of 1952. Eighty-four-year-old, William C. Nichols, the aged head of the Nichols family clan passed away on the 14th of July.[7] Ten of the twelve children born to William and Lizzie made their way home out in the McCollum community to comfort their weeping mother.

Pervie, who had baptized his father a couple years earlier, made the trip. Just a few weeks previous, he had left his work of two-and-a-half years in Greenville, Mississippi, and had moved his family to Macon, Georgia to preach for the Central church.[8] Most of the other siblings lived in the area around home. Three days later, the family gathered at the McCollum church of Christ for the funeral where W. A. Black (1904-1980) comforted the family. The body was then taken over into the edge of Fayette county where it was laid to rest in the White's Chapel church of Christ cemetery. What a day of celebration it was to his widowed wife and children to know that he had made preparations to meet his Lord in glory through his obedience to the gospel.

1954 - Funeral of Lizzie Nichols
L-R: Pervie, Carey Columbus, Zella Nichols Windham, Gus, W. A. Black, Charlie R. Nichols, Velma Virginia Nichols Boshell, and Hazey Mae Dozier.

Nineteen months passed all too quickly for the Nichols family when the call to return home came once again. This time, the summons was in view of the sad passing of the matriarch of the Nichols family, sister Velma Elizabeth "Lizzie" Wyers Nichols on the 22nd of February 1954.[9] At the age of eighty, this dear old sister to so many in the Kingdom, and precious mother, grandmother, and great-grandmother, was now and forever with the Lord. One hundred seven people were counted among her descendants at the time of her death. Among the endearing words sent in to the *Gospel Advocate* concerning her passing was the following,

> Her large family was not brought up in idleness, luxury and ease, but the hard way. She knew the full meaning of hardships, toil and economy. Yet she loved to labor and toil. She enjoyed her long hours of labor in the fields and garden, as well as in the

house, but she had to be industrious to help provide for the bare necessities of life for her large and growing family. In trials and triumphs of hardships too grim to be mentioned, she sacrificed all that was within her in order to keep her progeny together, healthy and happy. She had the rugged individualism demanded by the times just at the turn of the century.

By her devotion to her home and to the eternal principles of right, she so indelibly stamped her image upon her children that today she has five sons who are gospel preachers, as follows: Gus Nichols, of Jasper, Ala., Charlie Nichols, of Columbus, Miss., Carey C. Nichols, of Fayette, Ala., Archie Nichols, of Pinson, Ala., and Pervie Nichols, of Macon, Ga. Four grandsons and five others who have come into her circle of relatives by marriage are also gospel preachers, making fifteen in all. No other mother among churches of Christ in all the world is known to have been connected with so many gospel preachers. These preachers have started others out to preach, and some of these still others; until today no doubt there are more than fifty preachers out preaching the true gospel because this unassuming mother lived and wrought as she did in this world. Hundreds and thousands are now Christians because she had high ideals and impressed them upon her children to be passed on to others.

She loved flowers and good people. She also loved to work. Her quest and utmost desire was for peace—peace of mind and heart—peace with everybody and everywhere. She was free-hearted and generous, even to the point of great and joyful sacrifice, and especially toward those who were worthy. She was modest and retiring, yet stout hearted and brave. None of her faults were of the baser sort. She was an inspiration unto many, but most especially unto her children, who now "rise up and call her blessed."

She was baptized by C. F. Cannon in Fayette County, Ala., out of denominationalism into the body of Christ nearly forty years ago. Her husband preceded her in death at the age of eighty-four July 14, 1952. She was buried at White's Chapel in Fayette County, Ala., beside her husband. The funeral services were conducted by W. A. Black at McCollum church of Christ.[10]

ENDNOTES

1 Note: The Sigma Rho Social Club seems to have been the society of choice by all eight of the Nichols kids when they attended Freed-Hardeman College.

2 Note: At the time of this writing, four grandchildren have passed away: Sharon, Eddie, Janet, and Paul.

3 Gus Nichols, *Gospel Advocate*, 17 July 1958, p. 459.

4 Phone interview with Vicki Blackwood, 17 August 2015.

5 Note: After the passing of brother Nichols the parsonage was transformed into office space for the church and has continued in this fashion to the present.

6 Phone interview with Nick Hamilton, 18 August 2015.

7 Obituary, *The Mountain Eagle*, 24 July 1952, p. TWO-A.

8 Pervie Nichols, *Gospel Advocate*, 15 May 1952, p. 324.

9 Ed., "14 County Deaths Reported During Week," *The Mountain Eagle*, Thursday, 4 March 1954, p. SIX-A.

10 Gus Nichols, *Gospel Advocate*, 18 March 1954, p. 215.

- 37 -

Speaking The Truth In Love

Therefore, my beloved brethren, be ye steadfast, unmovable, always abounding in the work of the Lord, forasmuch as ye know that your labor is not in vain in the Lord.
— Paul, 1 Corinthians 15:58

THE HARDEMAN MEETING

In 1954, N. B. Hardeman (1874-1965), then in his 80th year, preached a meeting in April for the Fifth Avenue church. The retired college president was still very active in his preaching appointments, and second to none in his ability to move the crowd with the gospel message. Gus reported ten baptisms and said, "The dullest moment in one of his discourses surpasses in interest the highest flights of the average preacher in our generation. Brother Hardeman is right now at his best."[1] Hear the genuine admiration expressed for the expertise and power in the elder preacher's eloquence,

N. B. Hardeman

> He makes no effort at oratory, yet he is so gifted by nature and so richly endowed by learning and experience that he could not preach without flights of oratory which sweep his audience with him in thought and feeling and bear them away to the throne of God. His word pictures are as visible to the mind as in the president's features in TV. He is a master of two things which stand out like Stone Mountain through all his sermons—words and simplicity. He either gets the best word in the dictionary or yokes up with it another one making the two do double duty. Then he is always natural and at ease in the pulpit. There is nothing about him nor his delivery which attracts attention away from the truth being presented. But every word and expression add to the luster and natural

beauty of the truth itself. There is nothing in his discourses to drive away any honest soul, yet the truth is presented without apologies, without fear or favor, just in the love of the truth and of souls to be saved thereby.

Natural wit and humor were used fittingly to hold attention and to drive some folly or foible into the background that the truth might be seen in its own light. Then the speaker would sweep down upon the audience rapt in attention and drive his point home to the conviction of all honest in heart. However, his preaching is not a cold, heartless presentation of matter to fill up time and carry out a program as an hireling his day. But he preaches with the joy and gladness of youth, and with an inward earnestness intentionally restrained, but never fully concealed. He has the power and pathos of youth combined with the wisdom and ability stored up through the long years of the past.[2]

With such words of kindness, it is easy to see that there was no greater admiration and respect one could have for another brother than Gus Nichols had for N. B. Hardeman. The two enjoyed a friendship that very few could claim to enjoy.

N. B. Hardeman Revival and Radio Ad

MEETINGS AND APPOINTMENTS

Beginning with the early 1950s, brotherhood papers reported less and less on the activities of Gus Nichols. This was not because he was less busy. In fact, if anything he was more active, going more places, and being involved in more programs and series than he had time to report. In 1955, it was related that he was conducting "eight or ten meetings each year,"[3] but these were only a small part of his nearly continuous labor. Annual appearances on several university lectureships were added to his endeavors. Generally, the year began at Freed-Hardeman College. From there, trips followed to David Lipscomb College in Nashville, Alabama

Christian College in Montgomery, and then occasional trips were made out to Abilene for the lectureship of the Christian college there.

Of the meetings Gus preached that were reported in 1954, one took place in June at the East Tupelo church in Mississippi where J. C. Choate (1932-2008) was the preacher. There were "seventeen baptisms and four restorations"[4] enjoyed during the course of the effort. In late August, he was at Warrior, Alabama where, "several obeyed the gospel, and some were restored."[5] There was also a meeting at Rayville, Louisiana, where Wendell Winkler (1931-2005) was the preacher at that time. Ten responded to the invitation in that meeting.[6] In the same report another meeting at Old Cedar Creek, in Walker County, initiated eight baptisms and eight restorations. From there a meeting was conducted at Mulga, Alabama resulting in two baptisms and two restorations.[7] In October, Gus attended to a meeting in Nashville, Tennessee, at the Highland Avenue congregation. Two were baptized during that engagement.[8]

1950s - Gus Nichols

In 1955, he spoke at Freed-Hardeman College on "God, And What It Means To Know Him." Then he made his way out to Abilene, Texas, for ACC's lecture series again. He spoke on, "Withdraw Yourselves From Those Who Walk Disorderly."[9]

Willard Collins (1915-2007) conducted the annual spring gospel meeting at Fifth Avenue that year with twenty-six being baptized and ten restored. They had to install a loud speaker on the lawn outside the building to take care of the overflow crowd at the latter part of the meeting. Collins revealed, "The brethren in Jasper plan to build a new building in the very near future which is sorely needed."[10]

Before the end of the year, Gus made his way down to Piedmont, Alabama to preach a meeting for the Piedmont Avenue church.[11] A few weeks later, he returned to assist the congregation in an appointment ceremony for elders and deacons. The preacher there, Johnny Payne (1910-1992), wrote a report of the events praising brother Nichols for his work in this effort. He said,

On Sunday night, October 23, Brother Gus Nichols of Jasper, Alabama appointed elders and deacons here in one of the most impressive services I have ever attended. The Church as a whole feel that untold good will come as a result of it.

Many visitors were present from neighboring towns and were deeply impressed with the seriousness of the occasion. For nearly two hours the large audience was so quiet it was simply amazing....Brother Nichols is one of the best in the brotherhood to conduct a service of this kind. His outstanding knowledge of the elder question, his wide experience as an evangelist plus his natural love for people makes him easily one of the top men among us to conduct a service of this kind. He reminded us of the great responsibility that we as elders must accept. He read to us from the Bible what God expects of us. Then turned to the congregation and read to them their duties and obligations to the elders.

1955 - Willard Collins

They confirmed it by rising to their feet and standing until asked to be seated. He asked each elder and deacon point blank if they willingly accepted the position to which each replied in the affirmative. Several prayers were offered during the service by Brother Nichols and the elders and deacons. This service will be long remembered by all who attended.[12]

Early in 1956, Gus celebrated his sixty-fourth birthday. It was business as usual that winter with his visit to Freed-Hardeman College for the Lectureship. He preached on "The Unity For Which Jesus Prayed."[13]

NEW BROADCAST

For ten years, Gus conducted a broadcast on Radio Station WWWB. The program was from 8:00 to 8:30 every morning, seven days a week. In all that time, it had been a great success to the church and community. When another station in town made him aware of a lunch time slot being available he jumped at the opportunity to begin broadcasting.

So, the *Words of Truth* broadcast began in 1956 on radio channel WARF in Jasper. The mid-day program was similar to the early broadcast.

Only events among churches of Christ were reported, but in addition to church activities and gospel meetings, birthdays, anniversaries, and the like, followed by a message from the Scriptures. Several preachers in the area assisted in conducting the program when Gus had to be away.[14]

SPEAKING THE TRUTH IN LOVE

Early in the spring of 1956, Gus and Matilda made their way out to Lamesa, Texas, to visit Carrie, W. T. and the grandchildren. Their granddaddy was also there to begin a gospel meeting for the congregation where W. T. was the preacher. Sixteen lessons were delivered between the fourth and eleventh of March, with each lesson being recorded. Among the various subjects where titles like, "Rightly Dividing the Word," "The Lord's Day," "Who Is a Christian?" "Problems of Marriage and the Home," and "What If I Am Lost?"

1956 - Gus Nichols

The humility of the man was demonstrated when W. T. lavished upon him great kindnesses in his introduction on the first evening. To this his father-in-law stated in his opening remarks,

> I shall not be able to live up to the introduction that has just been given me. It reminded me of an introduction once given me at Freed-Hardeman by Claude Gardner. He presented me as a "model preacher of modern times." Of course, this was embarrassing to me; but I told the audience that I had decided not to object since the dictionary says a "model" is a "miniature or small representation of a thing." And that is what I feel that I am—a small imitation of the real thing.[15]

During the meeting, it was suggested that the lessons were so good that each should be transcribed and put in book form. The outcome was a book entitled, *Speaking The Truth In Love*, and was produced and copyrighted in 1956 by Nichols Brothers Publishing Co. Copies were sold for $3.00. The publication was affectionately dedicated to Matilda with the words,

> Unto my faithful and beloved Christian wife,

Who has given herself in service with a smile:
Whose devotion to me and our home through life,
Has exemplified the doctrine of, "The Second Mile,"
Is this volume affectionately dedicated by
Gus Nichols.[16]

The book included the sixteen lessons he preached, as well as three lectures delivered to Bible Classes. The introduction gave a brief presentation of the life of the preacher written by W. T. The book was promoted among the brotherhood papers and enjoyed a good circulation.[17]

A NEW ELDER

When the Nichols moved to Jasper, the organization of the congregation was not complete, as it had no elders. Not long after the Friday evening classes began in the winter months of the year, an eldership finally was formed, with faithful men being appointed. A good number of years later, during the process of transition to the new building on Sixth Avenue, more men were needed to fill the role. In the twenty-third year of his service as minister, the church pressed Gus Nichols into the service of elder. He entered the office in the 64th year of his life and served in that role the rest of his days.

SIXTH AVENUE CHURCH OF CHRIST

When the church of Christ in Jasper set out to build a church building on Fifth Avenue in 1927, it took $15,000.00 to raise the structure that could seat around 500 people. The thinking was that it should be more than sufficient for many, many years. But, when Gus Nichols began preaching for the little church five years later, the rapid growth of the congregation challenged their initial thinking. Over the next twenty-two years, many were added to the body of Christ from the area. Bringing in the best preachers in the brotherhood for gospel meetings, annual Vacation Bible School programs, the occasional debates, along with other special events, it served to stretch the building's capacity. With only five classrooms, there seemed always to be a need for more space. The building was finally paid off the 19th of June 1943, and very soon the need for expansion loomed tall on the horizon.

Early in 1956, one-half a block of property was purchased one block to the southwest of the building on the corner of 15th Street and 6th Avenue. Immediately, a committee was formed for planning a new building to be constructed as soon as possible. Church leader, K. L. Jones took the lead in the planning program, along with two elders, H. G. Dill and C. M. Karrh. Others on the committee included members, Andrew Posey, A. C. McGlaun, Harry Sherer, Sam Evans, Donald Lackey, Gus Nichols, and his son-in-law, Rile Blackwood.

Speaking The Truth In Love

An architect from Atlanta, Georgia, Morris Hall, produced drawings, and bids were taken from various builders. Local contractors, Construction Engineers, Inc. offered a bid of $188,700.00, which was approved on the 8th of August. Commitments from several of the brethren were in excess of $40,000.00, and the balance was to be procured through a bank loan. On the 14th, a groundbreaking ceremony took place on the new property with the press, community leaders and many church members in attendance. A photo and report appeared in the following issue of *The Mountain Eagle*, as building was underway.

Erecting a new place of worship has a way of adding new excitement to a work. People are always willing to dig deep for a cause they can see.

Ground Breaking for Jasper Church Building

Sixth Avenue Church Building

The Nichols had always given liberally to the Lord's work, but when the church was asked to give, they determined to increase their contribution. For years, Gus and Matilda had quit giving Christmas presents to one another. Instead, they took the money they would have spent and gave it to a particular mission work or a benevolent cause. One year, they were audited by the Internal Revenue Service. When all the canceled checks written to the church were added up by the auditor, he was surprised to see how they could give 28% of their income to the church when they were on such a small income. Long after the building was finished they continued to give sacrificially to the work of the Lord.[18]

In a little less than twelve months, the building was completed close to the time for the summer gospel meeting. Sunday morning, the 21st of July 1957, was the first assembly of Christians in the new auditorium that could seat 700. Gus preached in the morning. A dedication service was planned for the afternoon to coincide with the beginning of the gospel meeting with B. C. Goodpasture (1895-1977) doing the dedicatory speech. Over 800 were in attendance at the afternoon gathering.

And thus, Fifth Avenue church of Christ became known as Sixth Avenue church of Christ, with Gus Nichols preaching there in his 24th year.

A TRACT BRINGS CONTROVERSY

Gus visited Henderson, Tennessee, fulfilling his annual appointment on the F-HC Lectureship early in February 1957. He spoke on "Conditions of Election," during the program. Early in the following month, he made his

Churches

Sixth Avenue Church History

Sixth Avenue Church Of Christ

By: Dawn Calloway

Back in 1924, the first Sunday night in October, Mr. Gus Nichols, the preacher at the Church of Christ in Cordova, came to Jasper to hold a meeting in the hope of starting a congregation. Mr. Forney Roberson and Mr. S.J. Oakley obtained the Odd Fellows hall over what was known as the Phillips and Stanley building in downtown Jasper for the meeting. Sixteen were present at that first meeting. Others followed later, but, "by the close of that meeting, fourteen members had taken their stand and expressed their determination to work and worship together as a congregation: Brother and Sister Forney Roberson; Brother and Sister S.J. Oakley; Brother and Sister John Ellis; Brother and Sister Jack Tirey; Brother and

arrow pointed upstairs. I followed on and wound my way around, and around, until I came to a door upon which was tacked a notice which said GOSPEL MEETING — SERVICES 7:30 P.M. EACH EVENING. WELCOME. That night my wife and I with our 3 babies were present."

Therefore, the Church of Christ of Jasper was born. A lot was bought on Fifth Avenue and a building was erected (which is now the Bible Missionary Church) and the dedication sermon was given by L.R. Wilson the first Sunday in October, 1927.

The first Elders were: Avery Fike, G.W. Hall, and C.M. Karrh. Other past Elders were H.D. Hill, A.C. McGlaun, R.W. Staggers and many more.

Blackwood, two of Gus Nichols' eight children. Mrs. Young said, "He loved people, no matter what their color or creed, and he impressed me so. The day after my mother was baptized, my sister and I ages 2 and 4, decided to baptize her baby chickens while she and Daddy were working in the field. She came home and asked, 'What happened?' because we had baptized them in a pen, then laid them out across the porch to dry," she says, laughing. "The poor things were dead, of course, but we just laid them out in a neat little row."

Mrs. Young and Mrs. Blackwood recall how hard their father worked as a farmer, a miner, and a preacher. "When he went to preach in his wagon, he'd already be tired from a day's work, so Kate, his mule, would take him there, and then daddy would turn her towards home and sleep until she stopped. Then, he knew he was home," Mrs. Young said.

A thirty minute radio program was started on November 1, 1946, by Gus Nichols, and has been on each day since.

On July 21, 1957, the Fifth Avenue Church of Christ moved to the new Sixth Avenue Church of Christ building. The opening sermon was given by B.C. Goodpasture at two o'clock, and the house was filled to overflowing with a seating capacity of 800 or

more.

Marlin Wade was the first person to be baptized in the new building, and Joan Wade and William Kimbrell were the first couple to be married in the new church.

Mr. David Wade, who is now the Evangelist at Sixth Avenue Church of Christ, has been there for two years with his wife, Helen, and three boys. Mr. Wade had this to say about the church, "The Sixth Avenue Church of Christ is a caring church in a growing community. It is our aim to restore New Testament Christianity in the 20th century. The congregation is active in evangelism, benevolence, and supports many good works at home and abroad."

The present Elders are: David Beaird, Paul Dozier, Sam Evans, Lincoln Herzig, Dempsey Jones, John Panter and Wayne Primm.

Deacons are Wayne Brown, Rodger Burleson, John Campbell, C.S. Deavours, Sam Drummond, Neil Evans, Robert Fields, W.S. Ferrell, Danny Latham, Joe Looser, Brack O'Rear, Jr., Reonld Pulliam, Bob Roberts and Ray Wallace.

The Secretary is Linda Harrison.

The oldest living member of Sixth Avenue Church of Christ is Matilda Nichols, 95 years of age, the wife of the late Gus Nichols.

The Old Fifth Avenue Church of Christ Building. The Insert Is A Picture of Gus & Matilda Nichols.

Sister Craig; Sister Columbus Deason (the daughter of Brother C.A. Wheeler); Brother R.O. Connor; Brother and Sister Avery Fike," it states in Avery Fike's *A Brief History of the Fifth Avenue Church of Christ*.

Mr. Fike continues, "Wednesday after the meeting started, I was walking down the street and in front of the Christian Church, I saw an arrow drawn on the sidewalk with crayon which said GOSPEL MEETING, FOLLOW THE ARROW. This had an interesting ring to it, and through curiosity, I followed the arrows around the block to the foot of the stairs where the

From 1929 until 1933, several 'young preachers' lent assistance including John McCleskey, A.M. Plyler and W.A. Black. Mr. Gus Nichols returned to Jasper from Milport in 1933, and lead the Church of Christ for 43 years. He was well known throughout the United States, and lectured and preached in 30 of those states.

Among his many accomplishments, he authored books and preached at Christ's Tomb in the Holy Land on May 20, 1962. His work influenced not only the people he met in his travels, but also his family.

I talked to Mrs. Gracie Young and her sister, Bertha

Sixth Avenue Church of Christ Today, Located At 1501 Sixth Avenue In Jasper.

way to Montgomery for the lecture series at Alabama Christian College. On Tuesday evening he spoke on, "The Blood of Christ."[19]

At 2:00 p.m. on the 23rd of April, brother Nichols presented a keynote address to the Tuesday afternoon crowd at the Lipscomb Spring Lectures. His discourse was entitled, "New Testament Principles For Caring For The Needy."[20] At the completion of the speech, very quickly over 350 requests came in for copies of the recording. Willard Collins (1915-2007) reported,

> Due to this great demand, arrangements have been made with the *Gospel Advocate* Company for this speech, which is almost seventeen legal-sized pages in length, to be printed in booklet form. Those who order the speech at Lipscomb will be the first ones to receive the booklet when it is printed.[21]

1957 - FHU Annual Bible Lectureship
Henderson Church Building
1957 FHC *Treasure Chest*

The *Advocate* produced the 20-page tract and distributed it widely at 15 cents a copy. It was believed by some to be the best explanation of why churches should support orphanages. The tracts were dispersed quickly until it was reported in June of a reprinting of the booklet.[22]

Late in December, an article written by Gus Nichols appeared in the *Gospel Advocate* entitled, "My Tract, A Letter, And A Reply."[23] Brooks C. Webb, the preacher for the church in Greenwood, Mississippi, wrote a letter to brother Nichols in which he criticized some of the comments made in his speech/tract over supporting children's homes. In it, he accused Gus of misrepresenting the suggestion made by some preachers, in particular, Yater Tant (1908-1997), that churches might be able to support orphan homes if they would put a "box in the vestibule," in which members could give individually to orphan homes rather than have the church support them through the church treasury. Webb suggested that Tant's comment should have been considered as being the lesser "evil"[24] rather than a real alternative.

In response, brother Nichols explained that Yater Tant had been in a Gospel Meeting down at Zion church of Christ in Walker County before he gave the speech at Lipscomb, and that while in Jasper he had spoken on Gus' radio broadcasts during his visit but did not discuss the subject at hand on the air. Further, he said that on the last day of Tant's meeting, he and Walker County preacher, Asa M. Plyler (1902-1991), were visiting in the Nichols' home, and it was there when Tant suggested that he would promote Childhaven, and the like, if Nichols would encourage brethren to do it on an individual basis. It was at that meeting that the "box in the vestibule" was suggested to him as a way that brethren could support the children's homes. Further, it was said that brother Webb was not aware of Tant's declarations during this meeting.

In the article, Gus once again explained his understanding that the question among churches was not *if* orphan's homes should be supported, but *how*. And, since the Bible has not made it clear as to how, then it was the duty of each congregation to determine the best way in keeping with the will of God. His final words encouraged brethren that, "in matters of faith let us have unity and uniformity; in matters of opinion and expediency let us have liberty, and in all things love."[25] Yet, not all heeded his plea.

LOOKING BACK, I'D DO IT AGAIN

A special issue for the *Gospel Advocate* was planned to appear on the 2nd of May 1957. It was to be devoted to preaching the gospel. The plan was that preachers like L. O. Sanderson (1901-1992), Rex A. Turner (1913-2001), Frank L. Cox (1895-1978), Frank Pack (1916-1998), Alan M. Bryan (1925-2006) and several others would write about the great blessing of preaching, and the encouragements they received in participating in such a great work. Gus Nichols wrote an article entitled, "Looking Back, I'd Do It Again." Later, the article was included in a short, fifty-page book entitled, *The Glory Of Preaching*.[26] This article beautifully represents Nichols' thinking at the height of his success as a gospel preacher, and is inserted here in its entirety.

> When I became a Christian, I made the greatest decision of my life. The decision to give one's life to God is the greatest decision that can be made. This choice largely determines all other choices

to be made at the forks of the roads along the way of life. Having once for all decided to follow Christ, one only needs to learn what the will of the Lord is. He has already determined to do whatsoever he learns to be right. Hence, the choice to become a Christian and follow Jesus all the way changes the whole course of one's life. He makes different decisions to those he would have made had he remained a sinner. He is then better prepared to choose his companion in marriage, the company he may keep and his life's vocation.

The decision to preach the gospel was my second greatest decision in life. It was in 1917 and I lived on a farm. We had just been blown away in a tornado which left death and destruction in its wake. It also left us closer to God. It showed us how quickly earthly treasures can be swept away. We had two little girls, and I had just registered for military duty, subject to call in the near future, if the war should continue much longer. World War I was then raging, and it seemed that the whole world had gone mad. As I saw the matter, the gospel of Christ was the only remedy for the sad plight of nations, as well as individuals. (Rom. 1:16.) Socialism, Catholicism, denominationalism and human wisdom had failed to save the world from hate and ruin. But the gospel and Christianity had not failed, in fact had not been extensively tried. Carnal nations had resorted to the use of carnal weapons in an effort to conquer and make the world better. "The sword of the Spirit, which is the word of God" (Eph. 6:17), had largely been discarded as being too weak to pull down the strong holds of evil.

For several years I had entertained the hope that I might be able to preach the gospel someday. On the day of my baptism, C. A. Wheeler who converted me had suggested that I could become a gospel preacher. This little seed-thought of inspiration had never died out in my soul. I was then twenty-five, and had been leading in song service, teaching Bible classes, leading in prayers and doing what I could to help establish a congregation at the schoolhouse in our community where I had obeyed the gospel several years before, and where I had come out of denominationalism.

I knew that the gospel call unto salvation (2 Thess. 2:14), was also a call to do in the Christian's life all that one can do for the glory of God. I often thought of James' statement that "to him therefore that knoweth to do good, and doeth it not, to him is it sin." (James 4:17.) I often meditated upon the fate of the man of one talent who was cast out because he did not use his one talent. (Matt. 25:14-31.) I also thought much about Paul's words, "Woe is unto me, if I preach not the gospel." (1 Cor. 9:16.) While I knew I never could preach like Paul, I believed I had some talent and ability for which I would be held responsible before God. When I had prayed over the matter for several days, the last day with fasting, I finally reached the decision that since I could preach the gospel I must do so, and that I would do it if the Lord willed to let me live and further prepare myself. To me, this was God's call to preach, and I could not further be a Christian and not preach the gospel. I must do it to be ultimately saved in heaven at last. With me it was a life and death proposition, and not a mere choice of a vocation.

I no longer dreaded the hardships and persecutions which I had expected to follow such a life. Rather I was anxious to get started, and was fully persuaded that whatever might happen to me and mine would be overruled of God for our good. This proved to be true. God has wonderfully blessed us. God gave us eight children and though I gave all my time to preaching the gospel, we never went hungry. Three of our four sons are full-time gospel preachers, and three of our four daughters married full-time gospel preachers. It was our desire and prayer that they might give themselves to God in this way, for preaching the gospel is the greatest work in the world. The joy of preaching the sweetest story ever told, and the thousands, which have turned to God under my feeble efforts, would be reward enough for me. If I were qualified to fill his office and had the opportunity to exchange jobs with the President of the United States, I would instantly spurn the temptation. I am doing what God wants me to do and what I want to do. If I had a thousand lives to live I would want to be a gospel preacher every time, and at the last would want to pray for a little more time in which to preach the gospel and reach a few more of those hungering for the truth. I have been preaching forty years now, and if I had life to live over I would do it again. May God give us more preachers of the word!"[27]

AMONG THE SAINTS

In addition to his regular lectureship appearances, some of the churches Gus assisted in 1957 included a trip in early June to Alexander City, Alabama to speak on a lectureship with, "Charles Marshall, Rex Turner, Bill Huggins, and John McKleskey."[28]

In August, he went down to Montgomery for a meeting with the Panama Street congregation. Nine were baptized and four were restored during the week. Rex A. Turner (1913-2001) said, "Brother Nichols was at his very best throughout the meeting."[29]

At the end of September, he returned to Montgomery to assist a struggling church. The Dalraida congregation was going through some inner conflict among some of its members which, "had led to envy, strife, hatred, etc. This had developed into factions that was leading to division in the church."[30] Gus was asked to sit on a panel with four other preachers, "E.C. McKenzie, H.C. Linderman, Kelton Whaley and J. M. Redmon."[31] For two days and two nights the brethren heard testimony of all parts. Heeding the suggestions of their mentors, the result was a wonderful time of prayer, forgiveness and reuniting of the brethren.

SECOND-CENTURY DRIVE WINNERS

The *Gospel Advocate* conducted its Second-Century Drive beginning the 1st of November 1956 and concluded it the following year at the end of October. At the close of the competition, prizes were rewarded to the winners. Guy N. Woods (1908-1993) won first place and was awarded $100.00. The second prize for $50 went to Gus Nichols.[32] The continued effort of promoting GA was a special part of his continued ministry, and the camaraderie he enjoyed between himself and other preachers in this outreach was always a pleasure.

Gus Nichols, B. B. James, H. A. Dixon

NO BETTER SCHOOL

Brother Nichols had the opportunity to visit the campuses of many brotherhood Christian colleges. But, none captured his heart quite like Freed-Hardeman College. A short letter appeared in the June, and again in the November issues of the school newspaper, *Freed-Hardeman Alumnograms*, with the following sentiments,

I am fully convinced that there is no better school than Freed-Hardeman College. It is doing a good and effective work in the training of young people for a better life. We have been blessed with eight children and all of them attended Freed-Hardeman College. In our modern and complex world, we cannot educate our children very well at home, and yet in our competitive age girls and boys must be educated better than ever before. Freed-Hardeman College takes up where the home ends and carries on to the glory of God and credit of the home. The teachers are Christians; they teach the truth about all things taught, and best of all, they set before the young people examples which are an inspiration to them as long as they live. Parents, be sure to send your children to a Christian school. They are worthy of the best in education.[33]

ENDNOTES

1 Gus Nichols, *Gospel Advocate*, 3 June 1954, pp. 429-30.

2 Ibid.

3 Willard Collins, *The Gospel Advocate Centennial Volume*, Nashville: Gospel Advocate Company, c.1956, p. 275.

4 J. C. Choate, *Gospel Advocate*, 12 August 1954, p. 637. Also reported in *Firm Foundation*, 17 August 1954, p. 14.

5 Gus Nichols, *Gospel Advocate*, 30 September 1954, p. 778.

6 Ibid., 26 August 1954, p. 674.

7 Ibid., 28 October 1954, p. 856.

8 Bruce C. Holt, *Firm Foundation*, 16 November 1954, p. 11. Also reported in *Gospel Advocate*, 2 December 1954, p. 955.

9 J. D. Thomas, "Timely Speeches on ACC Lectureship," *Firm Foundation*, 11 January 1955, p. 22.

10 Willard Collins, *Firm Foundation*, 31 May 1955, p. 358.

11 Johnny Payne, *Firm Foundation*, 9 August 1955, p. 526.

12 Ibid., 6 December 1955, p. 793.

13 Gus Nichols, 1956 Lecture Outlines, Volume 4, Annual Bible Lectureship, January 9-13. 1956, "The Unity For Which Jesus Prayed," Henderson: Freed-Hardeman College, pp. 5-12.

14 Note: Initially, several preachers in the area handled the broadcast with, Levi Sides, Paul M. Wylie (1933-2004), and others doing the preaching. When the influence of Non-Institutional brethren arose through their own radio programs, brother Nichols took over the broadcast to devote more time to answering their charges. In a phone interview with Levi Sides in February 2018, he recalled many times watching brother Nichols during the program put on by the McArthur Heights preacher, Thomas G. O'Neal (1938-2012) or the North Jasper brethren, Irven Powell Lee (1914-1991), both from the Non-Institutional persuasion. Gus would write copious notes during their programs that he planned to examine when he got his next opportunity to be on the air. Discussed further in chapter 39.

15 Gus Nichols, *Speaking The Truth In Love*, Chattanooga: Nichols Brothers Publishing Company, 1956, p. 11.

16 W. T. Hamilton, *Speaking The Truth In Love*, Chattanooga: Nichols Brothers Publishing Company, 1956, p. 3.

17 Note: The book went out of print for several years, but was reprinted by Hester Publications in Henderson, Tennessee in 2011.

18 Flavil Nichols, "Honor Thy Parents, Some Things I Learned From My Father, The Late Gus Nichols," 1990 Freed Hardeman College Lectureship, Henderson: Freed-Hardeman College, 1990, p. 194.

19 Advertisement, *Gospel Advocate*, 7 March 1957, p. 155.

20 Howard A. White, *Gospel Advocate*, 18 April 1957, p. 255.

21 Willard Collins, *Gospel Advocate*, "Nichols' Speech To Be Printed," 23 May 1957, p. 324.

22 Advertisement, "Good Booklets for the Tract Rack: 3. New Testament Principles of Caring for the Needy," *Gospel Advocate*, 20 June 1957, p. 389.

23 Gus Nichols, "My Tract, a Letter and Reply," *Gospel Advocate*, 26 December 1957, p. 825.

24 Ibid.

25 Ibid.

26 Advertisement, *Gospel Advocate*, 4 July 1957, p. 425.

27 Gus Nichols, *Gospel Advocate*, 2 May 1957, pp. 282-83.

28 John Payne, *Gospel Advocate*, 23 May 1957, p. 331.

29 Rex Turner, *Gospel Advocate*, 15 August 1957, p. 525.

30 Virgil L. Shelton, *Gospel Advocate*, 24 October 1957, p. 686.

31 Ibid.

32 B. C. Goodpasture, ed., "Congratulations!" *Gospel Advocate*, 28 November 1957, p. 754.

33 Gus Nichols, "Gus Nichols Says," *Freed-Hardeman Alumograms,* Vol. 9, No. 11, November 1957, p. 3.

- 38 -

I Discovered Gus Nichols

I have preached righteousness in the great congregation: lo, I have not refrained my lips, O Lord, thou knowest.

—David, Psalms 40:9

THE HERALD OF TRUTH

The Highland church of Christ in Abilene, Texas, began a national radio broadcast in February 1952 called *Herald of Truth*. Contracting with the American Broadcasting Company Network, within three years the outreach ministry was being played on over 300 radio stations from coast to coast. On May 2, 1954 the program entered the world of television on 42 stations across the nation.[1] James D. Willeford (1916-1992) and James W. Nichols (1927-1973)[2] were the speakers for both radio and television.[3]

Gus Nichols and a brother

The success that came from the growth and expansion of the program was not without criticism. As early as 1953, Glenn L. Wallace (1903-1988) led the charge in the pages of the *Firm Foundation* with two articles questioning whether the Scriptures authorize the program's existence. Controversy had arisen over whether churches could support the work from the church treasury, and even about whether the program's title, *Herald Of Truth*, was a scriptural name.[4] The extreme amounts of money used to produce it caused others to fear it would become another missionary society.[5]

There were also strong defenders of the program, like Cecil N. Wright (1908-1996) who wrote in the *Gospel Advocate* a stern rebuttal to the two articles in the Texas paper. Though an admirer of Wallace in the past, he sternly rebuked the criticisms saying, "If the *Herald of Truth* can be improved with constructive criticism, such is solicited by the Highland elders and should not be withheld. But I had ten thousand times rather be an all-out supporter of it as it is than to seek to 'kill' it. God prosper it, and bless all who contribute to its success!"[6] Cousin of Glenn Wallace, G. K. Wallace (1903-1988), jumped in with his own support, saying, "This is a type of program that is needed in America because it is designed to reach the man on the street."[7] Thus, for the next fifteen years, the Herald of Truth became another bone of contention among factions within the body of Christ.

1959 - Herald of Truth Dinner
J. Roy Vaughn, Gus Nichols, Wanda and Batsell Barrett Baxter

How did Gus Nichols feel about the *Herald of Truth*? On the 12th of April 1959 Sixth Avenue church of Christ in Jasper, Alabama was jettisoned to the national stage as *Herald of Truth* television cameras captured a worship service inside their building with Gus doing the preaching. When the event appeared over the air, those in America who had somehow not been aware of who Gus Nichols was, were introduced to his leadership among churches of Christ very quickly. More than anything, it was a joy for the congregation to be a part of a program where the word of God was able to reach the homes of so many of their fellow countrymen.[8]

It was no simple task for brother Nichols, as he felt very uncomfortable under the extra lighting and knowing he was being filmed. With his usual freedom in his sermons not to be tied to notes, part of the commitment to do the telecast was to submit a transcript of the sermon, well in advance of the filming. At one point in the sermon, the director stopped the service and told the preacher he was veering from his text. Finally, he made it through, and as they say in show business, "it was a wrap."

Later in the year, a representative of *Herald of Truth*, Paul Hunton, visited the Jasper congregation with video equipment and reel in hand. He reported,

> I spoke to the church in Jasper, Alabama on Wednesday night and showed the new film. When it was over, Gus Nichols said, "That is the best thing I have ever seen. I will give $100 in 1960. Ask who will promise to give above their regular contribution." Hands began to go up and $1,275 was promised that night. Brother Nichols invited me to speak on his radio program the next morning. Just as soon as the program was over, the phone began to ring and others who were not present the night before promised also to give. When we left, Brother Nichols asked for a film that he might show it to every church in the county.[9]

Before the end of the year, an article appeared from the pen of another representative of the program, John F. Reese. Entitled, "Brother Nichols' Radio Program,"[10] he wrote in elaborate terms of the good work of the Sixth Avenue church of Christ and its preacher of twenty-five years. He commended the radio work that was being done in the Jasper area, praising the great growth in the Lord's church that had followed with over fifty congregations in Walker county. This success was a perfect segue into promoting *Herald of Truth* with its potential of reaching the entire nation through radio and television. He further stressed that the same principle authorizing the local work in Jasper was the same being used to initiate and maintain the national program.

1959 - Four Preachers
Gus Nichols, George Bailey, Guy N. Wood, E. R. Harper

INDIANAPOLIS LECTURESHIP

Several weeks after the *Herald of Truth* TV episode was recorded, Gus made his way to Indianapolis, Indiana to participate in the Irvington Lectureship. The Irvington church, located in the eastern part of the city, was the home congregation for Restoration Movement historian, Earl Irvin West (1920-2011). The lectureship was organized in the spring of 1946, and over the years grew to be one of the strongest programs of its kind in the North Central United States. Gus was joined in the twelfth annual program with David Lipscomb President, Athens Clay Pullias (1910-1985), Batsell Barrett Baxter (1916-1982), Cecil N. Wright (1908-1996), Ben F. Taylor (1878-1987), and several others. The theme for the series was, "The Church Tomorrow."[11]

Nichols at John Dillinger's Grave
Crown Hill Cemetery, Indianapolis

Early in August, Gus conducted a meeting at the State Avenue congregation in Decatur, Alabama. Tommy Q. Vernon (1935-1990) was the preacher there at the time, and reported that brother Nichols, "spoke daily over WMSL here in Decatur."[12] In September, the East Hill church in Pulaski, Tennessee had him in for a meeting. Three were baptized during that effort.[13]

NICHOLS-SANDERS DEBATE

The new church building on Sixth Avenue was the setting for a four-night discussion between their preacher and a minister in the Church of God by the name of Ronald Sanders. Walker County and the surrounding area had several Holiness congregations, and Sanders was their voice on the polemic platform.[14]

> The first two nights Brother Nichols affirmed: "The scriptures teach that water baptism to a believing penitent is for or unto the remission of alien sins, or is a condition of salvation to alien sinners, and was administered and commanded in New Testament times, or in the days of the apostles. Mr. Sanders denied. Mr. Sanders affirmed: The scriptures teach that alien sinners are saved by Holy Ghost baptism by faith alone in answer to prayer

and that water baptism is not commanded or required under the New Covenant or New Testament." Brother Nichols denied.[15]

O. C. Lambert (1890-1972) served as moderator for the debate. It was reported that every night he, "read each of the rules for honorable controversy in a debate. Mr. Sanders was deeply disturbed when brother Nichols continued to press him concerning his positions."[16]

GUS NICHOLS, PRINCE OF PREACHERS

The annual lectureship programs at Freed-Hardeman College continued to thrust Gus into the limelight. At the 1958 series, held January 12-16, the theme was "The Church Through The Centuries." Jasper's finest addressed audiences daily at the 2:30 session on "Problems Facing The Church."[17]

In 1959, the lectureship was conducted between the 4th and 8th of January, and the theme was, "The Book of Books." Gus spoke at the 1:30 session on the subject, "The Book Of Ephesians."[18]

The new editor for the *Firm Foundation*, Reuel Lemmons (1912-1989), attended the lectureship for the first time that year. His purpose, in part, was to promote his paper's 75th anniversary of existence. Opportunities were given to him to encourage readership of the magazine, and help was requested to grow the work. He reported that H. A. Dixon (1904-1969) led the campaign for subscriptions with the promise of 250 and followed with, "Gus Nichols, prince of preachers from Jasper, Alabama volunteered for 'at least a hundred.'"[19] Lemmons' glowing depiction of brother Nichols illustrates the level of estimation perceived of him by an approving brotherhood. His talents made him the man for any occasion where the impartation of biblical truth was needed. In his day, he was the quintessential spokesman for righteousness, and most worthy of the assessment, "prince of preachers."

In February, Gus made his way out to Wichita, Kansas where he served as the keynote speaker for the lectureship at the Cleveland Avenue church. The fourteenth annual program focused upon the theme, "The Power of the Church." Speaking each night, as well as at three noon services, his lessons focused on purity, good deeds, and discipline. They stated, "We are happy that we can bring Brother Nichols to this section again."[20]

Alabama Christian College Lectures was next on the agenda. He was the evening keynote speaker at 8:30 on the 9th of March. His subject was, "The Death of Christ."[21]

Following was a trip to Nashville in April for the 32nd annual David Lipscomb College Lectures. He spoke on a special track with G. Mitchell Pullias (1895-1984) and B. Jack Boyd (1901-1978) on the subjects, "Christian Man—Husband, Father, Elder, Evangelist,"[22] and "Christian

Woman—Her Role And Her Reward."[23] Gus also taught a 9:00 a.m. daily class on, "Meeting Major Denominational Errors."[24]

His belief in supporting the Christian Colleges made Gus the perfect voice of reason to encourage support from others. In the age when the way business was conducted by the schools was called into question, he was ready to defend their practice when in keeping with biblical principles. This was especially true for Alabama Christian College. Being a board member, he felt an attack on the school was an attack on himself.

When inflammatory remarks of speculation about how the school solicited funds arose through the pen of Florence preacher, Charles Holt, in the *Gospel Gleaner*, and in his local bulletin, the *Contender*, Gus clarified the policy of Alabama Christian College concerning the receiving of funds from congregations. In an article that appeared in the school paper, *The Alabama Christian College Reporter*, and later in the *Advocate*, Gus expressed that the Board had determined not to solicit funds from churches but would allow the college to accept "unsolicited donations,"[25] from them. The policy was determined only after Co-President Rex A. Turner (1913-2001) asked the advice of John T. Lewis (1876-1967) and Gus Nichols. It was then that the Board of Trustees made its policy decision in 1946, thirteen years prior to Holt's stirrings.

B. C. GOODPASTURE APPRECIATION LUNCHEON

While in Nashville for the David Lipscomb College Lectureship, Gus was a participant in a special luncheon. For twenty years, B. C. Goodpasture (1895-1977) had been at the helm of one of the brotherhood's most prestigious papers, the *Gospel Advocate*. The Old South Room at the Maxwell House Hotel in downtown Nashville was the setting for the festivities where above 250 attendees gathered to extend their appreciation to the prodigious editor. The dignitaries present were among some of the brotherhood's most highly respected leaders. Batsell Barrett Baxter (1916-1982), head of David Lipscomb College's Bible Department, served as the master of ceremonies. His tribute to the editor was in the form of a comparison between he and another great church leader of a previous century. Calling Goodpasture, "The Alexander Campbell Of Our Day,"[26] his illustrative similarities were recorded for later transcribing and posting in the pages of the *Advocate*.

The main spokesman for the event was Gus Nichols. His speech, "An Excellent Editor, Wonderful Paper And A Good Work," was also later transcribed and published in full. Praise was given the great editor of GA for his difficult, but devoted task at decision making. In his own very unique way, he illustrated his editorial skills by telling a story of a farmer that hired a strong young man to work on his farm. He said,

For many weeks the young fellow enjoyed chopping wood, digging ditches and doing the heavy work made available. Finally, the old farmer became somewhat sorry for the young fellow and decided to give him an easier job. So he sent him to the potato barn to separate the rotting potatoes from the good ones. The young man came for his lunch that day and announced that he was leaving, and would work no longer. When urged to give a reason for his sudden change of mind and unhappiness, he admitted that his new job did not require the manual labor required in chopping wood and digging ditches, but declared his new job was killing him. When asked what it was, he shook his head and said, "It's them decisions!"[27]

Focus was given to the role journals have played in contributing to the strength of the body of Christ. He praised Alexander Campbell (1788-1866) and his efforts in *The Christian Baptist* to influence preachers of his day to know, "the way of the Lord more perfectly." In the same vein, *Gospel Advocate* had done similarly among its readership for over a century. He further demonstrated it by bringing up several examples of innovations that through the years have been successfully combated against in the pages of the *Advocate* concluding,

> Its power for good has been great, and never greater than now under the guidance of its illustrious editor, B. C. Goodpasture. Counting all its readers, which far exceed its large subscription list, perhaps a quarter of a million people read something good from its pages each year, most of them each week. It should go into every home in every congregation of the saints.[28]

PLACING MEMBERSHIP

Several articles continued to appear in the pages of the *Gospel Advocate* from the pen of Gus Nichols during this period. Being the queries editor for the paper led to numerous opportunities to answer questions on a wide range of topics. Between 1958 and 1960 over fifty subjects were addressed under the wisdom of his learned pen. Among the many answers to questions sent in, he dealt with such subjects as judging, serving on Jury Duty, elders, deacons, addressing the needs of orphans and widows, instrumental music in worship, issues surrounding death and eternity, cremation, women leading in worship, singing during the Lord's Supper, eating on the church grounds, marriage and many, many more.

Appearing as the front-page article for the 28 August 1958 issue of *GA* was an article by Gus Nichols entitled, "Placing Membership." What followed was a biblical and practical handling of a question concerning the authority for local congregations of the church to enforce such practice.

Bleeding into two more pages in the issue, the subject was so capably addressed by the queries editor that at the end of the article was the addenda, "This article will be printed in tract form and may be purchased from the Gospel Advocate Company. —Editor."[29]

In the October 3rd issue, the following advertisement appeared, "'Placing Membership,' Gus Nichols. Sound counsel and scriptural authority on the question of placing membership in a local congregation upon moving to a new place. 3¢ each; $2.25 per 100."[30] Advertised with a tract by another brother, the ad suggested, "Distribute them among the congregation...furnish them to Bible classes...display them in the church lobby for visitors to take and read."[31] With such distribution, it is easy to see how the influence of Gus Nichols became so widely experienced among brethren across the nation.

CONTROVERSIES CONTINUE

Disputes in the brotherhood continued to take its toll on unity throughout the end of the decade. Deep and abiding friendships that were longstanding were falling by the way with every passing month while the papers hammered out the issues. Accusations, pointed fingers, and reading between the lines, continued to break down long-enjoyed harmony. So, from where did the controversies arise? Gus reasoned,

> Not only do we have to face the old problems over and over, as they don a new dress, but new problems, real and imaginary, are constantly rising out of the minds of a restless, changing population. Many of our problems now plaguing the church had no real existence as such, until so many began to talk and write so much about them that the brotherhood to some extent has become confused.[32]

Perhaps a good illustration of this might be seen in an article written by Homer Hailey (1903-2000). It appeared on the front page of the 20th of November 1959 issue of *Gospel Advocate* entitled, "Keepers of Orthodoxy." In it, Hailey spoke about the present crisis in the brotherhood, steering clear of any particular personalities. He gave examples of great and charitable works that denominations had done in helping those in benevolent need; noting that it was not the church that was doing these things, but others. He followed by expressing concern that when some have sought to do something in a positive way they were often met with criticism by self-appointed keepers of orthodoxy, adding, "Then let someone raise a word of defense of the man for what he is doing, and he, too, becomes an outcast."[33] Zeroing in on the destructive threat of those who saw themselves as "keepers of orthodoxy," he attempted to get the brotherhood to see the big picture, how the "threat" was minimal in comparison to the over-all need for maintaining unity. He continued,

What have the members of the church done, aside from holding a few meetings over the country, building a few buildings, and conducting a few poorly arranged and directed Sunday morning Bible classes? They have built a half dozen colleges and are directing a half dozen orphan homes. What else? That is about it. And who have been instrumental in even this little? Not the "keepers of orthodoxy;" they have been too busy telling these few what is wrong with their methods and efforts to lead in anything constructive.[34]

With several appeals, Hailey closed his article by saying that as long as the church stands, there will be a need for men to,

Stand firmly and staunchly against innovations and against departures from the truth. But when contentions for the truth degenerate into personal feuds, characterized by vituperation, satire, sarcasm, and personal animosities, such "keepers of orthodoxy" then serve no good end. Their works become that of destruction, not of the error they set out to meet, that will have been forgotten, but of whatever good the church may have been doing, which, heaven knows, is little enough.[35]

Two weeks later, Gus was given the editorial page of the issue in which he gave comments under the title, "Homer Hailey's Article." In glowing and loving terms, he expressed his appreciation for Hailey's words, expressing that it was shameful that many great works had been left to denominations when the church should be doing these kinds of things. He said, "I was made glad and my eyes cleared up from the mist of tears to think that we had such a fine article from such a fine man as Homer Hailey."[36] Further in the piece, Gus expressed his desire as he read the Hailey article that he wanted to send him a letter to thank him for it,

But upon finishing the article, I was greatly let down, and it would be impossible for me to describe my feelings and deep emotions when I saw that this excellent article was written in 1952—more than six years ago. During these six years, many changes have taken place. Many fine men and wonderful gospel preachers have lined up with the very spirit and movement which Brother Hailey's article condemns, and have hindered the good works which Brother Hailey commended in his article. Had his article been written under a recent date, it would have carried with it tremendous weight and power. However, I am glad it was written and that somebody requested its reappearance in the *Advocate*. I love Brother Hailey because he is a lovable man and has not lost the milk of human kindness from his soul.[37]

Closing with a concern that had Hailey written the article today that he might not endorse every word of it, Gus assumed this in view of Hailey's transition to align himself with those leading in the present crisis. The church cooperation division continued.

PRAISE FOR FRIDAY NIGHT CLASSES

An article appeared in the February 12, 1959 issue of the *Gospel Advocate* praising the teaching work of brother Nichols. Written by Ernest Clevenger, Jr. (1929-2014), the piece gives a bird's-eye view of the kind of service that was being provided to the brotherhood through the Friday night classes that were being offered in Jasper, as well as the man behind it. The article, entitled, "I Discovered Gus Nichols," is reproduced here in its entirety.

Friday Night Classes

Ever since I can remember, I have heard of Gus Nichols, and can remember a few of the times when he preached in Chattanooga when I was a boy. Until moving to Alabama, I had never really known Brother Nichols, even though I had heard him in meetings and lectureships in several states.

One day, after I had been living in Russellville for a few months, a brother wrote me that a monthly class was being organized for preachers, and Brother Gus was to be the teacher. I inquired about this class from some who said they had been attending his weekly class, and from some "older" preachers who lived in North Alabama that had been driving the sixty to one hundred miles or more to Jasper two or three times a month to sit in his class. I decided that I, too, would go to see what "magic spell" this teacher could hold over preachers to make them travel so far for just a two-hour class. The day I went was the day I discovered Gus Nichols.

This writer has never heard anyone who can match the ability of Brother Nichols to put across the message of God's word in simple yet forceful terms and illustrations. He can wring more thoughts out of one verse than four or five "average" preachers can. But even more, he does what he preaches; he "wraps his message in love." His sermons on illustrating Bible truths by such things as a pencil, a watch, a hammer and a postage stamp are such that people who hear them, even from an inexperienced speaker cannot forget them easily. With many things today, within and without the church, to discourage and lead young preachers off the true pathway, Brother Nichols' life and teaching are an inspiration.

Each Friday night men from near and far gather at the Sixth Avenue church building in Jasper for the 7 o'clock class. The last Friday night in each month has been set aside for those who cannot attend but once a month. If you can go, it will not cost, it will pay.[38]

ENDNOTES

1 G. H. P. Showalter, "Further Report On Television," *Firm Foundation*, 25 May 1954, p. 5.

2 Note: No relation to Gus Nichols.

3 G. H. P. Showalter, ed., "Television Programs In Production," *Firm Foundation*, 9 February 1954, p. 9.

4 Glenn L. Wallace, "Questions About The 'Herald of Truth,'" *Firm Foundation*, 1 December 1953, p. 3. Note: Glenn L. Wallace (1907-1978) appears to have been one of the first, if not the first, critic to raise an eye-brow against the *Herald of Truth* in brotherhood papers. Others followed over time.

5 W. S. Willis, "A Perfect Pattern,"*Firm Foundation*, 2 March 1954, p. 11. Note: The American Christian Missionary Society was originated in 1849, and its great growth and power led to much division among churches of the Restoration Movement around the turn of the 20th century. It is beyond the scope of this work to delve deeply into a discussion of the controversy over the *Herald of Truth* program, or for that matter, many of the other issues that divided the churches other than the things that directly affected and involved Gus Nichols.

6 Cecil N. Wright, "The Herald Of Truth Discussion," *Gospel Advocate*, 1 April 1954, p. 251.

7 G. K. Wallace, "The Herald Of Truth," *Gospel Advocate*, 15 May 1952, p. 319.

8 *Winston County Church History*, unpublished, Special Resources Room, Carl Elliott Regional Library, Jasper, Alabama, p. 35.

9 Paul Hunton, "3,000 Souls for $1.00," *Gospel Advocate*, 26 November 1959, p. 757.

10 John F. Reese, "Brother Nichols' Radio Program," *Gospel Advocate*, 10 December 1959, p. 792.

11 Paul V. Dobson, "Irvington Lectures," *Gospel Advocate*, 6 May 1958, p. 286.

12 Tommy Q. Vernon, *Gospel Advocate*, 4 September 1958, p. 571.

13 Gilbert E. Shaffer, *Gospel Advocate*, 30 October 1958, p. 697.

14 Note: Ronald Sanders' meeting with Gus Nichols was the first of several encounters with other Alabama preachers among churches of Christ in years to come including Hiram O. Hutto (1923-2006) in Cordova in 1960, Tom Moody twice in Jasper and in Brilliant in 1973, and Thomas N. Thrasher in Decatur in 1973.

15 Reuel Lemmons, ed., *Firm Foundation*, 11 November 1958, p. 718.

16 Ibid.

17 Advertisement, *Firm Foundation*, 14 January 1958, p. 25.

18 Ibid., 9 December 1958, p. 781.

19 Reuel Lemmons, ed., "The Freed-Hardeman Lectureship," *Firm Foundation*, 20 January 1959, p. 34.

20 Advertisement, "Cleveland Avenue Plans Fourteenth Annual Lectureship," *Firm Foundation*, 10 February 1959, p. 94.

21 Advertisement, *Gospel Advocate*, 5 March 1959, p. 158.

22 Advertisement, "David Lipscomb College, 32nd Annual Lecture Series, *Firm Foundation*, April 19-23," 10 March 1959, p. 160.

23 Advertisement, *Gospel Advocate*, 2 April 1959, pp. 209, 222.

24 Ibid.

25 Gus Nichols, *Gospel Advocate*, 10 September 1959, p. 583.

26 Batsell Barrett Baxter, *Gospel Advocate*, 14 May 1959, p. 311.

27 Ibid., p. 313.

28 Ibid., p. 314.

29 B. C. Goodpasture, ed., *Gospel Advocate*, 28 August 1958, p. 555.

30 Advertisement, "Valuable Booklets For Every Individual And Congregation," *Gospel Advocate*, 2 October 1958, p. 633.

31 Ibid.

32 Gus Nichols, *Gospel Advocate*, 14 May 1959, p. 313.

33 Homer Hailey, "Keepers of Orthodoxy," *Gospel Advocate*, 20 November 1958, p. 737.

34 Ibid.

35 Ibid. p. 747.

36 Gus Nichols, *Gospel Advocate*, 4 December 1958, p. 770.

37 Ibid.

38 Ernest A., Clevenger, Jr., *Gospel Advocate*, 12 February 1959, p. 103.

Stalwart Defender Of The Faith

> They shall not hurt nor destroy in all my holy mountain: for the earth shall be full of the knowledge of the Lord, as the waters cover the sea.
> —The Messianic Prophet, Isaiah 11:9

MODERATING FOR THE WALLACE-HOLT DEBATE

A grammar school auditorium in Florence, Alabama served as host location for a debate between G. K. Wallace (1903-1988) and Charles A. Holt in mid-December 1959. Wallace was living in Henderson, Tennessee, at the time and working for Freed-Hardeman College. Holt was the local minister for the East Florence church of Christ.

The discussion centered on protests from some brethren about supporting orphanages like Childhaven, Boles Children's Home, and the like, out of the church treasury. Also, similar support of the national radio and television program, *Herald of Truth*, was being called into question. Moderating for brother Wallace was Gus Nichols.

There was some doubt up until time of the debate as to whether the event would take place. Previously, both participants had signed propositions, but Holt and the elders of the East Florence congregation continued making changes to the propositions. Wallace accused them of facilitating Holt, so he could lash out at orphanages by name and anyone else he chose. He protested, "At the same time they restrict me from even referring to *The Gospel Guardian*[1] and the East Florence Church where he preaches."[2] Brother Wallace determined only to debate according to the originally agreed upon propositions, and that if Holt and the East Florence elders did not like it they

Gus Nichols

did not have to show up for the exchange. He followed, saying that he would be there, and if no one showed, he would preach four nights on the agreed-upon propositions himself.

In the end, Holt and his followers did come to the debate. The moderator later wrote an extensive report on the proceedings illuminating the arguments made on both sides.[3] While orderliness prevailed throughout, Holt's presentations were somewhat pointed and severe. Wallace was praised for the way he handled both himself and the arguments of his opponent. The determination was to print the debate and make it available through the Gospel Advocate Company. Within a year the *Wallace-Holt Debate* was produced in book form.

Marvin Bryant, Gus Nichols, V. P. Black

THE CONVERSION OF MARVIN BRYANT

Hidden to most of the Judeo-Christian world is the unique and precious concept of New Testament Christianity. Those who have preached the restoration plea have provided the world with a gift from God not to be taken lightly. The recipients of this gift have attained to it out of a deep realization of something lacking in their own particular religious experience when compared to the Word of God. Drawing closer to the

Lord through a study of His Word will present an irresistible press toward a return to His way and nothing short of it will suffice.

Gus Nichols found this way; whether by intention or by being in the right place at the right time will be forever unclear; though in his thinking it was the providence of God. What is certain is that there was a burning desire within him for knowledge and clarity. When he was exposed to the truth of the gospel, and mixed it with a discerning spirit, the result was obedience. Participation in salvation and the church Jesus built in Acts 2 was the outcome.

Naturally, his devotion to preaching that message was to find people similar to himself—searchers! Searchers for truth! One such person among thousands was a man by the name of Marvin Franklin Bryant (1922-1997). A native of Stockton, Baldwin County, Alabama, Marvin grew up in the Presbyterian faith. Trained for the ministry at Columbia Theological Seminary in Decatur, Georgia, he served in his chosen denomination several years. While attending a term of study at the University of Edinburgh, Scotland, he devoted himself to a particular study on the worship of the church of the New Testament. This resulted in an effort on his part to see if just such a church existed today. Upon returning to the United States, he reached out to Curtis C. Cates (1910-2003),[4] a minister he had known when preaching for the Presbyterians down in Foley, Alabama some years previous. Cates, then the preacher at the West End church of Christ in Montgomery, Alabama was able to give him much insight as to the intent and purpose of those who seek the ancient order of things. Brother Cates introduced Marvin to Rex A. Turner (1913-2001). The two became fast friends and studied the Scriptures most frequently.

Marvin's search led him to attend the Freed-Hardeman College Lecture program in early January 1960. The theme of the program that year was "A Changeless Gospel In A Changing World."[5] As usual, Gus Nichols was there as a daily speaker on the subject of "Denomination Doctrines: A Corrupted Gospel." Intrigued by the study, he was introduced to Gus and several others. Studying with the man while in Henderson, he was invited down to Jasper to visit in the Nichols family home. After studying with Gus, Marvin determined that he must be baptized for the forgiveness of his sins and did so the 26th of January by the hands of brother Nichols.[6]

Marvin's elder brother in the faith became a great confidant, and he long held the Nichols family in highest esteem. Very quickly after his baptism he was preaching meetings among congregations of the church of Christ. He began a unique ministry of his own reaching out to denominational preachers and presenting to them the restoration plea. The outcome was that many church leaders from among several denominations gave up their ties to religious division in order to take on the New Testament order. His is one brief, but highly successful, example of one whose life was touched by the gospel through Gus Nichols, and through him and others continued to bless the Kingdom of Christ with other potential members.[7]

The sincere closeness to brother Bryant's "father in the faith," is demonstrated in the lines he wrote to sister Nichols years after the passing of his esteemed brother in Christ. The handwritten letter is entered in its entirety,

> January 26, 1989
>
> Dear Sister Nichols,
>
> It was January 26, 1960 that I drove to Jasper from Montgomery to spend the night with you and bro. Gus. My purpose in coming was to test my understanding of the scripture with him before I got baptized by bro Rex Turner who had primarily been my teacher.
>
> After supper this night he invited me to attend an elders' meeting with him and the end results was I was baptized there by him. No doubt even this, I believe, was providential. Every year thereafter on January 26th, I always wrote bro. Nichols and thanked him for the contribution that he had made in my life. I believe the year after his death I wrote to you.
>
> I spent so many happy nights in your home and you were always so gracious and good. You were a real complement to him and the great work that he did for God.
>
> I hope you are well and enjoying good health. I promise to remember you in my prayers and I wish to be remembered in yours.
>
> God Bless,
>
> Marvin Bryant

COLLEGE PROGRAMS

Gus continued to make his circuit among the Christian College lecture series. Being the queries editor for the *Gospel Advocate* made him the logical candidate for doing similar work among the colleges. In the spring of 1960, he conducted the daily Queries and Answers Sessions during the Special Classes at David Lipscomb College.[8] In 1961, he did the same during the August series. Of his work, Willard Collins (1915-2007) wrote,

> Gus Nichols, a member of the *Gospel Advocate* staff, probably holds the record for having appeared on more Lipscomb August

Stalwart Defender Of The Faith

lecture programs than any other speaker. He has lost count of the number in which he has participated but has been here nearly every year. He spoke in a special session on "Dangers Facing the Church" throughout the week. He and Mrs. Nichols announced that they expect to come back for every future Lipscomb August lectures as long as the Lord permits them to do so.[9]

Later in November, Gus made his first trip out to Searcy, Arkansas, to participate in the 38th Annual Harding College Lecture Series. During the program, the young and dynamic Arkansas preacher, Charles R. Coil (1929-1994), spoke on, "The Challenge Of Seeking The Lost At Home."[10] He illustrated the importance of telling the story of Jesus by saying,

The Lecturer

> Bro. Gus Nichols tells of the boy who appeared on a radio quiz program and was asked what was his greatest accomplishment. The boy replied that his greatest achievement thus far in life was to graduate from a certain school. Said Bro. Nichols sadly: "I knew then that this boy had never won a soul, for soul-winning is the world's greatest work."[11]

ONE-HUNDRED-SIX RESPONSES

The annual gospel meetings at Sixth Avenue were highlights of each and every year for the church. As has been noticed in the history of its existence, some of the finest preachers in the brotherhood stood in their pulpit and proclaimed the unsearchable riches of Christ. Without exception, in the spring of 1961, there was perhaps no greater voice for the cause of Christ than that of Willie Albert Bradfield (1910-1972). W. A. was known far and wide by his sheer presence in the pulpit. At well over six feet tall, his hands outstretched to nearly seven feet according to his biographer, Andrew D. Erwin. His deep booming voice, charismatic presence, and powerful ability to proclaim the Word, made him the perfect speaker for their outreach effort.

On the first day of the meeting, 397 attended. On the last night, before a crowd of 957, he stood proclaiming the message with great confidence. From Ephesians 2:12 he proclaimed, "If you are outside of Christ there is No Hope! No Hope! No Hope!"[12] As the song leader ascended the platform, people came pouring into the aisles. With occasional interruptions by the Tennessee preacher, song after song continued to be led. All the while, cries from the great speaker could be heard above the sound of the singing as he walked up and down the aisles searching the crowd for those who might respond. After an invitation that was said to have gone on for "one and one-half hours,"[13] the crowd was seated, and fifty-three souls had made their way to the front of the auditorium in response.[14] All together, one-hundred-six responded during the eight-day meeting with fifty-four baptisms and fifty-two restorations in potentially one of the greatest meetings in the history of the congregation. In glowing terms Bradfield reported on his visit to Jasper saying, "It was one of the richest experiences in my life to be associated with Gus Nichols and the Sixth Avenue church in Jasper, Ala."[15]

GA SUBSCRIPTION CHALLENGE

Early in January 1961, a "big" subscription drive kicked off at the *Gospel Advocate* with a formal challenge between two of the most well-known preachers in the brotherhood. Located at Madison, Tennessee, Ira North (1922-1984) was the minister of the largest congregation among churches of Christ in the world. He was also a professor of speech at David Lipscomb College. He challenged "Gus Nichols, minister of the church of Christ in Jasper, Ala., and champion of former subscription drives for the *Gospel Advocate*."[16] The gauntlet laid down was as follows:

> Whereas both you and I are deeply appreciative of the great good the *Gospel Advocate* has done for over one hundred years,
>
> Whereas we are both genuinely interested in seeing its influence for good extended,
>
> Whereas also you have been the champion subscription man for many years,
>
> I, therefore, challenge you to a friendly contest in 1961 to see who can bring in the most subscriptions to this grand old paper that has contended so earnestly for the restoration of New Testament Christianity for so long,
>
> And further suggest that you as the champion and I as the challenger look to our mutual friend, Willard Collins, as "umpire" and leave it to him to set down the rules of the great subscription war.
>
> Your devoted friend and younger admirer, Ira North."[17]

In similar fashion, the Jasper preacher picked up the gauntlet three issues later and the battle began. In a subsequent release, details of the contest were further explained,

> Gus Nichols, the stalwart defender of the faith, of Jasper, Ala., has accepted the challenge of Ira North, the dynamic preacher

of the Madison (Tenn.) church of Christ, to a friendly contest to see which can secure the greater number of subscriptions to the *Gospel Advocate* between now and December 31, 1961.[18]

Friends of both preachers were encouraged to send in subscriptions to support the competitor of their choice in the challenge. The winner at the end of the contest was to receive an award of $100 by the *Advocate*.

An update in early March described Nichols as the "champion," and North as the "contender."[19] People were again encouraged to send in clubs and individual subscriptions in the name of either of the two involved in the contest. On the 6th of April, both men made appeals to *GA* readers to help them win the challenge. Ira North wrote,

Gus Nichols' 77th Birthday

> I humbly solicit your help in the great subscription contest now underway between Brother Nichols and me. I am the underdog in this contest. Brother Nichols is older than I am. He has more knowledge. He has more wisdom. He has many contacts all over the country. He has been the champion subscription man for many years. However, what I lack in knowledge, wisdom, etc., I intend to make up with hard work. I am in the contest to win. I solicit your help. It is time for a change. My campaign is rolling and headed for victory in December. Your help and influence will be greatly appreciated.[20]

It was easily seen that the exchange between these two men was all in the spirit of friendly competition. Seeing the more jovial side of the champion, in similar banter, Gus responded to the challenge made by the young man thirty years his junior,

This is to solicit the help of every reader of the *Gospel Advocate* in my behalf in the subscription contest between Ira North and me, to end in December of this year. Brother North and hundreds of workers are working feverishly to unseat me. They are combing the nation for subscriptions to be counted in his favor. Brother North is a highly educated Christian gentleman, richly endowed with many talents and with a winning personality.

However, I wish to win this contest for the following reasons: (1) I desire to increase the circulation of the greatest and finest religious weekly magazine in all the world, a paper which has stood the test of the fiery trials for more than one hundred years. (2) I was raising clubs for the *Advocate* before my worthy opponent could read. (3) Furthermore, I am not living in the past. Just six years ago during the great Centennial Drive for subscriptions, I sent in more than fifteen hundred, and I am still the champion subscription winner. (4) Why should it be thought to be "time for a change," so long as I produce more subscriptions than any other? Why should I be laid on the shelf and have to "fade away like an old soldier?" (5) Brother North is young and after I am gone will have opportunity to taste the joy, which comes from winning. Trials and years have brought me through the school of experience until I am now better fitted than ever before for the mark of distinction in the goal set before us. However, this time I must depend upon others to help me. If my friends fail to get out and make up the clubs, I shall be defeated![21]

In April, the count was 1,091 to the contender and 976 to the champion.[22] By June, the numbers were 2,234 subscriptions by North and 2,192 by Nichols.[23]

On the 20th of that month, Gus found himself once again involved with the Gospel Advocate Appreciation Dinner. The 106th annual anniversary of the paper was conducted again on the campus of David Lipscomb College during its Summer Lectureship program. There were 206 who assembled for the event where the repartee between champion and contender continued, both appearing as the featured speakers.[24] At the banquet, Nichols was showing a slight lead with 2,671 subscriptions, and North with 2,653.

Progressing through the summer, the August report showed 3,401 for the North column and 2,760 in the Nichols column. In September, the number was 3,030 in favor of Nichols and 3,416 in favor of North.[25] By November, 3,500 subscriptions appeared on North's side, and 3,199 on the Nichols' side.[26] *GA* reported in mid-December, "The contest is close—

too close 'to be comfortable.' The final score will be announced early in January."[27]

On the 11th of January 1962, an article on the third page appeared with the banner, "Ira North Becomes Champion Subscription Man For *Gospel Advocate*."[28] Willard Collins reported that 4,761 subscriptions were sent in for the new champion, while Nichols came in at second with 3,838 subscriptions. The drive turned out to be a good marketing campaign for the paper, and further bolstered the place of both preachers in the hearts of a profoundly admiring brotherhood.

Gus Nichols

In a providential twist, the outcome of the contest became a greater blessing to the loser. When brother North was told he would receive the $100 for winning the contest, he determining to give the entire amount to the former champion by way of making the first contribution toward a potential Bible Lands tour for the elder preacher. As brother Nichols had never been to the Holy Lands, the excitement of such a trip was something the whole brotherhood could support.

An appeal was made to the readers of the *Advocate* to contribute to the "On To The Holy Land Brother Gus Nichols" travel fund. The offices of the *Gospel Advocate* agreed to be the collection point for anyone who wished to contribute toward just such a trip.

GOSPEL MEETING WORK

In 1960 and 1961 Gus traveled to several places in the country for gospel meeting opportunities. In early February 1960, he traveled to Ponca City, Oklahoma, to preach a meeting for the church there.[29] In May, he traveled over to Alexander City, Alabama for a meeting. Long-time friend, John Payne (1910-1992), was preaching there at the time and reported, "Eighteen responded to the invitation. The church was edified greatly."[30] A meeting followed in Milan, Tennessee, in early September with eighteen being baptized and one being restored. The preacher, O. D. Johns (1922-2002) said of brother Nichols, "He did some of the greatest preaching I have ever heard."[31] In mid-October he made his way to Memphis to participate on a lectureship program at the Getwell congregation.[32] From there he made his way to St. Louis, Missouri, to preach a meeting for the West End congregation.³³ He finished the year with a meeting at East Cullman, Alabama.³⁴

1961

As has been seen thus far in his preaching career, gospel meeting work was a highly significant ingredient in the ministry of Gus Nichols. Year after year to this time his meeting efforts were reported in the pages of brotherhood journals. However, in 1961, for the first time in his preaching life, no reports of his meetings were published. This is not to say that he was less busy. At the end of the Jasper meeting, W. A. Bradfield said, "Brother Nichols preaches nineteen sermons per week and is one of the finest co-workers that could ever be found. He has been preaching in Jasper for twenty-eight years."³⁵ Preaching two sermons daily over the radio for seven days a week made up the bulk of this number. Adding to these daily duties were his weekly obligations in the pulpit at Jasper as well as the many Bible classes, Friday night training sessions, funerals, weddings and other duties he conducted. Perhaps the reason for fewer reports was the sheer volume of involvement in the public eye at this point in his life. At 69 years of age, the man was busier than he had ever been in his younger years.

When Gus was not preaching he was writing. Nearly half the issues of the *Gospel Advocate* in 1961 contained his *Queries Answers* column. A vast array of subjects was under discussion, Divorce & Remarriage, appointing and trying elders, the work of the Holy Spirit today, baptism and sanctification, hermeneutics, and several others. With all these things being done on a regular basis, it is little wonder that he would be considered a stalwart defender of the faith.

THE GUS NICHOLS STORY

How do you sum up the life's work of a man like Gus Nichols? In March 1961, the first of three articles appeared in the pages of the *Gospel Advocate* devoted to an exchange with brother Nichols. In an interview format, many questions about Gus' life and experiences were asked.³⁶ Questions about his early life, conversion, study habits, and the like, gave him ample opportunity to give a most insightful look into his life. He revealed things about his work, such as the number of sermons he had produced were "several thousand outlines on paper and perhaps many more than that in mind."³⁷ He disclosed that he had "held up toward one hundred" debates, and that the preachers who had influenced him most were N. B. Hardeman (1874-1965), H. Leo Boles (1874-1946) and the writings of the old Indiana preacher, Ben Franklin (1812-1878). He explained that he had trained at least 34 preachers from his Friday Night Class sessions over the years. He told how many of his family were preaching saying there were, "four of us brothers who preach, four of my

The Gus Nichols Story

sons preach, three sons-in-law, and about six or seven others who are in the realm of kinship."[38]

He was asked about his father's conversion, and his most "unusual" but successful radio program. Photos appeared showing the man at work as well.

The major questions of discussion in the interview centered on the "dangers facing the church" and those promoting division within it. In Gus' thinking the four greatest threats were, "first, modernism and liberalism on the one hand, and secondly, anti-ism on the other hand."[39] He completed the list with materialism and complacency. When asked about those who caused division, he singled out Roy Cogdill (1907-1985) and Yater Tant (1908-1997) who were the editors of *The Gospel Guardian*.

In the final section of the interview, he was asked, "What principle issues are involved in the present disturbances which face members of the church?"[40] His answer involved a discussion on how churches are biblically allowed to address the needs of widows and orphans. His first concern was the view that the church was all-sufficient for its work including being able to provide a home for widows or orphans. He said, "God never intended that the church should be a home."[41] And that, "God has never legislated as to where the needy are to be cared for."[42]

Another issue of disturbance he perceived was how some could hold to the idea that the church could not help non-Christians with benevolence. He used as example that if a cyclone came through and people were injured around the church building, the church could not help a child because he is not a "saint," or brother. Such thinking made no sense to him. Still another issue was that some believed that churches could not cooperate in evangelizing. He cited passages of Scripture to show how churches in the first century assisted each other in carrying out the work of the Lord and alluded to efforts like the *Herald Of Truth* program which plainly fall within the guidelines of these biblical precedents.

By in large, supporters of the *Gospel Advocate* were very pleased with the interview. One preacher wrote, "I hope you will put part three of your 'Gus Nichols Story' in tract form. It contains the most able treatment of the 'issues' that I have seen in print."[43]

However, not everyone was quite so pleased. A growing burr in the saddle of brother Nichols and cooperating brethren was a preacher who had moved into Walker County, Thomas Gaither O'Neal (1939-2012). Preacher for the McArthur Heights congregation south of Jasper, he had his own daily radio program, and devoted a generous amount of time attacking Gus Nichols, the Sixth Avenue church, the *Gospel Advocate*, and any other person or group on his radar screen who promoted institutional support and church cooperation.[44]

Beginning in the September 21st issue of *The Gospel Guardian*, O'Neal began a four-part run of his own, prefaced as a "review" of "The Gus Nichols Story."[45] Throughout the series, arrows were shot at the elder preacher. He made comments like, "The Sixth Avenue meeting house is the 'unofficial' headquarters of religious activity of churches of Christ in Walker County, Alabama."[46] Claims were made that Gus had been "reviewing" O'Neal's sermons on the radio for months, and charged him with being the "papa" of all the preachers in the county.[47] He charged Nichols as having used his influence to cause some of O'Neal's planned gospel meetings in the region to be canceled. His main thrust was accusing brother Nichols and his cooperating brethren of going beyond the authority of the Scriptures to support children's homes and joint mission efforts from the church treasury.

The attacks on brother Nichols broadened in 1963 when Irven Powell Lee (1914-1991), moved to Jasper to assist some brethren in establishing the North Jasper church of Christ. They built a small building just north of town on Highway 5.[48] Similar to O'Neal, Irven Lee had his own radio program where he continued to criticize brother Nichols and what he considered the dangers of institutional support. Both O'Neal and Lee were known at times to play taped sermons of nationally known non-institutional preachers, Yater Tant (1908-1997) and A. C. Grider (1912-1990), and, then accuse the brethren at Sixth Aveunue and their preacher of walking disorderly.[49] Often times as brother Nichols gave what seemed to be a daily defense, he referred to Lee and the North Jasper brethren as "the church a little north of the Bible."

With every passing month, with every subsequent issue of the brotherhood journals, and the daily regurgitations of the issues over the air, lines were being drawn in the sand and divisions among brethren prevailed. Alabama churches as a whole were being disturbed with division over the cooperation issues, and county by county it became easily discernable as to the direction that region would go based on how many of the individual congregations determined the camp in which they belonged.

At this stage of his life, brother Nichols was a household name throughout the brotherhood. Depending on your feelings over the issues of the day determined in a great way as to whether or not his name conjured up good feelings. The growing displeasure by some brethren, whom he had loved and

Gus and Matilda at Blue Ridge

Blue Ridge Encampment Attendees

Attendees at Blue Ridge Encampment
Photos by James S. Rickard (1920-2014)

cherished for many years, served to break his heart. However, he never relented in his resolve to stand for what he believed to be the truth, as the Gus Nichols story continued.

BLUE RIDGE ENCAMPMENT

Tucked away in the recesses of the Smokey Mountains are the grounds of the Blue Ridge Encampment. Located a few miles east of Ashville, North Carolina, in the little community of Black Mountain, is a conference center built and operated by the Y.M.C.A. The brainchild of J. W. Brents (1884-1963) and A. R. Holton (1891-1964) and others, the annual gathering began as a summer retreat for members of the church in 1951.[50] The program served to attract several church leaders like Ira North (1922-1984), Batsell Barrett Baxter (1916-1982), J. M. Powell (1907-2004), and many more. The first visit for Gus and Matilda was in the summer of 1961. Gus was asked to be a featured speaker and to handle questions and answers in what became known as the "Gus Nichols Hour."[51] For years thereafter, part of the Nichols' summer tradition was to attend the Blue Ridge Encampment.[52] Each year, they gathered what grandchildren were close by and carried them to Bible camp. Vicki, Karen, Eddie, Janet, and others recalled many summer visits to North Carolina.

TRAINING FOR SERVICE

The effort to increase education among churches goes back to the early 1930s when Jesse Parker Sewell (1876-1969) and Henry Eli Speck, Jr. (1885-1966) wrote a book entitled, "The Church and Her Ideal Educational Situation."[53] Sewell, Speck and others traveled among churches then to help build their Bible School programs. It was not until the mid-1950s that area-wide gatherings were planned to enhance the education program in churches. Some of the first "Training For Service" gatherings that became annual events were in Lubbock, Texas; Oklahoma City, Oklahoma; and at Madison church of Christ in Nashville, Tennessee. In Alabama, programs were conducted in Montgomery, Birmingham and in the Shoals. These programs were so well planned that thousands joined in from long distances to increase their teaching skills for the Bible School programs at home.

In November 1961, around thirty churches in the area surrounding Jasper cooperated in conducting a "Training For Service Series" of their own. Conducting the program were men from Nashville such as Paul M. Tucker (1914-2000), Neil S. Bryan (1915-1994) and Fred G. Allen, Jr. (1918-2000), who specialized in making teacher's aides for children's classes. Others included Lottie E. Novak (1917-2006) from Columbia, Tennessee; Levoy Bivens (1912-1983) of Montgomery, Alabama; Jon Jones of Alberta City, (Tuscaloosa) Alabama; and those from the Walker County area included Paul Wylie (1933-2004) of Goodsprings, Robert Lee Williams of Oakman, and Gus Nichols. The evening of the 13th was the marked beginning, and the series went on for the week day and night.[54] Hundreds attended each session, serving to build unity in a region where division was on the rise. Adding the Training For Service concept to the work in Jasper further demonstrates the aggressive spirit of her leadership to provide the very best the brotherhood had to offer in promoting excellence in leadership development. With it, the legacy of Gus Nichols continued to be advanced.

ENDNOTES

1 Note: *The Gospel Guardian* was a paper published out of Lufkin, Texas, and edited by Fanning Yater Tant (1908-1997). The paper long served as a voice of the anti-cooperation movement among churches of Christ. Charles A. Holt served as an associate editor for the paper during this period.

2 G. K. Wallace, "Wallace-Holt Debate," *Gospel Advocate*, 3 December 1959, p. 782.

3 Gus Nichols, "Wallace-Holt Debate," *Gospel Advocate*, 28 January 1960, pp. 54-55.

4 Note: Curtis Crum Cates (09.14.1910-07.21.2003) was a long-time preacher in south Alabama. He attended Alabama Christian College and Harding School of Religion. He preached at Foley in the early 1950s, at West End in Montgomery, but mostly for his home congregation at Flomaton. His son, Curtis A. Cates (1941-2013) also preached, and served several years as Director of Memphis School of Preaching. The Cates are buried in the family cemetery near Fort Deposit, Lowndes County, in the Little Sandy Ridge Cemetery.

5 Advertisement, *Firm Foundation*, 6 October 1959, p. 636.

6 Rex A. Turner, "Former Presbyterian Minister Embraces New Testament Christianity," *Gospel Advocate*, 3 March 1960, pp. 133-34.

7 Note: A long-time friendship existed between the Bryants and your author's family, the Harps. Many times, our paths crossed with Marvin and Johnnie while my dad, Richard T. Harp, was preaching at the Chisholm church in Montgomery in the mid-1960s and thereafter. While my family was serving as missionaries in New Zealand in the early 1990s, the two visited in our Auckland home for a few days while they were traveling. Great conversations were enjoyed with them about Marvin's wonderful and appreciative memories of the early days of his Christian walk, and all those who blessed his life during that period since.

8 Advertisement, *Gospel Advocate*, 18 February 1960, p. 111.

9 Willard Collins, *Gospel Advocate*, 31 August 1961, p. 554.

10 Note: Charles R. Coil was born in Flint, Michigan, December 11, 1929. He grew up near Salem, Arkansas. He attended Harding Christian University, Oklahoma State University, Harding School of Theology, and received the Doctor of Laws from Freed-Hardeman University in 1982. He preached for several years in Bristow, Oklahoma, and later at Salem, north of Florence, Alabama. In 1971, he became president of International Bible College, now Heritage Christian University. In 1990, he became Chancellor of the college. He passed away December 1, 1994, and was laid to rest in the cemetery at Mt. Zion church of Christ, near Florence.

11 Charles Coil, Harding College Bible Lectures 1961, Austin: Firm Foundation Publishing Company, 1961, p. 104.

12 Andrew D. Erwin, *You've Been A Good Brother Willie: The Life And Sermons of W. A. Bradfield*, Delight: Gospel Light Publishing Company, 2011, p. 53.

13 Ibid. p. 54.

14 W. A. Bradfield, "106 Responses In Alabama Meeting," *Firm Foundation*, 25 April 1961, p. 268.

15 W. A. Bradfield, *Gospel Advocate*, 27 April 1961, p. 268.

16 Willard Collins, "Ira North Challenges Gus Nichols In Securing Advocate Subscriptions," *Gospel Advocate*, 19 January 1961, p. 40.

17 Ibid.

18 B. C. Goodpasture, ed., "The Big Subscription Contest Is On," *Gospel Advocate*, 16 February 1961, p. 98. Note: Clubs were clusters of subscriptions sent in, as opposed to individual subscriptions.

19 B. C. Goodpasture, ed., "Special To Club Senders," *Gospel Advocate*, 2 March 1962, p. 142.

20 Ira North, "Special Message To Advocate Readers," *Gospel Advocate*, 6 April 1961, p. 210.

21 Gus Nichols, *Gospel Advocate*, "Special Message To Advocate Readers," 6 April 1961, pp. 210, 215.

22 B. C. Goodpasture, ed., "Score North-Nichols Contest," *Gospel Advocate*, 6 April 1961, p. 214.

23 Ibid., "Score Nichols-North Contest," 1 June 1961, p. 342.

24 Ibid., "Record Attendance Present For 106th Anniversary Dinner For *Gospel Advocate* During Recent June Lectures At Lipscomb," 20 July 1961, pp. 456-57.

25 B. C. Goodpasture, ed., "Score Nichols-North Contest," *Gospel Advocate*, 28 September 1961, p. 613.

26 Ibid., "Score Nichols-North Contest," *Gospel Advocate*, 2 November 1961, p. 693.

27 Ibid., "Score Nichols-North Contest," *Gospel Advocate*, 14 December 1961, p. 795.

28 Willard Collins, "Ira North Becomes Champion Subscription Man For *Gospel Advocate*," *Gospel Advocate*, 11 January 1962, p. 19.

29 James C. Bays, *Gospel Advocate*, 28 January 1960, p. 61.

30 John Payne, *Gospel Advocate*, 28 July 1960, p. 476.

31 O. D. Johns, *Gospel Advocate*, 29 September 1960, p. 620.

32 Alan E. Highers, *Gospel Advocate*, 17 November 1960, p. 734.

33 Sterl A. Watson, *Gospel Advocate*, 8 December 1960, p. 778.

34 James W. Clark, *Gospel Advocate*, 5 January 1961, p. 12.

35 W. A. Bradfield, *Gospel Advocate*, 27 April 1961, p. 268.

36 Note: The interview was conducted during a visit to Jasper by Paul Hunton, Vice-President of Gospel Press. The material was used by Willard Collins in the

form of the three articles that appeared 2 March, 6 April and 20 April 1961 in the *Gospel Advocate*.

37 Willard Collins, "The Gus Nichols Story," *Gospel Advocate*, 2 March 1961, p. 136.

38 Ibid.

39 Ibid., p. 138.

40 Willard Collins, "The Gus Nichols Story, Part III," *Gospel Advocate*, 20 April 1961, pp. 244-45.

41 Ibid.

42 Ibid.

43 J. Curtis Manor, *Gospel Advocate*, 11 May 1961, p. 301.

44 Note: Thomas G. O'Neal was born in Washington D.C., but grew up in Lawrenceburg, Tennessee. He began preaching when he was 16. He attended Freed-Hardeman College and preached for churches in Tennessee, Florida, and Alabama. He served the McArthur Heights church of Christ in Jasper from 1960 to July 1964, when he departed to the Azalea City church in Orlando, Florida, according to *Searching The Scripture*, September 1964, p. 10. He passed from this life while living in Tampa, Florida, 16 June 2012, and burial followed in his hometown of Lawrenceburg, in the Mimosa Cemetery.

45 Thomas G. O'Neal, *The Gospel Guardian*, 21 September 1961, p. 309.

46 Ibid., 5 October 1961, p. 339.

47 Ibid. "The Gus Nichols Story," *The Gospel Guardian*, Vol. 13, No. 22, 5 October 1961, p. 3, 11b.

48 Note: Irven P. Lee was born 26 July 1914 in Wilton, Arkansas. He was baptized in 1928 by Texas preacher, Horace Busby (1884-1965). Lee was a preacher and an educator. He taught at: Dasher Bible School, Valdosta, Georgia; Athens Bible School, Athens, Alabama; and Mars Hill Bible School in Florence, Alabama. His preaching was mostly in Alabama. Several years he was in Russellville. He spent a short time in Jasper in 1963, but soon moved to Hartselle, where he preached for many years. He passed from this life 4 May 1991, and was buried in the Roselawn Cemetery in Athens, Alabama.

49 Flavil Nichols, "In Memoriam: Gus Nichols," *Words of Truth*, 15 November 1985, p. 3.

50 W. T. Cato, "J. W. Brents' Seventy-Fifth Birthday," *Gospel Advocate*, 5 March 1959, p. 152.

51 Advertisement, "Plan Your Vacation With Christians," *Gospel Advocate*, 1 March 1962, p. 136.

52 Note: The final week of the Blue Ridge Encampment took place in late July 2014. Spanning 64 years of encouragement to hundreds of families for two

generations, it was one of the longest running camps of its kind in Restoration Movement history.

53 Advertisement, *Firm Foundation*, 28 March 1933, p. 6.

54 Gus Nichols, "Training For Service Series," *Gospel Advocate*, 9 November 1961, p. 716.

- 40 -

Where The Savior Trod

And looking upon Jesus as He walked, he saith,
Behold the Lamb of God!
—John, The Immerser, John 1:36

Three-score and ten was the age of his life on the twelfth of January 1962. Still as sharp as ever, the sage of Jasper was deemed by most of the brotherhood as a constant. The precipitous volume of his industry was feeding a generation of Christians a steady diet of unbiased and unadulterated truth. His anchor, plunged deeply into the bedrock of God's Word, was keeping those of his influence steadfast and unmovable, always abounding in the work of the Lord. Ever ready to give a defense for the way of Christ, his days were filled with opportunities to guide the erring back to the Light, while assisting the man in the pew with increased godliness. No stranger at his door was turned away from a meal at Matilda's table, no mail was left unopened, no phone call ignored, and no listener to his sermons was left disappointed. At seventy, the life of the man was the fullest it had been in all his forty-five years of preaching.

Active seems to be such an inadequate word to describe his busy schedule. Often, he was seen in town. Twice daily, his voice was being heard over the airwaves from two different radio stations. Each issue of Jasper's *Daily Mountain Eagle* newspaper contained short evangelistic articles or sermons from his pen. In the summertime, you could still see him out cutting his own grass, wearing a white shirt, tie, and hat. Most often when Matilda had meals prepared, she was known to say, "Tell the preacher it is time to eat!" Gus was always ready—always the professional Christian! In the minds of many, he was the complete man of God.

Is such a man worthy of praise? Many thought so. For twenty-five years, the impact of his presence had been felt in the halls of Freed-Hardeman College. Chapel Hall, in what is now endearingly referred to as Old Main, with her walls displaying the great preachers and educators of the past, all looking on in silence, while the room time and again was being filled with the words spoken by the preacher from Jasper, Alabama, cried out for some sort of acknowledgement. Certainly, he of all preachers deserved recognition.

While planning the 26th annual Freed-Hardeman Lectureship, H. A. Dixon (1904-1969), the college President; W. A. Bradfield (1910-1972), the director of Public Relations; G. K. Wallace, Executive Assistant to the President; W. Claude Hall (1883-1967); and others on the lectureship

26th Annual Lectureship, *Skyrocket*

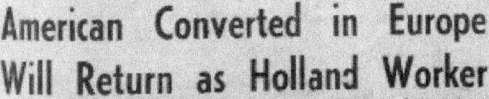

1962 - *Christian Chronicle,* Feb. 23

committee, deemed it significant to give honor to whom honor is due. In the history of the Special Courses and Lecture programs no such esteem had been laid upon any of its speakers to the level of what was being planned during this year's event. But then, who had been worthier?

Within weeks of Bradfield's return from his successful Jasper meeting the previous year, the event was being promoted in the *Gospel Advocate*. He wrote,

One of the big special features that is being planned for the annual Bible Lectureship at Freed-Hardeman College February 5-9, 1962, is the Gus Nichols Appreciation Dinner, February 8. This will be the twenty-fifth lectureship at Freed-Hardeman College in which Brother Nichols has participated. Relatives and friends of Brother Nichols everywhere are invited to be in Henderson for this occasion. It will be necessary for reservations to be sent in early. Facilities will accommodate only about two hundred fifty people. The cost to each person attending will be approximately $1.50.[1]

Similar advertisements appeared throughout the remainder of the year producing growth in anticipation by the lectureship's attendees.

On the appointed day, many of Gus and Matilda's children, and their families, were seen around the college campus, making their way to their intended destination at the appointed hour. The Booster Club organized and sold out all the tickets for the dinner weeks in advance. Late in the afternoon of Tuesday the 6th of February, people began making their way into the crowded college student center where the festivities were to begin at 5:00 p.m. Two hundred eighty-eight well-wishers packed the small hall.[2]

Only the consummate preacher would enlist such a group of dignitaries to speak on such an occasion as this. Men excelling in their fields of expertise were selected to speak about the man they knew intimately as one who excelled in all the areas that were featured that evening.

After the meal, the excellent gospel meeting preacher and emcee of the program, W. A. Bradfield, mounted the podium, welcoming all in the room. He then introduced the great church planter and educator, Albert R. Hill, Sr. (1890-1983), at that time the preacher for the church in Louisville, Mississippi, to be the after-dinner speaker. Several

men very close to brother Nichols followed with short recollections and acknowledgments. Son, Flavil Nichols, at that time living in Mayfield, Kentucky, spoke briefly on, *Gus Nichols—Early Life and Family*. Then, from Scottsboro, Alabama and Nichols' son in the faith, W. A. Black (1904-1980) came to the microphone and focused on *Gus Nichols—The Preacher*. Following, was the *Gospel Advocate* editor from Nashville, B. C. Goodpasture (1895-1977), who arose to speak on, *Gus Nichols—The Writer*. The debater, Guy N. Woods (1908-1993), from Memphis, was next. He expounded upon, *Gus Nichols—The Debater*. A late addition to the roster, G. K. Wallace (1903-1988), expounded upon *Gus Nichols—And Freed-Hardeman Lectureships*. This was followed with *Gus Nichols And Christian Education*, by the president of Alabama Christian College in Montgomery, Alabama, Rex A. Turner (1913-2001).[3]

> **GUS NICHOLS WILL BE HONORED**
>
> by W. A. Bradfield
>
> Gus Nichols, veteran gospel preacher of Jasper, Ala., and participant for the 25th year in the annual Freed-Hardeman College Bible Lectureship Feb. 5-9, will be honored at a special appreciation dinner February 8 at 5:00 P.M. in the College Student Center.
>
> Tickets to the dinner cost $1.50. More than 250 are expected to attend.
>
> The program will include an after dinner speech by Albert Hill of Louisville, Miss.; welcome and Emcee—W. A. Bradfield, Henderson, Tenn.; "Gus Nichols, Early Life and Family"—Flavil Nichols, Mayfield, Kentucky; "Gus Nichols, the Preacher"—W. A. Black, Scottsboro, Ala.; "Gus Nichols, the Writer"—B. C. Goodpasture, Nashville, Tenn.; "Gus Nichols, the Debater"—Guy N. Woods, Memphis, Tenn.; "Gus Nichols and Christian Education"—Rex Turner, Montgomery, Ala.; "Gus Nichols, A Tribute and Presentation"—H. A. Dixon, Henderson, Tenn.; The Response, the Honoree—Gus Nichols, Jasper, Ala.
>
> Those planning to attend should send $1.50 for each ticket desired to W. A. Bradfield, Henderson, Tenn.

Several presentations were made as the evening progressed. H. Graden Dill, a member of the Sixth Avenue church, representing the aldermen of the city of Jasper, Alabama presented the Nichols with a silver service with the inscription, "In grateful appreciation for 30 years of service to Jasper, Ala. and its citizens, City Commissioners, Feb. 8, 1962."[4] Then, Sam Evans, one of the elders at Sixth Avenue, made a presentation to the Nichols on behalf of the congregation.[5] H. A. Dixon made the final tribute and a presentation. He unveiled two portraits of Gus Nichols. One was later hung at the bottom of the stairs leading to Chapel Hall in Old Main, and the other was given to brother Nichols to hang in his office.

Finally, the honoree made his way to the speaker's stand to greet his officiates and friends with all the humility befitting the occasion. He greeted each of his contributors with jovial, witty, and gratuitous praise, thanking all for what he considered unworthy honor.

All in attendance were deeply moved by the kindnesses expressed during the proceedings. It was a special time to give praise to one of Freed-Hardeman's most loyal supporters, and one of the brotherhood's finest voices for the Lord. Throughout the week devoted to the theme, "Building For Christ," brother Nichols had the opportunity to present four lessons in morning sessions on the subject of "Christian Fellowship."[6]

Reuel Lemmons (1912-1989) reported in the Texas paper that, "one of the highlights of the week was the Gus Nichols Appreciation Dinner."[7]

TO EUROPE AND THE MIDDLE EAST

With the completion of the subscription campaign at the *Gospel Advocate* in January 1962, and the lead taken by the contest winner Ira North (1922-1984) in giving his winnings of $100 as a contribution to the Gus Nichols Bible Lands Travel Fund, the push for funding the trip became the focus. Requests were sent to a beneficent brotherhood to help brother Nichols travel with the hope that sister Nichols would be able to attend as well.

Gus, Flavil, and Matilda Nichols
Traveling to the Middle East

The greatest push came during the appreciation dinner at Freed-Hardeman when $200 was given to the Nichols in cash along with a passionate appeal to give to the fund. Until that time, it was still uncertain if the Nichols would make the trip, but in his response that evening he said that if the brethren wanted them to go that he and sister Nichols would commit to going. In March, Willard Collins reported, "Since such a fine response was evident at the Gus Nichols Appreciation Dinner at Freed-Hardeman College in February, plans were made for Brother and Sister Nichols to go to the Holy Land this year. Over $3,200 was pledged at the dinner."[8]

The departure date was set for the 1st of May 1962, heading for New York, and beyond. The trip was to involve travel to, "London, Paris, Rome, Cairo, two weeks in the Holy Land, and then a trip to Athens."[9]

On the 5th of May, from aboard Air France, Flight 768, Gus sent a telegram to the offices of the *Advocate*, "With me are my wife, our son, Flavil, and W. Gaddys Roy. We left April 30 for a tour of Europe and the Holy Lands. Expect to return June 1. Each preacher spoke in New York. Sunday, April 29, before flying to London."[10]

Their time in the Holy Lands was relatively short. But, they used it wisely. W. Gaddys Roy (1916-2009) recalled, "We literally traveled from Dan to Beersheba."[11] They had travel guides to take them through the sites of old Jerusalem, to the ruins of ancient Megiddo, to the edge of the old Kishon River, and to the Sea of Galilee. They walked through the gravesite of King David, on temple mound where Abraham offered Isaac, and followed where the Savior trod on his way to the place of the skull.

Sunday Morning at the Empty Tomb

One Sunday morning, they met with others for worship sometime between seven and nine o'clock, "within sixty feet of the tomb at Gordon's Calvary just outside Jerusalem's walls."[12] It was there that brother Nichols preached on the subject of the resurrection of Jesus. He used for his text, "That I may know him and the power of his resurrection, and the fellowship of his sufferings, being made conformable unto his death" (Philippians 3:10).

They went to Egypt and saw the great pyramids of Giza, visited the prodigious Valley of the Kings, and experienced the seemingly boundless Nile River. More than tourists, they were learning—absorbing the culture, and never shirking an opportunity to comprehend and even to teach. Later, Gus recalled an engaging discussion with a tour guide about creation,

> While traveling in Egypt in 1962, we had as a guide back to the airport a man who was a graduate of a university and claimed to be a Christian. But he said that scientists are about to "create" life, and if and when they do, he said he nor any one else would ever believe in God after that. I replied that it obviously takes great intelligence to create life, that up to now the whole world has not been equal to the task, and that if great intelligence should someday be so assembled as to synthesize life it would prove that life comes from intelligence and creative power, and not from dead and lifeless matter by accident and chance. Our guide later said he felt "like a fool" after considering this application of the facts.[13]

The Nichols returned home around the first of June, and very quickly all were back into the work catching up on things that needed special attention. Before his departure, the congregation hired a young man to come in as an assistant minister beginning upon his return. Wade Isaac Johnson moved to Jasper to help in the work in June.[14]

Throughout the summer, brother Nichols showed slides taken by Flavil on the Holy Lands trip during meetings and special events. He preached a gospel meeting for the Highlands church in Russellville, Alabama and on the last evening showed the slides to "one of the largest audiences"[15] they ever had.

Soon after their return from the trip, Gus and Matilda headed to the thirty-fifth annual lecture program of David Lipscomb College. It was a busy week as usual. Again, he attended the Annual Dinner for the *Gospel Advocate*. Being the runner-up of the subscription contest that ended in January, plenty of photos were taken, and when given the opportunity to speak about the contest, he challenged Ira North once again to another subscription battle saying, "I believe I can lick him good."[16]

While on the Holy Lands trip, advertisements appeared scheduling Gus and Flavil to show the slides of their trip at the 15th Annual August Lecture Series at David Lipscomb.[17] He and Flavil were to report on the trip every afternoon at 2pm. Then at 3pm Gus was to speak on, "Memories of Bible

Lands."[18] These lectures were well attended. In a time when world travel was still somewhat novel, these lectures made it possible to add another dimension to one's understanding of the Bible.

In October, a lengthy, "Thank You, Every One," letter appeared in the *Gospel Advocate*. Recalling the kindnesses at the beginning with Ira North's generous gesture of giving him his $100 winnings of the *GA* subscription contest, and B. C. Goodpasture adding another $100 to get the fund started, and then the outpouring of thoughtfulness at the appreciation dinner at Freed-Hardeman, he expressed how thankful he and sister Nichols were for the kindnesses shown to them. Of course, the opportunity was also taken to promote the *Advocate* and readership of the magazine. He encouraged all to subscribe and to promote the magazine among their congregations. In the end, he expressed once again his appreciation saying, "All of this was so wonderful that it was to us a sort of an 'out of this world' experience."[19]

MEETINGS, LECTURESHIPS AND MORE

Interspersed with all the honoring and foreign trip development, the year of 1962 was filled with opportunities to minister in all the vast ways that had become common to the septuagenarian preacher. In March, he made his way to Alabama Christian College for their 20th annual lectureship. He spoke each morning on, "Religious Errors and How To Meet Them."[20] Then, on Friday night he joined B. C. Goodpasture in a special emphasis evening on the eldership. Gus spoke on, "The Responsibility of Elders For Vision and Leadership."

Reflecting on that evening, Goodpasture opened his editorial on the 12th of April with, "Gus Nichols and I were guest speakers at the concluding service of the Twentieth Annual Lectureship program of Alabama Christian College. This service was held in the City Auditorium. It seats about 2,300 persons."[21]

Also that night, Alabama preacher, and church-wide educator on stewardship, V. P. Black (1918-2007), stood before the "filled to capacity" crowd and engaged the gathering in a challenge to pay off the $80,000.00 indebtedness of the college by the 1st of May. This was all in view of the unveiling of a new plan by Gus Nichols, and the other members of the Board of Directors of the college, to purchase a 93-acre track of land about six miles from downtown Montgomery on the Atlanta Highway, and move the college to the new campus as soon as possible.[22] These were exciting times for the future growth and development of the Montgomery-based institution.

Later in March, the annual gospel meeting at Sixth Avenue welcomed J. Cliett Goodpasture as guest speaker. B. C.'s son not only following in his father's footsteps as a preacher, but he, too, worked on the staff of the *Gospel Advocate*. The meeting was well attended throughout the week. He conducted a morning service at 7am along with the regular evening service. Gus reported, "three baptized and two restored," and adding that, "he did a masterful job of preaching the gospel in simplicity, purity and power."[23] Also mentioned was their intentions of having him back for a meeting again in four years.

In early April, Gus traveled up to McMinnville, Tennessee, to conduct a meeting for the Bybee Branch church. The meeting ended on the 10th with the preacher, Buford C. Holt (1910-2001) reporting,

> People attended from at least forty-five congregations in this area and neighboring counties. One was baptized and two restored. Brother Nichols preached daily (except Saturday) over the radio stations and dealt with the liberal and "anti" views toward the Scriptures and showed how both are in error. On Saturday night he gave the clearest lesson I have heard on cooperation of churches in the Lord's work. If every congregation over the country could be taught for a few days by Brother Nichols the "anti" views would claim but a few people anywhere. May God continue to bless this great preacher with good health and opportunities to proclaim the gospel.[24]

Holt's mention of the "anti" issues reveals that the struggle among churches were continuing and growing stronger in the brotherhood. Churches who had communed and worked together jointly in the past were polarizing against one another with all too great rapidity.

A few weeks later, Gus penned an article that appeared in the *Advocate* entitled, "Are We Liberalists?" He named Roy Cogdill (1907-1985) and Yater Tant (1908-1997) as taking the lead in persuading brethren not to support orphan homes or cooperating with one another in evangelism, as well as charging those who do with liberalism. It was further revealed in the article that fifteen years prior, the brethren from twenty congregations in the Houston, Texas area worked together to have a joint meeting with Foy E. Wallace, Jr. (1896-1979). This was a meeting these men supported. He also mentioned the Hardeman Tabernacle meetings in Nashville in the 1920s when brethren cooperated to evangelize, as an example of what had long been practiced within the brotherhood. He then questioned that if they were wrong then, why they had not come forward and repented like they were suggesting "liberal" brethren should do today. Being charged as "liberal" was an insult to brother Nichols and other brethren who consistently through the years sought to do everything strictly according to the Scriptures.

Other inconsistencies from among the "antis" appeared as well. W. Ray Duncan (1911-1998) wrote of his visit to Walker County for a two-week meeting at the Zion congregation during the summer. He said, "I was associated with Gus Nichols in his radio work for eighteen days. The non-cooperative antis are cooperating in putting on a radio program aimed at disturbing and tearing down any work that Brother Nichols and faithful Christians of that area are doing."[25]

OTHERS SUMMER AND FALL ACTIVITIES

At the end of June, Gus and Matilda made their way once again over to the Blue Ridge Encampment in the Smokey Mountains. Held the week of the 24th through the 28th, he conducted the Gus Nichols Hour, answering biblical questions that were put forward by the campers. Also, participating that year, was B. C. Goodpasture, who was the daily chapel speaker, and Leslie G. Thomas (1895-1988), who conducted the Bible Classes, and others.[26]

In the fall, Gus made his way out to Abilene for a series of special classes at the Highland church. His lectures were on, "Children's Homes and Church Cooperation." Other preachers spoke at the event where two tents were set up that could seat up to 8000 people. The following day, local paper, *The Abilene News-Reporter*, revealed that "4,692 attended the Special Classes."[27]

Toward the end of October, he spoke on the Franklin Lectures in Franklin, Tennessee. The series marked the 129th anniversary of the founding of the Fourth Avenue church. On Wednesday night Gus spoke on, "The Christian's Relationship to the State."[28]

A couple weeks later, he made his way back to Searcy, Arkansas, for the annual lecture program at Harding College. Conducted November 19-22, the theme was: "The Authority of the Holy Scriptures."[29] Appearing on the forum with him were Batsell Barrett Baxter (1916-1982), H. A. Dixon (1904-1969), Don Gardner (1927-1996), Cleon Lyles (1914-1989) and others.

A BOOK OF SERMON OUTLINES

A new book of sermons by the Nichols Brothers Publishing Company was released at the end of 1961. Entitled, *Sermon Outlines by Gus Nichols*, the volume sold for $3.50.[30] A lengthy introduction appearing in the front of the work by Flavil, revealed his father's years of discipline in study and application of the Word of God. Over 120 sermons in outline format on many subjects were included with the explanation that many of the lessons were so rich in information that it would be impossible to preach them in one sermon.

The book was promoted throughout the following year in the *Gospel Advocate*. Ira North wrote about it in a report under the title, "Sermons That Stir And Save."[31] In the brief advertisement, he suggested that every preacher should own the volume, and that the sermon on the resurrection was worth every bit of the purchase price.

Gus Nichols' wisdom and advice continued to appear in his "Questions Answers" column in the *Gospel Advocate* throughout 1962. In the first issue of February, several questions about marriage, baptism and the work of the Holy Spirit were answered.[32] Later in the month, he explained what happens to a person when he dies and other questions centering around the subject of eschatology.[33] His column appeared with less frequency toward the end of the year, indicating his busy schedule and trip to the land where the Savior trod.

ENDNOTES

1 W. A. Bradfield, "Gus Nichols Appreciation Dinner," *Gospel Advocate*, 25 May 1961, p. 331. Note: The advertisement was repeated in 22 June issue of *GA*, p. 399.

2 Note: The location of the student center at that time is now the Draughon Music Building, located on the Freed-Hardeman University campus between Old Main Administration Building and the Hope Barber Shull Academic Resource Center and Libraries. The building was built in 1929 and served as a cafeteria/student center on the first floor. The upper floor had a gymnasium with seating up to 400 people. *Gospel Advocate*, 28 August 1929, p. 820.

3 Edgar Orman, Associate Editor, *Christian Chronicle,* 23 February 1962, p. 1. Note: The speech by G. K. Wallace was not in earlier advertisements of the special dinner. It is assumed that his role in the event may have been an afterthought, but no less essential to capture the significance of the man. The speech appeared verbatim in the *Gospel Advocate*, 07.01.1976, p. 424, and remains the only extant message from the various speakers during the event. The speech so clearly expressed the person of Gus Nichols, that it was deemed wise to place, in its entirety, at the front of this book to serve as the volume's Forward.

4 Note: The silver service is proudly displayed in the home of Gus and Matilda's daughter, Bertha Blackwood of Jasper, Alabama. I visited in her home 10 October 2011 where I was able to talk to her about her memories of her parents and see some of her precious keepsakes. One of her mementos is a copy of her father's Dickson Bible. Her father sold Dickson Bibles for a time, and her copy had sermon outlines on every spare blank page in the front and in the back of the precious volume.

5 W. A. Bradfield, *Gospel Advocate*, 22 February 1962, p. 127.

6 Gus Nichols, 1962 Lecture Outlines, Vol. 10, 26th Annual Bible Lectureship, Freed-Hardeman College, pp. 20-38. Note: Also in *Gospel Advocate*, 23 December 1961, p. 826.

7 Reuel Lemmons, "F. H. C. Lectures Successful," *Firm Foundation*, 6 March 1962, p. 159.

8 Willard Collins, *Gospel Advocate*, 29 March 1962, p. 196.

9 Ibid.

10 Gus Nichols, *Gospel Advocate*, 17 May 1962, p. 318.

11 W. Gaddys Roy, *Gospel Advocate*, 5 July 1962, p. 427.

12 Gus Nichols, *Great Preachers of Today—Sermons of Gus Nichols*, J. D. Thomas, editor, 1966, p. 67.

13 Ibid., p. 6.

14 Dona Karrh, "Sixth Avenue Church of Christ," *Words of Truth*, 5 October 1990, p. 2.

15 Ernest Clevenger, Jr., *Gospel Advocate*, 16 August 1962, p. 523.

16 Willard Collins, *Gospel Advocate*, 19 July 1962, p. 458.

17 Advertisement, *Gospel Advocate*, 10 May 1962, p. 304.

18 Ibid., 26 July 1962, p. 476.

19 Gus Nichols, *Gospel Advocate*, 4 October 1962, pp. 629-30.

20 Advertisement, *Gospel Advocate*, 1 March 1962, p. 141.

21 B. C. Goodpasture, ed., "Alabama Christian College," *Gospel Advocate*, 12 April 1962, p. 226.

22 Rex A. Turner, *Gospel Advocate*, 12 April 1962, pp. 228-29.

23 Gus Nichols, *Gospel Advocate*, 26 April 1962, p. 270.

24 Buford Holt, *Gospel Advocate*, 3 May 1962, p. 283.

25 W. Ray Duncan, *Gospel Advocate*, 16 August 1962, p. 524.

26 B. C. Goodpasture, ed.,*Gospel Advocate*, 12 July 1962, p. 440.

27 Report, *The Abilene News-Reporter*, 2 October 1962, p. 12D.

28 Advertisement, *Gospel Advocate*, 1 November 1962, p. 703.

29 Ibid., 20 September 1962, p. 597.

30 Gus Nichols, *Sermon Outlines* by Gus Nichols, Jasper: Nichols Brothers Publishing Company, 1961.

31 Ira North, "Sermons That Stir And Save," *Gospel Advocate*, 8 February 1962, p. 95. Advertisements appeared in *GA* on 25.01, p. 62; 1.2, p. 78; 8.11, p. 717; and 6.12., p. 776.

32 Gus Nichols, "Queries Answers," *Gospel Advocate*, 1 February 1962, p. 71.

33 Ibid., 22 February 1962, p. 116.

Where The Nichols Boys Go, Things Grow

> Marriage is honorable in all, and the bed undefiled.
> —The Writer of Hebrews, 13:4a

"PEM"

William G. Pemberton (1886-1962) was a Missouri-born commercial artist. In his early years, he was a bit of a drifter, living in several locations around the country. In the late 1920s he moved to Winfield, Alabama where his main source of income was to paint murals for businesses in the area. His artwork appeared in restaurants, in people's homes, and often churches of various denominations would have him paint murals behind their baptistry.

One of his customers was Gus Nichols. Early in his preaching career, Gus saw the power of visualizing the message through illustrations. In the days before projection technology, a preacher could take a typical bed-sheet, some paint, and with a little imagination, produce the basic outline of his sermon in a most inviting and illustrative way. These sheet sermons were most helpful especially in gospel meeting settings where convincing the alien sinner of his precarious state was of critical importance.

When Gus became aware of the talents of Mr. Pemberton, "Pem," he approached him about producing a sheet sermon for him. Flavil explained, "Dad would trace out his sermon charts on a piece of paper and Pem would paint them. I would tell Pem to paint one for daddy and one just like it for me. The more careful and precise daddy was, the more precise Pem was."[1]

Pem and his wife were not Christians at the time and were known to be partakers of spirits on occasion. However, they were serious about their work, and were so very careful in the production process to make sure that the passages written on the paper were what appeared on the sheet. As instructed by brother Nichols, Pem had his wife look up the passages in the Bible and read them to him while he continued the work at hand. In time, faith entered the hearts of the artist and his dutiful spouse. Approaching the local preacher in Winfield he said, "My wife and I need help. We have read enough of Gus Nichols' sermon charts to know that 'repent' means we have to give up drinking and we must be baptized."[2] Upon their confessions they were baptized into Christ.

Progression in faith led Pem to enter the ministry. He helped establish congregations and built up the church for several years around Winfield. A good number of reports of his work appeared in the pages of the *Gospel Advocate* over the years of his ministry. Through the years, he continued to paint hundreds of chart sermons on sheets for preachers of the gospel. Many of those old charts survive to this day. Very few, however, were signed.

Chart painted by W. G. "Pem" Pemberton (1886-1962)

In 1946, the Pembertons moved to East Tennessee where he planted churches and worked among the saints near Knoxville. In 1953, one brother expressed of Pem,

> He has been a student of nature from childhood and became a scenic artist in which be served the public many years. Gus Nichols convinced him that he should use his talents in the Master's service. He has no little ability as a gospel preacher. His words of love and sympathy strike the tender cords of the heart and with his paint brush he has made sermon charts that are used in many parts of the world. . .The good he has done and the truth he has preached will live in the hearts of many for years to come.[3]

Not far from the Tipton Station church of Christ, a work he planted, is a little cemetery on Henry Haynes Road. Two small upright markers stand side by side in the center of the graveyard. One is inscribed, "PEM, Passed Away May 6, 62." The other simply reads, "MRS. 'PEM.'"

OPEN FORUM MODERATOR

The 1963 lectureship season kicked off with the annual trip to Freed-Hardeman College. Conducted February 3-8, the theme for the forum was, "Christianity In Our Time."[4] At this stage, Guy N. Woods (1908-1993) normally conducted the Open Forum. However, due to scheduling problems, this year he was unable to fulfill this commitment. Thus, falling back on their old reliable, brother Nichols handled the daily 3:30 session. Always ready! Always thorough in his explanation! The forum was in good hands in brother Woods' absence.

The next month's forum was in Montgomery. The Alabama Christian College Lectures were conducted March 4-8 on the theme: "They Shall All Be Taught of God—John 6:45."[5] Every morning at the 11 o'clock hour, Gus spoke on the topic, "Religious Errors," in the College Auditorium. The last day of the lectureship was conducted in Montgomery's largest venue, the Alabama State Coliseum.

CHRISTIAN SERVICE AWARD

In the early spring, Gus boarded a flight to Los Angeles, California, to participate in the 20th Annual Lectureship of Pepperdine College. Though his first trip that far west, there was some familiarity with a number of the brethren. Long had he been acquainted with the Tennessee preacher and school president, M. Norvel Young (1915-1998).[6] In the initial contact, his services were required for a special lesson they wished for him to preach as a part of their theme, "Christ Our Contemporary." He was totally unaware that they had plans to do much more.

Gus Nichols, right, is presented with the Christian Service Award for his years of service as a gospel preacher. Making the presentation is Pepperdine College President M. Norvel Young.

1963 - Christian Service Award

The new, but not quite complete, Friendship Hall was the place of gathering at 5 o'clock on Tuesday, March 19th, 1963, for the annual Elders-Preachers Dinner. Brother Young was the emcee for the evening's festivities. Before a filled room, the guest speaker was introduced, and brother Nichols came to the microphone to address, "Christ, Our Contemporary In Keeping The Unity Of The Spirit."[7] Upon completion of the message, President Young thanked him for the message, and preceded to confer upon brother Nichols the college's highest recognition, "designed to honor distinctive Christian service."[8] The Christian Service Award was given to the preacher from Alabama for his dedication to the cause of Christ, and how his life's work has blessed an indebted Kingdom of believers. Thousands throughout the week attended the lectureship, hearing many great speakers, but as one later recalled, "One of the highlights of the lectureship was the presentation of the college's Christian Service Award to Gus Nichols."[9]

GOSPEL MEETING WORK

The gospel meeting season began in 1963 with a visit to Jasper by Guy N. Woods (1908-1993) the third week in April. The west Tennessee preacher was a favorite among churches in the south. Advertisements for the meeting revealed that Woods was to speak each day at 10:20 a.m. and at 7:30 each evening. After each evening lesson, slides of the Nichols' Holy Land trip were shown for twenty minutes. Great crowds filled the Sixth Avenue building each evening.

As has been noted, by this stage in his life, Gus is seldom if ever sending reports about his meeting work. However, the recipients of his efforts were. For instance, Malcolm L. Hill (1934-2012)[10] was the young preacher in the small metropolitan Atlanta community of Forest Park. He moved there in June 1960 to work with a new congregation that had been recently planted by Hapeville's North Avenue church. In the first five months of 1963, seventy had responded to the invitation,[11] and the church was primed with anticipation of the coming of Gus Nichols for their meeting beginning the 12th of May. The meeting "closed with six baptisms and six restored."[12]

After the Georgia meeting, he was off to Little Rock, Arkansas, for a series with the Downtown congregation. The preacher there, Cleon Lyles (1914-1989), reported a good effort by the Jasper preacher. In June, he went to visit with his Bible Lands traveling companion from the year before, W. Gaddys Roy (1916-2009) in a meeting at Piedmont, Alabama. "Seven were baptized and eighteen restored," during the meeting.[13] At the end of the month, he traveled to Milan, Tennessee, for a meeting in which he co-preached with J. Walker Whittle (1921-2017). O. D. Johns (1922-2002), the Milan preacher, reported that five were baptized and ten were restored during the meeting.[14] Around the third week in June, the family took their annual trip to the Blue Ridge Encampment where he continued the Gus Nichols Hour, "with his now famous style of giving Bible answers from questions from the audience."[15] This was followed with a trip to Luverne, Alabama, just a little south of Montgomery, where five baptisms were reported.[16]

A. R. Holton

Rue Porter

Three preachers with long records of service to the brotherhood will deliver key addresses at the third annual Elders' Workshop at Abilene Christian College, August 5-7. They are A. R. Holton of Abilene, Gus Nichols of Jasper, Alabama, and Rue Porter of Neosho, Mo.

Holton will speak on "Inspiring and Training Preachers and Missionaries" and "The Elder and the Mission Outreach." Nichols will speak on "The Elder and Problems in the Local Church" and "Spiritual Growth." Porter's topics are "The Elder and Brotherhood Problems" and "The Value of the Gospel Meeting."

Aylesbury Mission Encourages Workers—23 Baptized

The sixty-two missionaries engaged in the Aylesbury, England, Mission conducted by the Hillsboro Church of Christ, Nashville, with the cooperation of sister congregations, were permitted to see some of the fruits of their labors. By the close of the meeting, June 21, twenty-three had been baptized and one restored.

All who had a part in the campaign for Christ in Aylesbury left for Wembley in the London area feeling that this was just the beginning of the harvest that would be reaped from their sowing. With the zealous work of members of the Aylesbury congregation, led by Len Channing, their

Speaker at ACC Elders' Workshop

TO ABILENE AND NASHVILLE IN AUGUST

In late August 1963, Gus headed to the campus of David Lipscomb College for their annual late summer series. He taught the "Adult Teaching Classes" daily during the forum. That summer, the school boasted a record breaking 1,400 attendees to their lecture program.[17]

In 1961, Abilene Christian College began an Elder's Workshop in the month of August. The purpose of the program was to "give elders and prospective elders an opportunity to come together and spend three days of intensive study on the problems of the eldership and in exchanging ideas for mutual profit of all, and a more effective work in the Lord's church."[18] Three speakers were featured at the third annual event on the mid-western Texas campus: A. R. Holton (1891-1964) of Abilene; Rue Porter (1897-1960) of Neosho, Missouri; and Gus Nichols. Gus was in his seventh year serving in the elder's role, and was well equipped for his topic of discussion, "The Elder and Problems In The Local Church."[19]

The conference was so well received that he was asked to continue discussing the eldership at the winter lectures at ACC in February 1964. The theme was on "Leadership in the Church." Potentially, no one was more qualified for the topic he was assigned, "The Elder's Family."[20] During the forum, he also spoke on "Motivating Young Men To Preach,"[21] and participated on a panel discussion.

SUPPORTING MISSION EFFORTS

Brother Nichols was a great supporter of the Lord's work everywhere. Calls came in from all over the country asking for advice and prayer. Occasionally, preachers in struggling mission efforts would call for his assistance. One such request came from a young state-side missionary in mid-1963. Richard T. Harp, a 1960 graduate from David Lipscomb College and native of Haleyville, up in Winston County, had moved his family to Lancaster, South Carolina, after graduation.[22] The work was small, struggling, and difficult. The church had purchased property on Dunlap Street, near downtown. It had an old dilapidated house on the lot, and a new building desperately needed to be built there. Seeking all the help the church could get, contact was made with brother Nichols to see if he could assist. A pleasant and helpful invitation was extended to the missionary to make a trip over to Walker County, Alabama and stay in the Nichols' home. In anticipation of his coming, Gus made several phone calls to churches in the region to set appointments for Richard to tell about his work and try to sell church bonds for building the structure the mission church so desperately needed.

A story this author has heard repeated several times over the years is how that upon his arrival in the Nichols' home, Richard was greeted with such kindness. He recalled being taken to the guest bedroom where he was to stay. Opening the closet to hang his clothing, he noticed a most peculiar sight in the floor just inside the door. There, before his eyes, was a tall stack of dry-cleaner cardboard inserts with writing on them. Stooping down for closer investigation, he noticed that sermon outlines and poetry were written on every one of the cardboard inserts in the stack. It became very clear that brother Nichols was both frugal and industrious. You see, in those days shirts were laundered, starched, and folded carefully around a piece of cardboard to look fresh and new, just like the day it was purchased. When the older preacher put a clean shirt on each day, he would never waste the cardboard, but sat down immediately and wrote a sermon outline or a few lines of poetry on it. In the floor of his closet were several hundred sermons on that tall stack of cardboard shirt inserts.

In the end, a good number of churches were contacted in Walker County and the surrounding area. The help and kindness of Gus and Matilda Nichols went a long way in accomplishing the financial help needed to build a church building for the small struggling South Carolina church.

Stories of experiences like this could be repeated over and over by so many people who were similarly blessed by the hospitality of the Nichols family. Both Gus and Matilda believed in the Lord's work and were always willing to give anything they had to promote it. To them it was never an imposition, but an honor to open their home to serve the needs of others.

WORDS OF TRUTH

Iconic representation of the Sixth Avenue preacher was seen on several fronts. As has been noted, people of the region heard his voice daily on the two *Words of Truth* radio broadcasts.[23] His articles often appeared in the *Daily Mountain Eagle*.[24] The brotherhood knew of his voice through meetings and writings in the *Gospel Advocate*. Then, in 1963, he began editing a paper out of the offices at Sixth Avenue that bore the name of his radio program. *Words of Truth* was a four-page weekly journal, designed to give deeper Biblical knowledge to its readers. Published forty-eight times a year by the *Northwest Alabamian* newspaper in Haleyville, the paper sold for five cents a copy. Within ten years, the paper was to enjoy a circulation of nearly 25,000 per week.

In the journal, brother Nichols consistently produced an editorial on present events important to the church. Treatment was given to many Bible topics. Staff writers include a long list of faithful gospel preachers like Robert R. Taylor, Jr., Bobby Duncan (1934-1999), Levi Sides, Glenn Posey, Don McWhorter (1932-2008), W. T. Hamilton (1921-1986), along with Flavil (1935-2018), Hardeman, Hudson, and others.

GOLDEN WEDDING ANNIVERSARY

On November 13, 1963, Gus and Matilda Nichols crossed the threshold of fifty years of marriage. A party was held at Rile and Bertha's home on Sixth Avenue to honor their beloved parents. In this time of their lives, many wonderful blessings had come their way, and plainly they had blessed so many. All their eight children were faithful Christians. Most of the boys were preachers, and most of the girls were married to preachers. On this great celebration, of marital faithfulness, long-time friend Ira North (1922-1984) wrote,

1963 - 50th Wedding Anniversary

> Congratulations to Mr. and Mrs. Gus Nichols on the recent celebration of their Golden Wedding Anniversary. Think what this couple has meant to the cause of Christ! Think how many souls have been led to Christ by their preacher sons! The Nichols family is one of the greatest in the world—they have done more than families who have given to the world statesmen, lawyers, doctors, and business executives. They have given sons and daughters who have given themselves in service as Christ's preachers and as preacher's wives. Let us thank God for this family and take inspiration from it. Also, congratulations to Hudson Nichols and the Iuka, Miss., congregation on the completion of their new building. Where the Nichols boys go, things grow.[25]

The added mention of Hudson's work is the perfect reflection of the success of the marriage of his parents. Like the works of his siblings, and their families, the Nichols family as a whole formed a powerful force for all that is good about the church of Christ. This was due fundamentally to the love for the Lord instilled in their hearts from their childhood by the example and guidance of their godly parents.

Jasper Couple Observes 50th Wedding Anniversary

Bro. and Mrs. Gus Nichols celebrated their Golden Wedding Thanksgiving Day with a reception at the home of a daughter, Mrs. G. Rile Blackwood, and Mr. Blackwood on Seventh Avenue.

Many floral tributes, hundreds of cards and telegrams and a flood of telephone congratulations added extra joys to the occasion of the day. Although gifts were asked to be unmitted, many friends felt that some token of appreciation to this minister and his faithful wife was indicated. Mr. Nichols has baptized over 10,000 in the past 47 years of ministry in this church.

Mrs. Nichols, gowned in blue crepe and wearing the white, golden throated orchid presented to her by her grandchildren, greeted the guests at the door with Mr. Nichols and Mr. and Mrs. Blackwood.

The dining room table was centered with an arrangement of golden mums and flanked with silver candelabra holding golden tapers. The three-tiered wedding cake decorated with golden spun rosettes and rose buds was placed at one end, while punch was served from a silver punch bowl at the opposite end, and coffee from another refreshment table. Daughters, Mrs. A. J. Kerr and Mrs. W. T. Hamilton, served the cake. Mrs. Hardeman Nichols and Mrs. Hudson Nichols served the punch and coffee.

Visiting their parents and assisting them in greeting their friends were all eight of their children and their families, Mr. and Mrs. Frank O. Young, Jimmy and Paul, of Bremen, Ga., Mr. and Mrs. A. J. Kerr and Pamela of Flint Mich., Mr. and Mrs. Flavil Nichols, Jimmie and Peggy of Mayfield, Ky., Mr. and Mrs. Fay Nichols, Carmen, Mike and Matilda Kay of Indianapolis, Ind., Mr. and Mrs. Hardeman Nichols, Judy and Beth, of Midland, Tex., Mr. and Mrs. W. T. Hamilton, Kathy and Nick, of Lamesa, Tex., Mr. and Mrs. Hudson Nichols, Sharon, Hudson Ray and Joe, of Iuka, Miss. Also on hand were grandchildren, Karen and Eddie Nichols, who

make their home with Mr. and Mrs. Nichols, and Sir. and Mrs. Blackwood, Vicki and John.

Miss Kahty Hamilton registered the host of friends who called between the hours of two and six.

Mr. Nichols is well known throughout the state, having served as Minister for the Sixth Avenue Church of Christ for 21 years. His daily radio program on WWWB has made him a familiar figure in the county. Today he counts 12 ministers in his family, including all four of his sons, three of his four sons-in-law, and four of his five brothers.

Mr. and Mrs. Nichols have applied the Golden Rule of "Do Unto Others As Ye Would Have Men Do Unto You" during their years of marriage and it seems to have worked well during these 50 years.

1963 - *Daily Mountain Eagle* Report

DON'T LOSE FAITH IN GOD
By Gus Nichols

Don't exchange faith in Almighty God
For faith in a mere human creature:
One who came from the dust of the sod,
Divinely formed in every feature.

Put your faith and trust in our Maker,
Not in created human beings.
Man would be a collossal faker,
To claim he created mind or seeing.

Believe the First words of the Bible –
"In the beginning, God created" –
Then you'll believe the rest reliable, –
To be true as therein related.

But those who are wise in their own conceits,
Wish to destroy faith in Jehovah.
History of God they try to defeat;
Therefore, they strive to make things over.

They wish to make man the supreme Being,
As though not of Divine creation,
Live by human wisdom and seeing,
And not by divine revelation.

But man's a mere created machine.
And needs the guidance of his Maker,
And he can't be saved by his own scheme:
Therefore, unbelievers are fakers.[26]

ENDNOTES

1 Tom Childers, "W. G. Pemberton," Frame 12: "interview with Tom Childers, 2003, in Flavil Nichols' home in Huntsville, Al." A presentation made at the annual lecture program at Southeast Institute of Biblical Studies, 24 February 2013.

2 Ibid.

3 G. C. Scarbrough, *Gospel Advocate*, 19 March 1953, p. 172.

4 W. A. Bradfield, *Gospel Advocate*, 5 July 1962, p. 431.

5 Advertisement, *Firm Foundation*, 26 February 1963, p. 140.

6 Note: Matt Norvel Young II was born in Nashville, Tennessee, 5 October 1915. He attended David Lipscomb College, Abilene Christian College, and Vanderbilt University. In 1938, he co-found the Nashville publication, *20th Century Christian*. He assisted in the planting of Lubbock Christian College in Lubbock, Texas, as well as helping to build Pepperdine College in Los Angeles. In 1957, he was appointed President of Pepperdine College and served in that role until 1971. He later served as Chancellor of Pepperdine University, and worked to build the institution the remainder of his life. He passed from this life 17 February 1998 and was interred in the beautiful Forest Lawn Memorial Park in northern Los Angeles, California.

7 Program, 1963 *Spring Bible Lectureship*, Pepperdine College, March 16-22, 1963, p. 10.

8 William S. Banowsky, "Pepperdine College Presents Award," *Gospel Advocate*, 16 November 1961, p. 734. Note: Initially, the *Christian Service Award* was given at monthly fellowship meals for the college, but later became an annual event. The first award was conferred upon George W. Bailey in 1961. Other early recipients were John Allen Hudson (1893-1962) in 1961, Andy T. Ritchie, Jr. (1909-1983) in 1965, and Marshall Keeble (1878-1968) in 1967.

9 Bill Youngs, *Gospel Advocate*, 25 April 1963, p. 269.

10 Note: Malcolm Lansden Hill (1934-2012) was born in Willow Grove, Tennessee, 12 January 1934. Sharing birthdays with Gus Nichols was the beginning of their connection. Nichols' best friend, B. C. Goodpasture (1895-1977), was a cousin to Malcolm's wife, Billie Ruth Bilyeu. He was also related to Albert R. Hill, Sr. (1890-1983). Malcolm later served as President of Southeastern Institute of the Bible, precursor to today's Heritage Christian University, in Florence, Alabama. Later, he served as President of Tennessee Bible College, in Cookeville, Tennessee. After a long battle with diabetes, Malcolm Hill passed from this life 26 June 2012, and was interred in Cookeville, Tennessee's City Cemetery. Gus Nichols was a close friend to the Hills and supporter of Malcolm's efforts through the years, especially as it had to do with the building of what is now Heritage Christian University.

11 Malcolm Hill, *Gospel Advocate*, 30 May 1963, p. 347.

12 Ibid., 11 July 1963, p. 444.

13 W. Gaddys Roy, *Gospel Advocate*, 4 July 1963, p. 429.

14 O. D. Johns, *Gospel Advocate*, 25 July 1963, p. 474.

15 W. S Blackman, *Gospel Advocate*, 29 August 1963, p. 552.

16 Willard W. Willis, *Gospel Advocate*, 22 August 1963, p. 540.

17 Willard Collins, *Gospel Advocate*, 12 September 1963, pp. 584-85.

18 Reuel Lemmons, ed., *Firm Foundation*, 13 June 1961, p. 380.

19 Advertisement, *Firm Foundation*, 9 July 1963, p. 445.

20 Ibid., "Four-Panel Discussions Set For ACC's Lectureship," 29 August 1963, p. 701.

21 Ibid., 21 January 1964, p. 48.

22 Note: The father of your author. I was two-years-old when we moved to Lancaster, South Carolina. It was the place of my earliest recollections.

23 Note: As has already been noted, the 8:00 a.m. program on WWWB was initially called, "The Gospel Broadcast." For a time it was called, "Truth In Love." Later, the name was changed to, "Words of Truth." The 12:15 session on WARF had no particular title. But, both were recognized as a part of the "Words of Truth," press releases of the Sixth Avenue church of Christ.

24 Note: *The Mountain Eagle* newspaper went through several name changes over the years. Today it is known as *Daily Mountain Eagle*.

25 Ira North, "What's Happening?" *Gospel Advocate*, 9 January 1964, p. 25.

26 *Words of Truth*, Vol. 9 No. 42, 9 May 1975, p. 42.

- 42 -

Solid Affiliations

> Now there was leaning on Jesus' bosom one of his disciples, whom Jesus loved.
> —John, John 13:23

"BROTHER POSEY"

The Sixth Avenue elders began a search for a new associate preacher early in 1964. Wade Johnson had departed, and someone was needed for the congregation due to the busy schedule of brother Nichols.

Just a few miles north of Jasper, the small, but solid, work at Lynn had produced a young man who was devoting his life to preaching the gospel. Born the 27th of October 1935 and raised in the Winston county town, Glenn Appleton Posey (1935-2018) was graduated from Lynn High School, and later Alabama Christian College. All his life he was exposed to many of the great preachers of the day, but none any more influential than Gus Nichols. Glenn married his high school sweetheart, Iris Holcomb. They grew up together in the church at Lynn and determined to dedicate their lives to the cause of Christ. For them, beginning their ministry at Jasper was a dream come true. Working with brother Nichols was a great blessing, but with home just several miles up Highway 5, it had all the makings of a perfect first work in ministry.

Glenn A. Posey

Estimating the task of assisting a man of the stature and standard of Gus Nichols is nothing short of impossible. When Glenn arrived, he felt well informed of his duties. However, only the half had been told. He soon realized that the main thrust of his work was to do the bidding of his elder counterpart. This was neither good nor bad—it was simply the fact. As a result, a deeper connection and friendship developed between the two that few men ever experience.

Arguably, no man had the opportunity to know Gus Nichols better than Glenn Posey. Yet, in his thinking, "no one knew Gus Nichols but Gus Nichols."[1] He had an office just down the hall from the elder preacher and was always at his beckoning call. While at the church building, several times in a day he would be busy at work in his office and would hear from down the hall, "brother Posey?!" Always professional, always esteemed, never was he referred to by his given name, but always the respectful "brother Posey." It was a level of honor of which he always felt unworthy to receive. However, with the call, he made his way to the preacher's office to hear of a new thing brother Nichols had learned, an interesting tidbit of information from a letter he just received, or something he wanted to hear the younger preacher weigh in on for discussion. Continually learning, constantly thinking of how the Word of God applies to all of life's situations, brother Nichols was the consummate student of the Scriptures. He helped Glenn to be the same.

The two men studied together daily. Always at the school of the Lord, they were ever learning, ever being challenged to know the way of Christ more fully. Gus knew the Bible, but it was the last thing he would comfortably admit. Call it humility if you will, but his thirst for knowledge seemed to force him forward in a never-tiring, ever-craving manner, in the thinking of his younger counterpart.

Glenn Posey Family
Iris, Glenn, Glenda, Mark Nichols

Brother Nichols loved to memorize the Scriptures. Since his days behind a plow, memorizing the Word of God was his greatest joy. He knew most all the Bible by heart and could quote the better part of it. One day, the two preachers started in the morning early in the book of Genesis. Glenn read a verse, and Gus quoted the verses before and after it. All day they continued. When they got to the chronologies and lists of names in the book of Numbers, they had not gone long until Glenn stopped and said, "brother Nichols, if you can quote these genealogies, there's not much point in us going further. You can quote all of it!"[2] At this point he began quoting on his own. He quoted seven chapters before stopping.

When Gus was away, Glenn was at home doing all of the things he was to do, as well as that of the senior preacher. Two radio programs a day, Bible classes to teach, sermons to preach, and even funerals and weddings to perform. "Busy" seems somewhat inadequate a word to describe his involvement. When brother Nichols was with him, there were times when they spent as much as 18 hours a day together, or in close proximity to one another.[3] In a time before the Internet, and mobile phones, it meant letters had to be written, or trips taken. Glenn seemed always to be on a mission on behalf of brother Nichols all over the county and region. Also, during the four years he was there, he traveled weekly to Harding Graduate School in Memphis to work on his Master's Degree. While the labor wore him out, it certainly prepared him for a lifetime of service.

Part of Glenn's work was assisting in the weekly production of *Words of Truth*. Still a new paper when he arrived, he quickly moved into the role of assistant editor. Writing, proof-reading, and getting the paper to the *Northwest Alabamian* in Haleyville for publication and distribution was very much part of his weekly duties.

Glenn served brother Nichols, but he was not a yes-man. The relationship was such that they could differ on various biblical topics and still hold the same amount of respect and appreciation. And, differ they did, occasionally. Yet, their differences only strengthened the fullness of their hearts toward each other. The level of intimate knowledge of the man very few if any had more than "brother Posey."

Gus and Glenn at a Gospel Meeting

The Posey family was so greatly influenced by the great love and character of brother Gus Nichols. They named their first-born, Mark Nichols Posey, in honor of the man of God from Walker County. A very talented and successful preacher of the gospel in his own right, Mark bears the name both in practice and in the influence of two great men, brother Nichols and his own father. Interestingly enough, Mark shares the same birthday as his elder friend and brother, Flavil Nichols, the 2nd of February.

CROSSING THE RACIAL DIVIDE

The Civil Rights movement in America brought much needed change in the social setting of our nation. The transition was difficult in many locations in both the south and the north. The gospel played a most important role in breaking down barriers and building relationships throughout the country. In the church, men like Marshall Keeble (1878-1968), R. N. Hogan (1902-1997), Levi Kennedy (1899-1970), and G. P. Holt (1923-2001) were among the greatest of the black preachers in the 20th century to help unite brethren of all races under the banner of the cross. There were many lesser-known preachers who did tremendous work among the black population to bring about growth in the Kingdom of heaven. John Harris (1922-2007) was a Louisiana born preacher living in Milan, Tennessee, who did much in the south. He often sent reports to the *Gospel Advocate* of the results of his labors. The following appeared in October 1963,

> Brother Gus Nichols, nationally-known evangelist of Jasper, Ala., selected me to conduct a meeting in Walker County, Ala. I baptized six at Carbon Hill, Ala. A retired schoolteacher, age sixty-six, was baptized. I also baptized the manager of the Blue Moon Cafe who had been a Methodist for forty years. I baptized three in Parrish, Ala., and five in Jasper, Ala. The last night of the meeting in Jasper closed with a packed house. Many Baptist preachers and deacons came to hear me. One was restored in Parrish. Brother Nichols allowed me to preach on his radio program thirty minutes a day for five days.[4]

Brother Harris returned the following year and enjoyed great success during that evangelistic campaign. In addition to speaking on brother Nichols' radio broadcasts again, he was involved in a two-night debate with a Baptist preacher by the name of George Horton. He reported,

> One of the highlights of the meeting was the night that Brother Gus Nichols and Brother Glenn Posey attended. Our entire audience was happy to see them. The colored brethren expressed to me personally their great love for Brother Gus Nichols and Brother Glenn Posey, who are ministers of the Sixth Avenue church of Christ.[5]

These reports demonstrate the great determination brother Nichols had in evangelizing among all people. It was with deep and abiding love for his fellow man that led him to promote the work among all races. For years, the Twenty-Fourth Street congregation and their preacher, Travis McCollum (1911-1994), enjoyed a good relationship with their Sixth Avenue brethren.

Brother Harris returned in 1965 for another visit. Several additions were enjoyed, and again he had the opportunity to preach on brother Nichols' program during the week of that event. This close communion gave brethren of both cultures a level of unity that made for a much more peaceable co-existence than was so often seen in many of the more urban centers in other parts of the country.

DR. GUS NICHOLS

For many years, George W. DeHoff (1913-1993), was a close friend to the Nichols family. In 1957, a new school was formed in Albion, Idaho, called Magic Valley Christian College. The Board of Trustees hired

DeHoff to be its first president. Serving several years in that capacity, his position carried with it the privilege of conferring upon people of high achievement the honorary Doctor of Laws degree. Well in advance of his departure from the office in June 1964, the decision was to bestow this honor on some brethren who accomplished much for the cause of Christ in their work. At least three recipients of the degree that year were B. C. Goodpasture (1895-1977),[6] Frank L. Cox (1919-1978),[7] and Gus Nichols.

The degree was conferred upon brother Nichols while DeHoff was on a visit to the southeastern part of the country early in the year. It was a blessing brother Nichols felt unworthy to receive, but one certainly merited in the eyes of the leadership at Magic Valley Christian College, and a much thankful brotherhood.

In May, a report appeared in the *Gospel Advocate* from Alabama Christian College. Groundbreaking of new construction took place on their new Atlanta Highway Campus. A photo appeared with dignitaries present for the occasion including Alabama's Lieutenant Governor. Noted among the dignitaries present was trustee of the school, "Dr. Gus Nichols."[8]

COUNSELING AND THE BIBLE

Jasper's preacher, like most, wore many hats while ministering to the flock. Being both elder and preacher, he was called on much more to be there to say the right word and encourage in the right way. Scrolls of proficiency in the field of counseling were not arrayed upon his office walls, but he knew the Word of God. Fully convinced of its power to address the needs of all people in all circumstances, he was ever ready to facilitate healing with its impactful truths. However, as the saying goes, "you can lead a horse to water, but you cannot make him drink." Such a mindset has always been the frustration of the preacher who shares the great pearls of God's wisdom before the swine of rebellion. Thus, being a man who was serious about sharing the healing power of the Great Physician, it was important to him, with the vast duties that laid claim to his time, that he knew those of his counsel were serious about doing their part in the process.

James D. Bales (1915-1995), Arkansas preacher and educator at Harding College, recalled Gus Nichols' approach to biblical counseling. He said,

> In a recent conversation with Gus Nichols he stated that in counseling with people he asked them two questions to begin with, First, are you willing to do the right thing? Do you want to do what is right? Second, are you willing to let the Bible decide what is right? If they are not, he talks with them about their attitude and about the Bible as the standard. For there is no need to discuss their particular problem unless they want to do

what is right, and unless they accept the right standard of right and wrong. Furthermore, Brother Nichols said that he did not read the scriptures to them but let them read the scriptures for themselves.⁹

Different variations of the questions have found their way in bulletin articles over the years. Sometimes with the added, "Are you willing to do it now" question has been recalled. In any case, such a simple approach to counseling has made it possible for many preachers and elders in the Lord's church to set this biblical standard as the format for their counseling practices ever since.

THE GOODPASTURES

The relationship that existed between Gus Nichols and B. C. Goodpasture (1895-1977) has already been illustrated to be as strong and committed as any that might be considered. Both men were equally so advanced in their fields of expertise that comparing the two would only serve to flatter both. However, it was their common love for the gospel of Christ that was the driving force in their ministry, and as far as they were concerned, in Him was their praise to be hidden.

Mr. and Mrs. B. C. Goodpasture

In 1964, Willard Collins (1915-2007) and John Cliett Goodpasture collaborated on a project to release a volume of sermons and lectures by the father of the latter. The publishing of the work was in view of commemorating 25 years of editorship of the *Gospel Advocate*, and included several tributes from various gospel preachers, one of whom was Gus Nichols. In an article entitled, "B. C. Goodpasture: In The Pulpit," he reminisced about the first time he heard brother Goodpasture preach, recalling the meeting that he held in Jasper back in 1936.¹⁰ In light of his great appreciation for the contributions of the man to the cause of Christ, he assessed,

> Personally, I consider B. C. Goodpasture as the greatest and best gospel preacher whom I have ever had the privilege of hearing. I doubt that any living preacher could excel several of his great masterpieces which I have heard under varying circumstances. He is truly a master of assemblies. His presence commands attention. His voice was rich and mellow with a pathos which at

times plucked the heartstrings of those who heard. His delivery was warm and fervent, with interest in his audience, whom he loved and admired. He always spoke deliberately and with ease— yes, and without notes. His vocabulary was always ready to lend him the right word, or phrase, or the right quotation, at the right time. His illustrative material made one think of the parables of Jesus. His power of exhortation and persuasion made his discourses and the invitation extended almost irresistible. But, as I view B. C. Goodpasture, he cannot be put into the molds and confines of a book of sermons. It will take the divine pictures of his whole life of loving and sacrificial service in the kingdom of God, both as a great preacher and editor of the *Gospel Advocate* to portray the greatness of this man whom I love and admire for his works sake.[11]

When the book was released, a copy was soon on its way to the waiting hands of Gus Nichols. He recalled,

When I first received my copy of these very timely and powerful lessons of divine truth, I started in to read them in very great haste. But I soon found myself landing upon some mountain-peak paragraph here, and a rich valley or lake of diamonds there, all such challenging matter that I soon found myself slowly reading and re-reading the whole book again and again several times, and each time with the same interest and spiritual refreshing.[12]

It is easy to see the depth of appreciation that existed in the heart of Gus Nichols for B. C. Goodpasture. His preaching, leadership, and direction for an entire generation of Christians meant the world to him and countless others.

Early in November, Gus received word of the passing of sister Goodpasture (1897-1964). Quickly, he made arrangements to make his way to Nashville to attend the funeral of his friend's dear wife of forty-six years. Upon his return home, he sat down and wrote a tribute that was preserved in a special issue of the *Gospel Advocate* dedicated to her life.[13] In his article, he compared Cleveland Cliett Goodpasture to the woman of Shunem whom the Holy Spirit inscribed as, "a great woman."[14] Further, he attributed to her five abundant qualities. He praised her intelligence as a mark of true greatness. He saw her as a woman of great faith, and one who loved so much. Her service was great, and he noted that her works will follow her after she is gone.[15] Truly the Goodpastures and Nichols enjoyed a bond that was deeply rooted in Christ. Their very visible connection and friendship illustrated for the onlooker a true sense of what the Lord intended the Christian community to be.

ENDNOTES

1 Interview with Glenn Posey, 10 October 2011.

2 Ibid.

3 Personal Interviews with Glenn Posey. Note: It has been the author's privilege to know the Poseys most of my life. I came to know their families when I preached for the Lynn Church of Christ a brief time during the mid-1980s. In preparation for this book, I had several visits with Glenn both on the phone and in person. He truly knew brother Nichols.

4 John Harris, "Among the Colored Brethren," *Gospel Advocate*, 10 October 1963, p. 665. Note: Brother Harris was affectionately called "Big John Harris," by those who knew and loved him. He was very tall, and his presence was so impressive to all who knew him. His occasions to come to Jasper to work with the 24th Street church of Christ, was always supported by brother Nichols and the brethren at Sixth Avenue.

5 John Harris, "Among the Colored Brethren," *Gospel Advocate*, 20 October 1964, p. 719.

6 Willard Collins, "B. C. Goodpasture Honored At Gospel Advocate Anniversary Dinner During Lipscomb Lectures," *Gospel Advocate*, 5 March 1964, pp. 152-53.

7 Gussie Lambert, *In Memoriam*, Shreveport: Self-Published, 1988, p. 59.

8 Rex Turner, "Ground Broken For Alabama Christian College," *Gospel Advocate*, 14 May 1964, p. 316.

9 James D. Bales, "Friends, Not Enemies," *Firm Foundation*, 5 May 1964, p. 288.

10 See footnote 11 in Chapter 20, "A Full-Time Preacher," concerning the correct year of the meeting as being in 1936 instead of what Gus reported as being in 1934.

11 Gus Nichols, *Sermons And Lectures*, "B. C. Goodpasture In The Pulpit," Chapter VII, pp. 29-31.

12 Gus Nichols, "A Timely Book to Grace Your Home and Bless Your Heart," *Gospel Advocate*, 23 July 1964, pp. 469-70.

13 B. C. Goodpasture, ed., *Gospel Advocate*, 10 December 1964.

14 2 Kings 4:8-10.

15 Gus Nichols, *Gospel Advocate*, 10 December 1964, pp. 791-92.

- 43 -

Controversy

> These are the things that ye shall do; Speak ye
> every man the truth to his neighbor; execute
> the judment of truth and peace in your gates.
> –The Prophet, Zechariah 8:16

The colorful and distinguished preacher from Jasper enjoyed a reputation of being able to give a defense for the truth at a moment's notice. By his seventieth year, his steadfastness and reliability enjoyed endorsement by a loyal body of believers. He was a stalwart of the faith, a defender of righteousness, and a voice for God not to be silenced. The pulpit had no superior, the printed page enjoyed no greater pen, and the air waves no more efficient speaker for the truths of God. Yet, with all these accolades few could be thought more humble. To Gus Nichols—in the opinion of the man—his perfection was found in the blood of Christ and not in himself.

Once during a gospel meeting, a woman expressed that she would give her life to know the Bible like he knew it. Respectfully, he responded that it was what she would *have* to do. As, it was exactly what he did! Adding to his daily study regimen was the sheer volume of duties that vied for attention every waking moment. His was a life-work.

He was prepared for a defense of the gospel, yet he sought to keep his mind open to the views of others even if he did not always accept them. Confrontation served to force him to think more deeply, which he loved. This is what led him to give up Calvinism when he first obeyed the gospel and continued to entice him toward a better understanding of the truth the rest of his life. His numerous debates were demonstrations of willingness not only to uphold the faith, but to absorb its saving power to the best of his ability. With it, he also wanted to understand every false way better than its most loyal defender in order that truth might prevail.

With every opponent he met on the polemic platform, he made it his business to know their arguments better than they. Many days before an impending confrontation he spent in complete solitude, stopping only to eat and sleep a little. At mealtimes, Matilda brought his food on a tray and sat it outside the closed door of his room of preparation, making sure he was not disturbed in any way.[1]

He appeared to have little or no fear in putting himself and his theology on the line. His preaching invited response, even if negative. His writing attracted praise and on occasion, disagreement. Yet, whether in debate or on paper, he was forever the student—forever the searcher—of that which made sense to him in keeping with God's word. If he saw the need to change his mind on a point of doctrine, he was willing to do so, if it meant staying true to what he was persuaded was correct.

Controversy was far from being his goal, but it was the outcome of his existence. And with it, at times, his views raised more than eyebrows among his brethren. Views he held on some subjects deemed controversial are the focus of the present chapter. All his teachings are not displayed here, but some that brought considerable reaction are here for our record of his life.

THE STATE OF THE RIGHTEOUS DEAD

Early in 1962, one of his *Queries Answers* columns in the *Advocate* was devoted to a series of questions having to do with eschatological, or end times, teachings in the Scriptures. Primarily, the question arose of what happens to faithful Christians when they die. As always, he set out to share what the Bible says. During the discussion, he veered from the prevalent thinking of most of his brethren on the subject. He wrote,

> The inspired apostle Paul expected and desired to "depart and be with Christ" at death, which he said was "gain" and "far better" than to "abide in the flesh" (Phil. 1:21-24). Paul also said he knew that we are "absent from the Lord" only "while" we are "at home in the body" (2 Cor. 5:6). He repeats his conviction in the matter in the next verses and says, "We are confident, I say, and willing rather to be absent from the body, and to be present with the Lord" (2 Cor. 5:8). Of course, the Lord is now in heaven (1 Pet. 3:22). This is why Stephen said at death, "Lord Jesus, receive my spirit" (Acts 7:59). He said he had just seen Jesus up in heaven (Acts 7:55.). . .Paradise is now transferred to heaven, and is no longer in "Hades," as before the ascension. We read that the "tree of life" is in the city of God, in heaven (Rev. 22:14). But again, we read that the "tree of life" is "in the midst of the paradise of God" (Rev. 2: 7). It follows, therefore, that "paradise" is now in heaven in the "city" where the tree of life is. This is where the souls of the slain saints were after death (Rev. 6:9-11). Paul identifies "paradise" with "the third heaven" (2 Cor. 12:1-7).[2]

According to brother Nichols, Jesus emptied "Paradise" after going there when he died. With purification offered at the cross, there was no need for Hades. So, when the church age began, faithful Christians went directly to heaven when they died.[3]

Controversy

Within weeks, Texas preacher, Guy W. Sims (1925-1983) rebutted with an article, the title of which, was taken from the second question in brother Nichols' column, "Where Will The Faithful Christian Go At Death?"[4] He began his comments with kind words of respect for brother Nichols though they had never met. Then, charging that he did "err

Guy Nichols and Guy Woods at FHC Open Forum

exceedingly" in his teachings on this subject, Sims countering Nichols' arguments in view of showing that the spirit of the Christian goes to the Paradise of the Hadean world until the Day of Judgment. For instance, he aligned Paul's statement in Philippians 1:21-24 concerning being absent from the body was to be with the Lord with his words in 2 Timothy 4:8. He said the apostle did not expect to receive his "crown of righteousness" until the last day, when all those who love his appearing receive theirs. He added that the slain saints of Revelation 6 were said to be under the alter and not in the "Holy of Holies." Then, adding that they entered the heavenly Jerusalem in Revelation 21:1-5 after the judgment. With several other points he countered Nichols' view on the subject.

Brother Nichols continued to hold to his beliefs on this subject but refused to make it a contest of faith. One example of this was on the occasion one year at the Open Forum at Freed-Hardeman Lectures. Guy N. Woods (1908-1993), was the moderator at that time. Someone asked a question about the state of the righteous dead. Brother Woods declared that when a Christian dies his spirit ascends to Paradise. With that, Brother Nichols immediately stood up and walked to the stage there at the Henderson church building, where it was conducted back then. He took sharp exception to brother Woods' position and insisted that they go directly and immediately to Heaven. They argued heatedly for several minutes. Then when they saw that they were at an impasse and brother Woods was about to terminate that discussion, brother Nichols walked over and stood close to his side, put his arm around brother Woods and said, "Guy, in spite of the fact that you're wrong about this, I still think you'll 'scarcely be saved.'" That's just the kind of sweet spirit he had.[5]

THE HOLY SPIRIT

Controversy within the brotherhood over the work of the Holy Spirit has long been a point of difference, especially as it has to do with the way in which He dwells in the life of the Christian. One view purported is that the Holy Spirit dwells in the Christian only through the Word, the Bible. The other view, held by many, including Gus Nichols, was that the Holy Spirit literally indwells the Christian, but with the added qualification that he in no way illuminates or reveals truth beyond the Scriptures.

Nearly all his preaching career, brother Nichols defended the Bible's teachings on the Holy Spirit against denominationalists. Several of his debates with Pentecostals and Calvinists were in view of dispelling falsehoods concerning the Spirit's work.

The year of 1967 began in typical fashion with a quick 170-mile trip to Henderson, Tennessee, for the lectures at Freed-Hardeman College. This year, Gus was to speak on two topics, "Holy Spirit and Denominational

Doctrines" and also "Instrumental Music and Current Issues." Alan Highers joined him in the discussion on, "The Holy Spirit and Tongue Speaking."[6]

Then, at the end of February, he was in Memphis for the Memphis Tennessee Lectureship hosted at the Getwell congregation. He presented lessons twice daily on the Holy Spirit.[7]

In June, the Nichols Brothers Publishing Company released a book entitled, *Lectures On The Holy Spirit*. In it was a series of eleven transcribed lessons, with corrections, that were recorded in a meeting he conducted at the Walnut Hills church of Christ in Dallas, Texas. This was the congregation where Hardeman was the preacher. With large crowds each morning and evening, brother Nichols taught on the subject with plainness and simplicity. The *Firm Foundation* critiqued the book that July in its "Books In Review" column, and was mildly critical. It read,

Lectures on the Holy Spirit

> Several good books have come on the market recently as a result of renewed interest in the Holy Spirit question...The reader will not agree with all the positions taken in this book, nor do we, but in the main they follow the main stream of thought among Bible students in the church. The quotation of practically every verse dealing with the Holy Spirit is typical of the author's preaching and writing. His dealing with each verse is painstaking, if traditional. Brother Nichols takes the position that the Holy Spirit does dwell in one in a manner distinct from the word, but that he does not guide us other than through the word.[8]

Six months later, the *Gospel Advocate* promoted the book, giving it much more flattering press. It was the "Book Of The Week," with Willard Collins (1915-2007) inserting the titles of each chapter to encourage the readers to lay down the $3.50 purchase price.

As was mentioned, not all agreed with brother Nichols on the subject. One who fell strongly in the "through the Word only" camp was his dear friend Guy N. Woods (1908-1993). Many, including this author, had the privilege of seeing the friendly banter between these two men on the stage at the annual Bible lectures at Freed-Hardeman. For over thirty years, brother Woods conducted the daily Open Forum. Many were the times during that period when questions arose about the work of the Holy Spirit. As soon as the topic was announced, and brother Woods began weighing in on the subject, just like clockwork, brother Nichols slowly arose from his chair to make his way to the speaker's stand. Many were drawn to attend the afternoon period in anticipation of seeing the two men discuss the issue with lively deliberation. Sometimes the discussion took up the better part of the hour. However, they always demonstrated a sense of respect and genuine love for one another, stating that some things in the Bible can be disagreed upon and fellowship continue to be maintained.

Another of his friends, one who saw himself as a student of brother Nichols yet stood in conflict with his position on the Holy Spirit was Franklin Camp (1915-1991). His book on the subject appeared in 1974 entitled, "The Work Of The Holy Spirit In Redemption." In it, he developed more fully the position that the Holy Spirit works through the Word of God in the life of the Christian.

REMARRIAGE OF THE GUILTY PARTY

Perhaps, the most controversial of all the subjects taught by brother Nichols was on the Bible's teaching on divorce and remarriage, in particular in the area of the remarriage of the "guilty party."

For most of his preaching career, his handling of the need for moral purity in the life of the Christian was seen by the brotherhood to be consistent with what the Scriptures teach. Queries surrounding marriage, and who can marry surfaced under his pen beginning in the early 1940s.

Someone sent in a question concerning a man who "marries four or five times" for reasons other than fornication and is baptized, can he stay with his last wife? To this, he responded in part by citing Matthew 19:9, and followed with,

> It is very likely that the young man mentioned has done entirely too much marrying. According to the foregoing Scripture, fornication is the only ground upon which he could have been justified in any remarriage during the life time of his first companion. Yet he married three or four times without the cause of fornication. His first marriage is still binding, and his others are only legalized adultery, and not recognized of God at all. But it is claimed that

he obeyed the gospel. This means very much more than is here claimed. Obedience to the gospel includes repentance. (Acts 2:38; 3:19.) And to repent means to turn from one's evil ways. (See Matt. 12: 41; Jonah 3:10.) One who continues to live in an adulterous wedlock has not turned from his evil ways and has not truly obeyed the gospel. A bootlegger cannot obey the gospel and go on peddling his liquor. A drunkard cannot obey the gospel and continue to be a drunkard. Those born of God do not commit sin—that is, they do not continue in the practice of it.[9]

In the 1953, "Truth In Love" series he preached at Lamesa, Texas he addressed the topic of repentance by saying,

> There is a new doctrine now, and I think its headquarters is Fort Worth, Texas, which teaches that one may be living in adultery with a tenth wife and be her tenth husband, and when they are baptized they will be forgiven of their sins of adultery and can go on living together as husband and wife. How can one repent of fornication and still live in it? There is no change of the mind for the better in that![10]

In 1961, someone wrote in to the *Gospel Advocate* and asked if a preacher could baptize a person living in adultery, to which he responded, "If he is living in adultery, or any other sin, and is not willing to give it up, he is not repenting, and his baptism would not be scriptural, and he would not be saved. (Matt. 3:7-10; Luke 13:3; Acts 17:30.)"[11]

In 1965, the *Gospel Advocate*, produced an issue especially to be distributed for free at the World's Fair in New York City. The issue was replete with sound and solid biblical teaching. It was intended to put a most Biblical and relevant face on the teachings of churches of Christ around the world. The April 15th issue included a special article by Gus Nichols under the title, "Questions On Re-Marriage." Once again, he demonstrated a consistent teaching on the subject with what he had previously taught in years past. The issue was so widely received as successful that it was reprinted in a special World's Fair Edition at the end of May with the cover in color. Again, thousands of copies of the issue were given away at the World's Fair.

It was around this time, that Gus began challenging some of his own thinking on the subject. He engaged the wisdom of some other preachers and scholars he respected in the process of determining whether his teaching of the past was truly in keeping with the spirit and teaching of Christ.

About six or seven months after the World's Fair issue, in early 1966, an article appeared on page three of the January 28th edition of *Words of Truth*, under the title, "May The Guilty Party Remarry?" This article was when a change in his thinking on the subject began to surface. After asserting that the "innocent party" could remarry he suggested,

> Why could the one remarry and not the other also? Is it because the two are still husband and wife in God's sight? If so, then the innocent person could not marry another for the reason she is already married, already has a companion or husband—is joined to another already. If the innocent one is loosed from the husband as though he were dead and can be married to another because she is no longer his wife, then IS HE ANY LONGER HER HUSBAND? How could he still be her husband if she is no longer his wife? But if he is no longer her husband, why could he not remarry another if she can?

> To use James D. Bales' illustration, if two mules are put into a small pasture and one breaks out and goes off to run with another mule and the owner brings back the fence-breaker and ties him hard and fast to the mule which stays in the pasture, then how could the man later loose the fence-breaker so the innocent mule is no longer tied to him, but so as to leave the fence-breaker tied to the innocent mule? If one is untied from the other, are not both equally untied? If not, why not?[12]

James D. Bales (1915-1995) was a long-time preacher, author, educator and professor at Harding College in Searcy, Arkansas. He was one of the most prolific and valiant defenders of the faith during his life. He and college President, George S. Benson (1898-1991) led the strongest battle of any of our brethren in the national fight against communism in America in the 20th century. Thousands of articles were written by brother Bales over the years to sustain the cause of Christ throughout the world.

Letters passed between brothers Nichols and Bales during this period of transition. In later years, brother Bales became a chief proponent of remarriage for the "guilty party," and produced a hotly debated volume entitled, "Not Under Bondage,"[13] where his views surpassed that of brother Nichols on the topic. However, Bales' influence on brother Nichols appears to be undeniable here.

In the last issue of July 1973, on page 2 of *Words of Truth*, he once again dealt with the issue of divorce and remarriage in his *Editorial* column. Amidst many other things about marriage and divorce he argued,

> "May the guilty party marry again?" I see no way in the world for it to be true that the "innocent party" may PUT AWAY *(emphasis his)* the "guilty party," and the guilty not really be put away. I see no way for the "innocent" to have a right to another marriage, but

the "guilty" have no such right. If the "guilty" is REALLY (emphasis Gus Nichols) "put away," he is no longer married to the "innocent party." How could the "innocent party" be loosed from the bonds of wedlock, and the "guilty person" still be tied to the "innocent?"

If one is handcuffed by an officer, with each hand locked and fastened to the other, how could the right hand be loosed from the left hand, so that it is no longer bound to the left hand, and yet the left hand still be bound to the right? "What therefore God hath joined together, let not man put asunder" (Matt. 19:6). HOW (emphasis Gus Nichols) could one of them be put asunder from the other, without the other being put asunder from that one? It seems to me impossible for the innocent to have the right to another marriage, and the guilty person not have such a right.[14]

The response to brother Nichols' change in views appears to have been relatively low-key. There were some who challenged him on his views, and some were interested in debating him. But, he never was willing to enter the debate arena on the issue. Perhaps the closest thing to a debate on the subject was a special interest discussion held at the Fall Lectures program on the campus of Harding School of Theology[15] in October 1973. The theme for the program was, "What the Christian Family Needs Today."[16] In the schedule, a doctrinal discussion was held on the question, "In Divorce Is The Guilty Party Free To Re-Marry?" Roy Deaver, Gus Nichols.[17] The answer of "Yes" to the question was defended by brother Nichols, and "No" by Texas preacher, and former President of Fort Worth Christian College, Roy C. Deaver (1922-2007). The discussion was well attended, and both speakers demonstrated a wonderful sense of candor and respect for each other.

Very little time did brother Nichols pursue the subject in the public eye. Only when it was brought to his attention did he deal with the question in a public setting. He sought not to be divisive or try pressing his thinking onto the brotherhood. His new re-marriage views on the subject never reached the pages of either the *Gospel Advocate* or the *Firm Foundation*. As noted, this interpretation appeared in his paper, *Words of Truth*, but then, not in a prominent way, and only in a couple of issues.

THE ELDERSHIP

Gus Nichols served as an elder in the Lord's church for many years. He worked alongside some great men during that period at Sixth Avenue who were equally committed to the body of Christ by serving in the office they filled.

At one point, during the 1960s, he and the eldership came under fire due to the installation of an elder who had no natural children of his own. Brother and sister C. M. Karrh were much beloved members of the congregation for many years. No two people were more highly esteemed by the membership or for that matter, the community. They both led in the congregation in every possible way. Brother Karrh worked in public education the greater portion of his working career. Sister Karrh was an elementary school teacher for over 30 years. He and sister Karrh fostered children in their home on different occasions as well, though they had no believing children of their own. Brother Nichols argued strongly that their experiences, their loving dispositions toward children and the care of them, made brother Karrh highly qualified to serve in the role of elder. In Nichols' thinking, Karrh fulfilled the principals regarding the eldership set out in 1 Timothy 3:4 and Titus 1:6.[18]

While his views on the eldership were deemed controversial, like some of his other views, they were not cast openly before the brotherhood for teaching purposes but were held as being in keeping with God's divine will.

Colorful, might be the word to describe the man as it had to do with his teachings on several biblical subjects. His reputation for soundness appears to have never wavered in the minds of an appreciative brotherhood, though some struggled to attribute such because of some of his views. Not always popular in the thinking of some, yet none doubted his sincerity when it came to his biblical interpretation. The nature of views espoused in any capacity are such as to invite discussion, disagreement, and potentially judgment. As strongly as anyone could teach, Gus Nichols held that he who judges all things is God, and it is for him to determine the destiny of us all.

DEACONS NOW REPLY
By Gus Nichols

Such excuses pile up very high,
But now the deacons make a reply:
Christ died and gave his own blood for you,
But unto him you're not being true!

You're not living for Jesus the Christ,
Who died for you and was sacrificed.
And you do not love the blessed Lord,
Nor live with the saints in one accord.

You love the world and its worldly ways,
You're wasting your life and all your days.
You go where ever you wish to go,
To the store, to the fair and the show.

Either you've gone astray into sin,
Or God's true children you've never been.
You've never obeyed God's blessed word,
Or you've turned away from what you've heard.

Backsliders to whom God's word is sent,
Too, must in godly sorrow repent,
And confess their many willful sins;
For that's where their remission begins.

Without excuses, and in all lands,
Those who love Jesus keep his commands:
Attend his worship; strengthen his church,
They live right and stay out of the lurch.

They love the church and one another,
And each one seeks to help his brother.
They do not hate, nor engage in strife,
But seek to live a much better life.

To reject the worship God commands,
Leads to a neglect of other demands,
Until such church members lose their faith,
Reject the rest of what scripture saith.

No, the Bible is ahead of date,
And points out the certain doom and fate,
Of all members of the Lord's church
Who hate the truth and themselves besmirch.

Come on then, and let us all faithful be,
I'll try to help you, and you help me,
To serve the Lord, and his word fulfill,
Be God's light, a city on a hill![19]

ENDNOTES

1 Reported in a conversation with Gary C. Hampton, Fall 2015.

2 Gus Nichols, "Queries Answers" *Gospel Advocate*, 22 February 1962, pp. 116-17.

3 Note: This position on where Christians go after death is not a new one. Several preachers have espoused this interpretation in the past. The train of thinking espoused in the article sounds much like that of Frank Gibbs Allen (1836-1887) in his book, *The Old-Path Pulpit*, initially released from Covington, Indiana in 1886. It had been re-released by The Gospel Advocate Company in 1940. Years later, Flavil reprinted Sermon Fourteen, entitled, "The State of Righteous Death," in which he prefaced that this was the material his father used "in his study and in his preaching." (*Words of Truth*, 31 March 1989, p. 1).

4 Guy W. Sims, "Where Will The Faithful Christian Go At Death?" *Gospel Advocate*, 19 April 1962, pp. 246-47.

5 Ken Joines, A recollection of the kind spirit of brother Nichols, even when sticking firmly to his beliefs. Email to the author, May 26, 2010.

6 Advertisement, *Firm Foundation*, 3 January 1967, p. 12.

7 Advertisement, *Gospel Advocate*, 16 February 1967, p. 111.

8 Reuel Lemmons, ed., "Books In Review," *Firm Foundation*, 4 July 1967, p. 430.

9 Gus Nichols, *Gospel Advocate*, 15 December 1949, p. 788.

10 Gus Nichols, *Speaking The Truth In Love*, "Repentance Unto Life," Chattanooga: Nichols Bros. Publishing Co., c.1956, pp. 146-47.

11 Gus Nichols, *Gospel Advocate*, 1 February 1962, p. 71.

12 Gus Nichols, "May The Guilty Party Remarry?" *Words of Truth*, 28 January 1966, p. 3.

13 James D. Bales, *Not Under Bondage*, Searcy: Self Published, 1979.

14 Gus Nichols, ed., "Editorial Answers," *Words of Truth*, 27 July 1973, p. 2.

15 Note: Formerly Harding University Graduate School of Religion and changed to Harding School of Theology July 1, 2011.

16 Advertisement, *Firm Foundation*, 16 October 1973, p. 13 [669].

17 Advertisement, *Gospel Advocate*, 18 October 1973, p. 674.

18 Phone Interview with James A. Horton, 2.3.2016. Note: James Horton was serving as an associate minister in the congregation while brother Karrh was serving as an elder. He recalled the controversy well, but said he knew of no greater people than brother and sister Karrh. He remembered well their love for children, and the efforts they made to live up to the high standard of God's Word in all things.

19 Gus Nichols, "Poems By Gus Nichols," *Words of Truth*, 26 March 1971, p. 3. Note: Even some of Gus Nichols' poetry can be said to have been controversial.

Mr. Walking Bible

> Thy word have I hid in mine heart, that I might
> not sin against thee. Blessed art thou, O Lord:
> teach me thy statutes. With my lips have I
> declared all the judgments of thy mouth.
> —David, Psalms 119:11–13

The mid-1960s continued to see Gus Nichols in great demand among schools and churches of Christ. Whether at home or away he maintained a schedule that men half his age would have struggled to sustain.

Touted as "Answer-Man" by the *Christian Chronicle*, he participated in the widely supported Mid-South Training for Service Series in Memphis in early March 1964.[1] Eight-thousand attendees were given the opportunity to sit at his feet and hear answers to Biblical questions during the week's event. He was joined in the program by some of the greatest gospel preachers of the day like E. R. Harper (1897-1986), Wyatt Sawyer (1924-2012), Carl McKelvey, Jack P. Lewis (1919-2018), and David Underwood (1928-2010), to name a few.

Between January 30 and February 5, 1965, he lectured daily at 8:00 a.m. on the book of Galatians at the Freed-Hardeman College Lectures in Henderson, Tennessee. W. A. Bradfield (1910-1972) later reported that it was one of the greatest lectureships in the history of F-HC. "The crowds were so large that the sessions had to be moved to Bader Memorial Gymnasium."[2] This was quite a transition from the more refined setting of Chapel Hall to sitting on folded chairs and bleachers when crowds were larger, but the program was growing with the likes of speakers, "Hugh Fulford, George Bailey, Batsell Barrett Baxter, Harold Hazelip, Otis Gatewood, Jay Lockhart, Garland Elkins, J. C. Davidson, Cliett Goodpasture, Roy Deaver, Guy N. Woods, Gus Nichols and Thomas B. Warren."[3]

ANSWER-MAN — Gus Nichols, minister from Jasper, Ala., taught a Bible question and answer class at the series. A preacher for over 50 years, Nichols will be given an honorary degree by Abilene Christian College in June.

The Answer Man

Toward the end of March, Gus headed out to Fort Worth to participate in the sixth annual lecture program at Fort Worth Christian College.[4]

He spoke the first night on the subject, "God Is!"⁵ For the five days of the program he also conducted a Queries and Answers forum in the auditorium.

Returning home, he readied things for the spring gospel meeting at Jasper. This year, Sixth Avenue hosted Guy N. Woods (1908-1993) for a series of sermons during the week of April 4-11. Twice daily, brother Woods preached on the radio in addition to morning and evening sessions in the church auditorium. Great attendance prevailed throughout the week.

In late June, Gus and Matilda made their annual summer trip to North Carolina for the Blue Ridge Encampment. Directed by J. M. Powell (1907-2004), the week's schedule included the regular Gus Nichols Hour for questions and answers. An added feature for the week was an "elder's workshop with Gus Nichols as chairman, and Ernest Clevenger, T. E. Burch, and L. R. Wilson as panelists."⁶

CHRISTIAN EDUCATION

Training preachers to preach the unsearchable riches of Christ was a great joy in the life of Gus Nichols. Hundreds attended his Friday Night Training Class over the years, many of whom had family obligations that forbade the ability to attend a Christian college. But, to say they were any less prepared for ministry by participating in the former is to underestimate the quality of education he offered.

Texas educator, Dr. Fred J. Barton (1911-2001), wrote an article for the *Firm Foundation* on the subject of "The Education Of Preachers." In the full-page address he praised the quality of education being offered by the Christian colleges. Then he added,

> Some 20th century preachers have felt the personal urgency of Paul's charge to Timothy and have themselves become teachers of preachers. For thirty years Brother Gus Nichols has conducted weekly classes for preachers in his home congregation in Jasper, Alabama.⁷ Brother Nichols has never thought of his work as being in competition with any other educational program. In fact, many of the men who first studied with him have been encouraged to go on to one of the colleges in the area for supplementary training. And, while Bro. Nichols is not himself a college graduate; perhaps no other preacher in the church today has been so widely used by the Christian colleges in lectureships and special training programs. And from all over north Alabama and northeastern Mississippi they have come, young men and older men, to study with this teacher-preacher. While earning their living at the sawmill or on the farm or in the coal mine, they

have studied the Bible and related areas of knowledge, and they have learned how to prepare and deliver sermons. Churches in the area have provided a sympathetic hearing as these men have learned, and as a result scores of useful ministers are at work today. More preachers need to read again and to ponder Paul's words to Timothy in 2 Tim. 2:2.[8]

Within days of the publishing of the article, the brethren at Sixth Avenue announced an expansion to the Friday night classes. The advertisement appeared as follows,

> Jasper Bible School - Gus Nichols - Our SATURDAY BIBLE SCHOOL will open at the Sixth Avenue Church of Christ, Jasper, Alabama at 9:00 A.M., October 2, 1965. Only the Bible and related subjects will be taught. THERE WILL BE NO CHARGE FOR TUITION. Your only cost will be your travel expenses, and your lunch which may be had in town, or brought with you. The school will be under the oversight of the elders of the Sixth Avenue Church of Christ, and classes will be offered to both young people and adults. We are prepared to offer additional classes if the attendance requires it. Each subject will be continued for THIRTEEN WEEKS, then other courses will be offered each quarter.
>
> CLASSES OFFERED THIS QUARTER
>
> 9:00 A.M. to 10:15
>
> THE BOOK OF ROMANS, By Franklin Camp of Birmingham, Ala.
>
> NEW TESTAMENT GREEK, By Douglas Harris of Birmingham. Ala.
> - RECESS PERIOD
>
> 10:30 to 11:45 A.M.
>
> BIBLE INTERPRETATION, By Gus Nichols, Jasper, Ala.
>
> THE BOOK OF JOHN By W. A. Black, Millport, Ala. - NOON PERIOD
>
> 1:00 P.M. to 2:15
>
> PERSONAL WORK, By Glenn A. Posey, Jasper, Ala.
>
> ENGLISH AND PUBLIC SPEAKING, By Marlin Howard, Cullman, Ala.
>
> BIBLE CHARACTERS, By Gus Nichols, Jasper, Ala.
>
> FUNDAMENTALS OF SINGING, By Paul Wylie, Goodsprings, Ala.
>
> We believe that most anyone who will take these Bible courses for four years will learn as much Bible as he would learn without such training in a life-time. Our work is not accredited by the State, and we are not in competition with "Our Christian Colleges." We are just trying to help the good heart which might otherwise be

neglected. The school will be conducted in the meetinghouse of the Sixth Avenue church. Bring your Bible, your notebook and pencil and come. Enroll in one or more of these classes. Talk to others and interest them in this SATURDAY SCHOOL.

Some have written that they are coming from all over our county, and other counties as well. You have long wanted to attend a Christian school. Here is your opportunity, and without charge to you.

(Editor's Note: The foregoing is an announcement from one of the great congregations of the brotherhood. This is not an entirely new work for this church, but rather an enlarged work. Many preachers have already been trained by Brother Nichols and the Jasper brethren.)[9]

In this vein, at the end of October an advertisement appeared in the *Advocate* announcing the Winter Lectures at Lipscomb in mid-January. Gus Nichols was scheduled to speak on the subject, "The Christian Companion in Christian Education."[10] There was no one more qualified to speak on this, or for that matter, most any other Biblical subject. He was that knowledgeable on such a vast base of teaching. The next year it continued to be seen when he spoke at Freed-Hardeman's lectures on "Preaching From The Overflow."[11]

After the new T. B. Larimore School of Evangelists started January 6, 1966 in Florence, Alabama, they planned to have special speakers come in who were leaders in the field of educating preachers. They did not use as example some great PhD from a major Christian College or University. They advertised, "Periodically, qualified speakers will be invited to come and speak to the students on essential themes. Gus Nichols is scheduled to lecture on 'Denominational Errors' January 27."[12]

GUS NICHOLS LIBRARY

The level of achievement one accomplishes in the course of life is often revealed by the level of estimation placed upon him or her by the host of admirers who have been recipients of their labor. This was certainly true with Gus Nichols and his admiring brotherhood. Though he never served as a university president, he was looked upon as the mouthpiece of biblical education. In the eyes of the church, no one knew the Bible or promoted the Bible any more than he.

In the spring of 1966, Alabama Christian College announced the plan to build a new library and learning center on its campus. The structure was to consist of two floors, at the cost of above $400,000. Marvin F. Bryant (1922-1997) was selected to be the National Campaign Chairman to raise funds for the building of the new learning center. The cover of the May 26th edition of the *Gospel Advocate* adorned a picture of the artist conception of the finished building along with a photo of Gus Nichols. In a lengthy article by Bryant, he introduced the plans for naming the library. He opened with the following, "The proposed new Library Learning Center to be constructed at Alabama Christian College, Montgomery, Alabama is to be named in the honor of Gus Nichols."[13] What followed was a brief biographical sketch on the life of the respected recipient. In a most concise catalog of accolades, he reported on many of brother Nichols' great successes as a gospel preacher. Among them included having preached in over 27 states in an innumerable amount of gospel meetings and baptizing over 11,000 people. More was written

Gus Nichols Library and Learning Center

to address brother Nichols' commitment to Christian education with his work as a board member at ACC, his Friday night and now Saturday school at the Sixth Avenue church, and much more. References were made to his having conducted over a hundred debates, authoring eight books, and conducted one daily radio program for twenty-seven years and another for eleven. He added, "Gus Nichols' personal library consists of some three thousand volumes, and he is known as, 'Mr. Walking Bible.'"[14] All these things and more showed beyond doubt of the worthiness of naming the library after Gus Nichols.

At the end of the article, B. C. Goodpasture (1895-1977) weighed in saying,

> We are happy to commend the Board of Directors of Alabama Christian College for their foresight and appreciation. It is

altogether fitting and proper that Brother Nichols be honored by this new Library Learning Center. We know of no one in the church who deserves such consideration more than the ever-busy and dedicated Gus Nichols. It is our conviction that brethren throughout the entire brotherhood will contribute to this noble undertaking.[15]

GREAT PREACHERS OF TODAY

Dr. James D. Thomas (1910-2004) edited a series of volumes entitled, *Great Preachers of Today* between the years 1960 and 1967. The series was meant to feature well-known and successful preachers throughout the brotherhood, by having them contribute a number of full-length sermons, following a particular theme for publication. The volumes, in turn, were intended to be historical demonstrations of all that churches of Christ had to offer the ages during that period of time. The preachers who were featured were well-known, successful and faithful—the elite among brotherhood evangelists.

Issued in 1960, the first volume was a presentation called, "The Sermons Of Batsell Barrett Baxter" (1916-1982). The second was entitled, "The Sermons of George W. Bailey" (1922-2017), in June 1961. The third, released in May 1962 was, "The Sermons of Athens Clay Pullias" (1910-1985). Between 1963 and 1964, three similar volumes appeared by M. Norvel Young (1915-1998), Frank Pack (1916-1998), and Willard Collins (1915-2007). The seventh and eighth volumes featured the sermons of Roy F. Osborne, Jr. (1922-2015) and John H. Banister (1910-1995). The tenth through twelfth volumes were by Jim Bill McInteer (1921-2010), William S. Banowsky, and B. C. Goodpasture.

Volume nine of the series featured, "The Sermons of Gus Nichols." Released in July 1966, it was a 275-page selection of forty-two full-length lessons under the main theme of "The Great Commission."[16] In the preface, Thomas referred to many of the accolades of brother Nichols including the naming of the new Gus Nichols Library Learning Center being constructed on the Alabama Christian College campus. Of this volume he wrote,

> We are especially happy to present this particular volume and to have Gus Nichols listed among our authors. We feel that this volume will probably take its place as one of the greatest, if not the greatest, book of sermons on first principles of all time. Brother Nichols' life and influence for the cause of Christ are adequate testimony to his character and ability and his knowledge of the gospel message. For a man to conduct a daily radio program over a period of 21 years should be an indication that he has

something to say that meets the needs of people. Probably few men living equal him in inspiring and training younger men to become gospel preachers.[17]

HYPOCRITICAL EXCUSES REBUKED
Gus Nichols

We live across town from church, you know,
And when weather's bad we just can't go.
Yes, we have a fairly good old car,
But then you know how most folks are.

We go to the fair, party or show,
In all sorts of weather, rain or snow.
We always go to places we like,
If we can't ride, we'll take a good hike.

But going to church is different, you know;
Perhaps others have done told you so.
When we all get straightened out just right,
We will all come, or have a big fight.

Church-going used to be much in style,
But not so now for a good long while.
You know we're living in a new age,
And are all forced to turn a new page.

Once there were no other places to go,
Religion's always a sort of show.
But we're now living in a new world,
Even the hair must be frizzled and curled.

Before the children can go to church,
We must get out and make a big search.
And you may think it sort of funny,
But church-going costs a lot of money.

Church folks think we just don't want to go,
They say we're hypocrites, but don't know.
We know we love the Lord and our church,
We used to go and the scriptures search.

But we're living in the latter days,
And things are changing in many ways.
Every body's saying here of late.
That the Bible is much out of date.

We used to take all the services in,
But now they say we are all in sin.
The children may start before too long,
And then we may also come along.

We've not attended in over a year,
But deacons come and put us in fear.
For they say they will not stay away,
Because there's coming a judgment day!

Preachers ought to stay in their pulpits,
And deacons look after hypocrites.
We can work out our own salvation,
Without all these abominations.[18]

ENDNOTES

1 "Pictures Tell Story Of Mid-South Training Series," *Christian Chronicle*, 17 April 1964.

2 W. A. Bradfield, *Gospel Advocate*, 25 February 1965, p. 127.

3 Ibid.

4 Note: This school began in 1956 under the presidency of Roy C. Deaver (1922-2007) and ceased its existence in 1971.

5 Advertisement, *Gospel Advocate*, 11 March 1965, p. 158.

6 J. M. Powell, "1965 Blue Ridge Encampment," *Gospel Advocate*, 22 July 1965, p. 472.

7 Note: The Friday Night Class was always in the northeast corner of the church auditorium, down front, to the right of the pulpit as you are looking from the pews.

8 Fred J. Barton, "The Education of Preachers," *Firm Foundation*, 19 October 1965, p. 661. Note: It should be recalled here that though Gus did not have an earned college degree, he finished three years of undergraduate work before Alabama Christian College in Berry, Alabama closed its doors in the spring of 1922.

9 Advertisement, *Gospel Advocate*, 28 October 1965, p. 690.

10 Ibid., 28 October 1965, p. 703.

11 Ibid., 4 November 1965, p. 816.

12 Albert Hill, *Gospel Advocate*, 25 November 1966, p. 761.

13 Marvin F. Bryant, "New Library Learning Center To Be Named In Honor Of Gus Nichols," *Gospel Advocate*, 26 May 1966, pp. 325, 330.

14 Ibid.

15 Ibid.

16 J. D. Thomas, ed., *Great Preachers of Today: Sermons Of Gus Nichols*, Abilene: Biblical Research Press, 1966.

17 Ibid. Preface, p. iv.

18 Gus Nichols, "Poems By Gus Nichols," *Words of Truth*, 26 March 1971, p. 3.

Brother Horton

> My son, keep my words, and lay up my commandments with thee. Keep my commandments, and live; and my law as the apple of thine eye. Bind them upon thy fingers, write them upon the table of thine heart.
> Say unto wisdom, Thou art my sister; and call understanding thy kinswoman.
> — Solomon, Proverbs 7:1-4

When Colbert County, Alabama-born James A. Horton, was in his second year at Freed-Hardeman, he had the opportunity to work with the Mt. Zion church in Hardin County, Tennessee. This was where he made his acquaintance with the preacher for the Savannah church of Christ, Hudson Nichols (1930-1995). Soon thereafter, he was invited to go and work with Hudson at the Savannah church for a time. When some problems arose in the congregation, Hudson made his way down to Jasper to get some advice from his father. While there, he discussed the value young James would be to the work at Jasper.

After four years of service at Sixth Avenue, Glenn Posey had departed the work to become the minister for the Hillview church in Birmingham. With it, the brethren at Jasper had already been putting feelers out to see who might come to the aid of brother Nichols and the congregation. At Hudson's suggestion, a visit was arranged with James and his wife, Rose.

James A. Horton

During their initial visit, Rose sat with sister Nichols at their home where they visited about the work while James met across the street at the church building with brother Nichols and the other elders. After a most satisfactory visit, the job of assistant minister was extended to him, to which he accepted. Arrangements were made to move his family down in early September 1966.

After accepting the position, some initial things made them concerned about their choice of works. For instance, one of the elders owned a cattle truck and drove it to Savannah to move the couple. Fortunately, it had been hosed out, but still was not the cleanest environment for moving their things. However, it became a memory for them—often recalling their move to Jasper in a cattle truck.[1]

The following February, great friend and successful evangelist, Willie A. Bradfield (1910-1972), stopped in for a Sunday visit at Sixth Avenue. He later recalled, "Last Sunday I preached at Jasper, Ala., where Gus Nichols has been preaching for thirty-four years. James A. Horton is now his able assistant. We had an area-wide meeting in the afternoon. There were thirty-five responses to the invitation. Including eleven baptisms."[2]

Over the next five years James learned much at the feet of brother Nichols. Like his predecessor, he made himself available to the elder preacher's beckoning call in every way possible. Often times, he made his way over to brother and sister Nichols' home when the elder Nichols was finishing up his breakfast. By this stage in their lives, sister Nichols had long since quit making biscuits from scratch but would always make canned biscuits.

Gus and Matilda at the New Preacher's Residence

Brother Nichols loved pouring sorghum syrup all over his hot biscuits and eating burnt sausage while instructing his young protégé on one matter or the other.

Part of his work was to assist brother Nichols in his morning radio broadcasts. It was brother Horton's daily task to take calls for the announcements portion of the show from 7:00-8:00 a.m. To assist him in it, the church installed a phone into his home. Then, after receiving the call-in notices, he presented them during the first part of the radio broadcast.

One day he did his announcements as usual, and brother Nichols had not shown up for the preaching part of the program. So, he prayed over the radio. He recalled that it was a long prayer. But still, he never came.

As James had nothing prepared in the way of a lesson, he quickly looked around and grabbed a copy of the Great Sermons series by George W. Bailey (1922-2017) and began preaching one of the sermons. He ended up doing the entire broadcast that morning. Later, brother Nichols told him he intended to be there, but someone from another congregation had called, and he could not get off the phone with them to attend to the radio program. He told young James that he knew he was more than capable of handling the difficult situation.

Being in his mid-twenties, the young associate held brother Nichols in such high esteem. The things he learned from him, and the good brethren at Sixth Avenue, made an indelible impression that stayed with he and his family all the days of their lives.

He recalled one Sunday morning, brother Nichols came in and sat down next to him on the front row before the worship services began. He leaned over and said, "brother Horton, give me a subject!" Responding with an inquisitive look, again he requested, "Give me a subject." Thinking about it, he turned and gave his senior partner a subject. Brother Nichols then went to the pulpit and preached a 45-minute masterpiece on that subject. He was truly a man prepared for any topic at a moment's notice.

An intimate bond developed between the two. Brother Nichols confided in him, sharing with him some of his most personal thoughts and concerns. More than co-workers, they were confidants, though their ages varied fifty years. One day, brother Nichols came out of his house, and ran into brother Horton on his way across the street to the church building, before the worship services. He had toothpaste on his lapel. James worked hard while they stood there trying to get the toothpaste off his suit. Ever the perfectionist, Gus always wanted, not only his heart, but to make sure his teeth and mouth were clean before he entered the pulpit to preach the Word of God.

Sometimes they traveled together to meetings and appointments. On one occasion a congregation in Cullman was having some troubles. They asked brother Nichols to come over and help them sort out their troublesome issues. When they entered the building, brother Nichols said, "Brother Horton, now you sit down right over there," off to one side of the meeting room. He guessed that this meant that brother Nichols wanting James to be seen, but not heard.

As a young preacher, he was greatly impressed at how brother Nichols displayed self-discipline. He often denied himself in the consumption of certain foods or desserts, especially the things he loved most. For instance, he loved good summer watermelons. For a time, while some construction was taking place at the church building, daily radio broadcasts were made from the Nichols' home across the street. One day, James noticed that brother Nichols had a watermelon cooling in the mudroom of the house. Several days passed and it was still in the same place. After a good while, curiosity got the best of him and he asked him why he had not eaten the watermelon. His determined older brother responded, "This one is not for eating—it is for self-discipline!" Asking what he meant he continued, "I have resolved not to each it. The more I see it, and want to eat it, I am determined not to do it to strengthen my will to deny myself of any fleshly cravings!" His determined and disciplined spirit made such a long-lasting impression.

James learned and appreciated so many other experiences he had while in Jasper. The older brethren taught him much about being a good preacher. One of the elders, brother E. R. Tarence (1905-1993), helped him greatly. One Sunday morning during worship, James sat in the pulpit before speaking, and crossed his legs. Brother Tarence came up after and kindly suggested to him that crossing his legs and showing leg hair was inappropriate. He explained that no one wants to look up a man's hairy legs during worship. He proceeded to say that preachers should be well groomed when they stand before the church. They should never wear a suit coat without a long-sleeve shirt, and his socks should always be pulled up. This advice helped James for over fifty years of preaching.

The Nichols had such an influence on the Hortons that they named their only child, James Nichols Horton, after brother Nichols. At his own admission, the influence of the Nichols family was so deeply embedded in his life that hardly a day has passed when he does not think of his wise mentor and his family. To this day, hardly a sermon is preached, or a lesson taught that the occasional illustration or a point is emphasized with words like, "Brother Nichols once said," or "Brother Nichols" did this or that. But, then, many of that generation could say the same.

Some of James' favorite memories were of stories he heard while working with Nichols family preachers. One story was an occasion when Flavil was a little boy and came down with a case of whooping cough. The small fellow was gravely ill, to the point that little hope was given that he would recover. The deep frustration, and inability to help, caused Gus to recall that he had read in the Bible about people so dedicated in prayer that they would fall to the ground, and throw dirt and grass and leaves into the air, as they poured out their hearts before the throne of God. His despair led him out into the back yard of his home where he fell to the ground prostrate and began praying with deep emotion. He spent the better part of the afternoon lying upon the cold earth as he poured his heart out before his heavenly Father. Later, when he came in, he received news that Flavil was showing signs of improvement. He really believed the Bible, and a God who hears prayer.

Another memory was when a stranger came to the door of brother and sister Nichols saying he was thinking of committing suicide and wanted to know if the good preacher would preside at his funeral. In quick response, Gus told the man that he would be happy to preach his funeral, and said he already knew the Scripture he planned to use, Luke 16, about the rich man who raised his eyes up in torments. Then, he told the man that this was exactly what was going to happen the very moment he killed himself. The sobering analogy quickly made its impression upon the inquiring man as he walked away from the preacher's door that evening. He decided suicide was not a good option. These were the kinds of things that were part of the making of the life of Gus Nichols, and so many who knew him throughout his life.

After five years of work, the Hortons left Jasper for the preaching position at Gloster Street church of Christ in Tupelo, Mississippi. But, it was not the last time he worked among the Nichols preachers. In addition to his previous association with Hudson a few years earlier, he worked with Hardeman in the Southside congregation in Fort Worth, Texas, as a youth minister for a several years. Still later, the offer came for him to work alongside Flavil when he was preaching in Mayfield, Kentucky. In the end, however, it did not come to fruition. Suffice it to say, the James Horton family enjoyed a life-long and positive relationship with the Nichols family.

CONVERSION OF SAUL
Gus Nichols

"Why tarriest thou?"
You should obey now!
Why wait another day?
There is no other way!
(Acts 22:16; Acts 9:5-6)

"Arise, and be baptized,"
(That's what Christ advised.)
"Wash away thy sins."
Here new life begins.
(Acts 22:16; Rom. 6:3-4.)

Paul did not delay
But obeyed that day
Was baptized into Christ,
Who was sacrificed.
(Acts 9:18; 22:16; 26:19;
Rom. 6:3; Gal. 3:26-27.)

His sins were washed away
He did not just pray,
But he was baptized,
As Christ advised.
(Acts 9:18; 22:16)

And Paul was BAPTIZED,
He was not rantized.
T'was a burial act,
An immersion FACT.
(Rom. 6:3-4; Col. 2:12.)

Paul was a Christian,
(Was not a Philistine)
Was in the Lord's church
Not left in the lurch.[3]

ENDNOTES

1 Conversation with James A. Horton, 2.3.2016. Note: Much of the subject matter from this interview and follow-up conversations make up the content of this chapter. His assistance in the writing of this volume has been most valuable and most appreciated by the author.

2 W. A. Bradfield, *Gospel Advocate*, 16 February 1967, p. 109. Note: He sent a similar report to the *Firm Foundation*, that appeared, 21 February 1967, p. 122.

3 Gus Nichols, "Poems By Gus Nichols," *Words of Truth*, 26 March 1971, p. 2.

- 46 -

A Master Preacher

> I have preached righteousness in the great congregation: lo, I have not refrained my lips, O Lord, thou knowest.
> — David, Psalms 40:9

RESPECT FOR BROTHERS LEWIS, DUNN AND NICHOLS

In February 1967, the brotherhood lost two influential giants, John T. Lewis on the 19th, and Gus A. Dunn, Sr. passed on the 28th. Both men departed just weeks prior to their 91st birthdays. Both preachers knew and influenced Gus Nichols in most powerful ways over the course of his lifetime. An article appeared in the *Gospel Advocate*, entitled, "Two Veteran Preachers." Written by Rex A. Turner, Sr. (1913-2001), praise was given to these great men of God and of their abiding influences in the church of their day. The level of respect held for these men by brother Turner was undeniable. When speaking specifically about the Texas preacher he said, "Brother Dunn, was a man of great intellect. He held two graduate degrees—the M.A. and the B.D. degrees. Except for Gus Nichols, I never knew a man who had committed to memory so much of the Scriptures and thus could call up the book, chapter, and verse that would express so accurately the point at hand."[1]

Gus Nichols

STILL VERY MUCH ON THE GO

During the winter and spring of 1967, Gus continued to maintain a rigorous schedule. As has been noted, in early February, he participated in the annual Lectures at Freed-Hardeman College, and then appeared in Memphis at the Getwell church, speaking on the Holy Spirit. During the third week in March, he was in Montgomery participating in the Alabama Christian College Lectures where he handled the daily, "Question Hour."[2]

A couple of gospel meetings of note: one, he conducted with Paul D. Murphy (1914-2003) in Pascagoula, Mississippi, with more than "500 in attendance;"[3] the other was for the Arlington church in Knoxville, Tennessee at the end of April.[4] The preacher there at the time, Oliver C. Cunningham (1916-1979), later gave a good report of the meeting,

Gus Nichols of Jasper, Ala., has closed a very successful revival for the Arlington church in Knoxville. Brother Nichols moved the entire congregation to a greater devotion to God. On Sunday night after the regular service he conducted a Question and Answer session, which was splendid. Arlington plans to have him back just for Question and Answer sessions.[5]

In late June, Gus and Matilda headed to North Carolina for the Blue Ridge Encampment where he conducted the annual Gus Nichols Hour answering biblical questions. He also spoke at the evening "fireside chats" held in the Robert E. Lee Hall. At the end of the month, he headed down to Birmingham for a three-day youth weekend at the Woodlawn church of Christ where Jerry Jenkins (1936-2010) was the preacher.[6]

THE NICHOLS-BATTS DEBATE

The City Auditorium in Anniston, Alabama played host to several evenings of discussions between Gus Nichols and a Church of God preacher from Chattanooga, by the name of Albert H. Batts (1903-2001). Over the years, Mr. Batts was as capable as anyone of their number in defending Holy Spirit baptism, and other teachings specifically related to his denomination.[7]

The event was scheduled for five nights, beginning on the evening of October 30th running through November 3rd. The first two nights, the discussion centered around, "The Holy Scriptures teach that baptism of the Holy Ghost is for all believers today as it was for the apostles and others in the days of the apostles."[8] On Wednesday and Thursday evenings the proposed study included, "The Holy Scriptures teach that water baptism to a penitent believer of the gospel is for or in order to the remission or forgiveness of alien sins."[9] The final night of the discussion, the two opponents squared off on, "The Holy Scriptures authorize the use of mechanical instrumental music in the worship of the church today."[10] Two-hour sessions each evening gave both speakers several fifteen-minute speeches in which to discuss the propositions.

The churches promoting the debate were the Calvin Street church of Christ and the Seventeenth Street Church of God. Howard A. Blazer, Sr., (1909-1995), wrote the report of the debate saying,

> Brother Nichols was at his very best in defending the truth. The first two nights Brother Nichols affirmed that "Water Baptism Is Essential to the Remission of Past or Alien Sins." He made an affirmation in the very beginning that in every passage of scripture where baptism and salvation are mentioned together baptism always comes before salvation. Mr. Batts never had the courage to attempt an answer. The next two nights, Mr. Batts

affirmed that "Holy Spirit Baptism Is for Us Today." Early in his affirmative he declared that there are no measures of the Spirit and that to receive the Holy Spirit in any manner was a baptism. Brother Nichols pressed him so on this until he later admitted that multitudes would be in heaven who had the Spirit but were not baptized in the Holy Ghost. Brother Nichols saw to it that he never recovered from that blunder. The last night Mr. Batts affirmed that "Mechanical Instruments of Music are Authorized in the Worship of the Church Today." It was apparent that he was his weakest in this affirmation, and Brother Nichols' able presentation of Truth stung with telling force.[11]

The debate was well attended with great cooperation from among the churches in the area. Flavil assisted his father as moderator each evening of the discussion, and Howard A. Blazer, Sr., served as the timekeeper. A book was published from the event that only included the last night's discussion, called, *Albert Batts and Gus Nichols: Debate on Instrumental Music in Worship*.

THE ARLINGTON MEETING

In late January 1968, Gus made his way out to Arlington, Texas, to participate in a meeting of the minds, so to speak. For many years, a melee of infighting among brethren over institutionalism plagued the unity of the Kingdom of Christ. Harsh words against brethren were strewn upon the pages of brotherhood papers, and "dirty laundry" had been heavily displayed upon the airwaves on radio broadcasts in nearly every little town and city where the church existed.

Firm Foundation editor, Reuel Lemmons (1912-1989) and Norman W. Starling, director of the Bible Chair at Southwest State College, San Marcos, Texas, organized a unity meeting of sorts at Buchanan Dam in Llano County, Texas. The first meeting was in April 1967. Nine men gathered in an informal setting for the purpose of telling each other the problems they had due to their positions on the Institutional question.

Then, in the fall, twelve brethren, six from both sides of the Institutional division, met at the same location to discuss the various points of difference. "The spirit was so good and the accomplishments were so rewarding,"[12] that a larger meeting was deemed in the best interest of the brotherhood.

Invitations were sent out about a planned meeting at Arlington Christian Youth Camp, near Arlington, Texas, for the end of January. From as far west as California and south as Florida, twenty-seven men, thirteen from each side, along with moderator, Norman Starling, met beginning on January 26th, and concluded on February 1st.

Breaking down into two teams, the first consisted of Gus Nichols, Hardeman Nichols, Jimmy H. Allen, H. A. (Buster) Dobbs (1926-2017), Lewis G. Hale, Alan E. Highers, Bill J. Humble, Hulen L. Jackson (1913-1997), Roy H. Lanier, Sr. (1899-1980), Reuel G. Lemmons (1912-1989), Johnny Ramsey (1930-2006), Eldred Echols (1920-2003), and J. D. Thomas (1910-2004). Team two, representing the other side of the issues were, James W. Adams, Roy E. Cogdill (1907-1985), Melvin Curry, Harold Fite, Clinton D. Hamilton (1924-1999), Stanley J. Lovett (1916-1989), Harry Pickup, Jr. (1924-2016), Franklin T. Puckett (1908-1975), Dudley Ross Spears, William Floyd Thompson (1910-1984), Robert F. Turner (1916-2007), Bryan Vinson, Sr. (1906-1989), and W. L. Wharton, Jr. (1914-2009).

Each man was given a topic to research, prepare, and present at the meeting. The first day, the focus was on establishing biblical authority. On the second day, the discussions turned to the question of distinction between church action and individual action. Then, on the third day, the subject was, "The Work Of The Church." W. L. Wharton, Jr. opened with a paper from the Non-Institutional model. Gus Nichols followed with a lesson under the same title representing the Institutional model. Others followed as well. "Cooperation of Churches" and "How To Attain and Maintain Fellowship" were discussed the last day. The closing remarks belonged to Reuel Lemmons. He thanked the brethren for their sense of kindness and love in sharing their messages. Following were great admonitions to all to maintain a sense of openness, and the pursuit of a better understanding.

A year later, the transcripts made from all the recordings went to print and was widely distributed by Roy Cogdill under the title, *The Arlington Meeting*.[13] To many, the meeting was a great success. But, despite efforts by all involved, the unity meeting bore no weight of authority beyond the efforts of those Christian brothers who gathered and discussed the issues that were dividing the body; most rejected the meeting.

Historically, the event and its preservation in print, is of great value. As long as it is available, it will be of great assistance to generations to come that research this era in restoration history. The appeals from both sides of the Institutional question were presented clearly and concisely.

Gus Nichols' participation in the Arlington Meeting demonstrates much about the man. First, his continued desire to preach the truth of the gospel, as he understood it, to anyone and everyone who would listen. He had fought this battle for nearly twenty years, yet, if he thought he could make some difference, he was ready to try. Second, was his great love for those who were out of fellowship with him. At this point in time, most men would have thrown up their hands in view of a perceived lost cause, but not so with him. He loved his brethren and was willing to do whatever possible to repair broken unity, even if it meant driving his car from Alabama to Texas just to meet a few of his brethren in the interest of repairing relationships.

Other events that year included his annual trip to Freed-Hardeman for the Lectureship program in early February. Daily, his topic of discussion was, "The Preacher And His Work."[14] Of particular excitement to him was the joy of being able to join others in saluting his long-time friend and co-worker G. K. Wallace (1903-1988) at the Appreciation Dinner. Gus led the benedictory prayer for the event.

From Henderson, he traveled out to Abilene, Texas, to speak on the Abilene Christian College's annual lecture program. Joining him in the schedule was his son, Hardeman. Gus spoke daily upon the subject, "Principles Of Biblical Interpretation."[15]

Then, in March, he headed back out to Texas for the Fort Worth Christian College Lectures. Every day, he moderated the Open Forum, and preached one evening on the topic, "Heaven, And What It Will Be Like To Go There."[16]

An early June announcement revealed that brother Nichols was to join several other church leaders to serve in an advisory role to the president of the Southeast Institute of the Bible.[17] At the helm of the new preacher training school in Florence, Alabama was Malcolm L. Hill (1934-2012). In the interest of building support from great men throughout the Shoals and distant regions, Hill reported the forming of the advisory group as follows,

> Charles Coil is chairman of the Preacher's Advisory Board, which consists of the following men: B. C. Goodpasture, Basil Overton, Thomas B. Warren, Kenneth Hoover, Bill Smith, Clarence Lavender, Willard Collins, James Bales, Gus Nichols, A. R. Hill, Guy N. Woods, V. P. Black, G. K. Wallace, Jack Gray, Eugene Clevenger, Larry Acuff, Paul Murphy, George Yates, J. V. Copeland, Steve Kepley, Jack Hazelbaker, Ray Frizzell, Ellis Coats, Alan Bryan.[18]

Other than the regular meeting work he did through the summer, Gus and Matilda made their annual trip in late June to the Blue Ridge Encampment in North Carolina. In addition to his conducting the Gus Nichols Hour of answering questions, he also taught the book of James in classes throughout the week.[19] The following year, he taught lessons on, "Christian Attitudes Toward People of Other Races."[20]

A MASTER PREACHER

When the 12th of January chimed in for the seventy-seventh time in Gus Nichols' life, there was no apparent let up in his stride. He continued his busy schedule of lectureship activity; work in the congregation at

Jasper, and meeting work. To demonstrate his amazing ability to stay the course, he preached a meeting in May in Knoxville, Tennessee, at the Karns church. The preacher at the time, John Waddey (1938-2014), wrote a lengthy biographical sketch for the *Gospel Advocate*, after the meeting. The introduction more than adequately describes the stature of the man even at his advanced age. He wrote,

> It was the privilege of the saints in the Knoxville area to hear Gus Nichols present a series on "Loyalty to Christ," May 23-25. At 77, Brother Nichols is truly "A master preacher" of the brotherhood. On Lord's day, he addressed the combined Bible classes on the theme of "Christian Homes." At the eleven o'clock service, he presented an hour's lesson on the analogy of Jesus and Adam. At 3:00 P.M., he spoke for an hour and forty-five minutes on "Dangers Facing the Church." Then from 7:30 to 9:30, he "preached his heart out," urging lost sinners to flee to Jesus for salvation. Few young men would have had the sheer physical strength to speak that much in one day. I have yet to hear another man that could hold his audience spell-bound as did Brother Nichols. In each sermon, Gus Nichols quoted more Scripture than many preachers include in a month's sermons. I say he quoted it! Not once did he open his Bible in the pulpit, yet not one thought was expressed that did not have a Bible proof-text to sustain it. Always, there was citation of the reference: book, chapter and verse. A highlight of the series was the "Open Forum" on Saturday morning. A fine audience gathered and submitted their queries. To each question, Brother Nichols gave an answer for the hope that within him lies. . . .To our young men who are presently preaching or who are planning to become gospel preachers, this great man of God is an example worthy of imitation. I think I can say that, because he is one who imitates Jesus. (1 Cor. 11:1.) Brother Nichols is great because he is rich in faith; pure and

Number 77

Matilda and Gus - His 77th Birthday

chaste in thought, speech and habits; diligent in his work, even at an age when most men have retired; humble in his success; fervent in his love for lost men and his zeal to save them; willing to help bear other's burdens; committed to defend the gospel of Jesus against its enemies and determined to go to heaven when he dies. Thank God for Brother Nichols and the privilege to sit at his feet.[21]

DEDICATION AND DOCTORAL DECREE

The Gus Nichols Library and Research Center was complete, and the doors opened on the campus of Alabama Christian College by the early summer of 1969. For the dedication ceremony on the 6th of June, many of the relatives and friends of brother and sister Nichols gathered on the college campus. Leading in the event was chairman of the Board for the college, Jimmy Faulkner (1916-2008). Amidst many words of kindness and appreciation, the library was officially opened. Granddaughter, Karen Nichols, who was a student in the college at the time, unveiled two beautiful oil portraits of brother and sister Nichols that were to hang in the lobby of the library.

Gus Nichols at Library Dedication

Following the ceremony, the festivities shifted to the J. L. Perry Cafeteria on campus for a meal and further honor of brother Nichols. The main speaker after lunch was visiting president of Oklahoma Christian College, Dr. James O. Baird (1920-1998).

That evening, Dr. Baird served as guest speaker for the 1969 graduating class commencement exercises. At the appropriate time, the name, "Bunion Augustus Nichols," was called. Arising in full graduation regalia, brother Nichols approached the platform where he was awarded by Oklahoma Christian College the Honorary Doctor of Laws Degree.

A day to remember! Honor to whom honor is due! The preacher, board member, educator, and a score of other outstanding titles, was being recognized yet again for a life of distinguished service to an admiring brotherhood. As the saying goes, the pure get purer. Those who knew Gus Nichols best recognized that such accolades meant little to the man. He was a servant of Christ, and to those in His Kingdom. After that, little else mattered.

THE WHOLE WORLD IS MINE
Gus Nichols

I thank the Lord, for I have much!
I'm not crippled and on a crutch.
Even if I were, I'd still be rich;
Men of faith don't fall in the ditch.

So thank the Lord for life and light!
For everything in reach and sight;
For the whole world's mine to enjoy!
God's praises shall my tongue employ.

My lungs partake of the common air;
My eyes drink in beauty everywhere.
I enjoy my neighbor's flowers,
Rejoice when others get showers.

The sun, moon, and stars are all mine
As if on me only they shined.
And so, the world belongs to me.
I partake of all that I see.

You see: My needs are so very few.
That title may belong to you.
Unto me, other people's things,
My great job and happiness bring.

If you prosper, I will rejoice.
For love always lifts up its voice
To give praise, and join in the fun
When a brother knocks a home run.

You see! If you love the human race.
When all are blessed, it shows in your face.
You partake of their blessings, too.
It helps way down inside of you![22]

1969 - Gus and Matilda Nichols

ENDNOTES

1 Rex A. Turner, "Two Veteran Preachers—John T. Lewis and G. A. Dunn—Are Dead," *Gospel Advocate*, 4 May 1967, pp. 278-79.

2 Advertisement, *Gospel Advocate*, 9 March 1967, p. 157.

3 Paul D. Murphy, *Gospel Advocate*, 13 April 1967, p. 235.

4 Oliver C. Cunningham, *Gospel Advocate*, 13 April 1967, p. 234.

5 Ibid., 22 June 1967, p. 398.

6 Jerry Jenkins, *Firm Foundation*, 15 August 1967, p. 522. Note: Jerry Austin Jenkins was born January 15, 1936, in Huntsville, Alabama. He spent his early years of preaching at Truman, Arkansas, and Hamilton, Alabama. He spent the last 45 years of his life at the old Woodlawn, later Roebuck Parkway church in Birmingham. He was co-founder of Jefferson Christian Academy in Birmingham, and founder of Maywood Christian Camp in Marion County, Alabama. He loved brother Nichols and considered it a joy to live and work with him in the Kingdom of the Lord. All who knew brother Jerry loved and respected his talents, his leadership, his love for the lost, and his friendship. He passed from this life the 26th of October 2010 and was laid to rest in Jefferson Memorial Gardens in Trussville, Alabama. Two of his sons, Jeff A. Jenkins and Dale Jenkins continue his legacy strengthening preachers and churches of Christ all around the world.

7 Note: He had faced off with other gospel preachers in debates including, S. H. Hall (1877-1961) in November 1947, A. C. Grider (1912-1990) in 1949, W. Curtis Porter (1897-1960) in May 1952, Harold Sain (1912-1980) in February 1965, and later in September of that same year with Carrol R. Sutton. Some time after his debate with brother Nichols, Batts met Guy N. Woods in a debate.

8 Howard A. Blazer Sr., *Gospel Advocate*, 17 July 1967, p. 524.

9 Ibid.

10 Howard A. Blazer Sr., "Debate Scheduled In Alabama," *Firm Foundation*, 15 August 1967, p. 523. Note: Another promotion of the debate appeared from the hand of Elbert G. Lewis in the 10 October edition on p. 651.

11 Howard A. Blazer Sr., "A Report On The Gus Nichols-Albert Batts Debate," *Firm Foundation*, 12 December 1967, p. 813.

12 Reuel Lemmons, ed., "Arlington Meeting Makes Serious Efforts To Resolve Issues," *Firm Foundation*, 20 February 1968, p. 122.

13 Roy Cogdill, *The Arlington Meeting*, Orlando: Cogdill Foundation, 1969.

14 Advertisement, *Firm Foundation*, 28 November 1967, p. 780.

15 Ibid., 2 January 1968, p. 10.

16 Ibid., 5 March 1968, p. 156.

17 Note: Precursor to International Bible College, and later Heritage Christian University.

18 Advertisement, "Southeast Institute of the Bible," *Gospel Advocate*, 13 June 1968, p. 375.

19 Ibid., 15 March 1968, p. 175.

20 Ibid., 9 January 1969, p. 31.

21 John H. Waddey, "Gus Nichols: A Master Preacher," *Gospel Advocate*, 3 July 1969, pp. 428-29.

22 Gus Nichols, "Poems By Gus Nichols," *Words of Truth*, 26 March 1971, p. 2.

- 47 -

These Old Soldiers

Thou therefore endure hardness, as a good soldier of Jesus Christ. No man that warreth entangleth himself with the affairs of this life; that he may please him who hath chosen him to be a soldier.
—Paul, 2 Timothy 2:3-4

Being old doesn't necessarily guarantee that one is right, but before we sound taps for these old soldiers like Goodpasture, Nichols, Wallace, and others, let's do our homework, brethren. If we will, we might discover that it is we who are standing in the chow line polishing our second lieutenant's bars and they who are out on the line firing. The old soldier who still hears clearly the trumpeter's call to battle wasn't named, but, old soldier, whoever you are, we salute you.[1]

GUS NICHOLS
Minister

1971 - Church Photo

Entering a new decade, the Sage of Jasper continued with more vim, vigor, and vitality than men half his age. With Baby Boomers, well into their teens and twenties, the seasoned preacher was still making a lasting impression on young minds. He was one of the few preachers who could preach well over an hour and keep crowds in rapt attention.

Of humorous note, a story was related over the years about how one time a man came to a gospel meeting to hear brother Nichols preach. After the service, as the preacher was shaking hands with the brethren at the door, the visitor said, "Brother Nichols, I have been wanting to hear you preach for a long time—but not that long!" The seasoned preacher was known for his lengthy expositions.

THE SPIRITUAL SWORD

The quarterly, *The Spiritual Sword* was initiated in October 1969. It was edited by Thomas B. Warren (1920-2000). The associate editor was the preacher at the Getwell church or Christ in Memphis, Rubel Shelley. Released under the oversight of the elders at Getwell, the publication was intended to be a voice for truth, admonishing faithfulness through well researched written material. Some of the best writers the brotherhood had to offer were asked to contribute articles on a vast array of topics. The second issue appeared in January 1970 under the theme, "The Inspiration of the Bible." The final article for the issue was, "The Bible Is The Infallibly Inspired Word Of God." The writer, Gus Nichols, was given the added postscript, "A special essay by a veteran preacher of the gospel."[2] In the April issue, he wrote on, "Jesus As A Miracle Worker." Several subsequent issues included articles by the inimitable Bible scholar.

In the January 1974 issue, the editor wrote a brief article entitled, "We Honor—Gus Nichols."[3] With a very brief biographical sketch, what followed were five specific areas in which brother Nichols should be so honored. He is a Christian, a friend of every good work, a writer and editor of good biblical material, a local preacher, and a defender of the faith. In the history of the paper, no other man was so honored in this way.

In another issue, Gus was heralded along with other great gospel preachers of yesteryear. The theme was "Precious Memories."[4] Flavil wrote a piece entitled, "Lessons From My Father, Gus Nichols." Some of the other preachers honored in the issue were N. B. Hardeman (1874-1965), G. C. Brewer (1884-1956), Foy E. Wallace, Jr. (1896-1971), Guy N. Woods (1908-1993), G. K. Wallace (1903-1988), and Franklin Camp (1915-1991).

The relationship Gus Nichols enjoyed with the Getwell church, *The Spiritual Sword*, and its staff, always exemplified the best of what makes New Testament Christianity both viable and appealing.

SPEAKING 800 TIMES A YEAR

The 1970 lectureship season kept brother Nichols busy throughout the winter and spring. In February, he spoke daily at Freed-Hardeman College on "Doctrine, Bible Authority, Tongues, and Final Authority."[5] With the nature of such a topic, in one of his lectures, he stated that a preacher could spend his entire life preaching the truth and still lose his soul because he failed to preach "the whole counsel of God."[6] At another point, he expressed that he was speaking in various venues and through different mediums over 800 times per year.[7] The printed volume of the lectures was so well received that year that the Gospel Advocate Company had to make a second printing in order to fulfill the requests.[8]

During the third week in March, he went down to Montgomery for the 28th annual lecture program of Alabama Christian College. His assigned topic was "Fifty-Three Years On The Firing Line."[9]

Gus Nichols Sunday School Class

The Southeastern College of the Bible in Florence held their lectureship in April with the theme, "Issues Past And Present." The program enjoyed a group of notable speakers including, "Gus Nichols, Basil Overton, Tom Warren, V. P. Black, Batsell Baxter, B. C. Goodpasture and Guy N. Woods."[10]

The year ended with a trip back to Memphis to participate in a two-day lecture program on the campus of Harding Graduate School of Religion, the 14th and 15th of December. The theme for the program was "Issues Facing The Church." Another list of well-known speakers at the podium included, "Bill Patterson, Jay Smith, Jack Lewis, Bill Humble, Bill Flatt, Clifton Rogers, N. Braden, Thomas, B. Warren, James D. Bales, Gus Nichols, E. Claude Gardner, Joe Hacker, Willard Collins, Harold Hazelip, Basil Overton, George Benson and Larry Swaim."[11]

GUS NICHOLS' PREACHER'S WORKSHOP

Beginning in the fall of 1970, V. P. Black (1918-2007), Billy D. Hilyer, Billy Lambert, and several others, organized a special program in south Alabama and Mississippi for recharging gospel preachers and church leaders. When Gus was approached about conducting the September program, he was excited about the prospects. The first event took place beginning Monday, the 28th of September, at the Gulf Coast Bible Camp facility in Lucedale, Mississippi. For the next five days, a busy schedule gave the elder preacher plenty of opportunities to teach classes, as he was the only teacher. Each afternoon there was a session devoted to questions and answers. The workshop was intended to be a faith building time for local preachers, with plenty of "time for relaxation and recreation"[12] added in for a truly holistic experience. The event became known as the "Gus Nichols' Preacher's Workshop."[13] Over fifty preachers attended the gathering the first couple of years. By the third year, women were invited to attend as well.[14]

Gus Nichols and Billy D. Hilyer

THE "FAMOUS" LECTURES AT FREED-HARDEMAN

Arguably, no person in the history of Freed-Hardeman College did more to promote it and its activities than did W. A. Bradfield (1910-1972). Before his premature death in early March of 1972, he had become the voice of the college to the brotherhood. His success as a preacher was second to none in gospel meetings. Aisles were often filled with responders after his sermons. It was often said in jest of him that he preached many sermons where he said at the close of a lesson that those who wanted to respond to the Lord should come sit in the pews to his left, and if they wanted to go to Freed-Hardeman College, they could sit on his right.

His aggrandizement of the school's lectureship program could always be counted upon at some stage of the year in the pages of the brotherhood papers. Always, he listed among the many speakers on the forum the name, Gus Nichols. In anticipation of the 1971 schedule, he attributed the popularity of the program to many of the "old soldiers." He said, "Such men as H. Leo Boles, Marshall Keeble, Gus Nichols, G. K. Wallace, B. C. Goodpasture, and Guy N. Woods have made these lectures famous."[15] That year, Gus spoke on "The Church, Its Worship, Singing, And The Lord's Supper" at the 8:00am sessions.

Some changes took place that year in the school with the departure of its Bible Department head, Thomas B. Warren (1920-2000) to Harding Graduate School of Religion. Of particular pride to brother Nichols was the appointment of William E. Woodson (1931-2010), his son in the faith, to the vacated chair. At the prospects of this promotion, Gus wrote a letter to college president, E. Claude Gardner (1925-2017), saying,

> I want to congratulate you and Freed-Hardeman College upon your choice of William Woodson for the responsible position for which he has been chosen at Freed-Hardeman. He is well qualified for the work and the place demanding a great man, strong in faith, richly endowed by good common sense and wisdom. Brother Woodson has great power in store for this position and has the will to work. He will put into his daily task his great talents and rich insights into the word of God by which he will be amply able to inspire faith and the zeal of the early Christians in the hearts of students and be a guarantee behind the already strong confidence of a great brotherhood often evidenced in Freed-Hardeman College.[16]

1970 - Board of Trustees
Alabama Christian College

In March, after conducting a one-day gospel meeting at Phoenix City, Alabama,[17] brother Nichols headed out to Texas to participate in the Fort Worth Christian College Lectures. He opened the program with a sermon entitled, "Inspiration of the Wonderful Word."[18]

He returned to Alabama after the forum and readied himself for the lectureship at Alabama Christian College, which took place March 22-

25. His assignment was to speak daily on the topics of past debates he had conducted with "teachers of false doctrine."[19] The first two days, he reflected on a debate he had in 1950 with Primitive Baptist, J. D. Holder, where they discussed the "Atonement," and "Conditional Salvation."[20] The following day, he spoke on the "Work of the Holy Spirit" from a debate he had with Pentecostal preacher, D. L. Welch, also in 1950. The last day, he presented a study on "Footwashing,"[21] from the debate he had with Holiness preacher, C. J. Weaver, in 1943.

In mid-April, brother Nichols headed back to Memphis to participate in the lectures at the Getwell church of Christ. Coined the "Memphis School of Preaching Lectures," Gus again took part in the program with several other well-known preachers.

From Memphis, he headed out to the north Texas panhandle town of Hereford, for a gospel meeting. The preacher, J. T. Marlin (1914-1993), reported one baptism and four restorations during the meeting and said, "The power of this man in preaching the gospel at age 79 is unbelievable."[22]

In July, brother and sister Nichols attended the Blue Ridge Encampment in North Carolina, where he spoke daily. At one of the great gatherings during the week, he was awarded the camp's Distinguished Service Certificate for his years of devotion to the success of the annual program.[23]

Later in the month, he traveled out to Poplar Bluff, Missouri. He taught daily in a Vacation Bible School program, and in the evenings preached a gospel meeting for the congregation. The preacher, C. B. Thomas (1897-1981), reported, "We have just had with us that great teacher, Gus Nichols."[24]

SADNESS IN THE FAMILY

Sorrow struck the Nichols family in early August when Gus' sister Virginia passed away on the 11th. Velma Virginia Boshell was a faithful member down at Zion church of Christ where the funeral and burial followed. She was eleven years younger than her oldest brother, and the first of the siblings to die in later years. Much loved by the children, Aunt Ginny's passing deeply saddened the family.[25]

Gus and sister Hazey Dozier and Zella Windham

Within a few days, he found himself at the preacher's workshop in south Mississippi before heading out to West Monroe, Louisiana, to participate in the "International Evangelism and Bible Lectureship,"[26] at White's Ferry Road. There he spoke on, "Christ, The Hope Of A World Plagued By Ignorance Of God's Word."[27]

Ever in demand, brother Nichols continued to move in the direction he was called to the best of his ability. More invitations came than could be attended to, but where he could, he was determined to use himself up for the cause of Him who gives all things. The year 1971 ended with another trip over to Memphis for the lectures at Harding Graduate School of Religion. The dates were December 5-7, and on this occasion, he spoke on, "The Christ Of The Scriptures."[28]

Recognition of his achievements continued to cast him into the limelight. That year, the American Biographical Institute listed Gus Nichols in their volume, "Personalities of the South." Published in Raleigh, North Carolina, the book included a brief biography on page 422.[29]

IS IT WRONG TO ARGUE?
Gus Nichols

"It is wrong to argue," so they say;
"We should defend the truth some other way."
Well, it's right for me, but wrong for them,
Because they practice what they condemn.

They argue that arguing is a sin,
But are right then arguing with men.
If it's right to argue about arguing.
Why is it wrong to argue about bargaining?

Is it wrong to argue against theft?
Or that it's no sin to be born deaf?
Or that Christ rose again on the third day.
Just as the divine record doth say?

If it's sin to argue for what's true,
Then tell me what you're going to do!
God tells us to "Contend for the faith"
Which means, "Argue for what the Book saith."

Jesus argued and disputed with men.
Do you think Christ committed sin?
Paul disputed daily—did Paul sin?
He argued with Jews and devout men.

Well, it is sin to argue for error.
That's what causes a world of terror.
Paul was set to defend the truth.
From early in life—even from youth.

It is sin to argue for false teaching.
That's wrong, even in debate or preaching.
It is wrong to be on the wrong side;
All men must in Christ's doctrine abide.

So don't argue before you know what's right.
The man who is wrong starts the fight.
But it's right to use the word of the Spirit.
Error has no rightful place or merit.

A wise man will not shoot in the dark,
Lest he ignite error with a spark.
If he finds himself against the truth,
He'll make amends back to his youth.

It is wrong to set destructive fires,
But right to fight them, even for hire.
It's wrong to spread disease germs, and sin.
But it's right to speak up and truth defend.

So, it's wrong to argue against the truth,
Whether one be in age, or a mere youth,
Only the truth can make us all free,
So, both sides are not alike, you see?[30]

ENDNOTES

1 Don Campbell, "Brethren, Let's Do Our Homework," *Gospel Advocate*, 25 March 1971, p. 182.

2 Thomas B. Warren, ed., *The Spiritual Sword*, January 1970, p. 55.

3 Thomas B. Warren, ed., *The Spiritual Sword*, January 1974.

4 Alan E. Highers, ed. *The Spiritual Sword*, January 1995.

5 Advertisement, *Gospel Advocate*, 8 January 1970, p. 28.

6 William S. Cline, Editorial, "Whole Counsel Of God," *Firm Foundation*, 10 December 1985, p. 2 [722].

7 Gus Nichols, "The Bible Is Complete." 1970 Freed-Hardeman College Lectures.

8 Advertisement, *Gospel Advocate*, 9 April 1970, p. 238.

9 Ibid., 12 March 1970, p. 173.

10 Ibid., 12 March 1970, p. 172.

11 Report, *Gospel Advocate*, 7 January 1971, p. 12.

12 V. P. Black, *Gospel Advocate*, 10 September 1970, p. 587.

13 Billy Lambert, *Gospel Advocate*, 16 September 1971, p. 588.

14 Ibid., 7 September 1973, p. 571.

15 W. A. Bradfield, *Gospel Advocate*, 26 November 1970, p. 764.

16 E. Claude,Gardner, "Woodson To Head Bible Department At Freed-Hardeman College," *Gospel Advocate*, 25 February 1971, p. 122.

17 Hoyt Bailey, *Firm Foundation*, 26 January 1971, p. 26.

18 Foy Kirkpatrick, *Gospel Advocate*, 21 January 1971, p. 47.

19 Advertisement, *Firm Foundation*, 9 March 1971, p. 156.

20 Advertisement, *Gospel Advocate*, 4 March 1971, p. 142.

21 Ibid.

22 Marlin, J. T., *Gospel Advocate*, 10 June 1971, p. 263. Also, repeated in *Firm Foundation*, 29 June 1971, p. 410.

23 *Daily Mountain Eagle*, Tuesday, 18 November 1975.

24 C. D. Thomas, *Gospel Advocate*, 5 August 1971, p. 490.

25 Note: A noted earlier, Gus' brother, Clarence, was born 5 October 1910 and died the same day. The following June, his brother, Troy, was born. He was born 6 June 1911 and lived three days. They were Gus' fourth and fifth brothers.

26 William E. DeLoach, *Gospel Advocate*, 21 October 1971, p. 668.

27 Advertisement, *Gospel Advocate*, 7 October 1971, p. 635.

28 Thomas B. Warren, *Gospel Advocate*, 11 November 1971, p. 711.
29 *Daily Mountain Eagle*, Jasper, Alabama, Tuesday, November 18, 1975.
30 *Words of Truth*, 26 March 1971, p. 2.

- 48 -

The Octogenarian

The hoary head is a crown of glory, If it be found in the way of righteousness.
—Solomon, Proverbs 16:31

Twelve days into the year 1972, the man of God in Jasper brought his eightieth year to completion. The unfaltering and unchanging Gus Nichols. He was as dependable and determined in his regimen as ever. He was a friend to all and enemy to none. His course remained honorable, true, and diligent. Everything he did was viewed through glasses colored by the gospel of Christ. To him, God's blessings flowed into every aspect of his world. Every nuance of human experience, in his thinking, should be seen in view of God's presence. Whether it be accolade or atrocity, celebration or catastrophe, everything initiated praise and adoration for the matchless Maker of all things.

1972 - Gus at 80 Years of Age

His significance to the brotherhood now was never more substantial. On the eve of his birthday, long-time friend and staff writer for *Words of Truth*, Robert R. Taylor, Jr., wrote a letter to him expressing, "There is no other man of our current acquaintance who has made the years count so much for the Lord and humanity as have you."[1] This feeling was shared by thousands of beloved brethren who saw, personally, the difference his presence made in their lives. It is little wonder he was held in such high esteem, as by his own estimation, he had stood before brethren over 75,000 times over the many years of his ministry.

Gus' health was very important to him, knowing that, "the Christian's body belongs to the Lord, and the Christian is obligated to take care of his body."[2] His doctor placed him on a special diet where he was to eat one egg a day, prepared in a certain way. He avoided greasy foods and made sure his bread intake was kept to a minimum. Walking was his daily choice of exercise. Getting out was pretty much impossible, because everywhere he went, he was usually stopped along the way and asked if he needed a ride. Where he and sister Nichols lived, there was a long hall leading from the living room to their bedroom at the south end of the house. Every morning he walked back and forth, up and down the hall, over and over for long periods. At times, he walked in figure-eight style in the living room, or he simply stepped in place while in his office or bedroom.

The voice of the octogenarian was still very strong. Two thirty-minute radio broadcasts continued to be a part of his daily regimen, not to mention his rigorous teaching and preaching schedule each week. During the annual lectureship at Freed-Hardeman, he stood in Bader Gymnasium at eight o'clock each morning speaking about, "The Bible and the Scheme of Redemption."[3] At the end of the very busy week, Ira North (1922-1984), preached at the closing Thursday evening session. Making the final remarks, college president, E. Claude Gardner (1925-2017), called brother Nichols to the stand to lead the attendees in *Amazing Grace* in honor of brother North's successfully televised program, *Amazing Grace Bible Class*.[4] In March, he spoke on a lectureship in Florence at the Eastwood church,[5] and daily on the lectureship at Alabama Christian College on "Counsel For Young Preachers,"[6] later in the month. In June, he spoke daily at the Blue Ridge Encampment on, "Problems Concerning The Holy Spirit."[7] In late September, he spoke several times at the third annual Gus Nichols Bible Workshop, at Gulf Coast Bible Camp.[8] In October, he preached on the lectureship at the Mastin Lake Road church in Huntsville, Alabama.[9] In November, he spoke on a similar program in Tampa, Florida at the Manhattan Ave. church.[10] In early December, both he and Hardeman spoke on the lecture program at Harding Graduate School of Religion in Memphis.[11]

1972 - Gus and Matilda Nichols 80th Birthday Celebration

Sleep seemed less essential the older he got. It did not take as much to keep him rested and sharp. He kept stacks of new books he was working through around the walls in his bedroom for when he woke up in the night. At this point, he was still studying five and six hours every day.

When attending lectureships or gospel meetings, he always had his trusty manual typewriter with plenty of paper. New sermons entered his mind all the time. Articles for *Words of Truth* or answering Bible queries for the *Gospel Advocate* needed writing and typing. Stacks of articles sent in by mail demanded proofing for publication. Whether at home or on the road, these things continued to demand his attention. He was known at times to preach a meeting sermon, go home and visit until late with his host family, and beg the use of their kitchen table to set up his typewriter for a little late-night work. Several mornings, families arose from their night's sleep only to see the preacher still in his white shirt and tie, hat on his head, at the table, hard at work.[12]

1972 - FHC Lectures

In his four-score years, he had seen so many changes. He was sixteen when he saw his first automobile. And with it, life seemed to transition into a faster and more intensive pace that never slowed. But, as far as he was concerned, one thing never changed—the Word of God. All need to study it and make it the foundation of their thinking and actions. Filling his days with ministry in the community, the congregation, and the brotherhood, he went about his schedule with inordinate swiftness and veracity. It is little wonder he needed help.

After his years of work with the Sixth Avenue congregation, James Horton and his family moved to a Tupelo, Mississippi, leaving brother Nichols in need of an assistant.

ALAN T. CLOYD

Very few Christians applied the sense of urgency in evangelism after their conversion more than Marvin Bryant (1922-1997). As has been noted, Gus Nichols immersed him in 1960. He immediately stretched his hand into the denominational ranks and found men at the top of leadership in their respective groups, planting the seed of first-century Christianity in the 20th century. And it worked! Many men were reached and converted in the process. One of these men was Alan Cloyd.

A native of Louisville, Kentucky, the twenty-six-year-old was a graduate of Cincinnati Christian University and associated with the Independent Christian Church. He had served for seven years in three different ministries among the Churches of Christ—Instrumental. His conservative leanings led him to attend the Freed-Hardeman College Lectures in February 1972. There, he was introduced to several brethren who showed great interest in assisting him in making the transition to mainstream churches of Christ. One of these was Gus Nichols.

After several communications with brother Nichols and the other elders at Sixth Avenue, the decision was made for Alan, his wife Molly, and their baby son, Joel, to move to Jasper and assist in the work there as the associate minister. Within six weeks of meeting, the Cloyds began their work on the fourth of April.[13]

THE PASSING OF BROTHER BRADFIELD

Potentially, there was no more thunderous voice for the gospel of Christ in meeting work in the 20th century than that of W. A. Bradfield (1910-1972). Buildings where he preached were always filled to overflowing. When news of his untimely death in early March came to the ears of an immediately saddened brotherhood, praise for his greatness as a pulpiteer and promoter of Christian education flowed from the journalist pen of many papers. The entire April 27th edition of the *Gospel Advocate* commemorated his excellence in Christian service. In his usual illustrative way, Willard Collins (1915-2007) spoke of brother Bradfield's work in helping Freed-Hardeman. Of the many things, he could have noted he chose to recall,

> The Appreciation Dinner for brother and sister Gus Nichols, Jasper, Alabama remains a climax in the lives of these two great Christians. It was the late W. A. Bradfield who arranged for this dinner and promoted it. The attendance was large, the program was excellent, and it was an experience in building the faith of the ones present.[14]

Though ten years had passed since the dinner, the memory of brother Bradfield was and always will be tied to his great works while at Freed-Hardeman, a part of which included that unforgettable evening in 1962 when Gus and Matilda Nichols were honored for their work in the cause of Christ.

ACKNOWLEDGMENTS THROUGHOUT THE YEAR

Thankful people seek ways to honor those who they appreciate, and not only from within the brotherhood. Gus Nichols was listed in the 1972 edition of "Who's Who in Alabama." His name and brief summary appears on page 299 of the volume.[15]

The influence of brother Nichols was felt on mission fields around the globe. For instance, the work in Anakapalle, India, was going strong during the 1960s and '70s. J. C. Bailey (1903-2001) and J. C. Choate (1932-2008), among other missionaries, reported on the successes of Bethel Christian School being operated there. For several years, it was reported of their having over a hundred students enrolled. In 1972, a library was completed and dedicated as the Gus Nichols Library.[16] Other accolades continued to come in as the man of advanced age persevered in his ministry for Christ at full speed.

lian Reporter   January 1972

Board Members Spotlighted

Gus Nichols Serves As Board Member, Has Preached 55 Yrs.

Gus Nichols

Gus Nichols has been a Gospel preacher 55 years, 39 of which have been with the Sixth Ave. Church of Christ in Jasper, Ala. He has received two honorary Doctor of Laws (L.L.D.) degrees from Christian colleges: Magic Valley Christian College, Albion, Idaho, 1964; and Oklahoma Christian College, Oklahoma City, 1969.

Nichols is the author of several books and is widely sought as a lectureship speaker, preachers' workshop lecturer and preacher. He has served as a member of the ACC Board of Trustees since 1956. He and his wife, the former Elizabeth Wyers, travel together to ACC and other meetings. Besides preaching fulltime for the Jasper church, Nichols is also an elder and teacher and has two daily 30-minute radio programs on WWWB and WARF radio stations in Jasper.

The 80-year old evangelist also edits the periodical Words of Truth, which was originally called Truth in Love. He has served on the Board of Trustees of Childhaven Home for Children and the Southeastern School of Preaching since the two organizations came into being and, since 1964, has been on the Board of the Blue Ridge Encampment. In 1963, Pepperdine College in Los Angeles presented him with its Christian Service Award. ACC named its new library for him in 1968.

The Nichols have four daughters—Mrs. Gracie Young, Mrs. Vodie Kerr, Mrs. Bertha Blackwood and Mrs. Carrie Hamilton—and four sons—Flavil, Foy, Hardeman and Hudson. They have several grandchildren and five great-grandchildren. Several of their grandchildren have attended ACC. Bro. and Sis. Nichols have been married 58 years.

(Editor's Note: January 12 is Bro. Nichols 80th birthday. We wish to take this opportunity and medium, on behalf of everyone at ACC, to wish this soldier of Christ a Very Happy Birthday, and many, many more!)

(Editor's Note: January 12 is Bro. Nichols 80th birthday. We wish to take this opportunity and medium, on behalf of everyone at ACC, to wish this soldier of Christ a Very Happy Birthday, and many, many more!)

News Clipping - Serving on the Board at Alabama Christian College

BELOVED FRIENDS
by Gus Nichols

What is more important than friends?
With loyal friends true life begins.
Friends mean more than silver or gold.
For they help us aim at higher goals.

A friend's closer than a brother,
And helps all to love one another.
The love of friends is free from strife.
And helps us live a better life.

Of course, Jesus is our best friend,
And He'll love us unto the end.
So, let us love and follow him,
And our pathway can ne'er grow dim.[17]

ENDNOTES

1 Robert R. Taylor, "Making The Years Count," *Words of Truth*, Vol. 7, No. 103, 28 January 1972, p. 1.

2 Roy Deaver, "A Visit With Gus Nichols," *Gospel Advocate*, " 14 December 1972, pp. 792-93. Note: This article was written late in brother Nichols' 80th year, but reflected his regimen in life at this stage.

3 W. A. Bradfield, "Freed-Hardeman College," *Gospel Advocate*, 30 December 1971, p. 830.

4 E. Claude Gardner, "Thanks For The Vote Of Confidence," *Gospel Advocate*, 2 March 1972, p. 138.

5 Malcolm L. Hill, "Eastwood's Faith Building Lectureship," *Gospel Advocate*, 24 February 1972, p. 123.

6 Advertisement, "Alabama Christian College Lectures,"*Gospel Advocate*, 9 March 1972, p. 158.

7 Report, "Wonderful Blue Ridge Encampment," *Gospel Advocate*, 10 August 1972, p. 504.

8 Billy Lambert, "Gus Nichols Bible Workshop," *Gospel Advocate*, 7 September 1972, p. 571.

9 Advertisement, *Gospel Advocate*, "Huntsville, Alabama Lectureship," 28 September 1972, p. 622.

10 John W. Franklin, "Lectureship-West Central Florida," *Gospel Advocate*, 19 October 1972, p. 668.

11 Advertisement, "Fall Lectureship Program Harding Graduate School of Religion," *Gospel Advocate*, 19 October 1972, p. 669.

12 Note: Such was the case of your author's experience with him. Once, he came for a gospel meeting at Forest Park, Georgia when my dad, Richard T. Harp, was the preacher. One night we came home from the meeting and brother Nichols did just as is mentioned above. I was but a young teen when we walked in for breakfast before school and there he sat, as if he had hardly moved an inch, since several hours before when we had seen him there before going to bed. His hat was still on his head, and the typewriter was still clicking away.

13 Bryant, Marvin, "Preacher Changes," *Firm Foundation*, 2 May 1972, p. 14 [286]. This report also appeared in the *Gospel Advocate*, 4 May 1972, p. 286.

14 Willard Collins, "W. A. Bradfield As A Promoter," *Gospel Advocate*, 27 April 1972, p. 267.

15 "The Golden Life of Gus Nichols," *Daily Mountain Eagle*, Jasper, Alabama, 18 November 1975, p. 2.

16 Note: At the time of this writing, Bethel Christian School is no longer in the hands of brethren. At one point, it was turned over to the government, but now it is uncertain if the school is still in existence.

17 Gus Nichols, "Beloved Friends," *Words of Truth*, Vol. 9, No. 8, 19 July 1974, p. 4.

The Sage Of Jasper

Canst thou bind the sweet influences of
Pleiades, or loose the bands of Orion?
—God, Job 38:31

The sun standing high on a cloudless day will cast its powerful presence into the deepest recesses of its earthly target. Similarly, the massive net of one's influence goes far beyond—far deeper—than is his ability to ascertain. Of a truth, Gus Nichols bore a name known in all households of Walker County, and potentially most of central Alabama. From the poor man on the streets in Jasper to the halls of the state capital in Montgomery, his influence was felt. Twice, Gus received recognition as Honorary Lieutenant Colonel Aide-de-Camp on the staff of Alabama's Governor, George C. Wallace (1919-1998). The distinction was complimentary in nature, but it served as a testimony to how his community and state held him in high esteem.

Gus, Matilda, Karen, Eddie

What made him truly a giant among God's spokesmen was how he made impact on the personal level. Little children were enamored by his presence, just like adults. His smile was decorated by a gold filling on one of his front teeth. Young and old alike enjoyed his unbroken attention any time they crossed his path. He had a way to make everyone feel important. His humble and holy sounding voice was so inviting, so personal—so down-to-earth. The sage of his wisdom was felt at home, in the pulpit and classroom, on the radio, and everywhere within the field of his milieu.

MAXCINE FELTON WHITE

The wife of Howard A. White, (1913-1991) President of Pepperdine University, was Maxcine Felton, an Alabama girl by birth. From the town of Hodges, in south Franklin County, she grew up in the shadow of the Sage of Jasper. When she graduated from high school, brother and sister Nichols encouraged her to go to Freed-Hardeman College. She attended there with Gracie and Vodie. Some years later Maxcine recalled,

> On September 15, 1936, I boarded the train for Freed-Hardeman College. I could not believe it, but there I was going to college

and all because Brother Nichols had shown me it could be done. I cannot mention all the Nichols family has meant to me, but I will always be grateful to them. Brother and Sister Nichols have been as parents to me, and the children have let me be one of them.[1]

After graduation from F-HC and later David Lipscomb, where she received her teaching degree, she returned to Jasper to teach in the public-school system. While there, she made her home in the Nichols household. During that period, "they had a profound influence on her and in many ways, she looked to them as a sort of second parents."[2]

When she later moved away, the Nichols were never far from her thoughts. She served for a time as Dean of Women at David Lipscomb College, and still later, married preacher and educator, Howard White. Her life took on a look much like that of the Nichols, in that, the field of her influence was widely felt. She soon found herself on the west coast deeply involved in education at Pepperdine College. When cancer took her life pre-maturely the 19th of January 1973, it was a few years before Howard was to be named the fifth president of the college.[3] After her passing, while going through some personal things in her wallet, among various pictures of her children and other family members was a photo of Gus and Matilda Nichols.

1973 - Sister Nichols Honored at IBC, August

THE FIRST LADY OF THE CHURCH

The legacy of Gus Nichols might never have risen to its great heights had it not been for his great helper in life, Matilda Brown Nichols. While the world's focus was on the man, those that knew the couple personally, knew and equally appreciated the force behind the man.

Thousands from all over the country poured into the Shoals area during the first week of August 1973 for the Summer Workshop at International Bible College.[4] On Tuesday evening, Gus served as the keynote speaker on the topic, "The Cross of Christ."[5] Following the close of the evening's session, the focus quickly shifted to a Special Services program honoring sister Nichols.

Among a great crowd of people, an array of well-wishers lined up to express their love and appreciation for the life of this good woman. College President, Charles R. Coil (1929-1994) served as emcee. Long-time family friend, William Woodson (1931-2010), was called to speak of his impressions of sister Nichols. Former associate minister at Sixth Avenue, James Horton, followed with his own stories and words of thanks, and expressed with deeply esteeming feelings, "She is truly the first lady of the Church."[6] Next, representing the grateful people of Walker County was the preacher from the Goodsprings congregation, Paul Wylie (1933-2004). Flavil, then stood before the crowd and read a poem that Gus had written about her and presented at their 50th Wedding Anniversary.

THE NICHOLS-KING DEBATE

Among the several controversies to face churches of Christ in the 1970s, one that fractured many congregations surrounded the study of eschatology, or what will happen at the end of time. Quite separate from the millennial discussion of the earlier part of the century was the teaching of some that Jesus' promised second coming took place in A.D. 70.

Several proponents arose saying when the Romans destroyed Jerusalem in A.D. 70., the Lord's promised "second coming" took place. With this, after His return then, there will be no other return. Touted by its chief proponent in the brotherhood as "realized eschatology," was Warren, Ohio, preacher, Max R. King.

Letters between brothers Nichols and King began to flow back and forth in anticipation of a potential debate on the subject. As part of his preparation, Gus made his thirty-seventh trip to Henderson, Tennessee, for the annual lectureship at Freed-Hardeman. He filled the 7:30 slot in Bader Gym each morning dealing with the subject "Christ & Last Things."[7] Each lesson served as the building of an apologetic from the Scriptures against the A.D. 70 doctrine.

Throughout the spring, communications continued between Nichols and King until agreement could be made concerning dates, location, formats, and most of all, propositions. The dates set for the debate was July 17-20, and Warren Western Reserve High School auditorium was reserved for accommodating a larger crowd. The week before the event, the *Firm Foundation* reported the propositions,

> King will affirm: "The Holy Scriptures teach that the second coming of Christ, including the establishment of the eternal kingdom, the day of judgment, the end of the world and the resurrection of the dead, occurred with the fall of Jerusalem in 70 A. D." Nichols will affirm: "The Holy Scriptures teach that the second and final coming of Christ, including the resurrection of all the dead, the day of judgment, the end of the World and the delivering of the kingdom to God the Father, is yet future in relation to us today."[8]

Flavil drove his father up to Ohio for the debate and served as moderator. During the exchange, both men were courteous as they presented their interpretations of the Scriptures. Good crowds attended each evening, and the debate was later published by the Parkman Road church where King served as the minister. The discussion raised awareness among the brotherhood as to the current dispute among brethren. Also, it was the last contest of Gus Nichols' debating career. Often reported during this period of his life was that he had held over one hundred debates.

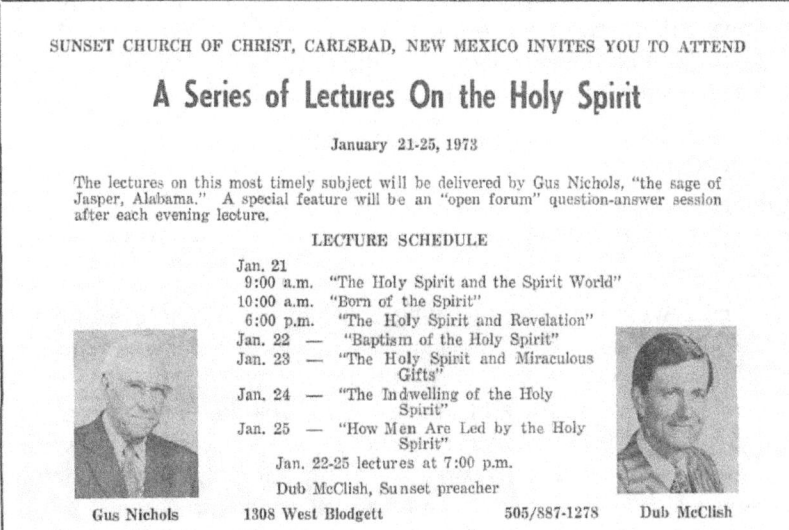

Lectures on the Holy Spirit

THE ERUDITE PROFESSOR

This volume could well be described as to how old school pragmatism meets new school elitism. Gus Nichols' education was old school. From standing behind a mule with only a pocket testament early in the 20th century, this lowly, humble farmer, climbed to the summit of educational instruction without so much as an earned Bachelor's degree. At eighty-one years of age, the calls continued to come from farther away; his teaching more widely demanded than was humanly possible to fulfill. Nearly every month of 1973 he was being featured on lectureships at different brotherhood congregations and college campuses, speaking on a wide array of topics. Whether lecturing on the Holy Spirit at the Sunset church in Carlsbad, New Mexico in January, or on Eschatology at Freed-Hardeman in February, or on how the Bible was used in the Restoration Movement at Alabama Christian in March, he continued to demonstrate his expertise in all fields. During the same week in early May, he spoke at York College in Nebraska on, "The Church, The Body of Christ," early in the week, then followed daily on the program of Memphis School of Preaching. In June, he spoke daily at the Blue Ridge Encampment, and in August on the summer lectures at International Bible College. In September, he conducted the Gus Nichols Bible Workshop at the Gulf Coast Bible Camp in southern Mississippi where a Greek Concordance was offered to the camper who brought with him the most denominational preachers.[9] In October, he spoke on the International Evangelism and Bible Lectureship at White's Ferry School of Preaching in West Monroe, Louisiana. And, then, in November, he discussed his controversial views on Divorce and Remarriage in a panel discussion with Roy Deaver (1922-2007) at Harding Graduate School of Religion in Memphis.[10]

HEAT EXHAUSTION

One would think that at such an advanced age, with an inordinate speaking schedule, it would take its toll on his health. Not so! It took a mid-August North Alabama sun to make a chink in his seemingly invincible armor.

The Sixth Avenue church had long engaged outside help to maintain their grounds around the building. Included in this was the continued offer to mow the lawn around the preacher's home across the street. However, Gus always refused the offer saying that he enjoyed pushing a lawnmower for exercise. As has been noted, at some stage each week of the summer, brother Nichols could be seen wearing his Stetson hat and long-sleeve starched white shirt and tie pushing the mower.

His exercise was cut short one day when he passed out. An ambulance was dispatched to his home to determine what needed to be done. A couple of weeks later, he penned a letter to be placed in the *Advocate*, where he explained,

> On August 15 I suffered complete heat exhaustion while mowing, and was in intensive care for two days and nights. All tests indicate

The Sage Of Jasper

I did not have a heart attack, and resumed my normal work load. I am grateful for all the prayers, cards, and telephone inquiries about me. Under medication I slept from sixteen to twenty hours a day, and thus my body was given some long-overdue rest.[11]

Within a short time, he was back to his regular preaching, radio, writing, lectureship, gospel meeting schedule, and mowing his lawn. With such commitment—such drive—it was little wonder that J. J. Turner surmised in an article entitled, "Is Gray Hair Beautiful?," "Some older gospel preachers are as productive today as they were years ago. Such men as Roy Lanier, Sr., B. C. Goodpasture, Gus Nichols, Foy Wallace, Jr., G. K. Wallace, J. C. Bailey, etc., are some of the most powerful writers and speakers of our day."[12]

RAY DUTTON

The Alan Cloyd family departed to other works around the fall of 1973, and it began time to search for another candidate to fill the shoes of associate minister for the Sixth Avenue church.

Ray Dutton was deeply familiar with Sixth Avenue having grown up in the congregation. Yet, at that time, he and his wife, Kaye, were living and working with the church in Belmont, Mississippi. Ray had just finished his Master's degree at Harding Graduate School of Religion in Memphis when he heard about the Cloyds leaving Jasper. Making inquiries about the position, it was not long before it seemed to all that Ray was the best fit for the position.

The Duttons moved home to Jasper around the beginning of the year 1974. At first, the plan was for he and brother Nichols to exchange pulpits week in and week out. However, the plan took a different look very quickly. You see, even at the age of 82, brother Nichols showed no signs of slowing down. As it turned out, several weeks went by when brother Dutton

Ray Dutton

was doing most all the preaching. So, the schedule became that when brother Nichols was in town, he did the preaching, and when he was away his younger counterpart filled the preaching responsibilities.

Classes and the radio schedule were determined much the same way. When brother Nichols was on the road, brother Dutton spoke at both broadcasts every day except Sunday, when they only conducted the 8am program. But, when they were together, as with his predecessors, brother

Dutton did the obituaries and other announcements, and brother Nichols preached the message.

A good relationship existed with the two preachers from the very start. There was such high esteem held for the older man by the younger, that their work together could hardly do anything other than blossom. Many were the times, when Ray finished the morning announcements, that brother Nichols would say, "Brother Dutton, what do we want to talk about today?" The first few times it startled the young man because he had no idea what brother Nichols needed to discuss. So, he just came up with a topic off the top of his head and announced a topic. Then, his co-preacher, without a single note, would preach a masterpiece over the airwaves on that subject. It was mesmerizing to Ray, not only brother Nichols' vast knowledge of so many topics, but that at his age, he was "sharp as a tack"—quick, and ready at a second's notice to preach the whole counsel of God.

One recollection brother Dutton had was sitting in an elders' meeting once when a younger elder came down pretty hard on brother Nichols for going overtime in one of his sermons. He usually preached forty-five minutes in his lessons, but apparently had gone an hour in the sermon being criticized. The young elder asked why it seemed to be so hard for him to work within the guidelines set by the elders for time to preach. Well, you could have heard a pin drop. Ray sat there, a young preacher, shocked, feeling quite defensive of his elder preaching brother, and quite disapproving of the elder's negativism. Brother Nichols, being an elder himself, sat there unmoved, calm, and never showing any negative reaction. He was quiet for several seconds, then he said, "Brethren, I have always sought to preach at any one time the things I felt God wanted me to preach for that occasion. I want this eldership to know that anytime you so desire to replace me, I will be gone yesterday." This was the last time his sermons were topics of elders' meetings.

Impressive about the man was his passion for preaching the truth. He taught Ray and all other preachers upon whom he had influence the need to preach when the opportunity presents itself. He later recalled,

> During the two years I was privileged to spend with brother Gus Nichols before his death, many times I heard him cry over the growing practice among many of our preachers to "lecture" rather than "preach the word." His complaint was that ever-increasing numbers of our preachers are refraining from reading and quoting the Scriptures and from giving book, chapter, and verse for statements they make.

On one occasion brother Nichols and I attended a funeral service where the preacher spoke some twenty minutes, and in that time never quoted or read from even ONE verse of the "holy scriptures" (2 Tim. 3:15). Later, as we discussed this matter, brother Nichols commented: "He talked and talked and talked, but he never let the Lord get a word in edgewise!"[13]

In his recollections, brother Dutton said, "I never found a chink in the man's armor. How he treated others, his attentiveness to the very least of his brethren, was impeccable. He was kind! Everything about him was genuine."[14] He said, "I never once ceased to be amazed at his love for others, his quiet humility, and his undying love for the Lord."[15] Like his colleagues of the past, he learned from brother Nichols things that went with him all the years of his ministry. In Gus Nichols was the sage of wisdom and knowledge that helped so many good people become great.

"Grace"

ARE YOU MAKING THE WORLD BETTER TODAY?
Gus Nichols

Say! Is your life being misspent,
With problems, worries, and discontent?
Why not straighten up, live for others,
And consider them your earthly brothers?

Resolve to help all others you meet.
Say kind words to all whom you greet.
Don't be a doubter. It will pay
Both now, and at the judgment day.

Remember the day is slipping fast!
Have you cheered those you met and passed?
Are they happier because they met you?
Remember: the day will soon be through!

How could you sleep in your bed
When not a good word you have said?
When you've ignored God and his plan
For you to help your fellow man?

Show your love; win souls for your prize;
For "He that winneth souls is wise."
"GO"—Don't waste another minute!
Win souls—put everything in it!

Then when you close your eyes at night,
You can say, "I've treated others right",
And I've obeyed God, walked in his way;
I've made the world better today!"[16]

ENDNOTES

1 Maxcine Feltman White, *Gospel Advocate*, 19 May 1955, p. 397.

2 Carroll B. Ellis, "A Tribute To Maxcine Felton White," *Gospel Advocate*, 30 August 1973, p. 558.

3 Ibid. Note: Maxcine Feltman White's influence was so widely felt by Pepperdine College that a women's dormitory was later designated in her name.

4 Note: Now, Heritage Christian University.

5 Advertisement, "Summer Workshop, International Bible College," *The World Evangelist*, July 1973, p. 12.

6 Bettye Beck, "Sister Gus Nichols Honored." *The World Evangelist*, September 1973, p. 7.

7 Advertisement, *Gospel Advocate*, 4 January 1973, p. 12.

8 Advertisement, "Debate Scheduled," *Firm Foundation*, 10 July 1973, p. 11 [443].

9 Billy Lambert, *Gospel Advocate*, 13 September 1973, p. 594.

10 Note: Discussed more fully in Chapter 43.

11 Gus Nichols, *Gospel Advocate*, 20 September 1973, p. 609.

12 J. J. Turner, "Is Gray Hair Beautiful?" *Gospel Advocate*, 27 December 1973, p. 825.

13 Ray Dutton, *Words of Truth*, "Let God Speak," 4 June 1976, p. 3. Note: This incident must have made a deep impression. He later used this same illustration in a different article for the *Gospel Advocate* entitled, "A Word In Edgewise," 18 October 1979, p. 657. Still later the illustration was reflected upon in an article written by James D. Bales (1915-1995) entitled, "Preachers And Bible Study," *Firm Foundation*, 18 March 1980, p. 8 [184].

14 Note: Most of the information shared in this section is from a phone interview with Ray Dutton, 10 April 2015.

15 Ray Dutton, "Brother Nichols Goes Home," Sixth Avenue church of Christ, bulletin article, 23 November 1975.

16 *Words of Truth*, "Poems By Gus Nichols," 26 March 1971, p. 2.

- 50 -

Honor To Whom Honor Is Due

> And he said unto him, Behold now, there is in this city a man of God, and he is an honourable man...peradventure he can shew us our way that we should go.
> —The Servant of Saul, 1 Samuel 9:6

Anyone who knew brother Nichols personally would easily say that he never looked for recognition and worldly praise. He was a soldier of the cross, always deferring to the Savior. When engaged in debate, he was tenacious in defending the truth of the Scriptures, constantly pressing his opponents mercilessly to give up their false positions for the sake of the truth. Like any warrior, he was valiant in defending the captain of his salvation. Because of his visible dedication, the man—the loyal man—enjoyed a tremendous following of thankful brethren.

DISTINGUISHED SERVICE MEDALLION

In late January 1974, brother Nichols made his way to Oklahoma City for the 24th annual lectureship series at Oklahoma Christian College. The series was devoted to "Neglected Bible Doctrine."[1] Adding to the excitement of participating in the lecture program was being able to spend time with Hardeman, who was scheduled as one of the keynoters during the week.

Brother and Sister Nichols

On Tuesday evening, college President James O. Baird (1920-1998) hosted the annual Preacher-Elder Fellowship Banquet. Amidst several comments, he made presentations to two great Christian leaders for their distinguished service to the church. One recipient was Reuel Lemmons (1912-1989), beloved preacher and editor of the *Firm Foundation*. Also, cited for his "outstanding Christian service," amidst great praise, was Gus Nichols.[2] Both these men were long held in high esteem for their life achievements, and most notably their service to the Kingdom of Christ.

A PAST CENTURY OF PREACHING

In February, Gus made his 38th consecutive annual trip to the lectureship in Henderson, Tennessee. He spoke daily in the 7:30am time slot, in Bader

Gym, about having the right attitude on, "Fellowship in the Church," "Truth and Error," "Faith, Expedience, and Opinion," and "Legalism and Compromise."[3] His expertise and reliability led him to be placed, "among Spiritual Zion's lovers of truth and practitioners of sound doctrine."[4]

Once again, the Nichols family experienced the sadness of loss at the passing of Gus' younger brother, Carey Columbus. At nearly five years his junior, Carey had led a duel life of farmer and preacher. Fayette County, Alabama had long been his home and the field of his labor. When he passed away the 22nd of February 1974, the family gathered together in Fayette for the funeral where his body was laid to rest in the Fayette Memorial Gardens. Only eternity knows the great good brother Carey Nichols contributed to the Kingdom of Christ.

7:30 at Bader Gym - FHC Lectures

In early March, Gus appeared in a lectureship over at Winfield where he spoke on Wednesday evening on the subject, "The End of Time."[5] Then, he crossed the Mississippi once again to go to Searcy, Arkansas, for Harding College's sixth annual Preachers Forum. The program was themed, "Modernism and Neo-Pentecostalism In The Church."[6] He closed out the program with the lesson, "A Past Century of Preaching."

Later in March, he again appeared on the annual lecture program of Alabama Christian College in Montgomery. This year he taught a class on, "When the Preacher Moves," which seemed a little outside his arena of expertise since he had been at Sixth Avenue for over 40 years. Yet, by this time in life, his wisdom was needed on a vast array of subjects which may or may not have been applicable to his own experience. He knew, not only how to quote the Bible, but how to apply its heavenly principles. He also appeared in a panel discussion on the subject of the Holy Spirit with Thomas B. Warren (1920-2000), Furman Kearley (1932-2003), and Leslie G. Thomas (1895-1988).[7]

TORNADO ALLEY

Northwest Alabama has long been familiar with the effects of inclement weather. Every spring, the threat of tornadoes and super storms are a menace to the region. People living there refer to their part of the country as Tornado Alley. Without doubt, the spring of 1974 is a major contributing factor to their thinking this way.

On April 3-4, an outbreak of super storms hit 13 states, spawning 148 tornadoes. At 7:57 p.m., as the Wednesday evening Bible Study at the Sixth Avenue church of Christ was about to adjourn, a F4 storm hit the downtown area of Jasper. Severe damage was sustained by several of the buildings, and over 100 people were reported as injured. Nevertheless, in all the mayhem, there were no casualties. It so happened that brother Nichols led the closing prayer that evening. Some later recalled that it was an unusually long prayer. After the tornado passed through, it was thought that if he had not prayed as long as he did, some of the members might possibly have been caught in the mayhem.[8]

Storms of this nature were not new to Gus Nichols. As calls came in from all over, much of his time was spent seeking ways to help those of his community, especially the membership at Sixth Avenue. In the wake of the devastation, he wrote an article in *Words of Truth*, entitled, "What About Tornadoes?" In it, he encouraged all to put their trust in God, knowing all things work together for good to those that love the Lord.[9]

With the demand of his attention at home, he had to cancel appointments to speak on the lectureship at Ohio Valley College along with some other previously made commitments.

TRIPS TO INDIANAPOLIS AND ATLANTA

In early May, Gus was back on the road, this time to Indianapolis, Indiana. Long time preacher in the area, W. L. Totty (1903-1982), of the Shelbyville Road congregation, played host for a series of meetings. In the spirit of earlier days when meeting reporting was more frequent, Totty wrote, "Gus Nichols preached five wonderful sermons for the Shelbyville Road church May 9-12. He preached the gospel in a plain, forceful manner. There were eight baptisms and one restoration."[10]

He continued a busy schedule through the summer including Matilda and his annual trip to the Blue Ridge Encampment in North Carolina in June.

In August, he drove over to Atlanta to participate in the graduation exercises of the Southeastern School of Religion. Hosting the school was the Chestnut Drive congregation, with director Charles Pledge organizing the event. Gus preached at the morning services and was involved in the commencement exercises in the afternoon. Pledge reported,

Brother Nichols is known, loved and used throughout the brotherhood by faithful congregations. His contribution in building up the cause of Christ has been of significance in this country and his influence has reached around the world. The part Brother Nichols has played in training men and encouraging men to preach the gospel of Christ will probably never be known and appreciated by people this side of eternity.[11]

Later in the fall, he returned to Atlanta to participate in the World Mission Forum, held at Forest Park. Organizer of the fourth annual event was minister of the congregation and long-time friend of the Nichols family, Richard T. Harp. The weekend was intended to raise awareness of the need for missions in the state of Georgia, as well as works being conducted all around the world. Seasoned missionaries were brought in from all over the world to report on and encourage missionary work. This particular weekend event culminated with an Atlanta city-wide worship service held at the Forest Park church building. Amidst a packed house, brother Nichols preached to the eager attendees on the subject, "What It Means To Be Lost."[12]

Sixth Avenue Church Members

107 YEARS OF EXPERIENCE

The fifth annual Gus Nichols Bible Workshop took place the last week in September 1974. The venue changed for the event this year from Gulf Shores Bible Camp in Mississippi to the campus of Alabama Christian College at the College church building. Previously, the program was primarily for the purpose of educating and encouraging preachers. This year, with more room available on the college campus, the program was expanded to include, "elders, deacons, and any interested male member of the church who would like to attend for the purpose of increasing his Bible knowledge."[13] In addition to having brother Nichols as the primary instructor for the event, the organizers added G. K. Wallace (1903-1988),

25 Years on the Radio

long-time preacher, and at that time, vice-president emeritus of Freed-Hardeman College. Hugh Fulford promoted the series in the *GA*,

> The names of Gus Nichols and G. K. Wallace are synonyms for Bible knowledge, gospel preaching, soundness in the faith, and the ability to impart spiritual knowledge. Brother Nichols has been preaching for fifty-seven years and Brother Wallace has been preaching for fifty years. They have been on the firing line for many, many years and are seasoned veterans in the army of the Lord. Both men serve as staff writers for the *Gospel Advocate* and have done so for many years. They have conducted gospel meetings throughout the length and breadth of the land, and have spoken on all our major college lectureship programs.[14]

Through the year, brother Nichols continued editing *Words of Truth*. He also submitted several articles to brotherhood papers. The sales of his preaching books, debates, and especially his volume on the Holy Spirit, continued to grow and be promoted. He was a man in demand for lectureships, meetings, teaching in his school, preaching, radio work, and just about anywhere his wisdom and sage advice could be utilized. That year, the American Biographical Institute of Raleigh, North Carolina, listed him in their annual volume, *"Personalities of the South."* [15]

BEAUTY A LOVELY THING
by Gus Nichols

Beauty is a divine and lovely thing
Whether it be in a child or in a king.
Real beauty is very charming and sweet—
Is often satisfying and complete.

It is not always observed at first sight,
Unless it is seen in its own true light.
It is hard to reproduce in pictures,
And is best loved in the light of scriptures.

Beauty is most charming when properly dressed,
And when divine character is often stressed.
If beauty were to lose its modest blush,
It would be like a mud fence in the brush.

Pure innocence written in the human face,
Outshines all the stars up in heavenly space.
The thing called "Beauty" must be in the heart,
How to express it is the greatest art.

The prettiest picture in all the earth,
The loveliest picture, of greatest worth,
Is a picture of Jesus' marvelous life.
Painted by our living the Christian life. [16]

Congrats Mrs. Gus Nichols
Matilda with her adopted sister, Pearly Ellis

ENDNOTES

1 Advertisement, *Firm Foundation*, 1 January 1974, p. 12.

2 David R. Owens, "Oklahoma Christian College," *Gospel Advocate*, 21 March 1974, p. 189.

3 Coleman Crocker, "Freed-Hardeman College Lectureship," *Gospel Advocate*, 10 January 1974, p. 30.

4 Robert R. Taylor, "The 1974 F-HC Lectureship," *Gospel Advocate*, 2 May 1974, p. 281.

5 Advertisement, "Winfield Lectureship Program." *Words of Truth*, Vol. 8, No. 38, 1 March 1974, p. 2.

6 Stan Green, "Harding College," *Gospel Advocate*, 24 January 1974, p. 62.

7 Advertisement, "Alabama Christian College Lecture Program," *Gospel Advocate*, 21 February 1974, p. 125.

8 Note: While no one died in the tornado that hit Jasper, other areas in Alabama were not so fortunate. Of the 319 deaths recorded from all the storms during those two days, Alabama experienced the most with 77 deaths. Long will the people recall the devastation to the little town of Guin, a few miles west of Jasper, that was nearly destroyed with an F5 tornado. The 1974 weather event stood as the worst outbreak of super storms in U.S. history until 2011 when a bigger series of storms hit the region killing 362.

9 Gus Nichols, "What About Tornadoes?" *Words of Truth*, Vol. 8, No. 44, 19 April 1974, p. 3.

10 W. L. Totty, *Gospel Advocate*, 20 June 1974, p. 398.

11 Charles Pledge, *Gospel Advocate*, 1 August 1974, p. 492.

12 Richard Harp, *Gospel Advocate*, 17 October 1974, p. 669. Note: It was your author's joy as a teenager to be at this forum every year in my youth. My father organized the World Mission Forum, and the annual event continues to the present.

13 Hugh Fulford, "The Gus Nichols Bible Workshop," *Gospel Advocate*, 19 September 1974, p. 601.

14 Ibid.

15 "The Golden Life of Gus Nichols," *Daily Mountain Eagle*, 18 November 1975.

16 "Beauty A Lovely Thing," *Words of Truth*, 26 October 1973, Vol. 8, No. 22, p. 4.

51

A Servant Goes Home

I have fought a good fight, I have finished my course, I have kept the faith.
— Paul, 2 Timothy 4:7

Mr. and Mrs. Gus Nichols

IF WE STAY ALIVE, IN SEVENTY-FIVE

If my wife and I stay alive
In the year nineteen seventy five;
And if it's the will of our dear Lord,
We'll spread his word in one accord.

We'll live for Jesus every day
Keep plodding up the narrow way.
We'll not slow down, nor will we stop
Until we reach the mountain top.

We'll teach and preach God's holy word,
The sweetest story ever heard;
As long as God may give us health,
Either in poverty or in wealth.

The battle's on between right and wrong
And we're still fighting very strong.
But not a duty will we shun
Until the victory is won.

We're in the battle until death,
To serve the Lord till our last breath;
We'll teach and pray and toil and strive
As long as able and alive.

We teach thousands in radio land
Are winning souls on every hand.
Many thousands read *"Words of Truth"*
Adapted to the aged and youth.

I preach for churches, large and small,
But I cannot help all who call
We're just doing the best we can
Strictly following the Lord's plan.

I preach at home with smiles and tears
Where I have preached forty-two years.
And if you search, and search, and search,
You may not find a better church.

We love the church at Sixth Avenue
To God's word, it strives to be true
We all strive to work together
And love as birds of a feather.

If one can't go to heaven with us,
The chances are he wants to fuss,
Or may not have been converted,
Or his heart may be perverted.

Thank God for the year SEVENTY FOUR,
And may we all have many more
In which we all may serve the Lord,
Looking for his eternal reward.

Attend all services of the church,
The Holy scriptures daily search;
Work hard and keep sweet as honey,
And if you can, give more money.

This past year of Christian living,
Should increase our liberal giving
Every year of our spiritual life
Should free us from more sin and strife.

Let us all strive to win more souls,
And set for ourselves higher goals.
Let's love and cherish each other
Treat each member as a brother.

Let us make ourselves do our best,
God and others will do the rest,
Let's face the year - SEVENTY FIVE
All fully awake and alive.

Don't look back to worry and fast;
You can't live now in this YEAR PAST
Forget the things that are behind;
Look ahead, or you will be blind.

You can't drive, always looking back,
And you will have no goal, in fact
Make plans with God for SEVENTY FIVE;
Say, "I will if God keeps me alive."

Each one should purpose in his heart,
What he will give - then do his part.
Daniel purposed he would not sin
That will make a new life begin.

We'll do better in SEVENTY FIVE
If God will let us stay alive.
We mean to do our very best,
And trust in God to do the rest.

We will the scriptures daily search,
And will live for Christ and his church.
At last we hope to hear him say,
You've travelled well the narrow way.

-Gus Nichols, January 10, 1975[1]

Two days after these words were published in the pages of *Words of Truth*, the Sage of Jasper turned 83. Who would dare to consider the man to be beyond his prime? Still as vibrant as ever—still coupled with his ministry! Married to Christ were Matilda and he. Together, they unrelentingly devoted themselves to the cause of Jesus. Servants—to the very end!

THE FOUR WAR-HORSES

For the thirty-ninth time, brother Nichols attended the Freed-Hardeman Lectures in Henderson, Tennessee. In anticipation of the first full week in February, college president, E. Claude Gardner (1925-2017) promoted in the *Gospel Advocate*,

> Four "war-horses"—Gus Nichols, B. C. Goodpasture, G. K. Wallace, and Guy N. Woods—will again be in the harness, as they have been for decades, at our big Bible Lectureship, February 3-7, 1975...It truly will be a blessing for us to hear the great Gus Nichols discuss the theme "Upholding Sound Doctrine" and to hear the courageous G. K. Wallace defend the faith in his discussion on "Threats to the Church Today" and to enjoy the sage comments in the Open Forum of the renowned scholar and preacher, Guy N. Woods, and to hear the last lecture in the series with the godly and eloquent B. C. Goodpasture, Editor of the *Gospel Advocate*, who will discuss the theme, "Take Along a Little Honey."[2]

At one point in the program, the college bestowed upon brother Nichols the Outstanding Contribution To F-HC Lectureship Award for his many years of promoting the program and serving it in a most practical and beneficial way.

ACC LECTURESHIP

With no signs of letting up, in late February, Gus made his way out to west Texas for the annual lecture series at Abilene Christian College. Reports of the event appeared in *The Abilene Reporter-News Daily*. After speaking at the 7:30 hour on the first evening, pictures of the two Sunday speakers, Gus Nichols and Dr. Paul Southern, appeared in the paper under the title, "47th Bible Lectureship Gets Underway at ACC." Reported were the words of brother Nichols, "I'd rather have the blood of Jesus, and all that it means to me, than to own all the worlds which God by Christ created in the beginning. . . .Furthermore, I'd rather have the salvation and the hope of heaven which I have because of the precious blood of Christ than to be given a million worlds like this." Also, noted from the sermon, "I love to live in this beautiful and lovely world, but not without God, nor his beloved Son. If I were offered a world like this one for every day that I would live in the sinning business, I would consider (it) a grand insult." Other similar comments followed concerning his lesson on the "Blood of Christ."[3]

IF I COULD GO BACK

In June, brother Nichols entered a recording studio for the purpose of reading several examples of his poetry from over sixty years of writing. The poems were spiritual in nature, produced on a record, with many tracks of his poetic genius entitled, "If I Could Go Back." On the dust jacket was a beautiful color photograph of the noble author sitting in a parlor with a Bible in his hand. It captured beautifully the man as he was known by a devoted brotherhood. Advertisements appeared in several of the brotherhood papers.[4]

25TH ANNUAL BLUE RIDGE ENCAMPMENT

Few could recall ever a time when Gus and Matilda took a vacation. The closest thing to a time of relaxation was the annual trip to Blue Ridge, North Carolina. Though more informal and therapeutic in nature, the event still laid demands upon brother Nichols to teach his daily Nichols' Bible Hour class, as well as other sessions which he was called upon to teach. The July 1975 session was unique in that the camp was celebrating its twenty-fifth year. It was also special because B. C. Goodpasture was being honored by the attendees for his many years of service. At the celebratory dinner, Gus and Matilda sat at the table of honor with the Goodpastures, along with J. M. Powell, brother and sister Jim Foster, and brother and sister Archie Luper. Flourishing words of fanfare were poured upon the editor of the *Gospel Advocate* by Gus and the other participants.

B. C. Goodpasture and Gus Nichols

AN IMPORTANT CHECK

When he turned eighty years of age, Gus had been a member of the Board of Trustees for Alabama Christian College for many years. Most of the members of the Board were very capable business men whom God had blessed with success along with great personal fortunes. While brother Nichols may not have had the wealth of his fellow counterparts, he excelled in his commitment to raise money and contribute personally to the college. He made a five-year commitment that year to give the college a thousand

J. M. Powell and Gus Nichols
Blue Ridge Encampment

dollars a year. When he told Hardeman about it, his son shared his concern that he might not be able to fulfill the obligation at his advanced age. To this, he answered that when he made the same commitment at the age of seventy-five, the Lord saw fit to keep him alive in order that he might fulfill it. It was his hope that making the same commitment again at eighty, that the Lord would see him through this promise as well. During the summer of 1975, he wrote the check for the third installment of his five-year commitment—several months before it was due. It served to be the last check he ever wrote. To him, it was most essential to stay true to his commitments no matter what transpired with his life.[5]

The Nichols Bible Hour

TIAS

Early on a warm Sunday morning in August, Gus woke up to begin his regular regimen for the Lord's Day as he had so many times in the past. Only, something seemed different. Many times in the past he had woken up tired, but generally always pressed on with the things before him. This morning something was not right. He did not feel very well. Still, he pressed forward. As the morning progressed, it just seemed he was feeling worse. The pressure to attend to the events of the day was nothing short of rote for him, as he had missed no more than four Sundays in fifty years, and those times were due to sickness. Finally, he was forced to tell Matilda he thought he needed to go to the hospital. She called for the ambulance to come. As he was placed upon the stretcher, he sought to reassure her. In his calm and soothing voice, he said, "Now, Mother, don't worry about me. No matter what happens, everything is going to be alright, because I am a Christian."[6]

He was taken to the Emergency Room at Peoples Hospital in Jasper for initial triage. Very quickly, it was determined that he could get better care in Birmingham. He was taken to Brookwood Medical Center in Homewood, where he underwent several tests. It was determined by doctors there that he was suffering from Transient Ischemic Attacks (TIA's), or mini-strokes. Soon, he was placed in a room for continued observation and treatment. Matilda was with him at every turn.

The children were contacted quickly. They were spread out all over the country. The closest to them were Bertha and Rile, who lived just up the street from them. Flavil and Mary lived on the way to Birmingham, in Sumiton. The rest of the children were quite distant but began arranging trips to attend to their parents' needs. Gracie and Frank were living in Memphis, where Frank was teaching in the Memphis School of Preaching. Vodie and A. J. were up in Decatur, Illinois. Foy was in Indianapolis. The others were in Texas, Carrie and W. T. in Waxahatchie, and Hardeman and Virginia were living in Ft. Worth. Hudson and Marilyn were at Gastonia, North Carolina. As the days turned into weeks, each of the children made their way home to help sit with their father, ferrying Matilda back home for breaks, and assisting in whatever way they could.

Peggy and Don Champion, Flavil's daughter and son-in-law, lived in Birmingham at the time. Numerous trips were made by them to the hospital. On Sundays they took the Lord's Supper and served it. Don would preside over the feast, and from the bed, their granddaddy would preach a sermon from his vast memory. Sundays were always precious days, as loyal friends and loved ones made their way to his bedside.

Bertha and Rile's daughter, Vicki, had just moved to Montgomery to teach at Alabama Christian in the elementary school. Every weekend she made her way back home to be with the family and visit her granddaddy. She related one experience of how her granddaddy asked her if she had any prospects for marriage. She said she was dating some but had none of which to speak. He told her she had let all the good ones get away, and that she needed to find someone seven years younger than her to marry. His thinking was that usually women live seven years after their husbands die. If she married a younger man, the chances were great that they would live to a ripe old age and die about the same time. Of course, Vicki found that pretty shocking since she was twenty-four. When she told her cousins what he had said, they all thought it was so funny, as that would mean she should be dating seventeen-year-olds.

During his stay, the family protected their father, allowing brief visits at the hospital. People came from all over to express their love. Preachers came daily but were encouraged to stay for a brief visit and prayer. On the 3rd of September, after 25 days in the hospital, Gus was able to go home.

His bedroom, at the end of the hall, very quickly became his office. Too weak to attend worship services, he was still thinking about the Lord's work that needed to be done. Very quickly, books began to stack up next to the walls that surrounded his bed, as he read constantly when not sleeping.

CHARLIE R. NICHOLS

For a number of years, Gus' brother, Charlie, had been living over in Lowndes County, Mississippi. At ten months younger than his oldest

A Servant Goes Home

brother, his health had been deteriorating for quite some time. He had been doing a little preaching, but certainly not as much as in earlier days. At 82 years, 10 months and 6 days, Charlie went quietly to be with the Lord, the 9th day of September 1975.

When word reached Gus, he was still very much battling with his own health. He had only been home from the hospital less than a week, and the trip for the funeral was just not possible.

Hudson had come in on Monday and was going to have to return to Gastonia by the weekend. Not anticipating his uncle's passing, he did not bring a suit to wear. As the Sixth Avenue church had a benevolence clothes closet, he went over and found a suit of clothes to wear to the funeral.

Charlie's body was laid to rest in a family plot in the old Lone Oak church of Christ cemetery amidst many adoring and saddened loved ones.

Charlie R. Nichols

INCREASED STRUGGLES

The mini-strokes continued. Some worse than others, ambulance calls continued until finally the doctors told Gus that pneumonia had ravaged his lungs. It did not look as if he was going to get better. While nothing within the man said, "give up," he knew he was declining. Never willing to quit, he pressed on in mind and spirit to serve God.

In the meantime, brother Dutton pretty much took over all the preaching duties at Sixth Avenue, along with the two daily radio programs. Some assistance came from preachers in the area, offering to help him bear what seemed to continue to be an insurmountable task. Who, but Gus Nichols could keep such a pace? Yet, the young preacher made a most faithful and valiant effort. Ray was a home boy. Brother Nichols had been his preacher. Now he was honored to return the favor.

Flavil was already serving as the Associate editor of *Words of Truth*. So, he quite naturally assumed full editorship while his father's illness prevailed. Of his father's condition he wrote,

> During his conscious moments, he still is lucid and clearly appreciates the interest and love of the brotherhood which is evidenced in the countless prayers, hundreds of phone calls,

and more than one thousand cards and letters. For him and the family, we gratefully thank you. Whatever may be the immediate outcome, we say with the full assurance of faith which he taught us, "Everything is going to be alright."[7]

The need for Flavil to be more and more involved with his father's decline made it necessary to be closer. The elders at the East Walker congregation were most accommodative, allowing him the time necessary to attend to his parents' needs. Several years later he recalled,

> The very last day Dad was able to get to the dining room, he invited brother and sister W. A. Black to come for lunch. As we helped him back to his bed, he asked me and Willet to read to him every passage we could think of about heaven. Knowing. . . death was imminent, he did not want family or friends to pray for him to recover for he knew that was impossible! Instead, he asked us to pray, that if it be in harmony with divine grace and wisdom, God would grant him freedom from pain, or (at least) that his pain might be kept at a minimum—if this, too, might be in harmony with the will of a gracious heavenly Father. He did not want to suffer; but he prayed that his passing might be quick, always submissively saying, ". . .not as I will, but as thou wilt" (Matt. 26:39). He stated that it is a mistake to withhold from a faithful Christian who is terminally ill the precious promises and sweet assurances of the scriptures! Share with them such passages as: "In thy presence is fulness of joy; at thy right hand there are pleasures for evermore" (Psa. 16:11). Dad found special comfort in, and shared, Paul's attitude, "Having a desire to depart, and to be with Christ; which is far better" (Phil. 1:23). "Thanks be to God, which giveth us the victory through our Lord Jesus Christ" (1 Cor. 15:57).[8]

No matter how much his health declined, Gus Nichols was instinctively a gospel preacher. Several days after he was committed to the bed, he finally reached the point where very few words came from his lips. He was sleeping most of the time and was taking hardly any nourishment. He began getting agitated, pulling the covers off and trying to get out of bed. At this stage, it was not normal. Flavil said, "Daddy, what's wrong? You can't get up now. Lie still!" In a weak and struggling tone, he mustered, "Got to get up." Again, he was told, "No Daddy, you can't get up right now. Please stay in bed." Brother Nichols again said, "Got to get up. . . got to go preach. . .the gospel!"[9]

Cards and letters came in bundles daily. The hall leading to his bedroom was literally covered from floor to ceiling with hundreds of cards from an adoring and prayerful public. Food and visits were a daily happening. The

A Servant Goes Home

children were so dutiful to protect their parents. Well-wishers were met at the door with kindness and more than adequate explanations of their father's situation.

When their father was no longer able to get out of bed they asked that preachers and elders who dropped in, would make their visits short, and that they not try in engage their father in conversation. They were encouraged to come in and read one passage of Scripture and have a prayer.

At one point, long after he had quit communicating with anyone, day in and day out he laid nearly lifeless before a loving and caregiving family. A preacher came to visit. He was asked to pray. During the prayer, they began hearing movement under the sheet. Brother Nichols' hands had not moved in days, yet they were slowly moving from the bed across his lap. Under the bedsheet, it was clear for all to see what he was doing. His hands were making their way together—a long and familiar sight, for he always had prayed with his pressed firm together in humbleness before his God.

As the body of the Lord's old soldier was failing, the family knew the time was very near. Even the gold tooth that so long had illuminated his wonderful smile had to be pulled for fear that he might choke on it. Dr. Mike Drummond, who grew up at Sixth Avenue congregation, was the family dentist who came and caringly extracted the tooth. Flavil later recalled,

> Little by little he lost more and more use of his body until it was absolutely—totally!—motionless. His heart was beating, and he was breathing—but he could neither wiggle a finger, nor a toe, nor blink his eyes, nor even swallow. We fed him through a tube and continued to talk to (or at) him, but do not know if he heard anything—for he was incapable of indicating any response! The family doctor sat with us for nearly two hours as he died peacefully at home on Sunday afternoon November 16, 1975.[10]

ENDNOTES

1 "If We Stay Alive, In Seventy-Five," *Words of Truth*, Vol. 9, No. 26, 10 January 1975, p. 2.

2 E. Claude Gardner, "Four War-Horses And Freed-Hardeman College Lectureship," *Gospel Advocate*, 23 January 1975, p. 57.

3 "47th Bible Lectureship Gets Underway at ACC," *The Abilene Reporter-News*, Monday Morning, 24 February 1975, p. 10-A.

4 Note: The idea for the album of poetry was introduced to brother Nichols by a young college student by the name of Dan Bowers. When the art work for the album was being determined, Dan came to Jasper for a photo shoot. Brother Nichols posed in several locations. The photo selected was while sitting in a chair in the parlor of the Bankhead home, Sunset. Special thanks to Dan Bowers for providing the photo used on the front of this book, one of many he took of brother Nichols that day.

5 Flavil Nichols, "Supporting Christian Education," *Words of Truth*, Vol. 21 #46, 16 November 1984, p. 2.

6 As reported by Ray Dutton, email, 24 March 2017.

7 Flavil Nichols, "Editor Stricken," *Words of Truth*, Vol. 10 No. 18, 26 September 1975, p. 1.

8 Flavil Nichols, "Lessons I Learned From My Father, Gus Nichols," *Spiritual Sword*, Vol. 26, No. 2, January 1995, pp. 13-14.

9 Note: This story was related to me and my father several months after brother Nichols' death. Flavil was in Atlanta staying in our home during a gospel meeting at the time. It was a heart-warming moment I have carried with me for over forty years.

10 Flavil Nichols, "In Memoriam: Gus Nichols," *Words of Truth*, 15 November 1985, page 3.

- 52 -

His Works Do Follow

And I heard a voice from heaven saying unto me, Write, Blessed are the dead which die in the Lord from henceforth: Yea, saith the Spirit, that they may rest from their labours; and their works do follow them.
—John, Revelation 14:13

Immediately, phone calls began spreading the news that the Sage of Jasper was now and forever with the Lord. William Woodson (1931-2010) made arrangements with choral director, Kelley B. Doyle (1925-2002) to take the members of the Freed-Hardeman College Chorus down to Jasper for a Wednesday funeral.

One of brother Nichols most beloved preacher friends was B. C. Goodpasture (1895-1977). Brother Goodpasture had started a gospel meeting at Riverdale, Georgia, just south of Atlanta, when the news came. Long had there been an understanding between Gus and B. C. that whoever of the two passed away first, the other would be called to preach the funeral. B. C. continued through Tuesday night, but departed early on Wednesday morning for Jasper, leaving the local minister, Virgil R. Richie (1913-2004), to complete the meeting.

Twenty-four hours before the funeral, the body lay in state in the building at Sixth Avenue. During that time, it was determined by some of the preachers in the area, that in fifteen-minute intervals, they would take turns, two at a time standing in place at the head and foot of the open casket of their dearly departed hero. As hundreds of preachers made their way to the building, many asked to participate to show their reverence for the occasion. Some of his grandchildren joined in and took their turns as well. How he was loved!

THE FUNERAL

The funeral was held on Wednesday afternoon. College presidents, preachers, elders, elected city officials, church members, neighbors, and friends made their way to join the grieving family. By early afternoon, the church house was filling to capacity.

At the two o'clock hour, Ray Dutton approached the podium where brother Nichols had preached for over a generation. He began the memorial service recalling the many times he sat with his elder brother in his office discussing the Word of God. He recalled times when he saw large tears rolling down brother Nichols' cheeks as he contemplated the power of the Scripture in view of how many people spoke against it. He then read 1 Thessalonians 4:13-17. Following with prayer, he asked God's comfort of the family and observed, "our loss is heaven's gain."

Paul Wylie (1933-2004), one of brother Nichols' preacher boys, and the minister of the Goodsprings congregation, then directed the Freed-Hardeman Chorus and all in attendance in brother Nichols' favorite song, "What A Friend We Have In Jesus!"

Emceeing the program, brother Dutton returned to the microphone saying he was the 36th preacher in the congregation there to be influenced by brother Nichols. He then introduced the first young man brother Nichols encouraged to preach, brother W. A. Black (1904-1980), who was then the preacher of his home congregation at Millport.

Brother Black recalled that it had been fifty years ago that brother Nichols had baptized him unto the remission of sins. He commended brother Nichols in that though he was not perfect, he could not recall anything he ever did wrong. He spoke of the wonderful way he had raised his children to be servants of the Lord, many of whom were preachers or preacher's wives. He was interested in his children, and the children of others. He wanted them all to do well. He was a friend to his neighbors. His greatest influence was on the church and encouraging young preachers. In preparation for the funeral, he listed seventeen preachers including himself, from Lamar County. Of the seventeen, fourteen attended Freed-Hardeman College. All learned from him in classes he taught at Jasper. One preacher he converted, converted twenty-five to thirty preachers, and they in turn converted others who became preachers. Hundreds are now preaching because of brother Nichols.

He recalled how he saw brother Nichols in attendance with a young preacher who stammered and struggled through his sermon. Noting how brother Nichols listened intently to it, after the services, he was one of the first to approach and praise the young man for his efforts. He was a busy man, but when not in debates or in preaching meetings, he attended meetings everywhere he could. He encouraged the preacher and churches in so doing. He cared for others and recalled his compassion and friendship even with his foes. Remembered was the occasion of one preacher he had debated several times, and when he was dying, brother Nichols went personally to his home and helped him when his life was in the balance.

William Woodson, head of the Bible Department of Freed-Hardeman College, and another of brother Nichols' preacher boys, then approached the podium. In gratitude, he spoke of the "very signal honor" given him by the family in allowing him to take part in the service. Further, thanks were given the Sixth Avenue church, "which over the years, made possible, the ways and means by which this great man of God, whose body lies before us, was able to achieve such heights of orators better than I could extol." He continued,

> Let me express appreciation to the churches of Christ in this community and elsewhere, who also made it possible for him, by providing encouragement, opportunity to speak, invoking his counsel, and endeavoring to follow that which he taught. Let me also speak for the common man, those who heard him so gladly, and who now, though they may not be able to say the words, deep down in their hearts are saying, "we walked with a Prince, but he made us to feel that we were Kings!"[1]

Words of tribute were read from different preachers of the past, including sentiments expressed by G. C. Brewer (1884-1956) in 1944 when he complimented greatly the capabilities and contributions of the then young Gus Nichols.[2]

Reporting other messages sent in, brother Woodson noted, "Some words by good friend, preacher and educator, J. D. Bales (1915-1995), who said, 'I guess the greatest contribution that I know of is his being a living demonstration of what Christ can do with the life which is dedicated to Him and His Kingdom.'" He continued with,

> Ben Holiday, elder of the church in Huntingdon, Tennessee, said, "I feel that his greatest contributions to the cause of Christ, have been his abilities, energies, and efforts that have been used so freely and willingly and ably to defend the Bible and the church against the inroads that have been attempted in the past two generations or more. By those inroads, I mean such things as anti-ism, liberalism, neo-Pentecostalism, and various other kinds of isms, that have crept in, that would not have been dreamed of in the church fifty years ago."

> Brother Jack Lewis wrote, "His love for the Lord, his integrity and the warmth of his personality cause me to understand why so many people love him. I never knew him to pull rank on a younger man. Rather, he made him feel important."

> Brother Hugo McCord, "If ever a human beside David could be a man after God's own heart, in my opinion, it would be Gus Nichols. How he loved his heavenly Father, and continually praised him because of His goodness in His greatness. And, because of His greatness in His goodness heaven will be richer for us all, because

of the influence of as a sincere and joyful a Christian who ever lived."

Willard Collins, of David Lipscomb College said, "Children felt close to him. I remember when he stayed in my home for a gospel meeting at Charlotte Avenue in Nashville, Tennessee, that my two little girls, who were at home then, would climb up and sit in his lap, and he would entertain them with many tricks. He was a man for all ages."

J. E. Choate, "Hudson Nichols was a student in freshman English class I taught at Lipscomb in the late 40s. I requested the students to write a biographical paper on the most memorable person he had ever been privileged to know in his life. Hudson responded like this, 'I know there are many good men in this world, but the best man I have known is my father. And, if there are just two people in heaven, my father will be one of them.'"

Restoration historian Earl West said, "I find it commendable that Gus Nichols was not cast in the role of an agitator. Instead, I noted that he helped to rescue many from the clutches of radicalism. It was evident during his lectures, that his keen edge, logic and common sense, buttress the structure of his biblical presentations. E. A. Elam often said that when his life came to a close he wanted it to be honestly said that he was always true to the Word of God. So, too, was brother Nichols true to the Word. This reminds one of the statement concerning a legend about Ignatius, an early martyr. It was said that upon his death, the martyr's heart was slashed away, and the name of Jesus were written in letters of gold upon each fragment. Who could have known Gus Nichols, and doubt that the name of Jesus was written in the right way upon his heart."

Brother Rex Turner said that as a young man he came to the Nichols' home unannounced, intending to study at the feet of brother Nichols. No announcement! No invitation! "Brother and sister Nichols greeted me and extended hospitality to me as if I had been their grandson, who they had not seen in a long time. But, the depression was on, and the Nichols had only eight children in their home. I've often wondered what my reaction would have been and what I would have done had I been in their place."

Lastly, brother Woodson referred to a letter written by Mr. Carl Elliott, Sr., a citizen of Jasper, but not a member of the church of Christ, who said,

I have been grieved, as have thousands of others in this area, over the critical illness of Gus Nichols, who has by all odds, been Walker County, Alabama's, single most influential citizen of this generation. Again, I think I was impressed most perhaps by him as an embodiment of the living Scriptures. His knowledge of, and ability to quote the Bible, literally astounded me. With that as a background, let me say I feel the greatest contribution made by Mr. Nichols to Jasper, has been the long-time Christian stability which he gave it. His was a continuing leadership and falling from it were all the fruits of that leadership both pastoral and organizational. His leadership crossed the formal boundaries of religion. As an organizer, he knew no peer. As one having the objectivity of the outsider it has been clear to me for a long time that Gus Nichols built the strongest church organization that North Alabama has ever seen. Most of the preachers of his church were men whose lives he had touched, and often they were men that he himself had led into the work of his church. Once they were into their ministerial jobs, he had the good sense to pull them back in and give them instruction in both faith and performance. Gus Nichols will live in this area for generations. Jasper's church of Christ edifice will itself, be a monument to all of us and our descendants for generations, that once upon a time there lived in Jasper a man named Gus Nichols; who spoke as with a sword of fire, and from the workshop of whose mind and hand there grew the seeds of modern miracles that continue to bear fruit. More than everything else I knew Gus Nichols as one whose dedication to his cause knew no bounds and no restraints. I don't expect to meet anyone else in this life who will excel Gus Nichols in drive, imagination or accomplishment.

Brother Woodson completed his thoughts by saying,

A second word is the word of resolution. I think the most impressive sermon I ever heard brother Nichols preach was entitled, "The Death of The Righteous." And, how often your hearts must have filled as he proclaimed it. In 1945 he wrote concerning this topic in the *Gospel Advocate* of January 11th. Just a few quotes here. 'It would have been more fitting if he (Balaam) had expressed the desire to the "life" of the righteous. . . .There is no substitute for an earnest desire to serve the Lord and be finally saved in heaven. . .Men can live right if they desire to do so—that is, if the desire to live right is stronger than the desire to sin. . .Men can find ways to do the "impossible" when they "hunger and thirst after righteousness." They can astonish the world with their rapid progress and learning and in the transformation of their character. The gospel taps the resourcefulness of men, unshackles and releases power for service hitherto unknown to them. Even their faith is overcoming power...Such a one can go onward and upward against the greatest difficulties and finally "die the death of the righteous."

Concerning my impressions and the influence of his life on me, I share with you a letter which I received from a dear and beloved Christian sister, wife of the late H. A. Dixon, of our school. She had this to say and she speaks for many, many of us. "I also wanted to tell you that brother G. C. Brewer was to my husband in many ways what brother Nichols has been to you. By the time of brother Brewer's death, he told me, he determined more than ever to fight the good fight of faith. He never swerved from that determination. I am persuaded that brother Nichols' death will affect you in the same way. And, I shall pray for you to that end."

Under the focus he called, "a word of hope," Brother Woodson completed his comments by drawing several parallels from the occasion in John 21 when Jesus fed his disciples, as being similar to what happens after life. Peter and the others had toiled all night to catch fish but failed. Jesus, at the dawn of the new day prepared food for them. They were all refreshed. Similarly, when the toil of this life is over, the Lord will have a feast prepared for all his people.

The Freed-Hardeman College Chorus followed with, "In The Sweet, By and By."

Brother Dutton then introduced B. C. Goodpasture. His words are as follows,

> We never know our limitations until we stand in the presence of death. Occasions like this remind us that the services we render are limited. They're in behalf of the living, rather than the dead. No word of ours can change the state of the dead. No word of mine can add peace to his ashes, or sweetness to his sleep. We are reminded by the things that have been read of the statement made by David concerning Abner. He said, "Know ye, that a prince and a great man has fallen in Israel today." I think those words very accurately describe our brother Nichols. He was a prince. He was a son of the King! He was a son of God Almighty—the eternal King.
>
> And not only that, he was a great man. On the ground that you recognize true greatness, he was great. He was great in the terms of the service he rendered. I think that this great audience is suggestive of the service he rendered—of the lives that he

touched for good. You know in St. Paul's there's a statement concerning the builder of the edifice, Sir Christopher Wren. If you would see his monument, look about you. And, if you would see the monument to brother Nichols, look about you. Look about the churches in this section of the state. Look about the lectureships of our colleges. And, look about the influence of our gospel preachers. Yes, he has erected a tremendous monument in that respect. We could call attention to that, but we can't call him back. We don't have the power that our Master had. On one occasion, you remember as He approached the little village of Nain. He met a funeral procession. It was exceedingly sad. The widow was carrying to the cemetery an only son. The father was dead. The son was dead. The family name would perish. It was an extremely heavy burden that this widow bore. Our Master caused the procession to pause. He restored the young man to life and to his mother and changed that funeral march into a procession of triumph.

Again, our Lord has spoken the words of life to Jairus' daughter and made happiness to dwell where sorrow had reigned. Our Master came into Bethany, where his friend Lazarus had laid lifeless for four days—dead. Our Master spoke to Lazarus, and he responded to his Master's summons. We have no such power as that now. We can only call attention to our Lord and His goodness—to what he does for his people. How he sympathizes with them, and how he helps them.

I like to think of brother Nichols in terms of a passage found in the 25th chapter of Genesis. It is a statement made concerning Abraham. We read that, "Abraham gave up the ghost, and died at a good old age, an old man and full of years, and was gathered unto his people." "He gave up the ghost." That means that body and spirit were separated. You know, James said, "the body without the spirit is dead." Man is a two-fold being. The inward man is a spirit being, and the outward man is material. As Solomon said in the twelfth chapter of Ecclesiastes, "when the dust returns to the earth, the spirit will return to God who gave it." Man is a two-fold being. And, so we read that, "Abraham gave up the ghost." That means that Abraham's spirit left his body—gave up the ghost and died. "The body without the spirit is dead." Death is the common lot of all men. We read that, "it is appointed unto man once to die, and after this the judgment." There have been and will be exceptions to that statement. But, that is the general truth. The general facts in reference to this matter, there were people who were raised from the dead. They died the second time, or else they are still living. There were exceptions to this statement that it is appointed unto man once to die. And, then again when the Lord comes the second time, Paul said, "we shall not all sleep, we shall not all die, but we shall be changed at a moment, in the twinkling of an eye." The last trump, when the Lord comes, they won't die. There are exceptions to the rule that it is appointed unto man once to die, but after this the judgment. So, we read that Abraham died, gave up the ghost, and died. The common lot of man. That is something we can't prevent. That's something we can prepare for. It is a part of wisdom for a man to prepare for that which he can't prevent. And, we believe that our beloved brother amply did that. We can't prevent death, but we can be prepared for it when it comes. Yes, "Abraham was an old man, gave up the ghost, and died. In a good old age." You know there is only one class of people that have a good old age. Only one! Some old men who lived in atheism, and agnosticism, and infidelity, have approached the end of life with terrible misgivings. One atheist said, "If I had an opportunity to live this life again as I have lived, or not to live at all, I'd select not to live at all." Another one said as he approached the end, though he was atheistic, he said, "Oh Lord, Oh God, but there is no God." But he said, "if there should be a God." And, that is the possibility that haunts the death couch of ever skeptic, of every agnostic. The thing he doesn't know may be the fact that Almighty God exists. He said, "If there should be a God, what will become of my poor soul?"

On the other hand, I like to think of Paul, the prisoner of the Lord. He was an old man in terms of the calendar—in terms of labors for Christ's sake—in terms of sacrifices and sufferings—in terms of spiritual growth and maturity. An old man in prison in Rome in the old Mamertine Jail–a dark and damp dungeon it was, with a sentence of death upon him. As we would say, he was on death row. And under those circumstances, "I have fought the good fight." Literally, I have fought for the good. Paul stood for something. Paul stood for truth and right. And those words are so reminiscent of brother Nichols. He stood for truth and right. He fought for the good. I have fought the good fight—fought for the good. So true of brother Nichols. "I have kept the faith." By the faith, of course, he means the teaching of Christ, the new covenant. There were two senses in which Paul kept the faith. In the first, Paul had kept it in the sense that he hadn't discarded any of it. He hadn't ceased to believe any of it. He hadn't rejected any of it, as some modern preachers have done. And, in the second place, Paul had kept it in the sense that he lived it. Yes, he debated. "Henceforth," he said, "there is laid up for me that crown of righteousness, which the Lord, the righteous judge, will give me in that day. And not unto me only, but all that love his appearing and His Kingdom." Paul was looking forward to a rich reward, was he not? And that reminds us again of the statement made concerning Abraham. "Abraham died in a good old age, and full of years, as an old man, and was gathered unto his people." I like that statement. He was gathered to his people. We read that Aaron died on Mt. Hor and was "gathered to his people." Now that doesn't mean that Abraham was buried where his father was buried. No doubt they were buried in the lower reaches of Mesopotamia. Abraham was buried in the cave of Machpelah. "Abraham was gathered to his people." What does that mean? That means that the spirit of Abraham was gathered to the company of his sainted dead. "Gathered unto his people." Isn't that a marvelous statement? I like to think of brother Nichols as being gathered unto his people, the people of God. I like to think of him meeting God's people on the other shore.

I like to think of what David said when his little child died. David, was in many respects, the greatest king Israel ever had. David had a little son. He became sick, and David fasted and prayed, and the child died. And after the child died, and David began ordering his life after the normal fashion. He took food and refreshed himself. And, his servants didn't seem to understand. They asked him why? He said, "While the child was sick and still alive, I thought God Almighty might spare him. But now," he said, "he is dead!" He said, "I cannot bring him back." There were many wonderful things David could do. David could play his harp so beautifully as to soothe the torn and distracted spirit of Saul. David could write psalms that would croon their message of comfort down through all succeeding generations. David could utter predictions that would be fulfilled a thousand years after he slept. And yet, he said, "I can't bring him back." "I can't do it." "I can't clothe his snow-white soul in the garments of mortality and bring him back to me." He said, "I can't do that." But, he said, "I can go to him." And, there the royal self found comfort. We can't bring brother Nichols back. But, thank God we can go to him. We can go to him. And, I believe brethren, that the reunion over yonder will be infinitely happier than the separation over here is sad. I believe that.

When John was on the loneliness of Patmos, he heard a voice. No doubt, John heard many voices. There was the ever present and noisy sea. There were the winds that swept the rocky isles.

There were other voices no doubt he heard. But, he said, "I heard a voice from heaven." The most authoritative of whom voices come. "I heard a voice from heaven saying, write." The message was too important to be entrusted to the memory of fallible man. It must be committed to writing. "I heard a voice from heaven saying, write!" Write! Preserve it! Humanity will need it! Write! "Blessed are the dead who die in the Lord." The word "blessed," means happy. You know it isn't often that inspiration draws aside the curtain and gives us a glimpse into the here-after. But, here, inspiration does. In the last book of the Bible, blessed are the dead—happy are the dead. We want our loved ones to be happy. Happy are the dead. Is brother Nichols happy? Happy are the dead who die in the Lord. "Yea, said the Spirit, they rest from their labors and their works do follow them." And, that was so true of brother Nichols. His work will follow him—his good work. A hundred years from now, you will be feeling the influence of his labors here. The world is better because he lived in it. We are all better because we knew him. God bless his memory. And, to the loved ones, I would commend you unto God, and the word of His grace, which is able to build you up, and give you the inheritance, among all them which are sanctified. God bless you![3]

At the close of the memorial service at the Sixth Avenue building, a long and slow procession made its way up Highway 5 toward the Walker Memory Gardens. Many stood as words of encouragement and prayer were offered by James A. Horton to console the grieving family. When the interment was complete, the Circle of Honor was covered with flowers all the way to the street.[4]

The golden life of Gus Nichols

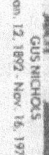

GUS NICHOLS
Jan. 12, 1892 – Nov. 16, 1975

Gus Nichols, a man of God who during his lifetime literally went from mudstock to superjet with the gospel, is dead at the age of 83.

A lengthy illness caused him to meet his Maker Sunday, Oct. 12, in the home he shared with his beloved wife, Matilda Frances Nichols, across the street from the Sixth Avenue Church of Christ. He founded the church in 1924, serving as its minister for 43 years.

His body will lie in state at the church until time of the funeral Wednesday at 2 p.m. Interment will be in the Fountain Garden in Walker Memory Gardens. Ministers of the Church of Christ conducting the service will be B.C. Goodpasture, W.A. Black and William Woodson.

Born in a log cabin near Carbon Hill Gus Nichols had little formal educational until later years. At the age of 12, he had to drop out of school to help support the growing family. His father William Calvin Nichols, "set him free" on his 16th birthday, and the next day he went back to school.

In his late 30's, with a wife and three children, he enrolled in Alabama Christian College, then located at Berry. Throughout his life he was a diligent student; he was an avid reader, accumulating a vast library.

In 1908, at the age of 17, Gus Nichols was baptized into Christ. He preached his first sermon in August, 1918, in a rural community schoolhouse. He supplemented his income by farming and working on a road mines. He often spoke of the hard 12 hours of work at $3 a day. The Nichols home was the first one destroyed by a tornado that swept through Carbon Hill May 27, 1917. Later he and his wife thanked God for that storm, for it had taught them not to trust in themselves, but to depend on God, who had "promised to make all things work together for good to his faithful children." Rom. 8:28. Subsequently he prayerfully resolved to preach fulltime. With his wife's encouragement: "Tho' I make a two-by-four preacher, but be a good one–the best you are capable of being," he went on to be just that.

He went by muleback, by wagon with his family beside him, by car, by train, and then by jet from coast to coast as well as over seas to preach the gospel.

The minister never sought controversy, yet in his later years, he received many honors due to his writings, recordings, lectures on college campuses and schools and evangelical campaigns.

Freed Hardeman College awarded him its 1975 award for outstanding contribution to its lectureships. He was awarded two doctor of law degrees, honorary, one by Magic Valley Christian College, Albion, Idaho (1964) and the other by Oklahoma Christian College, 1969. In 1971 and 1974 he was listed in "Personalities of the South," bearing American leaders. He is listed in the 1972 edition of "Who's Who in Alabama," and was twice commissioned an honorary lieutenant colonel aide-de-camp on the staff of Alabama Gov. George Wallace.

Pepperdine University at Los Angeles, Calif., awarded him its Christian Service Award in 1973. He received the Distinguished Service Award from Oklahoma Christian College in 1974 and a Distinguished Service Certificate in 1975 for the annual service to Blue Ridge Encampment. In 1969 Alabama Christian College at Montgomery, (on whose Board of Trustees he has served since 1956) honored him by naming its modern library "The Gus Nichols Library and Learning Center." In 1971 a library was named in his honor on the campus of Bethel Christian School, Anchipatki, India. A cottage for children at Childhaven, Cullman bears Gus Nichols' name in honor of his service as a member of the board of trustees since it began in 1949. A plaque was awarded for his encouragement and of her contributions toward the development of Indian Creek Youth Camp near Jasper.

Many of his sermons, lectures, debates, even poetry, have been published or are on cassette tapes. Two television films featuring him on "Herald of Truth" were seen nationwide and are seen in several cherished libraries. One is a filmed service of the Sixth Avenue Church of Christ as he preached and the other entitled "The Gus Nichols Story," depicts biographical events of his life.

In his later years, he contrast what he believed to be truth with error. He felt that such material is rubbed, the brother's

He preached the truth as he saw it on his daily radio program each morning beginning in 1961 although in the last few weeks others have taken up the task for his church. He made this program a most popular one in Walker County by mentioning illnesses, deaths births and items of general interest to his "high-born." For many years he wrote a column for the Mountain Eagle.

In addition to Jasper, he served congregations in Millport, Berry and Cordova, as well as small rural communities.

The work of Gus Nichols lives on in the work of others he has influenced. Three of his sons became fulltime ministers, and the fourth preaches part-time, three of his daughters married fulltime ministers, the other a Christian businessman. Four of his brothers became preachers and one grandson is a fulltime minister. Among his relatives (including in-laws) at least 30 became preachers of the gospel. For 43 years he conducted annual training classes from which have gone continual lines of leaders. Several dozen of men are now fulltime ministers due to his direct influence in their decisions.

Survivors include his wife of 62 years, Matilda Frances (Brown) Nichols, and their eight children: Mrs. Frank D. (Gracie) Young, Memphis, Tenn.; Mrs. A.J. (Audie) Kerr, Decatur Ill.; Flavil H. Nichols, Sumiton, Mrs. G. Ellis (Bertha Blackwood) Jasper; Mrs. W.T. (Carrie Hamilton Wasalberdo, Tex.; Foy W. Nichols, Indianapolis, Ind.; Hardeman Nichols, Fort Worth, Tex.; and Hudson Nichols, Gastonia, N.C. 15 grandchildren, six great-grandchildren; two sisters, Mrs. Will (Zilla) Windham, and Mrs. Paul R. (Hazy) Dodier, both of Jasper, three brothers, Archie Nichols, Birmingham, Perrie Nichols, Jackson, Miss., and Tim Nichols, Fayette.

Grandsons will be pallbearers.

The family suggests that memorials may be made to Sixth Avenue Church of Christ, Childhaven at Cullman, Christian Colleges or to Indian Creek Youth Camp.

Daily Mount Eagle: Report on the passing of brother Nichols

ENDNOTES

1 William Woodson, Audio recording of Gus Nichols' funeral, 19 November 1975.

2 Note: These comments came from an article that appeared in the *Gospel Advocate*, 3 August 1944, p. 508. The article was in praise for the way Gus Nichols conducted himself in his debate with C. J. Weaver in Huntsville. The words read in the funeral are included early in this book in chapter 27, entitled, "Rising To The Defense Of The Gospel."

3 B. C. Goodpasture, ed., "Gus Nichols Funeral Eulogy," *Gospel Advocate*, 19 November 1975.

4 Note: Some years previous, the owners of Walker County Memory Gardens built, in front of their offices, a Circle of Honor. It was intended as a group of plots designated for some of Walker County's most beloved citizens. A fountain was placed in the center of the section, and the plots of honor were placed there around it. When brother Nichols passed, the cemetery asked the Nichols family if they would allow them the honor of hosting the body of Gus Nichols as its first citizen to be interred in the Circle of Honor. The gift of four plots were accepted by the Nichols family. For over twenty-five years the circle only hosted the bodies of brother Nichols, and later sister Nichols. The children were given the opportunity to award the other two plots. It was decided that Flavil and Mary would have those plots. And, at the time of this writing, sister Mary Nichols is buried in the circle. When Flavil died, the 28th day of April 2018, he was the last of the four to be buried in the Nichols plot, between his mother and his wife.

- 53 -

Thank God For Brother Nichols

> Be ye followers of me, even as I also am of Christ. Now I praise you, brethren, that ye remember me in all things, and keep the ordinances, as I delivered them to you.
> —Paul, 1 Corinthians 11:1-2

From the cemetery, the family made their way back to the preacher's home at Sixth Avenue to relax, regroup, and discuss their plans for the future. At eighty-one years of age, Matilda Nichols had never lived alone. She left the home of her parents at the age of nineteen, and within two weeks of her husband's funeral, they would have celebrated their sixty-second wedding anniversary.

From this point on, life would take on a much different pace—a much different way of living. The first thing decided among the family was that their mom would not have to be alone. Within a few weeks, an apartment near the church building was rented. She wanted her independence, but most every night one of her children spent the night with her. For a time, she traveled around and stayed in the homes of children weeks at a time. This was always good and looked forward to by the family.

FREED-HARDEMAN LECTURES

The February gathering of the 1976 Freed-Hardeman Lectureship took on a new tone with the passing of Gus Nichols. The 7:30 a.m. slot that he had been conducting each morning passed to Franklin Camp, who had been at the 8:30 a.m. slot, now in newly built Loyd Auditorium. Chairman of the program, William Woodson, wrote a moving piece in the front of the lectureship book in memory of brother Nichols. He wrote, "It is most appropriate and very well deserved that the Lectureship and the Lectureship book of 1976 should be dedicated to this great servant of God."[1]

EXCELLENCE IN CHRISTIAN MASS COMMUNICATION EVANGELISM

At the end of February, Hardeman traveled to Abilene to receive a special presentation on behalf of his late father. The gathering on the campus of Abilene Christian University was the fourth annual Mass Communications Evangelism Symposium. At a special ceremony, on behalf of the ACU Center for the Study of Mass Communications Evangelism, Dr. Fred Barton, presented the first annual award for Excellence in Christian Mass Communication Evangelism to Gus Nichols.

The posthumous award accompanied a defining list of successes that few people could possibly attain. For instance, Dr. Barton noted that "counting his lectures, sermons, and radio broadcasts, Gus Nichols delivered about 900 sermons a year."[2] Further, he noted that the 83-year-old preacher from Jasper had not only ministered for the same congregation beginning in 1932 until his death, but he conducted two radio programs daily, organized and taught a preacher's training school for 42 years, wrote for "several religious journals," and spoke on several college lectureships each year, including the previous year on ACU's Lecture program.

GUS NICHOLS PAVILION

Brother Nichols was for many years a supporter of Indian Creek Youth Camp. Lying in the southern part of Walker County, just off old Highway 69, the camp had for several years been a blessing to summer youth campers and their families. Every year brother Nichols made his way out to the camp as often as possible to speak to the young campers. On September 15, 1976, at the gathering of the camp organizers, the main hall was formally dedicated.

In the summer previous to brother Nichols' passing, the organizers of the camp determined to have a walk-a-thon to raise money for a swimming pool and a pavilion. Ray Dutton organized the fund-raiser. The walk was to begin at the Sixth Avenue church building and end at the camp, seventeen miles to the south.

Levi Sides - Nichols Cottage
Childhaven, Cullman, Alabama

On May 3, 1975 the walk commenced. As the day progressed, rain set in, but it did not deter the walkers in the least. Bertha Blackwood drove her daddy down to the camp in the afternoon. As they drove past over a hundred walkers, she noticed tears flowing from the face of her sweet father as he thought about all those kids walking in the rain to raise money for the camp. Little did he know that a little over a year later, the pavilion they hoped to raise money for was complete and dedicated, the Gus Nichols Pavilion.

THE GUS NICHOLS MEMORIAL ISSUE OF THE GOSPEL ADVOCATE

The deep bond that existed between Gus Nichols and B. C. Goodpasture, the editor of the *Gospel Advocate*, has been demonstrated time and again in this volume. Yet, in the 25 March 1976 edition, the highest compliment the paper could make to the great preacher from Walker County, Alabama was to devote the entire issue to the person of Gus Nichols. With his picture indelibly placed upon the cover of the magazine, nine close friends and family sent in articles to pay tribute to a man who had given them and the brotherhood more than could be placed into words. Yet, they made a valiant effort. E. R. Brannon wrote on "Gus Nichols, The Man." Flavil Nichols (1919-2018) wrote, "Gus Nichols As A Father." Frank Pack (1916-1998) wrote, "Gus Nichols, a Great Man of God." Rex A. Turner (1913-2001) wrote, "Gus Nichols As I Knew Him." Malcolm L. Hill (1934-2012) wrote, "Gus Nichols As I Knew Him." W. A. Black (1904-1980) wrote, "Gus Nichols Was A Friend To All." Willard Collins (1915-2017) wrote, "Gus Nichols As A Friend." J. D. Thomas (1910-2004), under the title, "Gus Nichols," expressed briefly the impressions brother Nichols made on Abilene Christian College.

Gospel Advocate Gus Nichols Issue

INDIAN CREEK YOUTH CAMP HALL OF FAME

Thirty-seven years after the passing of brother Nichols, his spirit and contribution to Indian Creek Youth Camp continued to be recognized. Not only through the Gus Nichols Pavilion that still serves as a worship center for hundreds of campers each year, he was further recognized in a ceremony of induction into the camp's Hall of Fame. For generations to come, his name and his influence will continue to make its mark on the young people and camp leaders who work to make this successful camp program a blessing to the cause of Christ.

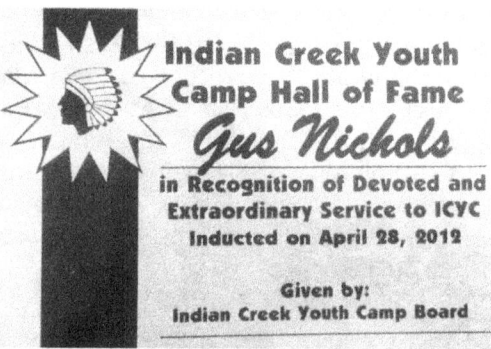

Indian Creek Hall of Fame

1976 - Open House - Nichols Library
Alabama Christian College, Montgomery, Alabama
Standing: Hardeman, Virginia, Vicki, Ray, Marilyn. Hudson, Bertha, Flavil, Mary
Seated: Joe and Matilda

THANK GOD FOR BROTHER NICHOLS

Thank God for brother Nichols! He has the truth to tell
When others are stumbling and stammering for words,
He's doing very well.
There are times when he is called upon to stand for that which is level,
And you can be sure of one thing:
He's always chasing the Devil!

Thank God for brother Nichols! He's converted many men!
And if you give him half a chance, you'll be included in!
He tells the story of Jesus the way it should be told;
He allows no addition or subtraction, therefore it never becomes old!

Thank God for brother Nichols! The orphan and poor he truly loves,
For he believes the Bible, and wants them too, to go above.
There are times when men accuse him of misguiding the BRETHREN;
But he knows the Lord will say in that great day,
"Gus Nichols, Come on in!"

Thank God for brother Nichols!
Very willing to the Lord he has given his life.
But, you know: perhaps he would not have made it,
if it had not been for his wife!
Truly Pearl of Pearls, and Gem of Gems, this Christian lady be!
For out of this family came four gospel preachers,
ready and willing also, you see!

"Yes!" Thank God for brother Nichols!
Great treasures and rewards are his yet to unfold,
All because this great man loved the Lord enough to save many precious
souls.
—Charles Crump (1938-2017)[3]

ENDNOTES

1 William Woodson, ed., *Freedom: Heritage, Accomplishments, and Prospects In Christ*, Freed-Hardeman College 1976 Lectures, Henderson: Freed-Hardeman College, 1976, p. 3.

2 "Gus Nichols Award At ACU," *The Christian Chronicle*, March 1976, p. 6.

3 Charles Crump, "Thank God For Brother Nichols," *Words of Truth*, Vol. 10, No. 18, 26 September 1975, p. 2.

Addendum #1
Time-line of Gus Nichols

November 23, 1890
Will and Lizzie Nichols marry – the parents of Gus Nichols.

January 12, 1892
Birth of Bunion Augustus "Gus" Nichols in a log cabin near Carbon Hill in Walker County, Alabama.

November 3, 1892
Charlie R. Nichols, the younger brother of Gus Nichols is born.

March 29, 1894
Birth of Matilda Francis Brown in Fayette County, Alabama.

December 18, 1896
Carey Columbus Nichols, the third child of Will and Lizzie Nichols born.

January 18, 1898
Zora Nichols, the fourth child of Will and Lizzie born.

1898
Christian Church founded in Jasper, Alabama.

May 10, 1900
Hazey Mae, fifth child of Will and Lizzie Nichols born.

February 22, 1903
Velma Virginia, sixth child of Will and Lizzie Nichols born.

January 23, 1906
William Archie, seventh child of Will and Lizzie Nichols born.

1908
Gus Nichols joins the Baptist Church at the age of 16.

February 16, 1908
Katie Ozella, eighth child of Will and Lizzie Nichols born.

August, 1909
Gus Nichols baptized by Charlie A. Wheeler in the creek at Iron Mountain Schoolhouse.

1910-1911
Two children of Will and Lizzie, Clarence & Troy die in infancy. (9th and 10th children)

January 12, 1912
Gus Nichols turns 20 years of age. His father sets him free to his own pursuits. Finishes 7th, 8th, and 9th grade classes within 6 weeks.

June, 1912
Alabama Christian College in Berry, Alabama opens under the direction of Gus A. Dunn (1876-1967) School continues until 1922.

October 18, 1912
Pervie Nichols is born, the youngest brother of Gus Nichols, the 11th child of Will & Lizzie Nichols.

November 30, 1913
Gus Nichols and Matilda Brown are married in her parent's home by Charlie A. Wheeler.

April 27, 1915
Gracie Nichols was born to Gus and Matilda. Their 1st child.

September 16, 1916
Vodie Nichols was born to Gus and Matilda, Their 2nd child. 2nd daughter.

December 16, 1916
Hubert Titus, the 12th and last child of Will and Lizzie is born.

May 27, 1917
Tornado destroys Gus and Matilda's home. He determines to devote himself to preaching.

June 10, 1917
Gus Nichols begins preaching at Iron Mountain Schoolhouse. Around this time registers for the U.S. Draft.

Late Summer, 1917
Matilda Brown Nichols is baptized by Charlie Wheeler in the creek at Iron Mountain Schoolhouse

February 2, 1919
Birth of Flavil Hall Nichols, 3rd child and 1st son of Gus and Matilda Nichols.

August, 1919
Gus Nichols enrolls as a student at Alabama Christian College in Berry, Alabama. Hal P. McDonald directing.

Addendum #1

October 1, 1920
Bertha Nichols Blackwood born. 4th child and 3rd daughter of Gus and Matilda Nichols.

August 16, 1921
Gus Nichols moderates for a debate the Charlie Wheeler has with D. B. Salter (Missionary Baptist) at Vernon, Alabama. Salter is later converted and becomes a gospel preacher.

June, 1922
Gus Nichols finishes his third year at Alabama Christian College, and with it the closing of the school.

March 11, 1923
Carrie Nichols is born. 5th child and 4th daughter of Gus and Matilda Nichols.

End of 1923
Gus Nichols reports 70 baptisms and 50 restorations for the year.

January, 1924 – December, 1926
The Nichols family sell the farm and move from Berry to Cordova, Alabama (35 miles).

Late Fall, 1924
Gus Nichols plants a congregation in the IOOF building at Jasper, Alabama.

January, 1926
The Nichols family moves to Millport, Alabama to begin mission work in Lamar County, Alabama and supported by three churches: Mt. Pleasant, Kingsville and Millport. Gus reports having preached 354 times and baptized 112 the previous year. Soon thereafter he begins a little paper called, *The Gospel Way*.

1926
Gus Nichols holds his first debate.

1926
A lot is purchased on Fifth Avenue and Fifteenth Street in Jasper for the purpose of building a church building.

October 15, 1926
Foy Wallace Nichols is born to Gus and Matilda. He is their 6th child and 2nd son.

March 16, 1928
Hardeman Nichols is born to Gus and Matilda. He is their 7th child and 3rd son.

End of 1928
Gus Nichols reports having completed two years of work in Lamar County. He regularly conducted five Bible classes a week. During 1928 he preached 336 times.

June 1929
Charlie Nichols debates Holiness preacher R. E. Higdon

End of 1929
Reports the preaching of 13 meetings, 310 sermons, 86 baptisms, and 184 discourses at mission points.

January 29, 1930
Willett Hudson Nichols is born. He is the 8th child and 4th son of Gus and Matilda.

1930
Has a meeting at Cordova with 53 baptisms.

July 3, 1930
Gus Nichols' first article appears in the pages of the *Gospel Advocate*.

January, 1933
The Nichols family moved to Jasper, Alabama to work with the Fifth Avenue church of Christ. He reports that during his seven years of living in Lamar County he preached over 2500 times and baptized more than 1000 souls, having baptized 228 in, 1932. The Jasper church had 20 members. They live there for the next 43 years.

1933
Nichols-Wright Debate —At the theater building in Dora, Alabama he debated a Church of God preacher named Alonzo Wright. Note: They met in three debates, one at Cordova and two at Dora in 1933.

Late 1933
Rex Turner, Sr., went and knocked on the door of Gus Nichols without so much as an invitation and asked Gus Nichols to teach him how to preach.

December 1933
Gus Nichols met E. Wright, of Dora, Ala., in three discussions — the first at Cordova and the last two at Dora.

Addendum #1

December 7-8, 1933
Gus Nichols debate with Rev. J. L. Scott, D.D., of Chattanooga, Tenn., at Carbon Hill, Ala. Discussed Holy Ghost baptism and signs and miracles.

June 7, 1934
Christian Chapel church of Christ begins in Lamar County. Gus Nichols given the honor of naming it. The church had been meeting since the work was planted by Nichols in the front yard of Golden and Ruby Curry in the mid-summer of 1928.

March 29, 1934
Gus Nichols met B. G. Dodd, Missionary Baptist, in a three nights' discussion, at Old Macedonia, on Black Water Creek, about ten miles out from Jasper. He affirmed the direct work of the Spirit in conversion, and salvation by faith in answer to prayer before baptism. Gus Nichols affirmed the possibility of apostasy.

May 13, 1934
Flavil Nichols preached his first sermon on the front porch of Walter Gurganus' home in Dovertown.

August 16, 1934
G. C. Brewer states in *Gospel Advocate* that there are 32 congregations in Walker County, Alabama. Preached the Fifth Avenue church of Christ summer gospel meetings in July 1934 and returns in 1935.

December 16, 1934
William Christopher Columbus Brown, father of Matilda, dies at Carbon Hill, Alabama. Buried at Pleasant Grove Cemetery.

Fall 1934
Gus Nichols begins Friday night classes at Fifth Avenue church of Christ to train men for the eldership and deaconship. The class is open to anyone in the area who wants to attend. Soon preachers from all over attend this Fall-Winter Class each year.

December 27, 1935
C. R. Nichol holds a debate with T. D. Dixon (Free-Will Baptist) – Gus Nichols serves as brother Nichol's moderator. Held at Boston, Alabama.

October 22-26, 1935
Gus Nichols meets R. E. Higdon (Holiness) in a four-day debate at Christian Chapel church of Christ in Lamar County, Alabama (Gus Nichols met Higdon 7 times).

November 1935
Gus Nichols co-edits a new brotherhood paper out of Birmingham, *Truth In Love*. Other editors include Gardner S. Hall, John D. Cox and Jack Meyer.

1936
Eldership appointed at Fifth Avenue church of Christ. Avery Fike, G.W. Hall, C. M. Karrh. R. W. Staggers came in a little later.

February, 1936
Gus Nichols releases "What Must I Do to be Saved?" - A 32 page tract: A sermon on the plan of salvation interesting and convincing.

Summer 1936
Gus Nichols meets B. C. Goodpasture who comes for a meeting at Fifth Avenue. Begins a life-long friendship. (Note: Goodpasture and his biographer later reflects that the meeting was 1934. However, it was in the summer of 1936.)

January 1937
Freed-Hardeman College begins Special Courses Session for three weeks. Gus Nichols did not speak at the first one, but within a year or so he is a regular speaker, and attends 39 sessions over the remainder of his life.

April 29, 1937
Charlie A. Wheeler dies. Gus Nichols preaches the funeral; burial in Dutton Hill Cemetery. Flavil Nichols is one of the pall bearers.

August 1938
While in a gospel meeting at Chisholm church of Christ in Montgomery, C. Leonard Johnson and Gus Nichols go to Kilby Prison and witness the electrocutions of two prisoners on Death Row. Writes a letter of the event to his family.

May 3, 1939
Gracie marries Frank Young. George W. DeHoff presides.

July 16, 1939
Vodie marries A. J. Kerr. Her father presides.

November 28, 1939
Flavil marries Mary Hardin. His father presides.

September 10-11, 1940
Debate between Gus Nichols and O. G. Lodge in Vinemont, Alabama. Lodge was from High Point, GA. He preached in the Church of God. Debate was on the New Testament Church.

January 14-23, 1941
Gus Nichols participates in F-HC Special Courses with a daily session called, "Query-Box Discussion." Met C. D. plum in a mock debate on the Operation of the Holy Spirit in the Christian. Gus Nichols took the negative. He also took the negative in another mock debate with B. L. Douthitt on "Essentiality of Baptism."

May 26, 1941
Gus Nichols conducts a six-nights debate with Mr. Glenn V. Tingley, or the "Christian Missionary Alliance." In debate at Oak Grove church of Christ, near Flat Creek, Alabama. Tingley affirmed the direct operation of the Spirit upon sinners in their conversion and that salvation is by faith alone before and without water baptism. Gus Nichols affirmed that water baptism is a condition of salvation or remission of sins to alien sinners. Two
night sessions and two hours to be given to each proposition.

January 1942
W. C. Graves purchases *Truth In Love* paper. Gus Nichols steps down as co-editor, but continues contributing articles.

January 15, 1942
Mock debate at F-HC Special Course on Premillennialism. E. R. Harper affirmed. Gus Nichols denied.

September 1942
Truth In Love sold to Marion Davis of Fayette, Alabama and Gus Nichols became editor of the paper.

June 1942
Gus Nichols conducts 4-night debate with O. G. Lodge (Holiness) at Bessemer, Alabama.

July 14-17, 1942
Gus Nichols conducts a debate with Charles V. Headrick (Baptist) at Lincoln church of Christ in Huntsville.

January 1943
Gus Nichols begins contributing weekly articles to local paper, *The Mountain Eagle*.

May 3-7, 1943
Gus Nichols begins debate with C. J. Weaver (Holiness) in Huntsville, Alabama. Four subjects. Probably his most known debate. Book is still in print.

March 6-9, 1944
Gus Nichols debates J. D. Holder (Primitive Baptist) at Tallasee, Alabama. Rex A. Turner moderates for Gus Nichols.

April 3-8, 1944
Gus Nichols speaks for the first time on the lecture program of Montgomery Bible College, in Montgomery, Alabama.

April 27, 1944
Gospel Advocate announces that Gus Nichols will become a staff writer for the paper.

June 22, 1944
Nichols-Weaver Debate goes on sale. Published by The Gospel Advocate Company, it sells out by the end of the year and enters its second printing.

August 1944
Fourteen-year-old, Hudson Nichols preaches his first sermon. Decides to be a preacher.

January 18, 1945
Gus Nichols appears the first time on the David Lipscomb Lectures.

September 18, 1945
Carrie Nichols marries W. T. Hamilton of Texas.

October 1, 1945
Paul Young is born to Gracie and Frank Young; the 1st grandchild of Gus and Matilda.

February 7, 1946
H. Leo Boles dies in his Nashville home. Gus Nichols surmises, "I reached the conclusion some years ago that Brother Boles was the greatest man known to me in all the brotherhood." (*Gospel Advocate*, 28 March, 1946, p.258)

July 30, 1946
Kathy Hamilton - Carrie and W. T. Hamilton's daughter is born; 2nd grandchild of Gus and Matilda.

Addendum #1

November 4, 1946
WWWB goes on the air in Jasper. The third hour of broadcasting began with the voice of Gus Nichols. He began "The Gospel Broadcast," thirty minutes a day, seven days a week with announcements, news, and preaching. The program continues to this day.

December 12, 1946
Bertha Nichols marries Rile Blackwood; her father presides.

January 27-31, 1947
Gus Nichols attends and appears on the David Lipscomb College Lectures in Nashville, Tennessee. Book is printed with his lecture on page 109 "Dangers Facing The Church."

February 24 – March 1, 1947
W. Curtis Porter meets Glenn V. Tingley in a debate in Birmingham. Gus Nichols moderates for Porter.

June 22, 1947
Eddie Nichols, Foy and Sarah Ann McCullough's 1st son; 3rd grandchild of Gus and Matilda was born.

July 11, 1948
Karen Nichols, Foy and Sarah Ann McCullough's 2nd child; 4th grandchild of Gus and Matilda is born. They later adopt and raise Eddie and Karen in their home.

August 5, 1948
Hardeman marries Virginia Montgomery.

End of 1948
Gus Nichols and the church at Fifth Avenue bind all the articles submitted to *The Daily Mountain Eagle* newspaper that year and begin selling it under the title "Sermons" by Gus Nichols. 66 sermons.

December 2, 1948
Gus Nichols becomes editor of the Queries Department at the *Gospel Advocate*, taking over from G. C. Brewer and a great line of great gospel preachers.

June 11, 1949
Gus Nichols "Nick" Hamilton is born to Carrie and W. T. Hamilton; Gus and Matilda's 5th grandchild is born.

Fall 1949
Gus Nichols becomes a founding board member of Childhaven Children's Home in Cullman, Alabama. Pervie Nichols baptized their father Calvin Nichols, into Christ, at the age of 82.

December 20, 1949
Janet Young is born to Gracie & Frank Young; Gus and Matilda's 6th grandchild is born.

End of 1949
Sermons by Gus Nichols - Vol. 2 – released.

May 15-19, 1950
D. L. Welch (Pentecostal Holiness) and Gus Nichols debate was conducted in Pensacola, Fla., May 15-19. (Gus Nichols met Welch as many as five different occasions.)

June 26-29, 1950
Gus Nichols debates Wes Busby (Pentecostal Holiness Church) under a large tent in Greenville, Mississippi. Pervie Nichols moderates for Gus Nichols.

July 29, 1950
Gus Nichols baptizes William Woodson.

September 11-15, 1950
Gus Nichols met Mr. J. D. Holder (Primitive Baptist) of Corinth, Miss., for the second time in a four nights' discussion. It took place in Medina, Tennessee. The crowd was so large they had to meet in a barn.

September 10, 1950
Judy, Hardeman and Virginia's 1st child, is born; Gus and Matilda's 7th grandchild.

End of 1950
Sermons By Gus Nichols And Others – volume released

September 11-14, 1950
Gus Nichols engages in a debate with J. D. Holder, Primitive Baptist, under a "pack shed" in Medina, Tennessee.

October 8, 1950
Hudson Nichols marries Marilyn Harwell.

February 6, 1951
Vicki, Rile and Bertha's 1st child, is born; Gus and Matilda's 8th grandchild.

Addendum #1

February 20-23, 1951
Gus Nichols met D. L. Welch (United Pentecostal Church). Held in the City Auditorium in Montgomery, Alabama.

May 3, 1951
Jimmy, Flavil and Mary's 1st child, is born; Gus and Matilda's 9th grandchild.

1951
John T. Lewis releases a 34-page tract called Childhaven, from a series of articles he wrote in the Ensley local paper. The name Gus Nichols is mentioned thirty-five times.

January 7-13, 1952
Gus Nichols met Frank Mullins for a four-night discussion on Premillennialism. First two nights in Gallatin. Second two nights in Nashville.

May 7, 1952
Beth, daughter of Hardeman and Virginia, is born; Gus and Matilda's 10th grandchild.

July 14, 1952
William Calvin Nichols, Gus' father dies and is buried at White's Chapel church of Christ. W. A. Black presiding.

September 16, 1952
Gus Nichols met D. L. Welch (United Pentecostal Church) in a debate in Bastrap, Louisiana.

November 9, 1952
Hudson and Marilyn Nichols lose a little boy in childbirth. He is buried at Oak Hill Cemetery, north of Jasper; Gus and Matilda's 11th grandchild.

December 8-12, 1952
Gus Nichols is the guest speaker at the second annual, Lectures on Preaching held at Abilene Christian College. Brought 10 lessons. Preached afternoon and evening from Monday to Friday.

December 15, 1952
Peggy, Flavil and Mary's daughter, is born; Gus and Matilda's 12th grandchild.

February 22, 1954
Velma Elizabeth "Lizzie" Nichols, the mother of Gus, dies and is buried by husband Calvin at White's Chapel. W. A. Black presiding.

October 7, 1954
The Nichols Brothers Publishing Company releases the *Nichols-Holder Debate*.

December 18, 1954
Sharon, daughter of Hudson and Marilyn, is born; Gus and Matilda's 13th grandchild. (Sharon died in a car accident in July 16, 1979.)

May 10, 1955
Gus Nichols' picture and biographical sketch appears in the 500 Club (turned in 500 subscriptions) - in the *Gospel Advocate Centennial Volume*.

December 13, 1955
Pam, A. J. and Vodie's daughter, is born; Gus and Matilda's 14th grandchild.

1956
A second 30-minute broadcast begins at noon on WARF radio in Jasper with area preachers doing the work, but primarily the work of Gus Nichols.

1956
Gus Nichols releases the volume, *Speaking The Truth In Love*, a 16-sermon series presented March 4-11 in Lamesa, Texas. Published by Nichols Brother Publishing Company.

July 21, 1957
Gus Nichols preaches the first sermon in the new Sixth Avenue church of Christ building.

Spring 1958
Lectures at David Lipscomb College, Gus Nichols lectures on "New Testament Principles For Caring For The Needy" – The Lecture was put in tract form by *Gospel Advocate* and sold for 15 cents a copy.

1958
Gus Nichols joined the Board of Trustees of Alabama Christian College. He served on this board the remainder of his life.

April 12, 1958
Broadcast of worship services of Sixth Avenue church of Christ on *Herald of Truth* national broadcast. America hears Gus Nichols preach.

Addendum #1

November, 1958
Gus Nichols met Mr. Ronald Sanders (Holiness) for a four-night debate at the church building of Sixth Ave. church of Christ. O. C. Lambert moderated for Gus Nichols.

April 14, 1959
Ray, Hudson and Marilyn's son, is born. Gus and Matilda's 15th grandchild.

December 8-11, 1959
G. K. Wallace and Charles A. Holt met in a debate in Florence, Alabama. Gus Nichols served as Wallace's moderator. The subject was Church Cooperation.

1960
Gus Nichols baptized Marvin Bryant. Bryant begins a ministry converting denominational preachers.

March 19, 1960
John, Rile and Bertha's son, is born; Gus and Matilda's 16th grandchild.

1961
Gus Nichols Sermon Outlines, Released, Nichols Brothers Publishing Company

March 2, 1961
"The Gus Nichols Story" series of articles released in *Gospel Advocate*. Interview with Gus Nichols about his family and work. Additional parts were released in the April 6th and April 20th issues.

June 1961
Gus and Matilda Nichols attend their first week of camp at Blue Ridge Encampment. Continued every year until 1975. Conducts an annual Q&A Session and lectures on various subjects.

Between 1961 and 1964
Gus Nichols debated Thomas G. O'Neal - Among the "anti-cooperation," and the "anti-orphan home" men with whom Gus Nichols discussed these issues were Irven Lee and Tom O'Neal, who moved into Walker County. When on their radio programs they presented (either in person or by tapes) such men as Yater Tant and A. C. Grider, Gus Nichols responded to them also. But with Lee and O'Neal he kept up a continual radio debate. For three weeks he and Thomas G. O'Neal discussed specific propositions, which debate was tape-recorded and is available on cassettes.

February 8, 1962
Gus Nichols Appreciation Dinner at F-HC. / In 1962, Gus Nichols filled in for Guy N. Woods at the Open Forum who had a conflict in his schedule, GA p.431, July 5, 1962. Tom L. Childers report, (Email correspondence – 12.10.2012)

May 5 – June 12, 1962
Gus, Matilda, Flavil and W. Gaddys Roy made a six-week tour of Europe and the Middle East at the expense of a loving brotherhood.

May 20, 1962
Gus Nichols preached a sermon in front of the assumed tomb of Christ from Philippians 3:10

October 2, 1962
Gus Nichols preached on Abilene Christian lectures to above 4,000.

January 1963
Gus Nichols begins editing *Words of Truth*

March 19, 1963
Gus Nichols speaks at the Elders and Preachers Dinner at the Pepperdine Spring Bible Lectures, on "Christ Our Contemporary In Keeping The Unity of the Spirit" in Friendship Hall – Presented the college's Christian Service Award.

April 24, 1963
Joe, Hudson and Marilyn Nichols' son, is born; Gus and Matilda's 17th grandchild and 16th to grow into maturity.

1964
Glenn Posey becomes associate minister of the Sixth Avenue church of Christ – serves in this role until 1968.

February 1964
Gus Nichols awarded the Doctor of Laws degree by George W. DeHoff, president of Magic Valley Christian College.

October 2, 1965
Jasper Bible School began a Saturday School – Franklin Camp, W. A. Black, Gus N., Douglas Harris, Glenn A. Posey, Paul Wylie, and Marlin Howard teaching – Free school at Sixth Ave. church of Christ.

1966
Great Preachers of Today, Volume IX was released – This volume represents a series of sermons written by Gus Nichols on the theme of

Addendum #1

The Great Commission, giving a full overview of the message of the Bible from the Existence of God to the life of the Christian as it relates to the Great Commission.

October 30 – November 3, 1966
Gus Nichols conducts a debate with Albert Batts (Church of God) – held at the City Auditorium in Anniston, Alabama. 500-800 in attendance each night.

November 1967
Gus Nichols debate with Albert Bates on Holy Spirit baptism and instrumental music.

1967
Lectures On The Holy Spirit released by Nichols Brothers Publishing Co.

1969
"The Gus Nichols Library and Learning Center" is dedicated on the campus of Alabama Christian College, and that evening Gus Nichols is awarded his second Doctor of Laws degree, this time from Oklahoma Christian College. Presented by President James O. Baird.

1971-1973
Gus Nichols conducted Gus Nichols Bible Workshop for preachers and Gulf Coast Bible Camp near Lucedale, Mississippi. After his death, the workshop was moved to Jasper, Alabama and merged with the *Words of Truth* Lectureship.

1971
The American Biographical Institute listed Gus Nichols in their book "Personalities of the South." Published in Raleigh, NC. A brief biography appears on page 422 in the 1971 volume. Also, presented in 1974.

June 1971
Distinguished Service Certificate is given to Gus Nichols for his annual service to Blue Ridge Encampment.

1972
Gus Nichols is listed in 1972 edition of "Who's Who in Alabama" page 299. Also, in 1972 a library was named in his honor on the campus of Bethel Christian School, Anakapalle, India.

July 17-20, 1973
Gus Nichols met Max R. King in a debate in Warren, Ohio, on A.D. 70 Doctrine. Gus Nichols' last debate.

1973
Flavil Nichols reported that the volume, *Nichols-King Debate,* was released.

August 7, 1973
At 7:00 p.m. – International Bible College in Florence, Alabama honors "Mrs. Nichols as a great and worthy woman." Speakers in order are: William Woodson, James Horton, Paul Wiley, Flavil Nichols, Hardeman Nichols, Alan Bryan.

February 22, 1974
Gus' brother, Carey Columbus, dies in Fayette County. Burial in Memorial Gardens, Fayette, Alabama.

1974
Gus Nichols receives the Distinguished Service Award from Oklahoma Christian College.

February 4, 1975
Freed-Hardeman College awards Gus Nichols its 1975 award for outstanding contribution to its lectureships. College President, E. Claude Gardner, says that in the lectureship Gus Nichols announced that it was his 39th visit to the FHC lectures. He came to the first one in 1937. E. C. gives him the title, "Man of the Book."

June 1975
Gus and Matilda attend the 25th Annual Blue Ridge Encampment. He speaks in the chapel service. B. C. Goodpasture honored that year for his years of service. The Nichols sit at the table with the Goodpastures, along with J. M. Powell, Mr. and Mrs. Jim Foster, and Mr. and Mrs. Archie Luper.

August 10, 1975
Sunday, Gus Nichols suffers the first of several Transient Ischemic Attacks "TIAs" or stroke-like symptoms that leaves his right side completely paralyzed and severely impairs his speech. Taken to hospital in Birmingham where surgery is performed and stays 25 days before returning home.

September 9, 1975
Gus' younger brother, Charlie, dies. Burial is in the Lone Oak church of Christ Cemetery, in Caledonia, Mississippi. Gus is unable to attend due to illness.

Addendum #1

September 19, 1975
Returns to hospital. This time he is diagnosed with pneumonia. Report in *The World Evangelist* that he had already received "countless prayers, hundreds of phone calls and more than 1,000 cards and letters."

November 16, 1975
Sunday - Gus Nichols dies in his home after a lengthy illness. Lies in state at 6th Ave. building until the funeral on Wednesday.

March, 1976
Posthumous award to Gus Nichols for Excellence in Christian Mass Communication Evangelism from Abilene Christian College. Dr. Barton said Gus Nichols spoke, including radio, lectures, preaching meetings, classes etc. 900 times per year.

October 6, 1991
Matilda Francis Brown Nichols dies.

UNAVAILABLE DATES

Nichols-Abercrombie Debate
Brother Cecil Abercrombie opposed Bible classes, uninspired literature, and women teachers. Gus Nichols and he engaged in several discussions. Among the first was at Kansas, Alabama and the last was at Piedmont, Alabama.

Nichols-Scott
At Carbon Hill, Alabama, he debated a Mr. Scott, PhD. of the Church of God with headquarters in Cleveland, Tennessee. This was the only Doctor of Philosopy he ever debated.

Nichols-Stewart
Another of his radio debates was with the local Nazarene preacher whose name was Stewart.

Nichols-Tallman
At the Brownsville Church of Christ, Pensacola, Florida, he met a member of the church, Dr. O. H. Tallman, Sr., who argued that all Christians are *baptized* with, or in the Holy Spirit.

Others
Gus Nichols debated a Church of God preacher with a Ph.D from Cleveland, Tennessee. The debate took place at Carbon Hill, Alabama. He debated a Baptist preacher named Brown at Woodbury, Tennessee, and two Mormon Elders at the Marion County Courthouse, Hamilton, Alabama. Other discussions included Catholics, Jehovah's Witnesses, 7th Day Adventists, Methodists, and Atheists.

Addendum #2
GUS NICHOLS: A GREAT MAN OF GOD

The following is a transcript version of a record produced by Freed-Hardeman College after the passing of Gus Nichols. It is comprised of excerpts of speeches made in the college Chapel the day after brother Nichols' death, November 17, 1975. Excerpts of the speeches include the college president at the time, E. Claude Gardner (1925-2017); the head of the Bible department, William Woodson (1931-2010); the head of the Mathematics department, Robert Witt (1912-1984); and the head of the Music department, Kelley B. Doyle (1925-2002).

Also, this record includes excerpts from the funeral of Gus Nichols held at the church building of the Jasper Church of Christ, November 19th, 1975. Excerpts of speeches included were that of Ray Dutton, associate minister of Gus Nichols at the time; W. A. Black (1904-1980), long-time friends and co-laborer; William Woodson, dear friend and son in the faith; and B. C. Goodpasture (1894-1977), editor of the *Gospel Advocate*, and dear friend to brother Nichols.

The record was 38 minutes and 35 seconds in length and narrated by William Woodson as follows,

> Lives of great men remind us
> we can make our lives sublime
> And on passing leave behind us
> footprints in the sands of time.

These words from a poet were often used by the late Gus Nichols, to encourage and admonish the development of a sterling Christian character. These words also serve to indicate something of the impact of this great man of God who lived and worked so faithfully in the cause of Christ.

In its beginning in 1937, the lectureship program at Freed-Hardeman College enjoyed the presences and the speaking of brother Gus Nichols. The 1976 lectureship is the first one since his beginning with us that he will not speak. Thousands of friends and brethren will miss him in our lectureship this year.

Freed-Hardeman College long enjoyed its association with this fine Christian gentleman, and with his beloved family. This year, as a tribute to him, we offer this recording of excerpts of comments made at Freed-Hardeman College and also presented at his funeral. In this series of excerpts, you will hear a tribute on the campus of Freed-Hardeman College on November 17. Brother Gus Nichols passed away on November 16th, the Lord's Day. The next morning, the chapel audience of the college, gathered for this tribute. Four men spoke in tribute to brother Nichols. The first was our esteemed president, E. Claude Gardiner." –Narrator

Since I first heard Gus Nichols, when he preached in a gospel meeting with the Henderson Church, when I was a student here in the early '40s, I have loved and appreciated him fully. I still recall his typewriter operating when he stayed in the guest room of Paul Gray Hall during that meeting. His sermons were so fervent and powerful, that they made such a deep impression on me, that I've tried to preach several of these sermons all through the years.

Many of his children, several of their spouses, and many of his grandchildren, attended Freed-Hardeman College. He has always been one of our staunchest supporters and counselors. As a preacher, he has had few equals. He has demonstrated the saying, "A rolling stone gathers no moss." Since 1933, he has preached for the Jasper church. He was in demand throughout the brotherhood until the very close of his life.

For many years he was one of our chief speakers and participants in the annual Bible Lectureship. He will be sorely missed. I have asked that for this year that we invite his sons and sons-in-law to speak in his 7:30 spot on the February Lectureship. His devotion for the college was expressed by him at the lectureship on February 4, this past year, or this past lectureship as follows. He said, "I could wish that we had many more wonderful schools like Freed-Hardeman College, that all of our schools were sound, and all of them as reliable as this model school has proved itself to be. You rarely ever hear of a gospel preacher going out from Freed-Hardeman College to be unsound. They are as sound as a dollar, as the old saying use to go, and we rejoice at the good work that is being done. I think Freed-Hardeman College is the model school in the brotherhood when it comes to soundness. And that the very attendance here at programs like this shows that it has the endorsement of the brotherhood in general. It shows that the people have confidence in Freed-Hardeman College."

Brother Gus Nichols was godly, wise, scholarly, faithful, good, successful, effective, powerful, influential, and in a word, a Christian. He has fallen, and younger men he has influenced, must pick up the armor and lead the battle for the Lord." —E. Claude Gardner

The next speaker at the Freed-Hardeman College tribute was William Woodson, chairman of the Bible Department.—Narrator

I spoke yesterday on the subject of *Things Which Make For Peace*. I believe that was an appropriate subject. I did not realize that my warm and good spiritual father, who baptized me in the Lord, had gone home. And yet I think it appropriate, that his passing occurred on the Lord's Day. And, I think it was something that I shall always rejoice in, that on the day of his passing, the greatest thoughts in my mind were concerned with the peace of God in the church of our Lord. We need that at this hour. He demonstrated to me in a way that perhaps no one else could have done the continuity of Christ's work on this earth, and that that work will always be done by his followers.

More than everything else, I knew Gus Nichols as one whose devotion to his cause knew no bounds and no restraints. I don't expect to meet anyone else in this life who will excel Gus Nichols in drive, imagination, or accomplishment. I thank God that I was privileged to know this man, a humble man, a man who could enjoy the presence and the counsels of the mighty, in both the political and the religious arena, and then in just a matter of a few moments, would gladly sit with pencil and pad in hand while a young preacher would perhaps preach his first sermon, would sally forth to proclaim his word.

Brother Roy Deaver said on one occasion, after he had had Brother Nichols to take many notes, he said, "Why do you take notes from me? You have known more in an hour than I will know in a lifetime." And Brother Nichols said, "Because my wife deserves a better husband than she's got. And I'm doing all I can to help her."—William Woodson

The next speaker, in the chapel service was Robert Witt, Chairman of our Mathematics Department and teacher of Bible.—Narrator

As far as I am concerned, I've lost one of my best friends. I've lost one of the most admired Christian men, beloved brother in Christ, and one of the best gospel preachers that I have ever heard. I would say in summary of brother Nichols life, that he certainly was a day and night servant of the Lord Jesus Christ. I heard that typewriter at 1:30 in the morning lots of times when he was typing out a new sermon. He was a constant-every-day servant of Jesus Christ for lo many, many decades of years of service.—Robert Witt.

The fourth speaker, in the chapel service was Kelley Doyle, Chairman of the Department of Music.—Narrator

Some quotes from brother Nichols, and I knew him, and appreciated him more as a song leader. That's a strange thing isn't it? But he used to say, "If its right to sing, its wrong not to learn how." Somehow I thought that was a good statement. And then, too, another statement from brother Nichols, I've heard him say when we get to heaven, there won't be a Lord's Supper, or preaching, or giving, but there will be singing in heaven. We will sing the song of Moses and the Lamb. Truly, a marvelous man, one that we appreciated so much, not a radical, not unreasonable, but a reasonable man. We'll miss him at the lectureship, because I think he served greatly in the sense of a balanced wheel. Keep things down on the ground, and running where they ought to run.—Kelley Doyle -28:30

Note: The Remainder of the record is taken from comments made at the funeral. These are detailed in chapter 52, *His Works Do Follow.*

Addendum #3

"He Walked Among The Mountains"
Robert R. Taylor, Jr.

Marvelous events of the Bible are frequently associated with majestic mountains. Noah's ark came to rest upon the mountains of Ararat (Gen. 8: 4.) The Decalogue was given from the summit of Sinai. (Ex. 20.) The mighty Moses breathed his final breath upon the peak of Pisgah. (Deut. 34.) Elijah met the proponents of Baalism upon the rugged beauties of Mt. Carmel (1 Kings 18.) The mighty prophet from Nazareth proclaimed the great sermon of Matthew 5, 6 and 7 upon the majestic mount possibly near the Sea of Galilee. Even earlier than this, our blessed Lord had been encouraged by Satan to fall before him and do him worship. This was upon an exceedingly high mountain. (Matt. 4: 8-10.) Upon a high mountain (possibly Mt. Hermon) our lovely Lord was transfigured before the "Inner Three." (Matt. 17.) The hill of Golgotha or the mount of Calvary was the place of his crucifixion. (Mark 15: 22; Luke 23: 33.) It was upon a Galilean mountain that Jesus gave the Great Commission. (Matt. 28: 16-20.) From the Mount of Olives he ascended back to the Palace of the Universe in Acts 1. By way of prophecy it was stated that the Lord's church would be established in the top of the mountains and its eloquent exaltation would ascend majestically above the hills. (Isa. 2: 1-3.) Acts 2 is the fulfillment of this precious promise, this powerful prophecy. Mountains therefore have an interesting and intimate connection with Bible events and Biblical personalities.

Just as mountains rise in splendor and majesty above the valleys, so the lives of a select few rise in splendor and majesty above the valleys where the multitudes congregate and live. It is no overstatement of fact to portray the late and lamented Gus Nichols as a majestic man who thrillingly treaded the mountains of spiritual greatness, of real eminence. We choose eight mountains which contained the useful presence of the noble Nichols as he tabernacled here for more than eighty-three years. This writer is among the great number who looked up to this marvelous man as he walked among the majestic mountains of Christian greatness.

The Mountain of Powerful Preaching

Brother Nichols was a man of manifold talents. He could do, and did do, many things well. He will be remembered for the books he authored, the hundreds of articles he penned, the personal and church related troubles he solved, the great family he led into vast areas of Christian fruitfulness and the numerous ones he befriended. But primarily and pre-eminently he was a preacher. He adorned the pulpit as a beautiful garment adorns a lovely Christian lady or a new suit adorns a handsome man. He fit the pulpit with dignity and delightful decorum. He was a Bible preacher. His sermons were saturated with Scripture. He preached Christ and him crucified. It is doubtful if any of his peers preached more sermons during the years from 1917 till 1975 than did Gus Nichols. The history of the church during the twentieth century cannot be written with a scholarly completion without telling the story of Gus Nichols and his wonderful work as a powerful preacher. He helped raise gospel preaching in this century to an exalted height. What a preacher he was in every sense of the term!

The Mountain of Steadfast Study

A devoted and dedicated life of steadfast study of the Sacred Scriptures paved the way for the great pulpiteer that brother Nichols became. From the very beginning of his life as a preacher in 1917, his faithful and godly companion freely took much of the family responsibility upon herself in order that he might be free to study. For about sixty years he studied about five hours per day. Truth to him was the pearl of great price. In the Bible he found an inexhaustible ocean filled with the precious water of abundant life. From the time the spiritual die was cast he never knew a day but that he panted after that life-giving water. He was a man of the Book. He lived by the Book. He pointed thousands of others to the beauties of the Book. He well earned the delightful designation that multitudes of brethren lovingly conferred upon him, "The Walking Bible." In him the Bible was personified; Christianity was eloquently exhibited in his patient pilgrimage through this life.

The Mountain of Saintly Service

A number of men go through life as servants but theirs is a service of a secular nature. Brother Nichols was a beautiful and benevolent man who served God, his family and his fellowman. The service he rendered so freely and sacrificially was performed as a saint of the most high God. He and sister Nichols spent a lifetime helping others. They fed the hungry, clothed the naked, took in the unfortunate, trained the young, consoled the sad and encouraged the despondent. Any benevolence done to the outward man was performed to open the door toward the rendering of a spiritual service. Jesus taught that the greatest will be servants. Brother Nichols was a man who served God and others before he slept the sleep of the sainted dead. Only eternity will reveal the vast number of spiritual services this humble man of God rendered to countless others. He was a spiritual multimillionaire in the good works laid to his abounding account. One of his great sermons through the years was on true riches. (Luke 16:11.) He was rich in the true sense of the term.

The Mountain of Courageous Controversy

"Soldiers of Christ, Arise!" found an eloquent exhibition and a positive personification in the courageous life of the noble Nichols. He was a militant warrior for right and truth. Like a massive mountain, the winds of error could not sway him from his stationary posture of sobriety, righteousness and godliness. He met many of the formidable foes of denominational error. Each one of them knew he had met a powerful man upon the polemic platform of honorable controversy. He was a successful debater himself and taught others to be of similar caliber. He feared no man because he went forth confidently with the Bible in his hand and truth upon his heart. Victory for truth—not self—was the only honorable reward he coveted in these verbal conflicts with the proponents of error. Brother Nichols knew how to battle for truth without becoming an aimless agitator. A valiant warrior in controversy he was; an agitator he was not. His opponents respected him. People loved him who differed with him religiously.

The Mountain of Family Faithfulness

Brother Nichols did some of his greatest work in the fervency of the family framework. He and Sister Nichols have produced one of the great families in the entire history of Christianity. The many in the family who preach, the women in the family who are married to preachers and the devotion to Christ that permeates the Nichols family are some of the most refreshing portraits of current home-life in an era that has majored in broken marriages, broken homes, broken lives and handicapped children. Christ reproduced in the family framework was the godly goal of brother and sister Nichols. A great and godly family rises up as a thrilling testimonial to the peaks of success they reached in this worthwhile endeavor. Hudson, his youngest son, said of his father many years ago, "If there are only two men in heaven, I believe my father will be one of them." What a beautiful tribute to lay at the feet of one's father.

The Mountain of Prolific Penmanship

Brother Nichols wielded a powerful pen. This is seen in the books he capably authored. It is seen in the Query Department for the *Gospel Advocate* that he edited for many years. He served as a distinguished staff member of the "Old Reliable" for a number of years. It is seen in the hundreds of great editorials he wrote for *Words of Truth*. He was a Biblical penman. His articles, like his stately sermons, were book, chapter and verse productions.

Scriptural logic flowed freely and gracefully as his pen touched the great themes of the Bible. His writings on "Generic and Specific Authority" were masterpieces of keen Scriptural analysis. What a great loss it would have been to all of us if he had never treaded on the mountain of religious journalism. His writings will live on and on. His pen was sharp and decisive for truth; it was deadly and destructive against any and all wrong, sin and isms of the day.

The Mountain of Heavenly Hope

Brother Nichols was a man with a mission. He was a stranger and pilgrim on earth. This world was not the real home he sought. It was simply the realm of a temporary sojourn, the place for his preparation for an eternal home. He was a man with heaven on his mind. This writer knows of no one who wanted to go to heaven any more deeply than did the Sage of Jasper. His sermons on heaven would bring freely flowing tears to his eyes and also to the eyes of his avid hearers. He spoke about heaven as one who stood upon its threshold. In full emulation of what Christ spoke in John 14:1-3, the noble Nichols believed in Jehovah God, in Christ and in the heavenly hereafter. These were the intense imperatives of his fervent faith.

The Mounts of Scriptural Similitudes

A similitude is a likeness or a comparison. Brother Nichols loved the Bible so deeply and lived so closely with its great characters that he became like them in his life. Like Abel he being dead yet speaketh. Like Enoch and Noah he walked with God. Like Abraham he taught his family to keep the commandments of the Lord. Like the Father of the Faithful he looked for a city "which hath foundations, whose builder and maker is God," (Heb. 11:10). Like Joseph he was a person of moral purity. Like Moses he was a powerful leader of men. Like Samuel he taught us what we should know and never ceased to pray for Jehovah's people. Like Joshua he was a conqueror and one who determined that he and his family would serve the Lord. Like the youthful David he sought to be a man after God's own heart. Like Isaiah he was stately as a man, as Jehovah's servant. Like Jeremiah he was sensitive of soul. Like Nehemiah he was a builder of walls—walls to keep truth in and error out. Like John the Baptist he was a great preacher and baptized multitudes. The number immersed by him stood in excess of twelve thousand. Like Jesus he loved righteousness and hated iniquity. Like the blessed Lord whom he loved so deeply and served so faithfully his meat was to do God's will. Like Peter he preached Christ. Like Paul he preached the whole counsel of God. Like the great apostle to the Gentiles he sought to know nothing save Christ and Him crucified. Like the apostle John he was surely a modern disciple whom Jesus loved. Like Timothy was charged to do, brother Nichols preached the word in season and out of season. Like Paul summed up his life in the old Mamertine Prison in Rome, brother Nichols could sum up his life and say he, too, had fought the good fight, he had kept the faith and he had finished the course. Like the Bible he loved, lived, preached and defended the force of his life was for the good and in absolute opposition to the wrong.

Conclusion

We cannot and would not bring him back though we miss him so much. If we are obedient to the faith till the end as we believe he was, then the separation from him and our other Christian loved ones is short and temporary. We look forward to clasping his hand on the shores of eternity where the redeemed will never know separation again.

Thank God brother Nichols lived. Both a prince and a great man has left our midst. What a priceless heritage he left us. What a noble imprint he left upon the mountains he treaded so nobly and courageously. Let us light the torch of truth he bequeathed us and never let it touch ground until we too pass from earthly scenes. That would be his wish for us; it should be our holy resolve. When the noble Nichols departed from this life he left a vast lonesome place across the sky. The mountains had lost a real man, a mighty man.[1]

ENDNOTES

[1] Robert R. Taylor, Jr., "He Walked Among The Mountains," *Gospel Advocate*, 18 December 1975, pp. 810, 815-17. Used by permission.

Addendum #4

Brother Nichols
Franklin Camp (1915-1991)

Does this seem to be a strange way to head an article in tribute to brother Nichols? I considered several ways to head the article, but I could not think of anything more appropriate. Brother Nichols was a man of varied and unusual abilities and I appreciated all of them, but when I thought of him, I always thought of him as "brother Nichols." This is one of the reasons that he was a great man. All the notoriety which he received never changed him from being "brother Nichols." It was my privilege to know him for forty years. He was "brother Nichols" the first time I met him, and he was still "brother Nichols" the last time I visited him while he was in the hospital. He was a living demonstration of Matthew 18:4, "Whosoever therefore shall humble himself as this little child, the same is greatest in the kingdom of heaven."

Brother Nichols was able to combine dignity and Christian humility as much as any man I ever knew. One never saw him without seeing in him Christian dignity at its best. When he walked into the pulpit, one could sense the dignity that separated him from people whose minds and hearts were centered on worldly things. When he opened his mouth to speak, one could immediately recognize his humility because of his unusual appreciation of the greatness and the majesty of God. His recognition of God's greatness made him humble and brother Nichols' humility made him great.

I recall vividly the first time I ever saw brother Nichols. It was the third Sunday of August 1935. He came to Munford, Alabama for a meeting. The first service began at 11:00 A.M. At about two minutes before eleven, he walked through the door and down to the front of the building. Only one person in Munford had ever heard him preach before this time. When the first service was over, those who had never heard before realized that they had been privileged to hear one of the great preachers of all time. The meeting lasted two full weeks with services twice each day. The crowds grew; the house ran over; people were standing; children were sitting around the rostrum and people were outside listening through opened windows. Thirty-seven people obeyed the gospel during the meeting. He stayed in our home and a friendship began which was to grow through a period of forty years.

I had preached my first sermon about three months before I met brother Nichols. My early association with him had a tremendous effect on me. I have learned many valuable lessons from him but the most important lesson he taught me was the importance of dedicated Bible study. In the first meeting where I heard him, he stated that he had studied the Bible five hours a day for twenty years. I realized that if a man like him needed to study five hours a day, I'd need to study even more.

I am grateful to God for having had the privilege of working with brother Nichols in a number of ways. The association and various endeavors gave me the opportunity to come under his influence more than it would have been possible otherwise. He preached in meetings where I worked and stayed in our home. This association was truly rich in every way. I had the opportunity to work with him in three meetings in Jasper. I preached in the first meeting in their new building and I helped in several Vacation Bible Schools in Jasper. I taught in the Saturday Bible School that he conducted in Jasper. I talked to him about serving on the Board of Alabama Christian College and he agreed to do so. I placed his name before the Board of Alabama Christian College to be considered as a member of the Board. I served with him on the Board for about fifteen years. The opportunity of being with him in all these ways gave me a chance to know him well and to recognize what an unusual man he was. No two people are alike, but brother Nichols was different in more outstanding ways than any man I had ever known.

When one considers the humble circumstances, which surrounded brother Nichol's early life, he is amazed at the heights which he attained. His formal education was limited, but his knowledge was abundant. He had more information in his mind that could be recalled at a moment's notice than any man that I've ever known. He knew more about different subjects than anyone I ever talked to. He knew the Bible, but he also knew other subjects just as well. He could talk about any subject one wanted to discuss just as well as he could discuss the Bible. He was acquainted with false doctrine of every kind and had a Bible answer for every one. He told me on one occasion that he could preach three thousand sermons without opening his Bible. I expect that is more sermons than most preachers could preach with notes.

Most of us have a potential we never reach. There are times that we do our best, but not always. In all the years that I knew brother Nichols, he was always at his best. It is my judgment that if he had his life to live over, he could not do any better. He is one man that I believe reached his potential. I never heard him preach a sermon when he did not preach to the very best of his ability. It is my firm conviction that he was the best preacher that is was possible for him to be. He was the best husband, the best father, and the best Christian that he could be. He did his best at whatever he did. He believed the admonition of Ecclesiastes 9:10, and put it into practice every day. "Whatsoever thy hand findeth to do, do it with thy might; for there is no work, nor device, nor knowledge, nor wisdom, in the grave, whither thou goest." If there are any that stand before God at the judgment, having reached their potential, brother Nichols will be among that number.

Brother Nichols was a man of the Book. The mention of his name would immediately remind one of the Bible. His love for the Bible and for truth was without equal. His favorite subject for discussion was the Bible. Some of the most pleasant and profitable hours of my life was spent in talking with him about the wonders of the Bible. The last time I was with him was when I visited him in the hospital here in Birmingham and practically all the time was spent in talking about the Scriptures. When I went into the room to visit with him, Gracie was sitting beside the bed taking notes on a sermon that he planned to preach when he got out of the hospital. Gracie left us to talk for a little while. While she was gone, brother Nichols went over the sermon with me; in fact, he preached the sermon to me. When he had finished preaching his sermon to me, he asked me what I had preached on the day before. He asked me to preach my two sermons to him. I had preached at Adamsville the Sunday prior to my visit with him and so I gave him the gist of the sermons which I had discussed. This is but a sample of his interest in the Bible. It was the one book that he was interested in more than anything else in life. It was the one book that he knew above every other book because his mind and heart was so full of it, it flowed from his mouth in a fluent way. It made no difference whether it was in the pulpit or riding in a car or visiting in the home, the Bible came from his lips.

I recall brother W. A. Black telling me of an incident when he and brother Nichols were returning from the David Lipscomb College Lectures. They picked up a man along the road and after a while the man asked brother Nichols what he did and brother Nichols said, "I preach." The man said, "What else do you do?" Brother Nichols said, "That's all I do. I preach." The man evidently had little knowledge and understanding of what is involved in preaching and especially a preacher being supported full time. Finally, brother Black handed the man the Bible and said, "Turn anywhere you want to and read one verse and let him quote the next verse." The man started thumbing through the Bible, reading a verse, and brother Nichols would quote the verse before and the verse after. This was done for quite some time and finally the man said, "I guess it's all right for the church to support a man like you to preach full time."

I also recall another conversation I had with brother Nichols which indicates his deep interest and dedication to the study of the Bible. He told me that whenever a question came up that he did not know the answer to, that he never closed his eyes in sleep until he had found the Bible answer to it. Few men that I have known in my life, were that determined to know God's will. I think this is one of the reasons that he was such an outstanding man. He was determined to find out what God wanted done and he was determined to do it to the very best of his ability. It is my firm conviction that if someone could have taken the Bible and convinced brother Nichols that in order to go to heaven, it would be necessary for him to walk around the world, he would have started that very day walking around the world. That is how determined he was to do what was right, to please God, and to go to heaven when he died.

There has been only one perfect man who has ever walked upon this earth and that man was Jesus Christ. He did not believe that perfection was simply an ideal to be thought about, but an ideal to strive toward. Every day of his life was spent in striving toward being a better person. He realized that one did not reach perfection here, yet this did not keep him from striving with might and main to reach onward and upward for perfection. Every day that he lived was a day dedicated to being better than he was the day before. Of all the men I have ever known in my life, brother Nichols was the best man that I have ever known. I have never known a man who had a more balanced life, whose life was characterized by more of the principles of the gospel than brother Nichols. It was not by accident that he was this kind of man. He was this kind of man because of his love for God, his love for truth, his determination to know the will of God, and his willingness to do what God wanted done, regardless of what the price might have been. Brother Nichols, like all of us, was interested in what others thought about him. But above all, he was concerned more with pleasing God. If he could please men and please God at the same time, he was happy. But if he could not please men and at the same time please God, he was determined to please God and let men think and do whatever they might.

Brother Nichols was a man of deep conviction. I believe that he would have given up life itself rather than sacrifice his convictions. Sometime when men have strong convictions, they have difficulty in being able to get along with other people. There are occasions when men have strong convictions that these convictions reach over into the realm of matters of judgment and expediency. Brother Nichols was a man who had deep convictions, but he also was a man of great wisdom. He had the ability to distinguish between things that were matters of faith and things that were matters of judgment. When it came to a matter of faith, he would stand like a stone wall. When it came to a matter of judgment, he was willing to lay aside his own personal preference for the sake of his brethren, peace, and unity. This is one of the ways where brother Nichols will be missed in the years that lie ahead. We are facing some difficult times in the church. There is a need for men with convictions such as brother Nichols had who will not sacrifice principles of faith upon the altar of the plaudits of the world. Yet at the same time there is a need for the wisdom that he had, to be able to distinguish in the areas of judgment and to know when to allow one's preference for a thing to be laid aside for the sake of peace and unity among brethren. We need to be careful in our struggle against modernism that has invaded the church to be sure that we do not allow matters of judgment to cause us to classify men as modernists who may differ with us in judgment. Brother Nichols was able to distinguish between a matter of faith and a matter of judgment. One could differ with him in a matter of judgment without there being any problem at all. It is my prayer that not only his stand for truth will continue to influence those of us who are left behind, but the wisdom that he used to distinguish between things that differ, and to walk hand in hand with loving hearts with those who may differ in matters of judgment.

Brother Nichols was one of the most unselfish men that I have ever known. Sometimes preachers can be about as selfish as anyone. With all the influence, the opportunities, and the prestige that brother Nichols attained as a preacher of the gospel, he continued to be a simple Christian and unselfish at heart. He did not believe that the accomplishment of others in any way detracted from the good he did in the kingdom of God. He rejoiced at the good that any could do. It made no difference whether they were small or great. One of the greatest inspirations a preacher could have was for brother Nichols to be in the audience. I have never known but one other man who was as good a listener as brother Nichols and that was my father. To have these two men in an audience was enough to make anyone preach his heart out. I recall the first meeting I preached in at Jasper. I agreed to go to the meeting with hesitation. I knew how great a preacher brother Nichols was. I knew my own limitations and I wondered what it would be like for me to be in the pulpit and brother Nichols in the audience. I remember the meeting well. There was some anxiety at the first service and the first sermon that I preached, but by the time the service was over, all anxiety had gone. Watching him as he listened was enough to make anyone forget about any problem of preaching with brother Nichols in the audience.

I recall another incident which is a manifestation of the unselfishness of brother Nichols. J. O. Jones was preaching at Clarksville, Tennessee. He was moving to Homewood, Alabama. The church in Clarksville was looking for a preacher. Brother Nichols was in a meeting in Clarksville. I received a call one night from brother Nichols. He said, "The church in Clarksville is looking for a preacher and I have recommended you for the work." He requested that I come up and speak for the church in Clarksville. I told him that I couldn't come that week but I would be glad to come the next week. The following week I went to Clarksville. Brother Nichols was still preaching in the meeting. I preached what is sometimes called a "trial" sermon in the middle of the meeting. I have often thought that that was one of the most unusual things I have ever done in my life—preach a sermon and be considered for a work in the midst of a gospel meeting that brother Nichols was preaching in. This indicates how unselfish he was. He was interested in every preacher doing his very best and anything he could do to encourage him, he was more than ready to do it.

This world is a better world because brother Nichols has lived in it. The state of Alabama, as well as the brotherhood in general, would indeed have been poorer spiritually had it not been for the life and the work of brother Nichols. The brotherhood in general and the state of Alabama in particular owe far more to this man than many will ever realize. Perhaps not until we stand before God in the judgment will we really appreciate and understand how much he has meant to the church in this area. He will truly be missed. Heaven will be a better place just because brother Nichols will be there. His smile, his enthusiasm and his joy will go with him into that world where joys are forevermore and where pleasures overflow. Brother Nichols lived life to its very fullest here on the earth and what a joy it will be for him to have the fullness of the joys that are provided in that world that lies beyond. He made the world brighter wherever he went. I believe that even heaven will be brighter just because brother Nichols will be among the redeemed.

Brother Nichols had a power in preaching that few men had. I have heard him preach through forty years. I have heard him on lecture programs. I have heard him in meetings. I have heard him at funerals. I have heard him preach in almost all the circumstances that one can conceive of. One of the unusual things about brother Nichol's preaching was his ability to preach in such a way as to make people want to be better. I have never heard him preach a sermon or speak on a lecture program but what he said made me want to live better. I know of no other man whose preaching had as much influence on me as that of brother Nichols. He understood fully the purpose of preaching. When he walked into the pulpit, it was his desire to lead men to hate evil and love righteousness. It is my conviction that he was more successful in doing this than any one I ever heard preach. Eternity alone will tell of the sins forsaken and righteous principles followed that resulted from his preaching.[1]

ENDNOTE

1 Franklin Camp, "Brother Nichols," *The Word Of Life*, Volume 5, Number 1, January 1976, pp. 1-3.

Bibliography

Alabama Christian Reporter, Montgomery: Alabama Christian College.

Armes, Ethel, *The Story Of Coal And Iron In Alabama*, Birmingham: The Chamber of Commerce, 1910.

Baxter, Batsell Barrett, and M. Norvel Young, eds., *Preachers of Today*, Vol. 1 & 2, Nashville: The Christian Press, 1952.

Boles, Leo Lipscomb and J. E. Choate, *I'll Stand On The Rock: A Biography of H. Leo Boles,* Nashville: The *Gospel Advocate Co.*, 1965.

Beattie, George William and Helen Pruitt Beattie, *Filson Club History Quarterlies*, "Pioneer Linns of Kentucky" Vol. 20, April 1946, Louisville, Ky.

Brewer, G. C., *Forty Years On The Firing Line*, Kansas City: Old Paths Book Club, 1948.

Bradfield, W. A., *Freed-Hardeman Alumnograms*, Henderson: Freed-Hardeman College.

Castleberry, Ottis L., *He Looked For A City*: A Biography of John T. Lewis, Fairmount: Cogdill Foundation Publications, 1980.

Choate, J. E., *The Anchor That Holds*: A Biography of Benton Cordell Goodpasture, Nashville: *Gospel Advocate* Publishing Co., 1971.

Claiborne, Winfred, ed. *1990 Freed-Hardeman College Lectureship*, "Honor Thy Parents: Some Things I Learned From My Father, The Late Gus Nichols," by Flavil H. Nichols, Nashville: 1990.

Cogdill, Roy, *The Arlington Meeting*, Orlando: Cogdill Foundation, 1969.

Cox, John D., *A Word Fitly Spoken*, Nashville: *Gospel Advocate* Co., 1962.

Coil, Charles, Harding College Bible Lectures 1961, Austin: *Firm Foundation* Pub. Co., 1961.

DeHoff, George W., *I See My Time Is Up*, Murfreesboro: DeHoff Pub. Co., 1989.

Erwin, Andrew D., *You've Been A Good Brother, Willie: The Life And Sermons Of W. A. Bradfield*, Delight, AR: Gospel Light Pub., 2011.

Fike, Avery, "A Brief History of the Fifth Avenue Church of Christ," Unpublished paper read at the mortgage burning of the Fifth Avenue church of Christ, Vertical Files, Genealogy Room, Carl Elliott Library, Jasper, Alabama. No Date.

Bibliography

Gurganus, V. Q., *A Brief History on the Cordova Church of Christ*, Upright Files in the Genealogy Room at Carl Elliott Regional Library, Unpublished.

Goodpasture, B. C., editor and president, *Gospel Advocate*, Nashville: Gospel Advocate Co.

Lambert, Gussie, *In Memoriam*, Shreveport: Gussie Lambert, Pub., 1988.

Lewis, John T., *Childhaven*, Birmingham: Star Pub. Co.

Lipscomb, David, ed., *Gospel Advocate*, Nashville: Gospel Advocate Company.

McGary, Austin, ed., *Firm Foundation*, Austin: Austin McGary.

Nichols, Aubrine A. and Dessie Ree Nichols, *Will and Lizzie Nichols Family Roster*, Unpublished document, 1995.

Nichols, Gus & C. J. Weaver, *Nichols-Weaver Debate*. Nashville: *Gospel Advocate* Co., 1944.

Nichols, Gus, *Sermons*, Jasper: Mountain Eagle Pub. Co., 1948.

---*Sermons by Gus Nichols and Others*, Mountain Eagle Publishing Company, 1949.

---*Sermons by Gus Nichols*, Volume 3, Jasper: Mountain Eagle Publishing Company, 1950.

---*Speaking The Truth In Love*, Chattanooga: Nichols Brothers Publishing Company, 1956.

---*Sermon Outlines by Gus Nichols*, Jasper: Nichols Brothers Publishing Company, 1961.

Overton, Basil, *The World Evangelist*, Florence: World Evangelist.

Patterson, Noble and Terry J. Gardner, Foy E. Wallace, Jr., *Soldier of the Cross*, Fort Worth: Wallace Memorial Fund, 1999.

Phone conversation with Glenn Posey, 02 November 2009.

Phone conversation with Flavil Nichols, 22 March 2011.

Phone conversation with James A. Horton, 02 February 2016.

Plyler, A. M., *Historical Sketches of the Churches of Christ In Alabama*, Henderson: Hester Pub., No Date.

Porter, W. Curtis and Glenn V. Tingley, *Porter-Tingley Debate*, Murfreesboro: DeHoff Publications, 1947.

Powell, James Marvin and Mary Nell Hardeman Powers, *NBH: A Biography of Nicholas Brodie Hardeman*, Nashville: Gospel Advocate Company, 1964.

Showalter, G. H. P., *Firm Foundation*, Austin: *Firm Foundation*, n.d.

Stone, Barton W. And John T. Johnson, *Christian Messenger*, 1832, Georgetown: L. N. Finnell at The Sentinal Office, Reprinted Fort Worth: Alvin Jennings, Star Bible, Dec. 1978.

The Heritage of Lamar County, Heritage of Alabama Series, Heritage Publishing Consultants, 2000.

Thomas, J. D., editor, *Great Preachers of Today—Sermons of Gus Nichols*, Abilene: Biblical Research Press, 1966.

Turner, Rex A., ed., *Sound Doctrine*.

Williams, Jennifer, reporter, "Words of Truth," *Daily Mountain Eagle*, (Jasper) August 4, 2008.

Whitehead, Larry, ed., *Alabama Restoration Journal*, Russellville: Clay Pub. Co., n.d.

Woodson, William, *The Restoration Movement And Unity, Freed-Hardeman College, Preachers And Church Leaders Forum, October 12, 1985*, Henderson: Freed-Hardeman College, 1986.

Underwood, Maude Jones, *C. R. Nichol: A Preacher Of Righteousness*, Clifton: Nichol Pub. Co., 1952.

Unpublished historical data on the history of the "The Church" in Jasper, in the Upright Files, Genealogy Room, Carl Elliott Library, Jasper, Alabama. n.d.

United States Census Records, 1870, Perry County, Alabama.

Wallace, Jr. Foy E., ed., *The Bible Banner*, Guthrie: Oklahoma Printing Co.

Woods, Guy N., *Questions And Answers: Open Forum*, Freed-Hardeman College Lectures, Vol. 1, Henderson, TN: Freed-Hardeman University, 1976.

1975 - Last Known Photo of Brother Nichols
Blue Ridge Encampment, June 1975
This is believed to be the last photo taken of Gus Nichols.
Photo was taken by James S. Rickard (1920-2014)

www.ingramcontent.com/pod-product-compliance
Lightning Source LLC
Chambersburg PA
CBHW060041230426
43661CB00004B/615